BIBLE CHARACTERS

BIBLE CHARACTERS

ALEXANDER WHYTE, D.D.

VOLUME TWO

NEW TESTAMENT

MARSHALL, MORGAN & SCOTT
London

MARSHALL MORGAN, AND SCOTT
116 BAKER STREET
LONDON WIM 2BB

Two Volume Edition 1952
Sixth reprint 1964
One Volume Edition 1967
This Edition 1972
Reprinted 1976

ISBN 0 551 05139 6

Printed in Great Britain by offset lithography by
Billing & Sons Ltd, Guildford, London and Worcester

672072W510

VOLUME TWO

THE NEW TESTAMENT

CONTENTS

FOURTH SERIES

JOSEPH AND MARY, TO JAMES THE LORD'S BROTHER

FIFTH SERIES

STEPHEN TO TIMOTHY

SIXTH SERIES

Our Lord's Characters

Fourth Series

JOSEPH AND MARY TO JAMES THE LORD'S BROTHER

LXX

JOSEPH AND MARY

Saint Matthew and Saint Luke, the first and the third Evangelists, tell us all that we are told of Mary. They tell us that she was the espoused wife of Joseph a carpenter of Nazareth, and that the Divine Call came to her after her espousal to Joseph and before her marriage. What a call it was, and what a prospect it opened up! No sooner was Mary left alone of the angel than she began to realise something of what had been appointed her, and what she must now prepare herself to pass through. The sharp sword that the aged Simeon afterwards spoke of with such passion was already whetted, and was fast approaching her devoted and exposed heart. On a thousand sacred canvases throughout Christendom we are shown the angel of the annunciation presenting Mary with a branch of lily as an emblem of her beauty and as a seal of her purity. But why has no spiritual artist stained the whiteness of the lily with the red blood of a broken heart? For no sooner had the transfiguring light of the angel's presence faded from her sight than a deep and awful darkness began to fall upon Joseph's espoused wife. Surely if ever a suffering soul had to seek all its righteousness and all its strength in God alone, it was the soul of the Virgin Mary in those terrible days that followed the annunciation. Blessed among women as all the time she was; unblemished in soul and in body like the paschal lamb as she was; like the paschal lamb also she was set apart to be a divine sacrifice, and to have a sword thrust through her heart. Mary must have passed through many dark and dreadful days when all she had given her to lean upon would seem like a broken reed. Hail, thou that art highly favoured of the Lord, the angel had said to her. But all that would seem but so many mocking words to her as she saw nothing before her but an open shame, and, it might well be, an outcast's death. And, so fearfully and wonderfully are we made, and so fearful and wonderful was the way in which the Word was made flesh, that who can tell how all this may have borne on Him who was bone of her bone, and flesh of her flesh; to whom Mary was in all things a mother, as He was in all things to her a son. For,

> Hers was the face that unto Christ had most resemblance.

Great is the mystery of godliness; God manifest in the flesh. A man of sorrows, and acquainted with grief. These are the beginnings of sorrows.

Joseph's part in all this is told by Saint Matthew alone. And as we read that Evangelist's particular account of that time, we see how sharp that sword which pierced Joseph's soul also. His heart was broken with this terrible trial, but there was only one course left open to him. Conclude the marriage he could not, but neither could he consent to make Mary a public example, and there was only left to him the sad step of revoking the contract and putting her away privately. Joseph's heart must have been torn in two. For Mary had been the woman of all women to him. She had been in his eyes the lily among thorns. And now to have to treat her like a poisonous weed—the thought of it drove him mad. Oh, why is it that whosoever comes at all near Jesus Christ has always to drink such a cup of sorrow? Truly they who are brother or sister or mother to Him must take up their cross daily. These are they who go up through great tribulation.

What a journey that must have been of Mary from Nazareth to Hebron, and occupied with what thoughts. Mary's way would lead her through Jerusalem. She may have crossed Olivet as the sun was setting. She may have knelt at even in Gethsemane. She may have turned aside to look on the city from Calvary. What a heavy heart she must have carried through all these scenes as she went into the hill country with haste. Only two, out of God, knew the truth about Mary; an angel in heaven, and her own heart on earth. And thus it was that she fled to the mountains of Judah, hoping to find there an aged kinswoman of hers who would receive her word and would somewhat understand her case. As she stumbled on drunk with sorrow Mary must have recalled and repeated many blessed scriptures, well known to her indeed, but till then little understood. "Commit thy way unto the Lord; trust also in Him, and He will bring it to pass; and He shall bring forth thy righteousness as the light, and thy judgment as the noonday. Thou shalt keep them in the secret of thy presence from the pride of men; thou shalt keep them in a pavilion from the strife of tongues." Such a pavilion Mary sought and for a season found in the remote and retired household of Zacharias and Elisabeth.

It is to the meeting of Mary and Elisabeth that we owe the Magnificat, the last Old Testament psalm, and the first New Testament hymn, "My soul doth magnify the Lord, and my spirit hath rejoiced in God my Saviour." We cannot enter into all Mary's thoughts as she sang that spiritual song, any more than she could in her day enter into all our thoughts as we sing it. For, noble melody as her Magnificat is, it draws its deepest tones from a time that was still to come. The spirit of Christian prophecy moved her to utter it, but the noblest and fullest prophecy concerning Christ fell far short of the evangelical fulfilment.

She is a happy maiden who has a mother or a motherly friend much experienced in the ways of the human heart to whom she can tell all her anxieties; a wise, tender, much-experienced counsellor, such as Naomi was to Ruth, and Elisabeth to Mary. Was the Virgin an orphan, or was Mary's mother such a woman that Mary could have opened her heart to any stranger rather than to her? Be that as it may, Mary found a true mother in Elisabeth of Hebron. Many a holy hour the two women spent together sitting under the terebinths that overhung the dumb Zacharias's secluded house. And, if at any time their faith wavered and the thing seemed impossible, was not Zacharias beside them with his sealed lips and his writing table, a living witness to the goodness and severity of God? How Mary and Elisabeth would stagger and reason and rebuke and comfort one another, now laughing like Sarah, now singing like Hannah, let loving and confiding and pious women tell.

Sweet as it is to linger in Hebron beside Mary and Elisabeth, our hearts are always drawn back to Joseph in his unspeakable agony. The absent are dear, just as the dead are perfect. And Mary's dear image became to Joseph dearer still when he could no longer see her face or hear her voice. Nazareth was empty to Joseph; it was worse than empty, it was a city of sepulchres in which he sought for death and could not find it. Day after day, week after week, Joseph's misery increased, and when, as his wont was, he went up to the synagogue on the Sabbath day, that only made him feel his loneliness and his misery all the more. Mary's sweet presence had often made the holy place still more holy to him, and her voice in the Psalms had been to him as when an angel sings. On one of those Sabbaths which the exiled Virgin was spending at Hebron Joseph went up again to the sanctuary in Nazareth seeking to hide his great grief with God. And this, I feel sure, was the Scripture appointed to be read in the synagogue that day: "Ask thee a sign of the Lord thy God;

ask it either in the depth, or in the height above. Therefore the Lord Himself shall give you a sign: Behold, a virgin shall conceive, and bear a son, and shall call his name Immanuel." Joseph's heart was absolutely overwhelmed within him as he listened to that astounding Scripture. Never had ear or heart of man heard these amazing words as Joseph heard them that day. And then, when he laid himself down to sleep that night, his pillow became like a stone under his head. Not that he was cast out; but he had cast out another, and she the best of God's creatures. Ay, and she perhaps—how shall he whisper it even to himself at midnight—the virgin-mother of Immanuel! A better mother he could not have. So speaking to himself till he was terrified at his own thoughts, weary with another week's lonely labour, and aged with many weeks' agony and despair, Joseph fell asleep. Then a thing was secretly brought to him, and his ear received a little thereof. There was silence, and he heard a voice saying to him, "Joseph, thou son of David, fear not to take unto thee Mary thy wife, for that which is conceived in her is of the Holy Ghost." Gabriel was sent to reassure Joseph's despairing heart, to demand the consummation of the broken-off marriage, and to announce the Incarnation of the Son of God. Did Joseph arise before daybreak and set out for Hebron to bring his outcast home? There is room to believe that he did. If he did, the two angel-chastened men must have had their own thoughts and counsels together even as the two chosen women had. And as Joseph talked with Zacharias through his writing table, he must have felt that dumbness, and even death itself, would be but a light punishment for such unbelief and such cruelty as his. But all this, and all that they had passed through since the angel came to Zacharias at the altar, only made the re-betrothal of Joseph and Mary the sweeter and the holier, with the aged priest acting more than the part of a father, and Elisabeth acting more than the part of a mother.

For my own part, I do not know the gift or the grace or the virtue any woman ever had that I could safely deny to Mary. The divine congruity compels me to believe that all that could be received or attained or exercised by any woman would be granted beforehand, and all but without measure, to her who was so miraculously to bear, and so intimately and influentially to nurture and instruct, the Holy Child. We must give Mary her promised due. We must not allow ourselves to entertain a grudge against the mother of our Lord because some enthusiasts for her have given her more than her due. There is no fear of our thinking too much either of Mary's maidenly virtues, or of her motherly duties and experiences. The Holy Ghost in guiding the researches of Luke, and in superintending the composition of the Third Gospel, especially signalises the depth and the piety and the peace of Mary's mind. At the angel's salutation she did not swoon nor cry out. She did not rush either into terror on the one hand or into transport on the other. But like the heavenly-minded maiden she was, she cast in her mind what manner of salutation this should be. And later on, when all who heard it were wondering at the testimony of the shepherds, it is instructively added that Mary kept all these things and pondered them in her heart. And yet again, when another twelve years have passed by, we find the same Evangelist still pointing out the same distinguishing feature of Mary's saintly character, "They understood not the saying which Jesus spake unto them; but His mother kept all these sayings in her heart."

And, again, if we are to apply this sure principle to Mary's case, "according to your faith so be it unto you," then Mary must surely wear the crown as the mother of all them who believe on her Son. If Abraham's faith has made him the father of all them who believe, surely Mary's faith entitles her to be called their mother. If the converse of our Lord's words holds true, that no mighty work is done where there is unbelief: if we may safely reason that where there has been a mighty work done there must have been a corresponding and a co-operating faith; then I do not think we can easily overestimate the measure of Mary's faith. If this was the greatest work ever wrought by the power and the grace of Almighty God among the children of men, and if Mary's faith entered into it at all, then how great her faith must have been! Elisabeth saw with wonder and with worship how great it was. She saw the unparalleled grace that had come to Mary, and she had humility and magnanimity enough to acknowledge it. "Blessed art thou among women: Blessed is she that believeth, for there shall be a performance of those things which were told her from the Lord." "Blessed is she that believeth," said Elisabeth, no doubt with some sad thoughts about herself and about her dumb husband sitting beside her. "Blessed is the womb that bare Thee," cried on another occasion a nameless but a true woman, as her speech bewrayeth her, "and Blessed be the paps that Thou hast sucked." But our Lord answered her, and said, "Yea, rather, blessed are they that hear the word of God and keep it." And again, "Whosoever shall do the will of My Father in heaven, the same is My brother, and sister, and mother."

LXXI

SIMEON

SIMEON was one of the Seventy. Simeon sat in the Jerusalem Chamber of that day. And it fell to the lot of the Old Testament company on which Simeon sat to render the prophet Isaiah out of the Hebrew tongue and into the Greek tongue. All went well for the first six chapters of the evangelical prophet. But when they came to the seventh chapter, and to this verse in that chapter, "Behold, a virgin shall conceive, and bear a son, and shall call his name Immanuel," Simeon at that impossible prophecy threw down his pen and would write no more. 'How shall this be?' demanded Simeon. And with all they could do, the offended scholar would not subscribe his name to the *parthenos* passage that so satisfied and so delighted all the rest. Till in anger he threw down his pen and went home to his own house. But at midnight an angel appeared to Simeon, and said to him: 'Simeon, I am Gabriel that stand in the presence of God. And, behold, thou shalt remain in this thy captivity till thou shalt see with thine own eyes the LORD's Christ, made of a woman, and till the virgin's son shall put his little hand into thine aged bosom, and shall there loose thy silver cord.' And it was so. And the same Simeon was just and devout, waiting for the consolation of Israel. And he was still waiting in the temple when his parents brought in the child Jesus, to do for him after the custom of the law. Then he took him up in his arms, and blessed God, and said: "Lord, now lettest Thou Thy servant depart in peace, according to Thy word: for mine eyes have seen Thy salvation."

I can only guess at Simeon's real meaning and whole intention when he said in the temple that day that his waiting eyes had now seen God's salvation. For salvation in that day, as in this day, had as many meanings as there were men's minds. Salvation had the very heavenliest of meanings to one man, and the very earthliest of meanings to another man. To one man in the temple that day the salvation of God meant salvation from Cæsar; while to another man it meant his salvation from himself. To one man it was the tax-gatherer, and to another his own evil heart. And, with all that we are so instructively told about Simeon, still it is not possible to satisfy ourselves as to what, exactly, that aged saint and scripture scholar had in his mind when he said that his eyes had now seen God's salvation. But it is not Simeon and his salvation who is our errand up into this temple to-night. It is ourselves. What, then, is our salvation—yours and mine? When we speak, or hear, or read, or sing about salvation, what exactly do we mean?—if, indeed, we have any meaning at all, or intend to have any. 'My son'—one of Simeon's sacred colleagues used to say to his scholars—'My son, the first thing that you will be examined upon at the day of judgment will be this: What was the salvation that you pursued after? What salvation did you study, and teach, and preach, and yourself seek after when you were still in time and upon the earth?' How happy will it be with old Simeon on that terrible day when he hears this read out over him before men and angels: "The same man was just and devout, waiting for the consolation of Israel, and the Holy Ghost was upon him." "Mine eyes," said Simeon, "have seen Thy salvation." And Joseph and His mother marvelled at those things which were spoken of Him.

And, being full of the Holy Ghost, Simeon went on to say: "Behold, this child is set for the fall and rising again of many in Israel." So He was in Israel, and so He is still. There are schools and systems of interpretation of Scripture; there are schools and systems of philosophy; and of this and that, in which this prophecy uttered by Simeon that day is still being fulfilled. They rise, and they stand, and they fall, just as they receive or reject Immanuel. But our question with this Scripture before us is not about schools and systems of theology and philosophy, but about our own souls. Has Mary's Son, then; has God's Son, been a stumbling stone to me? Or, has He been the one foundation laid in Zion for me? Has He, to my everlasting salvation, and to His everlasting praise, lifted me up from all my falls and made me to stand upon His righteousness as upon a rock? Simeon himself had at one time stumbled and been broken on this child, and on His too great name. But the steps of a good man are ordered of the Lord, and He delighteth in his way. Though he fall he shall not be utterly cast down, for the Lord upholdeth him with His hand. Now, unto Him that is able to keep you from falling, and to present you faultless before the presence of His glory with exceeding joy: to the only wise God, our Saviour.

"And for a sign that shall be spoken against." We wonder to hear that. We are shocked to hear that. We say in amazement at that: What did He ever say or do that He should be spoken against by any man? He did the very opposite. He went about doing and speaking only good. But that made no difference to those men in that day who spake so spitefully against Him. Some spake against Him out of sheer ignorance of Him. They had never seen Him. But they spake against Him in their distant villages as if He had come and done them and theirs some great injury. And many who saw Him every day spake against Him every day, just because they did not understand Him, and would not take the pains and pay the price to understand Him and to love Him. Some, again, were poisoned against Him by what other people, and people of power, said against Him; some through envy, and some just because they had once begun to speak against Him, and could never give over what they had once begun to do. And they went on so speaking till they were swept on to cry, Crucify Him! not knowing what they were saying, or why. Take good care how you begin to speak against any man, good or bad. The chances are that, once you begin it, you will never be able to give it over. When you have once begun the devil's work of evil-speaking, he will hold his hook in your jaws, and will drag you on, and will give you a stake and an interest in lies and slander, till it will enrage and exasperate you to hear a single word of good spoken about your innocent victim. "Judge not," said our Lord, feeling bitterly how He was misjudged Himself. And Albert Bengel annotates that in this characteristic way: *sine scientia, amore, necessitate*. "I spoke not ill of any creature," said Teresa, "how little soever it might be. I scrupulously avoid all approaches to detraction. I had this rule ever present with me, that I was not to wish, nor assent to, nor say such things of any person whatsoever that I would not have them say of me. Still, for all that, I have a sufficiently strict account to give to God for the bad example I am to all about me in some other respects. For one thing, the very devil himself sometimes fills me with such a harsh and cruel temper—such a wicked spirit of anger and hostility at some people—that I could eat them up and annihilate them." That was the exact case with the detractors of Jesus Christ. They had no peace in their hearts, or in their tongues at Him, till they had eaten Him up and annihilated Him. This is such a horrible pit of a world that not even the Son of God Himself could come down into it, and do the work of God in it, without being hunted to death by evil tongues. And with that awful warning, and after nineteen centuries of His grace and truth, no man of any individuality, and talent, and initiative for good, can, to this day, do his proper work without straightway becoming a sign to be spoken against. To this day some of the most Christlike of men among us have been the most written against and spoken against, till such speech and such writing may almost be taken as the seal of God set upon His best servants and upon their best work. "And for a sign that shall be spoken against," said Simeon, as he returned the Holy Child to His mother

LXXII

ZACHARIAS AND ELISABETH

HIGH up in the hill-country of Judea there dwelt a certain priest named Zacharias with his wife Elisabeth. They were no longer young; they had lived a long and happy lifetime together. The single shadow that had ever lain upon their serene and saintly life had been this that their house was childless. But all that was now long past—long past and quite forgotten. "For thus saith the Lord to them that choose the things that please me, and take hold of my covenant, even unto them will I give in mine house and within my walls a place and a name better than of sons and of daughters: I will give them an everlasting name, that shall not be cut off." And while the Lord spake thus to them both, Zacharias in his holy office spake thus to Elisabeth: 'Why weepest thou, and why is thy heart grieved? Am not I better to thee than ten sons?' Thus the God of Israel spake to them both, and thus they spake to one another, till Luke is able to record this of them both, that they were both righteous before God, walking in all the commandments and ordinances of the Lord blameless.

It is the fullness of time at last. It is at last the great day on which the New Testament has been predestinated to open. Zacharias has gone up to Jerusalem according to his course. The priestly lot has again been cast and has fallen this time on Zacharias. He is chosen of God and called upon to enter the Holy Place, to minister at the altar, and to make morning and evening intercession for the sinful people. Never before, in all his long lifetime, has Zacharias had this awful privilege; only once in a priest's whole lifetime was this great office put upon any son of Aaron. Clothed in his spotless robes, with his head covered and with his shoes off, this holy man and elect priest disappears within the golden doors of the Holy Place. As he enters he sees the golden candlestick, and the table of shewbread, and the altar of incense. From that altar there rises the sacred flame that had been lighted at the pillar of fire in the wilderness, and which has burned on unconsumed ever since. Taking his censer full of incense into his hand Zacharias pours it on the perpetual altar-fire, and says: Lord, let my prayer come before thee like this incense; and the lifting up of my hands like the evening sacrifice! And the whole multitude of the people were praying without at the time of incense. And there appeared unto Zacharias an angel of the Lord standing on the right side of the altar of incense. And when Zacharias saw him he was troubled and fear fell upon him. But the angel said unto him: Fear not, Zacharias; for thy prayer is heard, and thy wife Elisabeth shall bear thee a son, and thou shalt call his name John. And thou shalt have joy and gladness, and many shall rejoice at his birth. And many of the children of Israel shall he turn to the Lord their God: to make ready a people prepared for the Lord. Then follows Zacharias's fear, and doubt, and disbelief; and then his deafness and dumbness; and then the visit of Mary to the hill-country of Judah, where Zacharias and Elisabeth had hid themselves; and then the Magnificat, as we call it: and then the birth and the circumcision of Elisabeth's son; and then the opening of Zacharias's mouth and the loosening of his tongue, all wound up with his magnificent Benedictus. A splendid preface to a splendid book!

"They were both righteous before the Lord, and blameless." This excellent instance of the frank and fearless, if confessedly condescending, style of Holy Scripture. Holy Scripture has no hesitation lest it should contradict or stultify itself. Holy Scripture speaks out its whole heart on each occasion boldly, and leaves the reconciling and the harmonising of its strong and sometimes startling statements to those of its readers who feel a need and have a liking for such reconciling and harmonising. As a matter of fact that was the widespread good name and spotless character of Zacharias and Elisabeth. Zacharias among his brethren in the priesthood, and Elisabeth among her kinsfolk and neighbours in Hebron, were both blameless. Holy Scripture in saying this simply classifies Zacharias and Elisabeth with Abraham, and with Samuel, and with Job, and with all such Old Testament saints. And if such generous judgments are not so often passed on men and women in New Testament times, that is so for reasons that are very well known to every New Testament mind and heart. And if those noble tributes to Zacharias and Elisabeth stagger and condemn us; if we read of their righteousness and their blamelessness with envy and with despair; what is that envy and what is that despair but two of our finest

New Testament graces through which we are being led on to a righteousness and a blamelessness that shall not be economical and of condescension, but shall be true and perfect and everlasting. That righteousness, in short, and that blamelessness of which a New Testament apostle prophesies in these so comforting words: "Nevertheless we, according to His promise, look for new heavens and a new earth, wherein dwelleth righteousness. Wherefore, beloved, seeing that we look for such things, be diligent that ye be found of Him in peace, without spot, and blameless." Blessed are they which do hunger and thirst after righteousness, for they shall be filled.

And the angel said unto him: Fear not, Zacharias: for thy prayer is heard. Had the angel come with that answer forty years before he would have been welcomed and well entertained both by Zacharias and Elisabeth. But he has come too late. 'No,' said Zacharias; 'no. It is far too late. The time is past—long past. The thing is impossible—quite impossible. And, indeed—and let not my lord be angry—it is no longer desirable.' Zacharias had long outlived his prayer for a son. He had long retracted his prayer. He had a thousand times justified the Hearer of prayer for not hearing and not answering his too impatient prayer. He had long ere now seen some very good and sufficient reasons why he and Elisabeth should end their days together. And, even if it were still possible, Zacharias was not willing to be plunged back at this time of day into all the anxieties, and uncertainties, and responsibilities, and dangers he had now for so long left for ever behind him. 'My prayer is not to be heard,' Zacharias had long ago said to himself. 'Let me direct my prayer and look up for far better, and far more sure, and far more steadfast, and far more satisfying things. The will of the Lord be done,' he had said long ago. But behold, to Zacharias's confusion, his prayer has been heard all the time! All these long past years of prayer, and waiting, and ceasing from prayer and turning to other things—all that time Zacharias's answer has been ready before God, and has only been waiting till the best time for the answer to be sent down. Pray on, then, all you postponed and disappointed and impoverished people of God; pray on and faint not. Pray on: for the prayer is far better than the answer. And, besides, your answer may all the time be ready, as Zacharias's answer was. But other people's prayers and other people's providences may be so mixed up with yours that you will have to wait till their prayers, and their preparations, and their providences are all as ripe and as ready as yours. The fastest ship in the British fleet has to wait for the slowest, and that explains why that fine vessel is not led into battle and let home to harbour with its full and proper spoil. Zacharias and Elisabeth were ready long ago. But Joseph and Mary were not ready; they were still but new beginners in faith and in prayer, in righteousness and in blamelessness. And thus it was that, without knowing why, Zacharias and Elisabeth and John the Baptist had to wait in the hill-country of Hebron till Joseph and Mary were made ready for the Divine predestination and for their prayer away north in Nazareth.

And Zacharias and Elisabeth hid themselves up in the hill-country for the next five months. Look at them. Look at Zacharias with his writing table, and Elisabeth with her needle. And never one word spoken between them all that time, only smiles and tears. What, do you suppose, was Zacharias doing all that time with no altar to minister at, and no neighbours to talk to, and no tongue, indeed, to talk with? "I have no books," said Jacob Behmen, "but I have myself." And Zacharias had himself. Zacharias had himself, and the wife of his youth, who was also the light of his eyes: he had himself and all those past years of prayer, and waiting, and resignation, and peace of mind. And then he had these past overwhelming weeks also. Do you still ask what Zacharias was doing all that time? Has your New Testament a margin with readings? Your so instructive margin, if you will attend to it, will tell you the very Scriptures over which Zacharias spent his days and nights all that silent time in Hebron. All you have got to do some day, when you are in the mind, is to consult the margin over against Zacharias's prophetical song, and you are in that as good as looking over his shoulder at his writing table. You are as good as walking out alone with him when he goes abroad among the sunsetting rocks of Judea to wonder, and to praise, and to pray over Elisabeth and himself and their unborn son.

Zacharias and Elisabeth were sitting alone with their own thoughts one day when who should knock at their door but the Virgin Mary herself all the way from Nazareth. Luke takes up his very best pen as Elisabeth and Mary embrace one another. He had it all long afterwards from an eye and ear witness, so that we might know the certainty of all that took place that day in Zacharias's house up in the hill-country. With the embrace and with the authority of a prophetess Elisabeth saluted Mary, and said: "Blessed art thou among women, and blessed is the fruit of thy womb. And whence is this to me, that the mother of my Lord should come to me?" What a day! What a dispensation! What a meeting! What a household! What a predestination descended on that roof! What unsearchable riches! What great and precious promises! What prayers! What psalms! What laughter! What tears! And Mary said: "My soul doth magnify the Lord, and my spirit hath rejoiced in God my Saviour." And Mary abode with Elisabeth about three months, and then returned to her own house.

And it came to pass, that on the eighth day Elisabeth's neighbours and her cousins came to the circumcision of the child; and they called him Zacharias, after the name of his father. But his mother answered and said: "Not so; but he shall be called John," that is to say, The-Grace-of-God. And they said unto her: "But there is none of thy kindred that is called by that name." And they made signs to his father what he would have the child called, and he asked for his writing table and wrote, saying; "His name is The-Grace-of-God." And they marvelled all. They marvelled all because it was a new name to them, and it offended them to hear it. It was to them an outlandish and an unintelligible name. They had never prayed for a son, or for anything else. They had never been visited of an angel. They had never hid themselves five months. Their husbands had never been struck deaf and dumb for their doubt. No babe had ever leaped in their womb because they were filled with the Holy Ghost. No. None of all their kindred had ever been called by this so stumbling name. Fathers and mothers of new-born children, be like Elisabeth and Zacharias in the naming of your children. Be very bold, if need be, in the naming of your children. Be original and independent in the naming of your children. Be truthful. Be thankful. Be believing. Be hopeful, and be assured. Be not afraid to write an altogether new name in your Family Bible. Go back to your true ancestors for a name sometimes, and not to those of flesh and blood only. Fish no more for testaments in the waters of baptism. Or if for a testament at all, then secure, as far as your naming of him lies, that your son shall be an heir of God, and a joint-heir with the Son of God. Name the name of God over your son. Name over your son what God has done for your soul. Name over him some secret of the Lord with you. Name him something that God has showed you out of His holy covenant. Elisabeth was very bold. She named her little son after no man on earth, but, actually, after Almighty God Himself in heaven. And her husband Zacharias was of one mind with her in that, as soon as he got his writing table into his hands. The God-of-all-Grace was thus made Sponsor and Name-Father to Elisabeth's only son, who was born of her so out of all ordinary time. Elisabeth and

Mary had spent three months together since Gabriel's visit to them both. And all those three months—morning, noon, and night—when they talked together, it was about nothing else but about the angel, and his visits, and his messages. And among other things that they less talked about to one another than whispered to themselves, was the naming of their unborn sons. "Immanuel!" and "Jesus Christ!" Mary would whisper to herself, with an ever-increasing wonder and awe at the awful words. While "The-Grace-of-God" was Elisabeth's holy secret. And, then, how the two children were born, and how they were brought up, and how they both justified, and fulfilled, and adorned their new and unheard-of names, let Luke and his fellow-evangelists say. And they will tell you, to begin with, how John—The-Grace-of-God—grew and waxed strong in spirit, and was in the deserts till the day of his showing unto Israel.

LXXIII

JOHN THE BAPTIST

"What manner of child shall this be!" was the universal exclamation of the whole hill country of Judea over the birth of John. The old age of Zacharias and Elisabeth; the errand from heaven of Gabriel; the dumbness in judgment of Zacharias; and the strange things that he wrote on his writing table; all that made all who heard of it to exclaim, "What manner of child, we wonder, shall John, the son of Zacharias and Elisabeth, turn out to be!" And the whole manner and character and service of John's childhood and youth and manhood, down to the day of his death, turned out to be wonderful enough to satisfy the most wonder-loving of Elisabeth's neighbours, both in Jerusalem and in all Judea.

John was in the deserts till the day of his showing unto Israel, so Luke tells us. And from Luke, and from some other trustworthy sources, we can see John for the first thirty years of his sequestered life as well almost as if we ourselves had lived in the very next desert to his deserts. For you must always remember this about John that he was in the deserts, and was with the wild beasts, till he began to be about thirty years of age. He was in those terrible deserts that lay all around the Dead Sea. Up and down John wandered, and fasted, and prayed, where Sodom and Gomorrah had once stood till the Lord rained fire and brimstone upon all the inhabitants of those cities, and upon all that grew upon the ground. And John was clothed with camel's hair, and with a leathern girdle about his loins; and he did eat locusts and wild honey. A terrible man. A man not to come near. The very bitumen-miners, whom everybody feared, were afraid of John. It made them sober and civil to one another when John came down to visit them in their squalid settlements. It was not that John was a misanthrope. John was the right opposite of a misanthrope. It was because all other men were misanthropes; were hateful, and were hating one another, that John could not any longer dwell among them, either in Judea or in Jerusalem, either in Sodom or Gomorrah. You totally misread and misunderstand John if you think that it was either misanthropy or moroseness that made John what he was. It was simply John's extraordinarily deep insight into the holy law of God that made him such a monastic of fasting and self-flagellation and prayer.

Before his father Zacharias died, and as long as Elisabeth lived, John had heard things like this at their lips in family worship every day: "The Lord shall lay on Him the iniquity of us all. He shall be stricken, smitten of God, and afflicted. His soul shall be made an offering for sin." It was on such things as these that Elisabeth suckled her heaven-sent son till it sometimes seemed to him in his loneliness of soul and in his agony of heart that he himself had been made sin, and nothing but sin. And, indeed, in some ways, John came as near being made sin as any mortal man ever came to that unparalleled experience. John was the man of sorrows till the true Man of Sorrows Himself should come. All the appetites of John's body, and all the affections of John's mind and heart, were drunk up and drained dry by the all-consuming fires of his unquenchable conscience. If all sight and sense and conscience of sin had utterly died out of Israel in that day, it had only died out of all other men's hearts to rage like the bottomless pit itself in the great broken heart of Elisabeth's substituted son. And thus it was that the very robbers ran and hid themselves among the rocks of the hill-country when they saw that terrible man standing again over against the city, and crying out, "Oh Jerusalem! Jerusalem! how shalt thou abide the day of His coming? For, behold! that day shall burn as an oven. That great and terrible day, when all that do wickedly shall be as the stubble!" A man alone. A man apart. A great man. "A greater man has never been born of woman," said He who knew all men. "What went ye out into the wilderness to see? A reed shaken with the wind!" He who said that never smiled, say some. I see Him smiling for once as He says that. 'A man clothed in soft raiment! No; anything but that. And anything but a reed; and with anything on but the soft clothing that they put on in kings' houses!'

And, now, from such a divinity-student as that, and after thirty years of such a curriculum and probationership as that, what kind of preaching would you go to church to look for? A dumb dog that cannot bark? A trencher-chaplain? A soft thing of gown and bands and lawn sleeves? A candidate for a manse and a stipend? "O generation of vipers, who hath warned you to flee from the wrath to come? Bring forth, therefore, fruits meet for repentance. And now the axe is laid at the root of the trees. Therefore every tree that bringeth not forth good fruit is hewn down and cast into the fire. He that hath two coats let him impart to him that hath none; and he that hath meat, let him do likewise. Do violence to no man. Neither accuse any man falsely, and be content with your wages. He shall baptise you with the Holy Ghost, and with fire. Whose fan is in his hand, and He will gather the wheat into His garner, but the chaff will He burn up with fire unquenchable." The greatest preacher of the past generation when preaching to a congregation of young preachers said this to them: "He who has before his mental eye the four last things will have the true earnestness. He will have the horror and the rapture of one who witnesses a conflagration, or discerns some rich and sublime prospect above and beyond this world. His countenance, his manner, his voice will all speak for him in proportion as his view has been vivid and minute.

> Yea, this man's brow, like to a title-leaf,
> Foretells the nature of a tragic volume.
> Thou tremblest, and the whiteness in thy cheek
> Is apter than thy tongue to tell thine errand.

It is this earnestness, in the supernatural order which is the eloquence of saints; and not of saints only, but of all Christian preachers, according to the measure of their faith and love."

But why, I wonder, was the forerunner able to content himself all his days with being no more than the forerunner? Why did John not leave off his ministry of accusation and condemnation? Why did he not wait upon, and himself take up, the ministry of reconciliation? When he said to his disciples, Behold the Lamb of God! why did the Baptist not go himself with Andrew and the others and become, first, a disciple, and then in due time an apostle, of Jesus Christ? Zacharias's son would have made a better son of thunder than both of Zebedee's sons taken together. Why, then, did John not leave the desert, and the Jordan, and follow Christ? Well, to begin with, he could not help himself. Jesus did not call John any more than He called His own brother James. "Go you," John said to Andrew, and to Peter, and to James and John, the sons of Zebedee. "Go you: I am not worthy to enter under the same roof with Him. I will remain where I am. I will work at the Jordan. I will preach repentance, and He will teach you to preach pardon. The Kingdom of Heaven is soon coming, but I shall not live to see it. I shall not live to see Tabor, and Calvary, and Olivet, and Pentecost, like you. He and you, His disciples, must increase, but I must decrease." John was a great man and a great preacher, but, as we are wont to say, he never quite escaped out of the seventh of the Romans.

John the Baptist, like some much more evangelical men, was well-nigh smothered out of life in the slough of despond. 'Art thou He that should come, or do we look for another?' Why dost thou eat and drink with Scribes and Pharisees, and leave me lying here in this prison-house of Herod and his harlots? Why dost thou eat and drink and make wine out of water for weddings? Rather, surely, should all God's true servants put on sackcloth and ashes and mourn apart, every family apart, and their wives apart. Art thou He that should come, or do we look for another? Yes; this is Elias come back again. "I have been very zealous for the Lord," complained Elias in his cave in Horeb. "I only am left, and they seek my life. It is enough. Let me die, O Lord, for I am no better than my fathers." The God of all comfort be thanked for Elias, and for John, and for the slough of despond! They are all written for our rebuke, and for our learning, and for our sure consolation. Had these things not been written we would have turned away from our Bible in despair, saying: 'These men are giants and saints. These are not men of like passions as we are. Why,' we are often tempted to complain. 'Why is God's Kingdom so long in coming? What hinders it, if indeed Christ is on His throne and has all things in His hand? Why does He not burst open my prison-house and redress my cause? Why is my sanctification so postponed? Art thou He that should come, or do we look for another?' "Go and show John again those things that ye do see, and hear. The blind receive their sight, the lame walk, the lepers are cleansed, the deaf hear, the dead are raised up, and the poor have the Gospel preached to them. And blessed is he, whosoever shall not be offended in Me. He that believeth, and hopeth against hope, and endureth to the end, he alone shall be saved."

But by far the very best thing that the Baptist ever said or did was what he said to his jealous disciples: "A man can receive nothing," he said, "except it be given him from Heaven. He that hath the bride is the bridegroom. He must increase, but I must decrease." I would rather have had the grace from God to say that than have been the greatest man ever born of woman. For he who thinks, and says, and does a thing like that is born, not of blood, nor of the will of the flesh, nor of the will of man, but of God. And yet, when I come up close to it and look it in the face, this great utterance of the Baptist is not by any means so unapproachable as I took it to be at my first sight of it. I myself could have said and done all that John said and did that day. That is to say, had I been in his exact circumstances? For what were his exact circumstances? They were these, and much more than these. John had drunk in the Sonship and the Messiahship of Jesus of Nazareth with his mother's milk. And he had been brought up all his days on that same marrow of lions. His mother Elisabeth, you may be very sure, did not die, nor did Zacharias depart in peace, till they had both told over and over again to their forerunner-son every syllable they had to tell. And thus it was that for full thirty years John did nothing else but wait for the Messiah. John thought about no one else, and spake about no one else, for all these endless years, but the Lamb of God. And thus it was that when Jesus of Nazareth came south to the Jordan to be baptised of John, the Baptist remonstrated and refused, and said: "I have need to be baptised of Thee." No, there was nothing at all so great or so good in John's self-effacing speech to his disciples. The most envious-minded man in all the world does not envy a lion, or an eagle, or an angel. A beggar does not envy a king. He only envies his neighbour-beggar whose pockets are so full of coppers and crumbs at night. "Potter envies potter." And the more theology there was in John's first great utterance, "Behold the Lamb of God," the less morality there was in his second great utterance, "He must increase, but I must decrease." No thanks to John not to be jealous of the Son of God! But had Jesus been simply a carpenter of Nazareth, and John's cousin to boot, turned suddenly such a popular preacher with all men, and with all John's baptised disciples going after him; and had John, in that case, said all this about his own decreasing, then I would down on the spot and kiss his feet.

"I was to preach in Clackmannan, where the most of the people were already for me to be their minister, but some that had the greatest power were against me, as it ordinarily fared with me in the places where I used to preach. On the Saturday afternoon there came a letter to my hand, desiring me to give the one-half of the day to another probationer, whom those who were against me had their eye upon. In these circumstances, seeing what hazard I was in of an evil eye, I committed the keeping of my heart to the Lord that I might be helped to carry evenly. He got the forenoon, for so it was desired by his friends. I was, as I expected, terribly assaulted by the tempter. When I came home from church my heart was in a manner enraged against itself on that account, and I confessed it before the Lord, abhorring myself, and appealing to God's omniscience, that I would fain have had it otherwise. As I was complaining that Satan had winnowed me, and had brought up much filthy stuff out of my heart, it came to my mind: 'But I have prayed for thee that thy faith fail not.' And then, in the evening, after service, while I sat musing over the day, I proposed this question to myself: Wouldest thou be satisfied with Christ as thy portion, though there was no hell to be saved from? And my soul answered, Yes! Supposing, further, wouldst thou be content with Christ, though likewise thou shouldest lose credit and reputation, and see other men before thee, and meet with much trouble and trial for His sake? And my soul answered, Yes! This was the last sermon I preached in Clackmannan, for I was going out of the country; and neither of us two preachers of that Sabbath was the person that God had designed for that pulpit."

He that hath the bride is the bridegroom.

LXXIV

NICODEMUS

THIS, I feel sure, is not the first time that Jesus of Nazareth and Nicodemus of Jerusalem have met. The sudden and trenchant way in which our Lord receives the cautious old ruler's diplomatic certificates and civilities, and every single word of the whole subsequent conversation, all point unmistakably, as I feel sure, to some previous meeting. The meeting took place in this wise; it must have taken place in some such wise as this:

Nicodemus was one of the oldest and most honoured heads of that overawing deputation which was sent out to Bethabara by the Temple authorities to examine into the Baptist's preaching, and to report to the Temple on that whole movement. "Who art thou?" Nicodemus demanded. "I am not the Christ," the

Baptist answered. "Why baptizest thou then?" "I indeed baptize thee with water unto repentance, but, Behold the Lamb of God which taketh away the sin of the world, He will baptize thee, when thou comest to Him, with the Holy Ghost." And, had Nicodemus only been alone that day, there is no saying what he might not have said and done on the spot. Nicodemus was mightily impressed with all that he had seen and heard at the Jordan. But he was not free; he did not feel free and able to act as his conscience told him he ought immediately to act. He was at the head of that Temple embassy of inquisition, and he simply could not extricate himself from the duties, and the responsibilities, and the entanglements of his office. He and his colleagues had, by this time, seen and heard more than they well knew what to say to the Temple about it all. And, accordingly, glad to get away from Bethabara, they took up their carriages and set out for Jerusalem, compiling all the way home their perplexing and unsatisfactory report upon John and, especially upon Jesus of Nazareth.

The third chapter of the Fourth Gospel is in many things an absolutely classical chapter. In his third chapter the fourth Evangelist introduces us into an inquiry-room, as we would call it, in which our Lord is the director and counsellor of souls, and in which Nicodemus is the inquirer and the convert. Nicodemus had not slept soundly one single night, nor spent one single day without remorse and fear, ever since that scene when he saw Jesus of Nazareth baptized by John, and coming up out of the water. And thus it was that he stole out of the city that night, and determined to see in secret this mysterious man. I cannot put you back into Nicodemus's state of mind as he stumbled out to Bethany in the dark of that night. To you, Jesus of Nazareth is the Son of God, and your Saviour, and Lord, and Master. But to Nicodemus that night Jesus of Nazareth was—Nicodemus staggered and stood still—he was afraid to let himself think Who and What Jesus of Nazareth was, and might turn out to be. "Rabbi, we know that thou art a teacher come from God." But it took the old ruler's breath away when it was answered him in such a sudden and sword-like way: "Except a man be born of water and of the Spirit he cannot enter into the Kingdom of God." To me it is a most extraordinary and impossible hallucination. My whole mind and imagination and heart and conscience would have to be taken down and built up again upon an absolutely other pattern; my whole experience, observation, and study of all these divine things would have to be turned upside down before I could possibly believe in what is called "baptismal regeneration." No! there is no such thing. Believe me, whoever says it, and however long and learnedly and solemnly they have been saying it, there is no such thing. There could not be. And, certainly, there is no such materialistic, mechanical, immoral, and unspiritual doctrine and precept here. But there is in place of it a divine doctrine and a divine precept that goes at one stroke down into Nicodemus's self-deceiving heart, and cuts his self-deceiving heart open to the daylight. If our masters of Israel do not know what our Lord pointed at when he said "water" with such emphasis, Nicodemus could have told them. And had Nicodemus only been brave enough; had he only had brow enough for a good cause; had he only gone down into the waters of Jordan beside Jesus of Nazareth, we would have been counting up to-day Peter, and James, and John, and Nicodemus, as all apostles of Christ. And we would have had an Epistle of Nicodemus to the Pharisees, and in it such a key to this whole conversation as would have made it impossible for any man to preach regeneration by water out of it. But Nicodemus missed his great opportunity, and both he and the whole Church of Christ have been terrible losers thereby down to this disunited and distracted day. Nicodemus, ruler of Israel just because he was, he was not equal to face such a loss of reputation and of other things as would immediately have descended upon him on the day he was publicly baptized. And as he lay and tossed on his bed every night after Bethabara, he thought he had at last devised a compromise so as to get into sufficient step with this teacher come from God, or whatever else He was, and yet not needlessly break with the Temple and its honours and emoluments. But there is no deceiving of Jesus Christ. For, have we not been told just before Nicodemus knocked at Martha's door, that Jesus knew all men, and knew what was in all men? And thus it was that Nicodemus had scarcely got his lips opened to pay his prepared compliments to our Lord when he was met again with that dreadful "water," which had haunted him like an accusing spirit ever since he had not gone down into it at Bethabara. Nicodemus stood ripe and ready for his regeneration, and for his first entrance into the kingdom of heaven, and he was within one short step of its gate at the Jordan, but that step was far too strait and sore for Nicodemus to take. Nicodemus saw the pearl, and knew something of the value of it, but he could not make up his mind to sell all he possessed so as to pay the price. In our Lord's words, which He was always repeating, Nicodemus had not the strength of mind and heart to take up his cross and be born again. He was not able to be baptized—not into regeneration, there is no such baptism—but into evangelical repentance and the open loss of all things. And thus it was that our Lord, with all His affability, would not enter on any closer intimacy or confidence with Nicodemus till he had gone out to John at the Jordan. There were a thousand things that held Nicodemus back from John's baptism at his age and in his office, and our Lord saw and sympathised with every one of them. But, King of the kingdom of heaven as He was that night in Bethany, even He could not make the door of the kingdom one inch wider, or one atom easier, than it was out at Bethabara. 'No!' our Lord said to Nicodemus, as he lay struggling in the net of his old heart and life all that night—'No! We do not need to talk any more about my mighty works or your new birth. You know your first duty in this whole matter as well as I can tell you. John told you, and you would not do it. And I cannot relieve you of your first duty any more than I can do it for you. And you may go away to-night, again leaving your immediate duty undone, but mark my words, till the day of your death and judgment there will be no other way to a new heart and a new life for you but to go out to the waters of Jordan and be baptized of John and before all Judea and Jerusalem, and then come after Me and be My disciple.' Nicodemus, that blind leader of the blind, had always taken it for granted that when the kingdom of God should come to Israel he would be taken up to sit in one of the highest seats of it. It had never once entered his snow-white head to doubt for one moment but that he would sit on a throne up at the right hand of the Messiah. Imagine, then, what a sudden blow in the face it was to Nicodemus to be told, and that by the very Messiah Himself, that he had neither part nor lot in that kingdom, and could not have, until he had been baptized in Jordan confessing his sins beside the offscourings of the city.

At the same time, Nicodemus that night was in Martha's house beside Jesus Christ, and not out at the Jordan beside John the Baptist. And Jesus Christ did not open the door and dismiss Nicodemus as John the Baptist would certainly have done. The very opposite. Our Lord, with His utmost tenderness for the ensnared and struggling old man, took patience to put all John's best preaching over again to Nicodemus, and added some of His own best preaching to it, and, all the time, in His most attractive and most winning way. John had scoffed at Nicodemus's boasted birth from Abraham; but Jesus contented Himself with simply saying that Nicodemus must be born of water and of the Spirit. John had assailed the Temple representatives as a generation of vipers; and, while Jesus did not withdraw or apologise for one single syllable of His so outspoken forerunner, He veiled His forerunner's strong language somewhat under the sacramental and evangelical typology of the serpent in the wilderness. And, then, from that He went on to honour and to win Nicodemus with that golden passage that "Even so must the Son of Man be lifted up." And that golden passage was, I feel sure, Nicodemus's salvation that very night, as it has been the salvation of so many sinners ever since. And then, as He shook hands with Nicodemus just as the cock was crowing in Martha's garden, Jesus said to Nicodemus, with a look and with a manner that the old ruler never forgot, "But he that doeth good cometh to the light, that his deeds may be made manifest that they are wrought in God." John, our evangelist, was present all that night, and he has written this chapter also of his book so that we might believe that Jesus is the Christ, the Son of God, and that believing we might have life through His name. And this evangelist, after that ever-memorable day at Bethabara, and that equally memorable midnight and morning at Bethany, never lets Nicodemus out of his sight. And thus it is that we read this in John's seventh chapter: "Then Nicodemus said to the chief priests and to the Pharisees, Doth our law judge any man before it hear him, and know what he doeth?" And then as we read John's nineteenth chapter, we come on this. "And there came also Nicodemus, which at the first came to Jesus by night, and he brought a mixture of myrrh and aloes, about a hundred pounds weight."

"Now I saw that there would be no answer to me till I had entire purity of conscience, and no longer regarded any iniquity whatsoever in my heart. I saw that there were some secret affections still left in me, which, though they were not very bad in themselves perhaps, yet in a life of prayer, such as I was then attempting, these remanent affections certainly spoiled all." Just so. Just so in Teresa, and in Nicodemus, and in you, and in me. It was surely not so very bad in itself for Nicodemus to let himself be put at the head of that Temple embassy of inquisition upon the Baptist. It was surely not so very bad in itself for Nicodemus, once having set out, to keep true to his colleagues, even if that was done somewhat at the expense and the injury of John. It was not such a great crime, surely, for Nicodemus to yield to such strong pressure so far as to put his name to the somewhat unfriendly report that his less scrupulous colleagues wrote out for the Temple. And it could only be good, surely, and to Nicodemus's credit, that he went out to Bethany at an hour most convenient for a ruler of the Jews. And it is not so very bad surely in itself in you—everybody does it—to take up a distaste at some man or some movement that you know quite well you have absolutely nothing against. It is surely not enough to cost you in the end the loss of your soul for you to think first of your prospects in life, and how you will continue to stand with this great man and with that, according as you cast in your lot with this party in the state, or with that denomination in the church. Everybody does it. And who but John would denounce so fiercely and so contemptuously such secret affections as these are in you? But then, if John and then Jesus denounce, and despise, and deny you, what will it profit you if you gain the whole of this world? But, happily, there is a second lesson out of Nicodemus, and out of his subsequent history, and it is this: Though you have been a coward and a dark friend to truth and to duty up to this night, if God in His great goodness should give you yet another offer and opportunity, seize it on the spot. Jesus is still among his enemies in many ways. Recognise and acknowledge Jesus Christ, and stand up for Him in your Sanhedrim like Nicodemus. Do you know Him? ask them. Have you ever gone to where He lodges and seen and heard Him for yourselves? Have you read the book you speak against? ask them. Do you love the writer, and do you wish him well? ask them. Do you rejoice in an evil report? demand boldly of them. Or do you rejoice, to your own loss, in the truth? The whole Seventy will turn on you, and will rend you. But what of that? For unless you are rent here for His name's sake, the Son of man will be ashamed of you when He is suddenly revealed and suddenly descends on you in all His glory.

But for Nicodemus, and another timid friend to truth, the dead body of our Lord might have been taken out of the city and cast into the flames of Tophet, that type of Hell, along with the carcases of the two thieves. All the disciples had forsaken their crucified Master and had fled. But Joseph of Arimathæa and Nicodemus went boldly to Pilate and besought him to let them bury the dead body that all other men hid their faces from that day. And Joseph and Nicodemus took the body of Jesus and wound it in linen clothes with the spices, as the manner of the Jews is to bury their dead. It was the same Joseph of Arimathæa who had been a disciple of Jesus, but secretly for fear of the Jews; and it was the same Nicodemus, which at the first came to Jesus by night.

LXXV

PETER

THE Four Gospels are full of Peter. After the name of our Lord Himself, no name comes up so often in the Four Gospels as Peter's name. No disciple speaks so often and so much as Peter. Our Lord speaks oftener to Peter than to any other of His disciples; sometimes in blame and sometimes in praise. No disciple is so pointedly reproved by our Lord as Peter, and no disciple ever ventures to reprove his Master but Peter. No other disciple ever so boldly confessed and outspokenly acknowledged and encouraged our Lord as Peter repeatedly did; and no one ever intruded, and interfered, and tempted Him as Peter repeatedly did also. His Master spoke words of approval, and praise, and even blessing to Peter the like of which He never spoke to any other man. And at the same time, and almost in the same breath, He said harder things to Peter than He ever said to any other of His twelve disciples, unless it was to Judas.

No disciple speaks so often as Peter. "Depart from me, for I am a sinful man, O Lord. Lo, we have left all and followed Thee; what shall we have therefore? Be it far from Thee, Lord; this shall never be to Thee. Lord, if it be Thou, bid me come unto Thee on the water. Lord, save me. The crowd press Thee, and how sayest Thou, Who touched me? Thou art the Christ, the Son of the Living God. To whom can we go but unto Thee? Thou hast the words of eternal life. Lord, it is good for us to be here; let us make three tabernacles: one for Thee, and one for Moses, and one for Elias. How oft shall my brother sin against me, and I forgive him? Though all men deny Thee, yet will not I. Thou shalt never wash my feet. Lord, not my feet only, but also my hands and my head. I know not the man. Lord, Thou knowest all things: thou knowest that I love Thee." And, to crown all his impertinent and indecent speeches, "Not so, Lord, for I have never eaten anything that is common or unclean." And then, in that charity which shall cover the multitude of sins, "Forasmuch then as God gave them the like gift as he did unto us; what was I that I could withstand God?" These are Peter's unmistakable footprints. Hasty, headlong, speaking impertinently and unadvisedly, ready to repent, ever wading into waters too deep for him, and ever turning to his Master again like a little child. Peter was grieved because He said unto him the third time, Lovest thou me? And he said unto Him, Lord, thou knowest all things: Thou knowest that I love Thee.

The evangelical Churches of Christendom have no duty and no interest to dispute with the Church of Rome either as to Peter's primacy among the twelve disciples, or as to his visits to Rome, or as to his death by martyrdom in that city. If the Church of Rome is satisfied about the historical truth of Peter's missionary work in the west, we are satisfied. All that can be truthfully told us about Peter we shall welcome. We cannot be told too much about Peter. And as to his primacy that Rome makes so much of, we cannot read our New Testament without coming on proofs on every page that Peter held a foremost place among the twelve disciples. In that we also agree with our friends. Four times the list of elected men is given in the Gospels; and, while the order of the twelve names varies in all other respects, Peter's name is invariably the first in all the lists, as Judas's name is as invariably the last. The difference is this: The New Testament recognises a certain precedency in Peter, whereas the Church of Rome claims for him an absolute supremacy. The truth is this. The precedency and the supremacy that Peter holds in the Four Gospels was not so much appointed him by his Master; what supremacy he held was conferred upon him by nature herself. Peter was born a supreme man. Nature herself, as we call her, had, with her ever-bountiful and original hands, stamped his supremacy upon Peter before he was born. And when he came to be a disciple of Jesus Christ he entered on, and continued to hold, that natural and aboriginal supremacy over all inferior men, till a still more superior and supreme man arose and took Peter's supremacy away from him. We all have the same supremacy that Peter had when we are placed alongside of men who are less gifted in intellect, and in will, and in character, than we are gifted. Peter's gifts of mind, and force of character, and warmth of heart, and generosity of utterance—all these things gave Peter the foremost place in the Apostolic Church till Paul arose. But Peter, remarkable and outstanding man as he was, had neither the natural ability nor the educational advantages of Saul of Tarsus. His mind was neither so deep nor so strong nor so many-sided nor at all so fine and so fruitful as was Paul's incomparable mind. And as a consequence he was never able to come within sight of the work that Paul alone could do. But, at the same time, and till Paul arose and all but totally eclipsed all the disciples who had been in Christ before him, Peter stood at the head of the apostolate, and so leaves a deeper footprint on the pages of the Four Gospels at any rate, than any of the other eleven disciples.

John was intuitive, meditative, mystical. Philip was phlegmatic, perhaps. Thomas would appear to have been melancholy and morose. While Peter was sanguine and enthusiastic and extreme both for good and for evil, beyond them all. Peter was naturally and constitutionally of the enthusiastic temperament, and his conversion and call to the discipleship did not decompose or at all suppress his true nature; the primal elements of his character remained, and the original balance and the proportion of those elements remained. The son of Jonas was, to begin with, a man of the strongest, the most wilful, and the most wayward impulses; impulses that, but for the watchfulness and the prayerfulness of his Master, might easily have become the most headlong and destructive passions. "Christ gives him a little touch," says Thomas Goodwin, "of some wildness and youthfulness that had been in Peter's spirit before Christ had to do with him. When thou wast young thou girdest thyself and walkedst whither thou wouldest. But when thou art old, thou shalt stretch forth thy hands, and another shall gird thee, and carry thee whither thou wouldest not. Peter had had his vagaries, and had lived as he liked, and, Peter, says Christ to him, when thou art hung up by the heels upon a cross, there to be bound to thy good behaviour, see that thou, remembering what thou wast when young, show them thy valour and thy resolution when thou comest to that conflict; and Peter remembered it, and was moved by it.—2 Peter i. 14." Such, then, was Peter's so perilous temperament, which he had inherited from his father Jonas. But by degrees, and under the teaching, the example, and the training of his Master, Peter's too-hot heart was gradually brought under control till it became the seat in Peter's bosom of a deep, pure, deathless love and adoration for Jesus Christ. Amid all Peter's stumbles and falls this always brought him right again and set him on his feet again—his absolutely enthusiastic love and adoration for his Master. This, indeed, after his Master's singular grace to Peter, was always the redeeming and restraining principle in Peter's wayward and wilful life. To the very end of his three years with his Master, Peter was full of a most immature character and an unreduced and unbridled mind and heart. He had the making of a very noble man in him, but he was not easily made, and his making cost both him and his Master dear. At the same time, blame Peter as much as you like; dwell upon the faults of his temperament, and all the defects of his character, and the scandals of his conduct, as much as you like; I defy you to deny that, with it all, he was not a very attractive and a very lovable man. "The worst disease of the human heart is cold." Well, with all his faults, and he was full of them, a cold heart was not one of them. All Peter's faults, indeed, lay in the heat of his heart. He was too hot-hearted, too impulsive, too enthusiastic. His hot heart was always in his mouth, and he spoke it all out many a time when he should have held his peace. So many faults had Peter, and so patent and on the surface did they lie, that you might very easily take a too hasty and a too superficial estimate of Peter's real depth and strength and value. And if Peter was for too long like the sand rather than like the rock his Master had so nobly named him, the sand will one day settle into rock, and into rock of a quality and a quantity to build a temple with. If Peter is now too forward to speak, he will in the end be as forward to suffer. The time will come when Peter will act up to all his outspoken ardours and high enthusiasms. In so early designating the son of Jonas a rock, his Master was but antedating some of Simon's coming and most characteristic graces. His Divine Master saw in Simon latent qualities of courage, and fidelity, and endurance, and evangelical humility that never as yet had fully unfolded themselves amid the untoward influences round about his life. In any case, an absolute master may surely name his own servant by any name that pleases him; especially a Royal Master; for the Sovereign in every kingdom is the true fountain of honour. Whatever, then, may be the true and full explanation, suffice it to us to know that our Lord thus saluted Simon, and said to him, Simon, son of Jonas, thou shalt be called Cephas, which is, by interpretation, a rock.

Of the four outstanding temperaments then, Peter's temperament was of the ardent and enthusiastic order. And, indeed, a deep-springing, strong-flowing, divinely-purified, and divinely-directed enthusiasm is always the best temperament for the foundation and the support of the truly prophetic, apostolic, and evangelic character. For what is enthusiasm? What is it but the heart, and the imagination, and the whole man, body and soul, set on fire? And the election, the call, the experience, and the promised reward of the true prophet, apostle, and evangelist, are surely enough to set on fire and keep on fire a heart of stone. It was one of the prophetic notes of the coming Messiah's own temperament that the zeal of God's house would eat Him up. And there is no surer sign that the same mind that was found in Jesus Christ is taking possession of one of His disciples than that he more and more manifests a keen, kindling, enthusiastic temper toward whatsoever persons and causes are honest, and just, and pure, and lovely, and of good report; just as there is nothing more unlike the mind and heart of Jesus Christ than the mind and heart of a man who cares for none of these things. Let us take Peter, come to perfection, for our pattern and our prelate; and, especially, let us watch, and work, and pray against a cold heart, a chilling temper, a distant, selfish, indifferent mind.

Closely connected with Peter's peculiar temperament, and, indeed, a kind of compensation for being so possessed by it, was his exquisite sense of sin. We see Peter's singular sensitiveness and tenderness of spirit in this respect coming out in a most impressive and memorable way on the occasion of his call to the discipleship. Andrew was not an impenitent man. John was not a hard-hearted man. But though they both saw and shared in the miraculous draught of fishes on the sea of Galilee, Peter alone remembered his sins, and broke down under them, in the presence of the power and grace of Christ. "Depart from me, O Lord, for I am a sinful man." "No; fear not," said his Master to Peter, "for from henceforth thou shalt so catch men." Peter's prostrating penitence at such a moment marked out as the true captain of that fishing fleet that was so soon to set sail under the colours of the Cross to catch the souls of men for salvation. That sudden and complete prostration before Christ at that moment seated Peter in a supremacy and in a prelacy that has never been taken from him. And there is no surer sign of an evangelically penitent and a truly spiritual man than this—that his prosperity in life always calls back to him his past sins and his abiding ill-desert. He is not a novice in the spiritual life to whom prosperity is as much a means of grace as adversity. They are wise merchant-men who make gain in every gale; who are enriched in their souls not only in times of trial and loss, but are still more softened and sanctified amid all their gains and all their comforts both of outward and inward estate. Well may those mariners praise the Lord for His goodness whose ships come home sinking with the merchandise they have made in the deep waters. But still more when, with all their prosperity, they have the broken heart to say, He hath not dealt with us after our sins, nor rewarded us according to our iniquities.

It was Peter's deep and rich temperament, all but completely sanctified, that made Peter so forgetful of himself as a preacher, and so superior to all men's judgments, and so happy, to use his own noble words, to be reproached for the name of Christ. Can you imagine, have you come through any experience that enables you to imagine, what Peter's thoughts would be as he mounted the pulpit stairs to preach Judas's funeral sermon? Judas had betrayed his Master. Yes. But Peter himself; Peter the preacher; had denied his Master with oaths and curses. And yet, there is Peter in the pulpit, while Judas lies a cast-out suicide in Aceldama! 'O the depths of the Divine mercy to me! That I who sinned with Judas; that I who had made my bed in hell beside Judas; should be held in this honour, and should be ministering to the holy brethren! O to grace how great a debtor!' And again, just think what all must have been in Peter's mind as he stood up in Solomon's porch to preach the Pentecost sermon. That terrible sermon in which he charged the rulers and the people of Jerusalem with the dreadful crime of denying the Holy One and the Just in the presence of Pilate. While he, the preacher, had done the very same thing before a few serving men and serving women. You may be sure that it was as much to himself as to the murderers of the Prince of Life that Peter went on that day to preach and say, "Repent, therefore, that your sins may be blotted out; since God hath sent His Son to bless you, in turning away every one of you from his iniquities." The truth is, by this time, the unspeakably awful sinfulness of Peter's own sin had completely drunk up all the human shame of it. If they who know about Peter's sin choose to reproach him for it, let them do it. It is now a small matter to Peter to be judged of men's judgment. They sang David's Psalms in Solomon's porch; and that day Peter and the penitent people must surely have sung and said, "Wash me thoroughly from mine iniquity, and cleanse me from my sin. For I acknowledge my transgression, and my sin is ever before me. Restore to me the joy of thy salvation, and uphold me with thy free spirit. Then will I teach transgressors thy ways, and sinners shall be converted unto thee." And if preachers pronounced benedictions after their sermons in those days, then we surely have Peter's Solomon's-porch benediction preserved to us in these apostolic words of his: "Ye therefore beloved, seeing ye know all these things, beware lest ye also fall from your steadfastness. But grow in grace, and in the knowledge of our Lord and Saviour Jesus Christ, to whom be glory both now and for ever. Amen."

LXXVI

JOHN

John, fisherman's son and all, was born with one of the finest minds that have ever been bestowed by God's goodness upon any of the sons of men. We sometimes call John the Christian Plato. Now when we say that our meaning is that John had by nature an extraordinarily rich and deep and lofty and beautiful mind. John had a profoundly intuitive mind. An inward, meditating, brooding, imaginative, mystical, spiritual mind. Plato had all that, even more perhaps than John. But, then, Plato had not John's privileges and opportunities. Plato had not been brought up on the Old Testament, and he had only Socrates for his master. And thus it is that he has only been able to leave to us the *Symposium*, and the *Apology*, and the *Phædo*. Whereas John has left to us his Gospel, and his Epistles, and his Apocalypse. John has the immortal honour of having conceived and meditated and indited the most magnificent passage that has ever been written with pen and ink. The first fourteen verses of John's gospel stand alone and supreme over all other literature, sacred and profane. The Word was God, and the Word was made flesh. These two sentences out of John contain far more philosophy; far more grace, and truth, and beauty, and love; than all the rest that has ever been written by pen of man, or spoken by tongue of man or angel. Philo also has whole volumes about the Logos. But the Logos in Philo, in Newman's words, is but a "notion": a noble notion, indeed, but still a cold, a bare, and an inoperative notion. Whereas the Word of John is a Divine Person; and, moreover, a Divine Person in human nature; a revelation, an experience, and a possession, of which John himself is the living witness and the infallible proof. I have heard of him by the hearing of the ear, said Philo. But mine eyes have seen and mine hands have handled the Word of Life, declares John. And, with the Word made flesh, and set before such eyes as John's eyes were, no wonder that we have such books from his hands as the Fourth Gospel, the First Epistle, and the Apocalypse.

How did John sink so deep into the unsearchable things of his Master, while all the other disciples stood all their discipleship days on the surface? What was it in John that lifted him so high above Peter, and Thomas, and Philip, and made him first such a disciple, and then such an apostle, of wisdom and of love? For one thing it was his gift and grace of meditation. John listened as none of them listened to all that his Master said, both in conversation, and in debate, and in discourse. John thought and thought continually on what he saw and heard. The seed fell into good ground. John was one of those happy men, and a prince among them, who have a deep root in themselves. And the good seed sprung up in him an hundredfold. The first Psalm was all fulfilled in John. For he meditated day and night on his Master, and on his Master's words, till he was like David's tree that was planted by the rivers of water so that its leaf never withered, nor was its fruit ever wanting in its season. Meditate on Divine things, my brethren. Be men of mind, and be sure you be men of meditation. Mind is the highest thing, and meditation is the highest use of mind; it is the true root, and sap, and fatness of all faith and prayer and spiritual obedience. Why are our minds so blighted and so barren in the things of God? Why have we so little faith? Why have we so little hold of the reality and nobility of Divine things? The reason is plain—we seldom or never meditate. We read our New Testament, on occasion, and we hear it read, but we do not take time to meditate. We pray sometimes, or we pretend to pray; but do we ever set ourselves to prepare our hearts for the mercy-seat by strenuous meditation on who and what we are; on who and what He is to whom we pretend to pray; and on what it is we are to say, and do, and ask, and receive? We may never have heard of Philo, but we all belong to his barren school. The Lord Jesus Christ is but a name and a notion to us; a sacred name and notion, it may be, but still only a name and a notion. The thought of Jesus Christ seldom or never quickens, or overawes, or gladdens our heart. Whereas, when we once become men of meditation, Jesus Christ, and the whole New Testament concerning Him, and the whole New Jerusalem where He is preparing a place for us, will become more to us than our nearest friend: more to us than this city with all its most pressing affairs. Our conventional morning chapter about what Jesus did and said, and is at this moment doing and saying, will then be far more real to us than all our morning papers and all our business letters. Nor is this the peculiar opportunity and privilege of men of learning only. John was not a man of learning. John was described as an ignorant and unlearned man, though all the time he was carrying about in his mind the whole of the Fourth Gospel. My brethren, meditate on John's Gospel. Meditate on that which was not made without long, and deep, and divinely-assisted meditation. You may be the most unlearned man in this learned city to-night, and yet such is John's Gospel, and such is the power and the blessedness of meditation on it, that John will look down on you after your house is asleep to-night, and will say over you, as you now sit, and now stand, and now kneel with his Gospel in your hands—"That which we have seen and heard declare we unto you, that you may have fellowship with us; and truly our fellowship is with the Father and with His Son Jesus Christ."

Meditation with imagination. All that John writes is touched and informed and exalted with this divinest of all the talents. The Apocalypse, with all its splendours, was in God's mind toward us when He said, Let us make Zebedee's son, and let us make him full of eyes within. Do not be afraid at the word "imagination," my brethren. It has been sadly ill-used, both name and thing. But it is a noble name and a noble thing. There is nothing so noble in all that is within us. Our outward eye is the noblest of all our outward organs, and our inward eye is the noblest of all our inward organs. And its noblest use is to be filled full of Jesus Christ, as John's inward eye was. John did not write his Apocalypse without that great gift in its fullest exercise. And we cannot read aright what he has written without that same exercise. We cannot pray aright without it. We cannot have either faith or love aright without it. And just in the measure we have imagination, and know how to use it, we shall have one of the noblest instruments in our own hand for the enriching and perfecting of our whole intellectual and spiritual life. I do not say that the Book of Revelation is the noblest product of John's noble imagination. For, all that was within John, imagination and meditation and love, was all moved of the Holy Ghost up to its highest and its best in the production of the great Prologue to the Fourth Gospel. At the same time, it is in the Revelation that John's glorified imagination spreads out its most golden wings and waves them in the light of heaven. Only it will take both meditation and imagination to see that. But to see that will be one of our best lessons from this greatly-gifted and greatly-blessed apostle to-night.

And, then, as was sure to come to pass, the disciple of meditation and imagination becomes at last the apostle of love. At the Last Supper, and as soon as Judas had gone out, Jesus said to the eleven, "A new commandment I give unto you, that ye love one another. As I have loved you, that ye also love one another. By this shall all men know that ye are my disciples, if ye have love one to another." Eleven thoughtful and loving hearts heard that new commandment and the comfort that accompanied it. But in no other heart did that Divine seed fall into such good ground as in his heart who at that moment lay on Jesus' bosom. "Little children, love one another," was the aged apostle's whole benediction as the young men carried him into the church of Ephesus every Lord's Day. And when he was asked why he always said that, and never said any more than that, he always replied, "Because this is our Lord's sole commandment, and if we all fulfil this, nothing more is needed. For love is the fulfilling of the law."

LXXVII

MATTHEW

MATTHEW loved money. Matthew, like Judas, must have money. With clean hands if he could; but, clean hands or unclean, Matthew must have money. Now, the surest way and the shortest way for Matthew to make money in the Galilee of that day was to take sides with Cæsar and to become one of Cæsar's tax-gatherers. This, to be sure, would be for Matthew to sell himself to the service of the oppressors of his people; but Matthew made up his mind and determined to do it. Matthew will set his face like a flint for a few years and then he will retire from his toll-booth to spend his rich old age in peace and quietness. He will furnish a country-house for himself up among the hills of Galilee, and he will devote his last days to deeds of devotion and charity. And thus it was that Matthew, a son of Abraham, was found in the unpatriotic and ostracised position of a publican in Capernaum. The publicans were hard-hearted, extortionate, and utterly demoralised men. Their peculiar employment either already found them all that, or else it soon made them all that. "Publicans and sinners"; "publicans and harlots"—we continually come on language like that in the pages of the four Gospels. Well, Matthew had now for a long time been a publican in Capernaum, and he was fast becoming a rich man. But, over against that, he had to content himself with a publican's companionships, and with a publican's inevitable evil conscience. Matthew could not help grinding the faces of the poor. He could not help squeezing the last drop of blood out of this and that helpless debtor. His business would not let Matthew stop to think who was a widow, and who was an orphan, and who was being cruelly treated. The debt was due, it was too long overdue, and it must be paid, if both the debtor and his children have to be sold in the slave-market to pay the debt.

Jesus of Nazareth, the carpenter's son, knew Matthew the publican quite well. Perhaps, only too well. Jesus and His mother had by this time migrated from Nazareth to Capernaum. He had often been in Matthew's toll-booth with His mother's taxes, and with other poor people's taxes. Even if not for Himself and for his widowed mother, the carpenter would often leave His bench to go to Matthew's toll-booth to expostulate with him, and to negotiate with him, and to become surety to him for this and that poor neighbour of His who had fallen into sickness, and into a debt that he was not able to pay. The sweat of Jesus' own brow had oftener than once gone to settle Matthew's extortionate charges. "If he hath wronged thee, or oweth thee aught, put that to mine account. I, Jesu, the son of Joseph, have written it with mine own hand, I will repay it'—that would stand in Matthew's books over and over again, till Matthew was almost ready to sell the surety Himself. But by this time Jesus, first of Nazareth and now of Capernaum, who had been every poor widow's cautioner for her rent and for her taxes, had left His father's inherited workshop, and had been baptized by John into a still larger Suretyship. And thus it is that He is back again in Capernaum, no longer a hard-working carpenter, mortgaging all His week's wages and more for all His poor neighbours. But he is now the Messiah Himself! And Matthew in his toll-booth has a thousand thoughts about all that, till he cannot get his columns to come right all he can count. And till one day, just as He was passing Matthew's well-worn doorstep, a widow woman of the city, with her child in her arms, rushed up against our Lord, and exclaimed to Him: "Avenge me of mine adversary!" till she could not tell Him her heart-breaking tale for sobs and tears. And then, with that never-to-be-forgotten look and accent of mingled anger and mercy, our Lord went immediately into the publican's office and said to him: 'Matthew, thou must leave all this life of thine and come and follow me.' Matthew had always tried to stand well out of eyeshot of our Lord when He was preaching. He felt sure that the Preacher was not well disposed toward him, and his conscience would continually say to his face, How could He be? But at that so commanding gesture, and at those so commanding words, the chains of a lifetime of cruelty and extortion fell on the floor of the receipt of custom; till, scarcely taking time to clasp up his books and to lock up his presses, Matthew the publican of Capernaum rose up and followed our Lord.

Matthew does not say so himself, but Luke is careful to tell us that Matthew made a great feast that very night, and gathered into it a supper-party of his former friends and acquaintances that they might see with their own eyes the Master that he is henceforth to confess, and to follow, and to obey. What a sight to our eyes, far more than to theirs, is Matthew's supper-table to-night! There sits the publican himself at the head of table, and the erstwhile carpenter of Capernaum in the seat of honour beside him. And then the whole house is full of what we may quite correctly describe as a company of social and religious outcasts. An outcast with us usually means some one who has impoverished, and demoralised, and debauched himself with indolence and with vice till he is both penniless in purse and reprobate in character. We have few, if any, rich outcasts in our city and society. But the outcast publicans of that night were well-to-do, if not absolutely wealthy men. They were men who had made themselves rich, and had at the same time made themselves outcasts, by siding with the oppressors of their people and by exacting of the people more than was their due. And they were, as a consequence, excommunicated from the Church, and ostracised from all patriotic and social and family life. What, then, must the more thoughtful of them have felt as they entered Matthew's supper-room that night and sat down at the same table with a very prophet, and some said—Matthew himself had said it in his letter of invitation—more than a prophet. And, then, all through the supper, if He was a prophet He was so unlike a prophet; and, especially, so unlike the last of the prophets. He was so affable, so humble, so kind, so gentle, with absolutely nothing at all in His words or in His manner to upbraid any of them, or in any way to make any of them in anything uneasy. They had all supped with Matthew before, but that was the first night for many years that any man with any good name to lose had broken bread at the publican's table. He had given suppers on occasion before, but Jesus had never been invited, nor Peter, nor James, nor John. And it was the presence of Jesus and His disciples that night that led to the scene which so shines on this page of the New Testament. For there were Pharisees in Capernaum in those days, just as there were publicans and sinners. And just as the publicans were ever on the outlook for more money; and just as the sinners were ever on the outlook for another supper and another dance; so the Pharisees were ever on the outlook for a fresh scandal, and for something to find fault with in their neighbours. "Why eateth your Master with publicans and sinners?" the Pharisees of Capernaum demanded of Jesus' disciples. And the disciples were still too much Pharisees themselves to be able to give a very easy answer to that question. But Jesus had his answer ready. Grace was poured into His lips at that opportune moment till He replied: "They that be whole need not a physician, but they that are sick. I came not to call the righteous, but sinners to repentance." Long years afterwards, when Matthew was writing this autobiographic passage in his Gospel, the whole scene of that supper-party rose up before him like yesternight. 'Jesus, now in glory,' he said to himself, 'was sitting here, as it were. James and John there. Myself at the door, divided between welcoming my old companions and warning them off. Some Pharisees from the synagogue are coming up with their lamps. Then their loud and angry voices; and then His voice with more pity in it than anger, calling sinners to repentance.' It was a night to be remembered by Matthew.

When Matthew rose up and left all and followed our Lord, the only thing he took with him out of his old occupation was his pen and ink. And it is well for us that he did take that pen and ink with him, since he took it with him to such good purpose. For, never once did our Lord sit down on a mountain side or on a sea-shore to teach His disciples; never once did He enter a synagogue and take up the Prophets or the Psalmists to preach; never once did He talk at any length by the way, that Matthew was not instantly at His side. Till Matthew came to be known not so much as Matthew the disciple, or as the former publican of Capernaum, but rather as that silent man with the sleepless pen and ink-horn. It needed a practised, and an assiduous, and an understanding pen to take down the Sermon on the Mount, and to report and arrange the parables, and to seize with such correctness and with such insight the terrible sermons of his Master's last week of preaching. But Matthew did all that, and we have all that to this day in his Gospel. The bag would have been safe, and it would have been kept well filled, in Matthew's money-managing hands, but Matthew had far more important matters than the most sacred money matters to attend to. What a service, above all price, were Matthew's hands ordained to do as soon as his hands were washed from sin and uncleanness in the Fountain opened in that day! What a service it was to build that golden bridge by which so many of his kinsmen according to the flesh at once passed over into the better covenant, the Surety of which covenant is Christ! "The Gospel according to St. Matthew: the Book of the generation of Jesus Christ, the son of David, the son of Abraham." "Saintliness not forfeited by the penitent," is the title of one of our finest English sermons, and, it may here be added, neither is service.

"And Matthew the *publican.*" Now, we would never have known that but for Matthew himself. Neither Mark, nor Luke, nor John, nor Paul ever calls Matthew by that bad name. It is Matthew himself alone who in as many words says to us, "Come, all ye that fear God, and I will tell what He has done for my soul." It is Matthew himself alone who publishes and perpetuates to all time his own infamy. Ashamed of himself, both as a publican and an apostle, till he cannot look up, the text is the only footprint of himself that St. Matthew leaves behind him on the sands of Scripture. Our first Gospel is his holy workmanship, and this text, so deeply imbedded into it, is the sure seal of its author's Christian temper and Apostolic character. "Position and epithet are indicative both of natural humility and modesty, as well as of evangelical self-abasement."

"They that be whole need not a physician, but they that are sick." Happy intrusion, and fortunate fault-finding of the Pharisees which ended in these ever-blessed words of our Saviour! And then, these words also: "I am not come to call the righteous, but sinners to repentance." Sick and sinful men, do you hear that? Are you truly and sincerely sick with sin? Then He who has made you sick will keep you sick till you come to Him to heal you. Are you a sinner with an evil life holding you like a chain in a cruel, an unclean, a hopeless bondage? Then—

He comes! the prisoners to relieve,
In Satan's bondage held;
The gates of brass before Him burst,
The iron fetters yield.

He comes! from darkening scale of vice
To clear the inward sight;
And on the eyeballs of the blind
To pour celestial light.

He comes! the broken hearts to bind,
The bleeding souls to cure:
And with the treasures of His grace
T' enrich the humble poor.

Are you that prisoner? Are you held in Satan's bondage? Is your inward sight clogged up with the scales of vice? Is your heart broken? And is your very soul within you bleeding? Are you a publican? Are you a sinner? Are you a harlot? Look at Matthew with his Gospel in his hand! Look at Zacchæus restoring fourfold! Look at Mary Magdalene, first at the sepulchre. Look unto Me, their Saviour says to thee also: Look unto Me, and be thou saved also. And so I will!

Thy promise is my only plea,
With this I venture nigh:
Thou callest burden'd souls to Thee,
And such, O Lord, am I.

LXXVIII

ZACCHÆUS

THERE was a soft spot still left in Zacchæus's heart, and that soft spot was this: Zacchæus was as eager as any schoolboy in all Jericho to see Jesus who He was. And like any schoolboy he ran before and climbed up into a sycamore tree to see Jesus, for He was to pass that way. And simple things like that, childlike and schoolboy-like things like that, always touched our Lord's heart. Of such is the kingdom of Heaven, He was wont to say when He saw simplicity like that, and self-forgetfulness, and naturalness, and impulsiveness, or anything else that was truly childlike. We would not have done what Zacchæus did. We are too stiff. We are too formal. We have too much starch in our souls. Our souls are made of starch, just as Bishop Andrewes's soul was made of sin. But starch is more deadly than sin. Your soul may be saved from sin, but scarcely from starch. "Curiosity and simplicity," says Calvin, "are a sort of preparation for faith. Nay, it was not without a certain inspiration from heaven that Zacchæus climbed up into that sycamore tree. There was a certain seed of true piety in his heart when he so ran before the press, and so climbed up into that sycamore tree," so says on this subject the greatest of all the commentators upon it.

Had our Lord considered public opinion He would have looked straight before Him when He came to that sycamore tree, and would not have let His eyes lift till He was well past Zacchæus's perch. But our Lord was as simple and as natural and as spontaneous that day as Zacchæus was himself. Our Lord paid no attention to the prejudices or to the ill-will of the populace. The more ground there was for their prejudices and their ill-will the more reason there was to Him why He should stop under Zacchæus's tree and call him to come down. The windows and the walls and the roofs of Jericho were all loaded with sightseers that day, but our Lord did not stop under any of them. It was at Zacchæus's sycamore tree alone that our Lord stopped and looked up and said: "Zacchæus, make haste and come down, for to-day I must abide at thy house." All Zacchæus's past life, all his real blamefulness, all the people's just and unjust prejudices, and all the bad odour of Zacchæus's class, it all did not for one moment turn our Lord away from Zacchæus's house. Had our Lord asked Himself—What will the people think and say, He would not have imperilled His popularity in Jericho by sitting at the tax-gatherer's table. But one of our Lord's absolute rules of life and conduct was to make Himself at all times and in all places of no reputation. And thus it was that the thought of how Jericho would take it never for one moment entered our Lord's mind. Not for years had any man who wished to stand well with the people so much as crossed Zacchæus's threshold. Zacchæus, with all his riches, was a very lonely man. He was a well-hated and a universally-avoided man. And thus it was that our Lord's conduct that day towards him completely overcame Zacchæus. He could not believe his own eyes and ears. That this great Prophet, whose face he had been so breathless to see, should actually stop and call his name, and invite Himself to his house, and that He should actually be walking with him back to his house! Zacchæus was well-nigh beside himself with amazement and with delight. That halt under the sycamore tree, that summons of our Lord, that walk back together through the astonished and angry streets, and then the supper and the conversation over it and after it—all that entered into and at last completed Zacchæus's salvation. Are you a minister, or an elder, or a missionary, or a district visitor? Then, sometimes, invite yourself to the hospitality of the poor, and the outcast, and the sunken, and the forlorn. Knock civilly at their door. Ask the favour of a chair and a cup of cold water. Join them in their last crust. And see if salvation does not from that day begin to come to that house also.

I cannot get it out of my mind the deep share that Matthew the publican must have had in the conversion of Zacchæus. You remember all about Matthew. How he was sitting in his toll-booth one day when Jesus came up to him and said: "Follow me." And how Matthew left all and followed Him. And how Matthew made Him a great feast, and how the scribes and Pharisees found fault, and said to the disciples, Why do ye eat and drink with publicans and sinners? And especially, you can never forget our Lord's golden answer: "They that are whole need not a physician, but they that are sick." Well, do you not think that Matthew must have had an intense interest in Zacchæus that night? Even if the eleven supped and lodged elsewhere in the city that night, our Lord would be sure to take Matthew with Him in order to encourage and to advise Zacchæus. When two members of any craft come together you know how they draw to one another and forget the presence of all the rest, there is such a freemasonry and brotherhood between them. They have so many stories to tell, experiences to compare, confessions to make, and confidences to share, that those who are not of the same occupation know nothing about. It is now going on to three years that Matthew has been a disciple, but it is like yesterday to him to look back to his receipt of custom. And when Jesus suddenly stopped under the sycamore tree that day and said, Zacchæus, come down, and when Zacchæus dropped that moment at our Lord's feet, no one's heart in all the crowd went out to the trembling little tax-gatherer like Matthew's heart. And all that night the two publicans had scarcely broken ground on all they had to tell one another. 'If He calls you to leave all and follow Him, you must do it at once. You will never repent it. You have no idea of Him. What a man He is, and what a master; and, how it is all to end, God only knows. But if He invites you to join us, I beseech you not to hesitate for one moment.' 'Tell me all about yourself,' said Zacchæus. 'What did He say to you? And how did you manage to cut off, and leave for ever behind you, the work and the wealth of your whole life so soon and so completely?' And Matthew told Zacchæus all we know, and far more that we need not listen to, for we would not understand it. Till, what Zacchæus stood forth and said next morning before our Lord, and before all Jericho, was fully as much at Matthew's instance and dictation as at Zacchæus's own repentance and resolution. 'Behold, Lord, I have made up my mind overnight, and I wish you and all men to know it—the half of my goods I give to the poor; and if I have taken anything from any man by false accusation, I restore him fourfold. 'Brave little gentleman! By that noble speech of thine thou hast added more than many cubits to thy stature! Thy bodily presence, say they, is weak, and thy height contemptible; but all thine after life will be weighty and powerful!

"It is a determined rule in divinity," says a great divine, "that our sins can never be pardoned till we have restored that which we unjustly took away, or which we wrongfully detain. And this doctrine, besides its evident and apparent reasonableness, is derived from the express words of Scripture, which reckons restitution to be part of repentance, and necessary to the remission of sins. For these are the determined words of Scripture—If the wicked restore the pledge, and give again that he hath robbed, and walk in the statutes of life, without committing iniquity, he shall live; he shall not die. None of his sins that he hath committed shall be mentioned unto him; he hath done that which is lawful and right, he shall surely live."

LXXIX

LAZARUS

Lazarus of Bethany comes as near to Jesus of Nazareth, both in his character, and in his services, and in his unparalleled experiences, as mortal man can ever come. Lazarus's name is never to be read in the New Testament till the appointed time comes when he is to fall sick, and to die, and to be raised from the dead, for the glory of God. Nor is his voice ever heard. Lazarus loved silence. He sought obscurity. He liked to be overlooked. He revelled in neglect. You could have taken any liberty you pleased with Lazarus with the most perfect impunity. Our Lord and His twelve disciples often found where to lay their head in Martha's house as it was called. But where Lazarus laid his head at such times no one ever asked. The very evangelists pass over Lazarus as if he were a worm and no man. They do not give him the place of a man in his own house. But Lazarus never takes offence at that. 'He is a sheep,' said the men and the women of Bethany. And so he was. For, when Jesus of Nazareth and His twelve disciples came to Martha's house, Lazarus hewed wood, fetched water, and washed the feet of the whole discipleship; and then, when they were all asleep, 'though he was the staff and sustentation of the family, he supped out of sight on the fragments that remained. All Bethany was quite right, Lazarus was a perfect sheep. They laughed him to scorn, they shot out the lip at him, and he never saw it. At any rate, he never returned it. Let Martha sweat and scold; let Mary sit still and listen; and let Lazarus only be of some use to them, that he would never believe he was, and that was Lazarus's meat and drink. So much so, that the world would never have heard so much as Lazarus's name unless the glory of God had been bound up with Lazarus's sickness, and death, and resurrection.

Our Lord hath this happiness, that He loved all men whether they loved Him or no. But there were some men that he loved with a quite special and peculiar love. And Lazarus was one of the most eminent of those men. But, even in our Lord's love to His friend, Lazarus is pushed back almost out of sight. Martha and Mary always come in before their brother in our Lord's love, as in everything else. This evangelist, that bare record according as he saw, had seen his Master's love to Martha and Mary many a time; but it was only now and then that he had the opportunity of seeing either Lazarus's love to his Lord, or his Lord's love to Lazarus. Lazarus loved his Lord far more than they all. But his love had this defect about it that it was a silent love. It was what we call a worshipping love. It was a wholly hidden love. Only, Lazarus's love could not elude His eyes Who knows what is in man without man testifying what is in him. And He so loved Lazarus back again, and so expected all His disciples to love Lazarus also, that He was wont to call Lazarus their universal friend. "Our friend Lazarus sleepeth," He said. For Lazarus by that time, for the glory of God, and for the glory of the Son of God, had fallen into a fatal sickness. And Martha had despatched a swift messenger to Bethabara beyond Jordan to summon Him and to say, Lord, he whom Thou lovest is sick. 'Trouble not the Master,' Lazarus had said to his sister in his sickness. 'The Jews of late sought to stone Him, and wouldest thou bring Him hither again?' And with a great shame and a great pain at himself for so troubling his sister and his Master, and with a great hunger in his heart for his Father's house in heaven, Lazarus turned his face to the wall and fell asleep.

Lazarus is altogether left out by us as we read this heavenly chapter. We leave out Lazarus in glory even more completely than he was left out by all men in this life. We leave out of this chapter heaven itself also as much as if we were all Sadducees. And not till we have our eyes opened to the ascended Lazarus, and to his throne in glory, will we ever read this magnificent chapter aright, or at all aright understand why in all the world Jesus should groan and weep all the way to where Lazarus's dead body lay and decayed in the grave. Our Lord did not leave Lazarus out. No, nor his glory either. Our Lord knew what He was on His way to do, and He took to heart what He was on His way to do, and it repented Him to a groaning that could not be uttered, to work His last miracle for the awakening of Jerusalem at such a cost to Lazarus. He knew all the time how it would all end. He knew what Caiaphas would say. And He knew what Judas and Pilate and Herod and the people would do. And He groaned in His spirit because He so clearly foresaw that His friend Lazarus, like Himself, was to be such a savour of death in them that perish, and at such a price to Lazarus.

So o'er the bed where Lazarus slept,
He to His Father groan'd and wept:
What saw He mournful in that grave,
Knowing Himself so strong to save?

The deaf may hear the Saviour's voice,
The fetter'd tongue its chain may break,
But the deaf heart, the dumb by choice,
The laggard soul that will not wake,
The guilt that scorns to be forgiven:—
These baffle e'en the spells of Heaven:
In thought of these, His brows benign,
Not even in healing cloudless shine.

Jesus wept. Yes: and if you saw a friend of yours in glory, and then saw also that he was to be summoned to lay aside his glory and to return to be a savour of death to so many of your fellow-citizens, you could not but weep also. Even if you knew that it was the will of God, and for the glory of the Son of God, your friend was coming, you could not but weep. And our Lord wept because Lazarus, who had been but four days in glory, was to be summoned to lay aside his glory and to return to this world of sin and death, and that on such an errand; an errand, as it would issue, of exasperation and final hardness of heart to his enemies. Chrysologus, the Chrysostom of Ravenna, has it: "When our Lord was told of Lazarus's death He was glad; but when He came to raise him to life, He wept. For, though His disciples gained by it, and though Martha and Mary gained by it, yet Lazarus himself lost by it, by being re-imprisoned, re-committed, and re-submitted to the manifold incommodities of this life."

"This last and greatest of His miracles was to raise our Lord much estimation," says the distinguished John Donne, "but (for they always accompany one another) it was to raise both Him and Lazarus much envy also." And I will always believe that the sight of Lazarus's share in this terrible tragedy mingled with the sight of His own share. Dante wept when he saw that he had to return to envious Florence from the charity of Paradise, even though it was to compose *The Commedia* for God and for the world. And Teresa has it that Lazarus entreated his Master not to summon him back to this life for any cause whatsoever. But it was to be to Lazarus as it was to be to his Master, and that is enough. "Now is my soul troubled: and what shall I say? Father, save me from this hour; but for this cause came I unto this hour. Father, glorify Thy name."

And thus it was that scarcely had Lazarus sat down in his Father's house: he had not got his harp of gold well into his hand: he had not got the Hallelujah that they were preparing against the Ascension of their Lord well into his mouth, when the angel Gabriel came up to where he sat, all rapture through and through, and said to him: 'Hail! Lazarus: highly honoured among the glorified from among men. Thy Master calls up for thee. He has some service for thee still to do for Him on the earth.' And the sound of many waters fell silent for a season as they saw one of the most shining of their number rise up, and lay aside his glory, and hang his harp on the wall, and pass out of their sight, and descended to where their heavenly Prince still tarried with His work unfinished. And Lazarus's soul descended straightway into that grave, where for four days his former body had lain dead, and towards which our Lord was now on His way. And the first words that Lazarus heard were these, and the voice that spake was the voice of his former Friend—"Father, I thank Thee that Thou hast heard me. And I knew that Thou hearest me always. Lazarus, come forth." And he that was dead came forth bound hand and foot with grave clothes; and his face was bound about with a napkin. And Jesus wept at the contrast between heaven and earth, and said, "Loose him and let him go." Just where did Lazarus go? Like himself, he no doubt hid himself till his Master would not eat till Lazarus was called. For they made our Lord a supper again in those days, and Martha served again, and Lazarus this time was one of them that sat at the table with Him. But the chief priests consulted that they might put Lazarus also to death: because that by reason of him many of the Jews went away and believed on Jesus.

Whether they carried out their counsel and put Lazarus to death the second time we are not told. The evangelist to whom we owe Lazarus had not room within his limits to tell us any more about Lazarus. But a post-canonical author had these entries in his Arabic diary, which I will faithfully copy out for your satisfaction about Lazarus. The entries are abrupt, and unfinished, and broken off, and sometimes quite unintelligible, as you will see. 'The man had something strange and unearthly in the look of him.' 'He eyed the world like a child.' 'He was obedient as a sheep, and innocent as a lamb.' 'He let them talk.' 'A word, a gesture, a glance from a child at play, or in school, or even in its sleep, would startle him into an agony.' 'His heart and brain moved there, his feet stay here.' 'Often his soul springs up into his face.' 'The special marking of the man is prone submission to the will of God.' 'He merely looked with his large eyes on me.' 'He loves both old and young; able and weak; he affects the very brutes, and birds, and flowers of the field.' 'The man is harmless as a lamb, and only impatient at ignorance and sin.' You can construct for yourselves out of these authentic fragments what Lazarus's second life was as long as the chief priests let him alone.

God's great demands that He sometimes makes on His great saints, is the great lesson that Lazarus teaches us. As, also, that great lowliness of mind, and great meekness, and great self-surrender, is our greatest saintliness. And, accordingly, that God made His greatest demands on His own lowly-minded Son, the meekest and the most self-emptied of all men. And, after Him, on Lazarus the friend of His Son. A demand on Lazarus that made his divine Friend mourn and weep for him, as he came down to earth to comply with the demand. Lazarus was the most lamb-like of men in all the New Testament, next to the Lamb Himself; and his services and his experiences were, if after a long interval, yet not at all unlike the services and the self-surrenders and the self-emptyings of His Master. For Lazarus also laid aside his glory.

Now, God's work in this world demands this very same meekness, and lowly-mindedness, and self-emptiness, and laying aside of our own glory, from some men among us every day. And God's work stands still in our hands, and all around us, just because He has no men like-minded with Jesus of Nazareth and Lazarus of Bethany. Who will offer themselves to take up the kenotic succession? Some humiliation, some self-emptying, some surrender, as of heaven itself in exchange for earth, may be demanded of you as your contribution to the glory of God, and to the glory of the Son of God. Something that will make your best friends groan and weep for you, as Lazarus's best friend groaned and wept for him. Yes; God may have as terrible a service to ask of you, when you are ready for it, as when He asked His own Son to go down to Bethlehem, and to Nazareth, and to Gethsemane, and to Calvary. Some self-emptying and self-sacrifice like that He asked of the glorified Lazarus also, when He sent him back to Bethany which was so nigh unto Jerusalem. Are you able? Are you ready? Are you willing to be made able and ready? Let your answer be the answer of Jesus of Nazareth, and of Lazarus of Bethany: "Lo, I come. In the volume of the book it is written of me, I delight to do Thy will, O my God: yea, Thy law is within my heart."

LXXX

THE WOMAN WITH THE ISSUE OF BLOOD

OUR Lord was on His way to raise the ruler's little daughter from the dead. Now, this woman who overtook Him on the way was not actually dead like the ruler's little daughter, but she often wished she was, for she was worse than dead. She had tried everything for her deadly disease. There was not a physician far or near that she had not consulted as to whether he could cure her. She had spent all her living upon physicians, till to-day, she is beside herself with downright despair. And so am I. I am not dead, but I often wish I were. For I, too, am all my life sick to death. And I have tried everything. Every preacher, every author, every discipline, every medicine of the soul. And I am worse to-night than ever I was. I am in a strait betwixt two. I love my work more than ever. No man ever loved his family more than Martin Luther did, but all the time he told his hearers who had head enough and heart enough to understand him, that he had no real joy in his children because of his sin. And I, for one, am exactly like Luther in that.

But to return to the text. "And a certain woman, which had an issue of blood twelve years, and had suffered many things of many physicians, and had spent all that she had, and was nothing bettered but rather worse—when she heard of Jesus, came in the press behind, and touched the hem of His garment. For she said within herself, If I may but touch His clothes I shall be whole. And straightway the fountain of her blood was dried up, and she felt in her body that she was healed of her plague." Well, blood is blood; and blood is bad enough; but blood at its worst is not sin. Sin is SIN. Sin hath no fellow. Sin has no second, unless it is death and hell. Sin tries Christ Himself to His utmost, as this woman's bloody issue tried and found wanting all the best physicians in all the cities round about. Christ could cure a twelve year old issue of blood incidentally, and just by the way, as we say; ere ever He was aware He had healed that woman of her blood, but not for all her remaining life of her sin. All her days, you may depend upon it, she was nothing better of her sin, but rather worse. None of the three evangelists tell it, but it is as true as if they had all told it in the same words.

She followed Him about with her sin wherever He went. She went up to Jerusalem after Him with her sin. She was one of the women who were beholding afar off when He died on the tree for her sin. She often went out all her days to the Garden of Gethsemane, and lay all night on her face because of her sin. And sometimes at a passover season, and such like, she felt in herself as if she was going to be healed this time; but, before the sun set, she was worse with her secret sinfulness than ever. And, till her innermost soul ran pure sin day and night, and would not be staunched of heaven or earth. And all that is our own very exact case to a scriptural parable. Long after we have sold all to win Christ; long after He has begun at times to shed abroad all that He has promised to shed abroad in our heart; long after that we will still be nothing better, but infinitely far worse. One stolen touch was sufficient for an issue of blood; but a long and close lifetime of absolute clasp of Christ will not heal us of our sin. Oh, the malice of sin! Oh, the height, and the depth, and the hold, and the absolute incurableness, of sin! Only, with all that we must not despair. We must not go back. We must not give over. Even if it is incurable, let us not say so. It is; but let us not say it even within ourselves. Let us be like this bleeding woman. To-night, put out your hand and touch Christ. Never mind the gaping crowd pressing behind and before on Him and on you. They are nothing to you, and you are nobody to them. Never mind what they do, or do not do. They are not bleeding to death like you, and they are no rule to you. They did not come up here to-night on your errand. You are as good as dead, and this may be your last chance of Christ. Make a grasp at Him. Make a great grasp, however unceremonious and desperate, at the hem of His garment. Actually stretch out your hand where you now sit, and the stretch of your hand will sacramentally help your heart. Never mind the people in the same seat staring at you, and thinking you are mad. So you are, and you need not sit and look as if you were not. Never mind that you have not all your days till to-night so much as once touched Christ by faith. This woman had suffered enough to drive her beside herself for twelve years before she ever thought of the hem of His garment, and she went home that night healed of her plague. Press through, and grasp tight, and hold fast till you hear Him say, 'Somebody is detaining me.' And till you go home laughing in your guilty heart at your new-found peace and strength and joy. What a power you have, O sinner, and what an opportunity! "Somebody hath touched Me; for I perceive that virtue has gone out of Me."

And then, if you succeed in touching Him to-night, you must not do that once for all, and never again. You must touch Him every day; and if you will not call me extravagant, and carried away, I will say—Do the same thing every hour and every moment of the week. One thing all the week is needful. And that is to keep that hem firm in your hand. Even when you feel completely disenchanted of this scripture and this night and this house; even when you feel shame as you look back at your intensity to-night; even when you feel that this woman, and Christ, and this church, and the present preacher are all a piece of the same entire dream—still grope after His garment. Believe in Him and in His garment. Keep believing and keep praying when no one knows. Lift up your heart to Him even in the press of business, and among the cumber of the house, and week-day and all. And He will let down into your hand the hem of His High Priestly garment, all tingling with bells, and all laden with pomegranates, and all shining with strength and with beauty. And when again your evil heart runs with envy, and anger, and pride, and ill-will, and unkindness, and all the rest of the bad blood of hell,—all that the more grasp you at Him and at His garment. It is like the precious ointment upon the head, that ran down upon the beard, even Aaron's beard, that went down to the skirts of his garment: His grace and His salvation, that is. Here love runs down, and here joy in your neighbour's joy, and here sweetness of temper, and here humility of mind, and here goodwill, and here attraction to people, and here brotherly kindness, and all the rest of that holy oil.

The healing of His seamless dress
Is by our beds of pain;
We touch Him in life's throng and press,
And we are whole again.

Now, why was it, did you ever think, that when our Lord healed so thoroughly this woman's sick body, He did not in an equally immediate, and in an equally thorough way, heal her far more sick soul? Why did He stop short at her blood? Why did He not work a far better cure on her sin? Was it because she was not sick of sin? Was it because she had not come, with all those twelve years, to know the plague of her own heart? Or was it because He did not come the first time to this world with a full salvation? Or was it, and is it, because sin is such a mystery of iniquity that it takes not only both His first and His second comings to heal our souls of sin; but long time, and great labour, and great pain, and great faith, and great prayer on our part also, before even His Divine power can perform and pronounce a perfect cure? Yes, that is it. Be sure that it is. Even if this woman had come on a very much better errand than she did come; and with a far better kind of faith and love; even had she come as David and Paul and Luther came all their days; she would only have gone home to a more horrible pit in her own heart than ever, and to a more corrupt and abominable and burdensome body of death than ever, and to a loneliness that the happiest home in Canaan could not have comforted; to a lifelong death indeed, of which her twelve years' issue of blood was but a far off and feeble emblem. Did you ever read Richard Baxter's Reasons why the Rest that remains for the people of God is never entered on and enjoyed here? What a splendid debate that seraphic preacher holds with all those saints of God whose hearts are broken continually with an unalleviable pain and with an insatiable hunger after holiness. What depths, both in God and man, Baxter sounds on that great subject, and what heights he scales! O my brethren, be pleaded with to read almost exclusively the books that are pertinent to your sinful and immortal souls—such as *The Saint's Rest*. Listen to the great saints as they come together to tell and to hear from one another what God has done for their souls. And O, as many of you as are torn to pieces every day with the torture of sin, as well as covered with inward shame at the degradation and pollution of sin, keep yourselves in life by hope. You are saved by hope. Keep every day numbering your days, and forecasting that Great Day on which Christ shall come to you and shall make you perfect as He and His Father are perfect. Give reins to your imagination and think,—all sin for ever gone! Think of that! All sin gone clean out of your sinful heart for ever! I cannot believe it possible. All things are possible to me but that. I, for one, will not be the same man, if ever that crowning work of Omnipotence is wrought in me. I will not know myself, that it is myself. Now, nothing but sin and misery; and then, nothing but love, and holiness, and unspeakable blessedness. This horrible and loathsome incubus, myself, for ever cast off, and for ever cast down into the depths of hell, never to come up again. And I set free from myself for ever, and admitted to the New Jerusalem to walk with Christ and with His saints, in all the holiness and all the beauty of the Divine Nature! "Comfort ye, comfort ye my people, saith your God. Speak ye comfortably to Jerusalem, and cry to her that her warfare is accomplished, that her iniquity is pardoned. What are these which are arrayed in white robes? and whence came they? These are they which came out of great tribulation. And God shall wipe all tears from their eyes. And there shall be no more death, neither sorrow, nor crying, neither shall there be any more pain: for the former things are passed away. And He that sat upon the throne said to me: These things are true and faithful."

LXXXI

MARY MAGDALENE

THERE is a still unsettled dispute among New Testament scholars as to how many Marys there are in the Gospels, and then as to their identification. But our dispute will not be as to this Mary or that, but only as to ourselves. No, nor even as to who and what were the seven devils that at one time had made such a hell in Mary Magdalene's heart. Our whole dispute and debate shall be to let in some light from heaven on the bottomless pit of our own hearts, so as to scare out of our hearts some of the seven devils who still haunt and harbour there.

> Seven times
> The letter that denotes the inward stain,
> He on my forehead, with the truthful point
> Of his drawn sword inscribed. And, 'Look,' he cried,
> When enter'd, 'that thou wash these scars away.'

We do not know just what Mary Magdalene's seven scars were. But for our learning, Dante's own seven scars are written all over his superb autobiographical book. And Dante's identical scars are inscribed again every returning Fourth Day in Bishop Andrewes's *Private Devotions*. Solomon had the same scars also: "These six things doth the Lord hate. Yea, seven are an abomination unto Him." And, again: "When he speaketh fair, believe him not, for there are seven abominations in his heart." And John Bunyan has the very same number at the end of his *Grace Abounding:* "I find to this day these seven abominations in my heart." And then Bunyan is bold enough, and humble-minded enough, to actually name his scars for the comfort and encouragement of his spiritual children. Now, what are your seven scars? What are your seven abominations in your heart? What are the six things, yea seven, in your heart that the Lord hates? It is almost our whole salvation to ask and to answer that question. Because it is a law of devils; it is their diabolical nature, and it is a first principle of their existence and indwelling and possession of a man, that they never make their presence known in any man till he begins to name them and curse them and cast them out. He does not at all feel their full power, and the whole pain, and shame, and distress, and disgust of their presence till he is almost delivered from them. They rage and roar and tear and gnash our hearts to pieces when they begin to see that their time in us is to be short. But, till then, we are absolutely insensible to their very existence, either outside of us or inside. It was an old aphorism of the deep old divines, and they took it, if I mistake not, out of the deep old stoics: "All vices are in men; but all vices are not all extant in all men." As much as to say: 'All the seven devils are in every man's heart, but they do not all rage and rend equally in every man's heart: no, nor in the same man's heart at all times. The very devils have their times and their seasons like everything else.' Now, though Mary Magdalene is my text, it is of little real interest or importance to me who and what her seven devils were, unless in so far as that would cast some light in upon my own possession; yours and mine. But, on the other hand, if I have come by any means to know something of the terrible plague of my own heart, then, in that measure, I am a real authority as to the Marys of the four Gospels; and especially as to Mary Magdalene. To have grappled long, even with one inward devil, and to have had him at my throat day and night for years, and I at his—that is true New Testament scholarship. That throws a flood of light on all the Marys who followed our Lord about, and that makes Mary Magdalene a minister's own and peculiar field, and his specialised department of pulpit work. And the same inward experience is making not a few of my hearers far better genealogists, and harmonists, and exegetes, and demonologists, than all their teachers.

Pride, envy, anger, intemperance, lasciviousness, covetousness, spiritual sloth—these were Dante's seven scars on his sanctified head. I had a great dispute on the subject of Dante's scars the other day with one of the best Dante scholars in this country. He contended against me with great learning and eloquence that Dante's besetting sin was pride—a towering, satanic, scornful pride, to the contemptuous and complete exclusion of all possible envy. He had Dante on his side in one passage at any rate. I could not deny that. And I confess it seemed to me that Dante and he together had established the doctrine that any envy at all is absolutely, and in the nature of things, quite incompatible with such a lofty pride as that was which wholly possessed Dante's heart. Till, staggered, if not truly convinced, I gave in: so browbeaten was I between two such antagonists. But when I came to myself; when I left all books, the very best, about pride and envy, and when I was led again of God's Holy Spirit into the pandemonium that is in my own heart, I recovered courage, till, to-night, I have my harness on again to fight the battle of divine truth against any man, and all men, and even Dante himself. And the divine truth to me in this matter is this: That in my heart, if not in Dante's, both pride and envy have their full scope together; and that they never, in the very least, either exclude, or drink up, or narrow down, the dreadful dominion of one another. Now, what do you say to that? How is it with your heart? 'I have no books,' said Jacob Behmen. 'I have neither Aristotle, nor Dante, nor Butler, nor Brea, nor Shepard, nor Edwards; I have only my own heart.' You have none of these books either, but you surely have your own heart. Who, then, for the love of the truth, will so read his own heart as to take sides with me? Come away. Take courage. Speak out. Speak boldly out. You must surely know what pride is, and you must all know, still better perhaps, what envy is, and at whose payments and praises and successes and positions your heart cramps and strangles and excruciates itself. Do you not both know and confess all these things before yourself and before God every day? Do you not? O stone-dead soul! O sport and prey of Satan! O maker of God a liar, and the truth is not in you! I would not have your devil-possessed heart, and your conscience seared with a redhot iron, for the whole world. I would rather be myself yet, and myself at my worst, a thousand times, than be you at your best. Whether you are true enough and bold enough to be on my side or no, I shall not be so easily silenced in my next debate about these two devils. For a man is more to himself, on such inward matters, than the whole *Commedia* and the whole *Ethics* to boot, with all their splendid treasures of truth, and power, and experience, and eloquence. As I was saying, I have not the least notion as to who or what Mary Magdalene's seven devils were, and much less do I know how they could possibly be all cast out of her heart in this life. I do not know much, as you will see, about Mary Magdalene, but I would not give up the little knowledge I have of myself, no, not for the whole world. For what would it profit me if I gained the whole world of knowledge and everything else, and lost my fast-passing opportunity of having all this pandemonium that is within me for ever cast out of me?

I will confess it again: How the whole seven could possibly

be cast out of her heart in this present life, I, for one, cannot imagine; and I do not believe it. Complete, or all but complete, deliverance from two, say, of the seven I could easily believe, but the remaining five are quite beyond me. Two of the seven scars are on the surface. They are but skin-deep. Two of Dante's seven devils have their holes in the sand; in the soft earth and on the exposed outside of our hearts. Properly speaking, they are rather mole-heaps and rabbit-burrows than the dens of devils. Properly speaking, they are not devils at all. Till any man who is in any earnest at all can easily dig them out with a spade, and wring their necks, and nail their dead carcases up on the church door and be for ever done with them. But if you do that with those two it will only the more terrify and exasperate the other five. When the outposts of hell are stormed and taken and put to the sword, that only drives the real hell, with its true and proper devils, deeper down into their bottomless entrenchments. There are some wild beasts so devilish in their bite; they make their cruel teeth so to meet and lock fast in a man's flesh; that the piece has to be cut out if he is to be saved from their deadly hold. And the fangs of these five genuine devils must be broken to pieces in their heads with the hammer of God, and the flesh and bone into which they have locked their cursed teeth must be cut out and sacrificed before the soul is set free. And in this case the Surgeon with his hammer and his knife is Death, and the full science and success of his operations will not be all seen till the Resurrection morning. "Like as a lion that is greedy of his prey, and as it were a young lion lurking in secret places. Arise, O Lord! disappoint him, cast him down. As for me, I will behold Thy face in righteousness; I shall be satisfied, when I awake, with Thy likeness." It is better to enter into heaven with seven devils excavated out of our hearts as with a knife, than to have them gnawing in our hearts to all eternity.

Since ever there were women's hearts in this world, were there ever two women's hearts with such emotions in them as when Mary the mother of Jesus, and Mary Magdalene, stood together beside His Cross? Did you ever try to put yourself into His mother's heart that day, or into Mary Magdalene's heart? They stood and wept as never another two women have wept since women wept in this world, till John at Jesus' command took His mother away from Calvary and led her into the city. But Mary Magdalene still stood by the Cross. He dismissed His mother, but He kept Mary; she would not be dismissed, and she stood near to His crucified feet. All His disciples had forsaken Him and fled. And thus it was that there was no eye-witness left to tell us how Mary Magdalene stood close up to the Cross weeping, and how she did wash His feet with her tears, and did wipe them with the hairs of her head. And then, when He said, I thirst, how she took the sponge out of the soldier's hand and put it to His lips. When he bowed His head she saw Him do it, and she heard Him say, It is finished! It was not a place for a woman. But Mary Magdalene was not a woman; she was an angel. She was the angel who strengthened Him. She was the whole Church of God and ransomed bride of Christ at that moment in herself: she and her twin-brother, the thief on the Cross. How the next three days and three nights passed with Mary Magdalene I cannot account for her to you. But on the first day of the new week cometh Mary Magdalene early, when it was yet dark, unto the sepulchre. And Jesus saith unto her, Mary! She turned herself, and saith unto Him, Rabboni! Jesus saith to her, 'Touch me not with thy tears, nor with the hairs of thy head, nor with thy ointment.' And, had he not said that, she would have been holding His feet there to this day. And now that He has ascended to His Father's house, He is saying to His saints and to His angels to this very day the very same words that He said in Simon's house—"This woman since I came in hath not ceased to kiss my feet."

But the supreme lesson to me out of all Mary Magdalene's marvellous history is just the text: "He appeared first to Mary Magdalene, out of whom He had cast seven devils." As much as to say,—it was not to Peter, nor to James, nor to John, that He gave that signal favour and unparalleled honour. It was not even to His own mother. It was to Mary Magdalene. It was to her who loved Him best, and had the best reason to love Him best, of all the men and women then living in the world. While this world lasts, and as long as there are great sinners and great penitents to comfort in it, let Mary Magdalene be often preached upon, and let this lesson be always taught out of her, this lesson, —that no depth of sin, and no possession of devils even, shall separate us from the love of Christ. That repentance and love will outlive and overcome everything; as also, that there is no honour too high, and no communion too close, for the love of Christ on His side, and for the soul's love on her side, between them to enjoy. Only repent deep enough and to tears enough; only love as Mary Magdalene loved Him who had cast her seven devils out of her heart; and He will appear to you also, and will call you by your name. And He will employ you in His service even more and even better than He honoured and employed Mary Magdalene on the morning of His Resurrection.

Mary Magdalene! my sister, my forerunner into heaven till I come, and my representative there! But, remember, only till I come. Cease not to kiss His feet till I come, but give up thy place to me when I come. For to whom little is forgiven, the same loveth little. Give place, then; give place to me before His feet!

LXXXII

THE MOTHER OF ZEBEDEE'S CHILDREN

WHY does the Evangelist write the text in that round-about way? Why does he not write the text in his own simple and straightforward style? Why does he not simply say: Salome, the mother of James and John? I do not know for certain why the Evangelist writes in that ambiguous and intentionally obscure way, but I will tell you what I think about it. By the time that Matthew sat down to compose his Gospel, James, the eldest son of Zebedee and Salome, had already been a long time in heaven with Christ; and John, his brother, was a high and an honoured Apostle in the Church of Christ on earth. James had long ago drunk of Christ's cup and been baptized with Christ's baptism. While John was, by this time, as good as the author of the Fourth Gospel, and the three Epistles, and the Apocalypse. All the same, nay, all the more, John had not forgotten the sins and the faults and the follies of his youth; and, above all, he had not forgotten that for ever disgraceful day when he got his mother to beg the best throne for him and for his brother. That disgraceful day though now so long past was ever before John. And thus it was, as I think, that Matthew wrote in this round-about way about it. 'May my right hand forget its cunning,' said Matthew, 'before I bring back a single blush to that great saint of God! No enemy of Christ and of His Church shall ever blaspheme out of my book if I can help it.' And thus it was that this Evangelist took a garment, and laid it on his shoulder, and went backward, till he had all but completely covered up the sin of Salome and James and John. 'Blessed Antonomasiast!' exclaimed John, when he read this chapter of Matthew for the first time. 'Yes,' said John; 'all Scripture is indeed given by inspiration of the Spirit of God: and God is love!' And it was so certainly with this special Scripture. For Matthew's heart of love and honour for John had taken his inspired pen out of his hand at the opening of this passage till this stroke of sheltering style was struck out before the writer knew what he is doing. Dante is full on every page of his of this same exquisite device. Dante, indeed, is the fullest of this exquisite device of any of the great writers, either sacred or profane. But the Bible had this exquisite device, as it had all Dante's exquisite devices, long before he was born. And still the Bible is by far our finest education in morals, and in manners, and in love, and in letters, as well as in our everlasting salvation.

'Leave it to me, my sons,' said Salome; 'leave it to me. Do not be in any doubt about it. It will all come right. I am not to be His mother's sister for nothing, and I have not followed Him about all this time, and ministered to Him out of my substance, for nothing. Blood is thicker than water,' she said, 'and you, my sons, will see that it is so. Leave it to me. Who is Andrew? And who is Peter? And who is their father? And who is their mother, I would like to know, that they should presume to be princes over my sons? It shall never be! Leave it to me, my sons; leave it to me.' "Then came to Him the mother of Zebedee's children with her sons, worshipping Him, and desiring a certain thing of Him. And He said to her, What wilt thou? She saith unto Him, Grant that my two sons may sit, the one on Thy right hand and the other on the left, in Thy Kingdom." Well done, Salome! Well done! As long as this Gospel is preached this splendid impudence of thine shall be told of thee! 'Let the sons of all the other mothers in Israel sit, or stand, or lie as they like; only, let my two sons sit high above them all, and have their feet on the necks of all the ten.' Had Salome's presumption been less magnificent, our Lord would have been very angry at her. But the absolute sublimity of her selfishness completely overcame Him. He had met with nothing like it. The splendid humility of the Syrophœnician woman completely overcame Him, and now He is equally overcome with the splendid shamelessness of Salome's request. Her cold-blooded cruelty to Himself also pierced His heart as with a spear. This is the Monday, and He is to be betrayed on the Thursday, and crucified on the Friday. All the same, Salome went on plotting and counter-plotting for a throne for her two sons that only existed in her own stupid and selfish heart. And it was the sight of all this that made our Lord's rising anger turn to an infinite pity, till He said to her two sons: 'Are ye able to drink of My cup, and to be baptized with My baptism?' And what do you think the two insane men said? They actually said: "We are able!" In such sin had their mother Salome conceived them. In such stupidity of mind. In such hopeless selfishness, combined with such hard-hearted presumptuousness. And then, that it should be John! That it should be the disciple who had been chosen to such a coming sanctification and to such a coming service! That it should be John, who had been so loved, and so trusted, and so leaned upon, and so looked to! And at this time of day, that John should be so deep in this miserable plot. Our Lord often spoke about a daily cross. Well, that was His cross that Monday, and a very bitter cross it was. More bitter to His heart by far than all the thorns and nails and spears of next Friday. What a cup of red wine that miserable mother and her two sons like her, made our Lord to drink that day! 'O Salome,' He said, 'and O James and John her sons, you little know the baptism you are all baptizing Me with. But your own baptism, also, will soon come. And mine is at the door.'

A little imagination, with a little heart added to it, would have saved Salome and her two sons from making this shameful petition. Salome should have said to herself something like this. She should have said this, and should have dwelt on it, till it made her shameful petition to be impossible. She should have said: 'But Andrew, and Peter, and all the ten, have mothers like me. All their mothers are just as ambitious for all their sons as I am for mine. And they will feel toward me and toward my sons just the same suspicion, and jealousy, and envy, and hatred, and ill-will, that I feel toward them. And what would I think of them if they took advantage of their friendship with Christ, as I am taking advantage of my friendship with Him, in order to get Him to favour them and their sons at our expense? And what would I think of Him if He was imposed upon, and prevailed upon, to overlook, and neglect, and injure my sons, at the shameful plot of some of their mothers?' Had Salome talked in that way to her own heart; and, especially, had she brought up her sons to look at themselves and at all their fellows in that light; she would then have been as wise a woman as she now was a fool, and as good a mother as she now was a bad. Where had Salome lived all her days? What kind of a mother had she herself had? In what synagogue in all Israel had she worshipped God? Who had been her teachers in the things of God? What had she been thinking about all the time our Lord had been teaching and preaching in her hearing, as He did every day, about seeing with other people's eyes, and feeling with other people's hearts, and doing to other mothers and to their sons as she would have them do to her and to her sons? How could she have lived in this world, and especially in the day and in the discipleship of Christ, and how could she have borne and brought up her sons to be His disciples, and still be capable of this disgraceful scheme? Had she possessed one atom of experience of the world, not to say of truth and wisdom and love, she could never have petitioned for a place of such offence and such danger for her two sons. Even if Christ had asked it of her, she would have shrunk from exposing her two sons to the envy and the anger and the detraction of all the ten, and of many more besides. 'Employ my sons in Thy service,' she would have petitioned; 'but let it be in some secluded and obscure place. Make them Thy true disciples even to death; but, I do beseech Thee, if it be Thy will, hide them in the secret of Thy presence from the pride of men, and keep them secretly in Thy pavilion from the strife of tongues.' She would have kneeled and worshipped and so spoken if she had had a mother's eye and a mother's heart in her bosom. But instead of that, this cruel woman to her own flesh and blood was for exposing her two sons to every possible shaft and spear of envy, and anger, and ill-will, and injury. 'How great they will be, if I can help it,' the heartless creature talked to herself and said: 'What titles they will wear! What power they will exercise! And how all Galilee will hear of it, and how they will all envy Salome!' Till she said: 'Leave it to me, my sons; leave it to me.' And James and John left it to her, and they both knelt down beside her as she said: 'Lord, I have a certain thing to ask of Thee.'

It was our Lord's continual way to make Scriptures out of His disciples, and to have those Scriptures written and preserved for our edification. And He made this Scripture for us out of Salome and James and John and the ten; this solemn Scripture: "It must needs be that offences come, but woe to that man by whom the offence cometh!" Woe to Salome and to her two sons, that is, for she made herself a great offence to the ten that day. She would have been offence enough simply with her so-near relationship to Christ, and with her so-gifted and so-privileged sons. But not content with that, she must needs take and lay both her sons as sheer rocks of offence right in the way of the headlong ten. Just because she was His mother's sister; just because James and John were His cousins; she and they should have kept in the background of the discipleship, and should never have come out of that background but with tender and slow and softly-taken steps. But it will take all the tremendous disenchantment of the coming Thursday and Friday to bring James and John and the others to their sober senses. And oh! you who are not come to your sober senses yet, with all Salome's shame all written for that purpose,—what, in the name of God, is to bring you to yourself? Oh, born fools and blind, not to see what stumbling-stones and what rocks of offence you are to other men, just as they are to you! Not to see the broken bones that other men take from you, just as surely as you take the same from them. Salome could not help it that she was His mother's sister. And James and John could not help it that they were their mother's sons. And you may be as blameless and as innocent as they were in that, and yet you may be a stone of stumbling down to death and hell to many men around you. At every talent that has been committed to you; at every added talent that you make for yourself and for the Church and for Christ; at every sweet word of praise that sounds around your honoured name; at every step you are summoned to take up to higher service; there are men all around you eyeing you with an evil eye. It is the same evil eye, with the same javelin in it, that Saul threw at David. It is the same evil eye with which both Peter and Judas shot hatred that day at James and John. And all the time, and till the javelin sang past their heads and stuck fast in the wall just beyond them, the two besotted brothers were in uttermost ignorance of what they and their mother had done, and what they had led the ten into doing, and what shame and pain they had caused their clear-eyed and pure-hearted Master. And even had James and John got their two thrones, would they, do you think, have got one-thousandth part of the pleasure out of their thrones that Peter and the nine would have got pain? And your own cup of honour, and praise, and what not, is not half so sweet to you as it is bitter as blood to the Peters and the Judases who see it in your hand. There is nothing but the merest and the sourest dregs in your cup, but they who see it at your lips do not know that. "It is impossible but that offences will come; but woe unto him through whom they come!"

LXXXIII

THE WIDOW WITH THE TWO MITES

SHE was a widow. And she was surely the poorest widow in all the city that day. But she had this—that she was rich toward God, and that He was rich toward her. For she loved the house of God. She was another Anna. Only, Anna lodged in the precints of the temple, and departed not from the temple night and day, whereas this poor widow somehow and somewhere had an impoverished house of her own. "O God, thou art my God," she kept saying to herself all the way up from her own impoverished house with the two mites in her hand; "my soul shall be satisfied as with marrow and fatness; and my mouth shall praise Thee with joyful lips, when I remember Thee upon my bed, and meditate on Thee in the night watches." When one after another of her neighbours and her kindred railed on her for going up to the Court of the Women in her deep poverty, she answered them not again. Only, she did not turn back, nor did she lose hold of her two mites. "Two mites," says Mark, "make a farthing." She had no great temptation to let her left hand know what her right hand had intended to do. And thus it was that without once lifting her eyes off the temple steps she cast her contribution into the temple-chest, and passed on into the the temple to offer her morning prayer, and then went down to her own house. She had seen nobody, she had spoken to nobody, and nobody had seen or spoken to her. And she does not know to this day what we know. Nor will she know till that day when everything shall be known and made manifest. What would she have thought if she had been told Who had watched her that day, and what He had said about her, and that we would be reading about her to-night in this far-off island of the sea? As also that her two mites would multiply, all down the ages, into millions upon millions of gold and silver, the same Eyes still watching the process all the time? And what will she think and what will she say when all that is told from the housetop on that day about her, and about her two mites, by the Judge of all? And still He sits over against the treasury in this temple to-night, and calls unto Him His disciples among us, and says to us, 'Verily I say unto you also.' And as He sits and speaks to us, and points us to this poor widow, we lay to heart from Him many lessons.

In every department of merely secular finance money is just money. The Chancellor of Her Majesty's Exchequer does not care one straw what our feelings toward him and toward his office are when he sends us in our income-tax schedule. He does not interrogate us as to our political principles, or even as to our loyalty to the throne. Only pay your taxes promptly and he will not trouble you again till next year. But it was very different from that in those communities where Paul was the collector of the contributions of the apostolic churches. "Brethren," he wrote, "we do you to wit of the grace of God bestowed on the churches of Macedonia, who first gave themselves to the Lord. For ye know the grace of our Lord Jesus Christ, that, though He was rich, yet for your sakes He became poor. Therefore, see that ye abound in this grace also." And, as our Lord sat over against the thirteen chests in the temple that day, and all thirteen for the temple upkeep in one way or another, it was not the money so much as the mind of the contributors that He watched and weighed. And thus it was that this poor widow's mind weighed out for her this never-to-be-forgotten approval and applause of our Lord, "Verily I say unto you, that this poor widow hath cast more in than all they which have cast into the treasury." Because, as Paul has it, she had first cast in herself. That, then, is our first and fundamental lesson in all church finance. It is ourselves first; and then, after ourselves, it is our time, and our money, and our work. Two mites of mind and intention outweigh out of sight a million of mere money in the balances of the sanctuary.

"For if there be first a willing mind, it is accepted according to that a man hath, and not according to that he hath not." And thus it comes about that such a noble and ennobling equality is established in the Church of Christ. Why, our very Lord Himself, though He was rich, yet for our sakes had become so poor that the poor widow was richer than He was that day. He had absolutely nothing; not so much as two mites, to call His own that day. He had literally and absolutely nothing but a willing mind. And thus it was that He sat so near the treasury enjoying the sight of the liberality of those who had both the willing mind and money also. He had no money. He had only Himself. And as they cast in their money, He again cast in Himself. All the time the poor widow was coming up the street singing to her own heart the sixty-third Psalm, our Lord was sitting in the treasury singing to His Father the fortieth Psalm. "Sacrifice and offering Thou didst not desire. Mine ears hast thou opened; burnt offering and sin offering hast Thou not required. Then said I, Lo, I come. In the volume of the book it is written of me, I delight to do Thy will, O my God; yea, Thy law is within my heart." I have an ancient friend in this congregation who, also, has God's law in this respect within her heart. Like Paul's Macedonian saints she has very little more than a willing mind. She puts on her old bonnet once a year and is announced into my study with five shillings in her hand. Where she gets it I cannot imagine, but this is what she does with it. I have another fellow-communicant who calls on me annually with a pound But the five-shilling one touches me most For her little room looks to me when I visit it as if she had far more need, not of five shillings, but of five pounds every year either from me or from the poor's box. But she has always a clean chair and a cup of tea for me when I call to see her. "A shilling," she said to me the other day when she came on her annual errand, "for Armenia. A shilling for the Jewish schools in Constantinople. A shilling for the miners' mission. A shilling for the Zenana ladies. And a shilling, over and above Dr. Chalmers's penny a week, for the Sustentation Fund." I would be a brute if I refused to take it. I would have yet to learn the first principles of the grace of God if I were tempted to say to her to take it away and to buy coals with it. For all the coals in the bowels of all the earth would not warm her heart and mine; and, shall I not say it, her Master's heart, as her love for these causes of His warms His heart, and hers, and her minister's heart. A well-to-do worshipper sent to me a hundred pounds as a special donation, over and above the hundred he gives in monthly instalments to his deacon. For more reasons than the coming dividend in May I was mightily delighted with his noble and timeous donation. But the five shillings melted my heart far more. He who sits over against His treasury here also, will Himself tell you in your hearing that day what He has to say about these two, and all such princely minds. "That"—it was said by a great preacher in a land of vineyards and olive yards in illustration and in enforcement of this very same subject of a willing mind—"that which comes from His people at the gentle pressure of their Lord's simple bidding, comes as the fine and sweet and golden-coloured olive oil which runs freely from the fruit, almost before the press has ever touched it. That, again, is as the dark and coarse dregs, which is wrung out by the force of a harsh constraint at the last." "When I was in France," says Bacon, "it was said of the Duke of Guise that he was the greatest usurer in all the land, because he had turned all his estates into obligations; meaning that he had left himself nothing, but only had bound great numbers of persons in life-long indebtedness to him." It is not for the lip of mortal man to say it, but it is true, that Almighty God holds Himself under obligations to us all, corresponding to all the estates, great or small, that we have spent upon Him and upon His house. And if it is only the inward estate of a more and more willing mind, what usurers we are, and what an obligation will He acknowledge and repay!

Mutatis mutandis, as the Latin lawyers said; making all allowance, that is, for the immense change of dispensation and of all other circumstances, the thirteen temple-chests of our Lord's day were just the Endowment Funds, and the Augmentation Funds, and the Sustentation Funds of our own land and day.

There were special chests elsewhere in the temple for the poor, and for the education of the children of the poor, but the treasury chests over against which our Saviour sat that day were just the Deacons' Courts of our own Free Church and other churches. It is doing no exegetical or homiletical violence to this exquisite scene to transfer every syllable of it to ourselves as a congregation and a court. Indeed it would take some blindness of mind and some pulpit ineptitude to lead us past the outstanding lessons and applications of this delightful Scripture. For our own Sustentation Fund is just that very same temple treasury over again exactly. By means of those chests the temple worshippers by their daily and weekly and monthly and yearly contributions supported the priests, the doctors, the readers of the law, and all the other office-bearers of the sanctuary. And, like our Sustentation Fund also, all classes contributed to the support of the sacred house; from the rich among the people down to this poor widow. Just as with ourselves where some give to this one fund hundreds of pounds a year and others a penny a week. And then out of our great central fund an equal dividend is made every May to every minister of the Free Church, from John O'Groats to Maidenkirk. So much so, that wherever you see a Free Church door open on a Sabbath morning, in town or country, and the people flocking up to it, you have had a hand in opening that door, and in sustaining that minister, and in preaching the unsearchable riches of Christ, to that congregation. And if, under God's hand, you are such a widow that you have nothing to give to your deacon but a willing mind, and a word of God-speed, that is quite enough. You are a rich contributor and a true pillar of the Free Church. It is no irreverence, but only a becoming gratitude and love to say it, that as I sit at the head of the monthly table of our Deacons' Court I have something in my heart not unlike what was in His heart who sat that day in the treasury of the temple. As I see our deacons coming in and laying down on the table, one a few shillings, and another hundreds of pounds, like Him I rejoice at the sight, and a little like Him I hope, I give myself again to the service of God and to the service of His people. If you could all see, as I every first Monday of every month see, our splendidly-equipped and splendidly-managed Deacons' Court, the sight would both move, and inflame, and sanctify your heart also. Tens and twenties of the finest young fellows in the city; arts, law, medical, and divinity students; young merchants, young bankers, young advocates, young tradesmen,—all tabling the income of their districts, and all received with the applause of the elders sitting around. And if you could hear the treasurer's monthly report, and then the censor's so stringent monthly scrutiny, and then the thanksgiving psalms and prayers, you would give far more to this so sustaining and so sanctifying Fund than you have yet given. And you would see, not by any means to perfection, but to a certain honest approximation, what a modern treasury-chest of the Lord's house ought to be, and what it will yet be in every congregation in the coming days of the Church of Christ in Scotland. For it is not by any means the enormous wealth of this congregation that has given to Free St. George's its honourable place at the head of this honourable Fund. It is, I shall say it in your presence, the exceptional intelligence in church matters and in personal religion that has all along, with all its drawbacks, characterised Dr. Andrew Thomson's and Dr. Candlish's congregation. And, taken along with all that, its absolutely unique and unapproached Deacons' Court.

LXXXIV

PONTIUS PILATE

It was Pontius Pilate who crucified our Lord. But for Pontius Pilate our Lord would not have been crucified. In spite of Pontius Pilate our Lord might have been stoned to death before the palace of the high priest that passover morning. Or, lest there should be an uproar among the people, He might have been fallen upon and murdered when He was on His knees in the Garden of Gethsemane that passover night. The assassins of the city might have covenanted with Caiaphas that they would neither eat bread nor drink water till they had killed Jesus of Nazareth. The whole council of the scribes, and the elders, and the chief priests had finally determined that Jesus of Nazareth, one way or another, must be put to death; but, with all that, it was Pontius Pilate who put Him to the death of the cross.

Pontius Pilate was the Roman governor. He was the Roman procurator placed at that time over Judah and Jerusalem. He was Cæsar's representative and viceroy. What Tiberius himself was in Rome, all that Pontius Pilate was in Jerusalem. The Emperor Tiberius had made a special selection of Pontius Pilate, and had sent him east with special instructions to govern, with his very best ability, the very difficult province of Judea. Pilate's was a much-coveted post among his rivals in Rome, but he had not found it to be a bed of roses. For, as the Jews had been the hardest to conquer, so had they continued to be the hardest to hold down, of all the races that ever writhed under Cæsar's heel. The conquest of Jerusalem, and the military occupation and civil management of that city and the surrounding country, cost the Roman Empire far more men and far more administrative anxiety than all that Jewry was ever worth. But the Roman statesmanship was not to be baffled, nor were the Roman eagles to be chased out of Jerusalem, by that malignant remnant of the Hebrew race. And thus it was that a procurator of such sleepless vigilance and such relentless temper as Pontius Pilate was selected and sent out to mingle the blood of all Jewish insurrectionaries with their sacrifices. And it had demanded all Pilate's personal astuteness, and all his practised statecraft, and it had called forth no little of his proverbial cruelty also, in order to stamp out one outbreak of the insurgent Jews after another. Till it would be hard to tell which of the two was by this time the more exasperated at the other: Pontius Pilate at the rulers of Jerusalem, or the rulers of Jerusalem at Pontius Pilate. The rage and the revenge of the rulers of Jerusalem against Pontius Pilate burn to this day like the coals of juniper in the pages both of Philo and of Josephus.

But of all the problems and responsibilities that had arisen in his province during Pilate's procuratorship, nothing had so much perplexed him, nothing had put him so completely out of his depth, as this widespread and mysterious movement originated by John of Jerusalem, and carried on by Jesus of Nazareth. Pilate had often wished that he could detect one single atom of danger to the Roman domination in John or in Jesus, or in any of their disciples, or in any of their doctrines or practices. But, absolute wolf for Jewish blood as Pilate always was, he was not wicked enough nor wolf enough to murder an innocent man merely because he could not comprehend him.

'Divine and Most Illustrious Tiberius,' so ran one of Pilate's procuratorial reports about this time, 'all is quiet here. I have 'had my troubles with this insufferable and ungovernable 'people, but neither watchfulness nor firmness has been wanting 'on my part. Only, the former matter of Jesus the son of David 'still perplexes me. I sometimes wish that a wiser man than I 'am were in my place, so that he might better report to you 'about this mysterious movement among this people. Had this 'Jesus been an ordinary Jewish zealot, or an insurrectionary of 'an everyday order, my duty to my master would soon have been 'fulfilled. But, as a matter of fact, Jesus the Christ, as he is 'called, is worth more to my administration than any legion of 'my armed men. He is the most peaceable and inoffensive of 'men. I know what I say, for I have had him and his discipleship 'watched and reported on in all places and at all times. Not only 'so, but it was only last week that I determined to be a spy upon 'him myself, so perplexed was I with all that I had heard about 'him. I accordingly most effectually disguised myself, a thing I 'had never done before, and went to where he dwelt and told 'him that I had for long been a secret disciple of his. I am come 'by night, I told him, for fear of his enemies and mine. But 'instead of his royal descent from David, or his Hebrew Messiah-'ship, or any pretensions or expectations of his of any kind, he 'would speak to me about nothing and about no one—David 'nor Solomon, Cæsar nor Caiaphas—but only about myself. Jew 'or Roman, or whatever I was, I must be born again, he insisted. 'I must be baptized in Jordan, confessing my sins. Till I was so 'born again, I, like all men, loved the darkness rather than the 'light, because my deeds were evil. And, that the only way to 'know the truth, and to be sure of the truth, and not to be 'afraid or ashamed of the truth, was just to do my duty to the 'truth, and to do nothing else. And when I asked him why he 'did not leave this so untruthful and so unfriendly land, and go 'and open a philosopher's school about all these things in Rome 'or Athens or Alexandria, his only reply to me was that he was 'not sent but to the lost sheep of the house of Israel. And, then, 'his eyes and his hands as he dismissed me from his presence 'were absolutely the eyes and the hands of a king. I shall not lift 'a single finger against this "King of the Jews," as his disciples 'call him, till I am commanded by Cæsar so to do.'

Well, it was while Pontius Pilate's procuratorial despatch was still on its way to Rome that the case contained in it came to a head in Jerusalem. It was the morning of the passover, and it was still early, when Jesus of Nazareth, with His hands bound behind His back, was led up by the whole Sanhedrim to Pilate's judgment-seat. As soon as he had sat down on his seat of judgment Pilate demanded of the rulers of Jerusalem, "What accusation bring ye against this man?" They answered and said, 'If he were not a malefactor, and indeed deserving of the death of the cross, we would not have brought him before thee. We found this fellow perverting the people and forbidding the people to give tribute to Cæsar, saying that he himself is Christ a king, and the Son of God.' When Pilate heard that, he took the prisoner apart, and asked Him, "Whence art Thou?" Pilate's heart was made of Roman iron, and his Roman heart had never failed him before. But, altogether; what with all he had heard and seen of our Lord already; and what with all he heard and saw of Him that morning; Pilate's heart absolutely stood still as he ventured to put to Him the staggered question: "Whence art Thou?" And Pilate's secret fear became downright terror when his prisoner looked up at him with such eyes, but answered him nothing. It was at that very moment that Pilate's wife exclaimed to her husband: 'How dreadful is this Roman Prætorium to me this passover morning! Let us arise and return to Cæsarea! Have thou nothing to do with this just man, for I have suffered many things this whole past night in dreams and in visions because of him!' Just what shape her great sufferings had been all that night we are not told. She, too, may have had reports brought to her about the preaching of John and Jesus. She, too, may have had her spies set upon Him. She, too, may have had told her some of His tremendous sermons that very passover week. For all Jerusalem—from top to bottom—was ringing with those terrible passover parables of His. And, out of all that she had seen and heard and apprehended,—what sufferings may not have come to Pilate's wife in her divinely-ordered dream that so awful night? She may have seen the Son of Man coming in His glory, and all His holy angels with Him. And she may have seen the kings of the earth, and the great men, and the rich men, and the mighty men, and her husband among them, hiding themselves in the dens and in the rocks of the mountains: and saying to the mountains and the rocks, Fall on us, and hide us from the face of Him that sitteth on the throne. 'Have thou nothing to do with that just man,' she said, 'for I have suffered some fearful sights this night because of Him!' "Wife," said the gaoler of Derby, with a doleful voice, "I have seen the day of judgment: and I saw George Fox there, and I was afraid of him, because I had done him so much wrong, and had spoken so much against him in the taverns and the alehouses."

With all his heart would Pilate have fallen in with his wife's warning, had it been possible for him to do so. He did not need her urgent message. He knew far better than she did that the prisoner at his bar was a just man, and something more than a just man, but that only tied up Pilate's hands all the tighter. "Have thou nothing to do with that just man!" Yes; but how is Pilate to get rid of that just man, hunted to death as both that just man and his judge both are by those inhuman hyænas who fill the palace court with their bloodthirsty cries? 'Tell me,' was Pilate's despairing reply to his trembling wife; 'tell me how I am to wash my hands of this just man: tell me how I am to set him free, and at the same time to satisfy his enemies, who have both him and me in their power?' But as their clamour still went on Pilate caught at one of their cries and thought he saw in it a loop-hole for himself at any rate, if not for his prisoner. "He stirreth up the people from Galilee to this place!" they cried. Now, as Pilate's good planet would have it, who should be in Jerusalem that passover morning but Herod Antipas, under whose jurisdiction all Galilee was, and Jesus therefore, as a Galilean. And the tetrarch was vastly pleased with the unexpected recognition of his royal sceptre, when this Galilean prisoner was sent by Pilate to receive Herod's sentence on him. And all the more so, that Pilate and Herod had had so many quarrels together about this very matter of Herod's jurisdiction. But here is the Roman governor, in his own city, and at his own instance, recognising in the most open and handsome way the too-oft invaded rights and prerogatives of the king of Galilee. "And the same day," says the Evangelist, "Pilate and Herod were made friends together again." And made friends, as that poor fox little knew, at such a cheap price on Pilate's part! But Pilate was not so easily rid of our Lord as all that. Herod Antipas was more of a circus-master than a serious-minded monarch; and, instead of taking up the case that had been referred to his jurisdiction, all that Herod aimed at was to get some amusement out of the accused. 'He is the King of the Jews, is he? He is a candidate for my royal seat, is he? Then put the white coat of a candidate upon him, and send him back to Pilate. The Governor will enjoy my jest: and it will somewhat cement our recovered friendship!'

It is impossible for us to enter into all our Lord's thoughts as He was dragged up and down the streets of Jerusalem that passover morning. Dragged in cords from Gethsemane to Caiaphas, and from Caiaphas to Pilate, and from Pilate to Herod, and from Herod back again to Pilate. And all the time with all the shame and insult heaped upon Him that the evil hearts of His enemies could devise. Our Lord's thoughts and feelings at all times are a great deep to us. But Pilate was a man of like passions with ourselves, and we can quite well understand what his thoughts and his feelings were when the chief priests were back again with their prisoner at the prætorium. What is Pilate to do? With all his power and with all his diplomacy what is Pilate to do next? You all know what he did next. He put up Jesus to the vote of the people against Barabbas, trusting that the gratitude and the pity and the sense of fairplay among the common people would carry the day. But, difficult as it is to explain, they all suddenly turned round and cried out with one voice, "Away with Him! Away with Him, and release to us Barabbas!" "Why?" demanded Pilate, with indignation and exasperation, 'What evil has this man ever done? Neither Herod nor I have found the shadow of a fault in Him.' You have seen the vote taken at an election-time in your own city. And you have seen how ill-will, and envy, and personal spite are so much more active at such times than justice, and gratitude, and goodness, and truth. Ignorance, and prejudice, and pure maliciousness, will come out to the polling-booth on their crutches and will need neither your canvasser nor your carriage to come for them. "Not this man, but Barabbas!" cried the rulers of the Jews; and to a man the rabble of the people cried out with them, "Away with Him! Away with Him! Crucify Him! Crucify Him!"

Whatever the wicked spirit may have been that took possession of the populace of Jerusalem that awful passover morning, the Holy Ghost Himself witnesses to us that it was the wickedest spirit in all hell that had come up and had taken possession of Caiaphas and his colleagues now for a long time. And we knew it before it was told us. We have seen it coming all the time. And Pilate saw it that morning, and had seen it coming all the time, and had told Tiberius about it. Our Lord's life and teaching and wonderful works, and the multitudes that were attracted to Him by all that;—it would have been the New Jerusalem above, and Caiaphas would have been a sanctified saint in heaven, not to have had his heart burned up with envy within him at our Lord's popularity with the people. It is at this moment in the Passion Play at Ober-Ammergau that the chorus comes forward with this warning to us:

> 'Tis envy—which no mercy knows,
> In which hell's flame most fiercely glows—
> Lights this devouring fire.
> All's sacrificed unto its lust—
> Nothing too sacred, good, or just
> To fall to its desire.
> Oh! woe to those this passion sweeps
> Helpless and bound into the deeps!

Pilate had never heard of the Jerusalem that is above, but no man knew better than he did the Jerusalem that was yelling like all the furies all around him. Caiaphas had put on his holiest of masks that holiest of mornings, and he had demanded swift execution to be done on this traitor against Cæsar and this blasphemer against God. But Pilate was not a child. Heathen as Pilate was, and hardened as a stone in his heart as he was, he both saw down into, and despised and detested every high priest, and scribe, and elder of them all. It was a noble hyperbole that was put upon Plato's tombstone: "Here lies a man too good and too great for envy." But that literally true epitaph, and no hyperbole, could not have been written even on Joseph's new tomb as long as Caiaphas remained alive in Jerusalem. Our Lord Himself was neither too good nor too great for Caiaphas's envy and ill-will, nor for Pilate's selfish cowardice and open sale of truth and justice. For, all this time, with all his power, and with all his pride, and with all his astuteness, and with all his resource, the chain of his terrible fate was fast closing around Pontius Pilate. And his rage, and his pain, and his pride drove him well-nigh demented. Never, surely, since mortal man was first taken and held fast in the snare of Satan, was any miserable man more completely seized and carried captive of his past sins and his present circumstances, than Pontius Pilate was that passover morning. And it all came to a head, and the fatal chain was all riveted round Pilate for the last time, when the savage threat was spat up at him: "If thou let this man go, thou art not Cæsar's friend!" That was enough. For at that Pilate took water, in his defeat and despair, and washed his hands before the multitude, and said: 'I, at any rate, am innocent of the blood of this just person: See ye, his murderers, to it.' And they saw to it.

All that is not the half of the history of that awful morning to Pontius Pilate, and of all that he went through. But that is enough to set Pilate sufficiently before our eyes in the hour and power of his fatal temptation. And all that is told us in order that we may turn our eyes inward and ask ourselves what we would have done that passover morning had we been in Pilate's place; had we stood between the deadly anger of Cæsar at us on the one hand, and with only a just man to be scourged and crucified on the other hand! We would have done just what Pilate did. To protect ourselves; to stand well with our masters, and to preserve our paying post; we would have washed our hands, and would have scourged Jesus, righteous man and all. Who here, and in this hour of truth, will dare to cast a stone at Pontius Pilate? What self-seeking, what self-sheltering, what truth-selling, what soul-selling man?

O break, O break, hard heart of mine!
  Thy weak self-love and guilty pride
His Pilate and His Judas were:
  Jesus, our Lord, is crucified!

I know all the old legends, sacred and profane, about Pontius Pilate, and about his miserable end. But I shall not believe any of them. I shall continue to hope against hope for poor Pontius Pilate. If my sale of my Saviour, and of my own soul, has so often chased me up to the Cross of Christ, so I think Pilate's remorse must have chased him. And as he washed his hands in water that passover morning, so I shall hope he washed his hands and his heart ten thousand times in after days in that Fountain for sin which he had such an awful hand in opening. The world would not contain the books if all the names of all the chief priests, and scribes, and inhabitants of Jerusalem; and all the governors, and centurions, and soldiers of Rome, who came to believe on Christ crucified were to be written in them. "Ye men of Israel, hear these words: Jesus of Nazareth, a man approved of God, Him ye have taken, and by wicked hands have crucified and slain. And now, brethren, I wot that through ignorance ye did it, as did also your rulers. But unto you first, God, having raised up His Son Jesus, has sent Him to bless you, in turning away every one of you from his iniquities." Who can tell? With that glorious Gospel preached far and wide, and with the Redeemer's prayer offered with His own blood to back it on the Cross, Father, forgive them: who can tell? I, for one, shall continue to hope for Pontius Pilate, as for myself. For—

O love of God! O sin of man!
  In this dread act your strength is tried,
And victory remains with love:
  Jesus, our Lord, is crucified!

LXXXV

PILATE'S WIFE

Our men of natural science are able sometimes to reconstruct the shape and the size of a completely extinct species from a single bone, or splinter of a bone, that has been quite accidently dug out of the earth. And in something of the same way Pilate's wife rises up before us out of a single sentence in Matthew's Gospel. We see the governor's wife only for a moment. We hear her only for a moment. But in the space of that short moment of time she so impresses her sudden footprint on this page of this Gospel, that as long as this Gospel is read, this that Pilate's wife said and did that Passover morning shall be held in remembrance for a most honourable memorial of her.

Both Pilate and his wife, in Paul's words, were Gentiles in the flesh, being aliens from the commonwealth of Israel, and strangers from the covenants of promise, having no hope, and without God in the world. Both Pilate and his wife were perfect heathens, as we would say. They were still at what we would call the pre-patriarchal period of divine revelation. They were still very much what Abraham himself was when God chose him, and spake to him, and said to him, "Get thee out of thy country, and from thy kindred, and from thy father's house, unto a land that I will show thee." As regards many of the good things of this life; learning, civilisation, refinement, and such like; the Roman governor and his gifted wife were very far advanced; but as regards what our Lord estimates to be the one thing needful for all men, they were not unlike Terah, and Nahor, and Abram, when they still dwelt in old time on the other side of the flood, and still served other gods. Both Pilate and his wife were still at that stage in which God was wont to speak to men at sundry times and in divers manners; and, among other manners, in the manner of a dream. For, till Holy Scripture came to some fullness and to some clearness, we find God revealing Himself in a dream, not only to Abraham, and Pharaoh, and Nebuchadnezzar; but even to Jacob, and Joseph, and Solomon, and down even to such New Testament men as Peter, and Paul, and John. Almighty God has complete control and continual command of all the avenues that lead into the soul of man, and He sends His message to this soul and to that at the very time and in the very way that seems wisest and best in His sight. And Elihu's remarkable description of the manner and the matter of one of his own divine dreams may be taken as a prophetic forecast of this passover dream of Pilate's wife: "In a dream, in a vision of the night, when deep sleep falleth upon men, in slumberings upon the bed: then He openeth the ears of men, and sealeth their instruction, that He may withdraw man from his purpose, and hide pride from man. He keepeth back his soul from the pit, and his life from perishing by the sword. He is chastened also with pain upon his bed, and the multitude of his bones with strong pain." A perfect picture of Pilate's wife's dream in the Prætorium that night, and of its divinely-intended purpose toward Pilate himself, which was to withdraw Pilate from his purpose, and to keep back his soul from the pit.

Long before that passover morning Pilate's wife had made up her mind about Jesus of Nazareth. With all the wealth and all the rank of the city against Him; with all the temple learning and all the temple authority against Him; with, without exception, every responsible ruler and every influential man in all Jerusalem against Him; and with all her own and all her husband's original interests and natural instincts strongly prejudicing her against Him—she had overcome all that, and had deliberately and resolutely taken up His side. She had made up her mind that whatever else He was, or might turn out to be, at any rate up to the present moment, He had been a blameless man. He had gone about doing good. The procurator's palace was the centre and the seat of everything. All the telegraph wires ran up and delivered themselves there. Everything that took place in the province was instantly reported at the Prætorium. Not a word of rebellion was whispered in closets, not a zealot stirred a foot in the greatest stealth, not a sword was sharpened at midnight in all the land, but it was all as well known to Pilate and to his wife as to the intending insurrectionary himself. And, though the Roman procurators were wont to leave their wives at home when they set out to their provinces, Pilate's wife was far too meet a help to him to be left behind when he was wrestling for his life with those rebellious and treacherous Jews in Jerusalem. And it was so. The procurator's wife shared all her husband's anxieties, all his responsibilities, and all his apprehensions. She was with him in everything with her keen mind and her noble heart. And with all her swift divination she had come to the sure conclusion long ago that Jesus of Nazareth was all and more than He seemed to be. Her Hebrew maid could not assist her Roman mistress to dress, but, one way or other, the same subject of conversation continually came up—what He had last said, and what He had last done. She could not drive out through the gate of the city but there was His congregation covering the highway. She could not return home that He was not healing some sick man at the door of the temple. And, all that passover week,—what with her husband's spies, and what with her own, she knew as well as Annas and Caiaphas themselves knew what they had determined to do. She had watched out of her window what we now know as the entry into Jerusalem. She had heard coming over the valley the voices of the children in the temple crying out and saying, "Hosanna to the Son of David!" till she wished that her children were among them. The last thing that absolutely carried her whole heart captive was Martha and Mary and their brother Lazarus. And it had needed all her own self-command, and all her husband's command over her as her husband, to keep her from going out to Bethany to see Lazarus with her own eyes. She had often read of such things in her own ancient books at home, but such a thing as this had never come so near her before. And then, when the report came to the Prætorium that Lazarus's friend had been betrayed and taken prisoner, and was all that night to be under trial before Caiaphas and the council; and then, that it would all roll in upon her husband the next morning—if a dream cometh through the multitude of business—no wonder that Pilate's wife dreamed about Jesus of Nazareth all that passover night!

Just what shape her dream took that passover night, I would give something for myself to know. And it is not mere and idle curiosity that makes me say that, for it would be to me a great lesson in the first principles of divine revelation to the Old Testament Church, as well as to this Roman matron's soul, and to my own soul. It would be as good as another disinterred manuscript of the Acts of Pilate, did we know something of the multitude of this business about Jesus that had gone that night to make up that so suffering and so opportune dream. With the books of the Hebrew prophets on her table, and with the echoes of John's preaching and Jesus' parables filling the air all around her, what may the governor's wife not have seen and heard in the visions and voices of that ominous night? She may have seen a hand coming out and writing it on the wall of the Prætorium, "Mene, Mene, Tekel Upharsin." She may have seen the same sight that made Daniel himself to be troubled, and his countenance to change. She may have seen the Ancient of days, with His throne like the fiery flame, and His wheels as burning fire, and the judgment seat, and the books opened. She may have seen one like the Son of Man come with the clouds of heaven, till His kingdom was an everlasting kingdom, and His dominion that shall not be destroyed. Till, 'For God's sake,' she said, 'have thou nothing to do with that dreadful man?' Now, among all your dreams and visions on your bed do you ever dream about Jesus Christ? You dream every night about this man and that woman that you love or hate. Do you ever dream about your Saviour? Do you love and fear Him to that extent? If He were actually engaged with you on the salvation of your soul, the multitudinous business connected with that inward work would surely make you think about Him all day till you would dream about Him all night. Do you ever do it? Will you be able to say to Him at the last day, 'Lord, Thou knowest that I often thought about Thee all day and dreamed about Thee all night, and told my husband my dreams about Thee in the morning?' Will you have as much as Pilate's heathen wife will have to say for herself and for him? Will you; or will you not? What do you think? What do you say?

And then, this will be openly acknowledged and admitted in the day of judgment that Pilate's wife was fearlessly true and faithful to all her light. Her best light was as yet but candle-light. It was but as rush-light. But, even candle-light, even rush-light, even the faintest reflection of candle-light or rush-light is, all the time, the very same light as the light of the noonday sun. All light of all kinds comes, in one way or another, from one and the same source. And the lurid light of Pilate's wife's dream that night all came to her and to him from the Light of the world. The identical same Light that is lighting you and me with such brilliance and beauty in this house to-night, that very same Light struggled within that Roman lady's soul on her bed and in her dreams in Jerusalem that night. And nothing in divine things is more sure than this, that they who love the light—be it candle-light or be it sun-light—shall have more light sent to them, till they have all the light that they need. To them their path shall shine more and more to the perfect day. They who love the light, and walk in what light they have, they shall never lie down in darkness. You may absolutely depend upon it that the True Light Himself, who stood under such a cloud before Pilate's bar that daybreak, both overheard and laid up in His heart the noble message that came out to the procurator. You may rely on it that He who had already sent her so much of His own light, continued to send her more, till she became one of those princess-saints of Cæsar's household, whom Paul so saluted in long after days. And may we not hope that Pilate himself was at last completely won with the holy walk of his wife, as he beheld her chaste conversation coupled with fear?

LXXXVI

HEROD THAT FOX

JACOB BEHMEN says that a man is sometimes like a wolf, cruel and merciless, and with an insatiable thirst for blood; sometimes like a dog, snappish, malicious, envious, grudging, as a dog is with a bone that he cannot himself eat; sometimes like a serpent, stinging and venomous, slanderous in his words, and treacherous in his actions; sometimes like a hare; timorous and starting off; sometimes like a toad, and sometimes like a fox, and so on. The

Teutonic philosopher has a whole incomparable chapter on "The Bestial Manifestations in Man." "My dear children in Christ," he proceeds, "my sole purpose in writing in this way to you is not to revile you or to reproach you with your fallen and bestialised estate. What I here write to you is the simple and naked and open truth. I am as certain as I live that it is the truth of God, because I have the daily experience of it all in myself. Every day, and every hour of every day, I have the bondage of it all, and the shame of it all, and the degradation and the guilt of it all, in myself, and not in another. And therefore, your embruted estate is here told you not to exclude any of you from the hope of salvation. The most wolf-like man among you, the most dog-like man among you, the most toad-like man among you, the most fox-like man among you—all such men are invited, and, indeed, commanded, to arise every moment and flee from themselves into the new birth in God. And, moreover, it was for this very purpose that the Son of God was manifested. It was to turn us all from being beasts and devils everlastingly, and to make us all with Himself, the new and born-from-above sons and daughters of the living God. Jesus Christ, the very Mouth of Truth Himself, called Herod a fox, not to sentence him, and to fix him for ever the fox that he was, but it was in order, if possible, to turn him from all his guiles, and all his lusts, and all his lies, and to make him even yet a child of God, and an heir of everlasting life." So writes "the illuminated Behmen" in his *Election of Grace*.

All the historians and all the biographers of that time, both sacred and profane, agree about Herod Antipas. They all agree that Antipas was his father's son in all that was worst in his father's character. Old Herod, with all his brutalities and with all his devilries, had at the same time some of the possibilities in him that go to the making of a great man. But by no possibility could his second son ever have been a great man. Antipas was a weak, cruel, sensual, ostentatious, shallow-hearted creature. He is known to the readers of the New Testament first as the dupe of a bad woman, and then as the murderer of John the Baptist, and then as one of the judges of Jesus Christ. He was that fox who tried to frighten our Lord to flee from His work; and at last he was that puppet-king, and reprobate sinner, to whom our Lord would not answer one word. His licentious life, his family miseries, his political manœuvres, his sycophantic and extravagant expenditures, his ruinous defeats, both in war and in diplomacy, his fall from his throne, and his banishment from his kingdom, are all to be read in the books of Josephus, who is an author altogether worthy to chronicle the deeds, and to tell the exploits, of such a hero. Avoid giving of characters. says Butler in his noble sermon on "The Government of the Tongue." At the same time, as Bengel says, the truth must sometimes be spoken, and must sometimes be all spoken. Sometimes a dog must be branded to all men to be a dog, and a serpent advertised to be a serpent, and a swine to be a swine. 'Go back,' said our Lord, 'to that fox which sent you, and tell him what I have said about him: tell him the name I have denounced upon him.' And we understand and accept both what our Lord and His two servants have said on this subject of the giving of characters. It is a large part of our daily lesson and discipline and duty in this life, to be able to give the proper characters, and to apply the proper epithets, to men and to things; and to do that at the right time and in the right temper. It is a large and an important part of every preacher's office especially, to apply to all men and to all their actions their absolutely and fearlessly right and true names. To track out the wolf, and the serpent, and the toad, and the fox, in the men in whom these bestialities dwell, and to warn all men how and where all that will end; no minister may shrink from that. All the vices and all the crimes of the tetrarch's miserable life, and all the weakness and duplicity of his contemptible character, are all summed up and sealed down on Herod Antipas in that one divine word that day: "That fox."

But what makes Herod Antipas such a poignant lesson to us is not that he was a fox, it is this rather, that he began by being a fox, and ended by being a reprobate. You know what reprobation is, my brethren? This is reprobation. "As soon as Pilate knew that this prisoner belonged to Herod's jurisdiction, he sent Him to Herod, who was in Jerusalem at that time. And Herod questioned Jesus with many words, but He answered him nothing." That is reprobation. It is our reprobation begun when God answers us nothing. When, with all our praying, and with all our reading, and with all our inquiring, He still answers us nothing. Herod's day of grace had lasted long, but it is now at an end. Herod had had many opportunities, and at one time he was almost persuaded. At one time he was not very far from the Kingdom of Heaven. But all that is long past. Herod had smothered and silenced his conscience long ago, and now he is to be for ever let alone. Nay—and let all beginning reprobates attend to this—not only was Herod let alone, but when he put many eager questions to our Lord, He answered him nothing. It is here that the real horror and the awful fascination to me of all Herod's case comes in. It is in this: because we also go on exactly like Herod, cheating ourselves, and thinking, poor self-entrapped foxes that we are, that we are all the time mocking God also, till it is too late; for God is not to be mocked by any man. David has drawn out this solemnising lesson, and has set it in a singularly impressive Psalm of his, and in never-to-be-forgotten words: "If I regard iniquity in my heart, the Lord will not hear me." Now, it was just because this lewd and cruel fox had so defiantly, and so flagrantly, and so criminally, and for so long, regarded the greatest iniquity in his heart and in his life, that now at last when he put so many questions to our Lord He answered him nothing. We all know the same thing ourselves. Fox-like, Antipas-like, Doth God see us? we say. Surely the darkness shall cover us, we say. Just this once more, we say. At a more convenient time I will reform myself, we say. We take our own way and our own time, and, fox-like, we have many tricks in our eye by which we will escape the trap. We have all gone on in that way, till these words of reprobation—"no answer"—describe to perfection many of us in this house to-night. In Herod it was murder and incest, never repented of and never forsaken, that so absolutely shut our Lord's mouth toward Herod and toward all his requests and all his questions. There are no controversies so dark and so terrible between God and our souls as the murder of John the Baptist. But God may be as silent and as angry at all our prayers and questions and casuistries as ever He was at Herod's. Nobody would believe, but those of us who have come through it, the little things, the trivial things, that will stop God's ear, and shut His mouth, and make Him our enemy. Somewhat too much money spent on ourselves, and somewhat too little spent on the Church of Christ and on His poor will do it. Too little time and strength spent in closet and intercessory prayer will do it. A secret ill-feeling entertained at somebody will do it. A debt not paid and with interest will do it. A prejudice nursed and not surrendered in time will do it. A grudge kept up will do it. An apology not made will do it. A too long and too free tongue will do it. An impertinent book, and the time and money spent upon that book will do it. A second sleep in the morning more than is necessary will do it. A pipeful of doubtful tobacco will do it. A daily glass or two of inexpedient wine will do it. A knuckle of too-savoury mutton will sometimes do it, as Dr. Jowett was wont to say. Nobody could tell, nobody who has not himself come through it all could imagine or believe if it were told them, the triviality, and the absolute immateriality, of the things that will in some men's cases do it. God has kept up a life-long controversy with some of His saints about little things that they could not put words upon, so unlike Almighty God and so beneath Him, as one would say, is the whole dispute. The truth is, when Almighty God is bent upon the absolute sanctification of some elect sinner, no autobiography, no *Brea,* no *Reliquiæ,* no *Grace Abounding,* no amount of imaginative genius and a corresponding style, could possibly convey to another man all the controversies, great and small, that all through his life go on between God and that elect sinner's soul. There are some terribly predestinated saints. There are some elections that almost consume those chosen souls to dust and ashes in the awful furnace of their sanctification. The apostle had this same terrible election, and sin-consuming ambition, for his Thessalonian converts. "And the very God of peace sanctify you wholly: and I pray God your whole spirit, and soul, and body be preserved blameless unto the coming of our Lord Jesus Christ." You have it all there. It is as much as to say, the very God of peace turn a deaf ear to your most importunate and agonising prayers, as long as there is a single speck of sin secretly staining any part of your soul. The very God of peace crucify every remaining lust in your body, and every remaining affection in your spirit, and every remaining thought, and feeling, and passion, in your soul, till you are absolutely blameless in His consumingly holy sight. The very God of peace empty you from vessel to vessel, and prune you to the quivering quick, and keep you in a sevenfold-fire, till the coming of the Great Refiner in the glory of His Father. And, in like manner, the very God of peace demands of you also every moment of your time, and every mite of your money, and every word of your mouth, and every beat of your heart. And not till He gets all that from you will He answer you one word; no, not for all your prayers, and all your sweats, and all your tears. It is not lawful for a child of God to have it, He will say, till He will make your disobedient life a burden to you past bearing, a torture, and one long agony. No! He denies you, till you can hear nothing in all your conscience but these angry words with you. No! it is not lawful for you. It is not right. It is not safe. It is not seemly. It is not expedient. It may be for others, but it can never now be for you. And as long as God in your conscience says that to you about anything whatsoever, you may debate, and question, and pray, and seek for marks and evidences till your dying day, but the very God of peace will answer you nothing.

And then there is this complication also: there are things that it is not lawful for one man to do, that his very next-door neighbour may do every day, and walk with God and talk with God all the time. There are things that are unpardonable in the sight of God in one man, but which are not only entirely innocent and inoffensive, but are positively virtuous and praiseworthy in another man. There are things that will be the ruin of one man's soul, that may all the time be the very sweetness and strength of his neighbour's soul. I may have to deny myself, on the pain of reprobation, every day, what you may eat and drink every day and ask a blessing on it. I may have to spend all the rest of my redeemed life in this world in a daily battle and a nightly self-examination against habits of body and mind that you cannot so much as imagine. I may have to sit up at my salvation every night of the week, while you are sleeping like an innocent child. I may have to meditate on David's Psalms continually, and on nothing else any more, while you are doing nothing else all your time and thought but either telling or hearing some new thing. I may have, till the day of my death, to fight against a slavery that makes you, in your lush liberty, say that I am beside myself. I may have iniquities in my heart absolutely shipwrecking all my prayers: iniquities that even David in his very best Psalms knew nothing about: iniquities that did not even exist in David's day, because the Holy Ghost was not yet given. So beset behind and before are some New Testament men, and some men far on in the life of grace, that God scarcely ever answers them one word from one year's end to another. Then king Herod questioned with Jesus in many words; but He answered him nothing. But, sings David, verily God hath heard me. He hath attended to the voice of my prayer.

LXXXVII

THE PENITENT THIEF

The two malefactors who were crucified with Christ had been ringleaders in Barabbas's robber band. And had Barabbas himself not been pardoned by Pilate that morning, he also would have carried his cross out to Calvary that day and would have been crucified upon it. But when Barabbas and his band are called thieves and robbers it is but due to them to give them the benefit of the doubt. In our noble British law and administration there is a deep and a fundamental distinction taken between ordinary criminals against all civilised society, and political criminals against this or that foreign government for the time. We give up swindlers and murderers when they flee to our shores, but we provide a safe and an honourable asylum for political refugees and state criminals, as we call them. Now all the chances are that Barabbas and his band had begun simply by being rebels against Rome, as, indeed, all the Jews were everywhere in their hearts. Though no doubt their repudiated, outlawed, exasperated, and hunted-down lives had by degrees made Barabbas and his band desperate and reckless, till they had become in many cases pure thieves and robbers. David in the cave of Adullam is not a bad picture of Barabbas at the beginning of his life of outlawry. For every one that was in distress came to David, and every one that was in debt, and every one that was discontented, and he became a captain over them; and there were with David about four hundred men. Only, no doubt, David was a far better captain than Barabbas ever was. David, no doubt, kept his men in far better hand, till he turned them out such splendid specimens of soldiers and mighty men of war, and the best law-abiding citizens in all Israel. But David had only Saul to overthrow, whereas Barabbas had Cæsar.

The Evangelist Luke had perfect understanding of all things from the very first. And no doubt he knew all about the early life of Barabbas and his band. And especially, I feel sure, he would make every possible inquiry concerning the early days of this remarkable man who is discovered to us in this Gospel as the penitent thief. But it would have been out of place in Luke to have gone into this man's whole past life at the moment when he is fixing all our eyes on the crucifixion of our Lord. At the same time, it is as clear as daylight to me that this is not the first time that this crucified thief has seen our Lord. He knew both our Lord's life and teaching and character quite well, though he had cast it all behind his back all his days up till now. He knew that our Lord had done nothing amiss all the time that he and his companions were fast ripening for the due reward of their deeds. There was not a Sabbath synagogue, nor a passover journey, nor a carpenter's shop, nor a tax-gatherer's booth, nor a robber's cave in all Israel where the name, and the teaching, and the mighty works of Jesus of Nazareth were not constantly discussed, and debated, and divided on. And Barabbas and his band must have had many a deliberation in their banishment about Jesus of Nazareth. Is He indeed the promised Messiah? Is He really David's Son? Is this really He who is to overcome and cast out Cæsar? If it is, we shall join His standard immediately, and He will remember us when He comes into His kingdom. Week after week, month after month, year after year, this went on till their hearts became sick and desperate within them. A hundred times Barabbas and this one and that one of his band had disguised themselves as fishermen and shepherds to come down to hear our Lord preach and to see the mighty works that He did. Nay, for anything we know, this man may at one time have been one of our Lord's disciples, quite as well as Simon Zelotes and Judas Iscariot. In his early, and enthusiastic, and patriotic days he may have been one of John's disciples. He may have seen Jesus of Nazareth baptized that day. He may have been baptized himself that day. He may have heard the Baptist say: "Behold the Lamb of God!" He may have been among the multitude who sat and heard the Sermon on the Mount. He may actually have closely companied with our Lord for a season. Till he was at last one of those who went back and walked no more with Him, because our Lord would not be taken by them and made a king. But, go back to Barabbas's band as he did, I defy him ever to forget what he had seen and heard down among the cities, and the villages, and the mountain-sides, and the supper-tables of Galilee and Jewry. This man, and many more like him, went back to their farm, and to their merchandise, and to their toll-booth, and to their robber-cave, but they took with them memories, and visions, and hearts, and consciences, they could never forget. As we see was the case conspicuously with this thief on the cross.

And all this went on: our Lord finishing the work His Father had given Him to do, while Barabbas and his band were fast ripening for their cross; till, as God would have it, our Lord and Barabbas, with these two of his band, were all taken and tried, and were sentenced to be crucified all four on the same passover morning. Now, when a man is on his way out to his own execution he would be more than a man if he paid much attention to the circumstances attending the execution of his neighbours. At the same time, this thief was no ordinary man. 'This is Jesus of Nazareth,' he would say to himself. 'This is the carpenter-prophet I used to steal into His presence to hear Him preach. I once thought to be one of His men myself to deliver Israel.' And then as men among ourselves do on the morning of their execution, the psalms and hymns of his boyhood came back into his mind. Till he did not hear the mockery and the insults of the people who filled the streets as he went on and said to himself: "Remember not the sins of my youth, nor my transgressions. For thou writest bitter things against me, and makest me to possess the iniquities of my youth. Thou puttest my feet also in the stocks, and lookest narrowly unto all my paths; thou settest a print upon the heels of my feet. We lie down in our shame, and our confusion covereth us; for we have sinned against the Lord our God; we and our fathers, from our youth even unto this day, and have not obeyed the voice of the Lord our God." Till, by that time, the terrible procession had got to Golgotha. And all the way, as already in the high priest's palace, and in the Prætorium, and now at Golgotha, all hell was let loose as never before or since. And Satan entered into the two thieves, and into this thief also. And no wonder that they both cursed and blasphemed and raved and gnashed their teeth and spat upon their crucifiers, as all crucified men always did, so insupportable to absolute insanity was the awful torture of crucifixion. And all the time God was laying on His Son the iniquity of us all, and all the time He was dumb, and opened not His mouth. "Save Thyself and us!" the two crucified and maddened men both cried to Him; the one in fiendish ribaldry, and the other out of a heart in which heaven and hell were fighting with their last stroke for his soul. Till this one of the two thieves at last came to himself. And the thing that made him come to himself was this: Our Lord had never opened His mouth. He had neither cursed, nor gnashed His teeth, nor spat at His crucifiers and revilers. But, at last, He also spoke. And it was the same voice—the thief had never heard another voice in all the world to compare with it! For, looking up into the fast-darkening heavens, our Lord exclaimed, "Father, forgive them; for they know not what they do." That benediction of our blessed Lord did more to benumb the agony of body and mind in this thief than all the wine mingled with myrrh the women of Jerusalem had made for him and for his fellows to drink that morning. "Father, forgive them!"—it absolutely broke the thief's hard heart to hear it. And as his hardened companion still reviled our Lord hanging beside him, the now penitent thief looked across and said to his old companion and fellow-malefactor the words that all the world knows.

John Donne, in a Lent sermon that he preached at Whitehall, dwells on what he calls "The despatch of the grace of God in the case of the penitent thief." The *per saltum* character of the thief's repentance and faith, and the full and immediate response of our Lord to his so-sudden repentance and faith, make a fine sermon. The kingdom of heaven suffered violence that day at this thief's so suddenly repentant and so believing hands. He took heaven, so to speak, at a leap that day. The swiftness of the thief's repentance, and faith, and confession, and pardon, and sanctification, and glorification, is something very blessed for us all to think about, and never to forget; and, especially, those of us who must make haste and lose no more time if we are to be for ever with him and with his Lord in Paradise. Let all old and fast-dying men have this written up, like Augustine, on the wall over against their bed—"There is life in a look at the crucified One." For we may not have time nor strength for more than just one such look of despatch.

And, then, if you would see the most wonderful believer this world has ever seen, come to the cross of Christ, and to that cross beside it, and look at the penitent thief. He was a greater believer than Abraham, the father of believers. Greater than David. Greater than Isaiah. While Peter, and James, and John, with all their privileges and opportunities, are not worthy to be named in the same day with this thief. For they had all forsaken their Saviour that awful day and had fled from Him. It was of the thief, and of his alone and so transcendent faith, that our Lord spoke in such praise and in such reproof to Thomas eight days afterwards, and said, 'Blessed is he in heaven with Me this day, who saw nothing but shame, and defeat, and death in Me, and yet so believed in Me, and so cheered Me that day.' For our Lord never, all His life, got such a surprise and such a delight as He got on the cross that day,—not from Peter, not from the Syrophœnician woman, not from the centurion, not from Mary Magdalene, as He got on His cross that morning from the thief who hung beside Him. There was nothing, after His Father's presence with Him, that held our Lord's heart up all His life on earth like faith on Him in any sinner's heart. And now that His Father also has forsaken Him; now that He is so absolutely deserted and so awfully alone; it is this thief's faith, and love, and hope that is such a cup of cold water to our Lord's fast-sinking heart. All faith and all hope on Christ were as dead as a stone in Peter's heart and in John's heart. Mary Magdalene herself, with all her love, had given Him up as for ever dead. But not the thief. It was at the very darkest hour this world has ever seen, or ever will see, that this thief's splendid faith flashed up brighter than the mid-day sun that day. Some say that Paul will sit next to Christ in Paradise. I cannot but think that Paul will insist on giving place to this very prince and leader of all New Testament believers. Anybody could have believed and laboured all their days after being caught up into the third heaven, and after seeing Christ sitting there in all His glory. But Christ was still on His cross, and His glory was as black as midnight, when all the faith of the church of God found its last retreat and sure fastness and high tower in the thief's unconquerable and inextinguishable heart. Paul deserves a high seat in heaven, and he will get all he deserves, and more. But the penitent thief could say, "I am crucified with Christ" in a sense that even Paul could not say that. And however high the thief's throne in heaven is, the whole church of angels and saints will acclaim that he is worthy. Well done! O greatest and bravest-hearted of all believers! Well done!

LXXXVIII

THOMAS

The character of Thomas is an anatomy of melancholy. If "to say man is to say melancholy," then to say Thomas, called Didymus, is to say religious melancholy. Peter was of such an ardent and enthusiastical temperament that he was always speaking, whereas Thomas was too great a melancholian to speak much, and when he ever did speak it was always out of the depths of his hypochondriacal heart.

It was already the last week of his Master's life before we have Thomas so much as once opening his mouth. And the occasion of his first melancholy utterance was this: Lazarus was sick unto death in Bethany. And when Jesus heard that His friend was so sick, He said to His disciples, "Let us go into Judea again." "Master," they answered, "the Jews of late have been seeking opportunity to stone Thee to death, and goest Thou thither again?" And it was when Thomas saw that his Master was walking straight into the jaws of certain destruction that he said, in sad abandonment of all his remaining hope, "Let us also go, that we may die with Him." Thomas felt sure in his foreboding heart that his Master would never leave Judea alive; Thomas loved his Master more than life, and therefore he determined to die with Him. And, indeed, that determination was not very difficult for Thomas to take. Life had not yielded much to Thomas. And its best promises, more and more delayed, and more and more deluding him, were taking less and less hold of Thomas's heart as the years went on. We see now that the disciples of Jesus of Nazareth had the very best cause for high hope and full assurance. But at that time, and especially that week, Thomas had only too good ground for all his anxiety, and despondency, and melancholy. And a whole lifetime of melancholy, constitutional and circumstantial, had by this time settled down on Thomas, and had taken absolute and tyrannical possession of him. The disciples were all sick at heart with hope deferred; as also with the terrible questionings that would sometimes arise in their hearts, and would not be silenced; all kinds of questionings about their more and more mysterious Master; and about His more and more mysterious, and more and more stumbling sayings, both about Himself and about themselves. And then His certainly impending death, and the unaccountable delay and disappearance of His promised kingdom: all that doubt, and fear, and despondency, and despair, met in Thomas's melancholy heart till it all took absolute possession of him. And till he sometimes said to himself that it would be the best thing that could happen to him if he could but die at once and be done for ever with all these difficulties and delays and bitter and unbearable disappointments. The discipleship-life, at its very best, had never been very satisfying to Thomas's heart; and, of late, it had been becoming absolutely unbearable to this melancholy and morose man. "Let us go," he said, "that we may die with Him."

The next time that Thomas speaks is when Jesus and His disciples are still in the upper room where the last passover had just been celebrated and the Lord's Supper instituted. "In My Father's house are many mansions: I go to prepare a place for you. And whither I go ye know, and the way ye know." The other disciples may know whither their Master is going, and they may know the way, but Thomas knows neither. The other disciples, as a matter of fact, know quite as little, and even less, about this whole matter than Thomas knows: only they think they know, when they do not: they have not knowledge enough to know that they know nothing. 'His Father's house?' said Thomas to himself. 'What does He mean? Why does He not speak plainly?' Thomas must understand his Master's meaning Thomas is one of those unhappy men who cannot be put off with mere words. Thomas must see to the bottom before he can pretend to believe. Thomas was the first of those disciples, and a primate among them, in whose relentless minds

doubt,
Like a shoot, springs round the stock of truth.

At the same time, Thomas in his melancholy candour and saddened plainness of speech was but ministering an opportunity to his Master to utter one of His most golden oracles. Jesus saith unto Thomas, "I am the way, the truth, and the life: no man cometh unto the Father but by Me." We cannot much regret that restless and realistic melancholy of Thomas since it has procured for us such a satisfying and ennobling utterance as that. "All His disciples minister to Him," says Newman; "and as in other ways, so also in giving occasion for the words of grace which proceed from His mouth."

Ten days pass. But what days! The betrayal, the arrest, the trial, the crucifixion, the burial, and the resurrection of Thomas's Master. What days and nights of trial, and that not for faith and hope only, but for reason herself to keep her seat! All the faith and all the trust of the disciples have not only fallen into a deep doubt during those terrible days and nights: all their faith and all their trust have been actually crucified and laid dead and buried, and that without a spark of hope. For as yet the disciples knew not the Scripture, that their Master must rise again from the dead. "Then the same day at evening, being the first day of the week, came Jesus and stood in the midst, and saith unto them, Peace be unto you. And when He had so said, He showed them His hands and His side. Then were the disciples glad when they saw the Lord." But Thomas was not with them when Jesus came. Where was Thomas that glorious Sabbath evening? Why was he not with the rest? How shall we account for the absence of Thomas? It could not have been by accident. He must have been told that the ten astounded, overwhelmed, and enraptured disciples were to be all together that wonderful night; astounded, overwhelmed, and enraptured with the events of the morning. What conceivable cause, then, could have kept Thomas away? Whatever it was that kept Thomas away, he was terribly punished for his absence. For he thereby lost the first and best sight of his risen Master, and His first and best benediction of peace. He not only lost that benediction, but the joy of the other disciples who had received it filled the cup of Thomas's misery full. The first appearance of their risen Master, that had lifted all the other disciples up to heaven, was the last blow to cast Thomas down to hell. The darkness, the bitterness, the sullenness, the pride, that had its seat so deep down in Thomas's heart, all burst out in the pre-presence of his brethren's joy. Thomas would have none of their joy. Thomas would not believe it. They were dreaming. They were deluded. They were mad. And the pride, and jealousy, and bitterness of his heart, all drove Thomas into a deeper rage and a deeper rebellion. "Except I shall see in His hands the print of the nails, and put my finger into the print of the nails, and thrust my hand into His side, I will not believe." We all understand Thomas's misery. We have all been possessed by it. It is the jealousy and the rage of a guilty conscience. It is the jealousy and the rage of a disappointed and a revengeful heart. When any good comes to others that we should have been sharers in, when we are absent through our own fault, and when those who were present come to tell us about all that we have lost, we have all been like Thomas. We said, I do not believe it. It was not all that you say it was. You are exalting yourselves over me. You are boasting yourselves beyond the truth. And if the truth cannot be hid from us, or denied by us, we hate them, and the thing we have lost, all the more. Thomas is told us for our learning. We see ourselves in Thomas as in a glass. Thomas, in all his melancholy and resentment, is ourselves. Unbelief, and obstinacy, and loss of opportunity, and then increased unbelief, is no strange thing to ourselves.

And after eight days the disciples were again within, and this time Thomas was with them. It had taken the disciples all their might all these eight days to prevail with and to persuade Thomas. And all of us who know what it is to wage a war with our own wounded pride, and with nothing but our own sullenness, and stubbornness, and mulishness to oppose to the pleadings of truth and love, we know something of what Thomas came through before he consented to accompany the other disciples to the upper room at the end of those eight days. "Then came Jesus, the doors being shut, and stood in the midst, and said, Peace be unto you. Then saith He to Thomas, Reach hither thy finger, and behold My hands; and reach hither thy hand and thrust it into My side, and be not faithless but believing." How Thomas would hate himself when his own scornful, unbelieving, contemptuous words came back to him from his Master's gracious lips! How utterly odious his own words would sound as his Master repeated them. And worst of all when his risen Master humbled Himself to meet Thomas's unbelieving words and to satisfy them! Thomas would have killed himself with shame and self-condemnation, had it not been given him at that grandest moment of his whole life to say, "My Lord and my God!" Jesus saith unto them, "Thomas, because thou hast seen Me, thou hast believed; blessed are they that have not seen, and yet have believed!"

Now, my brethren, do you clearly understand and accept this peculiar blessedness of believing without seeing? Do you clearly see and fully accept the blessedness of a strong and an easy acting faith in things of Christ? Faith is always easy where love and hope are strong. What we live for and hope to see, what we love with our whole heart, what we pray for night and day, what our whole future is anchored upon, that we easily believe, that we are ready to welcome. In that case our faith is to us nothing less than the substance of the thing hoped for; it is the evidence of the thing not seen as yet. What with Thomas's temperament of melancholy; what with his not having hid in his heart the things that our Lord had so often said about His coming death for sin and His resurrection for salvation; and then his hot jealousy and ill-will at the joyful news of the disciples; with all that Thomas's heart was in a state most deadly to faith. Had Thomas's heart been tender, had he had seven devils cast out of his heart like Mary Magdalene, he also would have gone out to the sepulchre while it was yet dark, and would have been the first of all the disciples to see his risen Lord. But, as it was, he was the last to see Him, and ran a close risk of never seeing Him in this world. Now, how is it with you in this same matter? Are you hard to convince? Are you slow of faith? Is your heart so set upon this world that you have no eyes or ears for the world to come? Are you able to dispense with Jesus Christ day after day till He dies out of your heart, and imagination, and whole life, altogether? Unbelief grows by what it feeds upon, just like faith and love. To him who has no faith in God, in Christ, in the Holy Scriptures, in the unseen world, and in the world to come, from him is even taken away the little faith that he had, till he has none at all. You know men in whom that awful catastrophe has taken place. You know it, in measure, in yourself. Your faith is all but dead. You do not wait for Christ's coming either to judge the world, or to take you to Himself, or to sanctify you, and comfort you, and answer your prayers. And then you are uneasy, and unhappy, and jealous, and angry, when you hear that He has been manifesting Himself in all these ways to them that believe. But you were not waiting for Him. You neither expected Him nor wished for Him: and He never comes to the like of you till He comes at last and too late. You will be horrified when it is told you what your whole life, and your whole heart, and all your desires and hopes say when words are put upon them. They all say, 'I will not believe until the last trump awakens me, and the graves are opened, and the great white throne is set.'

Now, from Thomas and his Lord that night let us learn this also, and take it away. Let us act upon the faith we have. Let us frequent the places where He is said to manifest Himself. Let us feed our faith on the strong meat of His word. And, since here also acts produce habits, and habits character; let us act faith continually on faith's great objects and operations. And, especially, on our glorified Redeemer. To Thomas He was crucified yesterday. But to us He is risen, and exalted, and is soon to come again. That the trial of your faith, being much more precious than of gold that perisheth, might be found unto praise, and honour, and glory at the appearing of Jesus Christ. Whom having not seen, ye love: in whom, though now you see Him not, yet believing, ye rejoice with joy unspeakable and full of glory.

> For all thy rankling doubts so sore,
> Love thou thy Saviour still,
> Him for thy Lord and God adore,
> And ever do His will.
> Though vexing thoughts may seem to last,
> Let not thy soul be quite o'ercast;
> Soon will He show thee all His wounds and say,
> Long have I known thy name: know thou my face alway.

LXXXIX

CLEOPAS AND HIS COMPANION

Cleopas and his companion were two men of Emmaus who had gone up the week before to Jerusalem to keep the passover. Cleopas and his companion were not exactly disciples of our Lord. That is to say, their names were not among the twelve; though the likelihood is that they were numbered and were well known among the seventy. And they had gone up to the feast in the hope that their Lord would be there, and that they would both see and hear Him as on former feast-days. It seemed to them like a year, like a lifetime, like another world, since last week when they walked and talked together so full of hope and expectation, all the way up from Emmaus to Jerusalem. For Jesus had come up to the passover, as they had expected He would. And they had both seen Him, and had heard Him speak. They had followed Him about in the streets of Jerusalem as He preached His last sermons, so terrible to them to see and to hear. They were not among the twelve, and they had not been invited to the upper room, but they had done the next best thing to that, for they had eaten their passover supper out at Bethany with their friend Lazarus, and with Martha and Mary his sisters. The whole of Bethany was absolutely overwhelmed when the news came out at midnight that Jesus had been betrayed by one of His disciples, and was at that moment in the hands of His enemies. And with their loins girt, and with their passover-staff in their hands, Lazarus, and Cleopas, and his companion, were abroad in the streets of Jerusalem all that night, and till after the crucifixion was finished next morning. And now the third day of that tremendous overthrow and shipwreck had come, when, with a sickness of heart indescribable, Cleopas at last said to his companion, 'Rise, and let us shake the dust off our feet against this accursed city, and let us escape to our own home.' True; certain women of their company had rushed into the city that morning, saying that they had seen a vision of angels who told them that their crucified Master had risen and left his grave; but to Cleopas all that was so many idle tales. 'No, no!' Cleopas said to his companion, 'come away home. Believe me, we have seen the last of the redemption of Israel in our day, at any rate.' Why, you will ask, was Cleopas in such a hurry to get home? Might he not have gone out to see the empty grave for himself? Might he not have waited in Jerusalem till the end of "the third day" that his Master so often foretold about Himself? As it was, Cleopas, like Pliable in the *Pilgrim's Progress,* was making a desperate plunge through the Slough of Despond so as to get out on the side next to his own house, when a man whose name was Help came and held out His hand to him, and to his companion, in the midst of the Slough.

Yes: Cleopas and his companion, like Mr. Fearing, had a perfect Slough of Despond in their own hearts that sunset as they walked down to Emmaus and reasoned together and were sad. 'Where did you see Him first? What was it that led you to think that He was the Christ? And, did you hear this sermon, and that? And this parable and that?' And then the arrest, and the trial and the crucifixion. No wonder they reeled to and fro, and staggered under their load of sorrow, till the workers in the fields said they were two drunken men on their way home from the feast. When a stranger overtook them as they halted, and reasoned, and debated together in their sadness. 'Peace be with you both!' said the stranger with a pleasant voice as he joined himself to their company. But Cleopas was scarcely civil. Cleopas scarcely returned the salute of the stranger, so overwhelmed was he with his sadness. And they walked on in silence, Cleopas and his companion, and the stranger. Till the sympathising stranger broke the sad silence with these confiding words: "What manner of communications are these that ye have one to another, as ye walk and are sad?" 'Art thou such a stranger in Jerusalem,' answered Cleopas, 'as not to know the things which are come to pass there in these days? Where wert thou all last week? Where wert thou last Friday? Thou canst not have been in Jerusalem, surely, for all Jerusalem was out at Calvary that morning. And if thou hadst been out there thou wouldst not wonder at our sadness.' The stranger did not say whether he had been out at Calvary last Friday morning or no. "What things?" He asked, bowing, as it were, to Cleopas's reproof and reproach at such unaccountable ignorance at such a time. And then we have Cleopas's reply in his own very identical words. For Luke, you must know, when he was preparing himself for his Gospel, and when he had read Mark's meagre verses about the Emmaus meeting, said to himself, 'I must be at the bottom of this! I must have a much fuller record of all this in my Gospel. I wonder if Cleopas is still alive?' And thus it is that we have before us, *verbatim et literatim*, the exact answer that Cleopas gave to the stranger when he asked, "What things?" 'I remember, as if it were but yesterday,' said Cleopas to Luke, 'the whole scene, and every word that He said to us, and that we said to Him. How could I ever forget a single syllable of it? It was all so burned into my heart that I have told it a thousand times.' And Cleopas took the Evangelist out of Emmaus and showed him the very spot just where the stranger joined them, and just where He said, "What things?" 'And just where I said—these were my very words to Him—I said, Concerning Jesus of Nazareth, which was a prophet mighty in deed and in word before God and all the people. And how the chief priests and our rulers delivered Him to be condemned to death, and have crucified Him. But we trusted, I went on in my folly, that it had been He who should have redeemed Israel: and beside all this, to-day is the third day since these things were done. And from that hour to this, I have never for an hour or may say never for a moment, forgotten the look He gave us when He said to us, "O fools, and slow of heart to believe!"' And then Cleopas continued to relate to Luke the rest of that never-to-be-forgotten conversation concerning the true Christ in Moses and the prophets. What an hour that was to Cleopas and to his companion! They did not know where they were. They forgot themselves. They were carried captive with the stranger's amazing knowledge, and with His supreme authority, and with His burning words. And no wonder. Many learned, and earnest, and eloquent men have expounded Moses, and David, and Isaiah since that Emmaus afternoon; but human ears and human hearts have never heard such another exposition of Holy Scripture as Cleopas and his companion heard at that stranger's lips.

For, this was an Interpreter, one among a thousand! When this Interpreter gave His first interpretation of Scripture in Nazareth three years before, there was delivered to Him the book of the prophet Isaiah. But they had no book to deliver Him on the way to Emmaus. Nor did He need a book. This stranger, whoever He was, seemed to Cleopas to have the whole book unrolled within Himself. He seemed to have Moses, and David, and Isaiah, and Jeremiah, absolutely by heart. And the way He spake to them called to His two companions' remembrance all that they had ever heard or read in Moses, and the Prophets, and the Psalms. The seed of the woman; the brazen serpent; the paschal lamb; the scapegoat; the thirty pieces of silver. My God, my God, why hast thou forsaken me? They part my garments among them, and cast lots upon my vesture. Reproach hath broken mine heart: I looked for some to take pity, but there was none: and for comforters, but I found none. They gave me also gall for my meat, and in my thirst they gave me vinegar to drink. He was wounded for our transgressions, He was bruised for our iniquities; the chastisement of our peace was upon Him: and with His stripes we are healed. He is brought as a lamb to the slaughter, and as a sheep before her shearers is dumb, so He opened not His mouth. 'O, fool, that I was!' Cleopas cried out to Luke. 'I had seen it all fulfilled the week before with mine own eyes. But, that evening, our eyes were somehow holden that we did not know Him again! At the same time how our hearts did burn as He spake these things to us. And then He said to us, appealing to us to reply: May not Jesus of Nazareth be the true Christ of God, and your own Redeemer after all? After all, may not Jesus of Nazareth be He who was to come? Do not all your own prophets tell you that the true Christ must be denied of His own, and delivered up to Pilate to crucify? Must not the Prince of Life, when He comes, be killed and raised from the dead on the third day? What think ye? What say ye? And have you not just told me yourselves that certain women of your own company were early this very morning at the sepulchre, and that the angels of heaven were descended there to testify that Jesus of Nazareth was alive again?' And so on, till their hearts burned within them like two coals of juniper.

O ye men still of Emmaus, now sitting and hearing all that in this house! I implore you to open your heart also to your Lord's burning words about Himself. To speak plainly, I implore you to seek out in this city that expounder, that one of a thousand preachers, who makes your heart to burn. If by chance, so to call it, you enter a church in this city of churches on a Sabbath day, with your heart sad, with your hopes ashamed, with your expectations a complete shipwreck, like Cleopas and his desponding companion, and the preacher so opens God's word to you, so sets forth the redemption of Israel and your own redemption, so sets forth a suffering Redeemer and His suffering people, that your heart is in a flame all that day, then, that is the preacher in all this world for you. That is my servant for you, says your God to you. I have made his mouth like a sharp sword for you. I have made him a polished shaft for you. I have hid him in my quiver for you. Hear him, said the Father, concerning his preacher-Son. And that preacher you have just heard may be as great a stranger to you as our Lord was to Cleopas on that highway that afternoon; but, if I were you, I would find out his name, and where God has given him his pulpit. If I were you I would have him for my minister, and for my children's minister, at any cost. I would sell my present house and buy another to be near that preacher. And if you never hear such a preacher; if no preacher has ever made your heart to burn; if there is not in all the city a single heart-kindling, heart-commanding, heart-capturing preacher for you, then, at any rate, there are not a few heart-kindling and heart-holding authors to be had. Authors, thanks be to God, that will make you all but independent of us lukewarm preachers. Do you know some of those authors' names? Do any of you almost owe your soul to some of them? Do you have a select shelf of them within reach of your chair and your bed? Could you say, if not of some spiritual preacher, then of some spiritual writer, what Crashaw says of Teresa: "The flame I took from reading thee." And what Cleopas said to Luke about this stranger's words, "Did not our heart burn within us?" I preached sin with great sense, says John Bunyan. And I warrant you that stranger preached the Messianic and the Atonement passages in David, and in Isaiah, and in Jeremiah, and in Zechariah, with great sense also, and for a very good reason.

> Yea, this man's brow, like to a title-leaf,
> Foretells the nature of a tragic volume:
> He trembles, and the whiteness in his cheek
> Is apter than his tongue to tell his errand.

Never did threescore furlongs seem so short since furlongs were laid out on the face of the earth. 'Come and sup with us,' said the entranced Cleopas to this mysterious stranger who had so over-mastered him, and so set his heart on fire. "Abide with us, for the day is far spent." And when they had sat down to supper,

Cleopas naturally asked the stranger, as you would have done, to say grace. What grace did that stranger say in that supper-room in Emmaus, I wonder? John Livingstone tells us that John Smith of Maxtown in Teviotdale had all the Psalms of David by heart, and that, instead of our curt and grudging grace before meat he always repeated to his attentive table a whole Psalm. Would it be at Emmaus the twenty-third Psalm. Would it be the twenty-seventh and the twenty-eighth verses of the hundred and fourth Psalm? Or, would it be Job's every Sabbath morning and every Sabbath evening grace and blessing? Or, would it be something that the stranger made up on the spot? Would it be this, at the hearing of which Cleopas's heart would kindle again? "Except ye eat the flesh of the Son of Man, and drink His blood, ye have no life in you. For My flesh is meat indeed, and My blood is drink indeed." Whatever the grace was that He said, you may be quite sure He did not say it as we say our graces. He did not mumble it over so that nobody could hear it. He did not say it as if He was ashamed of it. He did not say, Amen! with His hand down already in the dish. Neither did Cleopas and his companion sit down and begin to eat before the grace was finished. No! for the truth is, the three men got no further than the grace that night. That sacred supper, with such a grace said over it, stands on that table to this day. It is not eaten to this day. For as the stranger handed to Cleopas and to his companion the bread He had blessed and broken, they could not but see His Hands! And the moment they saw His Hands, He had vanished out of their sight.

XC

MATTHIAS THE SUCCESSOR TO JUDAS ISCARIOT

In the opening chapter of the Acts of the Apostles we are introduced into the first congregational meeting, so to call it, that ever was held in the Church of Christ. There are a hundred-and-twenty members present in the upper room, and the Presbytery of Jerusalem are met there with the congregation: moderator, clerk, and all. Peter presides; and he discharges the duties of the day with all that solemnity of mind and all that intensity of heart which we seldom miss in Peter. The solemnity of the meeting would solemnise any man. It would melt a far harder heart than the heart of the emotional son of Jonas ever was. For Judas Iscariot, a member of the Presbytery, so to call him, has turned out to have been the son of perdition all the time. For thirty pieces of silver he had become guide to them that took Jesus. Peter himself had wellnigh gone down into the same horrible pit with Judas: and he also would have been in his own place by this time, had it not been that his Master prayed for Peter that his faith might not fail. And thus it is that Peter is now sitting in that seat of honour and influence and authority, and is conducting the election of a successor to Judas, with all that holy fear and with all that firm faith which makes that upper room, under Peter's presidency, such a pattern to all vacant congregations to all time. Considering her age and her size, the Church of Jerusalem had a large number of men any one of whom could quite well have been put forward and proposed for the vacant office. But Peter and his colleagues, with a great sense of responsibility, had prepared a short leet of two quite outstanding and distinguished men; Joseph, who was surnamed Justus, and Matthias. And then one of the eleven led the congregation in prayer in these well-remembered words—"Lord, Thou knowest the hearts of all men: show whether of these two Thou hast chosen." And the lot fell upon Matthias, and he was numbered with the eleven apostles.

Now, somewhat remarkable to say, never before the day of his election, and never after it, is Matthias's name so much as once mentioned in all the New Testament. At the same time, we have Matthias's footprints, so to speak, oftener than once on the pages of the four Gospels. And a man's mere footprints, and the direction they point to, will sometimes tell us far more about the real character and capacity of the man than whole volumes of printed matter about him. The first time we see one of Matthias's footprints is on the sands of Bethabara beyond Jordan, where John was baptizing. Like Andrew and Simon the sons of Jonas, and like John the son of Zebedee, Matthias was a disciple of the Baptist at that time, confessing his sins. The next day John seeth Jesus coming to him, and saith to Matthias, Behold the Lamb of God. And Matthias heard him speak, and he followed Jesus, along with John and Andrew. And when Peter tabled Matthias's name on the day of the election, he certified all these things about Matthias to the ten, and to the women, and to Mary the mother of Jesus, and to His brethren, and to the whole hundred-and-twenty. And more than that, Peter certified to the whole congregation that, when many who had been baptized, apostatised and went back and walked no more with John and Jesus, Matthias, said Peter, has this to his praise, that he has endured and has persevered up to this very present. Not only so, but this also, that Matthias had been a witness with the eleven of the resurrection of the Lord. And these, added Peter, are the two indispensable tests of fitness for this vacant office; a three years' conversion and faithful discipleship, and this also, that he had seen the risen Lord with his own eyes. And the lot fell upon Matthias.

Now, it is sometimes not very unlike that when you yourselves meet to call a minister. Tremendous as the moment is: everlasting as the issues are that hang upon that moment: you may never have heard so much as the name of that candidate for the pastorate of your immortal soul. You may never so much as have heard him once open his mouth either to pray or to preach. Not one of the hundred-and-twenty had ever heard this stranger man Matthias once open his mouth. But Peter has had his eye on Matthias all along. Peter knew far more about Joseph and Matthias than they could have believed. Peter was all ears and all eyes where a future apostle and pastor was concerned. And so it is sometimes still. All you really know about your future minister you have to take sometimes on the best testimony you can get. As one of our own elders once said when we were calling our young minister: "I would rather trust to those two capable men who know him and have heard him preach, than I would trust to my own ears." And he spake with both wisdom and humility in so saying. Like the hundred-and-twenty, little as you know about your future minister, you know this much, that when all the other young men at school and college were choosing learning, and philosophy, and medicine, and law, and the army, and the navy, and trade, and manufactures, and so on; this youth now in your offer was led to choose the word of God, and the pulpit, and the pastorate, for his life-work. And, with all that, you may with some assurance, put your hand to his call, after you have made your importunate and personal prayer about this whole momentous matter to Him who knows the hearts of all men. For He knows your heart better than you know it yourself: and He knows just what kind of a minister your heart needs: your own heart and your children's hearts. And, then, He knows the hearts of all those probationers also, and whether their hearts are properly in their Master's work or no. As also what motive it was that made them ministers at first, and with what motive and with what intention they are laying out their future work among you. How well it is, both for congregations and candidates, that He knows all men's hearts, and that all men's hearts are in His hands.

Three years ago Matthias had come through a very sharp trial of faith, and love, and patience, and perseverance. At his conversion and baptism Matthias had prepared his heart to leave all and to follow Christ. But instead of being invited to do what with all his heart he wished to do, Matthias was deliberately passed over by our Lord in His election of the twelve. Matthias had been in Christ, as Paul says, a long time before some of those men who were lifted over his head; and here was he as good as set aside and clean forgotten. And, just suppose, what is more than likely, that Matthias knew Judas's secret heart and real character quite well; what a shock it was to Matthias's faith, and love, and whole religious life, to see such a deceiver as Iscariot was, deliberately chosen by Christ, when Matthias would have shed the last drop of his blood for the Master who had refused to employ him. But Matthias, for all that, did not let his heart sour. He accepted being set aside as his proper place. He found in himself only too many reasons why he was so set aside. He was like the defeated candidate in Plutarch who, departing home from the election to his house, said to them at home that it did him good to see that there were three hundred men in Athens who were better men than he was. And thus it was that when many men would have turned away and gone after another master, Matthias said to himself: 'Office or no office, election or rejection, call or no call, to whom else can I go?' Nay, not only did Matthias keep true to his Master through all these humiliations and disappointments, but he continued to behave himself and to lay out his life just as if he had been elected and ordained. So much so, that without ordination he worked harder at the out-of-the-way work of the discipleship than some of those did who were elected, and ordained, and honoured, and rewarded men. And thus it was that Peter was able to certify to the hundred-and-twenty that Matthias had been as true and as loyal to his Lord all those three years as the very best of the eleven had been. 'And thus,' said Peter, 'if there were some who were numbered among us who were not at heart of us, there were others who were at heart and in life really of us, though they were not as yet written down among us.' So have I myself seen heaven-born and highly-gifted ministers of Christ passed over in the day when this and that vacant charge met to cast their lots. And, like Matthias, I have seen such men left out at the beginning only to be the more promoted and employed in the end. But then, to be sure, they were like Matthias in this also, that all their days they were men of staunchest loyalty to their Master, and men of sleepless labour for His cause. When a door shall open, and where, is not the true servant's business, nor his anxiety. It is the true servant's part to be ready; which the truest of all servants never feels that he is. And disappointments and procrastinations to all such men are but extended opportunities to enable them to be somewhat less unready for their call when it comes. If Matthias had been a modern probationer you would not have found him going about complaining against this committee and that congregation. You would not have seen him going about idle all the week, and then turning up at each new vacancy with the same old and oft-fingered sermon. No. You may shut all your doors on some candidates, but you cannot shut them out from their books, and from the hidden and unstipended work that their hearts love. You cannot, with all your ill-cast lots, either embitter or alienate a truly elect, and humble-minded, and diligent disciple of Christ. And with all your ill-advised elections the stone that is fit for the wall will not always be let lie in the ditch.

But is there anything possible to our very best probationers that can at all be compared to this qualification of those days—to have companied with the Lord Jesus all the time He went out and in among His disciples? Yes; I think there is. Nay, not only so; but when we enter into all the inwardness and depth of this matter we come to see that our students of divinity and our probationers have actually some great advantages over the twelve disciples themselves. Our Lord's words are final, and full of instruction and comfort to us, on this matter. His words to Thomas, I mean. Jesus saith to him. "Thomas, because thou hast seen, thou hast believed; blessed are they that have not seen, and yet have believed." And you will all recall Sir Thomas Browne's noble protestation: "Now, honestly, I bless myself that I never saw Christ nor His disciples. I would not have been one of Christ's patients on whom He wrought His wonders. For then had my faith been thrust upon me, nor should I enjoy that greater blessing pronounced to all that believe and saw not. I believe He was dead and buried, and rose again: and desire to see Him in His glory, rather than to contemplate Him in His cenotaph or sepulchre. They only had the advantage of a bold and noble faith who lived before His coming, and who upon obscure prophecies and mystical types could raise a belief and expect apparent impossibilities." To have seen and handled the Word of Life; to have had Him dwelling among them, full of grace and truth, as John says; to have had Him going in and out among them, as Peter says, was a privilege incomparable and unspeakable. At the same time, let any student in our day read his Greek Testament, with his eye on the Object: let him be like John Bunyan:—"Methought I was as if I had seen Him born, as if I had seen Him grow up, as if I had seen Him walk through this world, from the Cradle to the Cross: to which, when He came, I saw how gently He gave Himself up to be hanged and nailed on it for my sins and wicked doings. Also, as I was musing on this His progress, that dropped on my spirit, He was ordained for the slaughter," and so on. Let any of our students company with Christ all the time He went in and out in that manner, and he may depend upon it that the beautiful benediction which our Lord addressed in reproof to Thomas will be richly fulfilled to that wise-hearted student all his happy ministerial days, and through him to his happy people. Now, if there were a divinity student here I would ask and demand of him out of this Scripture for students—Are you so companying with Christ while you are still at college? Do you see with all your inward eyes what you read in your New Testament? Do you believe and believe and believe your way through the four Gospels? Is your faith the very substance itself of the things you hope for, and the absolute and conclusive evidence of the things you do not as yet see? Do you pray your way through the life of Christ? Do you put the lepers, and the sick, and the possessed with devils, and the dead in their graves, out of their places, as you read about them; and do you put yourself into their places, and say what they say, and hear and accept what is said to them? For, if so, then you will receive, all your preaching and pastoral days, the end of your faith, the salvation of your own soul, and the salvation of the souls of your people.

Then, again, could any of our probationers be put forward by his proposer as Matthias was still put forward by Peter? No. It could not possibly be said of any man living in these dregs of time of ours that he had been an actual witness of the resurrection of Christ. And yet I am not so sure of that. Strange things can be said when you come to speak about a true probationer. With man it is impossible; but not with God. With God all things are possible. I myself know probationers who are witnesses of the very best authority that Christ is risen indeed. Let such a young preacher come to your vacant pupit with Ephesians i. 19 to ii. 1 for his Sabbath morning exposition; and let him set forth with Paul, that the spiritual quickening of a soul dead in trespasses and sins is done by the same mighty power that quickened and raised up Christ, and you will soon see if he knows what he is speaking about. And if he does: if he makes your hearts to burn with the noble doctrine of his and your oneness with the risen Christ, then you have in your offer a living witness of apostolic rank for Christ's resurrection. You might have the angel who rolled away the stone and sat on it for your other candidate, but he should have no vote of mine. Give me for my minister, not Gabriel himself, but a fellow-sinner who has been quickened together with Christ, and who can describe the process and the experience till my death-cold heart burns within me with the resurrection-life of Christ. Give me a minister whom God hath raised from the dead, and you may have all the sounding brasses and tinkling cymbals in heaven and earth for me. And I am glad to say that there are not a few probationers abroad of that experience. Only, are you sure you will recognise them when they appear and preach in your pulpit? For—

> A jest's prosperity lies in the ear
> Of him that hears it, never in the tongue
> Of him that speaks it.

Let the hundred-and-twenty take heed how they hear.

XCI

ANANIAS AND SAPPHIRA

THEMISTOCLES tossed all night and could not sleep because of the laurels of Miltiades. And Ananias was like Themistocles because of the praises poured upon Barnabas by Peter, and by all the apostles, and by all the poor. Ananias and Sapphira could not take rest till they, like Barnabas, had sold their possession, and laid the price of it at Peter's feet. 'Lay it at Peter's feet,' said Sapphira to her hesitating husband, 'and say that you are very sorry that the land did not sell for far more. And after I have made my purchases, I will come to the Lord's Supper with you. Keep a place for me at the Table, and I will join you there in good time in breaking of bread and in prayers.' And Ananias did as Sapphira had instigated him to do. Only, Ananias was not at all happy in his approach to Peter's feet that day. Somehow or other, Ananias could not summon up that gladness and that singleness of heart with which all the other contributors came up that day. With all he could do there was a certain awkwardness and stumblingness of manner that Ananias, somehow or other, could not shake off all that day. You who are collectors for churches and charities are well accustomed to all Ananias's looks and ways of speaking that day. You often hear from us the very same explanations and apologies and self-defences. 'There had been a great fall in the rent of land in Judea of late. And thus the old estate had not nearly yielded its upset and expected price. But what it had yielded, Peter was welcome to it.'

Everything fell to Peter in those days. The offices and services of the early Church had not as yet been divided up and specialised into the apostleship, and the eldership, and the deaconship, and, till that was done, Peter had to be everything himself. Peter was premier apostle, ruling elder, leading deacon, and all. It was like those country congregations where the minister has to do everything himself, till he has neither time nor strength nor spirit left to give himself continually to prayer, and to the ministry of the word. But Peter was a perfect Samson in the Israel of that day. He was a minister of immense capacity, gigantic energy, endless resource, and overpowering authority. And thus it was that it had fallen to Peter to sit over against the treasury, and to enter the Pentecostal contributions that day. And it struck Ananias like a thunderbolt, when Peter, instead of smiling upon him and praising him, denounced and sentenced him so sternly. "Ananias, why hath Satan filled thine heart to lie to the Holy Ghost?" And the young men arose, and wound him up, and carried him out, and buried him. And then, three hours after, just as Peter was shutting up his books to go to dispense the Lord's Supper, at that moment Sapphira appeared. 'You sold your farm for so much, your husband tells me?' 'Yes, my lord, for so much.' And the young men came in and found her dead, and they buried Ananias and Sapphira in Aceldama, next backbreadth to Judas Iscariot, the proprietor of the place. That the prophecy of Isaiah might be fulfilled: "They shall go forth, and look upon the carcases of the men that have transgressed against me; for their worm shall not die, neither shall their fire be quenched, and they shall be an abhorring unto all flesh." And that the prophecy of Daniel also might be fulfilled: "Many of them that sleep in the dust of the earth shall awake, some to everlasting life, and some to shame and everlasting contempt."

What a world this is we live in! What a red-hot furnace of sin and sanctification is this world! How we all tempt and try and test and stumble one another in everything we say and do! Barnabas cannot sell his estate in Cyprus and lay the price of it at Peter's feet, but by doing so he must immediately become the sudden death of Ananias and Sapphira. But for the Pentecostal love, and but for Barnabas's baptism into that love, Ananias and Sapphira would have lived to see their children's children and peace upon Israel. They would have sat down together at the Lord's Table till Peter preached their funeral sermon and held them up as two pattern proprietors of houses and lands. But Barnabas and his renowned name became such a snare to Ananias and Sapphira that they were buried on the same day and in the same grave. *Ama nesciri* has been the motto of more than one of the great saints. Seek obscurity, that is. Subscribe anonymously, that is. Do not let your collectors and the advertising people print your name or your amount, that is. Say, A Friend. Say, A Well-wisher. Put a star, put a cross, put anything but your name, not even your initials. Or, if you are a popular author, say, and not a landowner in these days; publish your books without your name. Employ another name. You may miss something that is very sweet to you by doing that; but it will be made up to you afterwards when all your royalties come in, and all your last day reviews. Think of Ananias and Sapphira when all men praise your generosity, or your Shakespearian genius, or your enormous emoluments. Be sure of this, that all Peter's praises of Barnabas did not refresh Barnabas's heart half so much as they caused that sinful sleeplessness, and all its consequences, to Ananias and Sapphira.

"Satan hath filled thine heart, Ananias." That was a terrible salutation for a man to be met with who had just sold a possession and laid such a large part of the price at the apostle's feet. But Peter knew all Satan's processes. Peter knew by experience what he was speaking about. And that is the reason why Peter speaks with such assurance and severity and indignation and judgment. And had Ananias at that moment gone out and wept bitterly, we would have been drawing far other lessons to-night out of that terrible Communion morning. Do you know the premonition, the sensation, the smell, so to say, when Satan approaches you to fill your heart? And what do you say to him? What do you do to him? Do you set chair for him? Do you lay a cover and set glasses for him? Do you share your pillow with him? "Ah! you are there again, my man!" So an old saint in the congregation salutes Satan as often as her practised nostrils catch the beginning of his brimstone on her stairhead. "But you are too late this time. I am engaged to-day. There is Some One with me. And you had better flee at once. Come sooner next time!" Luther threw his ink-bottle. What do you throw? What do you do? Or is Satan in on you, and are you in his hands and at his service, in money matters, and what not, before you know where you are? "Ah, sir, you are there again, are you? But my heart is as full to-day as it can hold of Another," calls out my stairhead friend by reason of her exercised senses.

The stroke was sudden, and, as we say, severe. But even at this distance of time and place we can see some good and sufficient reasons for the severity of the stroke. *Pœna duorum doctrina multorum,* is the epigrammatic comment of an old writer. On two hands that sore stroke would tell for long. On the one hand, on those who were tempted to join the Christian community in order to share in the Pentecostal charity. For, then as now, a crowd of impostors would dog the steps of the open-hearted and open-handed church. On the other hand, we all give very much as others have given before us. We measure our givings, not by our duty nor by our ability, but by what others have done, and by what is expected of us. We wish to impress you. We wish to have your approval. We say with Ananias: 'This is all I can spare; indeed, this is all I possess.' Our sin, and our danger of death in our giving, lie not so much in that we have given less than we could have given, but in that we have not told the truth. "Yea, for so much," we say, till the feet of the young men are almost at our door. The stroke was sudden and severe to the onlookers, but it was not at all so sudden or so severe to Ananias and Sapphira themselves. It was not unexpected and without warning to them. There were many provocations and aggravations on their part of which we are quite ignorant. Ananias may at one time have been a poor man's son, and when he came up to Jerusalem in his youth to push his fortune, he may have knelt down on the side of Olivet and said, 'Thy vows are upon me, O God. And if Thou wilt give me bread to eat, and raiment to put on, and a wife and children in Jerusalem, then the Lord shall be my God, and the God of my household.' Or, again, in some time of adversity he may have said, "The pains of hell gat hold upon me; but I will pay that which my mouth spake when I was in trouble." Or, again, in those sweet but soul-deceiving days when they were bridegroom and bride together; in those Beulah days—"As for me and my house, we will serve the Lord. Like David, we will walk with a perfect heart in all our household affairs at home." Ah, yes; God was no doubt quite sufficiently justified to Ananias and Sapphira themselves, when He judged them so swiftly that day. At the same time, Jeremy Taylor, who has given immense learning and intellect to all such cases, says that God sometimes accepts a temporal death in room of an eternal. And that, to some persons, a sudden death stands instead of a long and an explicit repentance. While Augustine, I see, and some other great authorities, are bold to class the awful case of Ananias and Sapphira under that scripture of the apostle where he assures us that some church members are delivered unto Satan for the destruction of the flesh, so that the spirit may be saved in the day of the Lord Jesus. Let us join with Augustine and Taylor in their burial-service over Ananias and Sapphira in the trembling hope that they were struck down in a sanctifying discipline, rather than in an everlasting condemnation. And that they so died that we might learn of them so to live as not to die. Let us hope that both husband and wife had the root of the matter in them all the time; and that we shall see them also saved in that day, in spite of Satan and all his fatal entrances into their hearts. The Lord rebuke thee, O Satan, is not this a brand plucked out of the fire?

And now to come home to ourselves. As you all know, we have an institution in full operation in the Free Church of Scotland which is based and built up and worked out on exactly Pentecostal and Barnabas principles. Dr. Chalmers's conception of the Sustentation Fund was derived and developed from the spirit and the example of the Apostolic Church of Jerusalem. The same Pentecostal spirit was poured out at the Disruption of the Established and Endowed Church of Scotland, to support the Free Church of Scotland under her injuries and her impoverishments for Christ's sake, and for the sake of His people. And thus it was that the ministers and deacons' courts of the Free Church were then, and are still, all of one mind and spirit, and have all things in common. And that same Pentecostal spirit breathes and burns, and that same Apostolic institution still stands and extends and expands, to this day. And still the Prophetic and Apostolic benediction is pronounced over the Free Church and her liberal-hearted people—"Bring ye all the tithes into the storehouse, saith the Lord of Hosts, and prove Me now herewith, if I will not open the windows of heaven, and pour you out a blessing, that there shall not be room enough to receive it."

"Prove Me now herewith," said the Lord. And He has promised that when we prove Him with our tithes, all manner of prosperity will follow our practice of that Scriptural rule and pattern. And the rule is not a Scriptural one only. Somehow or other, the tithe, the tenth part, fills all classical literature, as well as the whole of Holy Scripture. And yet, with all that before our eyes, plain as plain can be, here we are, at this time of day, blundering about and telling lies, many of us, like Ananias and

Sapphira, without any method, or principle, or rule in our givings, any more than if Scripture had never spoken on this matter, or as if a rule of love and common-sense had never been laid down. Till we waken up, and take the Patriarchal, and Mosaic, and Prophetic, and Apostolic, and even Pagan way of taxing our income, and laying aside a definite and a liberal part of it for church and charity, we need never expect to inherit the promises, or to enter into that liberty of heart and hand which awaits us and our children. It is surely time that we found out some better way than our present haphazard way of dealing with this great and pressing matter. For everything comes on us in this city. All Scotland, all Ireland, and many parts even of rich England; France, Switzerland, Italy; churches, manses, missions—everything comes on Edinburgh, and on a limited field of Edinburgh. When some great financial genius, say, like Dr. Chalmers, arises in the Church to expound and enforce this disastrously neglected law of God, a new day will dawn on our whole religious and charitable exchequer. Then the Christian child will be brought up to tithe his pocket-money of sixpence a week for Jesus his Saviour's sake. And his father his pound a week, or his ten pounds, or his hundred, or his thousand. And, then, all we shall have to do, without straining our hearts or souring our tempers, will be calmly, and at our leisure, to exercise our best discretion as to the proportion and the destination of the stewardship-money we have had intrusted to us. And, when that Apostolic day dawns, our successors in the churches and charities of the land will look back with amazement at our poverty-stricken ways of collecting church money, leaning on State endowments, and all such un-Pentecostal expedients. And all because our eyes had, somehow, not been opened to Scriptural wisdom, and to Scriptural love, and to Scriptural liberality, in this whole matter of our Lord's money.

XCII

SIMON MAGUS

But who, to begin with, was Simon Magus? And how did it come about that he believed, and was actually baptized by Philip the evangelist; and then was detected, denounced and utterly reprobated by the Apostle Peter? How did all that come about?

Well, you must know that Samaria, where Simon Magus lived and carried on his astounding impositions, was a half-Hebrew, half-heathen country. Samaria had just enough of the Hebrew blood in its veins to make it full of the very worst qualities of that blood, mixed up with some of the very worst qualities of the heathen blood of that day also. And Simon Magus was at once the natural product, and the divine punishment, of that apostate land in which we find him living in such mountebank prosperity. Simon Magus was a very clever man, and he was at the same time a very bad man; till, by his tremendous pretensions, he had the whole of Samaria at his feet. There was something positively sublime about the impudence and charlatanry of Simon Magus, till he was actually feared and obeyed and worshipped as nothing short of some divinity who had condescended to come and take up his abode in Samaria. But the whole man and the whole situation is best set before us in the two or three strokes of the sacred writer. "There was a certain man called Simon, which beforetime in the same city used sorcery, and bewitched the people of Samaria, giving out that himself was some great one. To whom they all gave heed, from the least to the greatest, saying, This man is the great power of God. And to him they had regard, because of that long time he had bewitched them with sorceries. But when they believed Philip preaching the things concerning the kingdom of God, and the name of Jesus Christ, they were baptized, both men and women. Then Simon himself believed also; and when he was baptized, he continued with Philip and wondered, beholding the miracles and signs which were done."

Philip had extraordinary success in his evangelising mission to Samaria. It was like New England, or Cambuslang, or 1859-60, or Moody and Sankey's first visit to Scotland. For the people with one accord gave heed unto those things that Philip spake, hearing and seeing the miracles which he did. And there was great joy in that city. 'The very devil himself has been converted and has been baptized by me,' Philip telegraphed to Jerusalem. 'I actually have the name of Simon Magus on my communion-roll.' At the hearing of that, the apostles sent two of their foremost men down to Samaria to superintend the great movement, and God sent the Holy Ghost with them, till the whole of Samaria seemed to have turned to God and to the name of Jesus Christ. Only, Simon Magus was all the time such an impostor that in his conversation and baptism he had completely deceived Philip. Nay, I think it but fair to Simon Magus to say that he had completely deceived himself as well as Philip. I think so. I am bound in charity to think so. When Simon Magus came up out of the water, had a voice from heaven spoken at that moment, it would surely have been heard to say, 'This is an arch-deceiver, deceiving, but, at the same time, being deceived.' Some men have far more self-discernment than other men, and self-discernment is the highest and the rarest science of all the sciences on the face of the earth. And, usually, there is united with great self-discernment, and as a reward and a premium put by God upon its exercise, the power of deeply discerning other men's spirits also. Now, although Philip was a prince of evangelistic preachers, and a good and an able man, at the same time he was far too easily satisfied with his converts. Philip was far better at preaching than he was at catechising. And thus it was that it fell to Peter and John to purge Philip's communion-roll of Simon Magus immediately on their arrival in Samaria. At the same time, this must be said, that Simon Magus had never come out in his true colours till after Peter's arrival, and till after all the true converts had received the Holy Ghost.

The circumstances were these: It was part of the Pentecostal equipment of the apostles to possess for a time some of the miracle-working powers that their Divine Master had exercised in order to arrest atention to His advent, and to secure a hearing to His ministry. And thus it is that we find the apostles speaking with tongues, healing the sick, opening the eyes of the blind, casting out devils, and many suchlike miracles and signs. Now, Simon Magus, like everybody else in Samaria, was immensely impressed with all that he saw and heard. No man was more impressed than Simon Magus, or more convinced of the divine mission of the apostles. But, with all his wonder and with all his conviction, he was never truly converted. The love of money, and the still more intoxicating love of notoriety, had taken such absolute possession of Simon Magus that he simply could not live out of the eyes of men. He must be in men's mouths. He must have a crowd around him. Themistocles could not sleep because of the huzzas that filled the streets of Athens when Miltiades walked abroad; and the crowds that followed Peter and John were gall and wormwood to Simon Magus. For, still greater crowds used to take him up and carry him on their shoulders in the days of his great power before Philip came to Samaria. Now, Peter had never liked the look of Philip's great convert, and it completely justified Peter's incurable suspicions when Simon Magus came one night into Peter's lodgings, and, setting down a bag of money on the table, said, 'What will you take for the Holy Ghost? If you will show me the secret of your apostleship so that I may work your miracles like you, I have plenty of money, and I know where there is plenty more.' The sight of the bag, and the blasphemous proposal of the owner of the bag, nearly drove Peter beside himself. And the old fisherman so blazed out at the poor mountebank that the page burns red to this day with Peter's denunciation. "Thy money perish with thee, for I perceive thou art still in the gall of bitterness, and in the bond of iniquity!"

"Giving out that himself was some great one." That is our first lesson from this Holy Scripture about Simon Magus. Let those take the lesson to heart who specially need it, and who will humble themselves to receive it. It may be sorcery and witchcraft like that of Simon Magus; it may be in the honours of the kingdom of Heaven like the sons of Zebedee; it may be in preaching sermons; it may be in making speeches or writing books; it may be in anything you like, down to your children's possessions and performances; but we all, to begin with, give ourselves out to be some great one. Simon Magus was but an exaggerated specimen of every popularity-hunter among us. There is an element and first principle of Simon Magus, the Samaritan mountebank, in all public men. There is still a certain residuum of Simon left in order to his last sanctification in every minister. But the most Simon Magus-like of all sanctified ministers I know is Thomas Shepard, and that just because he is the most self-discerning, the most honest, and the most outspoken about himself of us all. Popularity was the very breath of life to that charlatan of Samaria. He could not work, he could not live, he could not be converted and baptized, without popularity. And there is not one public man in a thousand, politician or preacher, who will go on living and working and praying out of sight, and all the time with sweetness, and contentment, and good-will, and a quiet heart. All Samaria must give heed to Simon Magus from the least to the greatest. And so still with his successors. A despairing missionary to the drunken navvies on a new railway, complained to me the other day that one of our great preachers, who was holidaying in the neighbourhood, would not give an idle Sabbath afternoon hour to the men loitering about the bothy door. It was the dregs of Simon Magus in the city orator; he could not kindle but to a crowd. "Seek obscurity" was Fénelon's motto. Whether he lived up to his motto or no, the day will declare; if he did, there will not be many wearing the same crown with him on that day. But Richard Baxter will be one of them. "I am much less regardful of the approbation of men, and set much lighter by contempt or applause, than I did long ago. All worldly things appear most vain and unsatisfactory when we have tried them most. But though I feel that this hath some hand in the effect, yet the knowledge of man's nothingness, and of God's transcendent greatness, with whom it is that I have most to do, and the sense of the brevity of human things, and the nearness of eternity, are the principal causes of this effect, and not self-conceitedness and morosity, as some suppose." These things will help to do it, but above all these things a completely broken heart will alone cast Simon Magus out of us ministers. A heart broken beyond all mollification or binding up in this world; but not even a broken heart, unless it is daily broken. Nothing will root the mountebank out of us ministers but constant self-detection, constant self-contempt, constant self-denunciation, and constant self-destruction. Oh, my friends, you do not know, and you are not fit to be told, the tremendous price of a minister's salvation. It is this that makes our crucified Master say to us ministers continually, "Few of you there be that find it."

You will not know what a "law-work" is; but Simon Magus was simply lost for want of a law-work. You never nowadays hear the once universal pulpit word. The Romans and the Galatians are full of the law-work, and so have all our greatest preachers been. Those two great evangelical Epistles were not yet written, but there was enough of their contents in the Pentecostal air, if Simon Magus had had any taste for such soul-searching matters. I must not allow myself to say a single word as to Philip's mismanagement of his catechumens' and young communicants' classes. Only, the sorcerer must have sadly bewitched the evangelist before Philip put Simon Magus's name down on his communion-roll. Philip knew his business and his own heart. I dare not doubt that. Only, somehow or other, he let Simon Magus slip through his hands much too easily. Believing, baptism, communion-table and all, Simon Magus had neither part nor lot in this matter of the work of the law. I would not keep either a young communicant or an old convert away from the table because he was not deeply learned in all the Pauline doctrines; but I could not undertake to recommend his name to the kirk-session unless he gave me some evidence of what the masters of our science call the law-work. He might never have heard the word, and I would never mention it to him unless, indeed, he was a man of some mind. But it is mocking God, and deluding men, to crowd the table with communicants like Simon Magus, who do not know the first principles either of sin or of salvation. The best law-work comes to us long after conversion and admission to the table; but neither before his so-called conversion, nor after it, did this arch-imposter know anything about it—"for thy heart," said Peter, tearing it open to its very core, "is not right in the sight of God."

"Fictus," that is to say, a living and breathing fiction, was the name given to such converts as Simon Magus in those early days. Ignorance, Temporary, Pliable, and Turnaway, were some of their names in later days. Now, you are not an impostor by profession like Simon Magus. You do not make your living by deluding other people. But there may very easily be an element of fiction, of self-delusion and self-imposition, in your supposed conversion, as there was in his. Calvin's moderation, saneness of judgment, and spiritual insight, carry me with him here also. "I am not of their mind," he says, "who think that Simon Magus made only a semblance of religion. There is a middle ground between saving faith and sheer dissimulation. Simon Magus saw that the apostles' doctrine was true, and he received the same so far; but the groundwork was all along wanting; that is to say, his denial of himself was all along wanting." Just so. I see and feel Calvin's point. Your religion is not all a sham on your part. You are not a pure and unmixed hypocrite. But neither is your religion of the right kind. It is not saving your soul. It is not making you every day a new and another man. Your heart is not right in the sight of God. It is not, and it never will be, till, as Calvin says, and as Christ says, you deny yourself daily. And that, every day, to your heart's blood, and in the matter of the sin that so easily besets you. With Simon Magus it was the praise of men, and their crowding round him, and their adulation of him. Now, what he should have done, and what Philip should have insisted on him to do, was to discover to himself and to confess to himself his besetting sin, and every day to drive another nail of self-crucifixion into it. Another new nail every day, till it gave up the ghost. Instead of that the poor impostor tried to get Peter to share his apostolic popularity with him for thirty pieces of silver! If you are a platform, or a pulpit, or any other kind of mountebank, seek obscurity, for your soul's salvation lies there. If you are a popular preacher, flee from crowded churches, and hold services in bothies, and in poorhouses, and in barns, and in kitchens. Never search the papers to see what they are saying about you. Starve the self-seeking quack that is still within you. Beat him black and blue, as Paul tells us he did, and as Thomas Shepard tells us he did, every time he shows his self-admiring face.

Simon Magus put the thought of his heart into the form of a money-proposal to Peter. But, bad as the proposal was, it was not so much the proposal that Peter so struck at as the heart of the proposer. "If perhaps the thought of thine heart may be forgiven thee." Now, answer this, as we shall all answer it one day—What about the thoughts of your heart? Are the self-seeking, self-exalting thoughts of your heart dwelt on and indulged, or are they the greatest shame to you, and the greatest torment to you, of your life? Do you hate your own heart as you would hate hell itself, if you were about to be cast down into it? Do you beat your breast and cry out, Oh, wretched man that I am! Has the law entered, and is the law-work deep enough, and spiritual enough, to make all the Simon Magus-like thoughts of your hearts to be an inward pain and shame to you past all knowledge, and past all belief about you, of mortal man? His thoughts, that is, of self-advertisement, self-exaltation, and self-congratulation? Does the praise of men puff you up, and make you very happy? And is their silence, or their absence, something you cannot get over? Is he a good man who follows you about, and believes in you, and applauds you: and is he an unpardonably bad man who prefers Philip, and Peter, and John to Simon Magus? Then, be not deceived, God is not mocked, and neither are the self-discerning men round about you. Both your happiness and your sadness: both your love and your hatred of men; are quite naked and open to those with whom you have to do. "For I perceive that thou art still in the gall of bitterness, and in the bond of iniquity." "We may conjecture," says Calvin, "that Simon Magus repented." Whereas Bengel leaves it to the last day to discover that and to declare that.

XCIII

THE ETHIOPIAN EUNUCH

Our Lord gave the Pharisees of His day this praise, that they would compass sea and land to make one proselyte. Now, this Ethiopian eunuch was one of their proselytes. Like the Scotch and English of our own day, the Jews of our Lord's day compassed sea and land to make money; but, almost more, to make converts to Moses and Aaron. Bent as their hearts were on making a fortune, the Jews of that day were almost more bent on spreading the faith of Abraham, and the hope of their fathers. And it would be in his business relations with the heads of some of the trading and banking houses that the Jewish merchants had set up in Ethiopia, that Queen Candace's treasurer came into contact with the worshippers of Jehovah, till it all ended in his becoming a proselyte of the gate. Think, then, of this Ethiopian treasurer and his royal retinue coming up all the way from the far south to pay his vow, and to seek the face of the Lord in His holy temple. Think you see his conversion in Ethiopia, his sojourning for a season in Jerusalem, and then his returning home; and these pictures of him in your mind will greatly help you to understand and appreciate this remarkable man and his remarkable story.

Now, what the Ethiopian eunuch saw and heard in Jerusalem, and took home with him from Jerusalem, would almost entirely depend on the introductions he brought with him, and on the houses to which he took those introductions. If an eastern prince were to come, say at an Assembly time, to our own city, his impressions of the city and of the country would entirely depend on the hands into which he fell. We are so partitioned off into churches, and sects, and sub-sects; into professions, and political parties, and social castes; into likes and dislikes; into sympathies and into antipathies; that, if the Ethiopian eunuch had his first introduction into any of those hot-beds of ours, he would return home a total stranger, and almost an enemy, to many of the best men and to much of the best life of our city and our country. Unless, indeed, he had brought from his bitter experience of controversy, and faction, and party spirit in Ethiopia, that open and liberal mind, and that humble and loving heart, which no designed introduction will mislead, and no invidious patronage or privilege will poison.

Had this been an ordinary Ethiopian eunuch he would have spent his holiday among the theatres, and circuses, and bazaars, and other Roman amusements, of Pilate's procuratorship. As it was, he may, for anything we know, have brought an introduction to the Roman Procurator, and may have been entertained by Pilate's wife herself in the Roman Prætorium. On the other hand, it is much more likely that he was directed and recommended to some of the heads of the Temple: to Annas, or to Caiaphas, or to some other ecclesiastical dignitary. You may make use of your own knowledge of the condition of Jerusalem, and of the rank of the eunuch, and of his religious errand, to choose for yourselves just where the Ethiopian eunuch was lodged, and just in what light he saw the life of Jerusalem. Only, I fear, with all his ability, and with all his insight, and with all his seriousness of mind, the eunuch's furlough came to an end before he had well begun to see daylight on the Pharisees and the Sadducees, the Essenes and the Herodians, the Zelots and the Publicans, the devotees of Moses, and the disciples of Jesus Christ.

Was the Book of the prophet Isaiah the parting gift of his Jerusalem host to this eastern prince on the day of his departure home? And did the donor of the sacred book, with an earnest look and with delicate kindness, point out to his guest as he mounted his chariot steps, the fifty-third and fifty-sixth chapters of the evangelical and ecumenical prophet? Or was the sacred book this good enunch's own selection? After he had purchased some of the rarest specimens of recent Roman art for his royal mistress, did he seek out the sacred scriptorium and price for himself the richest-set roll of the prophet Esaias that the scribes possessed? In whatever way he had come by the fascinating book, he was away out of the city, and well on to the border of the land, before he was able to take his eyes off his purchase. The Ethiopian eunuch will be summoned forward with his Isaiah in his hand at the last day to witness against us all for the books we buy and read, and for the way we murder time, both at home and on our holidays, as well as on our long journeys. Did you ever see any one reading his Bible in a railway carriage, or on the deck of a steamboat? Did you ever see Isaiah, or Paul, in text or in commentary, exposed for sale on a railway book-stall? Oh, no! the very thought is profanity. We load our book-stalls, and our newsboys' baskets, and our travelling bags, with all the papers of the morning and the evening; and with piles of novels of all colours; and with our well-known Protestant reticence and reverence for divine things, we reserve our Bibles for home, and give up our Sabbath-days to Paul and Isaiah. One in a thousand will break through and will re-read on a railway journey his Homer or his Virgil; his Milton or his Shakespeare; his Bacon or his Hooker; his Â Kempis or his Bunyan; while one in a hundred thousand will venture to take out his Psalms or his New Testament. "The great number of books and papers of amusement, which of one kind or another, daily come in one's way, have in part occasioned, and most perfectly fall in with, and humour, this idle way of reading and considering things. By this means time, even in solitude, is happily got rid of, without the pain of attention. Neither is any part of it more put to the account of idleness—one can scarcely forbear saying is spent with less thought, than great part of that which is spent in reading." If that accusation was laid against the readers of 1792, how much more have we laid ourselves open to it in 1899?

But, all this time Philip is wandering up and down the wilderness, thinking that he must have mistaken his own imagination for the voice of the Lord. Caravans of pilgrims come and go: merchants of Egypt and of Arabia and cohorts of Roman soldiers: but all that only makes the evangelist the more lonely and the more idle. But, at last, a chariot of distinction comes in sight, and as it comes within earshot Philip hears with the utmost astonishment the swarthy master of the chariot reading aloud. Philip was not astonished at the distinguished man reading aloud, but his astonishment and admiration were unbounded when he began to make out at a distance what the dark-skinned stranger was reading. "He was led as a sheep to the slaughter; and like a lamb dumb before his shearer, so opened he not his mouth." "Understandest thou what thou readest?" said Philip, as the chariot came to a standstill. All this took place in the simple, unsophisticated, hospitable East; and it must not be measured by our hard and unbending habits of intercourse in the West; and, especially, in dour-faced Scotland. It would be taken as the height of intrusion, and, indeed, impudence, among us if one man said to another sitting over his book on a journey, "Are you understanding what you are reading?" But if we sat beside a foreigner who was struggling with one of our complicated guide-books, and was just about to start off in a wrong direction, it would be no intrusion if we leaned over and said to him, 'I fear, sir, that our barbarous language is not easily mastered by foreign scholars; but English is my native tongue, and I belong to this country. Can I be of any use to you?' "How can I," said the eunuch, "except some man should guide me?" And he desired Philip that he would come up and sit with him. Had the eunuch come to Jerusalem last year at this passover time, as he had been urged to come, and as he had at one time intended to come, he might have had Philip's Master sitting beside him to-day and reading Isaiah with him. But the eunuch had missed that opportunity by putting off paying his vow for another year. He was a year too late for ever seeing Jesus Christ in the flesh, and hearing Him open up Isaiah concerning Himself. But, better late than never. Better meet the meanest of His servants, than miss the Master altogether.

Was it the eunuch's own serious instincts, I wonder, that led him to the fifty-third of Isaiah? Or had he heard that profound and perplexing chapter disputed over by Stephen and Saul in one of the synagogues of Jerusalem? I cannot tell. Only, it strikes me, as it struck Philip, as a remarkable fact that out of the whole Old Testament this utter stranger to the Old Testament was pondering over its most central chapter, and its most profound prophecy, as he rode home in his chariot. When Augustine was a catechumen in Milan, and was just at the eunuch's stage in the truth, Ambrose directed his pupil to the study of Isaiah. "But I, not understanding my first lesson in that prophet, laid it by to be resumed when I was better practised." Bunyan also tells us that when he was beginning to read his Bible he much preferred the adventures of Joshua and Sampson and Gideon to Isaiah or Paul. But, explain it as we may, this Ethiopian neophyte was already far ahead of Bunyan, and even of Augustine. For he held in his hands the most Pauline page in all the Old Testament, and he would not lay it down till he got to the bottom of it. "I pray thee, of whom speaketh the prophet this? of himself, or of some other man?" What struck the imagination and the conscience of the eunuch was this: the absolutely unearthly picture that the prophet draws of his own character and conduct: if indeed it is of his own character and conduct the prophet speaks. "He was led as a sheep to the slaughter," the eunuch read again, "and like a lamb dumb before his shearer, so opened he not his mouth." The eunuch knew not a few good, and humble, and patient, and silently-suffering, men in Ethiopia, but he know no one of whom the half of these things could be said. And, if this was the prophet himself, no wonder then at the reverence in which both the name of the prophet, and the name of his book, were held in Jerusalem. 'Oh, no!' said Philip. 'Oh, no, no! the prophet did not speak of himself, nor of any other mortal man. Oh, no, no! far from that! The prophet was a man of like passions with other men. He was a man of unclean lips, like all other men. Oh, no! the prophet did not speak of himself, but of another manner of man altogether. Thou art a stranger in Jerusalem, but thou must have heard something of the things that have come to pass there in these last days. Thou must surely have heard the name of Jesus of Nazareth?' 'I did hear that name,' answered the eunuch. 'I often heard it. Sometimes I heard that name blessed, and sometimes I heard it cursed. And I was warned that all the time I was in Jerusalem I must not once speak that name, nor listen to any one speaking it to me. But we are far from Jerusalem here; and of whom speaketh the prophet this?' "Should we make it our first aim in the pulpit to do full justice to the subject we have in hand; or should our immediate and sole endeavour be to do good to our hearers?" said one of my most thoughtful friends to me the other day.

What do you do yourself? was my reply to him. But we had to part before we had time to argue it out. Philip, at any rate, set himself in the first place, and with all his might, to do full justice to his great subject. And it was in the progress of that full justice that the eunuch got all the good that the best hearer even in our day could get from the best preacher. Sometimes the one way is best, in some hands, and sometimes the other, according to the preacher, according to the hearer, and according to the subject. For the most part surely, first the subject thoroughly studied down, and handled with our utmost ability and finish, and then application made with our utmost skill and urgency and love. "Mix your exhortations with doctrine," said Goodwin to the divinity students of Oxford. Better still, in our day at any rate, begin your exhortation well with doctrine, and then end your doctrine with its proper exhortation springing out of it. Only, the eunuch did not wait for Philip's exhortation. He did not give Philip time to wind up and round off his doctrine. Philip's sermon on the fifty-third of Isaiah is not finished to this day. "See, here is water!" broke in the eunuch. "I see it!" broke in a young Forfarshire farmer in the middle of my prayer with him in the minister's study late that night after a fine revival meeting conducted by Mr. Low of Fountainbridge, and Dr. Macphail of Liverpool. And my prayer lies there to this day, like Philip's sermon, never finished, and that is five-and-twenty years ago. "I see it!" and we both sprang to our feet; and, instead of the rest of my prayer to God I said to the farmer, "Never lose sight of it, then. Never lose sight of it in all your days!" He did lose sight of it, and went back, to the breaking of his minister's heart. But the backslider returned, and, as I was told, died in raptures, exclaiming, "I see it! I see it!" "See, here is water!" exclaimed the eunuch, cutting short Philip's sermon. "I see it!" exclaimed the farmer, cutting short my prayer.

"And when they were come up out of the water, the Spirit of the Lord caught away Philip, that the eunuch saw him no more; and he went on his way rejoicing." Rejoicing that those Jewish merchants had ever opened their warehouse in Ethiopia. Regretting that he had not come up sooner to Jerusalem, when he might have seen his Saviour's face, and heard His voice. But, all the more rejoicing that he had not put off coming to the passover altogether. Rejoicing also that he had not talked about the sights of Jerusalem all the way to Gaza, but had read all the way in the prophet Isaiah. And rejoicing, above all, that he had said in the moment it came into his heart to say it, "See, here is water!"

And, still, as the chariot travelled its long stages toward far Ethiopia, the eunuch thought with a humble and a holy joy of all the way his God had led him, and of the singular grace that had at last apprehended him. And who can tell but that Queen Candace, and a great multitude of her black, but comely people, will yet be seen by us stretching out their hands and casting their crowns at His feet of whom Isaiah spake, and of whom Philip preached!

Let it no longer be a forlorn hope
    To wash an Ethiope;
He's washed: his gloomy skin a peaceful shade
    For his white soul is made.
And now, I doubt not, the Eternal Dove,
    A black-faced house will love.

XCIV

GAMALIEL

READ for the first time, and looked at on the surface, Gamaliel's speech in the council of Jerusalem was both an able and a successful performance. The argument of the speech carried the consent of the whole council—not an easy thing to do—for Peter had just cut the whole council to the heart. But Gamaliel calmed the whole council; he reassured the most hesitating; and he all but satisfied the most bloodthirsty; till the whole Sanhedrim broke up that day with loud and universal congratulations pronounced upon the ability and the sagacity of Gamaliel's speech. But, in order to see what was the real and ultimate value of Gamaliel's speech; and, still more, in order to a true and ultimate estimate of Gamaliel himself, let us look with some closeness at the whole situation with which Gamaliel was called upon to deal that day.

Well, then, this was the situation. Gamaliel had brought forward Theudas, who had boasted that he was somebody; and Judas of Galilee, who had drawn away much people after him; and Gamaliel had made some good points in his speech by his references to those two dispersed men. But Jesus Christ was not a Theudas, nor a Judas of Galilee, nor a dispersed man. Jesus Christ was Jesus Christ. He was Himself, and not another. Jesus

Christ had been promised in every page of the law and the prophets and the psalms, all of which were in the daily text-books in Gamaliel's school. And Jesus Christ had come, and had fulfilled, and that a thousand times told, every jot and tittle of all that had been prophesied and promised concerning Him. And Gamaliel had been set in his high seat by the God of Israel in order that he might watch for the coming Messiah, and might announce His advent to the people of Israel. But, for some reason or other, instead of recognising and announcing the true Christ of God when He came, as, for instance, John the Baptist did; instead of casting in his lot with Jesus of Nazareth; instead of dissolving his school and sending Saul of Tarsus and all his other scholars to follow the Lamb of God, Gamaliel, for some reason or other, still kept his seat in the Sanhedrim all through the arrest, the trial, the crucifixion, the resurrection, and the ascension of Jesus Christ, and when Christ's disciples were on their trial for their lives this short speech contains all that Gamaliel has to say for them and for himself. We must, at all times, and to all men, do as we would be done by: and therefore it is that we seek again and again for some explanation, some excuse, some apology, for Gamaliel's remaining a member of the council that had tried and crucified Jesus Christ. But, with all our search, we can find nothing out of which to make a cloak for Gamaliel's case. Had Gamaliel been an ignorant and an unlearned man there might have been some excuse for him. But Gamaliel had not that cloak at any rate for his sin. So far as I can see it, the simple truth in Gamaliel's deplorable case was this. With all his learning, and with all his ability, and with all his address, Gamaliel had approached this whole case concerning Jesus Christ from the wrong side; he had taken hold of this whole business by the wrong handle. And we all make Gamaliel's tremendous and irreparable mistake when we approach Jesus Christ and His cause and His kingdom on the side of policy, and when we handle Him as a matter open to argument and debate. He is not a matter of argument and debate; He is an ambassador of reconciliation. We are simply not permitted to sit in judgment on Almighty God, and on His message of mercy to us. He who sends that message to us is our Maker and our Judge. And Gamaliel, with all his insight, and with all his lawyer-like ability, has turned all things completely upside down when he sits in judgment, and gives this carefully-balanced caution, concerning the Son of God.

Speaking philosophically and politically and ecclesiastically, Gamaliel was a liberal, and he has this to be said for him, that he was a liberal long before the time. He was all for toleration, and for a free church in a free state, in an intolerant and persecuting day. He was far in advance of his colleagues in observation, and in reading, and in breadth and openness of mind. He was tinctured with the Greak learning that so many of his class were now beginning innovatingly to taste. And we cannot but wonder whether, among all his stores of ancient instances, that of the Greek Socrates had come that day into his mind. "We ought to obey God rather than men," Peter had just said. "Whether it be right in the sight of God to harken unto you rather than unto Him, judge ye," he had also said. "Athenians," said Socrates, "I hold you in the highest reverence and love; but I will obey God rather than you. I cannot hold my peace, because that would be to disobey God." And Socrates continued so to obey God till his self-examining voice was put to silence in the hemlock cup. And much more must Peter summon all Jerusalem to repentance in spite of the prison and the scourge and the cross. The Athenians, in their philosophical and political liberality, would have let Socrates alone, if he would have let them alone; but not for his life could he do that. And Peter was under a far surer and a far stronger constraint than Socrates. The one was the apostle of truth as it is in the reason, and in the conscience, and in the self-examined heart; while the other was the apostle of the truth as it is in all that, and in Jesus over and above all that. The French, with their keen, quick, caustic wit, have coined a nickname for those politicians who neglect principles and study the skies only to see how the wind is to blow. They call all such public men by the biting name of "opportunists." Now, Gamaliel was the opportunist of the council of Jerusalem in that day. He was a politician, but he was not a true churchman or statesman. He was held in repute by the people; but the people were blind, and they loved to be led by blind leaders. And Gamaliel was one of them. For, at this supreme crisis of his nation's history, when there was not another moment to lose, this smooth-tongued opportunist came forward full of wise saws and modern instances. But the flood was out, and the time was past, if ever there was a time for such fatal counsellors as Gamaliel. His own opportunity has of late been passing with lightning-speed: and, now, when God, in His long-suffering, has given Gamaliel his last opportunity, he deals with God and with his own soul as we here see.

Erasmus and the Reformation always rise before me when I read of Gamaliel and study his character. Erasmus, the fastidious, cautious, cool, almost cold scholar. Always stepping lightly over thin ice, always calculating consequences, and always missing the mark. Convinced of the truth, but a timid friend to the truth. Clear-eyed enough to see the truth, but built without a brow for it. Lavater thus analyses Holbein's portrait of Erasmus, and as we read the remarkable analysis we see in it a replica of Gamaliel's portrait.—"The face is expressive of the man. There is a pose of feature indicative of timidity, hesitancy, circumspection. There is in the eye the calm serenity of the acute observer who sees and takes in all things. The half-closed eye, of such a depth and shape, is surely such as always belongs to the subtle and clever schemer. That nose, according to all my observation, is assuredly that of a man of keen intellect and delicate sensibility. The furrows on the brow are usually no favourable token: they are almost invariably the sign of some weakness, some carelessness, some supineness, some laxness of character. We learn, however, from this portrait that they are to be found in some great men." Altogether a man of maxims and not of morals; a man, as he said of himself, who had no inclination to die for the truth: a man, as Luther said of him, in whose estimation human things stood higher than divine things: a man, two men, Gamaliel and Erasmus, a large class of men. "Speak not of them," said the master, "but look at them and pass them by."

Young men! with your life still before you, Gamaliel, the fluent and applauded opportunist, is here written with a special eye to your learning. Make your choice. It is an awful thing to say, but it is the simple truth; God and His Son, His church and His gospel, His cause and His kingdom, all stand before your door at this moment, waiting for your choice and your decision. Gamaliel decided, and his day is past. and he is in his own place. And now is your day of decision. Everlasting and irremediable issues for you and for others depend on this day's decision. Make up your minds. Take the step. Take sides with Peter and John. Take sides with Jesus Christ. And, as time goes on, having taken that side, that step will solve for you a thousand perplexities, and will deliver you from a thousand snares. You will be the children of the light and of the day: and you will walk in the light when other men all around you are stumbling in darkness, and know not whither they are going. Suppose that you had been Gamaliel, and act now as you so clearly see how he should have acted then.

This is our sacrament evening, and we have come to Gamaliel, and to his choice, and to his speech, not inopportunely, as I think, for our ensample on such an evening. For, what is a sacrament, and a sacrament day, and a sacrament evening? Well, Gamaliel may very well have seen the sacramental oath taken by the young soldiers under the walls of Jerusalem. At any rate, if he had ever been at Rome on a deputation, he would to a certainty have seen and heard the Sacramentum sworn to on the field of Mars. For the Sacramentum was the well-known military oath that the young soldier took when he entered on his place in the world-conquering legions of Rome. It was his sacramental oath when he lifted up his hand to heaven and swore that he would follow the eagles of Cæsar wherever they flew; to the swamps of Germany, to the snows of Caledonia, to the sands of Arabia, to the Jordan, to the Nile, to the Ganges, to the Thames, to the Clyde, to the Tay. And we, this day, old soldiers of the cross, and new recruits alike, have called upon God and man to see us that we will not flinch from the cross, but will follow it to heat and cold, to honour and shame, to gain and loss, to life and death. We have eagles to fight under, of which the angels desire to be the camp-followers. Only, let us all well understand, and without any possibility of mistake, just where our field of battle lies; just who and what is our enemy, just who is our Captain, just what is His whole armour, and just what hope He holds out to us of victory.

Well, then, lay this to heart, that your battlefield is not over the seas: it is at home. It is in the family, it is in the office, it is in the shop, it is in the workshop, it is at the breakfast and dinner-table, it is in the class-room, it is in the council-chamber. Your battlefield is just where you are. Your battle follows you about the world, and it is set just where you are set. And that is because your enemy, and the enemy of your Captain, is yourself. It is no paradox to say that; it is no hyperbole, no extravagance, no exaggeration. "The just understand it of their passions," says Pascal. That is to say, they understand that their only enemy is their own sensuality, their own bad temper, their own hot and hasty and unrecalled words, their own resentment of injuries, their own retaliation, their own revenge, their own implacable ill-will, their own envy of their dearest friend when he excels them in anything—and so on. What a sacramental oath that is, to swear to take no rest, and to give God no rest, till He has rooted all these, and all other enemies of His and ours, out of our heart! But, then, let us think of our Captain, and of our armour, and of our rations, as in this house this day, and of our battle-cry, and of our sure and certain victory. And, then, eye hath not seen, nor ear heard, the things that God hath prepared for him that overcometh. "To him that overcometh will I grant to sit with Me in My throne, even as I also overcame, and am set down with My Father in His throne."

XCV

BARNABAS

BARNABAS, I am afraid, is little more than a bare name to the most of us. Paul so eclipses every one of his contemporaries, that it is with the utmost difficulty we can get a glimpse of any one but Paul. How much do you know about Barnabas? Who was Barnabas? Why was Joses called Barnabas? You would have some difficulty, I am afraid, in giving answers to all these questions. And I do not blame you for your ignorance of Barnabas. For, Paul is so great, that the very greatest and the very best men look but small when placed alongside of him. At the same time, there were great men before Agamemnon, and Barnabas was one of them.

"Barnabas, a Levite, of the country of Cyprus, having land, sold it, and brought the money, and laid it at the apostles' feet." Cyprus is a large and fertile land situated off the coast of Syria. In ancient times Cyprus was famous for its wines, its wheats, its oils, its figs, and its honey. To possess land in Cyprus was to be a rich and an influential man. Many men who possessed houses and lands sold them under the Pentecostal fervour, and laid their prices at the apostles' feet. But Barnabas stood at the head of them all, such was his great wealth, such was his great generosity, such was his high character, and such were his splendid services in this and in many other ways to the apostolic church.

As we read on in the Acts of the Apostles we come to the sad story of Ananias and Sapphira; then to the creation of the office of the deaconship; then to the great services and the triumphant translation of Stephen; and, then, the east begins to break in the conversation of Saul of Tarsus. And it is in the first rays of that fast-rising sun that we see for once, if not again, the full stature and the true nobility of Barnabas. It was but yesterday that Saul was seen setting out for Damascus, breathing out threatenings and slaughter against the disciples of the Lord. And, to-day, he has fled back to Jerusalem, the most hated, the most feared, and the most friendless man in all that city. And, with the blood of so many martyrs still on his hands, it was no wonder that the disciples in Jerusalem were all afraid of Saul, and would not believe that he really intended to be a disciple. Saul of Tarsus a disciple of Jesus Christ! Saul of Tarsus converted, and baptized, and preaching Jesus Christ! No! Depend upon it, this is but another deep-set snare for our feet! This is but another trap baited for us by our bitter enemies! So all the disciples said concerning Saul, and they all bore themselves to Saul accordingly.

Barnabas alone of all the disciples and apostles in Jerusalem opened his door to Saul. Barnabas alone held out his hand to Saul. Barnabas alone believed Saul's wonderful story of his conversion and baptism. Barnabas alone rejoiced in God's saving mercy to Saul's soul. "They were all afraid of Saul, and believed not that he was a disciple. But Barnabas took Saul, and brought him to the apostles, and declared unto them how he had seen the Lord in the way to Damascus, and that the Lord had spoken to him, and how he had preached boldly at Damascus in the name of Jesus Christ." If Barnabas had never done anything else but what he did in those days for Saul of Tarsus, he would deserve, and he would receive, our love and our honour for ever. Barnabas so firmly believed what Saul told him, and so nobly acted on it. He so stood up for Saul when all men were looking askance at him. He so trusted and befriended Saul when every one else suspected him, and cast his past life in his face. Barnabas staked all his good name in Jerusalem, and all his influence with the apostles, on the genuineness of Saul's conversion, and on the sincerity and integrity of his discipleship. Barnabas stood by Saul till he had so turned the tide in Saul's favour, that, timid as Peter was, he actually took Saul to lodge with him in his own house in Jerusalem. And Barnabas gave Saul up to Peter, only too glad to see Saul made so much of by such a pillar of the Apostolic Church as Peter was. With Saul staying fifteen days under Peter's roof, and with James treating Saul with his cautious confidence, Barnabas's battle for Saul was now completely won. Very soon, now, it will be the greatest honour to any house on the face of the earth to entertain the apostle Paul. But no proud householder of them all can ever steal this honour from Barnabas, that he was the first man of influence and responsibility who opened his heart and his house to Saul of Tarsus, when all Jerusalem was still casting stones at him. Barnabas was not predestinated to shine in the service of Christ and His Church like Paul; but Paul himself never did a more shining deed than Barnabas did when he took Saul to his heart at a time when every other heart in Jerusalem was hardened against him. Everlastingly well done, thou true son of consolation!

The scene now shifts to Antioch, which is soon to eclipse Jerusalem herself, and to become the true mother-church of evangelical Christianity. The apostolic preaching had an instantaneous and an immense success at Antioch, and it was its very success that raised there also, and with such acuteness, all those doctrinal and disciplinary disputes that fill with such distress the book of the Acts, and the earlier Epistles of Paul. Jerusalem still remained the Metropolitan Church, and the difficulties that had arisen in Antioch were accordingly sent up to Jerusalem for advice and adjudication. And, that the heads of the Church at Jerusalem chose Barnabas out of the whole college of the apostles to go down and examine into the affairs of Antioch, is just another illustration of the high standing that Barnabas had, both as a man of marked ability, and of high Christian character. "Who, when he came, and had seen the grace of God was glad, and exhorted them all, that with purpose of heart they would cleave unto the Lord. For he was a good man, and full of the Holy Ghost and faith; and much people was added unto the Lord." How full of the Holy Ghost Barnabas was we are made immediately to see. For Barnabas had not been long in Antioch till he became convinced that Antioch was very soon to hold the key of the whole Christian position. Already, indeed, so many questions of doctrine and administration were come to such a crisis in the Church of Antioch, that Barnabas felt himself quite unable to cope with them. And, worse than that, he could not think of any one in Jerusalem who was any better able to cope with those difficult questions than he was himself. In all Barnabas's knowledge of men, and it was not narrow, he knew only one man who was equal to the great emergency at Antioch, and that man was no other than Saul of Tarsus. But, then, Saul was comparatively young as yet; he was not much known, and he was not much trusted. And shall Barnabas take on himself the immense responsibility, and, indeed, immense risk, of sending for Saul of Tarsus, and bringing him to Antioch? And shall Barnabas take this great step without first submitting Saul's name to the authorities at Jerusalem? There were great risks in both of these alternatives, and Barnabas had to act on his own judgment and conscience and heart. There are supreme moments in the field when an officer of original genius, and of the requisite strength of character, will determine to stake all, and to do some bold deed, on his own single responsibility. He will take an immense and an irretrievable step without orders, and, sometimes, against orders. He will thus win the battle, and then he will not mind much either the praise or the blame that comes to him for his successful act of disobedience. Antioch must have Saul of Tarsus; and Barnabas, taking counsel with no one but himself, set out to Tarsus to seek for Saul. "Leaving France, I retired into Germany expressly for the purpose of being able to enjoy in some obscure corner the repose I had always desired, and which had so long been denied me. And I had resolved to continue in the same obscurity, till at length William Farel detained me at Geneva, and that not so much by counsel and exhortation, as by a dread imprecation, which I felt to be as if God from heaven laid His mighty hand upon me to arrest me. For after having learned that my heart was set upon devoting myself to my private studies, for which I wished to keep myself free from all other engagements, and finding that he could gain nothing by entreating me, he proceeded to utter an imprecation that God would curse my retirement, and would blast my selfish studies, if I should refuse to come to Geneva when the need was so great." John Calvin was Saul of Tarsus over again. William Farel was Barnabas over again. And the reformed city of Geneva was the evangelised city of Antioch over again. "Then departed Barnabas to Tarsus to seek for Saul. And when he had found him, he brought him to Antioch." To have the heart to discover a more talented man than yourself, and then to have the heart to go to Tarsus for him, and to make way for him in Antioch, is far better than to have all Saul's talents, and all the praise and all the rewards of those talents to yourself. Speaking for myself I would far rather have a little of Barnabas's grace than have all Saul's genius. Give me Barnabas's self-forgetful heart, and let who will undertake Saul's so extraordinary, but so perilous, endowments. Luther says that we cannot help being jealous of the men who are in our own circle and are more talented than ourselves. Perhaps not. But if Barnabas had to get over jealousy in connection with Saul's coming to Antioch, that jealousy, at any rate, did not hinder him from setting out to Tarsus to seek for Saul. He must increase, but I must decrease, said Barnabas to himself and to his subordinates as he set his face steadfastly to go down to Tarsus. Barnabas had taken his own measure accurately, and he had taken Saul's measure accurately also, and he took action accordingly. Now, noble conduct like that of Barnabas is always its own best reward. Christlike conduct like that instantly reacts on character, and character like Barnabas's character manifests itself in more and more of such Christ-like conduct. Barnabas had done Saul a good turn before now, and that only made him the more ready to do him this new good turn when the opportunity was afforded him. "Barnabas was a good man, and full of the Holy Ghost and faith." And three times he publicly proved that; first when he sold his estate in Cyprus and brought the money, and laid it at the apostles' feet. And he proved that again when he took Saul in his friendlessness and brought him to the apostles in Jerusalem, and compelled them to believe in Saul, and to trust him, and to employ him. And still more conclusively did Barnabas prove his fullness of the Holy Ghost, when he set out to Tarsus to seek for Saul in order that Saul might come to Antioch, and there supersede and extinguish Barnabas himself.

But, as if to chasten our too great pride in Barnabas, even Barnabas, this so pentecostal and so apostolic man; even Barnabas, so full hitherto of the Holy Ghost and of faith—even he must fall at last, and that too all but fatally. For God speaketh once, yea twice, yet man perceiveth it not, that He may withdraw man from his purpose, and hide pride from man. We would have been too much lifted up to-night about Barnabas if we had not had his whole history written to us down to the end. For, what two chosen and fast friends in all the New Testament circle of friends, would you have wagered would be the last to fall out fiercely, and to turn their backs on one another for ever? Not Paul and Barnabas, at any rate, you would confidently and proudly have said. Whoever will quarrel, and fall out, and forget what they owe to one another, that can never, by any possibility, happen to Paul and his old patron Barnabas—so you would have said. But you would have lost your wager, and your confidence in the best of men to boot. "Let us go," said Paul to Barnabas, "and visit our brethren in every city where we have preached the word of the Lord and see how they do." And Barnabas determined to take with him John, whose surname was Mark. And Paul thought not good to take Mark with them. And the contention was so sharp between them that they departed asunder one from the other. And Barnabas took Mark, and Paul chose Silas. Has Paul forgotten all that he once owed to Barnabas? And why does Barnabas's so sweet and so holy humility so fail him when he is so far on in the voyage of life? "Mariners near the shore," says Shepard, "should be on the outlook for rocks." And Barnabas was so near the shore by this time that it distresses us sorely to see his ship strike the rocks and stagger in the sea in this fashion. Barnabas's ship strikes the rocks till one of the noblest characters in the New Testament is shattered and all but sunk under our very eyes. Who was right and who was wrong in this sharp contention I have no heart to ask. Both were wrong. Paul, and Barnabas, and Mark too—all three were wrong. And multitudes in the Apostolic churches who heard of the scandal, and took contending sides in it, were wrong also. And this sad story is told us to this day, not that we may take sides in it, but that the like of it may never again happen amongst ourselves.

> The grey-haired saint may fail at last,
> The surest guide a wanderer prove;
> Death only binds us fast
> To the bright shore of love.

The last time we see Barnabas, sad to say, Paul and he are contending again. But I will not draw you into that contention. We have had instruction, and example, and warning, and rebuke, enough out of Barnabas already. Instruction and example in Barnabas's spendid liberality with his Cyprus possessions. Instruction and example in his openness and hospitality of mind and heart toward a suspected and a friendless man. And still more instruction and example in his noble absence of all envy and all jealousy of a man far more gifted, far more successful, and soon to be far more famous than himself. And, then, this warning and this rebuke also, that at the end of such a life, even Paul and Barnabas should contend so sharply with one another that they scandalised the whole Church of Christ, and departed asunder never to meet again, unless it was to dispute again in this world.

> Let not the people be too swift to judge,
> As one who reckons on the blades in field
> Or ere the crop be ripe. For I have seen
> The thorn frown rudely all the winter long
> And after bear the rose upon its top;
> And barque, that all the way across the sea,
> Ran straight and speedy, perish at the last,
> Even in the haven's mouth.

The evening praises the day, and the chief grace of the theatre is the last scene. Be thou faithful unto death, and I will give thee a crown of life.

XCVI

JAMES, THE LORD'S BROTHER

I OFTEN imagine myself to be James. I far oftener imagine myself to be in James's place and experience, than in the place and experience of any other man in the whole Bible, or in the whole world. The first thirty years of James's life fascinate me and enthral me far more than all the rest of human life and human history taken together. And I feel sure that I am not alone in that fascination of mine. Who, indeed, would not be absolutely captivated, fascinated, and enthralled, both in imagination and in heart, at the thought of holding James's relationship to Jesus Christ! For thirty years eating every meal at the same table with Him; working six days of the week in the same workshop with Him; going up on the seventh day to the same synagogue with Him; and once every year going up to Jerusalem to the same passover with Him. For James was, actually, the Lord's brother. Not in a figure of speech. Not mystically and spiritually. But literally and actually—he was James the Lord's brother. Jesus was Mary's first-born son, and James was her second son. And the child James would be the daily delight of his elder Brother; he would be His continual charge and joy; just as you see two such brothers in your own family life at home. When Mary's first-born Son was twelve years old it was the law of Moses that He should be taken up to Jerusalem to His first passover. James was not old enough yet for his first passover, but you may be sure he missed nothing with his father and mother and Brother to tell him all about Jerusalem and the passover when they came home; James both hearing his elder Brother and asking Him questions. For the next eighteen years Joseph's door is hermetically shut to our holy curiosity. All we knew is, that one, at any rate, of Joseph's household was filled with wisdom, and the grace of God was upon Him. Not another syllable more is told us about Joseph or Mary, or any of their household, till the preaching of the Baptist broke in on that house, as on all the houses of the land, like the coming of the kingdom of heaven. John and his baptism was the talk of week-day and Sabbath-day in Nazareth, as in all the land, till at last a company of young carpenters and fishermen went south to Bethabara beyond Jordan where John was baptizing. And Jesus of Nazareth, known as yet by that name only, was one of them. You have by heart all that immediately took place at the Jordan. "Behold the Lamb of God, which taketh away the sin of the world. We have found the Messiah. We have found Him, of whom Moses in the law, and the prophets, did write, Jesus of Nazareth, the son of Joseph. Rabbi, Thou art the Son of God, Thou art the King of Israel. And Jesus returned in the power of the Spirit into Galilee. And He came to Nazareth where He was brought up; and, as His custom was, He went into the synagogue on the Sabbath-day and stood up for to read. And there was delivered to Him the book of the prophet Esaias. And when He had opened the book He found the place where it is written, The Spirit of the Lord is upon Me, because He hath anointed Me to preach the gospel to the poor; He hath sent Me to heal the broken-hearted, to preach deliverance to the captive, and recovering of sight to the blind, to set at liberty them that are bound, to preach the acceptable year of the Lord. And all bear Him witness, and wondered at the gracious words which proceeded out of His mouth." But, all the time, James His brother did not believe on Him. No, nor did James believe down to the very end. I wish I had the learning and the genius to let you see and hear all that must have gone on in Joseph's house for the next three years. The family perplexities about Jesus; the family reasonings about Him; the family divisions and disputes about Him; their intoxicating hopes at one time over Him, and their fears and sinkings of heart because of Him at another time. Think out for yourselves those three years, the like of which never came to any other family on the face of the earth. And, then, think of the last week of all; the arrest, the trial, the crucifixion, the resurrection of Mary's first-born Son—whose imagination is sufficient to picture to itself Joseph and Mary and James and the other brothers and sisters of Jesus all that week! Where did they make ready to eat the passover? What were they doing at the hour when He was in Gethsemane? Were they standing with the crowd in the street when He was led about all night in His bonds? And where were they while He was being crucified? For, by that time, no one believed on Him but the thief on the cross alone. All the faith in Christ that survived the cross was bound up in that bundle of smoking flax, the penitent and praying thief. The next time we come on James is in these golden words of Paul written concerning him long afterwards, "and that Jesus Christ was buried, and that He rose the third day according to the scriptures. After that, He was seen of James; then of all the apostles." He was seen of James somewhere, and to somewhat of the same result, that He was seen of Saul at the gate of Damascus.

Three years pass on, during the progress of which James has risen to be one of the pillars of the Church of Jerusalem. James's high character, and his close relationship to Jesus Christ, taken together with his conservative tone of mind, all combined to give him his unique position of influence and authority in the Church of Jerusalem. We have a lifelike portrait of James as he appeared to the men of his day which it will interest and impress you to look at for a moment. "Now, James was holy from his mother's womb. He drank no wine or strong drink. He ate no animal food. No razor ever went on his head. He anointed not himself with oil, and used not the indulgence of the bath. He wore no wool, but linen only, and he was such a man of prayer that when they came to coffin him his knees were as hard and as stiff to bend as the knees of a camel. On account of the sternness of his character he was called James the Just, and James the bulwark of the people." Now in that contemporary account of James may we not have a clue to the obstinacy of his unbelief, and to his all but open hostility to our Lord? For James was a Nazarite of such strictness and scrupulosity that he could not fail to be greatly offended at his Brother's absolute and resolute freedom from all such unspiritual trammels. James's eldest brother was no Nazarite. He was no Scribe. He was no Pharisee. And He must often have stumbled James, so far did He come short of a perfect righteousness, as James understood and demanded perfect righteousness. In His public preaching He was compelled to denounce what James scrupulously practised as the law of Moses and the law of God. The Scribes and the Pharisees were continually finding fault with James's Brother for His laxity in the traditions of the elders, and no man would feel that laxity so acutely as James would feel it. So rooted was James in the old covenant that, even after his conversion, he still continued to cleave fast to his unevangelical habits of thought and practices of life, in a way and to an extent that caused the greatest trouble to the rest of the apostles, and to Paul especially. In our Lord's words, James, all his days, was one of those men, and a leader among them, who continued to pour the new wine of the gospel into the old bottles of the law, till the old bottles burst in their hands and the new wine was spilled. Converted as he undoubtedly was, James was half a Pharisee to the very end. And, if ever he was a bishop at all, he was the bishop of a half-enlightened Jewish ghetto rather than of a Christian church. Still, when all is said, we have an intense interest in James; not so much for his position or for his services in the apostolic church, as for this, that he was the brother, the born and brought-up brother, of our Lord.

James was the born and brought-up brother of our Lord, and, by that, he being dead, yet speaketh. And the one supreme lesson that James teaches us to-night is surely this, 'Keep your eyes open at home, for I made this tremendous mistake. The unpardonable and irreparable mistake of my whole life was this, that my eyes were never opened at home till it was too late. I never once saw what was for thirty years, day and night, staring me in the face, if I had not been stone-blind. It never entered my mind all those years that He was any better than I was myself. Indeed, I often blamed Him that He was not nearly so good as myself. But I remember now: we all remember now endless instances of His goodness, His meekness, His humility, His lowliness of mind and heart. We often recall to one another how we all took our own way with Him, and got our own way with Him in everything. How silent He was when we were all speaking, and would not hold our peace. How obliging He was, how gentle, how sweet. But, all the time, we saw it not till it was all over, and it was too late.' The kingdom of heaven did not come with sufficient observation to James. Had his elder Brother been a Pharisee, had He been a Scribe, had He been a John the Baptist, had His raiment been of camel's hair, had His meat been locusts and wild honey, and had He had His dwelling among the rocks, James would have found it far easier to believe in his Brother. But the still small voice of a holy life at home made no impression on James. Yes: let us all acknowledge James's tremendous mistake, and let us all go home with our eyes opened lest the kingdom of heaven may have come to our own house also, and we may not see that till it is too late. A Christian character may be displayed before our eyes at home, and we may never discover it, just because it is at home. Ay, and let us beware of this, lest our hard ways, our proud ways, our selfish tempers and our want of love, may all be the daily cross and thorn of some child of God hidden from our eyes in our own homes, as James was to Jesus. Out of doors many began to believe in James's Brother, but no one indoors. In His own home, and among His own brothers and sisters, our Lord had no recognition and no honour.

And James is a warning to us all in this respect also, that he never, to the very end, became a true and complete New Testament believer. Whether it was that he had been too long an unbeliever, and never could make up for the opportunities he had lost; or whether it was that he yielded to his natural temper too much, and let it take too deep a hold of him; or whether it was that he was never able to suppress himself so as to submit at Paul's feet; or whether it was that he could never shake off the hard and narrow men who hampered and hindered him; or whether it was his life-long chastisement and impoverishment for neglecting the incomparably glorious opportunity God had given him for thirty-three years,—whatever was the true explanation of it, the fact is only too clear on too many pages of the New Testament, that James, all his days, was far more of a Jew than a genuine Christian. His canonical Epistle itself belongs more to the Old Testament than to the New. Luther felt afterwards that he had gone too far in what he had said in his haste about the Epistle of James. But every one who knows and loves and lives upon Paul's Gospel as Luther did, will sometimes feel something of Luther's mind about James and his Epistle. Though his risen Brother appeared to James as he appeared to Paul, at the same time, God could never be said to have manifested His Son in James as He had manifested Him in Paul. Account for it as we may: brother of our Lord, Bishop of Jerusalem, pillar of that Church as he was and all, James never came within sight of Paul as a New Testament saint of Christ and an evangelical apostle. James never entered himself, and he never led his people, into the glorious liberty of the sons of God. Surely a most solemn warning to us, that our natural tempers, our traditional prejudices, our early sympathies, the school of life and thought and worship in which we have been brought up, and our not ignoble loyalty to that form of doctrine into which we were in our youth delivered,—all that may stand in our way; all that may have to be fought against and conquered; if we are ever to come in the unity of the faith, and of the knowledge of the Son of God, unto a perfect man, unto the measure of the stature of the fullness of Christ.

Fifth Series

STEPHEN TO TIMOTHY

XCVII

STEPHEN

In the stoning of Stephen there was lost to the Pentecostal Church another Apostle Paul. Stephen was a young man of such original genius and of such special grace, that there was nothing he might not have attained to had he been allowed to live. His wonderful openness of mind; his perfect freedom from all the prepossessions, prejudices, and superstitions of his day; his courage, his eloquence, his spotless character; with a certain sweet, and at the same time majestic, manner; combined to set Stephen in the very front rank both of service and of risk. In all these things, and especially in the openness, receptiveness, and ripeness of his mind, Stephen far outstripped even such pillar apostles as Peter and James and John themselves. Stephen had anticipated also, and had forerun, and had all but carried off the apostolic palm from Paul himself. All these things made Stephen already all but the foremost man of his day, and, as a consequence, the first man to be struck at and struck down. Simple deacon and servant of tables as Stephen was, it was impossible that a man of such ability and such distinction should be confined and limited to that. His intellectual power, his spiritual insight and foresight, with the strength of his faith and the warmth of his devotion, were all such that he soon found himself deep in apostolic duty, as well as in the proper work of the deaconship. After his purely deaconship work was done, and springing immediately out of his way of doing it, Stephen felt himself constrained on many occasions to take a still more public part in the support and the defence and the edification of the infant Church of Jerusalem. But malice always follows eminence in this world, as Stephen soon found out to his cost. Ignorance, superstition, prejudice, ill-will, odium, all began to dog Stephen's footsteps and to raise their murderous misrepresentations against him in every synagogue into which he entered. And the better he spoke, and the more unanswerably, the more were the enemies that he raised both against himself and against the truth, till his enemies had their own way with him. "We have heard him speak blasphemous words against Moses, and against God." That was his indictment, as we say; and then we have his apology in the seventh chapter of the Acts, and a very remarkable piece of speaking it is in many ways.

As often as we hear of an Apology we always think of Socrates. On the other hand, our Lord, when on His trial, offered no Apology. He held His peace, insomuch that the governor marvelled greatly. What, I reverently wonder, would His Apology have been? You who are students of the New Testament might do worse, now that your college exercises are nearly over, than to continue your great studies and try to construct, with all your learning and ability and insight, the Apology that our Lord, had He seen fit, might have addressed to that same Council. An intelligent congregation would greatly delight in that supposed Apology for a Sabbath evening lecture, if you did it well. At any rate, if your sense of reverence will not let you put His Apology into your Master's mouth, you might do this: you might sometime take the trouble to compare the Apology that Plato puts into his Master's mouth with this Apology of Stephen that you have here in Luke. The one, the first great defence of truth and righteousness in the Pagan Dispensation; and the other, the first great defence of Christ and His infant Church in the Apostolic and Evangelic Dispensation. "Men, brethren, and fathers, hearken!" Stephen commences. Always commence by conciliating your audience, says Dante. In his introduction, says Augustine, Stephen practises the Quintilianian art of capturing the goodwill of his hearers, however stoutly and sternly and plain-spokenly he may have to end.

It almost looks as if we had Stephen's Apology verbatim in the Book of the Acts. His speech reads as well to us as if we had sat in the Council that day and had heard it with our own ears. The beloved physician, when he turned Church historian, had a perfect understanding of all things from the very first; and, among other things, he supplies us with remarkably full reports of some of the great sermons and speeches and apologies of that all-important time. Sometimes a single word, sometimes an accent on a single word, sometimes the shaping and insertion of a single phrase, sometimes a quotation or a paraphrase of a quotation, sometimes what he does not say, as well as what he does say, sometimes what he manages to suggest without saying it at all: little things like these will discover and proclaim the true orator. And that is the case again and again in Stephen's Apology. Pericles, Plutarch tells us, never spoke that he did not leave a secret sting in the hearts of his hearers. And all Stephen's eloquent review of Old Testament history drew on and gathered itself up to drive this terrible sting through and through the hearts of the whole Council, "As your fathers did, so do ye! For ye have now been the betrayers and murderers of the Just One!"

Now, out of all that, quite a crowd of lessons and instructions and examples and warnings rise up before us, and press themselves upon us. Let us select two or three of those lessons, and leave the others for the present unspoken.

1. Up to this time the twelve had done everything with their own hands. They had been evangelists, preachers, apologists, pastors, ruling elders, session-clerks, servants of tables, and everything else, for the daily increasing congregations of Jerusalem and the whole country round about. But it was the money matters of the Pentecostal Church that completely broke the apostles down, and brought things to a perfect standstill. When thousands of people were contributing to a central sustentation fund, and were again, rich and poor, supported out of it; when the rich were selling their possessions and were laying the prices at the apostles' feet; and when the increasing crowds of poor members were receiving their daily dole directly from the apostles' hands; it is plain that all this would soon result in the serious encroachment of the secular side of their work, so to call it, on the purely spiritual side. Their public teaching and preaching, and certain still more important matters, would be seriously interfered with, till the twelve apostles took the wise step that is recorded in this chapter. It is not reason, they said, and we cannot go on with it, that we should leave the Word of God in order to serve tables to this extent. Wherefore, brethren, look out among yourselves seven men whom we may appoint over this business. And we will, all the more, give ourselves continually to prayer and to the ministry of the Word. And this proposal of the apostles commended itself to the common sense of the whole Church, and they chose seven select men and set them before the apostles for ordination. And we inherit the wisdom and the benefit of that apostolic example to this day. The Church of our day also says to her members and to her office-bearers something like this:—'It is utterly unreasonable that our ministers should all alone be expected to perform all the multitudinous work that arises out of a great congregation. It is quite preposterous that any one man should be expected to preach two or three sermons a week, keep in close contact with a thousand people, baptize our children, marry our sons and daughters, console our sick, bury our dead, find work for our unemployed, negotiate loans of money and gather gifts for our embarrassed members, get our aged and our orphaned into asylums and hospitals, besides many other things that can

neither be foreseen nor set aside by our ministers.' And thus it comes about that a compact is entered into and a division of labour is made. The young men take the financing of the congregation off their minister's hands, while the more experienced men share with him in the teaching and the ruling and the visiting of the flock. Never more than just at the present day did the Church see the divine wisdom of the apostolic institution of the deaconship, or feel more the need of adhering to it and extending it. And, then, the minister who honestly performs his part of the compact in prayer and in preaching will not lack, any more than Peter and John lacked, the willing and capable help of Stephen and of Philip. As James Durham says: "In all this we see what a minister's great task is, and wherein he should be taken up—secret prayer, reading, and meditation, and then the public preaching of the Gospel. We see also that though all ministers are virtually both elders and deacons as the twelve were, yet ought they to regulate both of these offices with respect to the former two of secret prayer and public preaching. As also that elders and deacons ought to have respect to keep ministers from being overburdened and too much toiled, that they may have freedom to follow their main work. Yea, even to have frequent and lengthened access to aloneness and solitariness, which is both most necessary as well as well becoming in a minister." And so on at great depth and fullness in 'The Dying Man's Testimony to the Church of Scotland.'

2. *Nomina debitta,* says John Donne; that is to say, 'Every man owes to the world the signification of his name, and of all his name. Every new addition of honour or of office lays a new obligation upon him, and his Christian name above all.' Now, when you name a man a deacon, as the apostles named Stephen, from the day you do so he begins to owe to the world and to the Church some new obligations. He is called and ordained and named because he is a man of honest report, and full of wisdom and devotedness; and all these graces grow in every new deacon as he goes on to exercise them. I do not know so well how it is with other Deacons' Courts, but I know to my continual delight and refreshment how it is with our own. I know how nobly our deacons fulfil the Pentecostal programme. And that is why our name as a congregation stands in such honour among the congregations of the land. It is our deacons who do it. It is the successors of Stephen and Philip who do it. Every penny of our Pentecostal thousands is collected personally by our deacons. And collected too with a spontaneity and a punctuality and a knowledge of what they are doing, and a love for what they are doing, that

make our monthly meetings one of the greatest delights and refreshments of my whole ministerial life. It all depends on our clerk and on our treasurer, and on our censor, and on our splendid staff; all our ability to serve the tables of our poorer brethren depends absolutely on our deacons. Take away our deacons, or let them stand idle while other people do their work, and we would very soon drop down from the front rank to which they and they alone have raised us. "Bring ye all the tithes into the storehouse, that there may be meat in Mine house, and prove Me now herewith, saith the Lord of Hosts, if I will not open you the windows of heaven, and pour you out a blessing, that there shall not be room enough to receive it." It is because our Stephen-like staff hear their Master saying that to them every month, that they purchase to themselves such a good degree, and purchase for Free St. George's congregation such a good degree also. Wherefore, all my brethren, look ye out among you men of mind, and men of heart, and men of business habits, and they will purchase a good degree for you also when you appoint them over this business. I only wish that every deacon in Scotland could come and see how our deacons in Edinburgh do their work.

3. And now to pass on to the day when Stephen finished his course, kept the faith, and resigned the deaconship. "Behold!" he exclaimed with the stones crashing about his head, "I see the Son of Man standing on the right hand of God!" But the Son of Man does not now any more stand, surely. For when He had by Himself purged our sins He surely sat down for ever on the right hand of God. "Sit, said the LORD to my Lord, at My right hand until I make Thy foes Thy footstool." But, with all that, He could not sit still when He saw them stoning Stephen. And so it is with Him always. He sits, or He stands, or He comes down to earth again, just according to our need, and just according to our faith. I see Him standing up, says Stephen. What a power, what a possession, is faith! For faith can make the Son of Man do almost anything she likes. As William Guthrie says of her, "Faith sometimes acts in a very wilful way upon her Lord." So she does. For look at what a wilful way the Syrophœnician woman acted upon her Lord, till, to get rid of her, He said to her, Take anything you like. Only go home to your daughter. And so still. The faith of His people gives Him absolutely no rest. Their faith makes Him stand up long after He has sat down. Their faith makes Him do everything and be everything that they need and ask. He did everything on earth, and He still does everything in heaven, by which He can be useful to poor souls. As for example.

Is the soul naked? Then Christ on the spot is fine raiment. Is the soul hungry and thirsty? Immediately Christ is its milk and its wine, its bread of life and its true manna. Is the avenger of blood at the heels of the sinner? Then just one step and the blood-guilty man is in the city of refuge. In one word, tell Him how He can help a poor sinner who has no other help, and all the high and honourable seats in heaven will not hold our Lord down. And, then, as He honours faith, so faith honours Him. Is He a bridegroom? Faith is in His arms. Is He a shepherd? Faith is at His feet. Is He a rock? Faith has already begun to build her house on Him for eternity. Is He the way? Faith runs with all her affections to the Father by Him. And they stoned Stephen, calling upon God, and saying, Behold, I see the Son of Man standing on the right hand of God. Lord Jesus, receive my spirit. And he kneeled down, and cried with a loud voice, Lord, lay not this sin to their charge. And when he had said this, he fell asleep. For they that have used the office of a deacon well purchase to themselves a good degree, and great boldness in the faith which is in Christ Jesus.

XCVIII

PHILIP: DEACON AND EVANGELIST

'THE more we are mown down by you, the more we multiply among you,' said Tertullian in his proud Apology. 'Every single drop of our blood springs up, in some thirty, in some sixty, and in some an hundredfold.' And thus it was that the banishment of Philip from Jerusalem was the salvation of Samaria, and thus it was also that the martyrdom of Stephen was the conversion of Saul. *Semen est sanguis Christianorum.*

Stephen was the first martyr, and Philip was the first missionary. The deaconship adorned itself and did nobly in those early days. Stephen and Philip were not apostles to begin with; they were simply deacons. They were not ordained, like the apostles, to prayer and to the ministry of the Word. But you cannot limit, and narrow, and bind down to the serving table two powerful and original men like Stephen and Philip. Paul had Stephen and Philip in his mind when he said to Timothy long afterwards, that they who have used the office of a deacon well, purchase to themselves a good degree, and great boldness in the faith which is in Christ Jesus. All of which both Stephen and Philip had emphatically done.

"And," writes Luke to Theophilus, "at that time there was a great persecution against the Church which was at Jerusalem; so that they were all scattered abroad throughout the regions of Judea and Samaria. And Philip went down to the city of Samaria, and preached Christ unto them. And there was great joy in that city." Now, just suppose for a moment that you had been Philip. Suppose that you had been scattered abroad like Philip and his colleagues. And suppose that you had escaped with the Gospel in your hands, and were chased into some half-heathen city that had just been touched on the surface with the knowledge of Christ. You would be sure to seek out those who had been so touched, and you would throw yourself on their hospitality and protection. And thus it was that Philip would certainly seek out the woman of Samaria that all the world knows about now, and in whose heart, and in whose house, there was now a well of water springing up into everlasting life. Peter and John would give Philip an introduction to her; and to reassure him about his reception, they would tell him, John especially, all about that oft-remembered day when their Master must needs go through Samaria, and when, being wearied on His journey, He sat thus on the well. And the woman would welcome Philip, and would say to him, Come in, thou blessed of the Lord, for when I was thirsty He gave me drink. And when Philip said to her, Sit down, woman, sit down and eat, she only served his table all the more hospitably, and said, I have meat to eat that thou knowest not of. Come to my house, she said also to all her neighbours, and see and hear a man who has come to my house from the very risen Christ Himself. And, taking his text from the woman's words, Philip preached the risen Christ in Sychar till there was great joy in that city. Luke is a scholar, and so is Theophilus. Luke is a student and an artist in his words, and Theophilus attends to what Luke writes. And thus it is that when Luke tells Theophilus that Philip preached 'Christ' to the Samaritans, and then that the same evangelist preached 'Jesus' to the Ethiopian eunuch, it is not for nothing; it is not of no consequence what Luke says, or how he says it. It is not without good reason that such a scrupulous composer as Luke is selects his names and his titles in this exact way for our Lord. Bengel is the very commentator for such a composer as Luke. And Bengel writes with his needle-pointed pen and says that "from the Old Testament point of view, progress is made from the knowledge of Christ to the knowledge of Jesus; while from the New Testament point of view, the progress is made from the knowledge of Jesus to the knowledge of Christ." "Not a single syllable," says Basil, "of all that is written concerning Jesus Christ should be left uninvestigated. The men who trace the hidden meaning of every word and even of every letter in the New Testament are those who understand best the end and nature of our Scriptural calling." Let our theological students, then, study out the fact of Philip's preaching 'Christ' in the city, and 'Jesus' in the desert, and make an Ellicott-like thesis for themselves and for their people on this subject, taking in Romans viii. 11.

Now, I must stop for a moment at this point to say how much I feel both impressed and rebuked by the noble conduct of Peter and John. Both Stephen and Philip were by far the subordinates of Peter and John. And there is no sin that so easily besets some of us ministers as just the sudden success of those who are by far our subordinates. There is nothing that more tries us and brings to the surface what we are made of at heart than just to be outstripped and extinguished by those who but yesterday were mere boys beside us. And it takes the strongest men among us and the holiest man all his might to behave himself with humility and with generosity to his late subordinates at such a time. But let us stop at this point and see how well both Peter and John came out of that furnace of theirs. They did not grudge, nor resent, nor suspect, nor despise the success of Stephen in Jerusalem, nor of Philip in Samaria. They did not say, The deacon has his proper place. They did not complain that he had so soon left the serving of tables. They did not say that Philip should attend to his proper work, and let preaching alone. They did not shake their heads and forecast that it would soon turn out to be all so much Samaritan excitement. They did not have it reported to them every word that Philip had at any time spoken that was out of joint. Far no. To their great honour be it told, they behaved themselves in all this temptation of theirs in a way altogether worthy of their apostolic office. They did not wait to see if the awakening was real and would last, as we would have done. But the twelve sent down Peter and John, their two best men, to assist Philip to gather in the results of his so suddenly successful mission. And Peter and John set to work with all their might to found a church out of Philip's converts, to be called the Church of the Evangelist, after the name of their deacon and subordinate. I, for one, must lay all that Samaria episode well to heart. I, for one, must not forget it.

Both Stephen and Timothy have made this impression also

upon me that they were born preachers, as we say. Born, not made. Born, not college-bred. Born, and not simply ordained. And if a man is a born preacher, you may set him to serve tables, or, for that matter, to make tables, but he will preach in spite of you. You may suborn men to bear him down. You may banish him away to Samaria, but I defy you to shut his mouth. Stephen and Philip were born with such a fire in their bones that no man could put it out. There is a divine tongue in their mouth that you cannot silence. The more you persecute them and cast them out, and the more tribulation you pass them through, they will only preach all that the better. Now, that there were two men of such rare genius among the first seven deacons is a remarkable proof of the insight of the congregation that elected them, as well as of the wealth of all kinds of talent in the Apostolic Church. I have often wished that I could have been one of the two Emmaus-men whose hearts burned within them as their risen Lord expounded unto them in all the Scriptures the things concerning Himself. And, then, after that I would fain have been the servant of the Ethiopian eunuch, so as to have sat beside him and heard him reading the prophet Esaias till Philip came up and said to him, Understandest thou what thou readest? How can I, except some man should guide me? And he desired Philip that he would come up and sit with him. And Philip opened his mouth, and began at the 53rd of Isaiah, and preached unto him Jesus. All this took place in the primitive, simple, unsophisticated east, and we must not measure any part of all this history by our western habits of intercourse. It would be resented as the height of intrusion and incivility among us if one man were to say to another over his book on the deck of a steamer or in a railway carriage, Are you understanding what you are reading? But look at it in this way. Suppose you sat beside a foreigner who was struggling with one of our English guide-books, and was evidently missing the sense, till he was starting off in a wrong direction; it would be no intrusion or impertinence if you made up to him and said to him something like this: 'I fear our barbarous tongue is not easily mastered by foreign scholars, but it is my native language, and I may be able to be of some use to you in it.' "How can I?" said the humble-minded eunuch, "except some man should guide me?" Now, we all think, because we know the letters of it, and are familiar with the sounds of it, that we understand the Bible: Isaiah, and John, and Paul. But we never made a more fatal mistake. There is no book in all the world that is so difficult to read, and to understand, and to love, as the Bible. Not having begun to understand it, some of you will turn upon me and tell me that even a little child can understand it. And you are perfectly right. "A lamb can wade it," said a great Greek expositor of it. But he went on to add that "an elephant can swim in it." And thus it was that, over and above the apostles, all the deacons of intellect and experience were drawn on to expound the Scriptures, first to the learned Council of Jerusalem, then to the sceptical men of Samaria, and then to the Ethiopian neophyte in his royal chariot. And thus it is still that the Church collects into her colleges the very best minds she can lay hold of in all her families, and trains them up under her very best teachers, and then when they are ready says to them, Go join thyself to this and that vacant pulpit, and make the people understand what they read. And you must often have both felt it and confessed it to be so. How different the most superficially familiar chapter looks to us ever after some great expounder, by tongue or by pen, has opened it up to us! A book of the Bible read in routine chapters in the pulpit or at family worship, how dull, and unmeaning, and immediately forgotten it is! Whereas, let an interpreter, one of a thousand, open it up to us, and we never forget either the chapter or him. "The Spirit of God maketh the reading, but especially the expounding of the Word, an effectual means of convincing and converting sinners, and of building them up in holiness and comfort, through faith, unto salvation." "It is mainly by the institution of expounding and preaching," says John Foster, "that religion is kept a conspicuous thing, a public acknowledged reality. If we are told that we should rather say that it is public worship that has this effect, we have to answer that public worship, apart from expounding and preaching, has a very small effect in favour of religion. It is quite certain that where the conductors of that worship have not knowledge and religion enough to expound and preach, that worship will be little more than a ceremonial routine of idle forms."

Years and years and years pass on. Philip has for long been a married man, and is now the father of four grown-up daughters. His wife is a good woman. She is a grave woman, as Paul exhorted her to be. And, between them, Philip and his grave and faithful wife both ruled themselves well, and thus their four extraordinarily-gifted daughters. And with such a father and such a mother, I do not wonder that when such things were abroad in those days as gifts of tongues, and gifts of healing, and gifts of prophecy, and many other operations of the Holy Ghost, a double portion of some of those miraculous things came to

Philip's four daughters. Luke has a quick eye for everything of that kind, and thus it is that he interpolates this footnote in his history of Paul. "And the next day we came to Cæsarea, and we entered the house of Philip the evangelist, which was one of the seven; and abode with him. And the same man had four daughters, virgins, which did prophesy. And as we tarried there many days, there came down from Judea a certain prophet, named Agabus. And when he was come to us, he took Paul's girdle, and bound his own hands and feet, and said, Thus saith the Holy Ghost, so shall the Jews at Jerusalem bind the man that owneth this girdle," and so on. And thus it was that this strange Agabus was the last sanctification of Philip and his wife and his four prophetical daughters. To begin with, his own children had been gifted and employed and honoured far above Philip himself. And then Agabus arrived just at the moment to be gifted and employed and honoured far above them all. In the rich grace and manifold wisdom of God, outwardly and ostensibly and on the surface, Agabus's errand was to foretell Paul about his future arrest at Jerusalem. But, far deeper than that, Agabus had a finishing work of the Holy Ghost to perform on Philip, and on his four daughters, and on their mother, that grave woman. A work of humility. A work of resignation. An evangelical work. A work far above the best prophecy. A work of lowly-mindedness. A work of esteeming others better than themselves. A work of saying, Agabus must increase, and I must decrease. And a work that, no doubt, began by reproaches and rebukes and charging God foolishly, like this. 'Why were not my prophetical daughters employed to deliver this prophecy to Paul? Why was a stranger brought in over our heads in this way? We cannot ever again have the same standing and esteem in Cæsarea after this so open slight. What a strength it would have been to us in our pulpit and pastoral work had my daughters been honoured of the Holy Ghost to utter this prophecy concerning the Apostle. It would have established us and honoured us in our work in Cæsarea like nothing else.' Agabus was an evil enough messenger to Paul; but he was such a staggering blow to Philip and to his whole household that it took all Paul's insight, and skill in souls, and authority with Philip, and power with God, to guide and direct Philip so that he should get all God's intended good to himself and to all his house out of it.

Now, Agabus does not come to your house and mine in such open and such dramatic ways as he came to Philip's house; but he comes. Agabus of Jerusalem came to Jonathan Edwards's grave and godly wife in Northampton in the shape of a young preacher. "On Monday night, Mr. Edwards being gone that day to Leicester, I heard that Mr. Buell was coming to this town. At that moment I felt the eye of God on my heart to see if I was perfectly resigned with respect to Mr. Buell's expected success among our people. I was sensible what great cause I had to bless God for the use He had made of my husband hitherto, and I thought that if He now employed other ministers more I could entirely acquiesce in His will. On Tuesday night there seemed to be great tokens of God's presence at Mr. Buell's meeting; and when I heard of it, I sat still in entire willingness that God should bless his labours among us as much as He pleased, even though it were to the refreshing of every saint and the conversion of every sinner in the whole town. These feelings continued afterwards when I saw his great success. I never felt the least rising of heart against him, but my submission to God was even and uniform and without interruption or disturbance. I rejoiced when I saw the honour God had put upon him, and the respect paid to him by the people, and the greater success attending his preaching than had now for some time past attended my husband's preaching. I found rest and rejoicing in it, and the sweet language of my soul continually was, Amen, Lord Jesus. Amen, Lord Jesus. I had an overwhelming sense of the glory of God, and of the happiness of having my own will entirely subdued to His will. I knew that the foretaste of glory I then had in my soul came from God, and that in His time I shall be with Him, and be, as it were, swallowed up in Him." Agabus, and Mr. Buell, and another. But who is that other? And what is his name?

XCIX

CORNELIUS

Cornelius had been sent out from Rome to Cæsarea very much as our English officers are sent out to India. The Romans both despised and hated the Jews, as we, with all our proverbial pride, neither despise nor hate any of our subject races; and, sharing both that despite and that hatred, Cornelius had come out to his centurionship in Cæsarea. But Cornelius was no ordinary Roman centurion, and he soon discovered that the Jews of Cæsarea were no ordinary tributary people. The wide and deep contrast between Italy and Israel soon began to make an immense impression on Cornelius's excellent and open mind.

Israel's noble doctrine of Jehovah and His Messiah; the spotless purity of Israel's morality, with the sweetness and the sanctity of its home life; its magnificent and incomparable literature, even to a man fresh from Athens and Rome; and its majestic and overpowering worship;—all these things immensely impressed Cornelius, till, by the time we are introduced to him, Cornelius is already a devout man, and one that fears the God of Israel, and prays to the God of Israel always.

It was one of the conspicuous characteristics of Cornelius that all his servants, both domestic and professional, stood on such a friendly footing with their master. His family religion, as we would call it, was one of the most outstanding and attractive things about Cornelius. Long before Cornelius was a baptized man at all, this mind of Christ was already found in the centurion. "I call you not servants," said One whom Cornelius did not yet know. "For the servant knoweth not what his lord doeth; but I have called you friends: for all things that I have learned of my Father I have made known unto you." So did Cornelius. Cornelius was already one of those Christian gentlemen who hold their commissions in the army less for their own sake than for the sake of their soldiers; and their landed estates less for their own sake than for the sake of their farmers, and gardeners, and coachmen, and grooms; and their factories less for their own sake than for the sake of their factory-hands; and their offices less for their own sake than for the sake of their clerks; and their shops less for their own sake than for the sake of their shopmen and their shopwomen; and their houses at home less for their own sake than for the sake of their children, and their domestic servants, and their ever-welcome guests. Of all holy places in the Holy Land, few places, surely, were more the house of God and the gate of heaven in those days than just the Roman castle of Cæsarea, where the centurion of the Italian legion lived in the fear of God with all his household, and with all his devout soldiers, who were daily learning more and more devoutness from the walk and conversation of their beloved and revered centurion.

Well, one day Cornelius was fasting and praying all that day till three o'clock in the afternoon. It must have been some special and outstanding day in his personal life, or in his family life, or in his life in the army. We are not told what anniversary-day it was; but it was a day he had never forgotten to commemorate in prayer: and he has never forgotten it in alms nor in thanks-offerings since: no, nor ever will. It had just struck three o'clock in the afternoon, when an angel descended and entered the barrack-room where Cornelius was on his knees. For are they not all ministering spirits sent forth to minister for them who shall be heirs of salvation? "What is it, Lord?" said Cornelius, looking up in holy fear. "Thy prayers and thine alms," said the angel, "are come up for a memorial before God." We have no Bible dictionary on earth that is able to explain to us the language of heaven, and thus we are left to compare Scripture with Scripture in this matter of a memorial. "This shall be told for a memorial of her," said the Master of angels, when the woman poured the alabaster box upon His head. And this remarkable and unique word stands in the text in order that we may exercise some understanding, and imagination, and encouragement, in our alms and in our prayers in our day also. There was joy in heaven—this is part of what a memorial in heaven means—over every good deed that Cornelius did, and over every good word that Cornelius spake, both to God and to man. They had their eyes upon Cornelius, those angels of God, because he had been pointed out to them as one of the heirs of salvation. And, you may be sure, they did not keep Cornelius's alms and prayers to themselves; but, the holy talebearers that they are, they sought out the prophets and the psalmists who had prophesied concerning the salvation of the Gentiles, and told them that the great work had begun at last in the conversion of the Ethiopian eunuch and the Roman centurion. And it was not left to their winged visits up and down with the last news from Cæsarea; but there were great books kept also, and one of them with Cornelius's name embossed on the back of it, with all his prayers, and all his alms, day and date, times and places, opportunities and people, with all their other circumstances and accompaniments. The memorial books are kept with such scrupulous care in heaven, because so much already turns there, and will afterwards turn there, on things that we might quite overlook down here. And those great volumes, kept with such insight and truth, lie open before the throne of God for a memorial, for the instruction of His angels, and for the joy of all the already saved. How it was decreed from all eternity that Cornelius should be a centurion; should be commissioned by Cæsar to Cæsarea; should be an open-minded man; should open his mind to the Old Testament and to the temple; should begin to pray, and should sometimes fast that he might the better pray; and should be always waiting to see what he ought to do;—all that was written in the book of his memorial concerning Cornelius. And, as time went on, Cornelius's memorial-volume grew till there was written in it how Peter came to him, and how he was baptized, and how he finished his course, and kept the faith, first at Cæsarea, and then at Rome, till it was said to him, that, as he had been faithful over a few things in Cæsarea, so let him come up to where his memorial was written, and he would be set over twelve legions of angels. "For," says John Calvin on Cornelius, "God keeps a careful memorial concerning all His servants, and by sure and certain steps He exalts them till they come to the top."

Now, the main point is, what about your memorial and mine? What about your alms and your prayers and mine? What about your fastings, and shut doors, and mine, in order that we may have a day now and then of undistracted, and concentrated, and self-chastening prayer? Has there ever been joy in heaven over your prayers and your alms and mine? Real joy in heaven among the angels and the saints of God? And do the faces and the wings of those messenger-spirits shine as they carry the latest memorial that has come up to heaven concerning us to tell the news of it to those in heaven who loved us on earth? Let us pray more, and give alms more, if only to add to the joy of God's angels and saints who remember us and wait for news about us in heaven.

But, a man of prayer, and a benevolent man, and a man with a memorial in heaven, as Cornelius was, he had still much to learn. He had still the best things to learn. He had still to learn CHRIST. And the difficulties that lay in the Roman centurion's way to learn Christ, you have simply no conception of. Till you read the Acts of the Apostles, as not one in a thousand reads that rare book; nay, till you have to teach that rare book to others, you will never at all realise what the centurion had to come through before he could be a complete Christian man. Ay, and what Christ's very best apostles themselves had to come through before they would have anything to do with such an unclean and four-footed beast as Cornelius was to them. It was twelve o'clock of the day at Joppa, and it was the very next day after the angel had made his visit to Cornelius about his memorial. And Peter, like the centurion, was deep that day in special prayer. Now, Peter must surely have been fasting far too long, as well as praying far too earnestly, for he fell into a faint as he continued to pray. And as he lay in his faint he dreamed, as we say; a vision was sent to him, as Scripture says. And in his vision Peter saw heaven opened above him, and a certain vessel descending unto him, as it had been a great sheet knit at the four corners and let down to the earth. Wherein were all manner of four-footed beasts of the earth, and wild beasts, and creeping things, and fowls of the air. And there came a voice to him, Rise, Peter, kill, and eat. But Peter said, Not so, Lord: for I have never eaten anything that is common or unclean. And the voice spake unto him again the second time, What God hath cleansed, that call not thou common. And scarcely had the sheet been drawn up to heaven, when three of Cornelius's servants knocked at the tanner's door, and asked if one Simon Peter lodged here. And when Peter saw the three men, and heard their message from Cornelius, he at once comprehended and fully understood the heavenly vision. And the vision was this. Cornelius and all his soldiers, devout and indevout, and all his domestic servants, and all the Roman people, good and bad, and all other nations of men on the face of the earth; all mankind, indeed, except Peter and a few of his friends, were bound up together in one abominable bundle. And Peter was standing above them, scouting at and spitting on them all. All so like ourselves. For, how we also bundle up whole nations of men and throw them into that same unclean sheet. Whole churches that we know nothing about but their bad names that we have given them, are in our sheet of excommunication also. All the other denominations of Christians in our land are common and unclean to us. Every party outside of our own party in the political state also. We have no language contemptuous enough wherewith to describe their wicked ways and their self-seeking schemes. They are four-footed beasts and creeping things. Indeed, there are very few men alive, and especially those who live near us, who are not sometimes in the sheet of our scorn; unless it is one here and one there of our own family, or school, or party. And they also come under our scorn and our contempt the moment they have a mind of their own, and interests of their own, and affections and ambitions of their own. It would change your whole heart and life this very night if you would take Peter and Cornelius home with you and lay them both to heart. It would be for a memorial about you before God if you would but do this. If you would take a four-cornered napkin when you go home, and a Sabbath-night pen and ink, and write the names of the nations, and the churches, and the denominations, and the congregations, and the ministers, and the public men, and the private citizens, and the neighbours, and the fellow-worshippers, —all the people you dislike, and despise, and do not, and cannot, and will not, love. Heap all their names into your unclean napkin, and then look up and say, 'Not so, Lord. I neither can speak well, nor think well, nor hope well, of these people. I cannot do it, and I will not try.' If you acted out and spake out all the evil things that are in your heart in some such way as that, you would thus get such a sight of yourselves that you would never forget it. And, for your reward, and there is no better reward, like Peter, you would one day come to be able to say, 'Of a truth I perceive that God is no respecter of persons. But in every nation, and church, and denomination, and party of men, and among those I used to think of as four-footed beasts of the earth, and wild beasts, and creeping things, God has them that fear Him, and that work righteousness, and that are accepted of Him.' And then it would go up for a memorial before God, the complete change and the noble alteration that had come to your mind and to your heart. For you would be completely taken captive before God by that charity which vaunteth not itself, is not puffed up, thinketh no evil, believeth all things, hopeth all things. And now abideth faith, hope, charity; but the greatest of these is charity.

Such are some of the lessons it is intended we should take to heart out of the story of Cornelius, the Roman centurion.

C

EUTYCHUS

THIS Eutychus is the father of all such as fall asleep under sermons. And he well deserves all his fame, for he fell sound asleep under an action sermon of the Apostle Paul. We do not know how much there may have been to be said in exculpation or extenuation of Eutychus and his deep sleep during that sacrament service. Eutychus may have suppered his horses four-and-twenty hours before, and given a boy a shilling to look after them till his return home from the Communion Table at Troas. Like an old friend of mine who used to do that, and then to travel all night from Glenisla to Dundee in order to be present at Mr. M'Cheyne's Communion. After which he walked home and took his horses out to the plough in good time on Monday morning. Only, I feel quite sure that Mr. M'Cheyne never needed to go down and raise my old friend to life again, as Paul had to go to the dead Eutychus. For he never fell asleep, I feel quite sure, neither under Mr. M'Cheyne's action sermon, nor during the three afternoon tables, no, nor under the evening sermon of Daniel Cormick of Kirriemuir, who used to preach not short sermons on such occasions, but never one word too long for St. Peter's, Dundee, in those pre-disruption days.

The sacred writer does not in as many words take it upon himself to blame the Apostle for his long sermon that night. Though what he does say so emphatically and so repeatedly would be unpardonable blame to any other preacher. What blame, indeed, could be more unpardonable to any of your preachers than what the Apostle was guilty of that night? The like of it has never been seen again since that night. To keep his hearers from the time of lighting the candles till the sun rose next morning! Matthew Henry would like to have had the heads of Paul's sermon that night. But my idea is that Paul's sermon had no heads that night. My idea is that as soon as the candles were lighted Paul recited his warrant for the celebration of the Lord's Supper, as we now read that warrant from his pen in First Corinthians. After which he would enter on the nature and the ends of the Supper, which would take some time to explain and exhaust. He would then diverge to tell the Troas people the never-ending story of how he came to be a catechumen and a communicant himself at first. He would then go on to the mystical union that subsists between Jesus Christ and all true communicants, during the deep things of which Eutychus would fall fast asleep. I know nothing so like that richest part of Paul's sermon as our own Robert Bruce's not short Sermons on the Sacrament, which Dr. Laidlaw has put into such good English, and Mr. Ferrier into such good buckram, for us the other day. And then, even after the accident to Eutychus, Paul was still so full of matter and of spirit, that he actually went on with his post-communion address till the sun rose on the cups still standing on the table, and on the elders standing beside them, and Paul still pouring out his heart from the pulpit.

Now, notwithstanding Paul's example, all our preachers should, as a rule, be short in their sermons. In Luther's excellent portrait of a good preacher, one of such a preacher's nine virtues and qualities is this, that he should know when to stop. So he should. Only, you have no idea how fast the pulpit clock goes when a preacher has anything still on his mind that he wishes to say. At the same time, every sermon is not to be cut according to the sand-glass. John Howe first attracted Cromwell by preaching for two hours and then turning the sand-glass for a third hour. And Coleridge in his notes on Dr. Donne, and on an hour and a half sermon of his preached at Whitehall, says: "Compare this manhood of our Church divinity with our poor day. When I reflect on the crowded congregations, and on the thousands who with intense interest came to those hour and two-hour sermons, I cannot believe in any true progression, moral or intellectual, in the minds of the many." And since I have Coleridge open at any rate, I must not deny you what Hazlitt says about Coleridge's own preaching: "It was in January, 1798, that I rose one morning before daylight, to walk ten miles in the mud, to hear this celebrated person preach. When I got there, the organ was playing the hundredth Psalm, and when it was done Mr. Coleridge rose and gave out his text. And his text was this: "He departed again into a mountain Himself alone." As the preacher gave out his text his voice rose like a stream of distilled perfumes; and when he came to the last two words of the text, which he pronounced loud, deep and distinct, it seemed to me, who was then young, as if the sounds had echoed from the depths of the human heart. The preacher then launched into his subject like an eagle dallying with the wind. For myself, I could not have been more delighted if I had heard the music of the spheres. Poetry and philosophy had met together, truth and genius had embraced each other, and that under the sanction of religion." Now, a preacher like Coleridge, and a hearer like Hazlitt, are not to be cut short by all the sand-glasses and pulpit clocks in the world. Sand-glasses and pulpit-clocks are made for such preachers and hearers, and not such preachers and hearers for sand-glasses and pulpit-clocks.

But another thing. Paul did not have his manuscript before him that night, and that circumstance was partly to blame for the too-great length of his sermon. I will be bold to take an illustration of that night in Troas from myself. When I am in Paul's circumstances; that is to say, when I have only once the opportunity to preach in any place, I never on such an occasion read my sermon from a paper. I just give out the Scripture text that I am myself living upon at that time, and then I speak out of such a heart as is given to me at that moment. But the danger of such preaching is just that which Luther has pointed out—I never know when to stop. Just as Paul did not know when to stop that night. And just as Luther himself, not seldom exceeded all bounds. Without a paper, not one preacher in a hundred knows when to stop. He forgets to look at the clock till it is far too late. With a paper, and with nothing more to say than is down on the paper, you stop at the moment. But not restricted to a paper, and with your mind full of matter, and your heart full of feeling, you go on till midnight. At home you hearers know what your minister is going to say, and you are able to settle yourselves down to sleep as soon as he gives out his text. But he has much more honour when he goes outside of his own congregation. And thus it is that you hear of how he preached so long, and was so much enjoyed, when away from home. That was Paul's exact case. If this was not his first and his only sermon at Troas, it was certainly his last. The Apostle would never see those Troas people again till the day of judgment; and who shall blame him if he completely forgot the sand-glass, and poured out his heart all night upon that entranced congregation. At the same time, and after all is said, Luther is quite right. A good preacher should know when to stop. In other words, as a rule, and especially at home, he should be short.

But, then, there are two sides to all that also. And your side is this. I never see any of you fall asleep at an election time. No, not though the speaking goes on till midnight. And, yet, I do not know that the oratory of the political candidates and their friends is so much better than the oratory of the pulpit. But this is it. Your own passions are all on fire in politics, whereas you are all so many Laodiceans in religion. Yea, what carefulness your politics work in you; yea, what clearing of yourselves; yea, what indignation; yea, what fear; yea, what vehement desire; yea, what zeal; yea, what revenge. So much so, that the poorest speaker on the party-platform will have no difficulty in keeping your blood up all night to the boiling point. At the same time, I frankly admit, few preachers preach with the passion, and with the issues at stake, that the politicians, or even the playactors, speak. And thus, on the whole, the sum of the matter is this—that, what between too long sermons, and too cold, the blame lies largely at every preacher's door.

And, then, even more than our sermons, our prayers should be short; our public prayers, that is. You may be as long as you like in secret, but not in public, not in the family, not in the prayer-meeting, and not in the pulpit. Bishop Andrewes, the best composer of prayers in all the world of prayers, is not short. His prayer for the first day of the week occupies fifteen pages. His prayer for the second day of the week covers eight pages. His three prayers on awaking take up six pages. His Horology five pages. His four Acts of Deprecation eleven pages, and so on. But then these not short prayers are printed in his *Private Devotions,* which his trustees could scarcely read, so kneaded into a pulp were they with Andrewes's sweat and tears. And no wonder, if you knew his history. William Law, on the other hand, was short and exact in his private devotions. But, then, to make up for that, he was so incomparably methodical, so regular, so punctual, and so concentrated, in the matter of his prayers. He was like

James Durham, of whom William Guthrie said that no man in all Scotland prayed so short in public as Durham did; but, then, "every word of Durham's would have filled a firlot." Look at Paul's short prayers also. Every word would fill a firlot. And so the hundred and nineteenth Psalm. Every single verse of that psalm is a separate prayer which might have been written by the laird of Pourie Castle. At any rate, we are saying that every night in our family worship at home at present. We take a different kind of Scripture in the morning when all the children are with us. But at night we just take one verse of that Old Testament James Durham, and every heart in the house is straightway filled like a firlot before God. The Lord's Prayer is short also, because it is not His prayer at all, but is composed for us and for our children. But His private devotions were not only far longer than Bishop Andrewes's, but are far more illegible to us with His tears and His blood.

And, then, if you ever rise to be an author, make your books short. You may be a great author and yet your books may all the time be very short among books. The Song is a short book. So is the Psalms. So is the Gospel of John. So is the Epistle to the Romans. So is the *Confessions*. So is the *Divine Comedy*. So is the *Imitation*. So is the *Pilgrim's Progress*, and so is the *Grace Abounding*. Brother Lawrence *On the Practice of the Presence of God* is so short that it will cost you only fourpence. I had occasion a moment ago to mention William Guthrie. Said John Owen, drawing a little gilt copy of Guthrie's *Saving Interest* out of his pocket, "That author I take to be one of the greatest divines that ever wrote. His book is my *vade mecum*. I carry it always with me. I have written several folios, but there is more divinity in this little book than in them all." "I am finishing Guthrie," said Chalmers, "which I think is the best book I ever read." And I myself read the whole of Guthrie in Melrose's beautiful new edition the other day between Edinburgh and London. All the greatest authors have been like Guthrie, and like Luther's best preachers, they have known when to stop. Let all young men who would be great authors, study and imitate all the short books I have just signalised. And though it is not a short book, and could not be, let them all read Professor Saintsbury's new book, out of which I borrow this last advice: "Phrynichus is redundant and garrulous; for when it was open to him to have got the matter completely finished off in not a fifth part of his actual length, by saying things out of season, he has stretched his matter out to an unmanageable bulk."

Now, after all that about preaching, and about prayer, and

about great authorship, Eutychus did not fall out of the window for nothing, if we learn from his fall some of these valuable lessons.

CI

FELIX

Our original authorities for the life of Felix are Luke in the Acts of the Apostles, Josephus in the *Antiquities* and in the *Wars of the Jews,* and Tacitus in the *Annals of the Romans.* Luke gives us one of his most graphic chapters about Felix; but he abstains, as the Bible manner is, from judging even Felix before the time. Josephus is graphic enough about Felix, but we are sure neither of Josephus's facts nor of his judgments. We cannot go very far either for or against any man on the word of such a witness as Josephus. But Tacitus scars Felix's forehead as only Tacitus's pen can scar. Tacitus, as his manner is, anticipates the very day of judgment itself in the way he writes about Felix. Felix began his life as a slave, and he ended his life as a king. But, as Tacitus says, there was a slave's heart all the time under Felix's royal robes. All what evil secrets lay hidden in Felix's conscience we do not know; but we have only too abundant testimony as to how savage, how treacherous, and how steeped in blood, Felix's whole life had been. Luke calls Drusilla the wife of Felix. Drusilla was a wife, but she was not the wife of Felix. Drusilla was still a young woman, but she had already come through wickedness enough to stamp her as one of the worst women in the whole of human history. Paul was lying in prison waiting for his trial at Felix's judgment-seat, when, most probably to satisfy Drusilla's guilty curiosity about Paul and Paul's Master, Felix sent for Paul to hear what he had to say for himself and for his Master. How the interview opened, and how Paul conducted his discourse, we are not told. But this we are told, that as Paul continued to reason of righteousness, temperance, and judgment to come, Felix trembled, and answered, "Go thy way for this time; when I have a convenient season, I will call for thee."

"The ears of our audiences must first be propitiated," says Quintilian in his *Institutes of Oratory*. And Dante but borrows from that fine book when he tells all public speakers in his *Banquet* that they must always begin by taking captive the goodwill of their hearers. Now, just how Paul managed to propitiate Felix's unfriendly ears that day, and to take captive his hardened heart, we are not told. But that the great preacher did succeed in getting a hearing from Felix is certain. And it was neither a short hearing nor a hostile that Felix gave to Paul that day. Felix sat in transfixed silence while Paul stood up before him, and plunged the two-edged sword of God's holy law into his guilt conscience, till the hardened reprobate could not command himself. A greater seal was never set to the power of Paul's preaching than when Felix shook and could not sit still under the Apostle's words. And a greater encouragement could not possibly be given to all true preachers than that scene in the palace of Cæsarea gives to them. What an ally, unseen but omnipotent, all true preachers have in the consciences of their hearers! "The conscience," says the prince of Puritan expository preachers, "is what the snout is in a bear, a tender part to tame him by. Conscience is acutely sensible to God's wrath. And hell-fire itself could not take hold of the soul but at this corner."

O conscience! who can stand against thy power!
Endure thy gripes and agonies one hour!
Stone, gout, strappado, racks, whatever is
Dreadful to sense are only toys to this.
No pleasures, riches, honours, friends can tell
How to give ease to thee, thou'rt like to hell.

If Felix had but sat still a little longer, Paul was just going on to tell him how to get ease to the hell that was beginning to burn in his bosom. But I suspect Drusilla at that moment. I cannot get over my suspicion that it was Drusilla who so suddenly cut short Paul's discourse, and sent him back to his prison. I do not read that Drusilla trembled. My belief about that royal pair is, that had Drusilla not sat beside Felix that day, Felix would have been baptized, and Paul would have been set free, before the sun had gone down. But Drusilla and her sisters have cast into their graves many wounded. Many strong men have been slain to death by them. Their house is the way to hell, and their steps go down to the chambers of death.

"Go thy way for this time," said Felix to Paul, "when I have a convenient season, I will call for thee." Felix never sat at a Communion Table. But many of us here to-night who sat at that table to-day have in effect said Felix's very words to-day to God and to our own consciences. Many of us trembled at the table to-day, but we recovered ourselves with this resolution—that we would repent and amend our ways at another time. More action-sermons and more table-addresses have been silenced and forgotten because of a postponed repentance than because of anything else. Felix did not really intend to shut Paul's mouth for ever. He did not intend to go before God's judgment-seat just as he was that day. And no more do we. We honestly intend to live righteously and temperately—after a time. When we are in other circumstances. When we have other companionships. When we have formed other and better relationships. After that happy alteration in our life to which we are looking forward, you will find us very different men. When I am old, says one. Not too old. But when I somewhat older and much less occupied. I will then have time to give to secret prayer. I will then have on my table, and near my bedside, some of those books my minister has so often besought me to buy and to read at a Communion season. I will then attend to God and to my own soul. Poor self-deceived creature that you are! Cruelty and uncleanness have slain their thousands; but a life like yours, a life simply of putting off repentance and reformation, has slain its tens of thousands.

But Felix, after all, was as good as his word, so far. Felix did actually call for Paul again, and that not once nor twice, but often, and communed with him in the palace. Only, it had almost been he had not done so, for he always did it with a bad motive in his mind. It was not to hear out Paul's interrupted discourse that Felix sent for Paul. The sacred writer is able to tell us what exactly Felix's secret motive was in so often giving the Apostle an audience. "He hoped also that money should have been given him of Paul, that he might loose him; wherefore he sent for him the oftener, and communed with him. But after two years Porcius Festus came into Felix's room; and Felix, willing to show the Jews a pleasure, left Paul bound." And it is because our motives in coming to church are so mixed that the years allowed us for our salvation pass on till some one else occupies our pew, and the preaching of salvation has for ever come to an end as far as we are concerned.

> Pulpits and Sundays; sorrow dogging sin;
> Afflictions sorted; anguish of all sizes;
> Without our shame; within our consciences;
> Yet all these fences, and their whole array,
> One cunning bosom sin blows quite away.

I have known a man come to a church for a slip of a girl; another as a stepping-stone to some great man's favour; another for the advantage of his shop; and another for the chance of a tippet and a chain and a hoped-for handle to his name, and so on. Felix sat under Paul's preaching because his household expenses in Cæsarea were so great, and his resources so low, and his debts so heavy. And because he had been told that Paul had such rich friends, that they could and would pay any price for his release. And who can tell how Felix's calculations might have turned out, had it not been that Cæsar so suddenly sent for Felix to come to Rome to give an account of his stewardship; and all that, most unfortunately, before Paul's rich friends had time to come forward. Many that sleep in the dust of the earth shall awake, some to everlasting life, and some to shame and everlasting contempt for the found-out reasons why they went to this church or to that.

It is like the fresh air of heaven itself to turn from Felix's church attendances in this matter of motive, and to turn to Paul. For, when the royal message summoning Paul to the palace was delivered to him in his prison, what was Paul's first thought, do you think? Paul was a great man. Paul was a noble-minded man. Paul was a true and a pure-hearted man. Paul never thought of himself at all. He never once said to himself how all this might tell upon his release and his liberty. Dear and sweet as release and liberty were to Paul. these things never once came into his mind that day. Felix and Drusilla alone came into his mind that day; Drusilla especially. For Drusilla was a Jewess; she was a daughter of Abraham; and Paul's heart's desire and prayer to God for long had been that Drusilla might be saved. And here, in this opportunity to him, was the answer to his prayer! And thus it was that all the way up from his prison to her palace Paul was thinking only of that wicked and miserable pair, with their fearful looking for of judgment. Till, with his heart full of all that, as Paul was led into the presence-chamber, Felix turned to Drusilla, and pointing to Paul, he as good as said to her—

> Lo! this man's brow like to a title-leaf,
> Foretells the nature of a tragic volume!
> He trembles, and the whiteness in his cheek
> Is apter than his tongue to tell his errand!
> Even such a man
> Drew Priam's curtain in the dead of night.

It was the snow-white purity of Paul's motives that gave to his words, and to his whole look and manner, such last-day power as he stood and spoke before Felix. Paul's eye was so single at that moment that the whole palace was filled to Felix as with the light of the great white throne itself. No other man knows with a full certainty any or all of his neighbour's motives. At the same time, I have come to think that the purity of a preacher's motives has very much to do with his success. Not always, perhaps; but sufficiently often to make it a good rule for all of us who are, or are to be, preachers. For instance, to speak of two very successful preachers who have lately gone to give in their account and reap their reward—Moody and Spurgeon. I have always attributed their immense and their lasting success to the singleness of their eye and the transparency of their motives. And therefore it is that I am always directing young probationers who are going to preach in a vacancy to read before they go Dr. Newman's sermon entitled, "The Salvation of the Hearer the Motive of the Preacher." I constantly tell them that this desired call, if it is to be a call to them from Christ, will largely lie in their motive that day. If the preacher makes the vacant congregation tremble like Felix till they forget themselves, that is the preacher for them, and that is the people for him. Let all probationers of the pulpit study that same great writer's noble lecture, entitled "University Preaching," and they will thank me for this instruction all their days.

And now to conclude. I can imagine no other night in all the year so convenient as just the night after a Communion day. I can imagine no night in all the year so acceptable to Christ, and so welcome to His Father. No day and no night in which our Redeemer so desires to see of the travail of His soul. No night in which he has so much joy in seeing either a sinner repenting, or a saint returning. It is a special night for new beginners, and it is famous for the restoring of backsliders' souls. This is the night, then, for us all to date from. It was that day, it was that night, when we had Felix, you will say all your days on earth. My Lord met me, you will say, in that house of His, and on that night of His. Come away then, and make a new start on the spot. Come away, and there will be a joy in heaven to-night that there will not be but for you. Oh! do come, and let this house have this honour in heaven henceforth, because this man and that man were born here. And, in saying that, it is not I that say it. Jesus Christ Himself singles you out of all the congregation and says to you, as if you were alone in this house, Come! Come, He says, and let us reason together. And if you are a very Felix and a very Drusilla; if your unrighteousness, and your intemperance, and your fearful looking for of judgment, are all as dreadful as were theirs, they shall be as white as snow. And though they be red like crimson, they shall be as wool. Who, then, this Communion evening, will come forward like the brave man in Bunyan, and will say to him who has the book and the pen and the ink-horn in his hand, Set down my name, sir! At which there was a most pleasant voice heard from those within, even of those who walked upon the top of the king's palace, saying—

Come in, come in,
Eternal glory thou shalt win.

So he went in, and was clothed with the same garments as they were clothed with. Then Christian smiled, and said, I think verily that I know the true meaning to me of this great sight, and the true intention to me of this great Scripture.

CII

FESTUS

A SINGLE word will sometimes immortalise a man. Am I my brother's keeper? was all that Cain said. And, What will you give me? was all that Judas said. One of his own words will sometimes, all unintentionally, sum up a man's whole past life. A man will sometimes discover to us his deepest heart, and will seal down on himself his own everlasting destiny, just with one of his own spoken words. By thy words thou shalt be justified, and by thy words thou shalt be condemned. And as Paul thus spake for himself, Festus said with a loud voice, Paul, thou art beside thyself; much learning doth make thee mad. With that one word Festus ever after it is known to us quite as well as if Tacitus himself had written a whole chapter about Festus. This is enough: Festus was that Roman procurator who said with a loud voice that Paul was beside himself. That one word, with its loud intonation, sets Festus sufficiently before us.

Their ever-thoughtful ever-watchful Lord had taken care to prepare His apostles for this insult also. The disciple is not above his master, nor the servant above his Lord. It is enough for the disciple that he be as his master, and the servant as his Lord. If they have called the Master of the house Beelzebub, how much more shall they call them that are of His household. And the loud and unbecoming outbreak of Festus would have staggered Paul much more than it did, had he not recollected at that moment that this very same thing had been said about his Master also. And that not by heathens like Pilate and Festus, but by those whom the Gospels call His friends. "And when His friends heard of it they went out to lay hold on Him, for they said, He is beside Himself." And many of the Jews, as soon as they had heard His sermon on the Good Shepherd, of all His sermons, had nothing else to say about the Preacher but this, He hath a devil, and is mad; why hear ye Him?

First, then, as to our Master's own madness. It is plain, and beyond dispute, that either He was mad, or they were who so insulted Him. For He loved nothing that they loved. He hated nothing that they hated. He feared nothing that they feared. Birth, wealth, station, and such like things, without which other men cannot hold up their heads; of all that He emptied Himself, and made Himself of no reputation. And, to complete the contrast and the antipathy, the things that all other men despise and spurn and pity He pronounces to be alone blessed. Meekness under insults and injuries, patience amid persecutions, poverty of spirit, humbleness of mind, readiness to serve rather than to sit in honour and eat,—these are the only things that have praise and reward of Paul's Master. The things, in short, we would almost as soon die as have them for our portion. And the things we would almost as soon not live at all as not possess, or expect one day to possess, Jesus Christ cared nothing at all for such things. Absolutely nothing. It was no wonder that her neighbours and kinsfolk condoled with His mother who had borne such a son. It was no wonder that they worked incessantly upon His brethren till they also said, Yes; He must be beside himself; let us go and lay hold on him.

Now, Paul came as near to his Master's madness as any man has ever come, or ever will come, in this world. For, what made Festus break out in that so indecent way was because Paul both spake and acted on the absolute and eternal truth of the things we speak about with bated breath, and only faintly and inoffensively affect to believe. Paul had been telling his royal auditors what he never wearied telling; his undeserved, unexpected and unparalleled conversion. His manner of life before his conversion also, when he put this very same word into Festus's mouth. I was exceeding "mad," he said, against the saints. And at midday, O king, he said, addressing himself with an orator's instinct to Agrippa, a light from heaven above the brightness of the sun, and a voice speaking to me in the Hebrew tongue—and so on, till Festus broke out upon him, as we read. Now, if you had come through half of Paul's experience, we also would have charged you also with being beside yourself. To have had such bloody hands; to have been carried through such a conversion; to have had, time after time, such visions and revelations of the Lord; and, especially, to have had such experiences and such attainments in the divine life—certainly, to us you would have been beside yourself. To have seen you actually and in everything counting all things, your very best things, your very virtues and very graces, to be but dung, that you might win Christ; to have seen you continually crucified with Christ; what else could we have made of you? How else could we have defended ourselves against you, but by calling you mad?

But Paul had more than one experience that made him appear mad to other men. And another of those experiences was his unparalleled experience and insight into sin. Paul's sinfulness of his own heart, when he was for a moment left alone with it, always drove him again near to distraction. As the sight of the ghost drove Hamlet mad, so did the sight of sin and death drive Paul. And not Paul only, but no less than our Lord Himself. If ever our Lord was almost beside Himself, it was once at the sight, and at the approach, and at the contact, of sin. We water down the terrible words and say that He was sore amazed and very heavy. But it was far more than that. A terror at sin, a horror and a loathing at sin, took possession of our Lord's soul when He was about to be made sin, till it carried Him away beyond all experience and all imagination of mortal men. And the servant, in his measure, was as his Master in this also. For, as often as Paul's eyes were again opened to see the sinfulness of his own sin, there was only one other thing in heaven or earth that kept his brain from reeling in her distracted globe. And the sight of that other thing only made his brain reel the more. And so it has often been with far smaller men than Paul. When we ourselves see sin; even such a superficial sight of sin as God in His mercy sometimes gives us; both body and soul reel and stagger till He has to hold us up with His hand. And were it not that there is a fountain filled with something else than rose-water, there would be more people in the pond than the mother of Christian's children. What a mad-house because of the sinfulness of sin the church of God's saints would be were it not for His own blood! And this goes on with Paul till he has a doctrine of himself and of sin, such that he cannot preach it too often for great sinners like himself. No wonder, with his heart of such an exquisite texture and sensibility, and continually made such an awful battle-ground, no wonder Paul was sometimes nothing short of mad. And why should it be so difficult to believe that there may be men even in these dregs of time; one man here, and another there, who are still patterns to God, and to themselves, and to saints and angels, of the same thing? Beside themselves, that is, with the dominion and the pollution of sin. Was there not a proverb in the ancient schools that bears with some pungency upon this subject? It is in Latin, and I cannot borrow it at the moment. But I am certain there is a saying somewhere about a great experiment and a great exhibition being made on an insignificant and a worthless subject.

I am old enough to remember the time when the universal London press, led by *Punch* and the *Saturday Review*, week after week, mocked, trampled on, cried madman at, and tried to silence young Spurgeon, very much as Festus tried to trample on and silence Paul. But *Punch* lived to lay a fine tribute on Spurgeon's grave. It was true of Paul, and it was true of Spurgeon, and it will be true, in its measure, of every like-minded minister, as well as of all truly Christian men, what old Matthew Mead says in his *Almost Christian*. "If," says old Matthew, "the preaching of Christ is to the world foolishness, then it is no wonder that the disciples of Christ are to the world fools. For, according to the Gospel, a man must die in order to live; he must be empty, who would be full; he must be lost, who would be found; he must have nothing, who would have all things; he must be blind, who would see; he must be condemned, who would be redeemed. He is no true Christian," adds Mead, "who is not the world's fool." And, yet, no! I am not mad, most noble Festus; but speak forth the words of truth and soberness.

CIII

KING AGRIPPA

King agrippa was the grandson of Herod the Great, and he had succeeded to the shattered throne of his fathers; or rather, he had succeeded to such splinters of that throne as Cæsar had permitted him to set up. Agrippa was a king, but he was a king only in name. The Jews, as they themselves once said, had no king but Cæsar. At the same time, Cæsar sometimes, for reasons of state, set up sham kings over certain portions of his great empire. And Agrippa was one of those simulacrum sovereigns. Bernice, who here sits beside Agrippa, was his sadly-spotted sister. If you wade deep enough into the sixth satire of Juvenal, you will find

Bernice more fully set forth in that pungent piece. As for ourselves, we will look in silence at Bernice, as Holy Scripture does, and will then pass her by. But take a good look at her brother Agrippa. Look well at King Agrippa, for he is the last king of the Jews you will ever see. There has been a long line of Jewish kings since Saul and David and Solomon, but this is the last of them now. The Jews are not to have even a shadow of a king any more. They are to have Cæsar only, till they cease to be. What a scene! Festus, Agrippa, Bernice, and the whole place full of Roman soldiers and civilians, with Paul standing in his chains, as a sort of holiday show and sport to them all. What a company! What a providence! What an irony of providence! Thou art permitted to speak for thyself, said the king to the prisoner. And the prisoner, after having spoken for himself, was led back to his cell, there to await the issue of his appeal to Cæsar. Great pomp and all, the ancient throne of David and Solomon is seen crumbling to its very last dust before our very eyes. While, bonds and all, Paul stands before Agrippa holding out, not his own hand only, but the very Hand of the God of Israel Himself, both to King Agrippa, to his sister Bernice, and to the whole decayed, dispersed, and enslaved house of Israel. So much so, that when Paul was led back to his prison that day Israel's doom was for ever sealed. We are now looking on one of the most solemnising scenes that is to be seen in the whole of human history.

It was the wonderful story of Paul's conversion, and that story as told by himself, that so deeply impressed King Agrippa and his sister Bernice in Cæsarea that day. Again, and again, and again, we have Paul's wonderful story fresh from his own heart. The story was new, and it was full of new wonderfulness to Paul himself, every time he told it. And it never failed to make an immense impression on all manner of people; as, indeed, it does down to this day. And no wonder. For just look at him, and listen to him. "My manner of life," said Paul, stretching forth his hand with the chain on it, "know all the Jews. For I verily thought with myself that I ought to do many things contrary to the name of Jesus of Nazareth." And then, how he did those things, and how he was still doing them, when a voice from heaven struck him down, and said, Saul, Saul, I am Jesus whom thou persecutest. And so on, with his wonderful story, till Festus could only shake off the spell of it by shouting out that Paul was mad. And till Agrippa, who knew all these matters far better than Festus knew them, confessed openly that, for his part, he believed every word of Paul's conversion; and, indeed, felt almost at that moment as if he were about to be converted himself. "Almost thou persuadest me to be a Christian like thyself!" confessed King Agrippa. And to this day nothing is so persuasive to our hearts as just the story of a personal experience in religion. So much so, that without this so persuasive element, somehow or somewhere in his preaching, all any preacher says will fall short of its surest power. Even if his testimony is not always conveyed in that autobiographic and dramatic form in which Paul always tells his story; yet, unless there is something both of the conviction and the passion of a personal experience, both the pulpit and the pen will come far short of their fullest and their most persuasive power. Unless in every sermon and in every prayer the preacher as good as says with the Psalmist, "Come, and hear, all ye that fear God, and I will declare what He hath done for my soul;" unless there is some such heartbeat heard as that, both our sermons and our prayers will be but lukewarm, and neither cold nor hot. "I preached sin with great sense," says John Bunyan. Which is just his fine old English for great experience, great feeling, and, indeed, great passion. And down to this very day we feel the still unspent surges of Bunyan's pulpit passion beating like thunder on the rocky coasts of his *Grace Abounding* and his *Holy War*. And, just as this narration of Paul's personal experience was almost Agrippa's conversion; and just as this and other like narrations of Paul's experience were not only almost but altogether Luther's conversion; and then just as Luther's experience was Bunyan's conversion and Bunyan's experience; and his incomparable narration of it your conversion and mine; so will it always be. "The judicious are fond of originals," says an anonymous author. So they are. And we are all judicious in that respect. And thus it is that original autobiographies, and diaries, and dramatic narrations: David's Psalms, Augustine's Confessions, Luther's Sermons, Andrewes's Private Devotions, Bunyan's Grace Abounding, Fraser, Halyburton, Boston, Spurgeon, and such like, are always so interesting, so perennially popular, and so fruitful both in conversion at the time, and in edification and in sanctification for long after. Let all our preachers then stretch forth their own hands, and not another man's; and let them answer for themselves in their own pulpits, and to their own people; and, whether their hands are bound or free,—"I often went to the pulpit in chains," says John Bunyan,—Felix, and Festus, and Agrippa, and Bernice among the hearers will be compelled, each in their own way, to confess both the truth, and the authority, and the power, of all such preachers of an original, and a passionately undergone, experience.

"The ears of our audiences must first be propitiated," says Quintilian, that great teacher of ancient oratory. And Dante but borrows from that old master when he warns all public speakers that they must always begin by endeavouring to carry captive the goodwill of their hearers. Now, we can never enter a Jewish synagogue, nor stand beside him in a judgment-hall, nor pass by him as he preaches at a street corner, without both seeing and hearing Paul practising the *captatio benevolentiæ* of the ancient oratorical schools. And that, not because he had ever gone to those schools to learn their great art, but simply because of his own oratorical instinct, inborn courtesy, and exquisite refinement of feeling. No such urbanity, and no such good breeding, is to be met with anywhere in all the eloquence of Greece and Rome. It was his perfect Christian courtesy to all men, taken along with his massiveness of mind, his overmastering message, and his incomparable experiences,—it was all that taken together, that lifted up Paul to the shining top of universal eloquence. Festus, fresh from the most polished circles of the metropolis of the world, behaved like a boor beside his prisoner. The only perfect gentleman in all that house that day stood in chains, and all the bad manners, and all the insolence, sat in Cæsar's seat. Let us all, and ministers especially, aim to be gentlemen like Paul. In the pulpit, in the Presbytery, and in the General Assembly; ay, and even if we are at the bar of the General Assembly, as Paul so often was; let us behave there also like Paul, as far as our natural temperament, and supernatural refinement of temperament, will support us in doing so. Let us learn to say in effect, I think myself happy, King Agrippa, because I shall answer for myself this day before thee. Especially because I know thee to be expert in all customs and questions among the Jews. And when Festus assails us with his coarse-minded abuse, let us learn to say with all self-command, No, Most noble Festus. Or, far better still, let us hold our peace. Let us turn in silence from Festus and his brutality to Agrippa and Bernice, and say to them,—I would to God, that not you only, but also all that hear me this day, were both almost, and altogether such as I am, except these bonds. Holding out his hands, "except these bonds." Beautiful and noble, beyond all Greek and Latin art. Is there a touch like that again in all the world? What a heart! What tenderness! What fineness of feeling! What gold would we not give for one single link of those iron bonds that day!

But Paul, with all his fascination, must not be permitted to draw our attention away from Agrippa. And that, because

Agrippa has lessons to teach us to-night that Paul himself, with all his eloquence, and even with his wonderful conversion itself, is not able to teach us. For Agrippa, you must know, to begin with, was half a Jew. By blood he was half a Jew; whilst by education, and by interest, and by sympathy, he was wholly a Jew; if it had only been possible for Agrippa to be outwardly, and openly, and honestly, what, all the time, he really was in his heart. And thus it was that Paul so fastened upon Agrippa and would not let him go. Thus it was that Paul so addressed himself to Agrippa: so passed by Festus and all the rest of his audience, and spoke home to Agrippa, and that with such directness and such power. And Agrippa felt Paul's full power, till he openly confessed that he felt it. So much so, that when Festus forgot himself, and broke out upon Paul in such an indecent manner, Agrippa interposed, and said, 'Not only is Paul speaking the words of truth and soberness, but he has all but persuaded me and my sister to take his side, and to be baptized.' But, before I come to that, what do you think about this scene yourselves? Applying your own common sense, and your own imagination, to this whole scene, what do you say about it yourselves? About Agrippa's speech, that is. Was Agrippa speaking ironically and mockingly when he said that Paul had almost persuaded him to be a Christian? Or did he honestly and sincerely mean what he said? There is a division of opinion about that. Did he mean that. King Agrippa as he was, and Festus's guest as he was, and Bernice's brother as he was, he was within a hairsbreadth of casting in his lot with Paul, and with Paul's Lord and Saviour? I, for one, believe that Agrippa was entirely honest and true and without any guile in what he said. And that Paul and Agrippa were so near shaking hands before Festus and all the court at that moment; so near, that their not altogether doing so on the spot makes that one of the most tragical moments in all the world. A tragical moment only second to that you will perpetrate to-night, if you feel what Agrippa felt, and say what Agrippa said, and then go away and do what Agrippa did. "Almost," is surely the most tragic word that is ever heard uttered on this earth or in hell. And yet, both earth and hell are full of it. Almost! Almost! Almost! An athlete runs for the prize, and he almost touches the winning-post. A marksman shoots at the target, and he almost hits it. A runner leaps for his life over a roaring flood, and he almost clears the chasm. A ship is almost within the harbour, when the fatal storm suddenly strikes her till she goes down. The five foolish virgins were almost in time. And Agrippa and Bernice were almost baptized, and thus their names almost entered into the Church of Christ. And so it is to-night with some of yourselves. Some of yourselves who were not, were almost, at the Lord's table to-day. You intended to be at it at one time. You were almost persuaded at the last Communion season. Now, just go down and ask Agrippa and Bernice what they would do if they were back in your place to-night. They have had experience of what you are now passing through, and of how it ends. But if you find that between you and them there is a great gulf fixed; so that they which would pass to inquire of them cannot, neither can they come back with their experience to you. In that case, I myself have had an experience not much short of theirs, and I will tell you with all plainness, and earnestness, and anxiousness, and love, what I think you ought to do to-night. Do not sleep; nay, do not so much as go home, till your name has been taken down altogether for the next Lord's table.

CIV

LUKE, THE BELOVED PHYSICIAN

We have in our New Testament two most important books from the practised pen of Paul's beloved physician. And if the style is the man in Holy Scripture also, then, what with Paul's great affection for his faithful physician, and what with his own sacred writings, we feel a very great liking for Luke, and we owe him a very deep debt. To begin with, Luke was what we would describe in our day as a very laborious and conscientious student, as well as a very careful and skilful writer. Luke takes us at once into his confidence and confides to us that what made him think of putting pen to paper at all, was his deep dissatisfaction with all that had hitherto been written about the birth, the boyhood, the public life, the teaching, the preaching, the death, and the resurrection and ascension of our Lord. And then in a right workmanlike way this evangelist sets about the great task he has with such a noble ambition undertaken. Luke has not given us what cost him nothing. He did not sit down to his desk till he had made innumerable journeys in search of all the materials possible. He spared neither time nor trouble nor expense in the collection of his golden contributions to our New Testament. Luke had never himself seen Jesus

Christ in the flesh, so far as we know, and the men and the women who had both seen Him and heard Him when He was on earth were becoming fewer and fewer every day. Invidious death was fast thinning the ranks of those who had both seen and handled the Word of Life, till Luke had not a moment to spare if he was to talk with and to interrogate those who had actually seen their Lord with their own eyes. Joseph, and Mary, and James, and Joses, and Simon, and Judas, and His sisters, and His kinsfolk, and His twelve disciples—so many of them as were still in life—Luke set forth and sought them all out before he sat down to write his Gospel. Mary especially. And Mary opened her heart to Luke in a way she had never opened her heart to any one else. What was it, I wonder, that so opened Mary's so-long-sealed-up heart to this Evangelist? Was it that old age was fast coming on the most favoured among women? Was it that she was afraid that she might suddenly die any day with all these things still hidden in her heart? Was it that she was weary with forbearing and could not stay? Were His words in her heart as a burning fire shut up in her bones? His words that were known only to God, and to His Son, and to Gabriel, and to Joseph, and to herself. Or was it Paul's great name, taken together with some of his great Epistles about her Son, that at last unlocked the treasure-house of Mary's heart and laid it open, full and free, to Paul's beloved physician and deputed secretary? Whatever it was, or however he got it, we have in Luke's Gospel as nowhere else, the whole hitherto hidden history of Mary's espousal, and Gabriel's annunciation, and the Virgin's visit to Zacharias and Elisabeth, as also Mary's Magnificat. And all up and down his great Gospel, and its so invaluable supplement, we have, on every page of his, fresh and abundant proofs both of Luke's industry and skill, as well as of his absorbing love, first for our Lord, and then for Paul. His characteristic Prefaces already prepare his readers both for his new and invaluable materials, as well as for an order and a finish in his books of an outstanding kind. There is an authority, and a presence of power, and, indeed, a sense of exhilaration, in Luke's two Prefaces, that only a discoverer of new and most important truth and a writer of first-rate skill, is ever able to convey. Exhaustive inquiry, scrupulous accuracy, the most skilful and careful work, the most exalted instruction, and the most assured and fruitful edification—yes; the style is the man.

Such is Luke's literary skill, so to call it, that he makes us see for ourselves just the very verse in the Acts where his materials cease to be so many collections and digests of other men's memoranda and remembrances. With the sixth verse of the twentieth chapter this remarkable book all at once becomes autobiographical of Luke as well as biographical of Paul. Could anything be more reassuring or more interesting than to be able to lay one's finger on the very verse where the third person singular ends, and the first person plural begins? We feel as if we were looking over Luke's shoulder as he writes. We feel as if we saw the same divine boldness that moment take possession of his pen that marks with such peculiar power and authority the opening of his gospel. Paul was like Cæsar, and like our own Richard Baxter, in this respect, that he went on performing the most Herculean labours, if not in actual and continual sickness, then with the most overpowering sickness every moment threatening him, and, not seldom, suddenly prostrating him. And since his was, out of sight, the most valuable life then being spent on the face of the earth, no wonder that the churches insisted that the Apostle must not any more make his journeys alone. And accordingly, first one deacon accompanied him and then another, till it was found indispensable that he should have a physician also always with him. And in all the Church of Christ that day a better deacon for Paul and a better doctor could not have been selected than just the Luke on whom we are now engaged. 'Only remember,' Paul would expostulate with the young scholar and student of medicine, 'remember well what our Master said about Himself on a like occasion,—the foxes have holes and the birds of the air have nests, but the Son of Man hath not where to lay His head.' But Luke was equal to the occasion. Luke was already a well-read man, and he had his answer ready, and that out of Holy Scripture too. "Entreat me not to leave thee, or to return from following after thee; for whither thou goest, I will go; and where thou lodgest I will lodge; where thou diest will I die, and there will I be buried; the Lord do so to me, and more also, if aught but death part thee and me." Till, when waiting for his martyrdom in Rome, Paul is able to write like this to Timothy, "I am now ready to be offered up, and the time for my departure is at hand. Demas hath forsaken me, having loved this present world, and is departed into Thessalonica. But Luke, and Luke only, is with me." "Honour a physician," says the Son of Sirach, "with all the honour due to him. Of the Most High cometh healing, for the Lord hath created him. And the healer shall receive honour of the King. The skill of the physician shall exalt his head, and in the presence of great men shall he be held in admiration." Luke had by heart the whole chapter, till, by the grace of God, he had it all fulfilled in himself, as Paul's beloved physician and our beloved third Evangelist.

Lessons, both literary and religious, offer themselves to us before we bring our short study of Paul's physician to a close. But chiefly religious. I do not know that there is any class of men in our day, scarcely the ministers of religion themselves, who have so much in their power, in some ways, as our medical men. Take a young medical man just settling down in a provincial town, or in a country district, and what an event that is in interest and in opportunity. It is scarcely second to the settlement there of a good minister. What sort of a man, I wonder, is he? And what place will he take among us? it will be anxiously asked. And if he at once attaches himself to the Church; if he at once becomes a Sabbath-school teacher, a deacon, an elder, an abstainer, and so on; then, as Jesus the son of Sirach, says, that physician will be honoured with all the honour due to him, and in the presence of all good men will he be held in estimation. And over and above his study and imitation of Paul's beloved physician, let every young doctor have always beside him the Autobiography, the *Religio Medici,* of that great writer and great honour to the medical profession, Sir Thomas Browne. And not his inimitable masterpiece only, but all his fascinating books, will make a rare shelf in any young doctor's library. If Sir Thomas Browne is such a ceaseless delight to such men of letters as Johnson, and Coleridge, and Carlyle, and Hazlitt, and Pater, what a life-long delight and advantage would he be to those who are of his own so beloved profession, if they are only of his still more beloved faith and hope. It is delightful to read of the towns of England competing and contesting as to which of them should have young Browne to settle down and practise among them: such were his attainments, and such was his character, in his student days, and in his early professional life, and such was the largeness and richness of his mind, taken together with the purity and the piety of his heart and his character. All of which purity and piety and true popularity is open to every young doctor everywhere. "Of the Most High cometh healing, for the Lord hath created the healer, The skill of the physician shall exalt his head, and in the presence of all men shall he be held in admiration," says the wise son of Sirach.

CV

ONESIPHORUS

ONESIPHORUS was an elder in the Church of Ephesus, and a better elder there never was. Paul is but taking Onesiphorus's portrait when he says that an elder must be blameless, vigilant, sober, humble-minded, given to hospitality, one that ruleth his own house well, having his children in subjection with all gravity; moreover, he must have a good report of them that are without. Altogether, a striking likeness of a rare and a remarkable man. Paul had been Onesiphorus's minister for three years, and they had been three years of great labours and great sufferings, on Paul's part, and you come to know your elders pretty well in three years like Paul's three years in Ephesus. The sacred writer has supplied his readers with Paul's farewell address to the elders of Ephesus, and a right noble address it is. "You know," he said, "from the first day I came into Asia, after what manner I have been with you at all seasons. Therefore, watch, and remember, that by the space of three years I ceased not to warn every one of you night and day with tears. And now, brethren, I commend you to God, and to the word of His grace, which is able to build you up, and to give you an inheritance among all them that are sanctified." And from that he goes on to give us the great scene on the seashore, when Onesiphorus fell on Paul's neck, and could not be torn off Paul's neck till the ship had almost sailed away without Paul. Onesiphorus sorrowing most of all at the words which Paul spake that he should see his face no more. And, no wonder at Onesiphorus's inconsolable sorrow, since it is a universal and an absolute law that you love a man, and cannot part from him, just in the measure that you have long loved him, and done him good, and suffered for his sake in time past. All the elders in Ephesus loved Paul, and had good reason to love him, but all taken together they did not love Paul as Onesiphorus did. For it was Onesiphorus, more than all his colleagues in the eldership of Ephesus, who had kept the apostle alive during those three years of such temptations and so many tears. Many and many a time Paul would have fainted altogether had it not been for Onesiphorus. It was one of those heartbreaking years of his in Ephesus that Paul was thinking when he said to Timothy that an elder must be vigilant, and hospitable, and not a novice. That is to say, Onesiphorus never let Paul out of his sight, day nor night, all those three trying years to Paul. "Night and day with tears," is Paul's own summing up of his three years' ministry in Ephesus. But, then, Onesiphorus always wiped away Paul's tears faster than Paul shed them, such was his extraordinary vigilance and hospitality towards Paul. Many were the nights when after a trying day and then a refreshing supper Onesiphorus would give out this well-selected psalm at family worship—

> Who sow in tears, a reaping time
> Of joy enjoy they shall.
> That man who, bearing precious seed,
> In going forth doth mourn,
> He doubtless, bringing back his sheaves,
> Rejoicing shall return.

It was of those many Sabbath evening supper-parties that Paul remembered and wrote to Timothy in his Second Epistle to him: "How oft Onesiphorus refreshed me, and in how many things he ministered to me at Ephesus, thou knowest very well."

Now before we leave Ephesus and go to Rome with Onesiphorus, there is a lesson and an example here both for ministers who would fain imitate Paul, and for elders who would fain imitate Onesiphorus. Our ministers all have their own tears and temptations like the apostle. All men, indeed, have their own temptations and tears, but it is ministers we have now in hand. Our ministers, over and above the tears and the temptations which they share with all other men, have their own peculiar tears and temptations which it takes all Onesiphorus's vigilance to find out, and all his hospitality to alleviate. But, with all that, none of these things must move our ministers. They must only all the more bury themselves in their work. They must let none of these things move them but to more and to better work. They must not let the praise of men, nor anything that man can do for them, be dear to them. Nothing must really be dear to our ministers but to finish their course with joy, and their ministry, which they have received of the Lord Jesus. At the same time, there is always plenty of scope for Onesiphorus, and for all his vigilance, alongside of every such ministry. I do not remember that it is in as many words in our elders' ordination oath, that they are always to refresh their minister's heart when he would otherwise faint. But

Onesiphorus did it out of his own vigilance of love, never thinking whether it was in his ordination oath or no. And I myself have been as well looked after as ever Paul was, and far better. I have always had elders myself, who, with all their own occupations and preoccupations, never let me out of their vigilant minds and hospitable hearts. I could give you their names, and I am tempted to do so in order to give point and authority to what I am now saying. But I daresay you all know the names of those elders yourselves. For such elders as Onesiphorus was do not content themselves with refreshing their minister's heart only; they carry out their holy office to all the flock over the which the Holy Ghost hath made them overseers. The whole world knows Onesiphorus's name now; and even in our own so unapostolic day, the house of Onesiphorus still holds on its vigilant and hospitable way.

But all that is years and years ago. And things have by this time come to this pass with Paul that he is now ready to be offered up, and the time of his departure is at hand. In other words, the apostle is just about to be brought before Nero for the second time, and everybody knows what that means. Now it is out of these circumstances that Paul pens these beautiful words to Timothy: "When Onesiphorus arrived in Rome, and was there, he sought me out with all the greater diligence that he knew I was in chains, till at last he found me." Now there are two interpretations of these words, and you are free to take either of those two interpretations that best commends itself to you. What do you think? How are you led to read this passage about Onesiphorus and his visit to Rome? Do you think it would be this? That Onesiphorus, being a business man, had some mercantile errand to Rome; and then, after his hands were free of that matter he bethought himself that he would like to see his old minister before he returned home to Ephesus? Or does your heart revolt from that poor and mean and contemptible interpretation? And do you stand up for it, that it was something far better than the very best business-errand that brought Onesiphorus all the stormy way from Asia to Italy? Was it not once more to see his dearest friend on earth with whom he had so often transacted the great business of the soul, till he had by this time a great treasure laid up in heaven? If any of you owe your own soul, or your children's souls, to any minister, that entitles you to interpret this passage to us, and to say whether it was business or religion, money or love, that brought Onesiphorus to Rome toward the close of Paul's second imprisonment. Like all other interpreters, you will understand

Onesiphorus just according to what you would have done yourself had you been in his place. Whatever it was that brought Onesiphorus from Ephesus to Rome, we are left in no doubt at all as to what he did before he left Rome and returned to Ephesus. Paul might be the greatest of the apostles to Onesiphorus, and he may be all that and far more than all that to you and to me, but he was only "Number So and so" to the soldier who was chained night and day to Paul's right hand. You would not have known Paul from any incognisable convict in our own penal settlements. Paul was simply "Number 5," or "Number 50," or "Number 500," or some such number. From one barrack-prison therefore to another Onesiphorus went about seeking for Paul day after day, week after week, often insulted, often threatened, often ill-used, often arrested and detained, till he was set free again only after great suffering and great expense. Till, at last, his arms were round Paul's neck, and the two old men were kissing one another and weeping to the amazement of all the prisoners who saw the scene. Noble-hearted Onesiphorus! We bow down before thee. What a coal of holy love must have burned in thy saintly bosom! Thou hast taught us all a much-needed lesson to-night. For we also have friends, and especially in the ministry, whose backs are often at the wall. whose names are often under a cloud, and who are forsaken of all men who should have stood by them. May we all come to be of thy vigilant and hospitable household! May we all have thy life-long and unquenchable loyalty to all those who suffer for righteousness' sake!

But now, my brethren, with all that, let us take very good care that the warmth of our present feelings over Onesiphorus does not all evaporate with this apostrophe to Onesiphorus. Let us not only admire and exalt Onesiphorus, let us forthwith imitate him. Let us, like him, seek out, and that too with all diligence, those who need, and especially those who deserve, our sympathy and our support. Ministers especially. Let us write them a letter of sympathy, let us make them a visit of sympathy, let us send them a gift of sympathy. Let us, in such ways as these, refresh them under their chains. Let us make them to feel that they are not so forgotten or so forsaken as they think they are. And this also. Like Onesiphorus also let us bring up our children to the same life of love. Let us take them with us sometimes when we go about doing good. Let them taste early the sweetness of doing good. And especially the sweetness and the reward of doing good to the suffering and the fainting in the household of faith. Let us set them to visit some godly and lonely old soul who will pray down present-day and last-day blessings on our head and on their heads, as Paul here does on the head of Onesiphorus and on the heads of his household. Send your children to the Sick Children's Hospital on the Sabbath afternoon with books and flowers. Send the older ones to the Infirmary and to the Incurable Hospital with the same and other gifts. And go to the prison yourself like Onesiphorus in Rome. And do it at once, before all this about Paul and Onesiphorus evaporates off your heart and leaves it harder than it was before. For if it all evaporates off your heart it had been better you had never heard Onesiphorus's noble name. We have all seen to-night Onesiphorus in Ephesus and in Rome, and we shall all see him at least once again; only, not in this world. We shall all see him again, but not till "that day," as Paul has it in the text. We have had too short time to give to him and to ourselves to-night, but there will be no such hurry on "that day." For that will be a long day. An immense amount of divine business will have to be taken up and gone through on that day. Do you think that the accounts of the whole world could be got through in a day such as we have hitherto counted days? Almighty God Himself will not be able to do it in a day of twelve hours. No, nor in twenty-four hours. And you may depend upon it He will not once rise off His great white throne till He is justified in all His judgments. There will be plenty of time that day. There will be all eternity to draw upon to make up that day. The sun will stand still as soon as he is well up, and he will not set till the last deed of mercy done on the earth has been sought out, and its reward made to run over. In spite of itself your left hand will be made to know on that day all that your right hand has hidden from it in this world: in Ephesus, and in Rome, and in Edinburgh. I was led a few moments ago to speak by way of illustration of some of our own Onesiphorus-elders. And one of them, who often refreshed his ministers, used to sit up there in the front gallery. I see him still as I now speak. It was dear Donald Beith. He will get a surprise on that day. He also will be found out that day. Nay, I have found him out myself before that day. And since he is not here to deny it, I will tell you what you will hear about him from better lips than mine on that day. This will be told in your hearing, and you will say that you once heard it before in your accepted time, in your day of salvation. More than one dark night my great friend sent his servant out to Fountainbridge and up a dark stair, where a godly old soul lived without food or clothes or coals. The servant had strict injunctions to lay the heavy parcels up against the door, and then to knock and knock till he heard the deaf old cripple crawling toward the door, when he was to escape down the stair and out into the dark night like a thief from a detective. Donald Beith was a wily old Edinburgh lawyer, but I found him out sometimes, and you will see him with your own eyes found out again, to his consternation, on that day. What a day of surprises that day will be! What a day of leaping of all kinds of secrets to everlasting light will that day be! No wonder Paul so often calls it "that day," and the "day of Christ," and many such-like great names. What a surprise, surprise after surprise, will Paul and Onesiphorus get on that day, and all stealthy and backstair men like Donald Beith. I think I see Paul, and Onesiphorus, and Donald Beith, and his Fountainbridge friend, all on one another's necks on that day, with their Saviour smiling over them as He sees of the travail of His soul in them, and proclaims that He is satisfied. O my God, may I be among them and one of them on that day; both I and all those whom Thou hast given me! The Lord grant unto me also that both I and they may find mercy of the Lord in that day!

CVI

ALEXANDER THE COPPERSMITH

THERE are some most interesting and most important questions of New Testament scholarship, and New Testament sanctification, connected with Alexander the coppersmith of Ephesus. And the first of those questions is this: Have we got in our present text the very and identical words that Paul penned in his parchment to Timothy? Have we got the literal and exact expressions, and discriminations of expressions, that Paul so studiously employed? Have we got the very moods and tenses, both in grammar and in morals, that were in Paul's mind and heart at the moment when he wrote these two so difficult verses about Alexander? That is a very interesting, important, and indeed indispensable, question. Only, the settlement of that question must be left in their hands who alone are able to grapple with such questions. But, meantime, a question and a lesson of the very foremost importance faces us and forces itself on the most unlearned and ignorant of us. And that question and that lesson is this. Suppose that Paul both thought and felt and wrote about Alexander as our version literally reads, what are we to do? Are we free to follow Paul, and to do what he here does? Are we free to execrate and denounce bad men, and hand them over to be rewarded according to their works? Are we free, and is it our duty, to imprecate God's judgments on those who do us much evil, and who withstand the work of God which has been committed to our hands? A whole controversy of New Testament scholarship, and another whole controversy of New Testament morals and religion, have arisen around this text concerning Alexander the coppersmith. But, taking the text just as it has been put into our hands to-night, what are we able to make of it? What shall we succeed in taking out of it to-night for our own guidance to-morrow, and for every day we live on the earth?

The first time we come on Alexander he is a Jew of Ephesus, and a clever speaker to an excitable crowd. By the next time we meet with Alexander he has thought it to be for his interest to be baptized and to be seen openly on Paul's side. But Paul's side did not turn out to be so serviceable to the coppersmith as he had expected, and thus it is that he is next discovered to us as having made complete shipwreck of faith and a good conscience. And, then, as no man is so implacable at you as a complete renegade from you, so there was no man, among Paul's many enemies, who so hated Paul, and so hunted him down, as just this Alexander the coppersmith.

To go back to his beginning. Alexander had this temptation, that he was fitted by nature to be much more than a mere coppersmith, he was so clever and so captivating with his tongue. Unless you are a man of a very single heart and a very sound conscience, it is a great temptation to you to be able in a time of public commotion to speak so as to sway the swaying multitude and to command their applause and their support. You rise on a wave of popularity at such a season, and you make use of your popularity for your own chief end in life. Many were the clever speeches the coppersmith made during his baptized days also; the Christians putting him forward to speak, just as the Jews were wont to put him forward when he was one of themselves. But, the wind working round and setting strongly in another direction, the coppersmith himself also instantly obeyed the law of the weather-cock he had fashioned with his own hands and had fastened on the roof of his workshop; for, as his copper creature did, so did he before the variable skies of those unsettled days. And thus it is, that when Paul is so soon to depart from all his false friends and all his implacable enemies alike, the Apostle writes this much-needed warning to his young and inexperienced successor, and says, "Alexander the coppersmith did me much evil, the Lord reward him according to his works, of whom be thou ware also, for he hath greatly withstood my words." Alexander did Paul and his apostolic work much evil, and that not out of ignorance and fanaticism, but out of sheer unmitigated malice. Sometimes malice is bought and sold in the open market, till everybody sees it and understands it. Sometimes a man is to be had for money, and he will write letters or make speeches for you as long as you pay him best. But genuine malice is a different article from that. There is no getting to the bottom of real and original and priceless malice. Its bottom is not here. Its bottom is in the bottomless pit. Unless Alexander sets himself, nay, unless God sets Alexander, to search in his own heart for the roots of his malice against Paul, no other man can come near understanding or believing the depth and the strength and the malignity of Alexander's ill-will. At the same time, Paul and the other apostles could not but see as clear as day, and every day, Alexander's ill-will and the malignity of it, so much was it thrust upon their painful experience continually. Alexander followed Paul about wherever he went, poisoning the minds and the hearts of all men to whom his tongue or his pen had access. One of our latest and best authorities thinks that Alexander even followed Paul to Rome, and did his best to poison Nero and his court still more against Paul. But, whether he made that malicious and superfluous journey or no, Alexander certainly did Paul and his good name and his divine work all the evil that his great gifts of speech and pen could do. It was no wonder that the constant presence of Alexander, and his implacable and sleepless malice, was almost too great a trial for Paul to bear. So studied, so systematic, and so persistent, were Alexander's evil words and evil deeds.

Now, surely there can be no question as to Paul's duty to Timothy in that case. Paul would have been sinning both against Timothy and against the Gospel had he not taken Timothy and warned him against the malignity of Alexander. True, Timothy had not yet suffered as Paul had suffered from the coppersmith. Alexander had not yet followed Timothy about poisoning the wells everywhere against him. But to prepare Timothy for what he might expect, and would be sure to meet with, Paul told Timothy, with all plainness and all pain, what his experience of Alexander and his malice had been. Now, what do you say? What do you do? Suppose such a man as Alexander the coppersmith has arisen in your community and is doing Alexander's very same work over again under your eyes every day, what do you do in that case? Do you content yourself with despising and detesting the mischief-making man in your heart? Should you not rather take some of his more wicked letters and speeches and point out to the simple and inexperienced the great lessons that lie on the face of such things? is malice and misrepresentation less important to point out to a young man entering on life, than bad grammar and slovenly composition? There are studies in sheer malignity set us every day, as well as studies in style; and a teacher of morals should treat the one kind just as a teacher of letters always treats the other. Why should we be so careful to point out solecisms and careless composition to our young people, and pass by studied malice, misrepresentation, perversion, and suppression of the truth? And malice, too, that is not limited and localised in its scope as Alexander's malice was in his day, but which has all the resources of civilisation in our day to spread it abroad. And resources also such that Alexander and his seed can do their wicked work in our day out of sight, and nobody know who they are till the day of judgment.

But by far and away our most important lesson out of Paul and Alexander is yet to come. Only, that lesson throws us back again on the previous question. Did Paul feel in his heart, and did he entertain and express to Timothy, all the anger and resentment that is expressed in the text? Did Paul actually say, "The Lord reward Alexander the coppersmith according to his evil works?" Whether he did or no, that makes no difference to us. Even if he did, we must never do so. Were another Alexander to rise in our day, ay, and were he to do all the evil to us and to our work that Alexander did to Paul and to his work, we must never say what Paul is here made to say, Paul was put by Alexander to the last trial and sorest temptation of an apostolic and a sanctified heart. And it is the last two-edged sword that pierces to the dividing of soul and spirit in ourselves, not to forgive insult and injury done to ourselves, but to forgive Alexander all that when he does it to the Church of Christ. Only, Christ Himself will have to be formed in you, and will have to live in you, and will have to think and feel and write in you, before you will be able to love that bad man, and to do him good, all the time he is doing, not you, but Jesus Christ Himself, evil. But when Jesus Christ truly dwells in you, then no malediction, and no revenge; nothing but good wishes and good words, will ever escape your lips or your pen. It is for this that bad men like Alexander are let live among us. It is first for their own repentance and reformation, and then it is that they may be the daily sanctification of men like Paul. Of men, that is, who would not be tempted by any less spiritual trial than anger and resentment at the enemies, not of themselves, but of the Church of Christ. And such men among us are sent to school, not to David on his deathbed, nor to Paul in his prison, but to Jesus Christ on His Cross; Who, when He was reviled, reviled not again; when He suffered, He threatened not; leaving us an example, that we should follow His steps. I once asked a friend of mine who had been subjected to more reviling than any other man of his land and day, how he thought such and such another man who had suffered still more reviling could go on with his public work under such diabolical ill-usage. "Oh," said he, "So-and-so always lives *in facie eternitatis.*" And nothing but the nearness of eternity and the nothingness of time, and the still more nothingness of either the praise or the blame of such men as Alexander; nothing but the constant presence of such things as these could support Paul and could keep his heart quiet and sweet under the malice and maltreatment of such a wicked man as the coppersmith. The face of eternity and the nearness of eternity will do it. The face of eternity and the nearness of eternity, and the face and the nearness of the Lord of eternity, that will do it.

Whether, then, this is some corruption in the text, as the scholars call corruption; or some of the remaining corruption in Paul's heart, as he would have called it himself, I do not know. But this I know, that it is the essence, and the concentration, and the core, of all corruption in my heart, when I again detect myself hating this man and that man for the love of God. Long after I am able to forgive this man and that man for what he has said or done against myself, I am compelled to cry out, O wretched man that I am! as often as I despise, or detest, or desire to hear of hurt to Alexander or to any of his widespread seed. I must not even let myself say, Vengeance is mine, I will repay, saith the Lord. No, I must rather say, 'Let thy vengeance fall on me rather. For I have been a disappointment to Alexander's ambition. I have been a provocation to him and an offence to him in many ways. He has stumbled and has been broken on me. I am not without blame in his shipwreck of faith and a good conscience.' Instead of cursing Alexander to God. William Law would the more have prayed for him late every night, according to that great man's life-long practice—'if you pray for a man sufficiently often, and sufficiently fervently, and sufficiently in secret, you cannot but love that man, even were he Alexander the coppersmith.' That ye may be the children of your Father which is in heaven; for He maketh His sun to rise on the evil and on the good, and sendeth rain on the just and on the unjust.

But all questions of corruptions in the text, and in Paul's heart, apart, let us part with Paul when he is indisputably at his very highest and his very best. And he is at his very highest and his very best in the very next verse to his two unhappy verses about Alexander. "At my first answer no man stood with me, but all men forsook me: I pray God that it may not be laid to their charge." Paul is at his very best in that; for it is not Paul at all who says that, but it is He speaking in Paul who, when He also was forsaken, said, "Father, forgive them." "I am crucified with Christ," says Paul when he is at his best. "Nevertheless I live: yet not I, but Christ liveth in me: liveth in me and forgiveth Andrew the coppersmith in me: and the life I now live in the flesh I live by the faith of the Son of God, who loved me, and gave himself for me."

CVII

PAUL AS A STUDENT

PAUL was not born in the Holy Land like Jesus Christ, and like Peter and James and John. But Paul was proud of his birthplace, as he might very well be. For Tarsus was a great city in a day of great cities. Athens was a great city, Corinth was a great city, and Ephesus was a great city. But Tarsus in some respects was a greater city than any of them. Jerusalem stood alone, and Rome stood alone; but Tarsus engraved herself on her coins as the Metropolis of the East, and her proud claim was not disputed. An immense industry was carried on in the workshops of Tarsus, and an immense import and export trade was carried on in her docks. Nor were the eminent men of Tarsus mere manufacturers and merchants; they were men of education and refinement of manners also. But Saul's father was not one of the eminent men of Tarsus. He was one of the Hebrew dispersion, and he was making his living by the sweat of his brow in that industrious Greek city. And thus it was that Saul his son was far better acquainted with the workshops of Tarsus than with its schools or its colleges. Saul of Tarsus was not born with the silver spoon in his mouth any more than was Jesus of Nazareth, his future

Master. It was one of the remarkable laws of that remarkable people that every father was expected, was compelled indeed, to send his son first to a school and then to a workshop. Rich and poor sat on the same school-seat; and rich and poor alike went from school to learn an honest trade. Rabbi Joseph turned the mill. Rabbi Juda was a baker. Rabbi Ada and Rabbi Jose were fishermen; and, may we not add, Rabbi Peter and Rabbi John? And so on: woodcutters, leatherdressers, blacksmiths, carpenters. And thus it was that Paul, again and again, held up his hands in the pulpit, and at the prisoner's bar, and said, 'These hands, as you see, are full of callosities and scars, because they have all along ministered to mine own necessities, and to the necessities of those who have been dependent on me.'

Saul of Tarsus, like Timothy of Lystra, from a child knew the Holy Scriptures. And thus, no doubt, there was found among his old parchments after his death a Table of Rules and Regulations for his college conduct in Jerusalem, as good as William Law's Rules for his college conduct in Cambridge; better Rules they could not be. But there is one possibility in Saul's student days in Jerusalem that makes our hearts beat fast in our bosoms to think of it. "And the Child grew," we read in a contemporary biography, "and waxed strong in spirit, filled with wisdom; and the Grace of God was upon Him. Now his parents went up to Jerusalem every year at the feast of the passover. And when He was twelve years old, they went up to Jerusalem after the custom of the feast. And it came to pass after three days they found Him in the temple, sitting in the midst of the doctors, both hearing them and asking them questions." Now Gamaliel would be almost sure to be one of those astonished doctors; and what more likely than that he had taken his best scholar up to the temple to explain the passover to him that day? And did not the young carpenter from Nazareth and the young weaver from Tarsus exchange glances of sympathy and shake hands of love that day at the gate of the temple? I, for one, will believe that they did. Are there sports of providence like that in the Divine Mind? asked one of his like-minded students at Rabbi Duncan one day. Yes, and No, was the wise old doctor's answer.

Now the first instruction, as I think, intended to us out of Saul's student days is this—that the finest minds in every generation should study for the Christian ministry. Perhaps the very finest mind that had been born among men since the beginning of the world entered on the study of Old Testament theology when Saul of Tarsus sat down at Gamaliel's feet. And all Saul's fine and fast maturing mind will soon be needed now. For a work lay before that weaver boy of Tarsus second only to the work that lay before that carpenter boy of Nazareth, though second to that by an infinite interval. At the same time, there has been no other work predestinated to mere mortal man to do for God and man to be spoken of in the same day with this weaver boy's fore-ordained work. For even after the Lamb of God had said of His work,—it is finished! how unfinished and incomplete our New Testament would have been without the life and the work of the Apostle Paul. There was a deep harmony pre-established from all eternity between the work of Jesus Christ, and the mind and heart of Paul His apostle. No other subject in all the world but the Divine Person and the redeeming work of Jesus Christ could have afforded an outlet and an opportunity and an adequate scope for Paul's magnificent mind. While, on the other hand, the law of God and the cross of Christ would have remained to this day but half-revealed mysteries, had it not been for God's revelation of His Son in Paul; and had it not been for Paul's intellectual and spiritual capacity to receive that revelation, and to expound it and preach it. Every man who has read Paul's Epistles with the eyes of his understanding alight, and with his heart on fire, must have continually exclaimed, What a gift to a man is a fine mind, and that mind wholly given up to Jesus Christ! Let our finest minds, then, devote themselves to the study of Christology. Other subjects may, or may not, be exhausted; other callings may, or may not, be overcrowded; but there is plenty of room in the topmost calling of all, and there is an ever-opening and an ever-deepening interest there. No wonder, then, that it has been a University tradition in Scotland that our finest minds have all along entered the Divinity Hall. The other walks and callings of human life both need, and will reward, the best minds that can be spared to them, but let the service of our Lord and Saviour Jesus Christ first be filled. To annotate the Iliad, or the Symposium, or the Commedia; to build up and administer an empire; to command in a battle for freedom by sea or land; to create and bequeath a great and enriching business; to conduct an influential newspaper; to be the rector of a great school, and so on,—these are all great services done to our generation when we have the talent, and the character, and the opportunity, to do them. But to master Paul, as Paul mastered Moses and Christ; to annotate, and illustrate, and bring freshly home to ten thousand readers, the Galatians or the Romans, or the Colossians; to have eyes to see what Israel ought to do, and to have the patience, and the courage, to lead a church to do it; to feed, and to feed better and better for a lifetime, the mind and the heart of a congregation of God's people, and then to depart to be with Christ,—let the finest minds and the deepest and richest hearts in every new generation fall down while they are yet young and say, Lord Jesus, what wilt Thou have me to do with my life, and with whatsoever talents Thou hast intrusted to me?

And, then, the best of all callings being chosen, the better his mind and the better his heart are, the more profit, to employ Paul's own word about himself, will be made by the true student. For one thing, the better his mind, the more industrious, as a rule, the student of divinity will be. And the absolutely utmost industry in this supreme department of study is simply imperative and indispensable. An unindustrious divinity student should be drummed out of the Hall as soon as he is discovered intruding himself into it. With what hunger for his books, and with what heavenward vows and oaths of work, young Saul would set out from Tarsus to Jerusalem! Our own best students come up to our divinity seats with thrilling and thanksgiving hearts, and it is only they who have such hearts who can at all enter into Saul's mind and heart and imagination as he descended Olivet and entered Jerusalem and saw his name set down at last on Gamaliel's roll of the sons of the prophets. Gamaliel would have no trouble with Saul, unless it was to supply him with books, and to answer his questions. 'In all my experience I never had a scholar like Saul of Tarsus,' Gamaliel would often afterwards say. And Saul's class-fellows would tell all their days what a help and what a protection it was to be beside Saul. "We entered the regent's class that year," writes James Melville in his delightful Diary, "and he took up Aristotle's *Logic* with us. He had a little boy that served him in his chambers, called David Elistone, who, among thirty-six scholars, so many were we in the class, was by far the best. This boy he caused to wait on me and confer with me, and well it was for me, for his genius and his judgment passed mine as far as the eagle the owlet. In the multiplication of propositions, in the conversion of syllogisms, in the *pons asinorum,* etc., he was as well read as I was in counting my fingers. This, I mark as a special cause of thankfulness." And young Saul of Tarsus would be just another David Elistone in Gamaliel's school. And you Edinburgh students of divinity must be as industrious and as successful as ever Saul was in Jerusalem, or little Elistone in St. Andrews. And you have far more reason. For you have far better teachers, and a far better subject, and a far better prospect, than ever Saul had. You are not eternally fore-ordained, indeed, to write the

Epistle to the Romans, or the Epistle to the Ephesians. But you are chosen, and called, and matriculated, to do the next best thing to that. You are called to master those masterpieces of Paul, so as to live experimentally upon them all your student life, and then you are to teach and preach them to your people better and better all your pulpit and pastoral life. You are to work with your hands, if need be; you are to sell your bed, if need be, as Coleridge commands you, in order to buy Calvin on the Romans, and Luther on the Galatians, and Goodwin on the Ephesians, and Davenant on the Colossians, and Hooker on Justification, and "that last word on the subject," Marshall's *Gospel Mystery of Sanctification;* and you are to husband-up your priceless and irrecoverable hours to such studies, as you shall give account at the day of a divinity student's judgment. You are to feed your people, when you have got them committed of Christ to your charge, with the finest of the wheat, and with honey out of the rock. And that, better and better all your life, till your proud people shall make their boast in God about you, as the proud people of Anwoth made their boast about that great genius, and great scholar, and great theologian, and great preacher, and great pastor, Master Samuel Rutherford.

"Give attendance to reading," was Paul's old-age reminiscence of his student days, in the form of a counsel to young Timothy. "Paul has not lost his delight in books, even when he is near his death," says Calvin. And I myself owe so much to good books that I cannot stop myself on this subject as long as I see a single student sitting before me. I have a thousand times had Thomas Boston's experience of good books. "I plied my books. After earnestly plying my books, I felt my heart begin to grow better. I always find that my health and my heart are the better according as I ply my books." But you will correct me that Paul could not ply the great books that Thomas Boston plied to his own salvation, and to the salvation of his people in Simprin and Ettrick. Well, then, all the more, ply your pure Bible as Paul and Timothy did, and your profiting, like Paul's profiting and Timothy's, will soon appear unto all. Plying your English Bible even, your profiting will soon appear in your English style, both spoken and written. It will appear in the scriptural stateliness and the holy order of your pulpit prayers also. Your profiting will appear also in the strength, and the depth, and the spirituality, and the experimentalness, and the perennial freshness of your teaching and your preaching. "Paul knew his Old Testament so well," says Dean Farrar in his splendid *Life of St. Paul,* "that his sentences are constantly moulded by its rhythm, and his thoughts are incessantly coloured by its expressions."

But, all the time—and it startles and staggers us to hear it—Saul was living in ignorance and in unbelief. They are his own remorseful words, written by his own pen long afterwards—ignorance and unbelief. The finest of minds, the best of educations, sleepless industry, blameless life, and all: with all that, the aged apostle shudders to look back on his student-days of ignorance and unbelief. What in the world does he mean? Strange to say, and it is something for us all to think well about, he declares to us on every autobiographic page of his, that all the time he sat at Gamaliel's feet, and for many disastrous years after that, he was in the most absolute and woe-working ignorance of the law of God. But that only increases our utter amazement. For, was it not the law of God that Gamaliel had opened his school to teach? What in the world, I ask again, can Paul mean? Have you any idea what the apostle means when he says, with such life-long shame, and such life-long remorse, that all his Jerusalem and Gamaliel days he was blind and dead in his ignorance of the law of God? It may, perhaps, help us to an understanding of what he means, if we try to mount up and stand beside him on the far-shining heights of his exalted apostleship, and then look back from thence on his student and Pharisee days in Jerusalem. For it was just in the law of God that Paul afterwards became such a master. It was just the complete abolition of his ignorance of the law of God that set him so high above even the pillar-apostles in their remaining ignorance of it. It was just the law of God that he so reasoned out, and debated with them, as well as taught and preached it with such matchless success in every synagogue from Damascus to Rome. It was his incomparable handling of the law of God that first discovered to himself, and to the enraptured Church of Christ, the apostle's unique theological and philosophical genius, and the whole originality, and depth, and sweep, and grasp, of his matchless mind. An absolutely new world of things was opened up to the Apostolic Church when Paul came back from Arabia with the full revelation of the law and the gospel in his mind, and in his heart, and in his imagination. It was of Paul, and of the law of God in Paul's preaching, that our Lord spake when He said, "I have yet many things to say unto you, but ye cannot bear them now. Howbeit when He, the Spirit of truth, is come, He will guide you into all truth,"—which He did when He led Paul into Arabia. And then, after those three reading, meditating, praying, law-discovering, self-discovering, Christ-discovering years, Paul came back to Damascus, carrying in his mind and in his heart the copestone of New Testament doctrine, with shoutings of grace! grace! unto it. It was Paul's imperial mind, winged as it was with his wonderful imagination, that first swept, full of eyes, over the whole Old Testament history, and saw, down to the bottom and up to the top, the whole hidden mystery of the Old Testament economies, from the creation of the first Adam on to the sitting down of the second Adam at the right hand of God. From the creation of Adam to the call of Abraham; and from the call of Abraham to the giving of the law four hundred and thirty years after; and from the giving of the law till the law was magnified in the life and death of Paul's Master. "I first of all mortal men have thought the Creator's thoughts after Him," exclaimed the great astronomical discoverer as he fell on his knees in his observatory. And the great discoverer of the whole mystery of God, in the law and in the gospel, must often have fallen down and uttered the very same exclamation. And his great revelations, and discoveries, and attainments, and experiences, are preserved to us in such profound, axiomatic, and far-enlightening New Testament propositions and illustrations and autobiographic ejaculations as these,—"The law entered that the offence might abound. By the law is the knowledge of sin. The law worketh wrath. Without the law sin was dead. I was alive without the law once. I am sold under sin. The law is our schoolmaster to lead us to Christ. By the works of the law shall no flesh be justified. But now we are no more under the law, but under grace. I am dead to the law, that being dead wherein I was held," and so on, through the whole of the Galatians and the Romans, and indeed throughout every Epistle of his. Yes, gentlemen, you may to-night be in as absolute ignorance of all that as the apostle once was; but, I tell you, there still lies scope and opportunity in all that for your most scholarly, most logical, and most philosophical, minds, and for your most eloquent, impressive, and prevailing preaching. Till you ascend for yourselves, and then lead your people up to this golden climax of the apostle concerning the law, and concerning Christ, and concerning himself in Christ—this golden climax—"For I through the law am dead to the law, that I might live unto God. I am crucified with Christ: nevertheless I live; yet not I, but Christ liveth in me: and the life I now live in the flesh I live by the faith of the Son of God, who loved me, and gave Himself for me."

CVIII

PAUL APPREHENDED OF CHRIST JESUS

THE first time we see Saul of Tarsus he is silently consenting to Stephen's death. Why the fierce young Pharisee did not take a far more active part in the martyrdom of Stephen we do not know; we can only guess. That a young zealot of Saul's temperament should be content to sit still that day, and merely keep the clothes of the witnesses who stoned Stephen, makes us wonder what it meant. But, beginning with his silent consent to the death of Stephen, Saul soon went on to plan and to perpetrate the most dreadful deeds on his own account. "As for Saul, he made havoc of the Church, entering into every house, and haling men and women, committed them to prison. Which thing I also did in Jerusalem; and many of the saints did I shut up in prison, and punished them oft in every synagogue, and compelled them to blaspheme. Beyond measure I persecuted the Church of God, and wasted it; I was a blasphemer, and a persecutor, and injurious." And thus it was that Saul actually went to the high priest in Jerusalem, and desired of him letters to Damascus, to the synagogues, that if he found any of this way, whether they were men or women, he might bring them bound to Jerusalem. And, accordingly, on that errand, out at the Damascus-gate of Jerusalem, he rode with his band of temple police behind him: out past Gethsemane: out past Calvary, where he shook the spear in the face of the Crucified, and cried, Aha, aha! Thou deceiver! and posted on breathing out threatenings and slaughter against the disciples of the Lord.

Gird Thy sword upon Thy thigh, O Most Mighty, with Thy glory and Thy majesty. Thine arrows are sharp in the hearts of the King's enemies, whereby the people fall under Thee!

And thus it was that, as Saul journeyed, and came near Damascus, suddenly there shone down upon him a great light from heaven. And he fell to the earth, and heard a voice saying to him, Saul, Saul, why persecutest thou Me? His eyes were as a flame of fire, and His voice as the sound of many waters. And out of His mouth went a sharp two-edged sword, and His countenance was as the sun shineth in his strength. Arise, go into the city, and it shall be told thee what thou shalt do. And Saul arose from the earth, and they led him by the hand, and brought him into Damascus. And he was three days without sight, and did neither eat nor drink. And Ananias entered the house where Saul lay, and putting his hands on him, he said, Brother Saul, the Lord, even Jesus, that appeared unto thee on the way as thou camest, hath sent me, that thou might receive thy sight, and be filled with the Holy Ghost. And immediately there fell from his eyes, as if it had been scales, and he received sight forthwith, and arose, and was baptized. Saul of Tarsus, I baptize thee in the name of the Father, and of the Son, and of the Holy Ghost. And there was great joy in the presence of the angels of God over the conversion and the baptism of Saul of Tarsus.

Now it is the suddenness of Saul's conversion that is the first thing arresting about it to us. It was literally, and in his own words, an "apprehension." "Suddenly," in his own word about it, as often as he tells us again and again the ever-fresh story of his conversion. The whole subject of conversion is a great study to those who are personally interested in the supremest of all human experiences. There is such a Divine Hand in every conversion; there is such a Sovereignty in it; taking place within a man, there is, at the same time, such a mysteriousness about it; and, withal, such a transcendent importance, that there is nothing else that ever takes place on the face of the earth for one moment to be compared with a conversion. And, then, there are so many kinds of conversion. So many ways of it, and such different occasions and circumstances of it. Some conversions are as sudden, and as unexpected, and as complete, as Saul's conversion was; and some are slowness itself. Some are such that the very moment, and the very spot, can ever afterwards be pointed out; while some other men are all their days subject to doubt, just because the change came so easy to them as to be without observation. They were born of the Spirit before they could distinguish good from evil, or could discern between their right hand and their left hand. A good sermon will be the occasion of one conversion, a good book of another, and a wise word spoken in due season of another. Hearing a hymn sung, as was the case one Sabbath evening in this very house; hearing a verse read, as was the case with St. Augustine. Just looking for a little at a dry tree will do it sometimes, as was the case with Brother Laurence. Hopeful saw Faithful burned to ashes; Christiana remembered all her surly carriages to her husband; and Mercy came just in time to see Christiana packing up. Their conversions came to Dr. Donne and to Dr. Chalmers long after they were ministers; and, after their almost too late conversion, those two great men became the greatest preachers of their day. A man of business will be on his way to his office on a Monday morning, and he could let you see to this day the very shop window, passing which, in Princes Street, he was apprehended. I was engaged to be married and she died, said a young communicant to me on one occasion. It was the unkindness of my mistress, said a servant-girl. Just as I am writing these lines this letter reaches me: "When the Lord opened my eyes the sight I saw broke me down completely. I tried to work myself right, till it turned out to be the hardest task I ever tried. But I would not give in till He took me by the coat-neck and held me over hell. Oh, sir, it was a terrible time! My sense of sin drove me half mad. But I kept pouring out my heart in prayer!" And then my correspondent goes on to tell me the name of the book that was made such a blessing to him. And then he asks that his mistakes in spelling be pardoned, and signs himself an office-bearer in the Church of one of my friends. But you will go over for yourselves all the cases of conversion you have ever heard about, or read about, and you will see for yourselves how full of all kinds of individuality, and variety, and intensity of interest, the work of conversion is, till like Mercy in *The Pilgrim's Progress,* you will fall in love with your own.

Some men put off their conversion because they have no sense of sin. But look at Saul. What sense of sin had he? Not one atom. He was an old and a heaven-ripe apostle before his full sense of sin came home to him. He was not groaning out the seventh of the Romans when he was galloping at the top of his speed on his way to Damascus. A sensibility to sin so exquisite and so spiritual as that of the apostle never yet came to any man but after long long years of the holiest of lives. To ninety-nine out of a hundred, even of truly converted men, it never comes at all. How could it? At the same time, who knows? your conversion, both in its present insensibility, and in its subsequent spirituality, may be to be of the same kind as Paul's was, if you will only on the spot submit to it. Accept your offered conversion, and go home and act at once and ever after upon it, and trust the Holy Ghost for your sense of sin. And if you belong to the same mental and moral and spiritual seed of Israel as Paul, your sense of sin will yet come to you with a vengeance. And, once it begins to come, it will never cease coming more and more, till you will almost be driven beside yourself with it. On the other hand, your conversion may not be to be of the heart-breaking kind. You may not be to be held over open hell by the coat-neck like my ill-spelling friend; your experience may be to be like that of Lydia. Like hers, your conversion may be to steal in upon your heart some night at a prayer-meeting,—be it of whatever kind it is to be, take it when and where it is offered to you. And if your conversion is of the right kind at all, and holds, you will in due time and in your due order, get your fit and proper share of that saving grace, of which you say you are so utterly empty to-night.

But not only had Saul no sense of sin to prepare him for his conversion: he had no preparation and no fitness for his conversion, of any kind whatsoever. He brought nothing in his hands. He came just as he was. He was without one plea. Poor, wretched, blind; sight, riches, healing of the mind. Read his thrice-told story, and see if there is any lesson plainer, or more pointed to you in it all, than just the unexpectedness, the unpreparedness, and the completeness on the spot, of Saul's conversion. With, on the other hand, his instantaneous and full faith, his childlike trust, his full assurance, and his prompt and unquestioning obedience. Yes, it is just the absolute sovereignty, startling suddenness, total unpreparedness, entire undeservingness, and glorious completeness, of Saul's conversion that, all taken together, make it such a study, and, in some respects, such a model conversion, to you and to me.

There is another lesson told us three times, as if to make sure that we shall not miss nor mistake it. Saul got his conversion out of that overthrow on the way to Damascus, while all his companions only got some bodily bruises from their fall, and the complete upsetting of their errand out of it. The temple officers had each his own story to tell when they returned without any prisoners to Jerusalem: only, none of them needed to be led by the hand into Damascus, and none of them were baptized by Ananias, but Saul only. All of which is written for our learning. For the very same thing will take place here to-night. One will be Saul over again, and those who are sitting beside him will be Saul's companions over again. One will go straight home after this service, and will never all his days have Saul's sudden and unexpected conversion out of his mind, such a divine pattern is it to be of his own conversion. While his companions will be able to tell when they go home who preached, and on what, the fullness of the Church, the excellence of the music, and the state of the weather on the way home—and that will be all. "And they that were with me saw indeed the light, and were afraid; but they heard not the voice of Him that spake with me. And I said, What shall I do, Lord? And He said unto me, Arise, and go into the city, and there it shall be told thee of all things which are appointed for thee to do."

'It is a trap set for us,' said Ananias. 'Lord,' he said, 'I have heard by many of this man, how much evil he hath done to Thy saints in Jerusalem. And how he has come here with authority to bind all that call upon Thy name. It is a trap set for our destruction,' said Ananias. 'Go to the street called Straight,' said the Lord, 'and if thou dost not find him in prayer, then it is a trap as thou fearest it is.' The mark of Saul's conversion that silenced Ananias was this, that Saul had been three days and three nights in fasting and in prayer without ceasing. Behold he prayeth, said Christ, proud of the completeness and the success of His conversion of Saul. Has Jesus Christ, with His eyes like a flame of fire, set that secret mark on your conversion and on mine? Does He point you out to His ministering angels and sympathising saints in heaven to-night, as He pointed out Saul to Ananias? How does your conversion stand the test of secret prayer? Behold, he prayeth! said Christ. And unceasing prayer, both for himself and for all his converts, remained to be Paul's mark, and token, and seal, down to the end of his days.

The best expositor by far that ever took Paul's epistles up into a pulpit, has said that the apostle never fell into a single inconsistency after his conversion. Now, with all submission, I cannot receive that even about Paul, any more than I can receive it about any other man that ever was converted on the face of this earth. That he never fell into a single inconsistency could only be said about One Man; and we never speak about His conversion. But the very fact that the profoundest preacher that I possess on Paul, and the profoundest preacher of conversion-consistency, has said such a thing as that, shows us what a splendid, what a complete, and what a consistent, conversion Paul's conversion must have been. How thoroughgoing it must have been at the time; and how holy in all manner of walk and conversation must Paul ever after have lived. Speaking here for myself, and not venturing to speak for any of you, when I read a thing like that, and a thing said by such a master in Israel as he was who said that, and then look at my own life in the searching light of that, I feel as if I can never up till now have been converted myself at all. Unless this also is a sure mark of a true conversion, which I have seen set down with incomparable power by this very same master in Israel, this,—that it is a sure and certain mark of a true conversion that no man ever understands what inconsistency really is till he is truly converted. To be all but entirely void of offence, as Paul said of himself; to be all but completely consistent in everything, was one of the sure and certain marks of Paul's conversion. But, then, to feel myself to be full to the lips of offence: to see and to feel myself to be the most inconsistent man in all the world, is, by this same high authority, offered to me as a mark of my conversion, as good to me as Paul's magnificent marks were to him. "The disproportion of man" is one of Pascal's most prostrating passages; and the offensiveness, the inconsistency, and the disproportion, of my heart and my life, are the most prostrating of all my experiences. Indeed, nothing ever prostrates me, to be called prostration, but these experiences. At the same time, the whole and entire truth at its deepest bottom is this. That both things are true of Paul and of his conversion. Paul was at one and the same moment, and in one and the same matter, both the most consistent, and the most inconsistent, of all Christ's converts. He was both the most blameless, and the most blameable; the best proportioned, and the most disproportioned, of all Christian men. Such was the holiness of his life, and such was the spirituality of his mind and heart. And both experiences, taken together, combine to constitute the most complete and all-round mark of a perfect conversion. Now, all that, and far more than all that, combine to make Paul's conversion the most momentous, and the most wonderful, conversion in all the world. And yet, no. There is one other conversion long since Paul's, that will, to you and to me to all eternity, quite eclipse Paul's conversion, and will for ever completely cast, even it, quite into the shade.

CIX

PAUL IN ARABIA

No sooner was Paul baptized by Ananias, than, instead of returning to Jerusalem, he immediately set out for Arabia. He had come down to Damascus with horses and servants like a prince, but he set out alone for Arabia like Jacob with his staff. For, all that he took with him was his parchments, and some purchases he had made in the street called Straight. A few of those simple instruments that tentmakers use when they have to minister to their own necessities, was all that Paul encumbered himself with as he started from Ananias's door on his long and solitary journey to Arabia.

What it was that took Paul so immediately and so far away as Arabia, we can only guess. If it was simply a complete seclusion that he was in search of, he might surely have secured that seclusion much nearer home. But, somehow, Sinai seems to have drawn Paul to her awful solitudes with an irresistible attraction and strength. It may have been an old desire of his formed at Gamaliel's feet, some day to see the Mount of God with his own eyes. He may have said to himself that he must hide himself for once in that cleft-rock before he sat down to his life-work in Moses' seat. I must see Rome, he said towards the end of his life. I must see Sinai, he also said at the beginning of his life. And thus it was that as soon as he was baptized in Ananias's house in Damascus, Paul immediately set out for Arabia.

Look at that weak bodily presence. But, at the same time, judge him not by his outward appearance. For he carries Augustine, and Luther, and Calvin, and Knox, in his fruitful loins. In that lonely stranger you are now looking at, and in his seed, shall all the families of the earth be blessed. Look at the eyes of his understanding as they begin to be enlightened. Look at him with his heart all on fire. See him as he unrolls his parchments at every roadside well, and drinks of the brook by the way. Thy word is more to me than my necessary food, and thy love is better than wine!

What a three years were those three years that Paul spent in Arabia! Never did any other lord receive his own again with such usury as when Paul went into Arabia with Moses and the Prophets and the Psalms in his knapsack, and returned to Damascus with the Romans and the Ephesians and the Colossians in his mouth and in his heart. What an incomparable book waits to be written about those three immortal years in Arabia! After those thirty preparation-years at Nazareth, there is no other opportunity left for any sanctified pen, like those three revelation-years in Arabia. Only, it will demand all that is within the most Paul-like writer, to fit him out for his splendid enterprise. It will demand, and it will repay, all his learning, and all his intellect, and all his imagination, and all his sinfulness, and all his salvation. Just to give us a single Sabbath out of Paul's hundred and fifty Sabbaths at Sinai—what a revelation to us that would be! It would be something like this, only a thousand times better. When first you fell in love: when first your captivated heart made you like the chariots of Ammi-nadib; the whole world was full of one name to you. There was no other name to you in all the world. Every bird sang that name. Every rock echoed with that name. You wrote that name everywhere. You read that name everywhere. You loved everybody and everything for the sake of that name. Now, it was something like that between Paul and Jesus Christ. Only, it was far better than that between Paul and Jesus Christ at the time, and it was far more lasting with them than it has been with you. Luther, who was almost as great a lover of Jesus Christ as Paul was, has this over and over again about Paul and Jesus Christ. "Jesus Christ is never out of Paul's mouth. Indeed, there is nobody and nothing now and always in Paul's mouth but Jesus Christ and His Cross." Now that is literally true. For, as often as Paul opens his Moses in Arabia, and finds the place he is seeking for, he cannot see the place when he has found it for Jesus Christ. Jesus Christ comes between Paul and everything. To Paul to read, and to meditate, and to pray, is Jesus Christ. So much so, that as soon as he finds the place at the very first verse of Genesis, he immediately goes off at the word, and exclaims, till the Arabs all around listen to his rapture,—the mystery! he exclaims, which from the beginning of the world hath been hid in God, who created all things by Jesus Christ. And at this,—Let there be light! For God, he exclaims again, who commanded the light to shine out of darkness, hath shined in our hearts in the face of Jesus Christ. And, does Adam burst out into his bridegroom doxology,—This is now bone of my bone, and flesh of my flesh! —than Paul instantly adds, Amen! But I speak concerning Christ and His Church. And before he leaves the first Adam he gets such a revelation of the second Adam made in him that the Corinthians had many a glorious Sabbath morning on the two Adams, all the way from Arabia, long afterwards. And, again, no sooner does God speak in covenant to Abraham about his seed, than Paul immediately annotates that He saith not to seeds as of many, but as of One, which is Christ. But, on all that Moses ever wrote, there was nothing that Paul spent so much time and strength, as just on this concerning the father of the faithful,— that Abraham believed in the Lord, and it was counted to him for righteousness. Now, said Paul, reasoning to himself over that revelation, and then reasoning to us,—Now it was not written for Abraham's sake only, that it was imputed to him, but for our sakes also, to whom it shall be imputed, if we believe on Him who raised up Jesus our Lord from the dead; who was delivered for our offences, and was raised again for our justification. And so on, till to have spent a single Sabbath-day with Paul at Sinai would have been almost as good as to have walked that evening hour to Emmaus. So did Paul discover the Son of God in Arabia: so did Paul have the Son of God revealed to him in Adam, and in Abraham, and in Moses, and in David, and in Isaiah, but, best of all, in Paul himself.

And, then, Paul's first fast-day in Arabia. Paul was never out of the Psalms on those days that he observed so solemnly at Sinai. Till his David was like John Bunyan's Luther, so old that it was ready to fall piece from piece if he did but turn it over. But he always turned it over at such sacramental seasons till he came again to that great self-examination Psalm, where he found it written concerning himself: These things hast thou done, and I kept silence. Thou thoughtest that I was altogether such an one as thyself. But I will reprove thee, and set them in order before thee. And it was so. For, there they stood, set in order before him, and passed in order before him and before God. The souls of all the men and women and children he had haled to prison, and had compelled to blaspheme, and had slain with the sword. And, then, as he hid himself in the cleft-rock—how the Name of the Lord would come up into his mind: and how, like Moses also, he would make haste and bow his head to the earth and say: Take me for one of Thy people. And, till God would again reveal His Son in Paul in a way, and to a degree, that it is not possible for Paul to tell to such impenitent and unprostrated readers of his as we are. And, then, far over and above those terrible sins of his youth, there was the absolutely unparalleled and absolutely indescribable agony that came upon Paul out of the remaining covetousness and consequent malice of his heart, and more and more so as his heart was more and more brought down under the ever-increasing and all-piercing spirituality of God's holy law. An agony that sometimes threatened to drive Paul beside himself altogether. And till, on the rocks of Sinai the shepherds would sometimes come on somewhat the same sweat of blood that the gardeners came on in the Garden of Gethsemane. For it was in Arabia, and it was under the Mount of God, that Paul's apostolic ink-horn was first filled with that ink of God with which he long afterwards wrote that so little understood writing of his, which we call the Seventh of the Romans. A little understood writing; and no wonder!

The Apostle came back from Arabia to Damascus, after three years' absence, absolutely ladened down with all manner of doctrines, and directions, and examples, for us and for our salvation, if we would only attend to them and receive them. Directions and examples of which this is one of the first. That solitude, the most complete and not short solitude, was the one thing that Paul determined to secure for himself immediately after his conversion and his baptism. And we have a still better

Example of all that than even Paul. For, over and above His thirty uninvaded years, no sooner was that "Glorious Eremite" baptized, than He went away and took forty days to Himself before He began His public life. "One day"—sings concerning Him one of His servants who loved seclusion also, and put it to some purpose—

"One day forth walked alone, the Spirit leading
And His deep thoughts, the better to converse
With solitude; till far from track of man,
Thought following thought, and step on step led on,
He entered now the bordering desert-wild,
And, with dark shades and rocks environ'd round,
His holy meditations thus pursued."

And thus it is that Holy Scripture is everywhere so full of apartness and aloneness and solitude: of lodges in the wilderness, and of shut doors in the city: of early mornings, and late nights, and lonely night-watches: of Sabbath-days and holidays, and all such asylums of spiritual retreat.

Down to Gehenna, and up to the throne,
He travels the fastest who travels alone.

But the Apostle's chief reason for telling us about Arabia at all is this, to prove to us, and to impress upon us, that it was not cities and colleges and books that made him what by that time he was made. It was God Himself who made Paul the Apostle he was made. I conferred not with flesh and blood, he protests. He had books, indeed, as we have seen: he always had. He had the best of books: he always had. But even Moses and David and Isaiah themselves are but flesh and blood compared with God. Even grace itself is but flesh and blood compared with Christ, says Thomas Shepard. And Paul is careful and exact, above everything, to make it clear to us, that not only was it God Himself who immediately and conclusively revealed His Son in Paul; but, also, that it was His Son that God so revealed. It was not Jesus Christ, so much, distinguishes Paul, that God revealed in him. Jesus Christ had revealed Himself to Paul already at the gate of Damascus, but God's revelation of His Son in Arabia was a revelation of far more than of Jesus Christ whom Paul was persecuting. For, this in Arabia is God's Eternal and Co-Equal Son. And that, not merely as made flesh, and made sin: not merely as crucified, and risen, and exalted, and glorified; but as He had been before all that, and during all that, and after all that. It was God's Essential and Eternal Son: it was God's very deepest, completest, and most crowning revelation possible of His only-begotten Son; that God, in such grace and truth, made in Paul in Arabia.

In me, says Paul. In my deepest mind and in my deepest heart: in my very innermost soul and strength. And thus it was that Paul underwent two grand revelations, over and above a multitude of lesser revelations which arose out of those two epoch-making revelations, and which both perfected and applied them. The one, that grand and epoch-making revelation made on the way to Damascus, and made immediately by Jesus Christ, whom Paul was at that moment persecuting. A revelation divinely suited to all the circumstances. A revelation outward, arresting, overpowering: taking possession of all the persecutor's bodily senses, and thus surrounding and seizing all the passes into his soul. The other, made within and upon Paul's pure and naked soul, and apart altogether from the employment of his senses upon his soul. A revelation impossible adequately to describe. A revelation made by God of His Son, most inward, most profound, most penetrating, most soul-possessing: most-enlarging to the soul, most uplifting, and most upholding: most assuring, most satisfying, most sanctifying: intellectual, spiritual, experimental, evangelical: all-renewing and all-transforming: full of truth, full of love, full of assurance, full of holiness, full of the peace of God, which passeth all understanding. Jesus of Nazareth appeared *to* Saul the persecutor, as He had already appeared to Mary Magdalene, and to the ten disciples, and to Thomas. But God the Father revealed His Son *in* Paul the Apostle, as He had never revealed Him before, and as He has never revealed Him since in mortal man. That is to say, with a fullness, and with a finalness, that has made all God's subsequent revelations of His Son, at their best, to be but superficial and partial, occasional and intermittent. Not that it need be so. Not that it ought to be so. For if we but gave ourselves up to God and to His Son, as Paul gave himself up, we also, no doubt, would soon reap our reward. But, as it is, Paul's apprehension of God's Son, Paul's comprehension of God's Son, and Paul's service of God's Son, have remained to this day, by far the first, by far the best, and by far the most complete, by far the most final, and by far the most fruitful, revelation of His Son, that Almighty God has ever made in any of the sons of men.

CX

PAUL'S VISIT TO JERUSALEM TO SEE PETER

PUT yourself back into Paul's place. Suppose yourself born in Tarsus, brought up at Gamaliel's feet in Jerusalem, and keeping the clothes of Stephen's executioners. Think of yourself as a blasphemer, and a persecutor, and injurious. And—then imagine yourself apprehended of Christ Jesus, driven of the Spirit into the wilderness of Arabia, and coming back with all your bones burning within you to preach Jesus Christ and Him crucified. But, all the time, you have never once seen your Master in the flesh, as His twelve disciples had seen Him. He had been for thirty years with His mother and His sisters and His brethren in Galilee. And then He had been for three years with the twelve and the seventy. But Paul had been born out of due time. And thus it was that Paul went up to Jerusalem to see Peter about all that. Paul had a great desire to see Peter about all that before he began his ministry. And you would have had that same great desire, and so would I.

At the same time, even with the prospect of seeing Peter, it must have taken no little courage on Paul's part to face Judea and Jerusalem again. To face the widows and the orphans of the men he had put to death in the days of his ignorance and unbelief. To Paul the very streets of Jerusalem were still wet with that innocent blood. Led in by Peter Paul sat at the same Lord's table, and ate the same bread, and drank the same wine, with both old and young communicants, who had not yet put off their garments of mourning because of Paul. Deliver me from blood-guiltiness, O God, Thou God of my salvation. Then will I teach transgressors Thy ways. Do good in Thy good pleasure unto Zion; build Thou the walls of Jerusalem. And thus it was that, to the end of his days, Paul was always making collections for those same poor saints that were in Jerusalem. Paul would have pensioned every one of them out of his own pocket, had he been able. But how could he do that off a needle and a pair of shears? And thus it was that he begged so incessantly for the fatherless families that he had made fatherless in Judea and in Jerusalem. Now, if any of you have ever made any woman a widow, or any child an orphan, or done anything of that remorseful kind, do not flee the country. You cannot do it, and you need not try. Remain where you are. Go back to the place. Go back often in imagination, if not in your bodily presence. Do the very utmost that in you lies, to repair the irreparable wrong that you did long ago. And, when you cannot redeem that dreadful damage, commit it to Him who can redeem both it and you. And say to Him continually:—Count me a partner with Thee. And put that also down to my account.

"To see Peter," our Authorised Version is made to say. "To visit Peter," the Revised Version is made to say. And, still, to help out all that acknowledged lameness, the revised margin is made to say, "to become acquainted with Peter." But Paul would not have gone so far, at that time at any rate, to see Peter or any one else. Any one else, but Peter's Master. But to see Him even once, as He was in the flesh, Paul would have gone from Damascus to Jerusalem on his hands and his knees. "I went up to Jerusalem to *history* Peter," is what Paul really says. Only, that is not good English. But far better bad English, than an utterly meaningless translation of such a text. "To interview Peter," is not good English either, but it conveys Paul's meaning exactly. The great Greek historians employ Paul's very identical word when they tell their readers the pains they took to get first-hand information before they began to write their books. "I went up to interrogate and to cross-question Peter all about our Lord," that would be rough English indeed, but it would be far better than so feebly to say, "to see Peter," which positively hides from his readers what was Paul's real errand to Jerusalem, and to Peter.

Had Landor been led to turn his fine dramatic genius and his ripe scholarship to Scriptural subjects, he would, to a certainty, have given us the conversations that took place for fifteen days between Peter and Paul. Landor's Epictetus and Seneca, his Diogenes and Plato, his Melanchthon and Calvin, his Galileo and Milton and a Dominican, and his Dante and Beatrice, are all among his masterpieces. But his Paul and Peter, and his Paul and James the brother of our Lord, and especially his Paul and the mother of our Lord, would have eclipsed clean out of sight his most classical compositions. For, on no possible subject, was Peter so ready always to speak, to all comers, as just about his Master. And never before nor since had Peter such a hungry hearer as just his present visitor and interrogator from Arabia and Damascus. Peter began by telling Paul all about that day when his brother Andrew so burst in upon him about the

Messiah. And then that day only second to it, on the Lake of Gennesaret. And then Matthew the publican's feast, and so on, till Peter soon saw what it was that Paul had come so far to hear. And then he went on with the good Samaritan, and the lost piece of silver, and the lost sheep, and the lost son. For fifteen days and fifteen nights this went on till the two prostrate men took their shoes off their feet when they entered the Garden of Gethsemane. And both at the cock-crowing, and at Calvary, Peter and Paul wept so sore that Mary herself, and Mary Magdalene, did not weep like it. Now, just trust me and tell me what you would have asked at Peter about his Master. Would you have asked anything? How far would you go to-night to have an interview with Peter? Honestly, have you any curiosity at all about Jesus Christ, either as He is in heaven now, or as He was on earth then? Really and truly, do you ever think about Him, and imagine Him, and what He is saying and doing? Or are you like John Bunyan, who never thought whether there was a Christ or no? If you would tell me two or three of the questions you would have put to Peter, I would tell you in return just who and what you are; just how you stand to-night to Jesus Christ, and how He stands to you: and what He thinks and says about you, and intends towards you.

And then if Mary, the mother of our Lord, was still in this world, it is certain to me that Paul both saw her in James's house, and kissed her hand, and called her Blessed. You may depend upon it that Mary did not remain very long away from James's house after his conversion. It was all very good to have a lodging with the disciple whom Jesus loved, till her own slow-hearted son believed. But I put it to you who are mothers in Israel, to put yourselves in Mary's place in those days, and to say if you would have been to be found anywhere, by that time, but in the house of your own believing son. And what more sure and certain than that God, here again, revealed His Son to Paul out of Mary's long hidden heart. 'I have the most perfect, and at first-hand, assurance of all these things from them that were eye-witnesses and ministers of the Word,' says Paul's physician and private secretary. Nowhere, at any rate, in the whole world, could that miraculous and mystery-laden woman have found such another heart as Paul's into which to pour out all that had been for so long sealed up in her hidden heart. 'Whether we were in the body, or out of the body, as she told me about Nazareth, and as I told her about Damascus and Arabia, I cannot tell: God knoweth.'

"From the Old Testament point of view," says Bengel in his

own striking and suggestive way, "the progress is made from the knowledge of Christ to the knowledge of Jesus. From the New Testament point of view, the progress is made from the knowledge of Jesus to the knowledge of Christ." And have we not ourselves already seen how Paul's progress was made? Paul's progress was made from the knowledge of Jesus of Nazareth risen from the dead, to the knowledge of the Son of God; and then from the knowledge of both back to the knowledge of the Holy Child Jesus, and the Holy Man Jesus, as He was known to His mother, to James His brother, and to Peter His so intimate disciple. Paul went "back to Jesus," as the saying sometimes is; but when he went back he took back with him all the knowledge of the Son of God that he has put into his Epistles, ay, and much more than the readers of his Epistles were able to receive. And God's way with Paul is His best way with us also. You will never read the four Gospels with true intellectual understanding, and with true spiritual appreciation, till you have first read and understood and appreciated Paul's Epistles. But after you have had God's Son revealed in you by means of Paul's Epistles, you will then be prepared for all that Matthew and Mark and Luke and John have to tell you about the Word made flesh in their day. Paul's hand holds the true key to all the mysteries that are hid in the Prophets and in the Psalms and in the Gospels. Take back Paul with you, and all the prophecies and all the types of the Old Testament, and all the wonderful works of God in the New Testament,—His Son's sinless conception, His miracles, His teaching and preaching, His agony in the garden, His death on the Cross, and His resurrection and ascension,—will all fall into their natural and necessary places. It is in the very same order in which the great things of God were revealed to Paul, and apprehended by Paul, that they will best be revealed to us, and best apprehended by us. First our conversion; and then the Pauline, Patristic, and Puritan doctrine of the Son of God; and then all that taken back by us to the earthly life of our Blessed Lord as it is told to us by the four Evangelists. Damascus, Arabia, Jerusalem,—this, in our day also, is the God-guided progress, in which the true successors of the Apostle Paul are still travelling, in their spiritual experience, and in their evangelical scholarship.

CXI

PAUL AS A PREACHER

When it pleased God to reveal the cross of Christ in Paul, from that day the cross of Christ was Paul's special, peculiar, and exclusive Gospel. The cross of Christ is "my gospel," Paul proudly and constantly claims, in the face of all comers. The cross of Christ, he declares, is the one and the only Gospel that he preaches, that he always preaches, and that he alone preaches. The cross of Christ was profitable to Paul for doctrine, for reproof, for correction, and for instruction in righteousness: and nothing else was of any real interest or any real profit to Paul. The cross of Christ was the alpha and the omega, the beginning, and the middle, and the end, of all Paul's preaching. Paul drew all his doctrines, and all his instructions, and all his reproofs, out of the cross of Christ. He drew his profound and poignant doctrines of the sinfulness of sin, and the consequent misery of man, out of the cross of Christ. He saw and he felt all that in himself, and in the whole world; but the cross of Christ gave a new profundity, and a new poignancy, to all that to him. He drew his incomparably magnificent doctrines of the grace of God and the love of Christ out of the cross of Christ: those doctrines of his in the preaching of which he bursts out into such rapturous doxologies. The whole of the life of faith also, in all its manifoldness, and in all its universalness, and his own full assurance of everlasting life,—all that, and much more than all that, Paul, by his splendid genius, and it all so splendidly sanctified and inspired, drew out of the cross of Christ. Take away the cross of Christ from Paul, and he is as weak as any other man. Paul has nothing else to preach if you take away from him the cross of Christ. His mouth is shut. His pulpit is in ruins. His arm is broken. He is of all men most miserable. But let God reveal the cross of Christ in Paul, and, straightway, he can both do, and endure, all things. Paul is henceforth debtor both to the Greeks and to the Barbarians; both to the wise, and to the unwise. Once reveal the cross of Christ in Paul, and you thereby lay a life-long necessity upon him. Yea, woe is unto him, ever after, if he preaches not the Gospel of the cross of Christ.

We preach not ourselves, Paul asserts with a good conscience in another sermon of his. And yet, at the same time, he introduces himself into almost every sermon he preaches. Paul simply cannot preach the cross of Christ as he must preach it, without boldly bringing himself in, as both the best pattern and the best proof of what the cross of Christ can do. Paul's salvation,—the absolute graciousness of Paul's salvation, and his absolute assurance of it,—these things are the infallible marks of their authenticity that Paul prints upon every Epistle of his. The cross of Christ, and Paul's salvation by that cross, are the two constant, and complementary, topics of Paul's pulpit; they are but the two sides of Paul's shield of salvation. The most beautiful English preacher of the past generation has told us that his conversion was so absorbing and so abiding that it made him rest ever after in the thought of two, and two only absolute and luminously self-evident beings, himself and his Creator. And so it was with Paul's conversion also. Only, in Paul's case it was not so much his Creator who was so luminously self-evident to Paul, it was much more his Redeemer. And thus it was that in Paul's preaching there were always present those two luminously self-evident subjects, Paul's sin and Christ's cross: Paul the chief of sinners, and Jesus Christ and Him crucified. And thus it is that Paul's so profound, and so experimental, preaching so satisfies us. And thus it is also that it alone satisfies us. When we are pining away under some secret disease if our physician comes and mocks at all our misery; if he treats our mortal wound as all imagination; if he rebukes and abuses us as if it were all so much melancholy, —our hearts know their own bitterness. But if we fall into the hands of a wise man and a sound and skilful physician, he at once takes in the whole seriousness of our case. Before we have opened our mouth about ourselves, he has already laid his hand on our hurt, and has said to us,—Thou art ill to death indeed. Thy whole head is sick and thy whole heart faint. And already we feel that there is hope. At any rate, we are not to die under the folly of a charlatan. And Paul is the furthest of all our physicians from a charlatan. Paul rips open all the dark secrets of our consciences, and all the hidden rottennesses of our hearts, till he is the one preacher of all preachers for us. And his the Gospel of all Gospels. At any rate, speaking for myself, as often as my own sin and misery, impossible to be told, again close in upon me till my broken heart cries out, Oh, wretchedest of men that I am! Paul is instantly at my bedside with the cross of Christ, and with his own case told to me to fetch back my life to me. Paul's prescription, as the physicians call it, never fails me.

Never. As often as seventy times seven, every mortal day of mine, the amazement and the misery of my sinfulness overwhelms me, Paul no sooner sets forth to me Jesus Christ and Him crucified, than a great light falls on my amazement, and a great alleviation on my misery. It is a dark light. It is a dreadful light. It is a light like a drawn sword. But it *is* light, where no other light from heaven, or from earth, could give a ray of light to me. At the cross, before the cross, under the cross, upon the cross, I am reconciled to God, and God is reconciled to me. I am reconciled to you also, and you to me. All the hand-writings in heaven and earth and hell, that were so bitter against me, are all blotted out by His blood. All my injustices to you, all my injuries, all my animosities, antipathies, alienations, retaliations, distastes, and dislikes, all are rooted up out of my heart by the cross of Christ. For I am slain to myself because of the cross of Christ. The one and only cause of all my unspeakable sinfulness and misery,—myself; I, myself, am slain to death for ever by the cross of Christ. My self-love, my self-will, my self-seeking, my self-pleasing; they are all slain; or what is as good they have got their sure deathblow by the cross of Christ. I am crucified with Christ: nevertheless I live; yet not I, but Christ liveth in me: and the life which I now live in the flesh, I live by the faith of the Son of God, who loved me, and gave Himself for me.

He alone is a "right divine" who can preach this faith of the Son of God properly, says Luther. He is a "right preacher" who can distinguish, first to himself, and then to his people, faith from the law, and grace from works, says the Reformer. Now Paul was a right divine and he was the first father and forerunner of all such. And never more so than when he is putting forth all his stupendous power to preach that divinest doctrine of his, that our best obedience, if offered in the very least measure for our salvation, is a complete abandonment, and a fatal denial of the cross of Christ. Some men will start up at that, and will protest at it, and debate against it. So did Paul as long as he was still alive, and kept the clothes of them that stoned Stephen. And so did I for a long time. But now that greatest and best of all Paul's doctrines of grace, as often as I come on it in its bud in Abraham, and in its full flower and fruit in Paul and in Luther, it makes my heart to sing and dance within me. And it comes to me from the God of my salvation a thousand times every day. Why was that blessed doctrine so long in being preached by some right divine to me? Why was I, myself, so long in learning and in preaching this first principle of the doctrine of Christ? And why do I go back so often, to this day, to Moses and to myself? I have a desire to depart and to be with Christ, says Paul to the Philippians. And so have I. But, before God, I lie not. He is my witness, that I beseech Him every day about this very matter, and about little besides. I beseech Him every hour of the day, that I may be spared for some more years yet, in order that I may grow, as I have never yet grown, into this selfsame faith of the Son of God. Into the faith that justifies the ungodly, and sanctifies the sinful, and brings love, and peace, and joy, and hope, and full assurance of everlasting life, to my soul. And to preach all that as I have never yet preached it: and, then, you would perhaps take my epitaph out of Luther on the Galatians, and would write this sentence over me—"Come, and see, all ye that pass by, for here lies a right divine." Why is it that this epitaph is so seldom to be read in any of our church-yards over our ministers? Why are there so few divines so right in Scotland as to satisfy Paul and Luther? Why are there so few of our young preachers who make Paul's determination, and stand to it? As often as I think of this great determination of his, I always remember Hooker's immortal sermon on Justification. Hooker, in this matter at any rate, was a right Pauline and Lutheran divine. And what does that master in Israel, and that equal master of an English style, say to us on this point? Every preacher of Christ, and of faith in the cross of Christ, should have this passage printed indelibly on his heart. "CHRIST HATH MERITED RIGHTEOUSNESS FOR AS MANY AS ARE FOUND IN HIM. AND IN HIM GOD FINDETH US, IF WE BE FAITHFUL; FOR BY FAITH WE ARE INCORPORATED INTO HIM. THEN, ALTHOUGH WE BE IN OURSELVES ALTOGETHER SINFUL AND UNRIGHTEOUS, YET EVEN THE MAN WHO IS IN HIMSELF IMPIOUS, FULL OF INIQUITY, FULL OF SIN; HIM BEING FOUND IN CHRIST THROUGH FAITH, AND HAVING HIS SIN IN HATRED THROUGH REPENTANCE, HIM GOD BEHOLDETH WITH A GRACIOUS EYE; PUTTETH AWAY HIS SIN BY NOT IMPUTING IT; TAKETH QUITE AWAY THE PUNISHMENT DUE THEREUNTO, BY PARDONING IT; AND ACCEPTETH HIM IN CHRIST JESUS, AS PERFECTLY RIGHTEOUS, AS IF HE HAD FULFILLED ALL THAT IS COMMANDED HIM IN THE LAW; SHALL I SAY MORE PERFECTLY RIGHTEOUS THAN IF HIMSELF HAD FULFILLED THE WHOLE LAW? I MUST TAKE HEED WHAT I SAY, BUT THE APOSTLE SAITH, 'GOD MADE HIM TO BE SIN FOR US, WHO KNEW NO SIN, THAT WE MIGHT BE MADE THE RIGHTEOUSNESS OF GOD IN HIM.' SUCH WE ARE IN THE SIGHT OF GOD THE FATHER, AS IS THE VERY SON OF GOD HIMSELF. LET IT BE COUNTED FOLLY, OR PHRENSY, OR FURY, OR WHATSOEVER. IT IS OUR WISDOM, AND OUR COMFORT: WE CARE FOR NO KNOWLEDGE IN THE WORLD BUT THIS, THAT MAN HATH

SINNED, AND GOD HATH SUFFERED: THAT GOD HATH MADE HIMSELF THE SIN OF MEN, AND THAT MEN ARE MADE THE RIGHTEOUSNESS OF GOD."

CXII

PAUL AS A PASTOR

IN his painstaking industry for Theophilus and for us, Luke has provided us with an extract-minute, so to call it, copied out of the session-books of Ephesus. Paul had been the minister and the moderator of the kirk-session of Ephesus for three never-to-be-forgotten years. But he has now for some time past been away preaching the Gospel and planting Churches elsewhere, and another elder of experience and of authority has all that time sat in the Ephesian chair that the Apostle used to occupy with such authority and acceptance. But Paul is now coming near the end of his life. He knows that, and he has a great longing, and a most natural longing it is, to see his old colleagues in Ephesus once more before he goes to be with Christ. And thus it is that at his special request an *in hunc effectum* meeting of kirk-session has been called, an extract-minute of which is to be read by the curious to this day in the twentieth chapter of the Acts of the Apostles. Now from this priceless little paper of Luke's we learn that, the session being constituted, Paul immediately took occasion to review those long past three years that he had spent in their city, and had sat at the head of their court. Paul had given three of the best years of his life to Ephesus, and it was only natural that he should take occasion to go over those three years and look at some of the lessons that those three years had left behind them, both for himself and for his successors in the eldership of Ephesus. And it is just those fine lessons that this first of Church-historians, with such an admirable literary instinct, and with such sanctified industry, has here supplied us with. Paul never spoke better. Paul simply excels himself. There is all that stateliness that never forsakes Paul. There is all that majesty that Paul bears about with him at all times and into all places. All united to a humility, and an intimacy, and a confidingness, that always carry captive to Paul the hearts of all men who have hearts. Paul is simply unapproachable in a scene like this. Paul has no equal and no second in the matters and the manners of the heart. Paul is almost his Master over again in these matters and manners of the heart, so much so, that when it was all over, we do not wonder that they all wept sore, and fell on Paul's neck, and kissed him, sorrowing most of all for the words which he spake, that they should see his face no more. In no other single passage in all Paul's Life by Luke, or in all his own Epistles even, do we see the finished friend and the perfect pastor as in this sederunt, so to call it, of the kirk-session of Ephesus. This sederunt, and this extract-minute of it, is a very glass in which every minister and every elder may to this day see themselves, and what manner of minister and what manner of elder they are, and are not.

"Serving the Lord," says Paul about those three years. And Paul always begins with that same thing. He begins every sermon of his, and every Epistle of his, with serving the Lord. I, Paul, the servant of the Lord, is his salutation and seal in every Epistle of his. And hence his stateliness, and hence his high seriousness, and hence his unparalleled humility, and hence his overpowering authority, and hence his whole, otherwise unaccountable, life, pastoral and all. No: the elders of Ephesus did not need to be reminded that Paul had not spent those three years serving and satisfying them. They got splendid service out of Paul, both for themselves and for their families, but all that was because Paul did not think of them at all, but only of his Master, There was a colossal pride in Paul, and at the same time a prostrate humility, such that they had never seen anything like it in any other man; a submissiveness and a self-surrender to all men, such that, as those three years went on, taught to all the teachable men among them far more for their own character and conduct than all his inspired preaching. If Paul had both forgiven and forgotten those unfortunate misunderstandings and self-assertions that will come up among the very best ministers and elders, they had not forgiven or forgotten themselves for those days, or for their part in them. And thus it was that when Paul said these words:—"Serving the Lord," those who had known Paul best were the first to say that it was all true. Now that it was all long past, they all saw and admitted to themselves, and to one another, how in this disputed matter and in that, Paul had neither served himself, nor them, but the Lord only.

We do not at first sight see exactly why Paul should be so sore, and so sensitive, and so full of such scrupulosity, about money matters. But he had only too good cause to say all he said, and do all he did, in that root-of-all-evil matter. It was one of the many most abominable slanders that his sordid-hearted enemies circulated against Paul, that, all the time, he was feathering his own nest. He is collecting money, they said, from all his so-called Churches, and is stealthily laying up a fortune for himself and for his family in Tarsus and Jerusalem. You all know how certain scandals follow eminent and successful men as its shadow follows a solid substance. We are ashamed, down to this day, to see Paul compelled to defend his apostleship and himself from such tongues and such pens; from such whispers and such backbiters. And yet, no. We would not have lost such outbursts as this for anything, or we would never have known Paul, or have loved him, or have believed in him and in his gospel, as we do, had we not been present at that table beside those men who had seen Paul with all their eyes day and night for three years. I defy you! he exclaimed, as he stood up in indignation and held out his callid hands—I defy you to deny it. I have coveted no man's silver, or gold, or apparel. Yea, ye yourselves know that these hands—and as he held them up, the assembled elders saw a tongue of truth in every seam and scar that covered them—these hands have ministered to all my own necessities, and to them that were with me. Noble hands of a noble heart!

Had his apostolic stipend been in their power to reduce it or to increase it; had a fund for his old age, or a legacy for his sister and her son been at all in Paul's mind; then, in that case, he might have been tempted to keep back some things in his preaching, and to put some other things forward. At the same time, though considerations of money had nothing at all to do with it, some other matters undoubtedly had to do with it. To me it is as clear as anything can be, that the apostle had been tempted, and even commanded, by those very men sitting there, to keep back some things out of his preaching that he was wont to bring forward into it. Paul would never have said what he did say at that heart-melting moment, and he would never have said it with the heart-melting emphasis he did say it, unless he had been speaking straight to the point. It was all long past now. He would never again either please or displease any of those elders, or any of their wives or children any more. And thus it is that he so returns upon his past temptations, and with a good conscience towards the truth, tells them that they may safely take all he had ever taught them and build upon it; for he had neither kept back anything that had been committed to his ministry among them, nor, on the other hand, had he added anything of his own to it. I kept back nothing that was profitable to you. I shunned not to declare to you the whole counsel of

God. In that also there is a glass held up for all ministers and all congregations in which to see and to examine both themselves, and all their past and fast-passing relations to one another, both in the pulpit and in the pew.

"And with all humility of mind." Evangelical humility, as Jonathan Edwards so splendidly treats it, lay deep down like a foundation-stone under all Paul's attainments as a Saint of God and as an apostle of Jesus Christ. Paul's Master had taken the proper precautions at the beginning of Paul's apostleship that he should be all through it, and down to the end of it, the humblest man in all the world. By that terrible thorn in his flesh; by a conscience full of the most remorseful memories; as well as by incessant trials and persecutions and sufferings of all conceivable kinds, Paul was made and was kept the humblest of all humble men. As all our preachers and pastors still are, or ought to be. For they too have each their own thorn in their own flesh, their own crook in their own lot, their own sword of God in their own heart and conscience. If it were nothing else, their daily work is the most humiliating and heart-breaking work in all the world. All other callings may be accomplished and laid down; may reward and may bring pride to those who follow them with all their might; but never in this world the Christian ministry. And not his defeats and disappointments among his people only; but still more, the things in a minister himself that account for and justify all those defeats and disappointments—all that makes his whole ministry to collapse, and to fall in on his heart continually, like a house that has been built on the sand. Till, whatever other gifts and graces a minister may be lacking in, it is impossible for him to lack humility. With all humility of mind, says Paul to the assembled elders of Ephesus. Humility of all kinds, he means; and drawn out of all experiences; and shown to all sorts of people. Till, both for a garment of office, and for a grace of character, a minister is clothed from head to foot with spiritual and evangelical humility.

"And from house to house warning every one night and day with tears." The whole of Ephesus was Paul's parish. And, not once in a whole year, like the most diligent of us, but every day, and back again every night, Paul was in every house. Paul was never in his bed. He did not take time so much as to eat. As his people in Anwoth said about Samuel Rutherford, Paul was always working with his hands, always working with his mind, always preaching, always visiting. "At all seasons," are Paul's own enviable words. At marriages, at baptisms, at feasts, at funerals, at the baths, and in the market-places. Now down in an old woman's cellar, and now up in a poor student's garret. Some men find time for everything. They seem to be able to manufacture time just as they need it. The sun and the moon and the stars all stand still in order that some men may get sufficient time to finish their work. It is for such men that sun and moon are created, and are kept in their places; they take their ordinances from such men, and from the Taskmaster of such men. Paul, I suppose, is the only minister that ever lived who could have read Richard Baxter's *Reformed Pastor* without going mad with remorse, and with a fearful looking for of judgment. "Another part is to have a special care of each member of our flock. We must labour to be acquainted with all our people. To know all their inclinations and conversation: for if we know not the temperament or the disease, we are likely to prove but unsuccessful physicians. A minister is not only for public preaching. One word of seasonable and prudent advice will do that good that many sermons will not do. See that they have some profitable moving book besides the Bible in each family; and if they have not, persuade them to buy some small piece of great use. If they be not able to buy them, give them some. If you cannot, get some gentleman, or other rich man that are willing to do good, to do it. Another part lieth in visiting the sick, and in helping them to prepare either for a more fruitful life, or for a happy death." There are few things in ministerial history that makes my heart bleed like the tragedy of Jonathan Edwards' breach with his congregation, and then his banishment from his congregation. And I never can get over it that, in spite of all else, had Edwards been a pastor like Paul, that terrible shipwreck could never have taken place. And, yet, I must frankly confess, that explanation does not satisfy every case, even in my own experience. For some of the best pastors I have ever known, have been the victims of the cruellest and most heartless treachery and ingratitude, and from some of their most pampered people.

Even the Apostle Peter makes the confession that he found some things in Paul's Epistles hard to be understood. And so have I. And not in the Romans and the Colossians only, but almost more in this kirk-session speech of his. I can understand him, even if I cannot compete with him, in his incomparable pulpit and pastoral work. I myself go about, in a way, preaching repentance toward God, and faith toward our Lord Jesus Christ. But after I am like to drop with my work; and most of all with the arrears of it; Paul absolutely prostrates me, and tramples me to death, when he stands up among his elders and deacons and says: "I take you to record this day that I am pure from the blood of all men!" I do not find his rapture into the third heavens hard to be understood, nor his revelations and inspirations, nor his thorn in the flesh, nor any of his doctrines of Adam, or of Christ, or of election, or of justification, or of sanctification, or of the final perseverance of the saints. It is none of all these things that I am tempted to wrest. But it absolutely passes my imagination how a horny-handed tent-maker, with twelve hours in his day, or make it eighteen, and with seven days in his week; a mortal man, and as yet an unglorified, and indeed, far from sanctified man, could look all his elders, and all their wives, and all their sons and daughters in the face, and could say those terrible words about their blood. Jesus Christ, who finished the work given Him to do, never said more than that. The only thing that ever I heard to come near that was when a Highland minister was leaving his parish, and said from the pulpit in his farewell sermon, that he took all his people to witness that he had spoken, not only from the pulpit, but personally, and in private, to every single one of his people about the state of their souls. Altogether, Paul was such a preacher, and such a pastor, and such a saint, that I cannot blame them for thinking in those days that he must be nothing less than the Holy Ghost Himself, who had been promised by Christ for to come. Such was Paul's character, and such was his work, and such was his success, both as a preacher and a pastor.

With all that, and after all that is said, I am still dazzled and absolutely fascinated with Paul's pastoral work. I cannot get it out of my imagination. I cannot get it out of my conscience. I cannot get it out of my heart. Above all his discoveries, when Professor Ramsay goes east to dig for Paul in Ephesus, I would like him to be able to disinter Paul's pastoral-visitation book. And with it the key to those cipher and shorthand entries about what he said and what he did in this house and in that, and day and night with tears. The hours he gave to it, his division of the day and of the night, the Psalms he read and opened up from house to house, the houses that made him weep, and the houses that sent him back to his tent-making singing. Did Paul make it a rule to read, and expound, and pray, in every house, and on every visit? Did he send word by the deacon of the district that he was coming? Or did he just, in our disorderly way, start off and drop in here and there as this case and that came up into his overcrowded mind? Till the learned Professor comes upon Paul's private note-book, for myself I will continue to interpret Paul's farewell address to the kirk-session of Ephesus with some liberality. Paul does not really mean me to understand that he was always weeping, and always catechising, and always expounding, and always on his knees in the houses of Ephesus. No; Paul was Paul in all parts of his pastoral work, as well as in everything else. Paul is the last speaker to interpret in a wooden way, far less in a cast-iron way. Paul, you may depend on it, was quite content some days just to have waved his hand in at that window, and to have saluted this and that man in the street, and to have been saluted in return by this and that gentlemanly little schoolboy with his satchel on his back. Paul would often drop in, as we say, not indeed to curse the weather, and to canvass the approaching marriages, like William Law's minister, but, all the same, to rejoice with the bridegroom and the bride, and to set down their exact date in his diary, so as to be sure to be on the spot in good time, and in his best attire. If you are a pastor, and if your visits up and down among your people help to keep your and their friendships in repair; to re-kindle and to fan the smoking flax of brotherly love; if your visits operate to the cementing and the stability of the congregation; then, that is already more than one-half of the whole end of your ministry, both pulpit and pastoral, accomplished. And, with all your preaching, and with all your pastoral work performed like Paul's in intention and in industry at least, you also will surely be able, with great humility as well as with great assurance of faith, to bid your people goodbye, and your kirk-session, saying —And now, brethren, I commend you to God, and to the word of His grace, which is able to build you up, and to give you an inheritance among all them which are sanctified.

CXIII.

PAUL AS A CONTROVERSIALIST

"Woe is me, my mother, that thou hast borne me a man of strife and contention to the whole earth," complained the sorrowful prophet. And the Apostle now before us might have made that very same complaint, and with much more cause. For Paul, from the beginning to the end of his apostleship, was simply plunged into a perfect whirlpool of all kinds of contention and controversy. Wherever Paul was sent to preach, north, south, east and west, thither his persecutors pursued him. Till, what Jeremiah exclaimed somewhat passionately and somewhat hyperbolically concerning himself, became literally true in the case of Paul. For Paul, without any exaggeration, was made nothing less than a man of strife and of contention to the whole earth.

But, then, this is always to be kept in mind, that Paul had a splendid equipment, both by nature and by grace, for his unparalleled life of apostolic controversy. Paul started out to face that life of temptation, as nearly crucified and completely stone-dead to himself, as any man can ever hope to be in this mortal life. It is our incurable self-love that is the bitter root of all our controversies, whether those controversies are carried on by the tongue, or by the pen, or by the sword. Once slay our incurable self-love, and once plant in its place the love of God and the love of our neighbour, and you have already as good as beaten our swords into ploughshares and our spears into pruning hooks. It is our self-idolatry and our self-aggrandisement; it is our greed, and our pride, and our intolerance, and our contempt and scorn of all other men, that is the one and only cause of all our contentions and controversies. Now, look at Paul. You cannot read Paul's Epistles without being constantly captivated with the extraordinary geniality, courtesy, humility, simplicity, and loving-kindness, of Paul. The Apostle Paul, it has been said at the cost of a certain anachronism and anomaly of speech, was the finest gentleman that ever lived. And if we take both the etymology, and the old English usage of that term, then it may quite well be let stand as a most succinct and a most expressive description of the Apostle's character. Coleridge says that while Luther was by no means so perfect a gentleman as Paul, yet the Reformer was almost as great a man of genius. And Luther gives us a taste both of his own genius and of his own gentlemanliness also, in what he says so often about Paul. Luther is always saying such things as these about Paul. "Paul was gentle, and tractable, and makeable, in his whole life. Paul was sweet, and mild, and courteous, and soft-spoken. Paul could wink at other men's faults and failings, or else expound them to the best. Paul could be well contented to yield up his own way, and to give place and honour to all other men; even to the froward and the intractable. In short, Paul's unfailing gentlemanliness is his constant character in all the emergencies of his extraordinary life." So speaks of Paul one of the most Paul-like men of the modern world. And an English gentleman, if ever there was one, has said of Paul in more than one inimitable sermon: "There is not one of any of those refinements and delicacies of feeling, that are the result of advanced civilisation, nor any one of those proprieties and embellishments of conduct in which the cultivated intellect delights, but Paul is a pattern of it. And that in the midst of an assemblage of other supernatural excellences which is the characteristic endowment of apostles and saints."

Now, all that arose, to begin with, out of Paul's finely compounded character by birth. After Mary, Paul's mother must surely have been the most blessed of women. And then after his birth in Tarsus there was his better birth from above. And then, with all that, there was the lifelong schooling that Paul put himself through, and the endless trials and temptations, contentions and controversies, of his apostolic life. By all these remarkable, and indeed unparalleled, means, Paul came more and more to be of that unequalled grace of fellow-feeling with all other men, and that noble temper of accommodation and adaptation to all other men, in which he stands out and unrivalled at the head of all the saints of God. Unrivalled. For no sooner has Paul come into the same room with you, than, that moment you feel a spell come over you, You do not know what it is exactly that has come over you, but you feel sweetened, and strengthened, and happy. It is Paul. You have never been in Paul's presence before, and therefore your present feelings are so new to you. For all the time you are together: all the time that he talks with you, and writes to you, and even debates and contends with you, Paul sees everything with your eyes, and hears everything with your ears, and feels everything with your feelings. It was this that so carried all men off their feet with Paul. It was this that made Paul such a preacher, and such a pastor, and such a friend, ay, and such an enemy. You could not have resisted Paul. You could not have shut Paul out of your heart, with all your prejudices at him, and with all your determination never to like him, and never to give in to him. Something like what Jesus Christ was to Paul, that Paul was to all men. You could not but give yourself up to Paul, he so gave himself up to you. Origen tells us that there were some men in the early church so carried captive by the Apostle that they actually believed Paul to be the indwelling Comforter Himself come in the flesh, and come into their hearts. And Origen confesses to having had a certain fellow-feeling with those heretics.

Now, my brethren, to come in all this to ourselves. For, here also, it is the old story, let a man examine himself. Well, Paul was born a gentleman already. Now, if you have not been so born, yet I have heard it said that grace will make the most unlikely of men a gentleman. I do not deny that; only, I must say I have never known a case of it. Tertullian has a saying to the effect that some men are as good as Christian men already, just by their birth of their mother. Now Paul was one of those happy men. Paul was born with a big and a tender heart, and divine grace had all that done to her hand beforehand in Paul. Persecutor and all, there was, all the time, the making of the most perfect Christian gentleman in all Christendom in Paul. Now, you will sometimes meet with men of Paul's noble begetting and noble breeding among ourselves. Not very often indeed, but sometimes, God has not left Himself wholly without a witness, even among ourselves. Men you cannot pick a quarrel with even when you try. Men you always get your own way with them. Men you always get a soft look and a soft answer from them. Men who, when you are a churl to them, are all the more gentlemanly to you. Men to whom you may be as self-opinioned and self-willed as you like, but it takes two to make a quarrel; and, after all, you are only one. Now, if any of you have any of that rare original in you, bless God for it every day, and bless all men round about you with it every day. For there is no greater blessing to men and glory to God in all this self-enclosed and alienated life. But, on the other hand, if you are not naturally a Christian gentleman, and yet truly wish to be such, then, know this, that God has surpassed Himself in fitting up and fitting out this present life for your transformation from what you are to what you wish to be. I did not say that the Holy Ghost could not make you, and make you behave like, a Christian gentleman, both at home and abroad. I took care what I said. I only said that I had not yet made your acquaintance.

Have you ever read that completely overlaid English classic, Paley's *Horæ Paulinæ?* In that incomparable specimen of reasoning the Archdeacon has a fine expression and a fine passage on Paul's "accommodating conduct." And that master of the pen has given us in that epithet a characteristically happy description of the apostle. For everybody who has read about Paul at all, knows this about him, that some of the greatest sufferings of his life sprang to him just out of his far too nobly accommodating conduct. Paul cast his pearls before swine. Paul's sweet and beautiful yieldingness in every matter that touched his own opinions or his own practices, taken along with his iron will in what was not his own; these two things must be taken together to know Paul. Luther, that evangelical genius almost equal to Paul himself, hits the whole matter here in a way that would have delighted Paul. "If two goats meet each other in a narrow path above a piece of water, what do they do?" asks Luther. "They cannot turn back, and they cannot pass each other; there is not an inch of spare room. If they were to butt at each other, both would fall into the water below and would be drowned. What then will they do, do you suppose? What would you do? Well, Nature has taught the one goat to lie down and let the other pass over it, and then they both get to the end of the day safe and sound." Now, Paul was always meeting goats on narrow ledges of rock with the sea below. And so are you, and so am I. And God ordains to you and to me our meeting one another in this strait gate and on that narrow way, and right below us is the bottomless pit. Will you lie down and let me pass over your prostrate body, and then we shall both be saved?

"Above all things the servant of the Lord must not strive." So said the Aged Apostle to Timothy, doing his best to put an old head on young shoulders. And I suppose every old minister who has learned anything in the school of life would say the same thing, to every young minister especially. Do not debate, said the greatest debater of his day, and one of the most masterly debaters in all literature. On no account, he said, enter into any dispute with any one, and especially about the truths of salvation. Give to all men every help to their salvation, but that of debating with them about it. And, according to my experience, William Law is wholly right. Far better let a man be demonstrably wrong in this and that opinion of his, than attempt to contradict and debate him out of it. You cannot do it. Far better a man be demonstrably ignorant in this and that even not unimportant matter, than that he be angry at you, and resentful at you, all his days, as nine out of ten corrected and contradicted men will certainly be. You will never set a man's opinion right if you begin by hurting his pride and crossing his temper. Cross a sinner and you will have a devil, said Thomas Shepard. That may be a little too strong, but few men are angels exactly for some time after they are crossed, and contradicted, and corrected. They are joined to their idol, let them alone. Oh, but you say, So-and-so will not leave you alone. Well, my argument is not that, but this. Let you him alone. "They say. What do they say? Let them say." Do not you even say so much as Paul said. Do not say that their judgment is just. Santa Teresa is not one of the ladies of our Scottish covenant, but this is what she says on the matter in hand: "The not excusing of ourselves is a perfect quality, and of great merit. It is a mark of the deepest and truest humility to see ourselves condemned without cause, and to be silent under it. It is a very noble imitation of our Lord. What about being blamed by all men, if only we stand at the last blameless before Thee!"

"Doing nothing by prejudice or by partiality," says the

apostle, still insisting on this same matter. Now, to be absolutely free of prejudice and partiality is, I fear, not possible to any one of us in this life. But we must both learn, and labour, and pray, to be delivered from the dominion of those wicked tempers, as much as may be. This passage is five-and-twenty centuries old, but it might have been written in London or Edinburgh yesterday. "No assurances, no pledges of either party, could gain credit with the other. The most reasonable proposals, coming from an opponent were received, not with candour, but with suspicion. No artifice was reckoned dishonourable by which a point could be carried. Every recommendation of moderate measures was reckoned either a mark of cowardice or of insincerity. He only was considered a completely safe man whose violence was blind and boundless; and those who endeavoured to steer a middle course were spared by neither side." We could all set the names of living men, ay, and of Christian men too, over against every line of that terrible indictment. But the design of the great historian in publishing that passage, as well as my design in preaching it, is to set before you and before myself, in every possible way, the mischief and the shame of such a state of things. And to determine, God helping us, to purge our hearts of all prejudice and partiality. The best political and literary journal ever published in this country, for many years held up a statesman of the last generation as a paragon of every public virtue and every personal grace. All that was noble, all that was grand and stately, all that was truly Christian, met in that minister of the Crown. But a crisis came when that hitherto peerless statesman saw it to be his duty to take a certain step in public life. And from that fatal day, nothing he ever said or did was right. Everything in him, and everything in his party, was as bad as bad could be. All who spoke against him in Parliament, or on the platform, or in the press, were so many Burkes come back to life. Eloquent, statesmanlike, unanswerable, were but three of the eulogistic epithets we read in every article. While, if any writer or speaker had a single word to say for that fallen idol and for his policy, they were either rogues or fools. It was a weekly lesson. And not a few of us learned the lesson. Indeed it was written so large that no one could miss learning it. It was as if it had been printed at the head of every page,—All you who would see prejudice and partiality, read what is written below. Speaking on this whole matter for myself, I owe a great debt to the conductors of that journal, and to Butler, and to Bengel. To Butler every day for that great saying of his—"Let us remember that we differ as much from other men as they differ from us." And to Bengel for this—*non sine scientia, necessitate, amore*: enter upon no controversy without knowledge, nor without necessity, nor without love.

CXIV

PAUL AS A MAN OF PRAYER

INTELLECTUALLY as well as spiritually, as a theologian as well as a saint, Paul is at his very best in his prayers. The full majesty of the Apostle's magnificent mind is revealed to us nowhere as in his prayers. After Paul has carried his most believing and his most adoring readers as high as they are able to rise, Paul himself still rises higher and higher in his prayers. Paul leaves the most seraphic of saints far below him as he soars away up into the third heaven of rapture, and revelation, and adoration. Paul is caught up so high into paradise in his prayers, that when he returns back into the body, he is not able to tell the half of the things that he has seen and heard in the presence of God. A great theologian, who is also a great devotional writer, has warned his readers against the dangers of an untheological devotion. Now, Paul's great prayers and great praises are the best examples possible of a devotion that is theological and Christological to the core. In the Ephesians and the Colossians especially, Paul's adoration flames up to heaven like the ascending incense of a great altar-fire. Paul's adorations in those two superb epistles especially reveal to us, as nothing else of Paul's composition reveals to us, the full intellectual strength, and the full spiritual splendour, of Paul's sanctified understanding. And then those unapproached adorations of his prove this also, that the Apostle's wonderful mind has found its predestined sphere and its sufficient scope in New Testament Theology, and especially in New Testament Christology. There may have been one or two as great intellects as Paul's in some of the surrounding dispensations of Paganism; but then those greatly gifted men had not Paul's privileges, opportunities, and outlets. God did not reveal His Son in those men. And thus it was that their fine minds never had full justice done to them in this life. But in Jesus Christ, and in Him ascended and glorified, Paul's profound mind had a boundless scope and a boundless satisfaction. The truth is, beyond the best adorations and doxologies of the

Apostle Paul, the soul of man will never rise on this side the adorations and doxologies of the Beatific Vision itself.

Now my brethren, there is a lesson here of the very first importance and the very first fruitfulness to you and to me. And that lesson is this. Let us put our very profoundest Christology into our prayers. One reason why so many of our prayers, both in public and in private, are so dry, and so cold, and so full of repetition, is just because there is so little Christology in them; so little New Testament Scripture, that is. I do not mean that there is too little New Testament language in our prayers; but there is too little both Old and New Testament language meditated on, understood, believed, realised, and felt. There is too little Scripture substance, Scripture strength, Scripture depth, and Scripture height, in our prayers. It was this that led Dr. Thomas Goodwin, by far the princeliest preacher of the Puritan pulpit, to counsel the divinity students of Oxford to "thicken" both their devotions to God, and their exhortations to their people, with apostolic doctrine. Now, even if you possess no students' books of apostolic doctrine, you possess the very Apostle himself in his Epistles, and I defy you to read his Epistles with the understanding and the heart, and not to be swept away, like their writer, into the most ecstatic and rapturous adoration. You will never be able to read in that way the doctrinal parts of the Romans, and the Ephesians, and the Colossians, or, indeed, any of Paul's Epistles, without being, now completely melted and broken, and now completely caught up into paradise, till you are a second Paul yourself. If your prayers hitherto have been a weariness to yourself, and to all men who have had to do with you, and to the Hearer of prayer Himself, get Paul's great Epistles well down into your understanding, and into your imagination, and into your heart henceforth, and out of your mouth, there will flame up doxologies and adorations as seraphic and as acceptable as Paul's own doxologies and adorations in his greatest Epistles.

The absolute unceasingness also of Paul's prayers immensely impresses us. In his own well-known words about himself Paul was "praying always with all prayer and supplication in the spirit." Now that, read literally, may well look to us like the language of a man gone into absolute exaggeration and extravagance about prayer. But it is not so. All that was literally true of Paul. Paul confessed sin for himself, and he interceded for other men; he adored also and broke out into doxologies, literally without ceasing. Do you ever employ an horology in your devotional life? You will find an excellent specimen of that apparatus and assistance to unceasing prayer on page 155 of Oliphant's edition of Andrewes's *Private Devotions.* Now just as if he had an horological tablet like that page hung up, now on his workshop-wall, and now on his prison-wall, Paul prayed night and day, and all the hours of every night and of every day, without ceasing. Like the genuine horologist he was, Paul introduced every day of his life with praise and prayer. When I awake I am still with thee! he exclaimed as he awoke. He had fallen asleep last night full of praise and prayer, and in the morning he just began again where he had left off last night. As Augustine says, Paul brought the word to the water-bason every morning and every night and made it a sacrament. Wash me, he said, and I shall be whiter than snow. I put on His righteousness, he went on, and it clothed me, it was to me for a robe and for a diadem. Thy Word—he remembered this also out of Job as he broke his morning fast—is more to me than my necessary food. And then as the day went on, every instrument he took into his hands, and every product he put out of his hands, was oratorical to Paul. Like his divine Master, everything was to Paul another speaking parable of the Kingdom of Heaven. Everything to Paul was another call to prayer and praise. Till literally, and without any exaggeration or hyperbole whatsoever, Paul prayed and sang praises unceasingly. Until you are as old as Paul you will have no idea what a large liberty, what a rich variety, what an inexhaustible resource, and what a full range and reward, there is in prayer. What an outlet for your largest mind, and for your deepest heart, and for your richest and ripest individuality. Instead of the life of prayer being a monotony and a weariness, as we think it, there is simply no exercise of the body, and no operation of the mind, and no affection of the heart, for one moment to compare with prayer, for interest, and for variety, and for freshness, and for elasticity, and for all manner of intellectual and spiritual outlet and reward. I sometimes speak to you about Bishop Andrewes, and I do so because his *Private Devotions* is by far the best book of that kind in all the world. As also because it is never out of my own hand; and, naturally, I would like it never to be out of your hand either. And all that because Andrewes is a man after Paul's own heart, for the freshness, and for the fullness, and for the richness of his prayers. Andrewes has a Meditation for every day of the week, and an Adoration, and a Confession of faith, and a Confession of sin, and a Supplication, and an Intercession, and a Thanksgiving, with no end of Acts of Commendation, Acts of Deprecation, Acts of Pleading, and such like. And then he has an Horology, composed exclusively out of Holy Scripture, for every hour of the day and the night. And much more of the same kind besides. What a rich, fruitful, nobly intellectual, and nobly spiritual, life Paul secured to himself, just by his habits and his hours of meditation and prayer. As Andrewes also secured in his measure. And many more who have given themselves to prayer as Paul and Andrewes gave themselves. And just because, with all that, we will not learn to pray, what a wilderness we all make this life to be to ourselves, till we lie down weary of it, and die and are buried in it. Lord, teach us to pray!

Now, just as Paul prayed always and without ceasing, so will we, if we take Paul for our master in divinity and in devotion; and if, like Paul, we go on, in all that, to make Jesus Christ our continual atonement for our sins, and our continual sanctification from our sinfulness. If we know sin at all aright, and Christ at all aright, then this will be the proof that we do so,—we will pray for pardon and for a holy heart, literally, without ceasing. How can any man cease, for a single moment, from repentance and prayer who has a heart full of sin in his bosom, and that heart beating out its sinfulness into his body and into his mind every moment of the day and the night? That man will never cease from prayer till he has ceased from sin, any more than Paul ceased. For, with that unceasingly sinful heart within him, there are so many men, and so many things, all around him, constantly exasperating his heart. You must all know that about yourselves. You are so beset with men whom you cannot meet in the street, or hear or see their very names, but you must surely, on the spot, flee to Christ to forgive, and heal, and hide you. Those men may never have hurt a hair of your head; they will never suspect what a temptation they are to you; but such is the rooted and ineradicable malice of your heart towards them, that, as long as you and they live in this world, you will have to pray for yourself and for them without ceasing. When you cease to pray for those men, you, that moment, begin again to sin against them; and that continually drives you back to the blood of Christ both for yourselves and for them. You will never acquit Paul of having gone extravagant, and of being beside himself about prayer, till you equal and exceed him in unceasing prayer, both for yourselves and for all men. And you will so exceed him when you take your exceedingly sinful heart in your hand, and hold it in your hand, watching its motions of sin, and its need of redemption, all the day. If it were possible, and, why, in the name of God, and of your immortal soul, should you not make it possible? If it were possible, I say, to take your private diary to-morrow, and to make a cross on the page for every time you have to flee from your own heart to the blood of Christ; and then to count up the number of the crosses at the end of the day,—if you did that, "always," and "unceasing," would be the weakest words you could use about your sin and your repentance to-morrow night. On the midday street to-morrow you would stop to make those sad marks in your book, at your meals you would make them, at business, at calls, and in conversation with your wisest, and best, and least sin-provoking, friends. At your work, at your family worship, in your pew on Sabbath, at the Lord's table itself; and, if you were a minister, in your very pulpit. "Always" and "unceasing." Paul made no exception, and found no discharge from that war. And neither will you, till you see Paul, and share his place with him, so close to his and your Master's feet, that sin will not reach you. An horology for one day like that would make you at night read both Paul's doctrines and his doxologies as you never read them before.

And I will be bold, and particular, and personal, at this point, and will say one thing of the foremost importance to you and to myself,—we must imitate Paul in this, and take far more *time* to prayer than we have ever yet taken. I am as certain as I am standing here, that the secret of much mischief to our own souls, and to the souls of others, lies in the way that we stint, and starve, and scamp our prayers, by hurrying over them. Prayer worth calling prayer: prayer that God will call true prayer and will treat as true prayer, takes far more time, by the clock, than one man in a thousand thinks. After all that the Holy Ghost has done to make true prayer independent of times, and of places, and of all kinds of instruments and assistances,—as long as we remain in this unspiritual and undevotional world, we shall not succeed, to be called success, in prayer, without time, and times, and places, and other assistances in prayer. Take good care that you are not spiritual overmuch in the matter of prayer. Take good care lest you take your salvation far too softly, and far too cheaply. If you find your life of prayer to be always so short, and so easy, and so spiritual, as to be without cost and strain and sweat to you, you may depend upon it, you are not yet begun to pray. As sure as you sit there, and I stand here, it is just in this matter of *time* in prayer that so many of us are making shipwreck of our own souls, and of the souls of others. Were some of us shut up in prison like Paul, I believe we have grace enough to become in that sequestered life men of great and prevailing prayer. And, perhaps, when we are sufficiently old and set free from business, and are sick tired of spending our late nights eating and drinking and talking: when both the church and the world are sick tired of us and leave us alone and forget us, we, yet, short of Blackness or the Bass-rock, may find time for prayer, and may get back the years of prayer those canker-worms have eaten.

And now to come to the last and the best kind of all prayer and the crown and the finish of all Paul's prayer, intercessory prayer, namely. We have little else indeed of the prayer-kind drawn out in any length from Paul's pen but prayer for other people. If you were to collect together and tabulate by themselves all Paul's prayers of all kinds, as Dr. Pope has done in his golden book, you would find that they all come in under the head of salutations, or invocations, or benedictions: intercession, in short, of one kind or other; with, now and then, such a burst of doxology as cannot be classified except by itself. What a quiet conscience Paul must have had, and what a happy heart, in this matter of intercessory prayer, compared with the most of us. For, how many people, first and last, have asked us to pray to God for them, whom we have clean forgot. How many children, sick people, heart-broken people, has God laid on our hands, and we have never once brought them to His mercy-seat. How happy was Paul, and how happy were those churches who had Paul for their pastor. How happy to have been his fellow-elder in Ephesus, his physician, his son in the Gospel. Speaking of Paul's physician, I shall close with a few lines on this subject, out of the private papers of Sir Thomas Browne, a man of prayer, not unworthy to be named with the Apostle himself: "To pray in all places where quietness inviteth; in any house, highway, or street; and to know no street in this city that may not witness that I have not forgotten God and my Saviour in it: and that no parish or town where I have been may not say the like. To take occasion of praying upon the sight of any church which I see, or pass by, as I ride about. To pray daily and particularly for my sick patients, and for all sick people under whose care soever. And, at the entrance into the house of the sick to say,—the peace and the mercy of God be on this house. After a sermon to make a prayer and desire a blessing, and to pray for the minister. Upon the sight of beautiful persons to bless God for His creatures; to pray for the beauty of their souls, and that He would enrich them with inward grace to be answerable to the outward. Upon sight of deformed persons, to pray Him to send them inward graces, and to enrich their souls, and give them the beauty of the resurrection." Had Sir Thomas Browne lived in Paul's day the praying Apostle would have ranked him with Luke and would have called them his two beloved physicians.

Brethren, pray for me, said Paul. Pray for my soul, said Arthur also,—

> Pray for my soul. More things are wrought by prayer
> Than this world dreams of. Wherefore let thy voice
> Rise like a fountain for me night and day.
> For what are men better than sheep or goats
> That nourish a blind life within the brain,
> If, knowing God, they lift not hands of prayer
> Both for themselves and those who call them friend?
> For so the whole round earth is, every way,
> Bound by gold chains, about the feet of God.

But that all-important matter of *time* comes back upon me, and will not let me go. Take *more time* to prayer, my brethren. Take one *hour* out of every twenty-four. Or, if you cannot spare an hour, take *half* an hour; or, if you would not know what to do or say for *half an hour,* take a *quarter of an hour*. Take from 8 to 9 every night, or from 9 to 10, or from 10 to 11, or *some part of that*. And, if you cannot fill up the time out of your own heart, take David, or Paul, or Andrewes, to assist you, and to show you how to pray in secret; for it is a rare, and a difficult, but an absolutely indispensable, art.

CXV

PAUL AS A BELIEVING MAN

The extraordinary concentration of Paul's faith upon the Cross of Christ is by far the most arresting and impressive thing about Paul. It is in the way that Paul lets go everything else in order that he may rivet his faith upon the Cross of Christ alone—it is this that makes Paul our model and our master in this whole matter of the Cross of Christ. For the sake of the Cross of Christ Paul denies himself daily in many other of the great things of Christ. What splendid visions of Christ there are in Paul's magnificent Christology! What captivating and enthralling glimpses he gives us sometimes into the third heavens! But we are immediately summoned back from all that to be crucified with Christ. There is a time and there is a season for everything, says Paul. And I am determined, he says, that so far as I am concerned you shall know nothing in this life, at any rate, save Jesus Christ, and Him crucified. A great Pauline divine, the greatest indeed that I know, was wont to say that there are many things in our Lord far more wonderful and far more glorious than even His Cross. But Paul never says that. Or, if he is ever carried away to say that, he instantly takes it back and says, God forbid that I should glory save in the Cross of Christ. Like the dove to its window, like the bird to its mountain, even after he has been caught up into the third heavens, Paul hastens back to the Cross of Christ. Once Paul is for ever with the Lord; once he is sat down finally with Christ in His kingdom; once he is at home in heaven, and not merely there on a short visit; once he is completely habituated to, and for ever secure in, glory, Paul will then, no doubt, have time and detachment to give to other things in Christ besides His Cross. And yet, I am not sure. At any rate, so long as Paul is in the flesh; so long as he is still carnal and sold under sin; so long as that messenger of Satan is still buffeting him, the Cross of Christ with its sin-atoning blood is the glory that excels all else in Christ to Paul. What grapples my own heart to Paul above all else is just the unparalleled concentration of Paul's experience, and of Paul's faith, and of Paul's preaching, upon the Cross of Christ.

Another thing in Paul's faith is the extraordinary way in which he identifies himself with Christ when Christ is upon His Cross. Christ and Paul become one sacrifice for sin on the Cross. Christ and Paul combine and coalesce and are united into one dying sinner on the accursed tree. It takes both Paul and Christ taken together to make up Christ crucified. Christ is apprehended, is accused, is condemned, and is crucified before God for Paul; and, then, Paul is crucified before God in, and along with, Christ. It is this transcendent identification of Christ with Paul and of Paul with Christ that the Apostle so labours, in the strength and in the style of the Holy Ghost, to set forth to us in his glorious doctrines of the suretyship and substitution of Christ, the imputation of Paul's guilt and pollution to Christ, and then the imputation of Christ's righteousness and the impartation of Christ's spirit to Paul. These great evangelical doctrines of Paul may be so divine and so deep that your heart does not yet respond to them. Paul's tremendously strong words about Christ and His Cross may stagger you, but that is because the law of God has not yet entered your heart. When it does, and when, after that, God reveals His Son in you, you will then become as Pauline in your theology and in its great language as

Luther became himself. I can very well believe that Paul's so original, so powerful, and so cross-concentrated faith, staggers and angers some of you. It does not stagger and anger any of you half so much as at one time it both staggered and positively exasperated Paul himself. But now, he says, I am crucified with Christ: with Christ who loved me, and gave Himself for me. And once Paul's faith is in this way concentrated on the Cross of Christ: and once Paul is so identified with Christ crucified: everything in Paul's experience—past, present, and yet to come —all that only roots the deeper and the stronger Paul's faith in the Cross of Christ. I often recall the evidence that Admiral Dougall gave at the Tay Bridge inquiry as to the direction and the force of the winds that blow down the valley of the Tay. "Trees are not so well prepared to resist pressure from unusual quarters," said that observant witness. "A tree spreads out its roots in the direction of the prevailing wind." Now Paul's faith was like one of the Admiral's wind-facing trees. For Paul's faith continually spread out its roots in the direction of the coming storm. Only, the wind that compelled Paul's faith to spread out its roots around the Cross of Christ blew down from no range of earthly mountains. It was the overwhelming wind of God's wrath that rose with such fury upon Paul's conscience out of Paul's past life. The blasts of divine wrath that blew off the bleak sides of Sinai struck with such shocks against Paul's faith in Christ, that, like the trees on the wind-swept sides of the Tay, it became just by reason of that wind so rooted and grounded in Christ crucified, that however the rain might descend, and the floods come, and the winds blow and beat upon Paul's faith, it fell not, for it had struck its roots, with every new storm, deeper and deeper into the Cross of Christ.

Down suddenly out of the dark mountains of Paul's past life of sin, the most terrible tempests would, to the very end of his days, burst upon Paul. You must not idolise Paul. You must not totally misread and persistently misunderstand Paul, as if Paul had not been a man of like passions with yourselves. Paul was a far better believer than you or I are. But as to sin there is no difference. And the very greatness of Paul's faith; the very unparalleled concentration and identifying power of his faith; all that only made the sudden blasts that struck at his faith all the more terrible to bear. Oh, yes! you may depend upon it Paul had a thousand things behind him that swept down guilt and shame and sorrow upon his head to the day of his death. The men and the women and the children he had haled to prison; the holy homes he had desolated with his temple hordes; the martyrdoms he had instigated, the blood of which would never in this world be washed off his hands; in these, and in a thousand other things, Paul was a child of wrath even as others. And that wrath of God would awaken in his conscience, and would assault his faith, just as the same wrath of God assaults your faith and mine every day we live: if, that is to say, we live at all. No, there is no difference. The only difference is that Paul always met that rising wrath with a faith in Christ crucified that has never been equalled. "I, through the law," he said, or tried to say, every time the law clutched at him as its prisoner—"I through the law am dead to the law. For I am crucified with Christ." When the two thieves died on their two crosses on Calvary, ay and even after their dead bodies were burned to ashes in Gehenna, there would still come up to the courts of justice in Jerusalem, complaints and accusations against those two malefactors from all parts of the land. 'He stole my ox.' 'He robbed my house.' 'He burned down my barn.' 'He murdered my son.' But the judge would say to all such too-late accusations that the murderer was dead already. 'He has been crucified already. He is beyond your accusations and my jurisdiction both. He has paid already with his life for all his deeds of robbery and of blood. His death has for ever blotted out all that can ever be spoken or written against him.' And so it was with Paul. All his persecutions, and all his blasphemies, with all else of every evil kind that could come up out of his past life,—it would all find Paul already a dead man. Paul is crucified. Paul has given up the ghost. Paul is for ever done with accusers and judges both: come up what will, leap into the light what will, it is all too late. A dead man is not easily put to shame, and no jailer carries a corpse to prison. Nay, Paul's case is far better than even that of the death-justified thieves. For, in Paul's case, two men are dead for one man's transgressions. And not two mere men, but one of them the very Son of God Himself. Truly the law is magnified and made honourable in Paul's case! Ten thousand times more honourable than if it had never been broken, since the Divine Lawgiver Himself has satisfied the broken law, and has Himself been crucified for Paul's transgressions.

And as it was with the thieves' past, and with Paul's past, so it is with your past and mine. With mine at any rate. "Let a man examine himself!" Paul kept saying to me all the week before last, and himself showed me the way. But indeed I did not need to examine myself, nor to be shown the way. My past, *of itself,* came down unto me like the thieves' past, and like

Paul's past, and like that Sabbath night's storm on the Tay train. From every city and village and house I had ever lived in, the wind blew and beat upon my conscience. Out of every relationship of life that God had ever set me in. Out of my pulpit, out of my pastorate, out of my family life, out of my closest and best friendships. Sins of omission and sins of commission. What I should have done, and did not. What I hated, and yet did. The temptation and the trial I had been to other men. The sin and the sorrow I had caused. The provocation and the offence I had been. The blame I had brought on the ministry,—and a thousand suchlike things. I could give you the names of the people and the places, only you would not know them. I leave the spaces blank for this reason also, that you may fill them in with the people, and the places, and the things, that sent you to the same Table in tears. What kind of a communion had you last Sabbath? I have no doubt many of you had both a better preparation and a better Communion Table than I had, though mine were by far the best I have ever had heretofore.

But Paul's peculiar and arresting form of speech in the text carries in it the secret of a great victory and a great peace. For mark well, what exactly Paul says. Paul does not say that he once was, or that he had been, crucified with Christ, but that he *is, at present,* so crucified. That is as much as to say that as long as Paul has any sin left so long will Christ be crucified. Not only is Paul's past sin all collected up and laid on Christ crucified; but almost more all Paul's present sinfulness comes up upon his conscience only to find Paul dead to his conscience, and to his sinfulness too, so truly and so completely is he crucified with Christ. It is impossible properly, or even with safety, to describe to a whole congregation Paul's experience. But those who have this blessed experience in themselves do not need it to be described to them, and their own tender hearts and holy lives are the best proof of its safety. I will attempt to describe to some of you what your life is, and the description will somewhat comfort and assure you concerning it. Your heart beats up its secret sinfulness with every pulse, so much so, that you would choke and consume and die with the guilt and the pollution of your heart, unless you were dead already. As it is, though nobody will believe it, or make sense of how it can so be, your unspeakable sinfulness never gets the length even of darkening your mind or imprisoning your conscience. And that is because your mind and your conscience are both in the keeping of Christ crucified. As Luther's conscience was. "The law is not the lord of my conscience," protested that Paul-like, that lion-like, believer.

"Jesus Christ is Almighty God, and He is the Lord of my conscience. He is the Lord of the law also, both unbroken, broken, and repaired, and He keeps the law out of my conscience by keeping my conscience continually sprinkled with His own peace-speaking blood." In Paul's words again, the true believer is "dead," both to the law, and to the sin and the guilt of his own corruption. A true believer's corruption of heart comes up into his consciousness not in order to produce there a bad conscience, but in order to find the believer crucified already for all that corruption with Christ. For myself, I could not live a day, nor any part of a day, were I not crucified with Christ. I would sicken, I would swoon, I would fall down on the street, I would die. Come up beside me, my brethren! There is room in Christ crucified for us all. I am sure you live a miserable life down there, and out of Christ. It is not a dog's life down there. Come up hither to peace and rest. Learn to say, and then say it continually till you say it in your very dreams,—I am crucified with Christ! And then you will be able to work in peace, and to eat and drink in peace, and to go out and in peace, and to lie down in peace, and rise up. Then you will be able to die in peace, and to awake for ever to Christ and his never-to-be-broken peace. "I am crucified with Christ, nevertheless I live, yet not I, but Christ liveth in me, and the life which I now live in the flesh I live by the faith of the Son of God, who loved me, and gave Himself for me."

"HIMSELF for *me,* HIMSELF for *me!*" There is a faith that for once surely, if never again, will satisfy even Jesus Christ, and will set Him free to do some of His mightiest works. If He went about all Jewry, and all Galilee, and even crossed over into Syrophenicia, seeking for faith, surely here it is to please Him at last. The SON OF GOD *for me!* Surely that must go to Christ's heart, and carry His heart captive. And we also will say it; I, at any rate, will say it with Paul. For as God is my witness I feel with Paul that nothing and no one but God the Son, and God the Son crucified, could atone for my sin. The Son of God on Calvary, with all heaven and all hell let loose upon Him,—He, and He alone: He and His blood alone, can meet and make answer to the guilt and the pollution of my sin. But His blood, THE BLOOD OF GOD,—It is surely able to speak peace in my conscience and comfort in my heart: in my curse-filled conscience, and in my hell-filled heart. "HIMSELF for *me!* HIMSELF for *me!*" For the shame, the spitting, the scourging, the staggering through the hooting streets, the bitter nails, the heart-gashing spear, the darkness of death and hell, all crowned by His Father forsaking Him,—Yes, *that* is the desert of *my* sin. *That* answers to *my* sin. *My* sin explains *all that*, and needs *all that*, and will be satisfied with nothing short of *all that*. *My sin* alone, in heaven, or earth, or hell, is the full justification of *all that*. *All that*, borne for me by my Maker, my Lawgiver, and my Redeemer. But it is best just as Paul has left it,—"HE loved *me*, and gave HIMSELF for *me*."

CXVI

PAUL AS THE CHIEF OF SINNERS

EVERYBODY knows what the most eminent saints of Holy Scripture think and say of their sinfulness. And here is what some of the most eminent saints who have lived since the days of Holy Scripture have felt and said about their own exceeding sinfulness also. And to begin with one of the very saintliest of them all—Samuel Rutherford. "When I look at my sinfulness," says Rutherford, "my salvation is to me my Saviour's greatest miracle. He has done nothing in heaven or on earth like my salvation." And the title-page of John Bunyan's incomparable autobiography runs thus: "Grace abounding to John Bunyan, the chief of sinners. Come and hear, all ye that fear God, and I will declare what He hath done for my soul." "Is there but one spider in all this room?" asked the Interpreter. Then the water stood in Christiana's eyes, for she was a woman quick of apprehension, and she said, "Yes, Lord, there is more here than one; yea, and spiders whose venom is far more destructive than that which is in her." "My daughters," said Santa Teresa on her deathbed, "do not follow my example; for I have been the most sinful woman in all the world." But what she most dwelt on as she died was that half verse, "*Cor contritum*—a broken and a contrite heart, O God, Thou wilt not despise." "Do not mistake me," said Jacob Behmen, "for my heart is as full as it can hold of all malice at you and all ill-will. My heart is the very dunghill of the devil, and it is no easy work to wrestle with him on his own chosen ground. But wrestle with him on that ground of his I must, and that the whole of my life to the end." "Begone! all ye self-ignorant and false flatterers," shouted Philip Neri at them; "I am good for nothing but to do evil." "When a man like me," says Luther, "comes to know the plague of his own heart, he is not miserable only—he is absolute misery itself; he is not sinful only—he is absolute sin itself." "I am made of sin," sobbed Bishop Andrewes, till his private prayer-book was all but unreadable to his heirs because of its author's sweat and tears. "It has often appeared to me," says Jonathan Edwards, "that if God were to mark my heart-iniquity my bed would be in hell." "I sat down on the side of a stank," says Lord Brodie, "and was disgusted at the toads and esks and many other unclean creatures I saw sweltering there. But all the time my own heart was far worse earth to me, and filthier by far than the filthy earth I sat upon." "This is a faithful saying," says Paul, "and worthy of all acceptation, that Christ Jesus came into the world to save sinners, of whom I am the chief." Well may our Saviour stop us and ask us whether or no we have counted the cost of being one of His out-and-out disciples!

I can very well believe that there are some new beginners here who are terribly staggered with all that. They were brought up positively to worship the Apostle Paul, and Luther, and Rutherford, and Bunyan. And how such saints of God can write such bitter things against themselves, you cannot understand. You would like to acquiesce in all that these men say about all such matters as sin and sinfulness; but you do not see how they can honestly and truly say such things as the above about themselves.

Fool! said my muse to me,
Look in thy heart and write.

Remember these two lines of the true poet. Though they were not written about sin they never come to their fullest truth and their most fruitful application till they are taken home by the sinner who is seeking sanctification. Yes; look well into your own heart and you will find there the true explanation of your perplexity about Paul, and Luther, and Rutherford, and Bunyan, and all the rest. For your own heart holds the secret to you of this whole matter. If you have any real knowledge of your own heart at all, this cannot possibly have escaped you, that there are things in your own heart that are most shocking and prostrating for you to find there. There are thoughts in your heart, and feelings, and wishes, and likes and dislikes; things you have to hide, and things you cannot hide; things that if you have any religion at all you must take on your knees to Jesus Christ every day, and things you cannot take to anything even in Him short of His sin-atoning blood. Well, you have in all that the true key to Paul's heart, and to the hearts of all the rest. So much so that if you advance as you have begun you will soon be staggering new beginners yourself with the Scriptures you read, and with the psalms and hymns you select, and with the petitions you offer ere ever you are aware; and, it may yet be, with the autobiography you will yet write to tell to all that fear God what He hath done for your soul. Just go on in the lessons of that inward school, and you will soon stagger us all by the passion that you, as well as David and Asaph, will put into the most penitential psalm.

"The highest flames are the most tremulous," says Jeremy Taylor. That is to say, the holiest men are the most full of holy fear, holy penitence, holy humility, and holy love. And all that is so because the more true spirituality of mind any man has, the more exquisite will be that man's sensibility to sin and to the exceeding sinfulness of sin. "The saints of God are far too sharp-sighted for their own self-satisfaction," says William Guthrie in his golden little book. So they are. For, by so much the holier men they become in the sight and estimation both of God and man, the more hideous and the more hopeless do they become to themselves. Such is their more and more sharpened insight into their own remaining sinfulness. Even when God is on the point of translating them to Himself because they so please Him, at that very moment they feel that they were never so near being absolute castaways. When all other men are worshipping them for their saintliness, and rightly so, those right saints of God are gnashing their teeth at the devilries that are still rampant in their own heart. They hate themselves the more you love them. They curse themselves the more you bless them. The more you exalt and enthrone them the more they lie with their faces on the earth. When you load them with honours, and banquet them with praises, they make ashes their bread and tears their drink. Their whole head will be waters, and their eyes one fountain of tears just at that moment when God is rising up in compassion, and in recompense, to wipe all tears from their eyes for ever.

And it is the sight of God that does it. It is the sight of Jesus Christ that does it. It is God's holy law of love entering our hearts ever deeper and deeper that does it. It is when I take my own heart, with all its wickedness-working self-love, and with all its self-seeking in everything, and self-serving out of everything and every one: with all its deceitfulness, and disingenuousness, and envy, and jealousy, and grudging, and malevolence, and lay it alongside of the holy heart of my Lord,—it is that that does it. It is then that I sit down at a stank-side with poor Lord Brodie. It is then that my midnight Bible begins to open at unwonted places, and I begin to make friends with unwonted people. It is then that I search the book of Job, say, not any more for its incomparable dialectic and its noble literature. All these things, as Halyburton has it, have now become comparatively distasteful to me. Or if not distasteful, then without taste and insipid, as Job himself says about the white of an egg. No: my soul turns in its agony of pain and shame and seeks an utterance for itself in such consummating passages as these. "I have heard of Thee by the hearing of the ear: but now mine eye seeth Thee. Wherefore I abhor myself, and repent in dust and ashes. Behold, I am vile: what shall I answer Thee? I will lay my hand upon my mouth." And from that my Bible begins to open at the right places for me in David, and in Asaph, and in Ezra, and in Daniel, and in Peter, and in Paul: and so on to all Paul-like men down to my own day. And thus it comes about that the authors who are classical to me now are not the ephemerids in religion or in literature that I used to waste my time and my money upon when I was a neophyte: my true classics now are those masterly men who look into their own hearts and then write for my heart. It is the sight of God that has made them the writers they are, and it is the same sight that is at last making me the reader that I, too late, am beginning to be. It is the sight of God that does it, till my sinfulness takes such a deep spiritualness, and such a high exclusiveness, and such a hidden secretness, that I can find fit utterance for all that is within me in David, and in David's greatest psalms, alone. As thus:—"Against Thee, Thee only, have I sinned, and done this evil in Thy sight. The sacrifices of God are a broken spirit: a broken and a contrite heart, O God, Thou wilt not despise. Create in me a clean heart, O God, and renew a right spirit within me."

It was their own sin; or to speak much more exactly, it was their own sinfulness, that so humbled Rutherford and Bunyan and Christiana and Teresa, and broke their hearts. Nothing at all humiliates; nothing really touches the hearts of people like them; but the inward sinfulness of their own hearts. We shallow-hearted fools would think and would say that it was some great crime or open scandal that those saintly men and women had fallen into. Oh, no! there were no men nor women in their day of so blameless a name as they. One of themselves used to say that it was not "so humiliating and heart-breaking to be sometimes like a beast, as to be always like a devil. But to be both!" he cried out in his twofold agony. The things of this world also that so humiliate all other men do not any more bring so much as a momentary blush to men like Rutherford, and women like Teresa. Just go over the things that humiliate and shame you in your earthly life and its circumstances; and then pass over into the ranks of God's saints, and you will there enter on a career of humiliation that will quite drink up the things that make you so ashamed now, till you will completely forget their very existence. What I am at this moment contending for is this, that sin alone truly humiliates a saint, even as holiness alone truly exalts him. It was sin, and especially sinfulness, that made those great saints cry out as they did.

A Greek fortune-teller was once reading Socrates's hands and face to discern his true character and to advertise the people of Athens of his real deserts. And as he went on he startled the whole assembly by pronouncing Socrates the most incontinent and libidinous man in all the city; the greatest extortioner and thief; and even worse things than all that. And when the enraged crowd were about to fall upon the soothsayer and tear him to pieces for saying such things about their greatest saint, Socrates himself came forward and restrained their anger and confessed openly and said, "Ye men of Athens, let this truth-speaking man alone, and do him no harm. He has said nothing amiss about me. For there is no man among you all who is by nature more predisposed to all these evil things than I am." And with that he quieted and taught and solemnised the whole city. Now in that again Socrates was God's dispensational apostle and preacher to the Greek people. For he was teaching them that there is, to begin with, no difference. That our hearts by nature are all equally evil. But that, as the Stoics taught, though all vice is equally in us all, it is not equally extant in us all. As also that he who knows his own heart will measure his own worth by his own heart and not by the valuation of the street and the market-place. As also that the noblest and best men in all lands, and in all dispensations, are those who know themselves, and who out of that knowledge keep themselves under, and wait upon God, till they attain in His good time to both a blameless heart, a blameless conscience, and a for ever blameless life.

Yet another use of this solemn subject is for the comfort of the true people of God. It is to lèt them see that they are not alone, and that no strange thing is befalling them, in all they are passing through. For myself, when I hear Paul saying this that is in the text, and Luther, and Rutherford, and Bunyan, and Andrewes, and Edwards, and Brodie, it is with me as it was with

John Bunyan's pilgrim in the valley of the shadow of death. "About the midst of the valley I perceived the mouth of hell to be, and it stood hard by the wayside, and ever and anon the flame and smoke, with sparks and noises, would come out in such abundance that Christian said, What shall I do? One thing I would not that you let slip. Just when he was come over against the mouth of the burning pit, one of the wicked ones got behind him, and stepped up softly to him, and whisperingly, suggested many grievous blasphemies to him, which he verily thought had proceeded from his own mind. This put Christian to it more than anything he had met with before, yet could he have helped it, he would not have done it, but he had not the discretion, neither to stop his ears, nor to know from whence these blasphemies came." And here comes our point. "When Christian had travelled in this disconsolate condition some considerable time, he thought he heard the voice of a man, as going before him, saying, Though I walk through the valley of the shadow of death, I will fear none ill, for Thou art with me. Then was Christian glad, and that for these reasons. First, because he gathered from them that some one who feared God was in the valley as well as himself. Second, for that he perceived God was with them, though in that dark and dismal state; and why not, thought he, with me? though by reason of the impediment that attends this place, I cannot perceive it. Thirdly, for that he hoped to have company by and by. So he went on, and called to him that was before, but that he knew not what to answer, for that he also thought himself to be alone. But by and by the day broke. Then said Christian, He hath turned the shadow of death into the morning."

CXVII

THE THORN IN PAUL'S FLESH

THE circumstances with Paul were these. To prepare Paul for his great Apostolic work he had been endowed with the most extraordinary gifts of mind. Paul was a man of genius of the very foremost rank. To my mind no man that I know, sacred or profane, is worthy for one moment to stand in the same intellectual and spiritual rank with Paul. And then nothing exalts a man, sacred or profane, in his own esteem like a great intellect. A towering intellect is perhaps the greatest temptation that can be put upon any mortal man. And then the unparalleled privileges and promotions that were added to all that in Paul's case, combined to make Paul's temptation to vainglory the most terrible temptation that ever was put upon any human being,—unless we call Jesus Christ a human being. But to keep to Paul. His election out of all living men for the greatest service and the greatest reward after the service and the reward of Jesus Christ Himself; his miraculous conversion; his unparalleled honours and privileges after his conversion far above all the greatest Apostles taken together; his labours more abundant than they all; and his transcending successes—all that was enough, according to Paul's own admission and confession afterwards, to exalt him above measure. Rightly received and rightly employed all these things ought only to have made Paul the humblest and the lowliest-minded of all men. But the very fact that He who knew His servant through and through saw it to be absolutely necessary to balance His servant's talents and prerogatives with such thorns and such buffetings, is a sure lesson to us that the humblest of saints is not safe from pride, nor the most heavenly-minded of men above dangerously delighting in the glory of this earth. In short, by far the best saint then living on the face of the earth was but half sanctified, and his Divine Master saw that to be the case, and took steps accordingly.

Now just what that thorn in Paul's flesh really was nobody knows. No end of guesses and speculations have been ventured about it, but with no real result. The Fathers and the Middle-age men for the most part took Paul's thorn to be something sensual, while the great body of Protestant and evangelical commentators hold that it must have been something wholly spiritual and experimental. Chrysostom thought he saw Hymenæus and Alexander in it. Whereas Calvin took it to be the lifelong impalement of Paul's inner man upon all kinds of trouble and trial. Mosheim again felt sure it was the ranklings of lifelong remorse out of Paul's early days; and so on. In our own day interpretation has taken a line of its own on this matter. Lightfoot holds strongly that it was epilepsy. And while Dean Farrar admits that there is something to be said for epilepsy, he decides on the whole for ophthalmia. And then Professor Ramsay, Paul's latest, and in his own field one of Paul's very best commentators, has no doubt at all but that it was one of the burning-up fevers so frequent to this day in Asia Minor. Whatever his thorn really was, we are left in no doubt as to what Paul did with it. And we are left in just as little doubt as to what his Master's mind and will were about it. And then all that leads us up to this magnificent resolve of the Apostle—"Most gladly, therefore, will I rather glory in my infirmities, that the power of Christ may rest upon me." A splendid parenthesis, in a splendid argument. An autobiographic chapter of the foremost instructiveness, and of all kinds of profit and delight, to read and to remember.

Now while it will be the most fruitless of all our studies to seek to find out what exactly Paul's secret thorn was; on the other hand it will be one of the most fruitful and rewarding of all our very best studies, both of ourselves and of Holy Scripture also, if we can find out what our own thorn is, and can then go on to make the right use of our own thorn. To be told even by himself just what Paul's thorn actually was would not bring to us one atom of real benefit. But if I have a thorn in my own flesh, and if I know what it is, and why it is there, and what I am to do with it—that will be one of the divinest discoveries in this world to me; that will be the salvation of my own soul to me. Never mind the commentators on Paul's thorn; no not the very best of them, lest they draw your attention away from your own. Be you your own commentator on all such subjects. Be you your own thorn-student, especially. What is it then that so tortures you, and rankles in you, till your life is absolutely intolerable to you? What is it that gnaws and saps and undermines all your joy in this life? What is it that makes you beseech the Lord thrice, and without ceasing, that it may depart from you? Tell me that, and then I will tell you Paul's thorn.

Oh, no! you exclaim to me, it was not his sore eyes. It was not his bad headaches. It was not even his frequent falling-sicknesses. Oh dear no, you say again. A thousand years of the most splitting headaches would not have laid you so low and so helpless; they would not have so taken the blood out of your cheeks, and so broken off all your interest and stake in life, and so cast you on your knees continually, as this thing has done that you point at so mysteriously, but with such evident assurance that you yourself have fallen into the same hedge of thorns with Paul. You cannot be absolutely and demonstrably sure, you admit, that it was not epilepsy, or ophthalmia, or a consuming fever in Paul. But you protest at us, as if we had been stealing Paul from you, that if it was either sore eyes, or a sick headache, or anything of that kind, then Paul was not the man that up till now you have taken him to be. But you will not let all the world, learned or ignorant, take away Paul from you. Almost as well take away his Master! No! you break out with Bunyan, Paul was that nightingale that sang his song from God to you because his breast was all the time pressed upon the thorn. You cannot sing like Paul, but you have not met with any man who follows Paul's song with more knowledge and with more enjoyment that you do; and therefore you reason that you have Paul's same thorn of God against your breast. And you speak so convincingly, and with such a note of assurance about it, that you almost persuade us that you have actually found out the riddle. Only, you are almost as mysterious about this whole matter as Paul was himself. There are some things, you say, that must remain mysteries, till each man discovers them for himself. No man ever discovered and laid bare Paul's thorn to you, and you will never open your thorn to any man who has not already suffered from, and so discovered, his own. You only wait till our breast is at our thorn also; and then by our singing you will know what has happened to us also. When we so sing, or so listen to such singing, you will enrol us with Paul and with yourself among those who have come to visions and revelations of the Lord. Oh, no, you smile at our innocence, and say to us: Don't you see that the grace and the strength of Christ are not prescribed anywhere else in Holy Scripture for epilepsy or ophthalmia? Luke was there with his balsams, and with his changes of air, and with his rests in a desert place, for all these ailments of the Apostle. Don't you see, you demand of us, that this very prescription proclaims the malady; the very medicine more than half discovers the disease. Iron: a little wine: sound sleep: nourishing food: a month at the baths up among the mountains; these things would cure the commentators. But the grace and the strength of Christ are reserved for far other thorns than Luke could extract, or even alleviate.

It is no wonder that the most learned men have been at their wits' end about Paul's thorn. No blame to them since the very Apostle himself made such a profound mistake about his own thorn. With all his clearness of intellect, and with all his spiritual insight, Paul was as much at sea about his own thorn as if he had been a commentator of the dark ages. If I may so, with my unsurpassed respect for so great an Apostle, he behaved like one of his own neophytes when his own thorn first came to him from Christ. By that time he ought to have been a teacher, but he had still need himself to be taught which be the first principles of personal religion, and had need of milk, and not of strong meat. For no sooner did the inward bleeding begin in Paul, no sooner did he begin to lose his night's rest because of the pain; no sooner did his heart begin to sink within him, than he fell to praying with all his well-known importunity that this whole thorn of his might be immediately taken away. Greatest of the apostles as he was; councillor almost of God Himself as he was; Paul's insight and faith and patience wholly failed him when his own thorn began its sanctifying work within him. You never made a greater mistake yourself than Paul made. With all his boasted knowledge of the mind of Christ, there was not a catechumen in Corinth or in Philippi with more of a fretful child in him than the so-called great Apostle was when his thorn came into his own flesh. For just hear his own ashamed confession long afterwards as to what he did. Without ever once asking either his Master or himself why that thorn had been sent to him; without ever looking once into his own heart for the sure explanation and the clear justification of the thorn, he instantly demanded that it should be removed. He acted as if his Master had paid no attention as to what befell His servant. He behaved himself as if his thorn had come to him out of nothing better than Christ's sheer caprice. 'This,' he said thrice, 'is so much pure and purposeless pain. This is so much quite gratuitous suffering that Thou hast let come upon me. Let this thorn only depart from me,' he cried 'and I will return to my faith, and to my love, and to my service of Thee and Thy people; but not otherwise. As long as this thorn lasts and thus lacerates me, how shall I serve Thee or finish Thy work?' But his Lord compassionately overlooked and freely forgave Paul all his unbelief and all his impatience and all his foolish charges, and condescended and said to him: My grace is sufficient for thee; for My strength is made perfect in weakness. Lord, exclaimed Peter in his precipitancy, not my feet only, but also my hands and my head. And Paul, a much stronger and a much less excitable man, said after he got his answer, and said it more and more all his days: 'Lord, not in one part of my flesh only, but plant those soul-saving thorns of Thine in all the still sinful parts of my body and my mind, in order that the power of Christ may rest upon me. For now as often as I am weak then am I strong. I am become a fool in my complaining. I still mistake my own salvation even when it lies at my door.'

But to come back to our riddle, and to set it over again to ourselves, so as to carry it home and work at it till we find out its true answer. What then is that thorn in the flesh of all God's best saints and of all Christ's best servants,—that thorn which still humbles, and humbles, and humbles them down, past all possible glorying in anything they are, or have ever been, or can ever be? Humbles the most heavenly-minded men in all the world down to death and hell, and so humbles such men only? What is it that Christ sends to stab His best servants deeper and deeper every day, and to impale them and buffet them till they are so many dead corpses rather than living and breathing and Christian men? And then on the other hand, what is that same thorn and stake and devil's fist that at every stab and stound and blow draws down the whole grace of Jesus Christ on the sufferer, till the sanctified saint kisses his thorn, and blesses his Lord, and would not part with the one or the other for all the world? Samson offered so many sheets and so many changes of raiment to any Philistine who within seven days would declare his riddle. And after John Bunyan had reset Samson's riddle to the readers of his *Grace Abounding* he felt sure that his sheets and his changes of raiment were all quite safe, for, after his offer to them, he said, "The Philistines will not understand me. But, all the same, it is written in the Scriptures, the father to the children shall make known in holy riddles the deep things of God." I give you therefore the next seven days and seven nights, Philistines and all, to find out Paul's great riddle. And as many of the children of light as shall have found out the only possible answer by this night se'ennight shall here receive, along with the grace and strength of Christ, a change of raiment. Now Joshua was clothed with filthy garments, and stood before the angel. And He answered and said to those that stood before him, saying: Take away the filthy garments from him. And unto him He said: Behold, I have caused thine iniquity to pass from thee and I will clothe thee with change of raiment. And I said, Let them set a fair mitre upon his head. So they set a fair mitre upon his head. And the angel of the Lord stood by. Such a reward still awaits all those who so plough with Paul's heifer as to find out his riddle. Yes; such a beautiful change of raiment awaits them, and such a fair mitre upon their head.

CXVIII

PAUL AS SOLD UNDER SIN

As often as my attentive bookseller sends me "on approval" another new commentary on the Romans I immediately turn to the seventh chapter. And if the commentator sets up a man of straw in the seventh chapter, I immediately shut the book. I at once send back the book and say, No, thank you. That is not the man for my hard-earned money. Just as Paul himself would have scornfully sent back the same book with this message to its author—If I have told you earthly things, and you have so misunderstood me, how shall I trust you to interpret my heavenly things? No, thank you, I say, as I send back the soon-sampled book. But send me for my students as many Luthers on the Galatians as you can lay your hands on, and as many Marshalls on Sanctification, in order that they may one day be preachers after Paul's own heart. But no, not that blind leader of the blind.

It is an old canon of interpretation that Paul alone is his own true interpreter. And the true student will take the canon down. *Non, nisi ex ipso Paulo, Paulum potes interpretari.* That is to say—There is no other possible interpreter of Paul, in all the world of interpretation, but only Paul himself. And I have come upon two other exegetical rules that have had the most profound results out of this present text; "the right context is half the interpretation." And this out of the same incomparable interpreter of Paul—"If a man would open up Paul, let him do it rationally. Let him consider well the Apostle's own words both before the text and after it." Now when we take Paul in this present text as speaking seriously and not in a sacred jest; and then when we take the whole context, we get an interpretation altogether worthy of Paul; altogether worthy of the depth and strength and majesty of the Epistle to the Romans: altogether worthy of the grace of God, and of the blood of Jesus Christ, as, also, altogether worthy of the Holy Ghost. Then the seventh of the Romans becomes henceforth to us, what it most certainly is, the most terrible tragedy in all literature, ancient or modern, sacred or profane. Set beside the seventh of the Romans all your so-called great tragedies—your Macbeths, your Hamlets, your Lears, your Othellos, are all but so many stage-plays: so much sound and fury, signifying next to nothing when set alongside this awful tragedy of sin in a soul under a supreme sanctification. The seventh of the Romans should always be printed in letters of blood. Here are passions. Here are terror and pity. Here heaven and hell meet, as nowhere else in heaven or hell; and that too for their last grapple together for the everlasting possession of that immortal soul, till you have a tragedy indeed; and, beside which, there is no other tragedy. Only, as Luther says, give not such strong wine to a sucking child.

"Did I see," says Dr. Newman, "a boy of good make and mind, with the tokens on him of a refined nature, cast upon the world without provision, unable to say whence he came, unable to tell us his birthplace, or his family connectison, I should conclude that there was some sad secret connected with his history." And did I hear or read of a man of refined mind, and of great nobility of nature that nothing could obliterate, and, withal, a truly Christian man; did I read or hear of such a man held in captivity by some vile, cruel, cannibal tribe in South America, or Central Africa, I would feel sure that he had a tale to tell that would harrow my heart. I would not need to be told by pen and ink the inconsolable agony of that man's heart. I could picture myself that poor captive's utter wretchedness. I could see him making desperate attempts to escape his horrible captivity, only to be overtaken and dragged back to a still more cruel bondage. And were that captive able by some secret and extraordinary providence to send home to this country so much as a single page out of his dreadful life, it would scarcely be believed, so far past all imagination of free men at home would be his incoherent outcries. But all that would be but a school-boy's story-book beside this agonised outcry of a great saint of God sold under sin. Yes, a great saint of God. For no soul of man is sold under sin to such an agony as this who is not, all the time, a heaven-born and a holy man: holy almost as God is holy. This is the slavery of the spirit in a supremely spiritual man: a slavery past all imagination of the commonplace Christian mind. You see that in the incredulous, uncomprehending, and utterly misunderstanding way, in which Paul's agonised outbursts are sometimes stumbled at, even by some of our masters in Israel.

And no wonder, for the most complete and cruel captivity, the most utter and hopeless slavery you ever heard of, falls far short of being sold under sin. There is a depth of misery in being so sold, there is a bleak and blank hopelessness in being so sold: nay, there is a certain self-revenging admission of justice in being so sold, that all goes to make up this uttermost agony of the self-sold slave. For he was not taken in honourable battle. He was not suddenly surprised and swept away into all this terrible captivity against his own will, and against all that he could do to resist and to escape. No. The gnashing agony of his heart all his days will be because he so sold himself. This will be the deepest bitterness of his bitterest cup. This will be the cruellest rivet of his most galling chain. And then to be sold under sin! The vilest and cruellest savage chief who makes God's earth the devil's hell to himself and others, is not sin. Sin has made him what he is, and it has made his slaves and his victims what they are; but both his cruelty and their misery fall far short of the full cruelty and the full misery of sin. Sin could bring forth ten thousand hells like that, and it could still go on bringing forth as many more. Sin is sin. And the true saint of

God feels that in his heart of hearts, till he scarce feels anything else. Till what all the whole life of a true saint sold under sin can be made in its agony, you may read in the seventh of the Romans; unless you have such agony in your own bosom that the seventh of the Romans sounds flat and tame beside it. "What I hate, that do I!" Oh, no! That is no man of straw. That is no studied artifice of Pauline rhetoric. That is no young Pharisee. Oh, no, that is Paul the aged himself. That is the holy Apostle himself in all his unapproached holiness. Tragedies! Tragedies of hatred and of revenge! If you would see hatred and revenge red-hot, and poured, not on the head of a hated enemy, but, what I have never read in any of your stage-tragedies, poured in all its red-hotness in upon a man's own heart; if you would see the true hatred and the true revenge, come to this New Testament theatre. Come to Paul for a right tragic author. Or far better, come to holiness and heavenly-mindedness yourself, and then you will have this whole agony enacted in your own heart; and that with more and more passion in your heart, all the days of your life on this hateful earth. My brethren, if you will believe me, there is nothing in heaven or on earth, there is nothing in God or in man, that from my youth up I have read more about, or thought more about, than just this text and its two contexts. And if the above interpretation is not the true interpretation of this text, then I just admit to you in the very words of St. Augustine—"I confess that I am entirely in the dark as to what the Apostle meant when he wrote this chapter." Only, I will add this. Unless Paul contradicts me himself, not all his commentators on the face of the earth will ever convince me that this seventh of the Romans is not to be taken seriously, but is to be taken as filled with the spiritual experiences of a man of straw.

Now this is another sure rule of interpretation that whatsoever things were written aforetime were written for our learning, that we through patience and comfort of the Scriptures might have hope. And eminently to my mind the seventh of the Romans was written that those who need the very greatest patience and the very strongest comfort and consolation, may have all that here. And in this way. If even Paul was sold under sin: if even Paul when writing the Romans was still carnal: if he that very day had said and done and thought and felt that he would not if he could have helped it: if he hated himself for what came upon him out of his heart even with his inspired pen in his hand: if sin still dwelt in him, till in his flesh there dwelt no good thing, and, then, if we delight in the law of God after the inward man, as he did: even if we find another law, as we every moment do find it, warring against the law of our mind, and bringing us into captivity to the law of sin, till we cry without ceasing, O wretched man that I am! and if all the time we thank God through Jesus Christ our Lord, and walk not after the flesh, but after the Spirit till there is therefore no condemnation to us—if all that is so, I would like you to tell me where I can find another chapter so full of the profoundest, surest, most spiritual, and most experimental, comfort. I have not found it. I do not know it, much as I need it. No. In its own wonderful way there is not a more comfortable and hopeful Scripture in all the Book of God than this. And for my part, I will not let any commentator of any school; no, not even of my own school, steal from me this most noble, and most divinely suited, cordial for my broken heart. As long as I am sold under sin I will continue to read continually this chapter, and all its context-chapters to myself, as all sent not to a man made of straw, but to a man made of sin, till he is every day sold under sin. "It was the saying of a good man, lately gone to his rest, whose extended pilgrimage was ninety-three years, that he must often have been swallowed up by despair, had it not been for the seventh chapter of Paul's Epistle to the Romans."

But if for the comfort and consolation of some men, this very same Scripture is written for the warning and admonition of other men. And I accordingly admonish you, as many as need this admonition, and will take it at my hands, not to praise yourselves because you are not yet sold under sin. "Don't speak to me," said Duncan Matheson on the market-square of Huntly to David Elginbrod, "I am a rotten hypocrite." "Ah, Duncan man," said old David, laying his hand on his friend's shoulder, "they never say Fauch! i' the grave." And Holy Writ itself says that where no oxen are, the crib is clean. My brother, do not boast that you do not know what it is to be sold under sin, and that you do not believe it about Paul either. A born slave, with a slave's heart, and a slave's habits, never complains that he is a slave. He knows nothing else. He knows nothing better. He wishes nothing more than that his ear be bored for ever to his master's door. Only a free-born, and a nobly-born, man, and a man who had been carried away captive, ever cries continually, O wretched man that I am! The Talmud-men denied the sinfulness of their sinful hearts as indignantly as any of you can deny yours. And they interpreted the sixty-sixth Psalm to their scholars in the same way that some commentators interpret the seventh of the Romans. "If I regard iniquity in my heart only, then the Lord will pass it by, and will not regard it," so they taught their scholars.

But to return once more to the inexhaustible comfort of this text, and then close. There is no shame and no pain in all this world of shame and pain for one moment to compare with the shame and the pain of the seventh of the Romans, as you do not need me to tell you, if you have that pain and shame in your own heart. But lift up your head, for it is to you and not to any other man, that God speaks in His holy prophet and says, "For your shame you shall have double. And for your confusion of face you shall yet rejoice in your portion. Therefore in your land you shall possess the double, and everlasting joy shall be unto you." Agrippa was shut up in a cruel and shameful prison for Gaius's sake; but no sooner did Gaius ascend to the throne than he had his friend instantly released and conferred upon him an office both of riches and renown. Moreover Gaius presented Agrippa with a chain of gold of double the weight with the chain of iron that he had worn in the prison for Gaius's sake. And so has Paul's Emperor done long ago to Paul. And so will He do before very long to you. To you, that is, who are now sold under sin for His sake. You will soon hear His voice speaking in anger to your jailors at your prison door and saying how displeased He is over all your affliction. And He will bring you forth with His own hand like Gaius; and for all your shame and pain He will bestow upon you double, with a chain of salvation round your neck that will make you forget all the sad years of your sold captivity.

He comes the prisoners to release
In Satan's bondage held,
The gates of brass before him burst,
The iron fetters yield.

CXIX

PAUL'S BLAMELESSNESS AS A MINISTER

Momus himself could have found no fault with Paul. Momus found fault with everybody, with one exception. But had he lived in Paul's day Paul would surely have been a second exception to the universal fault-finding. For Paul so magnified his ministry; he so gave himself up to his ministry; he so laboured in season and out of season in his ministry; and above all he so pleased all men in all things for their good to edification; he so went about doing good and giving none offence that he lifted both his ministry and himself clear up above all the fault-finding of all fair-minded men. So much so that Paul stands next to our Divine Master Himself as a blameless model for all ministers, as well as for all other men of God. And both his own ministry and that of all his successors were so much on Paul's mind, that in every new Epistle of his he has given us something fresh and forcible as to how all ministers are to attain to a blameless ministry, till they shall be able to give a good account of their ministry, first to their people, and then to their Master.

Now immediately following the text and intended to illustrate and to enforce the text, Paul lays down a remarkable map: it is a whole atlas indeed of all his past ministry. A moral and spiritual atlas that is. It is not a chartographer's atlas of all the parishes and presbyteries and synods in which Paul has lived and laboured. It is far more interesting and far more profitable to us than that. For it is nothing less than a faithful and feeling panorama of all the outstanding states of mind and passions of heart that he and his successive congregations had come through while he lived and laboured among them. Mr. Ferrier has lately given us an excellently-scaled and a most eloquent map of the parish of Ettrick. On that most impressive sheet we are shown the situation of the church and the manse; the farm-towns where all Thomas Boston's elders lived who had a brow for a good cause; the hamlets also where he held his district prayer-meetings, and so on. And every inch of that minute map is a study of the foremost importance and impressiveness for all the parish ministers of Scotland. But Paul's pastoral map bites far deeper, and with far sharper teeth, into every minister's conscience than even Boston's mordant map will bite, though it is warranted to draw ordained blood also. Paul does not engrave topographically indeed all the cities, and all the synagogues, and all the workshops, in which he lived and laboured. But he lays down with the greatest art the latitudes and the longitudes of all his trials, and temptations, and tumults as a minister. Instead of saying to us Here is Philippi, and here is Ephesus, and here is Corinth, and so on: Paul says to us Here were afflictions, and here were necessities, and here were troubles on every side. And just as in Thomas Boston's parish there are pillars and crosses set up to mark and to record to all time in Scotland his great victories won over himself, and his corresponding victories won over his people; so does Paul set up this and that great stone of ministerial remembrance and had had these instructive things engraved upon it: "by pureness, by knowledge, by long-suffering, by kindness, by the Holy Ghost, by love unfeigned, by the word of truth, by the power of God, by the armour of righteousness on the right hand and on the left." There are able and devoted divinity-students here tonight who look forward before very long to have a church and a manse and a pulpit and a people of their own. What would you say for a relaxation some day soon after the session is over to make a real geographical map of all the places where Paul was a preacher and a pastor; and then to distribute beside those sacred sites all the afflictions, the necessities, the distresses, the imprisonments, the tumults, and the labours of the text. And then on the other side of the sacred site, the pureness, the knowledge, the patience, and suchlike, by all of which your great forerunner and example-minister came out of it all having given offence in nothing, but with an everlastingly honoured name. Such an exercise, taken in time, and laid to heart in time, would surely help you to take in hand some hitherto unheard-of parish in Scotland, so as to make it an Anwoth, or an Ettrick, or suchlike. There are hundreds of parishes in Scotland up to this day absolutely nameless, but to some one of which some one of you may yet marry your name for ever, till your parish and you shall shine together for generations to come, like the brightness of the firmament, and as the stars for ever and ever. You still have it in your own hands tonight to do that. But in a short time it will be too late for you also. Go, my sons, in God's name and in God's strength, determined, as much as in you lies, to give your happy people disappointment in nothing, and offence in nothing, till their children shall bury your dust in your own churchyard, amid the lamentations of the whole country-side, and shall write it over your dust that you were absolutely another Apostle Paul to them, both in your preaching of Christ crucified, and in your adorning of that doctrine.

"In tumults," is Paul's own specially inserted expression; it is his own most feeling and most expressive description, for long periods and for wide spaces of his apostolic life. "In tumults," he says with especial emphasis. Now we all know in what New Testament books, and in what painful chapters of those books, all those tumults are written. But it would be no profit to us to go back to-night on Paul's tumults, unless it were in order that we might the better lay our own tumults alongside of his, and lay ourselves in our tumults, alongside of Paul in his tumults. Well, then, come away, and let us do that. Come away, and let us speak plainly. What, then, have some of our tumults been, yours and mine, as minister and people, since we first knew one another? Was it Disestablishment? Was it Home Rule? Was it some heresy case? Was it the Declaratory Act? Was it the Union? was it hymns, or organs, or standing at singing? or was it something else so utterly parochial, and petty, and paltry, that nobody, but you and I, could possibly have made a tumult out of it? Now whatever our tumult was, how did we behave ourselves in it? What are our calm thoughts about it, and about ourselves in it, now that it is all over? However it may be with you and me, it is certain that some men have gone to judgment, out of those very same tumults, with everlasting shame on their heads. How then do we stand in this matter of blame and shame? And blame and shame or no, are we any wiser men, and any better men to-day because of those tumults? Or after all our lessons are we just as ready for another tumult, and as ill-prepared for it as ever we were? Are we just as ill-read, and as ill-natured, and as prejudiced, and as hot-headed, and as full of pride and self-importance, as ever we were? What do you think? What do you feel? What do you say? You must surely see now as you look back, what a splendid school for Christian character, and for Christian conduct, all those tumults were fitted, and intended of God, to be to you. Well then, how do you think you have come out of those great years in those great and costly schools? Has your temper and your character come out of those terrible furnaces like gold tried in the fire? For all those tumults whatever you may have made of them, and they of you, they were all intended to be but means to a far greater end than their own end. That is to say, they were all intended to test and try and prove you and me as both ministers and men of God, and that by the only proof we can give to God or man. The proof, that is, of patience, and purity of motive, and sufficient knowledge, and long-suffering, and love unfeigned, and the word of truth, and the power of God. And to show to all men, as Paul did, that we have not received the grace of God in vain; because, amid our greatest tumults, we have given offence in nothing, and in nothing has our ministry been to be blamed.

My brethren, you are not ministers, thank God for that. But you will let your ministers tell you what is in their hearts concerning you, and concerning themselves, as they read this too-proud chapter of Paul's. If you were all ministers I would go on to say in your name, and you would agree with me, as to what a cruel chapter this is. For once—what a heartless chapter! Was it not enough for Paul that he should enjoy his own good conscience as a minister, but he must make my conscience even more miserable than it was before? What delight can it give him to pour all this condemnation and contempt upon me and my ministry? And, did he not know, did he not take time to consider, that he was trampling upon multitudes of broken hearts? I wonder at Paul. In so scourging the proud-hearted and uplifted Corinthians he must have forgotten all us poor ministers, who, to all time, would read his blameless and boasted ministry, only to be utterly crushed by it. It was not like Paul to glory over us in that way. But let us recollect ourselves, and say that it is all right. It is not for such as we are to be puffed-up, or even to be easy-minded, or to be anything else but bruised, and broken, and full of the severest self-blame. And, therefore, we will go back upon the ruins of our ministry with this self-condemning chapter in our hands, and will recall the tumults that so wounded the Church of Christ, and so many hearts in her, and all the unpardonable part we took in those tumults, that would never have been what they were had we not been in them. Our offences without number also in our very pulpits. Oh, my brethren, the never-to-be-redeemed opportunities of our pulpits; and the lasting blame of God and our people, and our own consciences, for our misuse and neglect of our pulpits! Rock of Ages, cleft for ministers! The "unedifying converse" of our pastorate, and so on: till we take up this terrible chapter, and read it continually, deploring before God and man, to our dying day, all that Paul was, and that we were not: and all that he was not, and that we were. But, with all that is for ever lost, there is one thing left that we shall every day do; and a thing that Paul did not do, on that day at any rate, when he wrote this proud chapter. We shall every day walk about amid the ruins of our past ministry, and shall say over it—Out of the depths have I cried unto Thee, O Lord. If Thou, O Lord, shouldest mark iniquity, O Lord, who shall stand! Deliver me from blood-guiltiness, O God, Thou God of my salvation; then will I teach transgressors Thy ways; and sinners shall be converted unto Thee. There is always that left to us, and that is better for us, and far more becoming in us, than the most blameless ministry.

Thomas Goodwin, that great minister, tells us that always when he was tempted to be high-minded and to forget to fear, he was wont to go back and take a turn up and down in his unregenerate state. Now, your ministers do not need to go so far back as that. All that we need to do is to open a few pages of our Communion-rolls and visiting books, and a short turn up and down those painful pages, with some conscience, and some heart.

and some imagination, will always make high-mindedness, and fearlessness, for ever impossible to us. You do not need to keep up our faults and failures and offences against us, for we never forget them for a single day. You may safely forgive us, for we shall never in this world forgive ourselves. How could we? No other man can possibly have such a retrospect of faults and failures and offences as a minister. It is impossible. The seventh of the Romans has been called the greatest tragedy that ever was written in Greek or in English. If that is so, some of our Communion-rolls and pastoral-visitation books are not far behind it. For the supreme tragedy of his own sad ministry is all written there by each remorseful minister's own hand. And such tragic things are written, or, rather, are secretly ciphered there, as to raise both pity, and fear, and terror, to all ministers, enough to suffice them for all their days on earth.

Now, you may well think that Paul has left nothing at all for you to-night, but for ministers only. Well, take this, as if Paul himself had said it. Find as little fault with your ministers as is possible. Blame them as little as you can, even when they are not wholly blameless. It is not good for yourself to do it, and it is not good for your children to hear you doing it. Be like Bacon's uncle with his family; reprehend them in private and praise them in public. That is to say, if you have a minister who will take reprehension, either in public or in private, at your hands. But, even when it must be done, do it with regret and with reverence. Be careful not to humiliate your minister overmuch. I am sure you will never intentionally insult him, however much you may have to remonstrate with him. I admit that this lesson is not literally within the four corners of the text, but it is not very far away from it.

And there is this also about offences, and fault-findings, and in a far wider field than the ministry merely. It is very humbling, when once we begin to discover it, that our very existence is an offence to so many men. We are like a stumbling-stone in their way: they fall on us and are broken, even when they could not explain or justify why that should be so; sometimes, again, our offensiveness will only be too easily explained both to them and to ourselves. But, at other times, they will need to go down into their own hearts for the real root of all this bitterness. And, then, when they do that, you will not be much more troubled with your offensiveness to them, or with their hostility to you. At the same time, walk you softly, as long as you are in this life. It is a dreadful thing to be the cause, guilty or innocent, of another man's stumbles and falls. "Love to be well out of sight," was the motto of more than one of the great saints. And, though that does not sound at first sight like great saintliness, yet it is. There are few better evidences of great and sure saintship, than just to "seek obscurity" for such reasons as the above. Keep out of people's eyes, and ears, and feet, and tongues then, as much as you can, and as long as you continue to cause so many men to stumble, and to fall, and to be broken over you.

And, then, both ministers, and all manner of men, never allow yourselves to answer again, when you are blamed. Never defend yourself. Let them reprehend you, in private or in public, as much as they please. Let the righteous smite you: it shall be a kindness: and let him reprove you: it shall be an excellent oil, which shall not break your head. Never so much as explain your meaning, under any invitation or demand whatsoever. They just wish to pick a quarrel with you, and you have something else to do. Now, I always like to seal down such a great lesson as this by some great name. A great name impresses the most hardened hearer. And I will seal down this great lesson by this out of a truly great name. "It is a mark of the deepest and truest humility," says a great saint, "to see ourselves condemned without cause, and to be silent under it. To be silent under insult and wrong is a very noble imitation of our Lord. O my Lord, when I remember in how many ways Thou didst suffer detraction and misrepresentation, who in no way deserved it, I know not where my senses are when I am in such a haste to defend and excuse myself. Is it possible I should desire any one to speak any good of me, or to think it, when so many ill things were thought and spoken of Thee! What is this, Lord: what do we imagine to get by pleasing worms, or by being praised by creeping things! What about being blamed by all men, if only we stand at last blameless before Thee!"

CXX

PAUL AS AN EVANGELICAL MYSTIC

THE two words "mystical" and "mysterious" mean, very much, the same thing. Not only so, but at bottom "mystical" and "mysterious" are very much the very same words. Like two sister stems, these two expressions spring up out of one and the same seminal root. Now, as to mysticism. There are more kinds of mysticism than one in the world. There is speculative mysticism, and there is theosophical mysticism, and there is devotional mysticism, and so on. But to us there is only one real mysticism. And that is the evangelical mysticism of the Apostle Paul. And that mysticism is just the profound mysteriousness of the spiritual life, as that life was first created by the Holy Ghost in Jesus Christ, and will for ever be possessed by Jesus Christ as His own original life; and then as it will for ever be conveyed from Him down to all His mystical members.

Now, to begin with, Christ Himself is the great mystery of godliness. Almighty God never designed nor decreed nor executed anything in eternity or in time, to compare, for one moment, for mysteriousness, with Christ. All the mysteries of creation,—and creation is as full as it can hold of all kinds of mysteries: all the mysteries of grace,—and grace is full of its own proper mysteries also: yet, all are plain and easy to be understood, compared with the all-surpassing mystery of Christ. Ever since Christ was set forth among men the best intellects in the world have all been working on the mystery of Christ. And, though they have found out enough of that mystery for their own salvation, yet they all agree to tell us that there are heights and depths of mystery in Christ past all finding out. Christ, then, that so mysterious Person who fills the Gospels and the Epistles with His wonderful words and works,—What think ye of Christ? Paul tells us in every epistle of his what he thinks of Christ, and it is this deep, spiritual, experimental, and only soul-saving, knowledge that Paul has of Christ, it is this that justifies us in calling him the first and the best of all mystics; the evangelical and true mystic: the only mystic indeed, worthy, for one moment, to bear that deep and noble name.

When you take to reading the best books you will be sure to come continually on such strange descriptions and expressions as these: Christ mystical; Christ our mystical Head; Christ our mystical Root; the mystical Union of Christ with all true believers; the mystical identity of Christ with all true believers, —and suchlike strange expressions. But, already, all these deep doctrines and strange expressions of evangelical mysticism are to be found in the deep places of Paul: and, in his measure, in the deep places of John also; and that because those two apostles, first of all spiritually-minded men, discovered all these mysterious and mystical matters in their Master. Ere ever we are aware we ourselves are mystics already as soon as we begin to read in John about the Living Bread, and the True Vine; and in Paul about the Head of the Church and His indwelling in us. But

Paul, after his great manner, goes on to show us that Christ is not the only mystical Head that this so mystically-constituted world of ours has seen. First and last, as that great evangelical and speculative mystic has had it revealed to him, there have been two mystical Heads set over the human race. Our first mystical Head was Adam, and our second mystical Head is Christ. Speaking mystically, says the most mystical of the Puritans, there are only two Men who stand before God; the first and the second Adam; and these two public Men have all us private men hanging at their great girdles. But, all the time, above Adam, and before Adam, and only waiting till Adam had shipwrecked his headship and all who were in it with him, stood the second Adam ready to restore that He had not taken away. And Paul so sets all that forth in doctrine, and in doxology, and in gospel invitation and assurance, that the Church of Christ in her gratitude to Paul has given him this great name of her first and most evangelical mystic. "And hath put all things under his feet," proclaims the great mystic, "and gave Him to be the Head over all things to the Church, which is His body." And again, "Him which is the Head, even Christ, in whom the whole body maketh increase unto the edifying of itself in love." And again, "And He is the Head of the body: for it pleased the Father that in Him should all fullness dwell."

But while Paul has many magnificent things to teach us about the mystical Headship of Christ over His Church, at the same time, it is the mystical union of Christ with each individual believer, and each individual believer's mystical union with Christ,—it is this that completes and crowns Paul's evangelical doctrine and kindles his most rapturous adoration. And all that is so, because all Paul's preaching is so profoundly experimental. Paul has come through all that he preaches. Goodwin, that so mystical and so evangelical Puritan, says that all the "apostolical and primitive language was at once mystical and experimental." But there is a more primitive and a more experimental and a more mystical language than even the apostolical. "I am the bread of life: he that cometh to Me shall never hunger; and he that believeth in Me shall never thirst. This is the bread that cometh down from heaven, that a man may eat thereof and not die. Verily, verily, I say unto you, except ye eat the flesh of the Son of Man and drink His blood, ye have no life in you." As also in our Lord's so mystical and so beautiful parable of the true vine and its true branches. And then in the next generation, Paul comes forward with his own so profound experience of all that, and with his own so first-hand witness to all that, in such sealing and crowning testimonies and attestations as these: —"I live, yet not I, but Christ liveth in me: and the life I now live in the flesh, I live by the faith of the Son of God." And, again, "To me to live is Christ, and to die is gain," and so on in all his epistles. Paul has so eaten the flesh and has so drunk the blood of Christ: he has been of the Father so engrafted into Christ, that he possesses within himself the very same life that is possessed by the risen Christ. The very identical life that is in Christ glorified is already in Paul, amid all his corruptions, temptations, and tribulations. There are very different degrees of that life, to be sure, in Christ and in Paul; but it is the very same kind of life. There is not one kind of spiritual life in Christ, and an altogether different kind of spiritual life in Paul. The same sap that is in the vine is in the branch. The same life that is in the head is in the member. But that is not all. Amazing as all that is, that is far from being all. The riches that are treasured up in Christ are absolutely unsearchable. For Paul is not content to say that he has in his own heart the identical and the very same life that is in Christ's heart: Paul is bold enough to go on to say that he actually has Christ Himself dwelling in his very heart. I,—you and I,—have in our hearts the very same life that was in Adam, with all its deadly infection and dreadful pollution; but, identified with Adam as we are, Adam does not really and actually dwell in our hearts. We still inherit the "fair patrimony" that he left us; but, I for one, both hope and believe, that Adam has escaped that patrimony himself. At any rate, wherever Adam dwells, he does not dwell in our hearts. But the second Adam is so constituted for us, and we are so constituted for Him, that He, in the most real and actual manner, and without any figure of speech whatever, dwells in us. Indeed, with all reverence, and with all spiritual understanding, let it be said, Christ has no choice; He has nowhere else to dwell. If Christ is really to dwell, to be called the dwelling, anywhere, it must be in Paul's heart, and in your heart, and in my heart. Christ is so mystical and mysterious: He is so unlike any one else in heaven or earth: He is such an unheard-of mystery, that He has *three* dwelling-places. To begin with, He is the Son of God; and as the Son of God He dwells in the Father, and the Father in Him. And, then, ever since His Incarnation, He has been the Son of Man also. And as the Son of Man, and ever since his ascension and reception, He has dwelt in heaven as one of God's glorified saints, and at the head of them. But, over and above being both Son of God and Son of Man: from the mystical union of the Godhead and the Manhood in His Divine Person,

He is the Christ also. And as He is the Christ, He dwells in His people, and can dwell nowhere else, in heaven or in earth, but in His people. Christ mystical is made up not of the Head only, but of the Head and the members taken together. And, as apart from the Head the members have no life; so, neither apart from His members has the Head anywhere to dwell. Nay, apart from His members, the Head has no real and proper existence. At any rate, as Paul insists, they are His fullness, and He is complete in and by them; just as they again are complete in and by Him. Paul, and you, and I, hung, originally, and in the beginning, at Adam's mystical girdle, and we have all had to take the consequences of that mystical suspension. But now we have all been loosened off from Adam, and have been united close and inseparably to Christ. Before God, we all hang now at Christ's mystical girdle. Ay, far better, and far more blessed than even that, Christ now dwells under our girdle, and dwells, and can dwell, nowhere else. That is to say, in simple and plain language, He dwells in our hearts by faith and love on our part, and by mystical incorporation on His part. I am crucified with Christ, nevertheless I live; yet not I, but Christ liveth in me. And, for this cause, I bow my knees unto the Father of our Lord Jesus Christ, that Christ may dwell in your hearts by faith.

Now, as might be looked for, a thousand things, mystical and other, follow from all that, and will, to all eternity, follow from all that. But take one or two things that immediately and at once follow from all that, and so close this meditation. And first, the mystical union between Christ and the soul is so mysterious that it is a great mystery even to those who are in it, and share it. As Walter Marshall, one of the greatest doctors in this mystery, has it: "Yes," says Marshall in his *Gospel Mystery*, "though it be revealed clearly in the Holy Scriptures, yet the natural man has not eyes to see it there. And if God expresses it never so plainly and properly, he will still think that God is speaking in riddles and parables. And I doubt not but it is still a riddle, even to many truly godly men, who have received a holy nature from God in this way. For the apostles themselves had the saving benefit of this mystery long before the Comforter had discovered it clearly to them. They walked in Christ as the way to the Father, before they clearly knew him to be the way. And the best of us know this mystery but in part, and must wait for the perfect knowledge of it in another world." So mysterious is this mystery of godliness.

But how, asks some one honestly and anxiously,—how shall I ever become such a miracle of Divine grace as to be actually, myself, a member of Christ's mystical body? Just begin at once to be one of His members, and the thing is done. Your hands do not hang idle and say,—How shall we ever do any work? Your feet do not stand still and say,—How shall we ever walk or run? Nor your eyes, nor your ears. They just begin to do, each, their proper work, and the moment they so begin, your head and your heart immediately send down their virtue into your hands and your feet. And so is it with the mystical Head and His mystical members. Just begin to be one of His members, and already you are one of them. Believe that you are one of them, and you shall be one of them. Just think about Christ. Just speak to Christ. Just lean upon, and look to Christ. Just go home to-night and do that deed of love, and truth, and humility, and brotherly-kindness, and self-denial, in His name, and, already, Christ is dwelling in you, and working in you as well as in Paul. Saul of Tarsus just said as he lay among his horse's feet,—Lord, what wilt Thou have me to do? and from that moment the thing was done.

Now, my brethren, if I have had any success to-night in setting forth Paul as an evangelical mystic, this also will follow as one of the many fruits of my argument. This fine word "mystical" will henceforth be redeemed in all your minds from all that dreaminess, and cloudiness, and unreality, and unpracticalness, with which it has hitherto been associated in your minds. "Vigour and efficacy" may not have been associated in many minds with the great mystical saints, and yet that is the very language that is used concerning them by no less an authority than Dr. Johnson. But just look at two or three of the greatest evangelical and saintly mystics for yourselves, and see if the great critic and lexicographer is not literally correct. Where is there vigour and efficacy in all the world like the vigour and efficacy of the Apostle Paul? Where is there less dreaminess or less cloudiness than in Paul? What a leader of men he was! What a founder and ruler of churches! What a man of business he was, and that just because of his mystical oneness with Christ. What an incomparably laborious, efficient, and fruitful life Paul lived! What a mystical conversation with heaven he kept up, combined with what stupendous services on earth! Take Luther also. There is not a more evangelically-mystical book in all New Testament literature than Luther's Galatians. And yet, or I should rather say, and therefore, what truly Pauline vigour and efficacy in everything! And take Teresa and her mystical deacon always at her side, John of the Cross. I would need to be a genius at coining right words before I could describe aright to you that amazing woman's statesmanship and emperorship in life and in character. Founding schools, selecting sites, negotiating finances, superintending architects and builders and gardeners; always in the kitchen, always in the schoolroom, always in the oratory, always on horseback. A mother in Israel. A queen among the most queenly women in all the world. And, unjust as Dr. Duncan is to William Law our greatest English mystic, Duncan is compelled to allow about Law that "he spoke upon the practical as with the sound of a trumpet. In practical appeals Law is a very Luther. Luther and Law were Boanerges." And, as Dr. Somerville, our west-end neighbour says, from whose fine book on Paul I have borrowed the title of this lecture:—"The intensity that characterised the religious life and experience of the late General Gordon, was all due to his evangelical mysticism. All associated in his case with extraordinary efficiency in the practical affairs of life and in the management of men." But why argue out such remote and historical instances when we have it all within ourselves? Let any man among ourselves carry about Christ in his own heart; let any man abide in Christ as the branch abides in the vine: let any man cleave as close to Christ as a member of our body cleaves close to its head: let any man say unceasingly every day, "I am crucified with Christ: nevertheless I live: yet not I, but Christ liveth in me;" and you will be absolutely sure to find that man the most willing, the most active, the most practical, and the most efficient man in every kind of Christian work. In one word, the more evangelically mystical any man is, the more full of all vigour and all efficacy will that man be sure to be.

CXXI

PAUL'S GREAT HEAVINESS AND CONTINUAL SORROW OF HEART

PAUL'S all-but complete blindness to the beauties of nature and to the attractions of art, as well as his all-but absolute indifference to the classic sites and scenes of Greece and Rome, has been often remarked on, and has been often lamented over. Paul's utter insensibility has been often set in severe contrast to our Lord's much-applauded love of nature. Calvin also has suffered no little vituperation for sitting all day over his

Institutes, and never once lifting up his eyes to give us a description of the Alps overhead. The prince of Scripture commentators will never be forgiven for never having once stood up in rapture over the sun-risings and the sun-settings on the eternal snows. Pascal also has come under the same condemnation because he could see no scenery anywhere much worth wondering at outside the immortal soul of man. And we are all at one in despising and spurning St. Bernard because he rode a whole day along the shores of the lake of Geneva with his monk's cowl so drawn down over his eyes that he had to ask his host at sunset where that famous water was which he had heard so many people talking so much about. Now, I am not going to put forward any defence or excuse of mine for Paul's limitations and insensibilities. The very most I shall attempt to do is to offer you some possible explanation of that great heaviness of mind, and that great sorrow of heart, which has lost Paul the full approval of so many of his best friends. How was it possible for Paul to travel through those so famous scenes, how was it possible for him to live in those so classic cities, and never to give us a single sentence about persons and places, the very names of which make our modern hearts to beat fast in our bosoms to this day?

> In vain to me the smiling mornings shine,
>   And reddening Phœbus lifts his golden fire;
> The birds in vain their amorous descant join,
>   Or cheerful fields resume their green attire.
> These ears, alas! for other notes repine;
>   A different object do these eyes require;
> My lonely anguish meets no heart but mine,
>   And in my breast the imperfect joys expire.

Right or wrong; praise Paul or blame him; try to understand him, and to feel with him and for him, or no; the thing is as clear as day, that some iron or other has so entered Paul's soul, and an iron such, that it will never depart from his soul in this world. And, till that rankling spear-head, so to call it, is removed for ever out of Paul's mind and heart in another world than this, say what you will to blame Paul, he has no ear left for the singing of your amorous birds, and no eye left but for that holy whiteness that so stains to his eyes both Mount Salmon and Mont Blanc. Master, said the holiday-minded disciples, see what manner of stones, and what buildings are here. But He turned and said to the twelve, I have a baptism to be baptized with, and how am I straitened till it be accomplished. The immense size of those stones, and the exquisite carving of their capitals, would have interested Him at another time, but His own time was now at hand: and so much so that He could see nothing else, all that terrible week, but Gethsemane and its cup, and Calvary and its cross. And, to come down to His great servant: when Mont Blanc was so full to him of the glory of snow and sunshine on many a Sabbath morning, Calvin was wont to boast it all back into its own place with this out of the Psalms,—"The hill of God is as the hill of Bashan; an high hill as the hill of Bashan. Why leap ye, ye high hills? This is the hill that God desireth to dwell in: yea, the Lord will dwell in it for ever;" and, so singing, Calvin went up again to Mount Zion. Cicero says somewhere that Plato and Demosthenes, Aristotle and Socrates, might have respectively excelled in each other's province, had it not been that each one of those great men was so absorbed in his own province. And Paul might have been a Christian Herodotus, and a New Testament Pausanias, had it not been for his own absolutely absorbing province of sin and salvation from sin.

All thoughts, all passions, all delights:
Whatever stirs this mortal frame;
All are but ministers of Love,
And feed His sacred flame.

Among all the heathenish doxologies of her voluminous devotees, nature has never had half such a noble tribute paid to her true greatness, as Paul pays to her, in three verses of his immortal eighth chapter. All the true lovers of nature: that is to say, all the true worshippers, not of nature, but of Jesus Christ; have by heart, and have deep down in their heart, the famous but wholly unfathomable tribute. Listen to nature's truest prophet, and truest priest, and truest poet, the Apostle Paul. "For the earnest expectation of the creature waiteth for the manifestation of the sons of God. For the creature was made subject to vanity, not willingly, but by reason of Him who hath subjected the same in hope. Because the creature itself shall be delivered from the bondage of corruption into the glorious liberty of the sons of God. For we know that the whole creation groaneth and travaileth in pain together until now. And not only they, but ourselves also, which have the first-fruits of the Spirit, even we ourselves, groan within ourselves, waiting for the adoption." Match that, if you can, for a tribute to nature's true greatness. Match that, if you can, out of all your sentimental stuff. You cannot do it. I defy you to do it. Pascal is constantly saying this of man, that man's great misery is the true measure of his greatness. Give me, therefore, Paul's profound lamentation over the bondage, and the vanity, and the groaning, and the travailing of nature; and over the shame, and the sin, and the misery of man her master. And, then, give me his magnificent prophecy over her evangelical future. To all of which profound pathos on the one hand, and to all of which magnificent hope on the other hand, your nature-worshipper's unbroken heart is utterly stupid and dead. Paul was such a great man, and such a great apostle of the Creator and Redeemer both of man and and of nature, that, in their present state of sin and misery, and on that account, like his Master, he was a man of inconsolable sorrows. And yet babes at the breast will wail out against the insensibility of that mighty mind and mighty heart; will wail out at his insensibility and indifference to those toys and trifles that so sanctify and satisfy them, as they so often assure us. Whatever may be the true explanation of your entire satisfaction with nature, and with art, and with travel, and with yourself, this is undoubtedly the true explanation of Paul's great heaviness and continual sorrow of heart. The tremendous catastrophe of the fall of man, and the fall of all nature around man,—that, to Paul, was so ever-present and so all-possessing, that there is no alleviation of his awful pain of heart on account of all that. At any rate, there is no alleviation of relief for him in the colour of the morning or evening sky, or in the shape of the hills, or in the music of the woods and the waters. Miserable comforters are all these things to Paul's broken heart; but most miserable of all, your mountebank comforters among men, who would thrust things like these upon Paul's profound and inappeasable sorrow. "A man in distress," says John Foster, "has peculiarly a right not to be trifled with by the application of unadapted expedients: since insufficient consolations but mock him, and deceptive consolations betray him." The whole truth about Paul, above all other mortal men is this. Paul is so intensely religious in his whole mind, and heart, and imagination, and temperament, and taste: he is so utterly and absolutely godly; he is such an out-and-out Christian man and Christian apostle: he is so consumed continually with his hunger and his thirst after righteousness: he is so captivated, enthralled, and enraptured with the beauty of holiness, that nothing will ever satisfy Paul, either for nature, or for art, or for travel, or for man, or for himself, short of the new heavens and the new earth. And until that day dawns, and that day-star arises in Paul's heart, whatever you and I may do, he will continue to look, not at the things that are seen, but at the things that are not seen; for the things which are seen are temporal, but the things which are not seen are eternal. Renan sometimes hits the mark in a manner that both surprises and rebukes us. "Paul," says that truly wonderful writer, "belongs wholly to another world than this present world. Paul's Parnassus and Olympus; his sunrises and his sunsets; his whole Greece, and Rome, and Holy Land itself, are all elsewhere, and not here."

But not amidst nature and art and travel only, but amidst far better things than these, men like Paul are often made men of sorrow and of a heavy heart. "How, now, good friends, whither away after this burdened manner? A burdened manner indeed, as ever I think poor creature had. Hast thou a wife and children? Yes; but I am so laden with this burden, that I cannot take that pleasure in them as I once thought I would. Methinks, I am as if I had them not." A bold passage, but a right noble passage. A Paul-like passage. Paul had neither wife nor child, but he could not have written a better passage than John Bunyan's above passage, even if he had had as many children as John Bunyan had, and had loved them, and had wept over them, as only John Bunyan could love and weep. At the same time, it would have been an additional relief, and a real and peculiar support to us, to have had a passage immediately from Paul's own pen on the heaviness of heart that cannot but accompany family life, when a man of Paul's sensibility, and of John Bunyan's sensibility, is at the head of that family. For Paul's most noble lamentation over the out-of-door creation is cold and remote, and is wholly without those bowels and mercies, that would have been stirred in Paul had he walked with a perfect heart before his house at home. But in the absence of Paul on the profoundest aspects of family life, I know nothing better anywhere than the Pilgrim's reply to Mr. Worldly Wiseman; and, some time after, to Charity. To Charity, who, though like the Apostle she has no children of her own body, yet like him, her love, and her imagination, and her genius for the things of the heart, all make her speak to us like a mother in Israel, and all make John Bunyan to speak in reply to her like a father in the same. As Thomas Boston also has it in one of his Shakespearian passages: "Man is born crying, lives complaining, and dies disappointed from that quarter. All is vanity and vexation of spirit. But I have waited for Thy salvation, O Lord."

Why are the ungodly generally so jocund? asks Thomas Shepard. Partly, he answers, their want of understanding. They may be very eloquent on scenery, and on travel, and on art, and yet the scales may be on their eyes and the shell on their heads all the time as to anything deeper than the surface of things. Most men, he asserts, remain total strangers to themselves, and to their true spiritual state, all their days. And a little after that, this pungentest of preachers goes on to ask why the truly godly are oft-times so much more sad and melancholy than other people? Among other deep answers he supplies himself and us with this deep answer,—It is not because they are too godly that they are so sad, but because they are not far more godly. They have grace enough to bring them off from casual and worldly delights, but not enough to enable them to live upon the spiritual and eternal world, and to fetch all their comforts from thence. Grace has for ever spoiled their joy in the creature, but they are not yet grown so spiritual as to live upon God, and hence it is that they are found so often hovering in sadness and dissatisfaction between earth and heaven. Thomas Shepard's *Ten Virgins,* and his *Zacchæus,* are perfect mines of the profoundest and most experimental truth. Lord Brodie also will give us his testimony on this same subject out of his heavy-hearted diary. Brodie was not Paul, nor Pascal, nor Bunyan, nor even Thomas Shepard, but he had sufficient heaviness of mind and sorrow of heart to purchase him a right and a title to be listened to on this matter now in hand. "I never could allow myself," he says, "much exuberant joy in any created thing. But I have always exercised myself to hold every such thing soberly and ready to be surrendered up." And a far better man, our own dear Halyburton, has much the same thing to tell us. "The strong power of sin that I found still remaining in me, and the disturbances thence arising, made life not desirable; and a prospect of final and complete riddance by death, made death appear much more eligible."

But to come back before we close to what we began with, that is to say, the true place of nature in the religious, and especially in the Christian, life. And instead of offering you my own weak words on such a high subject, take this classical passage out of the diary of Thomas Shepard's great pupil in the things of the soul, the greatest man, Dr. Duncan is inclined to think, since Aristotle. We all know the use that our Lord makes of nature in His preaching. Well, here are some examples of the uses that Jonathan Edwards makes of nature also. "Immediately after my conversation, God's excellency began to appear to me in everything—in the sun, in the moon, in the stars, in the waters, and in all nature. The Son of God created this world for this very end, to communicate to us through it a certain image of His own excellency, so that when we are delighted with flowery meadows and gentle breezes of wind we may see in all that only the sweet benevolence of Jesus Christ. When we behold the fragrant rose and the snow-white lily, we are to see His love and His purity. Even so the green trees, and the songs of birds, what are they but the emanations of His infinite joy and benignity? The crystal rivers and murmuring streams, what are they but the footsteps of His favour and grace and beauty? When we behold the brightness of the sun, the golden edges of the evening cloud, or the beauteous rainbow spanning the whole heaven, we but behold some adumbration of His glory and His Goodness. And, without any doubt, this is the reason that Christ is called the Sun of Righteousness, the Morning Star, the Rose of Sharon, and the Lily of the Valley, the appletree among the trees of the wood, a bundle of myrrh, a roe, and a young hart. But we see the most proper image of the beauty of Christ when we see the beauty of the soul of man." So far the greatest mind since Aristotle.

But, now that I have come to an end, I see now that I might have spared both you and myself also all this time and trouble. For our Lord's great words, "they began to be merry"; and the elder's great words that "God would wipe away all tears from their eyes"; those two Holy Scriptures, rightly understood, rightly imagined, and rightly taken to heart, would, of themselves, alone, have saved both you and me this long and superfluous discourse to-night.

CXXII

PAUL THE AGED

It is calculated that the Apostle must have been somewhere between fifty-eight and sixty-four when he wrote of himself to Philomen as Paul the aged. Certain difficulties have sometimes been raised over the text. It has sometimes been asked whether Paul would have spoken of himself as an old man, say, at sixty, or sixty-three. But a thousand things may come in to make a man feel either old or young at that, or at any other age. The kind of life a man has lived; virtuous or vicious, religious or irreligious, idle or industrious, for himself, or for God and his generation, the state of his health, the state of his fortune, his family life, his disappointed or fulfilled hopes in life, and so on. Cicero wrote his *Cato* at sixty-three, and the great orator's design in that famous dialogue was to brace up those men around him whose knees were beginning to tremble, and their hands to hang down about that time of life. And Cicero goes on to fortify first himself and then his readers, with such examples as those of Plato, who died at his desk at eighty-one; and Isocrates, who wrote one of his best books at ninety-four, and who lived another five years on the fame of it; and Gorgias the Leontine, who completed a hundred and seven years, and never to the end loitered in his love of work, but died leaving this testimony on his deathbed, "I have had no cause for blaming old age," he said. "I, myself," adds Cato, "supported the Veconian law at sixty-five with an unimpaired voice and powerful lungs." And, best of all, at the age of seventy, Ennius lived in such a heart as to bear nobly those two burdens, which are by most men deemed the greatest—poverty and old age. Ennius bore those two burdens with what seemed to all men around him the greatest goodwill. On the other hand, in annotating the text Bishop Lightfoot reminds us that Roger Bacon complained of himself at fifty-three as already an old man. And so too Sir Walter Scott lamented of himself at fifty-five as "a grey old man." Now it must be admitted that those two Christians do not come out at all well when set beside the brave-hearted heathens. Only, Dr. Samuel Johnson's shout must not be forgotten—Drink water, Sir, and go in for a hundred! And who himself drank water and went in for reading the best and writing the best, till he published his masterpiece after he was threescore and ten. Dante's old age in the Banquet begins at forty-five. But, on the other hand, Tacitus declares that if he had one foot in the grave, it would not matter, he would still be reading and writing the best.

Now, with all his love and loyalty to Paul, and with all his perfect understanding of everything connected with Paul, for some reason or other, Luke all but completely fails us as Paul's old age approaches. "And Paul dwelt two whole years in his own hired house in Rome, and received all that came in unto him, preaching the kingdom of God, and teaching those things which concern the Lord Jesus Christ, with all confidence, no man forbidding him." These are Luke's very last words to us about Paul. I wish I could believe that these beautiful words described Paul's very last days down to the end. But when Luke, for some reason or other, drops into absolute silence, Paul's own Epistles of the Imprisonment come in to supply us with such affecting glimpses into the Apostle's last days as these. "I, Paul, the prisoner of Jesus Christ. For whom I am an ambassador in bonds. Be not ashamed of me His prisoner. For my bonds are manifest. This also thou knowest that all those that are in Asia be turned away from me. But the Lord have mercy on the house of Onesiphorus, for he oft refreshed me, and was not ashamed of my chain. For I am now ready to be offered up, and the time of my departure is at hand. Demas hath forsaken me, having loved this present world. Only Luke is with me. The cloke that I left at Troas, when thou comest, bring with thee, and the books, but especially the parchments." With one foot in the grave, like Tacitus, Paul is still reading books and writing parchments. "At my first answer no man stood by me, but all men forsook me. Do thy diligence to come to me before winter." You see Paul forsaken, lonely, cold and without his cloke, chained to a soldier, and waiting on one of Nero's mad fits for his martyrdom. Well may Paul say, if in this life only we have hope in Christ, we are of all men most miserable. But Paul has such an anchor within the veil that, amid all these sad calamities, old age and all, he is able to send out such Epistles of faith and hope and love as the Ephesians and the Colossians and the Philippians and the Pastorals and Philemon. Comparing the *Odyssey* with the *Iliad,* Longinus says, "If I speak of old age, it is nevertheless the old age of Homer."

I really wish I could prevail with you who are no longer young to put aside, as Butler beseeches you, your books and papers of mere amusement, and to read Cicero's *Cato,* and some of the other old age classics, if only to make those fine books to serve for so many foils in a fresh perusal of the Epistles of the Imprisonment. It is our bounden duty to read a Greek or a Roman masterpiece now and then, such as the *Phædo* or the *Cato,* if only to awaken ourselves again to the immensity of the change that came into this world with the Incarnation and the Resurrection of our Lord. What a contrast between philosophy at its very best in Socrates and Cicero, and the Gospel of our salvation unto everlasting life in Paul's old age Epistles! The whole truth and beauty and nobility of such books as the best of Plato and Cicero is all needed the better to bring out the inconceivable contrast between this world at its very best before Christ, and the new heavens and the new earth that our Lord brought to this world with Him and left in this world behind Him. How such glorious passages as these shine out afresh upon us after we have just laid down the *Cato* and even the *Phædo.* Such well-known, but so little realised, passages as these: "Christ shall be magnified in my body, whether it be by life or by death. For to me to live is Christ, and to die is gain. For I am in a strait betwixt two, having a desire to depart, and to be with Christ, which is far better. For our conversation is in heaven; from whence also we look for the Saviour, the Lord Jesus Christ, who shall change our vile body, that it may be fashioned like unto His glorious body, according to the working whereby He is able even to subdue all things unto Himself. For I am now ready to be offered, and the time of my departure is at hand. I have fought a good fight, I have finished my course, I have kept the faith. Henceforth there is laid up for me a crown of righteousness, which the Lord, the righteous Judge, shall give me at that day; and not to me only, but unto all them also that love His appearing." What a man was Paul! If we did not know that this was Paul, we would certainly think that it was a Greater than even Paul. Really and truly, my brethren, it would be well worth your putting yourself to some expense and some trouble in order to read, say, the Consolations of Cato to your old age, and then to turn to Paul's consolations and comforts. Unless, indeed, you already read your Paul with such understanding, and with such imagination, and with such heart, that you do not need the assistance that Plato and Cicero were raised up and preserved to this day to give you.

Well; after repeated readings lately of the Cato, and the Epistles of the Imprisonment, and the Art of Dying Well, and Jeremy Taylor, and suchlike authors for old age, I will now tell you some of the reflections, impressions, and resolutions, that have been left in my own mind. And take first Paul's so touching message to Timothy about his cloke, and his books, and his parchments. For all that comes in most harmoniously after we have just been reading *Cato* about our keeping on reading and writing our best to the end. Lest you might not be able to lay your hands on what Calvin says about Paul's books, I will copy out the passage for you. "It is evident from this," says the prince of commentators, "that the Apostle has not given over study even when he is preparing himself for death. Where are those men then, who think that they have made so great progress that they do not need any more to persevere? Which of you will have the courage to compare yourself with the Apostle? Still more surely does this passage refute the folly of those fools who, despising books, and neglecting all study, boast of their spiritual inspiration." And if I might be bold enough to add one word after Calvin. I am not now, alas! a neophyte in these matters, and I will therefore take boldness to say this to you. Read the very best books, and only the very best, and ever better and better the older you grow. Be more and more select, and fastidious, and refined, in your books and in your companions, as old age draws on, and death with old age. I wonder just what books they were that Paul missed so much in his imprisoned and apostolic old age at Rome. It might have been the *Apology*. It might have been the *Phædo*. It might have been the *Cato Major*. It could not possibly have been Moses, or David, or Isaiah, or Micah. You may depend upon it, Paul did not forget his Bible when he was packing his trunk at Troas. You are far better off in the matter of books for your old age than Paul was with his Bible and all. Never, then, be out of your Old, and especially, never be out of your New Testament. As Paul says about prayer, read in your New Testament without ceasing. Never lay it down, unless it is to take up another letter of Samuel Rutherford, or another pilgrim's crossing of the river, or, if you have head enough left for it, another great chapter of the *Saint's Rest*. Nothing else. At least, nothing less pertinent and appropriate to your years and to your immediate prospects. Nothing less noble. Nothing less worthy of yourself. Nothing at all but just those true classics of the eternal world over and over again, till your whole soul is in a flame with them, and till your rapture into heaven seizes upon you with one of them in your hand.

You may remember how a great divine as he grew old was wont, for that and for some other reasons, to go back now and then and take a turn up and down in his unregenerate state. As Paul also was wont to do. For as Paul grew older and saintlier, he the oftener would go back upon the sins of his youth. Paul was like William Taylor, who when asked of God what He would choose for a gift in his old age, answered, repentance unto life. And thus it is that if you are well read in Paul's old-age Epistles you will find far more repentance unto life in his last years, than even in his years of immediate conversion and remorse. You meet with an ever deeper bitterness at sin, and at himself, as time goes on with Paul: and, then, a corresponding amazement at God's mercy. And you will do well to be followers of the Apostles, and the Puritan, and the Presbyterian, in this sinner-becoming practice. Go back, then, deliberately and at length, and take many a good look at the hole of the pit you had dug for yourself, and in which you had made your bed in hell. And come up from the mouth of that horrible pit, and up to that rock on which you now stand, and see if the result will not be the same in you that it was in Paul and in those two most Pauline of preachers and writers; see if it will not make you hate sin with a more and more perfect hatred, as also to make you long again, and as never before, to be for ever with the Lord.

And, not only read your very best, but pray your very best also, and that literally without ceasing. Yes, without one atom of exaggeration or hyperbole, always and without ceasing. If for no other reason than just to make up a little before you die for ever, for your long life, now for ever past, and in which you have found time for everything but prayer, and for every one but God. Or, have you no children or grandchildren to make up to them also for your neglect of their immortal souls? And have you in this matter ever considered God's acknowledged and accepted servant Job? How with him it always was so, that when the days of his children's feastings again came round, he sent and sanctified them, and rose up early in the morning and offered up burnt-offerings according to the number of them all. When do you offer up for your children, early in the morning, or late at night? Different fathers have different habits. Or, when you go back with Paul and take a turn up and down in your unregenerate state, do you ever come upon slain souls who are now under the altar, and who cry continually concerning you— How long, O Lord, holy and true, dost Thou not judge and avenge our blood on them that dwell on the earth! Pray, O unforgiven old man! Pray without ceasing, all the time that is now left you. And who can tell, if God will turn and repent, and turn away from His fierce anger against you, that you perish not.

And every day and every night over your Paul and your Bunyan and your Rutherford and your Baxter, and suchlike, practise, as they all did, your imagination and your heart upon Jesus Christ. Practise upon Him till He is far more real to you, and far more present with you, than the best of those people are who have lived all your days in the same house with you. Jesus Christ either is, or He is not. If He is not, then there is nothing more to be said. But if He is, then set aside every one else, and practise His presence with you, and your presence with Him. Imagine Christ. Make pictures by that splendid talent that God has given you for the very purpose of making pictures to yourself of Christ. Make pictures to yourself of your meeting with Christ immediately after death. Forefancy your deathbed, said Samuel Rutherford. Do you ever forefancy yours? It was the forefancying of his deathbed that was the conversion and salvation of that old man to whom Rutherford sent the letter. Do you ever forefancy your first meeting with Christ? How do you think He will look? How and where will you look? Rehearse the scene, and have your part ready. It is to the old alone, be it clearly understood, that these things are spoken. The young, and the middle-aged, and those who are busy with other things than preparing to meet with Christ, and with other books than the above—They have plenty of time. But neither you nor I. Let us, at any rate, be up and doing. Santa Teresa felt a thrill go through her every time the clock struck on the mantelpiece. The same thrill, as she had been told, that all our earthly brides feel each time their slow clock strikes. An hour nearer seeing Him! she exclaimed, and clapped her hands. Up, all you old people, and be like her. Up, and make yourselves ready. Up, and abolish death. Up, out of your bondage all your days through fear of death. Up, and practise dying in the Lord, till you take the prize. Up, and read Paul without ceasing, and pray without ceasing, till you also shall stand on tiptoe with expectation and with full assurance of faith. Yes; up, till you also shall salute His sudden coming, and shall exclaim, Even so, come quickly, Lord Jesus!

CXXIII

APOLLOS

THE founding and the naming of Alexandria, its matchless situation, its architectural beauty, the rare wisdom of its statesmanship, and the splendid catholicity of its sacred scholarship,—all these things greatly interest us and greatly impress us. And all these things tell at once upon the text and serve richly to illustrate the text. For Apollos, though a Jew, was born in Alexandria, and received his education in Alexandria. The repeated dispersions of the Jewish people had filled the Jewish quarter of Alexandria with tens of thousands of that expatriated people, but everywhere an industrious, enterprising, and successful, people. By that time the Jews of Alexandria had almost the half of the whole city given up to themselves, and the Jewish merchants, and bankers, and scholars of Alexandria were, in all their several walks of life, in the very foremost rank. And, without in any way forsaking or forgetting the faith of their fathers, the Jews of Alexandria had opened their own minds, and the minds of their children, to the best learning of that eminently learned city. Apollos, when an inquiring boy, would be taken up by his father to the famous synagogue every Sabbath day, where he would see the seventy elders sitting on their seventy thrones of gold, and where we would watch for the waving of the far-off flag that summoned the immense congregation to fall down at the same moment on their knees to say their Amen. On the week-days, and in spite of the fierce anathemas of the fanatical scribes of Jerusalem, young Apollos would be sent to school where he would learn to read Homer and Plato, as well as Moses and Isaiah. And in his holidays he would be taken out of the city to walk along the seven-furlong mole to the famous lighthouse island, on which the Sacred Septuagint had received its finishing touches. And as the talented boy became a student he would often find his way to the world-renowned library of Alexandria, into which had been collected the whole literature of the ancient world, sacred and profane; all the best books of Israel, as well as all the best books of Greece and Rome and Egypt and India.

It is not in our power to fix down the exact date of Apollos's birth, but we are quite sure of this, that he was a contemporary, and almost certainly a schoolfellow, of Philo the famous Hellenistic Hebrew of Alexandria. We possess no book of Apollos's authorship, unless Luther's bold guess is also a correct guess that Apollos wrote the Epistle to the Hebrews in his mature years. And unless that other guess is also correct that he wrote the Book of Wisdom in his Alexandrian years. These, to be sure, are only guesses at his authorship, but the guesses of men of learning and genius have often far more truth in them than the proofs and certainties that satisfy less learned and less imaginative men. At the same time, if it is but an illuminating guess that we possess anything at all from Apollos's pen, we are quite sure about the many extant works of Philo. And so much alike were those two great contemporaneous men, that we can almost transfer to the one what we are told about the other. For, just as of Philo it may with absolute certainty be said that "he was a Jew, born in Alexandria, an eloquent man, and mighty in the Scriptures," so, on the other hand, it is no great stretch of the imagination to picture Apollos to ourselves as the author of *The Allegories of the Sacred Laws, The Theology of Moses,* and *The Indictment of Flaccus.*

Paul was not what we would call an eloquent preacher. The Apostle's detractors were wont to set Paul aside with this contemptuous sentence, that his bodily presence was weak, and his speech contemptible. But his greatest enemies could not say that about Apollos. Depth of mind and fluency of speech do not always go together. They did not go together in Moses and Paul, the two greatest men of the Hebrew race. But Apollos was both a man of a deep mind and of great oratorical genius. Quintilian, another contemporary of Apollos, has a finer chapter on this theme, that a great orator is just a good man well skilled in speaking. Now, Apollos satisfied both parts of that excellent definition also. For Apollos was first a good man, and then he was a skilful speaker. No man in the Apostolic Church was nearly such a skilful speaker as Apollos was. And the sacred writer is careful to add concerning Apollos that he was "mighty in the Scriptures" also. In saying that the sacred writer intends what he says to be all but the very highest praise that can possibly be given to Apollos. A great mind alone will not make a man mighty in the Scriptures. A great gift of oratory alone will not do it. It is the moral and spiritual qualities of the sacred orator, when they are added to his intellectual qualities, that make men confess his might when he handles the Holy Scriptures. The acknowledged might of Apollos in the pulpit was the might of conviction and of character; it was the might that has its seat in the conscience and the heart of a good man, taken together with that other might of a great intellect and real eloquence. The great might of Aristotle and Quintilian combined would still have left Apollos weak as other men in the things of God, unless there had been united with all that the might of a conscience on fire against all unrighteousness, and of a heart on fire with the love of all truth and all goodness. Apollos has much still to learn, but this is a right noble foundation on which to build up a great preacher of the Gospel: "a Jew, born in Alexandria, an eloquent man, and mighty in the Scriptures"; so far, that is, as he as yet understands the Scriptures.

This then was the Alexandrian scholar and orator who came to Ephesus on an Old Testament mission immediately after Paul had left that city. Paul and Apollos had no acquaintance as yet with one another. They had never met, and though they were both great preachers, they did not at all preach the same Gospel. With all his Alexandrian learning, and with all his finished eloquence, and with all his knowledge of Moses and Isaiah and John the Baptist, Apollos knew nothing, or next to nothing, of Jesus Christ. How Apollos had come to know so much as he did know, we are not told; but we are told distinctly that his knowledge came to an end with the preaching and the baptism of John, the son of Zacharias and Elisabeth. It perplexes us to be told that about such a man as Apollos was. That such a universal student, and such a lover of all kinds of truth, and especially of revealed truth, should have lived so long in the very metropolis of all intelligence, and not have got beyond the school of John—that quite staggers us about Apollos. At the same time, we must remember that with all his marvellous activity and success, Paul had never been so far as Alexandria. If Paul had preached Christ even once in that magnificent synagogue, what a chapter we would have had in the Acts of the Apostles about Paul's conversations with Apollos. But as it was, Apollos was still preaching just as John had both preached and baptized twenty years before at Bethabara beyond Jordan. John's doctrines and exhortations were preached by Apollos with tremendous passion and impressiveness; with all John's own tremendous passion and impressiveness; and with a polish of manner and a perfection of style to which John was an utter stranger. But that was all the preaching that Aquila and Priscilla listened to Sabbath after Sabbath, as Apollos stood up in the pulpit of Ephesus. Sabbath day after Sabbath day, Aquila and Priscilla came up to the synagogue and listened to Apollos preaching John; and every returning Sabbath day they listened to him with increasing regret that he had not come to Ephesus in time to have heard Paul preaching Christ. With a weekly increasing distress they listened to what they heard, or rather, did not hear, till, at last, they took Apollos and expounded unto him the way of God more perfectly.

Such then is this so beautiful passage, and so full of all manner of lessons for students, for young preachers, and for old people. And first, for old people, and for people far on in the spiritual life. I can overhear Aquila and Priscilla on their way home from the synagogue Sabbath after Sabbath; or, rather, I can overhear them after their children are asleep. For you may depend upon it, Aquila and Priscilla did not discuss Apollos's sermons at the church door or at the dinner table. Was that a good sermon to-day, father? asked young Keble. All sermons are good, my son, answered his wise father. And Aquila was like old Keble. All the way home from church Aquila talked to his sons and daughters about Alexandria and her schools; about the Septuagint; about Apollos's great learning and great eloquence; about the work that he had laid out on that sermon; about his noble style; about his commanding manner, and about the great lessons to be learned from every sermon of his. And then, when the Sabbath was over, and they were alone, Aquila and Priscilla would open their minds quite freely to one another about the young preacher. Now how would we have done had we been in Aquila's and Priscilla's place? This is what we would have done. We would have let the whole congregation see what we thought of Apollos. We would have shifted about in our seat. We would have looked at the clock. We would have held down our head. We would have covered our eyes with our hands. We would have glanced at our neighbours to see how they were taking it all. We would have smiled sadly, so that all might see us. And then, at the door—"How did you like him? Poor boy! he does not know the very A B C of the Gospel!" And so on, till it would all have been told to Apollos, and till we had ruined our influence with him, and his influence with us and with our children for ever. How Aquila and Priscilla managed it I cannot imagine. But manage it they did, for "they took Apollos unto them," says the sacred writer, "and expounded unto him the way of God more perfectly." "An old and simple woman, if she loves Jesus, may be greater than our brother Bonaventure."

I admire all the three so much, that I really do not know which to admire the most; Aquila and Priscilla in their quite extraordinary wisdom and tact and courage, and especially love; or Apollos in his still more extraordinary humility, modesty, and mind of Christ. A shining student of Alexandria, a popular and successful preacher, not standing-room when he preached in the synagogue, followed about by admiring crowds, and with many seals to his ministry among them; such a famous man to be taken to task about his pulpit work by two old workers in sail-cloth and carpets, and to be instructed by them how to preach, and how not to preach—"the whole thing is laughable, if it were not for its impudence." So I would have said had I been in Apollos's place. But like the true Alexandrian he was, and the true preacher, and the true coming colleague and successor of Paul, Apollos instantly saw who and what he had in Aquila and Priscilla. In a moment he felt they were by far his superiors in the things of the pulpit at any rate, and he at once made it both easy and successful for them to say to him all that was in their minds and hearts. I would far rather have Apollos's humble mind and quiet heart at that supreme moment of his life than all his gold medals, first-class certificates, and all his crowds to boot; the noble young Christian gentleman that Apollos at that moment proved himself to be.

It was their own experience of the way of God that enabled and authorised Aquila and Priscilla to take Apollos and teach him that way more perfectly. It was not Paul's preaching that did it. Their own experience, in their case, went before Paul's preaching, accompanied it, and came after it. They knew the doctrine of Christ perfectly because they had lived the life of Christ perfectly. Tent-makers as they were, and wholly unlettered as they were, they received it as soon as it was written, and read and quite well understood the Epistle to the Ephesians, because they had all its deep mysteries already in their own hearts. Paul in his best preaching had only told Aquila and Priscilla, with all his authority, what they knew to a certainty before. Every true preacher comes on the same thing continually among his people. And every wide reader of such literature knows where to find illustrations of the same thing. Brother Lawrence, the humble cook, instructing the theologians of his day about the practice of the presence of God; Jacob Behmen enlightening William Law; Thomas Boston's old soldier giving his minister a loan of "The Marrow"; and Cowper's poor Cottager. But the classical passage is in *Grace Abounding*. "Upon a day the good providence of God did cast me to Bedford to work on my calling; and in one of the streets of that town I came where there were three or four poor women sitting at a door in the sun, and talking about the things of God; and being now willing to hear their discourse, I drew near to hear what they said, for I was now a brisk talker myself in the matters of religion. But I may say, I heard, but I understood not; for they were far above, out of my reach. Their talk was about a new birth, the work of God in their hearts, also how they were convinced of their miserable state of nature. They talked how God had visited their souls with His love in the Lord Jesus, and with what words and promises they had been refreshed, comforted, and supported against the temptations of the devil. And, methought, they spoke as if joy did make them speak; they spoke with such pleasantness of Scripture language, and with such an appearance of grace in all they said, that they were to me, as if they had found a new world, as if they were people that dwelt alone, and were not to be reckoned among their neighbours. Therefore I should often make it my business to be going again and again into the company of these poor people, for I could not stay away. And presently I found two things within me at which I did sometimes marvel; the one was a very great softness and tenderness of heart; and the other was a great bending of my mind to a continual meditating on them, and on all other good things which at any time I had read or heard of." All that might have been found in the best Alexandrian Greek among Apollos's papers after his death. Better Greek he could not have written, nor a better description of his experiences as he came and went to Aquila's and Priscilla's house in Ephesus. "By these things," adds Bunyan, "my mind was now so turned that it lay like a horse-leech at the vein, still crying out, give, give."

They complain that there threatens to be a dearth of candidates for the Christian ministry. But that can never be. For where can the flower of our youth find a field for their scholarship and for their eloquence like the evangelical pulpit? What other calling open to a talented young man can compete with spiritual preaching? What other occupation can possess and satisfy a pure mind and a noble heart, and that more and more, to the end of life? Where will our intellectual youth find a literature for one moment to compare with the literature of Jerusalem and Alexandria? And a sphere of work like a congregation full of such people as Aquila and Priscilla? How long halt the flower of our Scottish youth between two opinions? If the Lord be God, follow Him. But if Baal, then follow him. Choose ye this day whom ye will serve. Will ye also go away? Lord, to whom shall we go? Thou hast the words of eternal life.

CXXIV

LOIS AND EUNICE

THIS Lois was a God-fearing woman herself, and a woman of a strong and an unfeigned faith. But with all that she made the tremendous mistake of giving her only daughter in marriage to a man who was still an absolute heathen. How such a good woman, how two such good women, could have fallen into this tremendous trap, we can only guess. But, then, we can guess; ay, and that only too well. For Eunice's lover, like so many of our own lovers, would begin to attend the synagogue-services for her sweet sake, till he was almost persuaded to become a proselyte of the gate for her sweet sake. And, but for some pagan and overpowering influences holding him back, under the transforming influences of Lois's noble character and Eunice's holy beauty he would surely have become all that Lois and Eunice prayed for so unceasingly that he might become before the marriage. But let Lois only give her consent; let Lois only give her dear daughter to him in marriage; and she will never have to repent putting her great trust in his hands. And the young Greek lover was not a false-hearted and a designing cheat in so saying. He really and honestly intended, after he was married, to live a godly husband's life. He said so, and Lois and Eunice believed him, and I believed him. We have all come through it ourselves. We have all had our own experiences of this self-deceivingness of a young man's heart. We have all ourselves seen and come through enough to convince us that Eunice's lover was entirely honest and honourable, as we ourselves were, when he said what he intended to be and to do as soon as he was a married man. Yes, we have all seen all that a thousand times, till we can sympathise, with all our heart, with all the three. That is to say, with the ardent and almost sanctified Greek lover, and with the two still-hesitating, but fast-yielding, Hebrew women. Till at last when she could hold out no longer, Lois gave her long-withheld consent to the mixed marriage. And in this way Eunice, a daughter of Abraham, became the married wife of this still heathen man; his wife, and in due time the mother of his uncircumcised sons. And he became her husband and her lord and the father of her children, still remaining all the time the same heathen man he had always been. And, alas! not only the same heathen man he had always been, but as time went on, and as his married life became a familiar possession and a disenchanted experience to him, he went further away from God and from family religion than ever he had been before. Nor did Peter's beautiful promise ever come true so as to mend matters in that so mixed and so unequally-yoked marriage. Peter's so beautiful promise to all good women when they waken up to see how they have sold themselves, and where they have landed themselves. "Likewise, ye wives, be in subjection to your own husbands, that if any obey not the Word, they also may without the Word, be won by the conversation of the wives, while they behold your chaste conversation coupled with fear." For some reason or other, that so apposite promise was never fulfilled to that so mismanaged marriage. Whether it was that Lois failed in her part as a mother-in-law, as she had so conspicuously failed as a mother; or whether it was that Eunice failed in fulfilling her part of the Apostle's promise; or whether it was owing to the pride and the obstinacy of the heathen heart of her husband; whatever was the cause, the father of Eunice's godly child never came to walk with a perfect heart before his house at home. He was never won, as at one time he so solemnly promised that he would be won, and at that warm-hearted time actually was almost won, to his believing wife's Holy Scriptures and to her God and Saviour.

Now nine women out of ten would simply have accepted Eunice's fate, and would gradually have sunk down to their husband's unbelieving level. But neither Lois nor Eunice were such weak women as that. Instead of that, and especially after the birth of little Timothy, the two God-fearing women set themselves all the more to a far more Scriptural, a far more prayerful, and a far more obedient, life than ever before. They did not cast up the days of their husband's love-making to his accusing conscience. Neither did they thrust their own repentance and remorse too much in his face. But neither did they hide out of his sight that divine faith and that domestic piety which had been the mainstay of their hearts before ever they had seen his face, and which was more than ever their only mainstay now that he had so fatally misled them. And the daily growth of the uncircumcised child only made the broken law of God against all such mixed marriages as theirs had been the more poignant to their broken hearts: as also, the same law of God as to the proper nature and admonition of such unhappy children as their child was. The confirmed, and now hopeless, heathenism of the child's father, and the everpresent remorse of their own hearts, only made both Lois and Eunice determine to work with all their might in order to make up somewhat to their innocent child for the great wrong they had all three done to him. And that the two sorely chastened women succeeded in all but completely compensating their spiritually fatherless child, we have Paul's own testimony to that, and a testimony that Timothy must all his days have read with tears and thanksgivings. "Thou Timothy from a child hast known the Holy Scriptures, and that because of the unfeigned faith that dwelt first in thy grandmother Lois, and then in thy mother Eunice, and I am persuaded in thee also." And thus it came about that Timothy, unhappy enough in his birth, and handicapped enough in starting on the race of life, was more than compensated for all that through the labours and the prayers of his mother and his grandmother, and through the beneficial operation of that noble New Testament law,—"He is not a Jew who is one outwardly: neither is that circumcision which is outward in the flesh. But he is a Jew who is one inwardly: and circumcision is that of the heart, in the spirit, and not in the letter: whose praise is not of man but of God."

That noble passage also in which the Apostle describes to Timothy his own upbringing is a classical passage to all Christian households. "But continue thou in the things which thou hast learned, and hast been assured of, knowing of whom thou hast learned them. And that from a child thou hast known the Holy Scriptures, which are able to make thee wise unto salvation, through faith which is in Christ Jesus. All Scripture is given by inspiration of God, and is profitable for doctrine, for reproof, for correction, for instruction in righteousness. That the man of God may be perfect, thoroughly furnished unto all good works." "Wise unto salvation." There is a whole volume of the inner history of that Greek-Hebrew household in those four verses, and in those three words that shine like an apple of gold in a picture of silver, at the heart of those four verses. The Greek father's bad conscience because he had never even tried to fulfil to those two over-trustful women what he had so often so solemnly promised them; his bad conscience would often exasperate his temper at them, and at the Scriptures they were always reading. He had his own Scriptures; and he was not wholly without excuse for exalting them as he did. Only, all his Greek and Roman Scriptures taken together could not give him peace of mind for the wrong he had done those two women. Nor could Lois and Eunice get the comfort and support they so sorely needed, out of any other Scriptures but the Psalms of David, and the promises of the Hebrew prophets. It was with Lois and Eunice's son as it was with the son of another self-deceived wife and mother long afterwards. The handwriting which was against us, which was contrary to us, is blotted out. This assurance the Platonic writings contain not. Plato's pages, with all their beauty, and all their wisdom, present not the image of this piety—Thy sacrifice, O Lord, is a broken heart. No man sings in Cicero or Plato—From Thee cometh my salvation. No one hears this call out of those books—Come unto Me all ye that labour." Not that it was young Timothy's time as yet to understand such deep and such spiritual Scriptures as these. But his time is coming when all Plato, and all Cicero, and all else, will no more satisfy his soul than they satisfied the soul of Monica's son. But that is still in the far and the unknown future. Timothy is still at that early stage of soul of which John Bunyan writes: "Wherefore falling into some love and liking for those things, I betook myself to my Bible, and began to take great pleasure in reading it; but especially with the historical part thereof. For, as for Paul's Epistles, and such like Scriptures, I could not away with them." Paul's Epistles were not written as yet in Timothy's youth, and he had no temptation to contemn them. But many were the delightful Sabbath hours that Lois his grandmother spent with Timothy her dawning grandson, over Bunyan's favourite Scriptures; over Abraham, and Isaac, and Jacob, and Joseph, and David, and Solomon. When, as he grew in wisdom, she would show him how all those great men of his mother's and his grandmother's Scriptures became wise unto salvation. As also, where they became foolish, and risked their salvation. Especially Solomon, who was in everything, except his salvation, the wisest of them all. Little did Lois dream as she went on with her pious occupation that she was thereby writing her name so impressively on the immortal pages of our New Testament. Little did she dream that we would actually be reading about her, and about her daughter Eunice, and about her grandson Timothy, in this far-off island of the sea. Little did that devout and chastened saint think that many of us in this congregation to-night would carry home lessons of salvation from her house to our own house at home. Great and marvellous are Thy works, Lord God Almighty: just and true are Thy ways, Thou King of Saints.

There is a piercing cry in this connection that often comes to my own heart out of one of Lois's Hebrew Psalms. And that heart-piercing and heart-uttering cry is this, "O, when wilt Thou come unto me? I will walk within my house with a perfect heart." I know the man who first uttered that cry to God. I see his house at home, as well as I see my own. And, more than that, I see him before he had a house. I see, and hear, and share in all his holy dreams, and high hopes, and solemn vows, and in all his protestations and resolutions. I made them all myself, and far more. But no sooner did that Hebrew bridegroom get the desire of his heart than he soon became a still worse husband than Eunice's Greek husband, and a still worse father than Timothy's father. And now so beset is he behind and before with his badly performed part as a husband and a father, that, O wretched man that he is, he is every day doing and saying things he ought not to do and say; doing and saying things that drive him to downright despair. No reformation prospers that he attempts. Everything seems to be bent against him in his life at home. And nowhere else so much as in his life at home. Till we come on this heart-breaking cry of his in our hundred-and-first psalm. Just as Eunice's husband and Timothy's father would have cried all his days, had he begun to look at himself as a husband and as a father in the glass of his wife's Holy Scriptures. For those Scriptures, while holy in everything, are in nothing more holy than just in the incessant and the inexorable demands they make on every husband, and father, and master, who reads them. How hard it is, but how heavenly good it is, to look continually at ourselves as householders in this glass of God that stands at this moment shining before us and searching us! How wise unto salvation it will yet make both ourselves and our households, if we will lay up in our hearts and practise in our lives the lessons even of this one Scripture we have had from the God of families to-night. And this great good will begin to-night with those of us who are honestly asking ourselves before God, just what things they are, naming them, in which we have so sorely disappointed those who once so trusted us. Just in what things, and naming them, we have come so shamefully short of our marriage-vows, and of our honest, and at one time, warm-hearted, intentions. To accustom ourselves to make such an inquisition as that, will do this at any rate—it will teach us humility at home, and that is the beginning of all true reformation there. It will teach us patience also, which is so much needed at home. And it will give us a sore heart all our days for those whose unhappy lot it is to live all the rest of their days under our roof, and to have us for all the husband, and all the father, they are ever to have in this world.

And O you who are still full of promises, and vows, and fond intentions! You who cannot listen to God's severe truth to-night with patience, you are so full of ardent dreams about what a house of love, and honour, and religion, your house is to be! Begin, I beseech you, to-night, to make yourself what you are one day to make your happy house. It is far easier, believe me, to begin all these good things before your marriage than after it. I can tell you that; nobody better. But if you will not believe me, believe Lois and Eunice. For they are come here to-night to warn you against a mixed marriage like theirs. Be ye not unequally yoked! Both the grandmother and the mother are come here to-night to plead with you, with all their experience, and with all their authority.

But whatever other men and women, young and old, may do, this is what I, the present preacher, will do even if I do it alone—,I will sing of mercy and judgment. Unto Thee, O Lord, will I sing. I will behave myself wisely in a perfect way. O when wilt Thou come unto me? I will walk within my house with a perfect heart. I will often return to the days of my youth. I will often return to the days of my warmth of heart, and of my many prayers in this matter, and my many vows. I will tell to my own heart all the steps in which Thou hast led me up to this present time. I will say, As for me and my house, we will henceforth serve the Lord. And one thing will I do; I will keep my heart well broken before Thee, and before my house all my days. I will clothe myself with humility as I go in and out before my house. I will put a bridle in my mouth. I will keep the door of my lips. I will not provoke my children to anger. I will reprehend them in private, and praise them in public. I will look on all their faults as what they have inherited from their father; and on all that is good in them as having come to them from their mother, and from their Father in heaven. The sins of my children shall always be their father's sorest chastisement at the hand of God, and their gifts and their graces shall always be his highest ornament and his greatest renown. O when wilt Thou come unto me?

CXXV

TIMOTHY AS A CHILD

It was something like this. It was something not unlike one of our own Scottish households where the father is not a church member, and where the minister is so strict that he will not baptize the child to the mother. In which case the grandmother and the mother would say to one another—'Very well. At any rate we shall all the more see to it that if our child wants the outward ceremony he shall have that want more than made up to him in the inward substance. What he has not received in the mere sprinkling with water, he shall, if we can help it, have it more than made up to him by the Holy Spirit. For we shall give God no rest till he has had far more mercy on our innocent child than our cruel-hearted minister has had.' And it was so. Till the very heathenism of Timothy's father was far better for his uncircumcised child than if that Greek father had been such a Christian father as the most of our fathers are. For just because of the father's unbelief, the faith of the grandmother and the mother became all the more unfeigned, and prayful, and importunate. The blot they had all three had such a hand in bringing upon their innocent child, lay so heavy on the heart of his mother and his grandmother that they could take no rest till they had seen that blot more than removed by the washing of regeneration, and the renewing of the Holy Ghost.

With such an unfeigned faith as that the two lonely women set themselves to bring up their little fatherless son in the nurture and admonition of the Lord. And they succeeded, if ever unfeigned women succeeded. And such unfeigned women as they were have always succeeded, and will always succeed, till the last of such women shall be called up to get her full wages from God. Such women, such mothers in Israel, as Hannah, and Elizabeth, and Mary, and Monica, and Halyburton's mother, and Wesley's mother, and the mother of Jonathan Edwards's children, and the mother of Thomas Boston's children, and many more. And in all those mothers it was their unfeigned faith that did it. Their unfeigned faith laid hold, first on God, and then on their children. For, not to speak of God, this kind of faith, and this kind of faith alone, takes hold of a child's heart. You cannot feign faith before your children. Even while they are still children they will find you out to their great pain and shame on account of their feigning mother. You may go on feigning faith with some success before every one else, but not before your children. You must walk with an unfeigned faith, and with a perfect heart at home, if you have such a child's eyes set on you as were set on both Lois and Eunice. Whatever the husband and the fathers in our households may do let all wives and mothers live a life like the lives of Lois and Eunice, and they will have their reward. At this point, and in a spare moment, I was led to take down an old favourite of mine who has always something pertinent to say on this matter now in hand. "Before all things, let the talk of the child's nurse not be ungrammatical." He is discussing the best education for an orator. "Chrysippus wished that every such nurse should be, if possible, a woman of some liberality of education. For it is his nurse the future orator first hears speaking, and it is her words and her accents he will first imitate. We are by nature tenacious of what we have imbibed in our infant years, just as the flavour with which we scent our casks when they are new, remains in them to the end." With a few changes and substitutions you have Lois and Eunice in Quintilian's First Book, and their early education of a future apostle.

It is not for nothing, you may depend upon it, that Paul gives Lois and Eunice such a first-class certificate for their first-rate methods, and for their signal success in teaching Timothy to read, and so far to understand, the Holy Scriptures. Paul always, and to everybody, both spoke and wrote like the true gentleman he was. But these are not so many mere courtesies and compliments that the aged Apostle pays to these two Bible-teaching women. There is a studied descriptiveness, as well as all his own warmth of heart, in what Paul here says to Timothy about the wise and painstaking methods that Lois and Eunice took with him over Holy Scripture. It is of his early readings of Holy Scripture at home that Paul reminds Timothy when he exhorts him to divide the word of truth rightly, both in his own family, and in his catechumen's classes, and in his expository pulpit. I see Lois putting on her spectacles an hour before she summons in Timothy from the playground. I watch her as she selects with such care the proper passage she is going to read with him. I admire her as she reads and re-reads the passage to herself, in order to make sure that she understands it herself. After which she prepares, and tries them over on her own knees, two or three petitions proper for the child to repeat after her, and to which he is to say his intelligent and hearty Amen. There is much that is full of rebuke and instruction to us all in the manse of Ettrick. But there is nothing more full of rebuke and instruction to us than the way that Thomas Boston prepared himself for family worship before he rang the bell. And as a consequence and a reward he records it again and again in his grateful diary, how, after such preparation he often got light, and comfort, and strength, and guidance for himself, as well as for his family, out of "the exercise." 'Remember the wise methods of Lois and Eunice,' said Paul to Timothy, 'when you are at your own family worship at home, as well as when you are at the head of a congregation.'

But with all these most excellent preparations for it, the great change had still to come to Timothy. "Towardly child as Timothy was," says Thomas Goodwin, "he was all the time unconverted." Timothy was kept for Paul to finish the work that Lois and Eunice had so well begun. There is a great instruction here, and a great comfort. A very great comfort. For there are a great many young men among ourselves exactly like Timothy. Like Timothy they are richly talented, well educated, religiously educated, and every way well brought up, young men. Like Timothy also they have received all that two generations of mothers of an unfeigned faith can do for them. And yet all the time they have not themselves taken the great step. And this goes on till one day their day of grace at last comes to them, as Timothy's day of grace came to him. A new minister stands in the pulpit; a skilful and urgent evangelist like Moody, or Drummond, or Kelman, or M'Neil, or George Clarke, or Mackay, visits the city and specially addresses such young men; or they are led to read the right book at the right moment; or some special and personal dispensation of Divine Providence is sent to them. Till, in a day, in an hour, in a moment, the fine fruit that has for so long been slowly ripening falls at a touch into the husbandman's basket. Paul comes round and preaches one day at Lystra, and Timothy is converted on the spot. Keep up your hearts, Lois and Eunice. Keep up your hearts. Though it tarry, wait for it; because it will surely come, it will not tarry. Behold, the husbandman waiteth for the precious fruit of the earth, and hath long patience for it, until he receive the early and the latter rain. Be ye also patient; stablish your hearts; for the coming of the Lord draweth nigh.

At the same time, while I rejoice with Paul that he had Timothy for his spiritual son, I cannot but feel tenderly for Lois and Eunice in this matter. I feel for Eunice especially, that she was not blessed of God to bear her son in his second birth as well as in his first birth. Speaking for myself, I would value above all else that God can give me in this world to see all my children truly converted like Timothy. And I would rejoice to receive their conversion through any instrumentality that it pleases God to employ. A new minister; a passing-by evangelist; a good book; a dispensation of family or personal providence; or what not. But O! if it pleases God let me have all my children's souls myself! Let them all say in after days—"it was my father that did it." That would make my cup to run over indeed. And I will not despair of it. Why should I for one moment doubt of it? For He is a God that delighteth to make a man's cup to run over, in that way and in every other way. At the same time, while I most feelingly sympathise with Lois and Eunice in their loss of Timothy's soul to Paul, I have a creeping doubt in my conscience that, with all their excellent Bible-reading with him, they cannot have dealt closely enough with Timothy's very mind and heart about himself. "The Holy Scriptures, which are able to make these wise unto salvation," is the Apostle's deep, and, as I think, significantly situated, expression. I do not altogether know why it is, but I cannot get this question put to sleep in my conscience; this question: Did Lois and Eunice, after all, do all they ought to have done, to make Timothy wise unto salvation? Did they do all they ought to have done to bring home his own salvation to the very conscience and mind and heart and imagination of their little charge? I admit much, as I must, about Lois and Eunice in their training of Timothy. But, somehow, their not getting the full seal of God set on their training of Timothy, makes me doubt if, after all, they had made their training of Timothy ready for such a seal, "Wise unto *salvation*." Now, tell me, did Eunice, do you think, take her son Timothy, and show him till she made it plain to him, what it would be for her and for him to be saved, and what it would be for her and for him to be lost? And did she do that with all her tenderness and with all her lovingness? Did she see it herself, and did she show it to him, how the very tones of his little voice sometimes up and down the house, and how his little looks and actions, were the very things that salvation had been sent for? Did she show him how the holy name "Jesus" came home to their house, and spake of salvation to old and young within its walls? I may be quite wrong, and I may be doing both Lois and Eunice a great injustice in all this. But I am not without some compunction that they would have had Timothy's full salvation for their own wages if they had made it completely and convincingly clear to the thoughtful child, just what wisdom unto salvation would be in their case and in his case. At any rate, even if I am quite wrong in my reading of their case, it matters nothing to them now. Only, this disconcerting reading of their case may be blessed to make some of ourselves look somewhat more closely and conscientiously at our own case at home than we have ever yet looked at it. That is to say, are we at once clear-headed enough, and plain-spoken enough, and attracting and winning enough, with our children? Leave no suspicion, leave no doubt, in that direction undealt with, my brethren. Leave no stone unturned in seeking the salvation of your children. Go to the very root of the matter with them. Go to the very root of the word with them. Make thoroughly to understand both the word, and the thing, salvation. Make them to see it. Make them to feel it. Make them to admit, and to confess to you, that you have made them both see it and feel it. To see and to feel what it would be to be lost; and what it would be to be saved. And then when you have done that to the best of your ability, and with much prayer both with them and for them, there will be the less likelihood that some passer-by like Paul will come and carry off with him what would be the sweetest jewel in all your heavenly crown. Come, my brethren, and let us be so wise unto our own salvation, and unto the salvation of our children, that we shall be able to say to our God on that day—Here am I, and all the children Thou didst give me!

CXXVI

TIMOTHY AS A YOUNG MINISTER

We are come to-night to Timothy as a young minister. And though you are not ministers yourselves it cannot but interest you to be told how such ministers as Paul and Timothy and their true successors are made; how they make themselves; and how that self-making of theirs goes on all the time they live and labour among you.

"Till I come, give attendance to reading." This is one of Paul's outstanding exhortations to Timothy. Now if these words were addressed by an experienced minister to a new beginner in our day, something like this would be universally understood 'Attend to your studies. Be always at your studies. Grudge every moment that is stolen from your studies. Never sit down without a book and a pen in your hand. And let it never be an ephemeral, or an impertinent, or an unproductive, book. You have not the time. You have not the money. Read nothing that is not the very best of its kind. Neither in religion, nor in letters, nor in anything else. Be like John Milton in his noble youth, be both select and industrious in your reading.'

But there is another interpretation of these words, and that on high authority too. "Reading," in Timothy's day—so the text is sometimes interpreted,—would mean to him very much what is nowadays called expository preaching or "lecturing," as we say in Scotland. Timothy is here exhorted to read Nehemiah's autobiography and then to imitate that great reformer and his great colleagues in their exegetic and homiletic way of dealing with the law of God. The preachers of Nehemiah's day, so he tells us in his Memoirs of himself, stood upon a pulpit of wood, and read the law of God distinctly, and gave the sense, and caused the people to understand the reading. And this, many eminent exegetes assure us, is the "reading" to which Timothy is here commanded to attend. Whether that is the true interpretation of this text or no, as a matter of fact Nehemiah's method of handling Holy Scripture has been followed by all his successors in the pulpit, both in Bible times and in Church-history times. To begin with, Nehemiah's method was our Lord's method also as often as the Book was delivered to Him by the minister in the synagogue on the Sabbath day. And from the Acts we learn that this was the universal method of the Apostles also. Both the Greek and the Latin fathers followed this same Scripture method; expository lectures of Chrysostom and Augustine are extant to us to this day. Calvin also stood upon his pulpit of wood, and read the Word of God distinctly, and caused the people of Geneva to understand the reading. Just as he still causes us to understand the reading as often as we consult his incomparable commentaries. And that same labour-loving and labour-rewarding method of pulpit work made the Puritans in England and the Presbyterians in Scotland the two greatest schools of preachers and people the Church of Christ has ever seen. At the same time, and while I wholly accept that official interpretation, so to call it, my heart leans to the more personal application of Chrysostom and Calvin. Those two very foremost authorities here understand Paul to counsel Timothy not so much concerning his pulpit work, as concerning his own private and personal and devotional attention to the Word of God. Calvin, above all men, had ears to hear. And that master in Israel overhears Paul saying to Timothy something like this: 'Read distinctly, and exhort convincingly, in your pulpit. But above and before all else, let the Word of God dwell richly in yourself. Even after you have known the Holy Scriptures from a child, still continue to call them constantly to mind by your systematic and assiduous reading and meditation. And by so doing thou shalt both save thyself, and them that hear thee.' "What I owe to these two Epistles to Timothy," confesses Calvin, "can never be told."

"Rightly dividing the word of truth"; this is another of Paul's master-strokes in these masterly Epistles. And that master-stroke of the Apostle serves to set forth another of the many advantages of the consecutive and comprehensive exposition of Holy Scripture. In true expository preaching the right dividing of the whole word of truth is largely left to the Spirit of truth Himself. On no other method is it possible for any preacher to divide aright the whole consecutive and cumulative body of doctrines and duties, as well as of privileges and comforts, contained in the Holy Scriptures. There are multitudes of doctrines, and reproofs, and corrections, and instructions in righteousness, that the minister who preaches from detached and unconnected texts will never be able to divide out to his people. And even when such a preacher does come upon some of those instructions and corrections that his people need, his inconsequent method of preaching will be sure to tempt certain of his hearers to set down his words less to the wonderful perfection, and particularness, and individualisingness, of Holy Scripture than to some idiosyncrasy of the preacher; or, it may be, to some personal animus of his. The preposterous charge of a personal intention and animus will not always be avoided by the best methods of pulpit-work; but the preaching that consecutively overtakes all the perfection and point of the Word of God will best meet and silence that vanity of mind, and that rebellion of heart, among our hearers. Every humble-minded hearer must often have felt and confessed the divine power with which some reproof came home to him, when it suddenly and unexpectedly leapt out upon him from the depths of some hitherto overlooked and unexpected passage of the manifold Word of God.

Another way of rightly dividing the whole word of truth is most excellently set forth by Jeremy Taylor in one of his golden charges to his clergy: "Do not spend your sermons on general and undefined things. Do not spend your time and strength on exhortations to your people to get Christ, to be united to Christ, and things of a like unlimited and indefinite signification. But rightly divide the whole doctrine of Christ. Tell your people in every duty what are the instruments, and what are the particulars and minute bearings, of every general advice. For, generals not explicated, do but fill the people's heads with empty notions, and their mouths with perpetual unintelligible talk, while their hearts remain empty and themselves unedified." Yes; O wise-hearted and golden-mouthed overseer. But we would need all thy oceanic reading, and all thy capacious intellect, and all thy splendid eloquence, and all thy unceasing prayerfulness, in order to come within sight of thy great counsels. And, my brethren, with the very best of methods, how much is still left to the individual minister himself to do. What ability, what study, what courage, what wisdom, what love, is needed rightly to divide the word of truth, Sabbath after Sabbath, to all the ages, and to all the understandings, and to all the circumstances, and to all the experiences, of a listening congregation. What a sleepless, what a many-sided, what an all-talented, what an all-experienced race of men the preachers of the Word of God would need to be!

And then if the Apostle says it once, he says it fifty times: 'Shun controversy, like the bottomless pit, in the pulpit.' Richard Baxter will surely be listened to on this subject. "Another fatal hindrance to a heavenly walk and conversation is our too frequent disputes about lesser truths. A disputatious spirit is a sure sign of an unsanctified spirit. They are usually men least acquainted with the heavenly life who are the most violent disputers about the circumstantials of religion. Yea, though you were sure that your opinions were true, yet when the chiefest of your zeal is turned to these things, the life of grace soon decays within. Let every sure truth even have but its due proportion, and I am confident that the hundredth part of our time and contention would not be spent as it is spent. I could wish you were all men of understanding and ability to defend every truth of God; but still I would have the chiefest truth to be chiefly studied, and no truth to shoulder out the thought of eternity. The least controverted points are usually the most weighty, and of most necessary and frequent use to our souls."

But as we work our way through these trenchant and pungent Epistles, what can the Apostle possibly mean by commanding a young minister of such infirm health as Timothy was to work for his pulpit and in his pastoral duties "in season and out of season"? And so commanding him, under the most tremendous imprecations; till we begin to suspect that it was not so much Timothy's bad health, as something far worse, that Paul had in his eye all the time. Was it not because one of the besetting sins of the ministerial calling was already setting in upon the very Apostolic Church itself? It would almost seem so. "We seek apologies for our slothfulness," says one of the most unslothful of ministers. Be that as it may; let all ministers, both those who are slothfully inclined, and those who are really infirm in health, and all young ministers especially, give attendance to reading the autobiographies of two of the most infirm, but at the same time two of the most resolutely unslothful, of all our Puritan and Presbyterian ministers: The *Reliquiæ Baxterianæ,* and Thomas Boston's *Memoirs of himself,* the latter edited by a young minister of our own who is neither slothful nor infirm.

With all his ailments, and whatever they were, Timothy never touched wine, either for stimulus or for strength. Just what it was that had made Timothy such a stern total abstainer we are not told. Whether it was the self-denying example of some of the great saints of his mother's Scriptures, or the awful falls of some others of those saints, we are not told. Only, we find the aged Apostle interposing and recommending Timothy to relax his rule somewhat and to take a little wine now and then. Now I would not interfere if any old minister, or any able and devout doctor, were to say to some young minister of my acquaintance what Paul here says to Timothy about his health and his inability for his work unless he begins to take wine. But for my part, and in our day, I would make sure that any infirm young friend of mine had tried some other expedients before he betook himself to this last expedient of all. I would do my very best to make sure that he kept early and regular hours both night and morning. And if I could get the ear of his session I would plead with them to see that their young minister took a Sabbath off every five or six Sabbaths. As also that he got a generous holiday once every summer. But above all that I would charge himself before God not to leave off his Sabbath preparation till the Saturday night. For I have seen far more woe worked in the manse and in the congregation by that last evil habit than I have seen worked even by strong drink. A real love for our books, and a real love for our pulpits, and a real love for our people, all that is far better for us ministers, and for our infirm health, than the very best of wines.

"Let no man despise thy youth; but be thou an example in thy conversation." Pascal has made "the disproportion of man" a proverb in our highest literature. And Richard Baxter has made the same word a barbed arrow in the consciences of all his ministerial readers. "The disproportion," that is, between our office and our walk and conversation in our office. I suppose there is not a minister on the face of the earth who does not gnash his teeth at himself continually as he returns home again from a conversation in which he has displayed such a disproportion to his office, and has taken such a scandal-causing part. Our young ministers may neither have Taylor, nor Baxter, nor Boston, nor any such master of ministerial deportment; but, as Behmen says, they have themselves. And if they begin early to examine themselves in this matter, and to improve upon themselves every time they cross their own doorstep, they will soon, and without books, become themselves as great examples and as great authorities as any ministerial-deportment author of them all. Let no man despise the youth and far less the age of any minister because of his disproportionate character and his disedifying conversation.

And, "take heed unto thyself," is just all that over again in other words. Take heed to thy doctrine indeed, but, first and last, take most heed to thyself. Fix thy very best and thy very closest attention on thyself. This is thy main duty as a pastor. Do not set thyself forward as a pattern to thy people. Only, make thyself a perfect pattern to them. For that minister who constantly and increasingly takes heed to himself in his walk and conversation; in preaching better and better every returning

Sabbath; in discharging all the endless duties of his pastorate in season and out of season; in holding his peace in controversy; and in a life of secret faith and secret prayer; God Himself will see to it that such an apostolic minister will be imitated and celebrated both as a pattern minister and a pattern man; both before his people, and before all his fellow-ministers. All that, by the grace of God, may be attained by any minister who sets himself to attain it, even though his book-press is as poorly furnished as Thomas Boston's book-press was so poorly furnished. At the same time, you well-to-do people, whose Christmas and New Year presses are so full of the best books, and the best of everything else, you should at this season go over all the young ministers and all the poor ministers you know, and should see to it that, with the Pastoral Epistles, they have also the best commentary, for a Scottish minister at any rate, that was ever written on those Epistles; better even than Chrysostom or Calvin; I mean Thomas Boston's *Memoirs* of himself as a parish minister. That golden book for Scottish ministers is full of things like this: "The untender carriage of some ministers in Nithsdale was very wounding to me. As also meeting with a neighbouring minister his foolish talking afforded me heavy reflections on the unedifying conversation of ministers, and my own among others, as one great cause of the unsuccess of the Gospel in our hands."

Well might Timothy, and well may every living minister to-day, lay down these two terrible Epistles, and say over them—Who is sufficient for these things? For no mere man is sufficient for such high things as these. No mortal man is sufficient for such a holy ministry as that. But then no mere mortal man is expected to be sufficient. You must not go away and suppose that the arch-Apostle himself was sufficient for the half of the charges he laid, almost with a curse, on Timothy. Paul, you may be sure, threw down his pen again and again in the composition of these two pastoral Epistles, and betook himself to his knees and to the blood of Christ before he could finish what he had begun to write. And these two Epistles, so full of matter for ministerial remorse, are to this day put into our hands, not to drive us to despair and self-destruction, but rather to summon us out of our beds every returning Monday morning to give better and ever better attendance to our reading of the best books, and to our writing in connection with them. To our sick-visiting in the afternoon, and to our whole walk and conversation all the day, and all the week, and every week, till a Greater than Paul comes. And, more than that, these pastoral Epistles are not written to us who are your ministers only. But all you people are to read these Epistles and are to ponder them and pray over them continually, in order that you may have it always before you at what a cost a true minister of the New Testament is made. As also to teach you to value aright such a minister when he is intrusted to you, till he shall finish his ministry among you, both by saving himself and those among you who have ears to hear him.

Sixth Series

OUR LORD'S CHARACTERS

I

THE SOWER WHO WENT FORTH TO SOW

NOT only in Jerusalem, and at the passover, but in Nazareth, and on days of release from labour, we may well believe that something like this would sometimes take place. "Son, why hast thou thus dealt with us? Behold, thy father and I sought Thee sorrowing." But He would answer to His mother,—"How is it that ye sought Me? Wist ye not that I must be about My Father's business?" So would His mother say to Him, and so would He answer her, as often as she sought for Him among their kinsfolk and acquaintance; while, all the time, He was out in the fields; now with the ploughman, and now with the sower, and now with the reaper, and now with the husbandman who had his fan in his hand with which he was thoroughly purging his floor. And as He walked and talked with the ploughman, and with the sower, and with the reaper, the Spirit of all truth would descend into His heart and would say to Him that all that husbandry He had been observing so closely was in all its processes and operations, not unlike the Kingdom of Heaven in all its processes, and in all its operations, and in all its experiences. Till, as He walked about and meditated, He would draw out to Himself the manifold likenesses between nature and grace; between the husbandry of the farm and the husbandry of the pulpit; when He would lay up all His meditations in His mind and in His heart, till we see and hear it all coming out of His mind and out of His heart in the teaching and the preaching of the text.

And, accordingly, nothing is more likely than that He had led His disciples to the sea-side that day along a way that was well known to Him. A way He had often walked as He went to watch the operations of the husbandman to whom that field belonged. And it being now the seed-time of the year, as the sower that day sowed, some of the seed fell under the feet of the twelve disciples, while flocks of hungry birds swooped down and devoured whole basketfuls of the sower's best sowing. And thus it was that no sooner had our Lord sat down by the sea-side than He forthwith pointed His disciples back to the field they had just passed through. And not only did He recall to their thoughts what they themselves had just seen, but He told them also all that He Himself had seen going on in that same field, year in and year out, for many spring days and many harvest days, when His mother could not make out where He was, or what He was doing. But all those observations and meditations of His now bore their hundredfold fruit in this great sermon so full of all kinds of instruction and illustration, and all taken from the field they had just left behind them. And then, at the petition of His disciples, our Lord expounded His homely riddle about the sower and his seed, till we have both that riddle and its exposition in our hands to-night in this far-off island of the sea.

"The seed is the Word of God," says our Lord. That is to say every true preacher sows the Word of God with both his hands, and he sows nothing else but the Word of God. The true preacher must put nothing else into his seed-basket every Sabbath morning, but the pure and unadulterated Word of God. The Christian pulpit is not set up for any service but one: and that one and sovereign service is the sowing of the seed of God in the minds and in the hearts and in the lives of men. The platform and the press are set up in God's providence for the sowing broadcast of His mind and will also: but the evangelical pulpit has an exclusiveness and a sanctification about it altogether peculiar to itself. Six days shalt thou read and write history, and biography, and philosophy, and poetry, and newspapers, and novels, but this is the Day the Lord has made. And He has made this Day, and has specially sanctified and hedged round this Day, for the sowing of that intellectual and spiritual seed which springs up, and which alone springs up, to everlasting life.

"And as he sowed, some seeds fell by the wayside. This is he that heareth the Word of the Kingdom, and understandeth it not." Our Lord was a man of understanding Himself, and He laboured continually to make His disciples to be men of understanding like Himself. And all His ministers, to this day, who are to be of any real and abiding benefit to their people, must labour first to make themselves men of understanding, and then to make their people the same. And if the people are void of understanding their ministers are largely to blame for that. There are people, indeed, in every congregation that our Lord Himself could not make men of understanding: at the same time, it is the ministers who are mostly at fault if their people remain stupid in their intellects and dark in their hearts. "Understandest thou what thou readest?' said Philip the once deacon, and now the evangelist, to the dark treasurer of Queen Candace. "How can I?" answered that wise man from the East. And Philip went up into the chariot and sowed the seed of the Kingdom of Heaven in the understanding and in the heart of that black but comely convert to the cross of Christ. And the first duty of every minister is to make his pulpit like that chariot of Ethiopia. The first duty of every occupant of a pulpit is to sow the Word of God and the Word of God only, and his second duty is to see that the people understand what they read and hear. "And Ezra the scribe stood upon a pulpit of wood, which they had made for the purpose. And Ezra opened the book in the sight of the people: for he was above the people: and when he opened it all the people stood up. And he read in the book in the law of God distinctly, and gave the sense, and caused the people to understand the reading,"—till his reading was so distinct, and so full of understanding, that it brought forth fruit in some of his hearers an hundredfold. One of the last things that Sir Thomas Grainger Stewart said to me on his death-bed was this: —"Sometimes make them understand the psalm before you invite them to sing it, for we have often sung it in my time not knowing what it meant." It was a wise counsel and given in a solemn hour. But, then, there is no pulpit duty more difficult than just to say the right word of understanding at the right moment, and not a word too much or too little. Dr. Davidson of Aberdeen was the best at that one single word of explanation and direction of any minister I ever sat under. He said just one weighty word, in his own weighty way, and then we all sang in the West Church, as Paul made them sing in the Corinthian Church, with the understanding, and with the spirit also.

"And understandeth it not. Then cometh the wicked one and catcheth away the seed that has just been sown." There is a house I am sometimes in at the hour of family worship. In that house, after the psalm and the scripture and the prayer, the head of the house remains on his knees for, say, five or six seconds after he utters the Amen. And then he rises off his knees, slowly and reverently, as if he were still in the King's presence, with his eyes and his whole appearance full of holy fear and holy love. And I notice that all his children have learned to do like their father. And I have repeatedly heard his guests remark on that reverential habit of his, and I have heard them confess that they went home rebuked, as I have often gone home rebuked and instructed myself. There is another house I am in sometimes, which is the very opposite of that. They have family worship also, but before he has said Amen the head of the house is up off his knees and has begun to give his orders about this and that to his servants. He has been meditating the order, evidently, all the time of the prayer. It must have been in such a house or in such a synagogue as that in which our Lord saw the wicked one coming and catching away the seed that was sown in the worshippers' hearts. I think I have told you before about a Sabbath night I once spent long ago in a farm-house up among the Grampians. Before family worship the old farmer had been reading to me out of a book of notes he had taken of Dr. John Duncan's sermons when they were both young men. After worship I got up and spoke first and said—"Let us have some more of those delightful notes." "Excuse me," said my friend, "but we all take our candles immediately after worship." The wicked one was prevented and outwitted every night in that house, and he has been prevented and outwitted in the houses of all the children who were brought up in that rare old farm-house up among the Grampians.

And, then, the stony places is he that heareth the word with joy, yet hath no root in himself. I do not know any congregation, anywhere, that hears the Word of God with such joy as this congregation. As for instance. All last summer, every Monday, I got letters full of joy over the preaching that had been provided in this pulpit. And then when I came home, in every house and on every street I was met with salutations of joy over Dr. George Adam Smith's last sermon. The Professor's text was this,—"Lord, teach us to pray." Now, that is three weeks ago, and the seed has had plenty of time to take root. And I am sent here to-night to ask you whether that so joyful hearing that Sabbath night has come, in your case, to any fruit. Have you prayed more these last three weeks? Have you been oftener, and longer at a time, on your knees? Have you been like Halyburton's mother—have you prayed more, both with and for your son, these three weeks? I did not hear the sermon, and I could not get anybody to tell me very much about it, beyond—O the eloquence and the delight of it! But some of you heard it, and God's demand of you to-night is,—with what result on your heart, on your temper, on your walk and conversation, on your character? Or, is it written in heaven about you since that Sabbath night,—'This is he who hears sermons with such applause, but has never had any root in himself. This is he who thinks that sermons are provided by God and man for him to praise or blame as suits his fancy.' And, then, to keep His ministers from being puffed up with such idle praise as yours,

God says to them—"Thou son of man, the children of thy people are still talking of thee by the walls and in the doors of their houses. And they come to hear thy words, but they will not do them. Lo, thou art unto them as one that has a pleasant voice, and can play well on an instrument. For they hear thy words, and show much love, but they do them not. But the day will come when they shall give an account of all that they have heard, and then shall they know that a prophet of mine has been among them."

And then he that receiveth the seed among thorns is he in whom the Word of God is simply choked, till he becometh unfruitful. There is only so much room and sap and strength in any field; and unless the ground is cleared of all other things, the sap and the strength that should go to grow the corn will be all drunk up by thorns and briars. You understand, my brethren? You have only so much time, and strength, and mind, and heart, and feeling, and passion, and emotion, and if you expend all these, or the greater part of all these, on other things, you will have all that the less corn, even if you have any corn at all. The thorns in the fields of your hearts are such things as contentions, and controversies, and debates, and quarrels. All these are so many beds of thorns that not only starve your soul, but tear it to pieces as you wade about among them. And not thorns only, but even good things in their own places, if they are allowed in your corn-field, they will leave you little bread for yourself and for your children, and little seed corn for next spring. Rose-bushes even, and gooseberry-bushes, beds of all sweet-tasting, and sweet-smelling herbs, are all in their own place in your garden; but you must have corn in your field. Corn is the staff of your life. And after corn, then flowers and fruits; but not before. After your soul is well on the way to salvation, then other things; but salvation first. Lest the cares of this world, and the deceitfulness of riches, and the lust of other things, entering in, choke your soul, till it is starved and lost: your soul and you.

We are indebted to Luke for many things that we would not have had but for his peculiar care, and industry, and exactness, as a sacred writer. And he reports to us one otherwise unreported word of our Lord's about the good ground that has its own lessons for us all to-night. "That on the good ground are they, which is an honest and good heart, having heard the Word, keep it, and bring forth fruit with patience." An honest heart. Now, there are honest, and there are dishonest, hearts in every congregation. The honest heart is the heart of the hearer who has come up here to-night with a right intention. His motive in being here is an honest motive. This is God's house, and that honest hearer has come to hear what God will say to him to-night. His eye is single, and this whole house has been full of light to him to-night. Already, to-night, he has heard words that he intends to keep to-morrow: to lay them up in his heart and to practise them in his life. He is an honest man, and God will deal honestly by him. But there are others, it is to be feared, in every congregation. They were in our Lord's congregations, and they are in ours. Hearers of the Word, with hearts that are not honest. They are in God's house, but they are not here to meet with God, or to understand, and lay up, and keep, His Word. They are here to see and to be seen. They are here to meet with some one who is to be met with here. They love music, and they are here because the music is good. Or they have some still more material motive; their office or their shop brings them here. Now, when God's Spirit says, Thou art the man! Admit it. Confess it where you sit. Receive this word into a good and honest heart, and say, Surely the Lord is in this place; and I knew it not. Say, this is none other but the house of God, and this is the gate of heaven. Say that God has been found of one man, at any rate, who did not come here to-night to seek Him. And come up here henceforth with that same good and honest heart that you have created within you to-night, and you also will yet live to bring forth fruit thirtyfold, perhaps sixtyfold, and even an hundredfold.

II

THE MAN WHICH SOWED GOOD SEED IN HIS FIELD, BUT HIS ENEMY CAME AND SOWED TARES AMONG THE WHEAT

THE Son of Man lived in obscurity in Nazareth till He began to be about thirty years of age, growing in wisdom every day, and every day saying to Himself—

> —What if Earth
> Be but the shadow of Heaven, and things therein
> Each to other like more than on Earth is thought?

And one day in His solitary and meditating walks He came on a field in which blades of tares were springing up among the blades of wheat all over the field. When, meeting the husbandman, He said to him, "From whence hath thy field these tares?" "An enemy hath done it," said the heart-broken husbandman. "While men slept, mine enemy came and sowed tares among the wheat, and went his way." It was a most diabolical act. Diabolical malice, and dastardly cowardice, taken together, could have done no more. That enemy envied with all his wicked heart the husbandman's well-ploughed, well-weeded, well-sowed, and well-harvested, field, till he said within himself, Surely the darkness shall cover me. And when the night fell he filled his seed-basket, and went out under cover of night and sowed the whole field over with his diabolical seed. And when our Lord looked on the wheat-field all destroyed with tares, He took that field, and that husbandman's faith and patience with his field, and put them both into this immortal sermon of His. And here are we to-night learning many much-needed lessons among our tare-sowed fields also: learning the very same faith and patience that so impressed and pleased our Lord in this sorely-tried husbandman. And at the end of the world, when he is told about us, as we have been told about him, that husbandman will say, It was well worth a thousand fields of wheat to be the means of teaching a little patience and a little long-suffering even to one over-anxious and impatient heart. For, what that husbandman knew not about his field when he bore himself so wisely beside it, he will know when the harvest is at the end of the world, and when the reapers are the angels.

Then Jesus sent the multitude away, and went into the house; and His disciples came unto Him, saying, Declare unto us the parable of the tares of the field. And He gave them an interpretation of His parable, which was to be the authoritative and the all-comprehending interpretation from that time to the end of the world. At the same time, and in and under that interpretation of His, there are occasional, and provisional and contemporaneous, interpretations and applications of this parable, that are to be made by each reader of this parable, according to his own circumstances and experiences. I will not take up your time, therefore, with the Donatist controversy in the days of Augustine; nor with the great struggles for toleration and liberty of thought recorded for all time in the Areopagitica, and in such like noble arguments. Only, there will no doubt yet emerge and arise new Donatist debates, and new demands for toleration of opinion, even of erroneous opinion, and with that, new calls for the utmost caution, and faith, and patience, especially in church censures, and in church discipline. Occasions will arise, and may be at the door, when we must be prepared, both by knowledge and by temper, to play our part in them like this husbandman in his field. Occasions and opportunities when the discretion, and the patience, and the long-faith of this wise-hearted husbandman, will be memorable and will be set before us for our imitation and our repetition.

Occasions have often arisen in the past, and they will often arise in the future, when a great alarm will be taken at the new discoveries, the new opinions, and the new utterances, of men who are under our jurisdiction, as the tares were under the jurisdiction of the servants in the parable. Now, for what other purpose, do you think, was this parable spoken to us by our Master, but to impose upon us patience, and caution, and confidence in the truth, and to deliver us from all panic, and all precipitancy, and all sudden execution of our fears? This is a very wonderful parable. No parable of them all is more so. Very wonderful. Very startling, indeed. Very arresting to us. For, even when the wheat-field was all covered with real, and not doubtful, tares, the wise husbandman still held in the hands of his indignant and devoted servants. Even when, demonstrably, and admittedly, and scandalously, and diabolically, an enemy had done it,—No! said this master of himself, as well as of his servants,—No! Have patience. Let the tares alone. Lest while you gather up the tares, you root up also the wheat with them. Let both grow together till the harvest. And then I will give the reapers their instructions myself.

My friends, if any one but our Lord had said that, or anything like that, in the presence of any actual instances of real or supposed tares, what would we have said to him, and said about him? I will not, for reverence sake, repeat what we would have said. But if our Divine Lord actually uttered these great and wonderful words, full of such calmness, and such patience, and such toleration, and such endurance; such endurance even of evil,—shall we not take His wonderful words to heart, and humbly and believingly apply them, where it is at all possible; even erring, if err we must, on the safe side; and leave it to Him, when we at all can, to give His own orders about His own field at the end of the world? And, if we leave it to Him, it will be a sight on that day to see how He will vindicate our patience and His own parable.

Look back for a moment at what He Himself here calls some of the "scandals" in His Kingdom, and you will be fortified in your toleration of many things of that kind in time to come. Everybody has heard of the scandal of Galileo, to the shame of the Church of his day. And we are not without our own scandals in our own day. The highest dignitary now in the Church of England was, not very long ago, all but rooted up, as all but tares, both he and his beautiful writings. Whereas now he is where he is by universal acclamation. In Fitzjames Stephen's brilliant four-days' speech before the Court of Arches, that learned and eloquent counsel said,—"My Lord, such differences have always existed in the Church. I might quote in favour of the accused party, some of the highest names in the Church of England. Hooker was charged, in his day, with subverting the authority of Scripture. Cudworth was called an atheist. Tillotson's life was embittered by persecution. Bishop Burnet, whose work afterwards became a theological text-book, was actually twice censured by the Lower House of Convocation. . . . My Lord, the one party viewing history, and criticism, and science, accept these results with gladness, and with candour, and the other party tremble before them. The one party would say with Hooker that to detract from the dignity of these things is to do injury even to God Himself, who being that Light which no man can approach to, has sent us these lesser lights as sparkles, resembling, so far, the bright fountain from which they spring." I will not quote what Stephen said about the other party. But he went on to say, "That, my Lord, is the real scope, tendency, and design of this prosecution, and that, as I said before, is its explanation, but not its justification."

And a greater than Fitzjames Stephen, the Golden-mouth of the English Church himself, says in his Discourse of the Liberty of Prophesying—"Let all errors be as much and as zealously suppressed as may be: but let it be done by such means as are proper instruments for their suppression; by preaching and disputation, by charity and sweetness, by holiness of life, by assiduity of exhortation, by the Word of God and prayer. For these ways are the most natural, the most prudent, the most peaceable, and the most effectual, instrument for the suppression of error. Only, let not men be hasty in calling every disliked opinion by the name of heresy. And if men will say that in saying this I persuade to indifferency, there is no help for me; I must bear it as I can. And I am not without remedy, for my patience will help me, and I will take my course."

And on the same subject a greater than either Stephen or Taylor has said: has sung—

> Let not the people be too swift to judge,
> As one that reckons on the blades in field,
> Or ere the corn be ripe. For I have seen
> The thorn frown rudely all the winter long,
> And after bear the rose upon its top:
> And bark, that all the way across the sea
> Ran straight and speedy, perish at the last,
> E'en in the haven's mouth.

But all that will only the more provoke some of you to retort on me and to demand,—Do you really mean to say, that so and so are to be tolerated, and tolerated where they are? Now, I will not answer that which you put so passionately; for I am not debating with you; but am teaching to the teachable among you, a little of what I have been taught myself. And, moreover, what I have acted on more than once as I had opportunity, and have proved it to be true and trustworthy teaching, and have never repented it. And if, instead of debating about it, you also will receive it, and will act upon it, you also will live to prove it true. Now, with all this, I have not gone out of my way one inch to-night to seek out this wonderful parable, and its so timeous interpretation. Not one inch. For it met me in the very middle of my way to you. And, all I could examine it, and excogitate it, and go round about it, and look at it in every light, and indeed try to escape it—I could make nothing else out of it than what I have now said. But the day will declare both the eternal truth, and the present truth, about this parable of the wheat and the tares. On that day, He who preached this parable will winnow out, and will burn up all false interpretations of it, and mine among the rest. Only, may you and I be judged more tenderly and forgivingly by Him on that day when we have many a time judged other erring men!

The whole field of letters, also, is more or less like this husbandman's tare-tangled field. You can get at the pure truth in print scarcely in anything. You can with difficulty get a book of the past, and much less a magazine, or a journal, or a newspaper of the passing day, that is not all sown over with the author's own seed-basket; all sown over, now with partiality, and now with antipathy. That field in Galilee was a study in malice to our Lord: and there are fields all around us to-day of the same sickening spectacle. You are a public writer; and so many are the collisions of interests, and ambitions, and pursuits, and competitions; and such is the pure malice, sometimes, of your own tare-filled heart, that we cannot get from you the naked and real truth about that cause or that man. You simply will not let us get at the real, unadulterated, unvarnished, untampered-with, truth. And, besides, such are the resources and appliances of civilisation in our day, that you can sow your evil seed under cover of anonymity, and your best friend will never know whosc hand it was that stabbed him in the dark. You are reviewing a book by tongue or by pen. The author is not liked by you, or by your party, or by your employer; or, you are an author yourself, and the writer of the book before you has run away with your popularity and your profits. You would need to be a saint to review his new book aright. You would need to be an angel to say in your paper about him and about his book, what you would like him to say in his paper about you and about your book. And, indeed, considering what this world is, and what the human heart is, there is far more of such angelic saintliness abroad in it than you would expect to see, unless you were actually on the out-look for it. But, fair writing, and true writing, and loving writing, or no, we have no choice. We must act like this wise husbandman; we must take our history, and our biography, and our politics, and our art, and our law, and our criticism, and our morning and evening and weekly newspapers, as they are—tares and all. Lest if we forbid the tares entering our house we shut out both truth and love with them. Let them grow together until the harvest; and, meantime, make them all so many means of this and that grace to you. In one of his noblest papers Dr. Newman vindicates the study of the great classics—Greek, Latin, and English—in spite of the basketfuls of impurity that are sown so broadcast in some of them. And the old scholar and saint argues that in the interest of the very purity of mind and heart that we fear sometimes are so early poisoned in those shining fields. And now, before leaving this point, I will add this—I am not an author, nor a journalist, but a preacher, and I will therefore add this—that he is a happy preacher who has lived through many times and seasons of temptation, and has never sown some of the tares of his own temper, and of his own partial mind, in his preaching, and even in his prayers. And I, for one, am not that happy preacher. Thomas Boston used to say, that of all men who needed the imputation of Christ's all-round righteousness, preachers and pastors were those men.

And then to come still closer to ourselves than even that. Such is the versatility, and the spirituality, and the inwardness, of our Lord's words in this wonderful parable, that they apply with the very greatest support and comfort to the heart of every sinful man also under his own all-searching sanctification. The heart of a great sinner, under a great sanctification, is the field of all fields. All other fields are but parables to him of his own field. And in nothing more so than in Satan and his satanic seed-basket. And worst of all, and saddest of all, that satanic seed is here almost part and parcel of the very field itself. For, from the beginning, that poisonous seed was, somehow, insinuated, and was already buried deep in the very original ground and soil of the soul; and so insinuated, and so rooted, that with the best husbandry it is never got out of the soil of the soul in this world. It is like those poisonous weeds in his best fields that so vex the husbandman's heart. Let him plough and harrow, and plough and harrow again; let him change his seed, let him rotate his crops; with all he can do, there is the accursed thing always coming up, choking the wheat, drinking up the rain and the sunshine from the wheat, and mocking all that the husbandman and his servants can do; mortifying and indeed breaking his heart. But here also,—and startling and staggering to read it,— our Lord here again advises patience. *Why* he does not cleanse the honest and good ground with one word of His mouth, He knows Himself. But that He does not speak the word, and so cleanse the ground, all His best saints have learned to their bitter suffering, and their heart-breaking cost. And among all the counsels and comforts He speaks to our tare-tortured hearts, this wonderful, this even staggering, counsel is heard in and over them all. 'Be patient with thine own sanctification, as with some other things, till I come. Behold, the husbandman waiteth for the precious fruit of the earth. Be ye also patient; for the coming of the Lord draweth nigh. And then the Son of Man shall send forth His angels, and they shall gather out of His kingdom all things that offend. And then shall the righteous shine forth as the sun in the kingdom of their Father. Who hath ears to hear, let him hear.'

III

THE MAN WHO TOOK A GRAIN OF MUSTARD SEED, AND SOWED IT IN HIS FIELD

Our Lord's parables are all so many applications of what we sometimes call the Sacramental Principle. That is to say, in all His parables our Lord takes up something in nature and makes it a lesson in grace, and a means of grace. The kingdom of heaven is like that, He said, as often as He saw a field of wheat all sown over with tares; or a vineyard with a husbandman working in it; or a lost sheep; or a prodigal son; or a marriage procession; or a few little children playing at marriages and funerals in the market-place. Our Lord so lived in heaven: He had His whole conversation so completely in heaven: His whole mind and heart and life were so absolutely absorbed in heaven, that everything He saw on earth, in some way or other, spoke to Him about heaven, and thus supplied Him with His daily texts, and sermons, and parables, about heaven. There are some men who are full of eyes, as Scripture says. They are full of eyes within and without. Now, our Lord was one of those men, and the very foremost of them. He was full of eyes by nature, and, over and above nature, He had an extraordinary and unparalleled unction from the Holy One. And thus it was that He discovered the kingdom of heaven everywhere and in everything. Already as a child He had deep and clear eyes both in His mind and in His imagination, and in His heart. As a child He had often sown the least of all seeds in Joseph's garden, and had watched that mustard seed springing up till it became a great tree. And with what delight would He see the birds of the air building their nests in the branches of His own high mustard tree. And how He would feed them, and their young ones, with the crumbs that fell from His mother's table. And as He grew in wisdom and in stature, He would come to read in that same mustard tree yet another parable about His Father's house and His Father's business. Or, as we sometimes say, in our book-learned way, He would see in that mustard tree another illustration of that Sacramental Principle which was ever present with Him.

Now it was not so much the great size of the mustard tree

that took such a hold of our Lord's imagination. It was rather the extraordinary smallness of the mustard seed. And that was a very fruitful moment for us when that small seed first fell into our Lord's mind and heart. For there immediately sprang up out of that small seed this exquisite little parable. This little parable, so exquisitely beautiful in its literature, and so inexhaustibly rich in its applications and fulfilments in no end of directions.

To begin with, the kingdom of heaven in Old Testament times was like a grain of mustard seed in its original smallness, and then in the great tree that it ultimately became. Take the very first of all the mustard seeds of the kingdom of heaven on this earth,—the call of Abraham. What could be a smaller seed, at the time, than the emigration of the son of Terah out of Ur of the Chaldees and into the land of the Canaanites? Again, what seed could well be smaller than that ark of bulrushes, daubed with slime and pitch, and hidden away among the flags by the river's bank? And, then, what less likely to spring up into all the psalms and hymns and spiritual songs of the Church of God than those little snatches and sacred psalmody that a shepherd boy sang to his few sheep on the plains of Bethlehem? And to come to Old Testament institutions and ordinances also. What more like a mustard seed than those few drops of midnight blood sprinkled so stealthily on the lintels and the door-posts of those slave-huts in the land of Egypt? And yet all the passover-days in Israel, and all our own communion days in the Church of Christ, and the marriage supper of the Lamb in His Father's house, have all sprung up, and will yet spring up, out of that small mustard seed. And in like manner, all our divinity halls had their first original in that small school which Samuel set up on his father's little property at Ramah. Our own Oxford, and Cambridge, and Edinburgh, and Aberdeen, and many more such like schools of the prophets, are all so many great trees that have their long roots struck away back into Samuel's little mustard seed. As also when the carpenters of Jerusalem made a pulpit of wood for Ezra and his colleagues, standing on which they read in the book of the law distinctly, and gave the sense, and caused the people to understand the reading. There you have the first small seed out of which ten thousand pulpits have sprung up, down to our own day, and will spring up, down to the end of all evangelical time. Our Lord Himself stood upon a pulpit of the same wood; and so did Paul, and so did Chrysostom, and so did Augustine, and so did Calvin, and so did Thomas Goodwin, and so did Matthew Henry, and a multitude of pulpit expositors of the Word of God which no man can number.

Our Lord, you may depend upon it, had all those Old Testament instances in the eyes of His mind when He spake to His disciples this so charming and so instructive little parable. But, always remembering His own mustard-seed beginning, and always forecasting what was yet before Him, and before the whole world through Him, our Lord must always have looked on Himself as by far the most wonderful mustard seed that ever was sown. Would you see with your own eyes the most wonderful mustard seed that ever was sown in all the world? Come and look at that Holy Thing that lies in the manger of Bethlehem, because there is no room in the inn. Which, surely, was the least-looking of all seeds, but is now the greatest among herbs. And, then, what a seed of the same kind was the call of the twelve disciples, and the conversion of Saul of Tarsus, and the conversion of Augustine, and the conversion of Luther, and Wesley, and Chalmers, and General Booth. Paul's first mission to the Gentiles also, and the first missionary that landed on our shores, and the first printing-press, and the first sailing of the *Mayflower,* and so on.

But it is time to come to ourselves. And among ourselves that small mustard seed is eminently a parable for all parents. For every little word that a parent speaks to his child: every little action of a parent in the sight of his child: every little attitude even, and movement of his: every glance of his eye, and every accent of his voice—are all so many mustard seeds sown in the little garden of his child's mind and heart. Every little Scripture lesson learned together: every little prayer offered together: and, especially, alone together: every little occasional word to explain, and to make interesting, his child's little lesson and little prayer: every wise little word spoken to his child about his own and his child's Saviour—every such small seed dropped by a parent's hand will yet spring up to his everlasting surprise, and to his everlasting harvest. Let all parents, then, and all nurses, and all tutors, and all schoolmasters, and all who have little children in the same house with them, lay this little parable well home to their imagination and to their heart. Let them not despise the day of small things. Let them have a great faith, and a great assurance of faith, in such small things as these. Let them have a great faith in Him, and in His wisdom, and His love, and in His faithfulness, who is continually, both in nature and in grace, folding up the greatest trees in the smallest seeds. And never more so than in the way He folds up your child's whole future in your little acts of faith, and prayer, and love, and wisdom, and patience, and hopefulness, done at home. Despise it not, for a great tree is in it. A great, a fragrant, and a fruitful tree, under which you will one day sit rejoicing in the shelter of it, and in the sweet fruitfulness of it.

Long before your son is ready to read Butler for himself, he will be a daily illustration to you of Butler's great principle of acts, habits, character. A little wrong act, another little act of the same kind, and another, and another, and another, and another, and all of them so small, that not one parent's eye in a thousand can so much as see them, the thing is so infinitely small, and the child himself is still so small. But, oh! the tremendous and irreparable oversight for you and for him! Read Butler for yourself till you have that wisest of Englishmen by heart. And as soon as your son is able to read his father's best books, buy him a good Butler for himself; and, some day when you are taking a long holiday walk together, have a good talk with him about that great teacher, both hearing your son's mind, and giving him in return your own mind, on that great man.

Thomas à Kempis's genesis of a fatal temptation is another instance of a mustard seed. An evil thought; the smallest seed of an evil thought, is, somehow, sown in our minds. In a thousand unforeseen ways such small seeds are being continually insinuated into all our minds. And if they are let enter our minds; if they are for a single moment entertained in our minds; evil thoughts, especially if they are of certain kinds, will immediately spread themselves out in our imaginations, and will so colour, and so inflame, and so intoxicate, our imaginations, that our wills, and even our consciences, are completely carried captive before we are aware, till another deadly work is finished in body and in soul. A thought, says the old saint, then an imagination, then a delight, then a consent, and then our soul is sold for nought. The kingdom of hell also is like a grain of mustard seed, which, when it is grown, all the obscene birds of the bottomless pit come up and breed in the branches thereof. As the children's hymn has it long before they understand it,

So our little errors
  Lead the soul away,
From the path of virtue
  Far in sin to stray.

But, blessedly, there is another side to all that. There is a genesis and a genealogy of things far more joyful to dwell on than that. A little thought of goodness, and of truth, and of love, will be sown in the garden of the soul. A little thought, as it looks, of God, of Jesus Christ, of heaven, well watered and shone upon by the Spirit of God. And then that little thought will open and will spread out into visions of beauty that will sanctify and fortify the soul, till the young soldier of Jesus Christ will step forward and will say like the brave man in John Bunyan—Set down my name, sir! When the heavenly watchers, seeing all that, will raise their songs over him, and will sing—

Come in, come in,
Eternal glory thou shalt win!

And all from a small mustard seed of one good thought sown in a good and honest heart.

And so on, in a thousand other regions of religion and life. But I will close, with what will come home to us all,—how to make our own home happy. For, what is the real secret of a happy home: a life-long happy home? What but little mustard seeds of loving, and of loving-kindness? What but little acts, and little habits, and then a great herb of character? A little act of forethought. A little act of respect. A little act of reverence. A little act of honour. A smile. A glance of the eye. A word of tact. A word of recognition. A word of praise. A word of love. A little gift. A little flower in a little glass of water. And many more things too small to put into a sermon for grown-up men.

With smiles of peace and looks of love
  Light in our dwellings we may make,
Bid kind good-humour brighten there,
  And still do all for Jesus' sake.

Little deeds of kindness,
  Little acts of love,
Help to make home happy
  Like the heaven above.

IV

THE MAN WHO CAST SEED INTO THE GROUND AND IT GREW UP HE KNEW NOT HOW

Dr. Bruce is by far the best expositor of this exquisite little parable. Dr. Bruce is always himself. That is to say, he is always autobiographical, always experimental, always scientific, always masculine, always full of bone and blood, always strength itself, always satisfying. "A man's capacity," he says, "to expound particular portions of Scripture depends largely on his religious experiences. For here it holds good, as in other spheres, that we only find what we ourselves bring. The case is the writer's own. And therefore the parable to be studied has been to him for many years a favourite subject of thought, and a fruitful source of comfort. Viewed as a repetition in parabolic form of the Psalmist's counsel,—Wait, I say, on the Lord." Dr. Bruce's book on the Parables is, to my taste, his best book. And then the exquisite little parable now open before us, shows Dr. Bruce, as I think, at his very best. So much so, that if there is to be anything of the nature of harvest to you to-night, let it be well understood that Dr. Bruce was the man who first cast the seed into the ground, but who fell asleep before the seed had sprung up in you and in me.

At the same time, the originality, and the freshness, and the force, of Dr. Bruce's exposition, is all to be traced back to the originality, and the freshness, and the force, of the parable which he so excellently expounds. You sometimes say to me that you do not know what style is. You have never been taught, you complain, to recognise style when you see it. And you ask me never to pass a piece of what I would call real style without stopping and calling your attention to it. Well, learn this little parable by heart, and say it to yourselves, till you feel the full taste of it in your mouth, and till you instinctively spue out of your mouth, everything of a written kind that is not natural, and fresh, and forceful: everything that is not noble, and beautiful, and full of grace and truth, like this parable. "For the earth bringeth fruit of herself: first the blade, then the ear, after that the full corn in the ear." A little child might have said it. And He who did say it makes us all feel like little children, with the naturalness, and the simplicity, and the truth, both to nature and to grace, of His exquisite words. The style is the man.

If we only had the eyes to see it, there is not a little of our Lord's teaching and preaching that is autobiographical, and experimental, and is consequently of the nature of a personal testimony. For, in all He went through, He went through it all because He was ordained to be the Firstborn among many brethren. He was in all points put to school, and taught, and trained, from less to more, like as we are. He was Himself so led as to be made in due time the Leader and the Forerunner of the whole body of believers. Till He is able at every new step in His heavenward way to turn round and say to us,—"Follow Me. He that followeth Me shall not walk in darkness, but shall have the Light of life." I like to look for our Lord's own footprints in every sermon of His, and what I look for I almost always find. As here. For, as it is in so many of His sermons, and as it is in so many of His parables that illustrate His sermons, this fine parable has, as I think, its first fulfilment in our Lord Himself. The seed of the kingdom was cast into the good ground of His own mind and heart also, and that from a child. And the seed that Mary, and Joseph, and the doctors in the temple, and the elders in the synagogue, all cast into that good ground sprang up, they knew not how. Till, when the sickle was put in for the first time, there was already such a harvest of grace and truth that they knew not what to make of it. Yes. It was so in Himself also: there was first the blade. For did He not grow up before them as a tender plant? And was He not subject to them as a little Child in the Lord? And was it not so that the Spirit of the Lord rested upon Him, they knew not how, till He began to be about thirty years of age? Matthew Henry sees our Lord Himself in this parable, and I am glad to have that great commentator's countenance in dwelling, as I so much love to dwell, on this delightful side of this delightful scripture.

And what was true of the Holy Child Jesus, will be true, in their measure, of your children and of mine. And if God the Father submitted His Son to His own divine law of gradual growth, and slow increase, and an imperceptible ripening, then we must not grudge to submit both ourselves and our children to the same divine ordinance. We must not torment ourselves with too much solicitude and anxiety about our children. We must not look for old heads on young shoulders. We must not thrust in the sickle on the same day as we sow the seed. We must not expect our sons to come all at once to the stature of perfect men, any more than we did ourselves. We were not perfect patterns at their age any more than they are. We were not by any means so deep in the divine life when we were young men as we now are. With ourselves also it was first the blade, then the ear, and only a long time after that, the full corn in the ear. We really must not embitter our own lives, and our children's lives, because they are not shaped as yet into all our form of doctrine and manner of life. We must not demand of them that they shall sit up at night to read our favourite authors. They are still young, and they have their own favourite authors. Enough, if, say thirty or forty years after this, they are come to their full intellectual and spiritual manhood. Enough, if, when we are no longer here to enjoy such masterpieces with them, they are by that time discovering the hid treasure, say, of Rutherford's *Letters,* and Guthrie's *Saving Interest,* and Baxter's *Saint's Rest,* and Marshall's *Gospel Mystery,* and William Law's immortal treatises, and are winding up every night with Bishop Andrewes's *Private Devotions.* By the time that we are done with those great guide-books of ours, and are distributing our choicest treasures to our children, we will write their names under our own names in our favourite copies, and will leave it to God to see that they write their children's names one day on the same revered pages. It was only after He was more than thirty years of age that we come on the Son of God Himself giving up whole nights at a time to secret prayer. Be you patient, therefore, brethren. Behold the husbandman waiteth for the precious fruit of the earth, and hath long patience for it, until he receive the early and the latter rain. Be ye also patient, stablish your hearts: for the coming of the Lord draweth nigh. Be you very thankful for the smallest signs of grace in your children. Despise not the day of small things. Look at that green blade in the spring field stealing its way so timidly round the obstructing clods and stones, and lifting up its hands towards the sunshine and the rain. And look for the same thing in your own house, and be thankful. For, in your house also, there will be first the blade, then the ear, and after that the full corn in the ear. You may not live to see it. You will most likely have fallen asleep before you see it. But you will be awakened to see it. And you will see no sweeter sight that sweet morning than the seed you sowed on earth at last come to its full ear in heaven. Yes, so is the kingdom of God. For when the fruit is brought forth, immediately He putteth in the sickle, because the harvest is come.

And, then, what a heart-upholding parable this is for all over-anxious ministers. It should be called the parable for all impatient parents and pastors; pastors especially. Our Lord is so bent upon consoling and comforting His ministers that He almost staggers us with what He here says about the unbroken peace of mind that every minister of His ought to possess. At all hazards, our Lord will once for all, pluck up all over-anxiety, and all impatience with their people, out of the hearts of His ministers. So much so, that He startles us with the state of security, and almost of absolute obliviousness in sleep, that He would have all His ministers to enjoy. What a courageous comforter of His over-anxious ministers is Jesus Christ! Cast in the the seed, He says, and take no more trouble about it. Sow the seed, and be secure of the harvest. Look at this wise sower how he sleeps, says our Lord to us. Imitate him. For so is the kingdom of heaven. It is as if our Lord came into this house and said:— So is this congregation. It is as if the ministers should preach, and hold their prayer-meetings, and teach their classes, and visit their sick, and should then wait in confidence till the seed should spring up, they know not how. And so it is as a matter of fact. We cast the seed of God's word into the earth, and the earth takes it, that is to say, God takes it, and it springs up, no man knoweth how, and the sowers of the seed least of all. Comfort My ministers, saith your God. Speak ye comfortably to My ministers, and say to them that the earth bringeth forth her fruit of herself, first the blade, then the ear, after that the full corn in the ear. There is another side, of course, to supplement all that; but one side is enough for one sermon of His, in our Lord's manner of preaching the kingdom.

I chanced upon this in my reading only last night. "Nothing great," says Epictetus, "is produced suddenly, not even a grape or a fig. If you say to me that you want a grape or a fig *now*, I will answer you that you cannot have it; a grape takes time. Let it flower first, then it will put forth its fruit, and then ripen. And would you have the fruit of a man's life and character all in a moment? Do not expect it." And again, "Fruit grows in this way, and in this way only. If the seed produces the fruit before the jointed stem, it is a product of the garden of Adonis. That is to say, the thing is for show only; it has no root in itself. You have shot up too soon, my man. You have snatched at fame before your season. You think you are something, but you will come to nothing. Let the root grow, then the first joint, then the second, and then the third, and then the fruit will come forth of itself." So Epictetus taught the young men in his Greek lecture-room. God never leaving Himself without a witness.

When a sinner first sets out on his sanctification, he begins already to sharpen his sickle, and to bind and stack his sheaves. He confidently promises himself and other people both sweet and strengthening bread to eat immediately out of his harvest. But both he, and all who have to do with him, soon find out that that is not at all the way of the kingdom of heaven. Not at all. In the kingdom of heaven, and in the sanctification of its subjects, it is first the blade here also, then the ear, after that the full corn in the ear. And sometimes, indeed, it threatens as if it were to be all blade in this field and no ear at all. Ay, and far worse than that: the very blade,with all its promise in it, will sometimes seem wholly to wither and absolutely to die. Why is it that I am so slow in growing any better? Why is my heart as wicked as ever it was, and sometimes much more so? You pray, in a way. You watch unto prayer, now and then. You study all the great authorities on sanctification that you can hear about, or can lay your hands on. But as soon as your secretly besetting sin is again suddenly let loose upon you, that moment you are down again in all your old agony of guilt and shame. Ah, my brethren, the kingdom of heaven is a very different experience from what you had at one time supposed it was. In our Lord's experimental words about it, the sanctification of the soul is first in the blade, then in the ear, and it is never, in this world, any more: it is never in this world the full corn in the ear. Whereas, poor soul, you thought that it was going to be the full ear with you all at once.

A great and a genuine sanctification, you must know, is the slowest work in all the world. There is nothing in heaven or earth so slow. The thing is sure, indeed, but the time is long. It would need to be sure, for oh, yes, sirs, it is long, long. And it is as sore, and as sickening, as it is long. There is a true description of it in our great Catechism. It is described there as "dying daily." And so it is. That is your case, is it not? It is dying by inches, is it not? It is having the two-edged sword driven daily into your heart, and never in this life healed out of your heart. Death is a process of pain, and shame, and ignominy. All possible pain, and suffering, and all manner of humiliation to mortal man, is collected up into the idea of death. But our everyday death is not true death at all, compared with the pain, and shame, and ignominy of death unto sin. And it all seems such a stagnation of sin, sometimes, and to some men. As, for instance, to the man who expostulated thus—"O my God, the more I do, the worse I am!" And to the man who first sang thus—

> And they that fain would serve Thee best,
> Are conscious most of wrong within.

Till, you may depend upon it, our Lord had His eye and His heart on His saints who are undergoing a great spiritual sanctification when He spake this many-sided and most comforting parable. He spake it first of Himself, and of His own growth in strength of spirit, and in wisdom, as well as in all manner of Messianic perfection. And then He spake it of parents and their children, and then of ministers and their people. But above all, He spake it of all those elect souls who are being kept for all their days under a slow but sure sanctification. There is first the blade of true holiness, He said, after that the ear, and then the full corn in the ear. But when the fruit is brought forth, immediately He putteth in the sickle, because the harvest is come.

V

THE WOMAN WHO TOOK LEAVEN AND HID IT IN THREE MEASURES OF MEAL

Being the first-born son in His mother's house, it would fall to the Holy Child Jesus to perform the part laid down for the first-born son in the feast of unleavened bread. And thus it was that after Jesus had struck the lintel and the two doorsteps with the blood that was in the basin, and after the whole family had hurriedly eaten each a portion of the pascal lamb, and a piece of the unleavened bread, at that appointed moment the eldest son of the house came forward and said, Father, what mean you by this service? What mean you by the blood, and the unleavened bread, and the bitter herbs? And Joseph would say, It is the Lord's passover, because He passed over the houses of the children of Israel in Egypt, when He smote the Egyptians and delivered our houses. And Joseph, and Mary, and Jesus, and James, and Joses, and Simon, and Judas, and their sisters, all bowed their heads and sang the Hundred and Thirteenth and the Hundred and Fourteenth Psalms. And once every year till the Holy Child came to the full stature of the Christ of God: every returning passover He entered deeper and deeper into this great ordinance, both hearing Joseph and asking him questions. Till He came to be of more understanding about the feast of unleavened bread than all His teachers: and understood both the blood, and the bread, and the bitter herbs, far better than all the ancients.

As long as He was still a child, He spake as a child, He understood as a child, He thought as a child. And the *great haste* that the unleavened bread signified, was enough for His imagination and His mind and His heart as long as He was a child. But then, as time went on, He would watch His mother at her housewife-work, and would observe how her leaven *spread* till her three measures of meal was all leavened. And as He meditated on the process going on under His eyes, He would again see in the leaven and in the meal another parable of the kingdom of God. And He would lay up the leaven and the meal in His mind and in His imagination and in His heart for some of His future sermons. And thus it was that on that great day of teaching and preaching when He sat by the sea-side, He had already given out parable after parable, till any other preacher but Himself would have been exhausted; but He still went on as fresh and as interesting and as instructive as when He began in the morning. "I am full of matter," said Elihu. "The spirit within me constraineth me. I will speak that I may be refreshed." And our Lord was like Elihu in that. For though He had already that day illustrated and applied the kingdom of God by a long and splendid series of parables, His mind was still as full of matter as ever. And the more He tried to put the kingdom of God into this and that parable, the more He saw other things in that inexhaustible kingdom for which no parable had as yet been provided. And thus it was that at this point, and as if to teach them to keep their eyes always open for their own future preaching, their Master suddenly turned to His disciples and asked them whether any of them had any light to cast upon the subject in hand. As if He were asking some of them to help Him out with His great subject, He said to them—"Whereunto shall I go on to liken the kingdom of God?" And when none of them had a word more to say concerning the inwardness, and the hiddenness, and the all-assimilating power, of that kingdom, He called to mind a former reflection of His own which came to Him one day beside His mother's kneading-trough. He remembered that day her three measures of meal, and the way that she took to turn that raw meal into wholesome and palatable bread. "And so is the kingdom of God in some respects," He said. "It is in some respects like leaven which a woman took and hid in three measures of meal till the whole was leavened." And here we are to-night, and in this church, suddenly transported back into Mary's little kitchen in Nazareth, in order to learn there yet another of her Son's parables about the kingdom of God.

Beware of the leaven of the Pharisees, He said to His disciples on one occasion. Now, what did He mean by that saying, do you suppose? What would you say was the leaven of the Pharisees? I do not know any more than you do, but I will tell you what I think. Leaven, to begin with, is something that is hidden and inward, and then it works inwardly and secretly, till it works its way through the whole surrounding measures of meal. Now, what was the leaven of the Pharisees? It must have been something inward and hidden, to begin with. And then it had by that time worked its way through their whole heart and character till they were the Pharisees who were bent on our Lord's death and destruction. Well, a little lump of leaven that a woman can hold in her hand does not look to be much, nor to have much power in it. But wait and see. And a little self-esteem in a young man's heart is not very much to be suspected or denounced, is it? But wait and see. Let that young man set out on his life with that little lump of self-esteem in his secret heart, and, as sure as he lives, this will be his experience, and the experience of all who have to do with him. So many and so unavoidable are the oppositions, and the contradictions, and the collisions of life, that if his self-esteem is not by means of all these things, and by means of the grace of God co-operating with all these things, chastened and subdued and cast out, then all these collisions, and corrections, and contradictions, will only the more increase and exasperate his self-esteem, till he will end his days as full of self-righteousness, and pride, and hardness of heart, as very Lucifer himself. On the other hand, humility, that is to say disesteem of a man's self, is so much good leaven hidden in a good man's heart. These are the words of well-known master in Israel,—"Humility does not consist in having a worse opinion of ourselves than we deserve, or in abasing ourselves lower than we really are. But as all virtue is founded in truth, so humility is founded in a true and just sense of our weakness, misery, and sin. So much so, that he who rightly feels and lives in this sense of his condition lives in humility." That is to say, he who at all rightly knows himself is done for ever with all self-esteem. There is not left in all his inward parts so much as a single ounce of that leaven of the Pharisees. But that sect in Israel were so set against all introspection, as they called it: their doctors of the law so denounced that sanctifying habit of mind and heart, that their scholars ended with crucifying the Lord of Glory. To such a lump of villainy and wickedness will a little leaven of self-esteem grow under the fit conditions, and in the fit heart, and left fitly alone. Now our Lord saw, only far too well, that evil leaven already at work in His twelve disciples. I do not take it upon me to say how far it is at work in any of you. I will not insist that your self-esteem is eating through your whole heart and is destroying your whole life and character. I will not fall out with you about that. I will not insist on what you call introspection, but I for one both feel and confess the truth of His words when my Lord says to me—Preacher, Beware! lest having discoursed so beautifully on humility to others, you yourself, through your self-esteem, should be a cast-away from the kingdom of God. Till it has to be my prayer, with the candle of the Lord in my hand continually—Search me, O God, and know my heart: try me, and know my thoughts: and see if there be any of this wicked way in me, and lead me in the way everlasting!

The Apostle Paul also has this on this same parable: "Purge out therefore the old leaven. Know ye not that a little leaven leaveneth the whole lump? Therefore let us keep the feast, not with old leaven, neither with the leaven of malice and wickedness, but with the unleavened bread of sincerity and truth." Now, what is malice and wickedness? We have seen what self-esteem is, and how it works till it leavens the whole lump. But what is the leaven of malice? You may be old enough to know without being told. You may have enough of it in yourself, and you may have suffered enough from it in others; but there are new beginners in self-esteem, and in malice, and the word must be rightly divided to meet their case as well as yours. Now, you who are new beginners in morals and in religion—what think you is malice? For you cannot purge it out, nor keep it purged out, if you do not know it when you see it. Well, malice also is like leaven in this. Its first beginning is so small as not to be worth speaking about in a dignified pulpit. You do not like some one. Nothing is so common, surely, as that. Already, at school, at college, in the office, in the workshop, in the house, you do not like some one. Well, that is your first half-ounce of the leaven of malice. And your feelings toward that man, and your thoughts about him, and your words about him, and your actions toward him, are like the three measures of meal with the little leaven at its heart. You just dislike that man—that is all as yet. But then full-grown men are so leavened with that same dislike that they actually come to hate one another. And—"hates any man the thing he would not kill?" You see then where you are. You see on what road you are travelling. You are travelling on the road of the Pharisees. You are travelling on the road to hell. And there is no surer, no shorter, and no more inevitable, road to hell than hatred, which is just dislike, and umbrage, and a secret grudge, come to their three measures of meal. Malice is bad blood, as we say. It is ill-will. It is resentment. It is revenge. Till it is in God's sight very murder itself; hidden, as yet, it may be from your introspection in its three measures of surrounding and smothering-up meal. And it is while this red-handed murder is still at its early stages of dislike, and antipathy, and animosity, that Paul beseeches you to purge it out. But in order to purge it out, you must take a candle like this to the work. A clear candle like this. You have a neighbour. He may at one time have been a friend. He may never suspect but that he is still a friend. He may be befriending you all the time. But at heart you are not his friend any more. Something has happened to you. Something that you must search out and admit about yourself. However humbling, however self-condemning, however self-hating, it may turn out to be, you cannot be a good and a true man any more till you have found yourself out. Your friend forgot you on some occasion. Or he preferred some one else to you. Or he took his own judgment and conscience for his guide in some matter in which you demanded to dictate to him. Or he got some promotion, or praise, or reward, that you had not humility and love enough to stomach. Track out your heart, sir! Heaven and hell hang on your tracking out your heart in that matter. No. Hell does not hang upon it, for hell has possession of your heart already. That wicked heat in your heart at the mention of his name, that is hell. That blackness which we all see in your very look, that is the smoke of your torment already begun. Purge it out, implores Paul. Ah! it is easy saying purge it out. Did Paul manage to purge it out himself, after all his most earnest preaching about it? No: he did not. No more than you and I. And it was when he had lighted all the candles he could lay his hands on; and when with them all he could not get down to all the malice that was still hiding in his heart, it was then that his Master had mercy on

His miserable servant, and said to him, My grace is sufficient for thee: for My strength is made perfect in weakness.

And though Pharisaic self-esteem and diabolical malice are all the instances to which our Lord's parable is applied first by Himself and then by His best Apostle, yet the parable is equally true of all the other leavenings of the devil that are insinuated into our souls. A little of the leaven of pride—think it out, with home-coming illustrations, for yourself. A little of the leaven of anger—think it out, with home-coming illustrations, for yourself. A little of the leaven of suspicion, and of jealousy, and of envy—with illustrations and instances taken from yourself. A little of the leaven of sensuality—"the inconceivable evil of sensuality"—as Newman calls it—with a whole portfolio of illustrations taken from yourself. A foul thought, a foul hint, a foul innuendo, a foul word, a foul image; a foul-mouthed boy in the playground; a foul-mouthed man in the workshop, in the office, in the bothy; a foul-mouthed woman in the workroom, in the kitchen, in the field; a foul book, a foul picture, a foul photograph in a shop-window in passing,—think it out, with a thousand illustrations taken from your own experience, and you will be wiser in this universal leaven of sensuality than all your teachers. You will yet be a master in Israel yourself in such sickening, but at the same time necessary, self-knowledge.

It is surely very striking to discover that while our Lord says so plainly that the kingdom of God is like leaven, yet both He, and His best Apostle, descend into the kingdom of Satan for all their best instances, and all their most pungent applications of the leaven. They would seem in this to leave it to ourselves to apply and to verify the parable in its application to the things of the kingdom of God. Whereunto shall I liken it? He said to His disciples. As much as to say—find out more and better instances, and illustrations, and verifications, for yourselves. And His example, and Paul's example, would seem to say to all preachers—give your people one or two illustrations taken from things they are only too well acquainted with already, and then leave them to prosecute the parable further for themselves. Would, said Moses, that all the Lord's people were prophets! And I will leave this parable where our Lord and His Apostles left it, only saying over it and over you, Would that all the Lord's people were expositors and preachers, and that out of their own observation and experience!

VI

THE MAN WHO FOUND TREASURE HID IN A FIELD

It was good stories like this in His sermons that made the common people begin to hear Him so gladly. There was not a carpenter's shop, nor a village market-place, in all Galilee where such stories of treasure-trove were not continually told. Stories of the same kind are not altogether unknown in our own land. But in the East, and to this day, such great finds as this man made are not at all uncommon. In times of commotion timid men will hide their treasures sometimes in the walls or under the floors of their houses, and sometimes they will bury them in their gardens and in their fields. And it will sometimes happen that the owner will die and will leave his secret treasure wholly undisclosed. And then some lucky man will come on that buried treasure some day in the most unexpected and accidental way; like this lucky man. He was ploughing one day in his master's field; or, was he digging deep with his spade and his mattock? When, suddenly, he reeled with joy at the sight of the glittering hoard that his ploughshare had laid bare. In one moment his resolve was made. Carefully covering up the shining spot, before the sun had time to set, he had already sold all that he possessed, and had made such an offer for the field that it was handed over to him, with all that it contained, before he slept. All the old books of the ancient world are full of such intoxicating stories as this. Perhaps the most famous of all those stories is that which Tacitus tells us about Nero. How a bold impostor hoaxed the emperor about an immense mine, full of all kinds of precious treasure, that was to be found in a distant part of his dominions. And Nero believed the wild tale till he became the laughing-stock of the whole world. But this was no hoax, this true find in that field of Galilee. Our Lord would seem to have known the fortunate ploughman, and to have had his happy story from his own delighted lips. But the barest outline of the rich story is all that Matthew's pen has here preserved to us. We would far rather have had the whole sermon that our Lord preached from that fortunate man's find than we would have had all his furrow full of gold and silver. For the word of our Lord's mouth is becoming more and better to us than thousands of gold and silver. But it has seemed good to the Holy Ghost to have this man's story told to us in the shortest possible way, and then to leave us to find out all its heavenly likenesses for ourselves.

Well, the first and foundation likeness between this parable and the kingdom of heaven is surely this. Just as our Lord is the Sower in another parable, and just as He is the Planter of the mustard seed in another, and the Good Shepherd in another, and the Good Samaritan in another, so He is the happy ploughing Man in this parable. And as the field was the world in a former parable, so it is here. And the kingdom of heaven, says our Lord, is like the treasure hid in the field of this world. And the first man who found the treasure that lay hid in the field of this world was the Son of man. All the world knows that He was rich, yet for our sakes he became poor. All the world knows how that being in the form of God, He humbled Himself, and made Himself of no reputation, and became obedient unto death, even the death of the cross. All of which, taken together, was the price He paid for this field, and for the treasure hid in this field. Our Lord bought this world, so to say, for the sake of the elect souls that lay hidden in it, till He was able to say,—"As thou, Father, hast given thy Son power over all flesh, that He should give eternal life to as many as thou hast given Him."

Incomparable Thomas Goodwin,—incomparable to me, at any rate,—says that Paul will be the second man in heaven, the Man Christ Jesus being the first man. And every one here will already have thought of Paul as soon as this fine little parable was read out to him. For, if ever any man could be said to have had every letter of this fine little parable fulfilled both in him and by him, that man was Paul. If ever any man, after the Man Christ Jesus, sold all that he had that he might buy the field, that man was the Apostle. Which field, in his case, was nothing less than Jesus Christ Himself. Jesus Christ Himself, with His justifying righteousness, held in Himself like hid treasure. This so fortunate ploughman in our Lord's sermon sold his little cottage in Capernaum, with its little garden full of fruits and flowers, and with all its vines and fig trees, under which he was used to sit after his hard day's work was done. He determined to sell all those dear possessions and delights of his for the sake of the treasure his eyes had once got sight of in that enriching and entrancing field. And Paul, in like manner, was ploughing at his daily task, when, lo, his horse's foot suddenly sank out of sight into such a wealth of unsearchable riches, that he straightway counted all things but loss in order to buy that field. Yes, truly. If Jesus Christ was the first ploughing man of this parable, then, surely, Paul was the second.

But the kingdom of heaven is such a rich and various kingdom that there are many other fields with hid treasure in them, lying all around the central field. And in some of those adjoining fields there is no little treasure still lying hid and waiting for the first fortunate ploughman to lay it open and to make it his own. You are not ministers. But you cannot fail to see what a rich field, and full of what treasure, every evangelical pulpit is, with its pastorate of the same character spreading out all around it. Only, here again, that minister who would possess himself of the hid treasure of his pulpit and his pastorate must sell all he has in order to buy up those two gold-filled fields. "At his first coming to his little village, Ouranius felt it as disagreeable to him as a prison, and every day seemed too tedious to be endured in so retired a place. He thought his parish was too full of poor and mean people that were none of them fit for the conversation of a gentleman. This put him upon a close application to his studies. He consequently kept much at home, writ notes upon Homer and Plautus, and sometimes thought it hard to be called to pray by any poor body's bedside when he was just in the midst of one of Homer's battles." "Mr. Kinchin," says George Whitefield, "was a minister of Dummer in Hampshire, and being likely to be chosen Dean of Corpus Christi College, he desired me to take his place and officiate for him till that affair should be decided. By the advice of friends I went, and he came to supply my place in Oxford. His parish consisting chiefly of poor and illiterate people, my proud heart at first could not well brook it. I would have given all the world to be back in my beloved Oxford. But upon giving myself up to prayer, and reading Mr. Law's excellent Character of Ouranius, my mind became reconciled to such conversation as the place afforded me. I prosecuted Mr. Kinchin's plan, and generally divided the day into three parts; eight hours for study and meditation, eight hours for sleep and meals, and eight hours for reading prayers, catechising and visiting the parish. The profit I reaped by these exercises was unspeakable. I soon began to be as much delighted with their artless conversation as I had previously been with my Oxford friends, and I frequently learned as much by an afternoon's visit as in a week's study. I remained at Dummer till a letter came from Mr. John Wesley in which were these words: 'Do you ask what you shall have in Georgia? Food to eat, and raiment to put on, and a house to lay your head in, such as your Lord had not. And a crown of glory that fadeth not away.' Upon reading this, my heart leaped within me, and as it were echoed to the call."

As I was saying, a minister who would dig up the hidden treasure out of his pulpit and pastoral fields must sell all his time and all his tastes; all his thoughts by day and all his dreams by night. He must spend and be spent. He must be the servant of all men. He must become all things to all men. He must not strive. He must have no mind of his own, but the mind of Christ only. Both his books, and his table, and his bed, must all go to the hammer. By then, by that time, he will begin to have a people about him of whom he will be able to say—"What is my hope, or joy, or crown of rejoicing? Are not even ye in the presence of our Lord Jesus Christ at His coming?" And then that all-surrendered minister will be summoned forward at the coming of his Lord, not any more to shame and everlasting contempt, but his Lord will say to him on that day when He makes up His jewels—'That jewel is yours,' his Lord will say: 'for that soul and that would have been lost to Me, but for your self-denying ministry.' And then, on that day, the poorest parish in all Scotland, and the meanest mission-field in all the world, will be seen to yield up treasures that will dazzle the eyes of men and angels to see them. Then they that be wise in time shall shine as the brightness of the firmament; and they that turn many to righteousness as the stars for ever and ever.

And on the other hand, such a minister's ministry is the all-enriching field of his understanding and discerning people. A scholarly, studious, able, evangelical, experimental, preacher every Sabbath day; and then all the week an assiduous, unwearied, ever-mindful, all-loving, pastor,—what a field, and full of what treasure to his people, is such a minister and such a ministry! What treasures of grace and truth lie hid there for the proper people. Ay, and lie hid, sometimes, even from his very best people. For how can any one know, or even guess at, what God has done so as to enrich them and their children in His fitting up and furnishing of their minister's whole life and experience? Ten thousand personal and ministerial providences and experiences have all befallen him for their sake. As also his ever sleepless labours for their understanding and edification. The half of which could not be told, and would neither be beloved nor understood, even if it were to be told. Only, sometimes you will hear of one man in a thousand; sometimes you will meet with one rare and remarkable man who has sold not a little, in order to become possessed of that minister and his ministry. The multitude in every congregation stumble about lucklessly and unprofitably even among the richest of fields. But, here and there, and now and then, another manner of man will sometimes be met with. One happy man in a thousand runs his ploughshare down into the treasure-trove of that pulpit, and then takes action accordingly. An old office-bearer of this very congregation told me long ago, how he had lately summoned a conference of his whole household in order to make a great family choice and decision. He put it to his wife, and to his sons, and to his daughters, whether he would build a house for them away out of Edinburgh, with a park and a garden and stables, and all that. Or whether he would buy a house in a west-end Crescent so as to be still near this church, and so as to let him remain in the session, and so as to let his family continue to sit under Dr. Candlish's ministry. And the eyes of that happy ploughman of Capernaum did not glisten with tears of greater joy than did that old elder's eyes when he told me that he had determined on a house within reach of the pulpit to which he owed his own soul, and his children's souls. And his wife had been in Dr. Candlish's ladies' class. Things like that do not happen every day. But that is, largely, because there are not pulpits every day like Dr. Candlish's pulpit of those days.

And, then, all the more because you are not ministers, you have the gold-filled field of your Bible always before you. If you had been ministers you would have had a constant temptation in connection with your Bible that, as it is, you have clean escaped. If you had been preachers you would have been tempted to read your Bible almost solely with an eye to good texts. And, better not read your Bible at all, than just to make sermons out of it. What a promise! you say as your read alone, and you read no more that night. What a consolation! you say. What a psalm! and you say and sing it all that week after, and at all times and in all places. What a name for you is the Name of your God! you say. And, like Moses on the Mount, you make haste and bow your head and worship, and say,—Pardon our iniquity and our sin, and take us for thine inheritance. Moses did not say—What a text for next Sabbath! And you have no temptation to say that either. There is nothing of that kind to come in between you and your immediate application of the rich grace of God's word to the needs of your own soul. Yes. What a field of fields to the right reader is the word of God! What a grace-laden field is the Psalms. And again, the Gospels. And again, the Epistles. What solid gold lies hidden in all these several spots of this rich field. Happy ploughmen! O, my brethren, search deep in the Scriptures. For they are they which testify to you both of yourselves and of your Saviour.

And then the field of prayer. O, the milk and honey of which every rig and furrow of that field is full! He maketh me to lie down in the green pastures of it. He leadeth me beside the still waters of it. And then, the treasure hid in it. And then, the enterprise of prayer, the exploration of it, the ventures in it, the sure successes of it. Surely this is the field in which there is a vein for silver, and a place for the fine gold. Iron is here taken out of the earth, and brass is molten out of the stone. The very stones of it are the place of sapphires, and it hath its dust of gold. It cannot be gotten for gold, neither shall silver be weighed for the price of it. This is a field that cannot be valued with the gold of Ophir, with the precious onyx or the sapphire. The gold and the crystal cannot equal it; and the exchange of it cannot be for jewels of fine gold. No mention shall be made of coral or of pearls; for the price of prayer is above rubies. The topaz of Ethiopia shall not equal it. Neither shall it be valued with pure gold. Verily, verily, I say unto you, Whatsoever ye shall ask the Father in my name, He will give it to you. Hitherto ye have asked nothing in my name. Ask, and ye shall receive, that your joy may be full.

VII

THE MERCHANT MAN WHO SOLD ALL THAT HE HAD AND BOUGHT THE PEARL OF GREAT PRICE

THIS is one of those travelling jewellers of the East who compass sea and land in their search for goodly pearls. He is never at home. He is always on the look-out for more and more precious pearls. Till one day his long search is signally rewarded. He is engaged in exploring a certain market of precious stones, when suddenly his eye falls on a pearl the like of which he had never supposed to exist. Its great size, its perfect form, its exquisite beauty, its dazzling light—he had never expected to see such a gem. Ascertaining from its owner the great price of the pearl, the merchant man forthwith sells all that he possesses, and buys up on the spot that pearl of great price. We get a well-known word from the honourable name that is here given to this enterprising merchant man. Our Lord calls him an *emporium* man. And so he is. For he has spent his whole life in the search for the very best pearls, till his emporium is famous for the size, and the beauty, and the value of its pearls. And his famous emporium is now more famous than ever because of this splendid purchase he has made on his last enterprising journey.

Now, the world of books, to begin with, is not unlike a merchant man seeking goodly pearls. For every really good book that a really good judge of books discovers becomes a pearl of great price to him. Till as his reading life goes on, he as good as sells all his former books for the sake of this and that pearl of books which he has discovered in the course of his reading. A new beginner in books reads everything he comes across. All printed matter interests him, and a poor and passing book will for a time satisfy him, and even entrance him. But as time goes on, and as the real use of a good book, and the real rarity of a good book, become revealed to him, the true reader will be found giving up all his reading time, and all his reading outlay, to the really great and life-long books of the world, and to them alone. As, for instance, Dr. Chalmers.

During my Christmas holiday I have been renewing my acquaintance with that true pearl of a book, Dr. Hanna's *Memoirs of Dr. Chalmers*. And among a multitude of lessons I learned and laid up for myself and for my classes out of that treasure-house, Dr. Chalmers's ever-growing appreciation of the very best books was one of the best lessons I again learned. "Butler made me a Christian," said Chalmers, somewhat hyperbolically, to one of his early friends. "Pascal's," he wrote to another friend, "is more than all Greek and Roman fame." Before his eyes were opened, and before his taste was refined to distinguish pearl from paste, Chalmers actually denounced John Newton, and Richard Baxter, and Philip Doddridge, from the pulpit, and as good as forbade his people to read them. But the day was fast coming when this great merchant man of ours was to sell all that he had in order to buy the very pearls he had so scouted in the days of his disgraceful and guilty ignorance. For as I read on I came on such entries in his private journal as these: "Began Richard Baxter, which I mean to make my devotional reading in the evenings." "Sept. 13.—I have begun Baxter's *Call to the Unconverted,* and intend it for circulation." And writing the same year to a younger brother of his, he says, "I look upon Baxter and Doddridge as two most impressive writers, and from whom you are likely to carry away the impression that a preparation for eternity should be the main business and anxiety of time." "Nov. 11.—Finished this day the perusal of Foster's *Essays,* which I have read with great relish and excitement. His profoundly evangelical views are most congenial to me. O my God, give me of the fullness of Christ! May I never lose sight of Christ, that through Him I may pass from death unto life." "March 14.—I am much impressed with the reality and business-like style of Doddridge's intercourse with God. O Heavenly Father, convert my religion from a name to a principle!" You may remember that there is an old evangelical classic entitled *The Marrow*. Sell a whole shelf of your juvenile books and buy it, and you will be wise merchant men, if Dr. Chalmers is a good judge.—"Sunday, August 23.—I am reading *The Marrow,* and derive from it much light and satisfaction. It is a masterly performance. August the 24th.—Finished *The Marrow*. I feel a growing light in the fullness and sufficiency of Christ. O my God, bring me nearer and nearer to Thy Son!" And of another masterpiece of another master mind, he writes—"Read Edwards on the *Religious Affections*. He is to me the most exciting and interesting of all theological writers." "Who taught you to preach in that way?" asked David Maclagan one day long ago at Dr. Rainy in the vestry behind me here. "John Owen," was all the answer. Now, writing to Dr. Wardlaw, Dr. Chalmers says, "I am reading Owen just now on *The Person of Christ*. May the Spirit more and more take of the things of Christ and show them to me." And again, "Have finished Owen on *Spiritual-Mindedness*. O my God, give me the life and the power of those who have made this high attainment!" And again, "Have you read Owen on the Hundred and Thirtieth Psalm? This is my last great book, and I would strongly recommend it as eminently conducive to a way of peace and holiness." And of the very Doddridge against whom he had at one time warned his parishioners, he now writes—"I have been reading more of Doddridge, and do indeed find myself to be a very alienated and undone creature. But let me cleave to Christ so as to receive all my completeness from Him." And of another goodly pearl, whose title at least you all know, he writes, "I am on the eve of finishing Guthrie, which, I think, is the best book I have ever read." And at a later date—"I still think it is the best human composition I ever read relating to a subject about which it is my earnest prayer that we may all be found on the right side of the question." Romaine, also, was such a favourite with Chalmers as he grew in years and in grace, that I cannot begin to quote his constant praise of that fine spiritual writer. And to sum up with an extract from his *Journal* that bears on this whole question—"I breathe with delight in the element of godly books, and do fondly hope that their savour, at one time wholly unfelt by me, argues well for my regeneration." And at the very end of his saintly and splendid life—"I am reading Ebenezer Erskine on *The Assurance of Faith,* and I specially like it. Its doctrine is very precious to me." Such are some samples of the kind of books that Dr. Chalmers sold all in order to buy a taste for them, and a life-long enjoyment of them. Let every divinity student read Chalmers's *Memoirs* just before he is ordained, and once again every three or four years all his ordained days.

You may not be much of a merchant man in the world of books, and yet this parable may be found entirely true of you in some other world of your own. "I have no books," said Jacob Behmen, "but I have myself." And Apollo did not say, Know many books. What he kept saying continually was this, "Know thyself." Now, you may be this kind of a merchant man that not some book, but some doctrine, of the kingdom of heaven may be to you your pearl of great price. The true and full doctrine of New Testament faith, for instance. What New Testament, and evangelical, and justifying, and sanctifying, faith really is. What its true object really is, and what its true acts and operations really are. The true nature of Gospel faith has been a perfect pearl of great price to some great men when at last they found it. It was so to John Wesley. "Preach faith till you find it," said Peter Bohler, Wesley's Moravian master, to him; "and then preach it because you have found it." And all the world knows how John Wesley sold, so to speak, every other doctrine in order to hold and to preach immediate and soul-saving faith, and with what immediate and soul-saving results. Another will find his pearl of great price in the spiritual doctrine of holy love, as was the case with John Wesley's English master, William Law. As Law did also in a whole world of doctrines, and habits, and practices, connected with secret prayer. And as George Whitefield, John Wesley's predecessor in field-preaching, discovered such unsearchable riches to him in the Pauline doctrines of election, and assurance, and perseverance to the end. And as so many men of the Owen, and Goodwin, and Edwards type have discovered in the deep, spiritual doctrines connected with the entrance into their hearts of the holy law of God, and connected with the consequent sinfulness of sin, and then connected with the work of the Holy Ghost continually carried on within their hearts. And so on. Till every genuine merchant man has his own special pearls of divine truth; not to the denying or the despising of other men's purchases; but because his own pearls of great price have so attracted him, and have so enriched him.

But after all that has been said about pearls of great price and their purchase, every merchant man's own soul is his most precious pearl. And our Lord counsels us all to sell all our other pearls, good and bad, great and small, and buy up our own soul unto everlasting life. "What is a man profited," our Lord demands of every man among us, "if he shall gain the whole world and lose his own soul? Or what shall a man give in exchange for his soul?" Our Lord was the last to undervalue the world which He has made, and of which He is the Heir, and yet He says that if many man should have this whole world in one hand, and his immortal soul in the other hand, he will be a fool of the first water if he holds to the whole world and lets go his immortal soul. Yes. The pearl of all pearls to you and to me is our own immortal soul. And we do not have to compass sea and land in search of this pearl of great price. We have it in our hand already, and all we have to do in order to be the richest of merchant men, is to keep a good hold of it. Unless, indeed, we have already lost hold of it. As we have. Alas, as we all have. Oh, what a fatal market is that which goes on all around every man who has a soul to sell to his everlasting loss, or to keep to his everlasting enriching. Oh, what a mad market that is in which men's souls, worth more than the whole world, are sold away every day for nought, and for far less than nought. And thus it was that our Lord was not content with warning us as to the value of our souls; but He entered the soul-market Himself, and bought back our souls at a price that has for ever put His immense estimate upon them. He who alone knows the exchangeless value of our immortal souls, He came and redeemed our souls at a price which was worth far more than the whole world, and all our souls to the bargain. For He redeemed our souls at the price of His own precious blood.

But then all that only ends, as every parable of His has ended, in making our Blessed Lord Himself THE PEARL of all pearls to us. All these partial, and, as it were, preliminary, pearls take their value to us entirely from Him. They all run up their values into Him. All good books are really good books to us, just in the measure that they speak to us about Jesus Christ. If they speak not to us about Him—take them away. Light the fire with them. They are not worth their house-room. All our doctrines also of whatever kind; doctrines of science, of politics, of letters, of art, of theology, of morals—all are sound and safe for a man to go by himself, and to teach his children to go by, only in the measure that Jesus Christ is in them. It was really, and all the time, the Preacher Himself who was the goodly Pearl of that sermon and that day. "To whom can we go," said Peter when he was under the illumination of the Father,—"but unto Thee? Thou hast the words of eternal life." All of you, then, who are seeking for goodly pearls, whether in the world of books, or of doctrines, or of any other kind of good things; here, under your very eye; here, to your very hand, is the greatest and the best Pearl in all the world. For Jesus Christ gathers up into Himself all the truth, and all the beauty, and all the satisfaction, that your heart has for so long been seeking in vain. He is the Father's Pearl of great price. He is the one perfect Chrysolite of heaven on sale on earth. Who, then, on the spot will sell all that he has, and will be for ever after the wisest of merchant men? Nay, who will take away with him to-night God's greatest Pearl as God's free gift, without money and without price? For the gift of God is eternal life, through Jesus Christ our Lord.

VIII

THE MAN WHO WENT OUT TO BORROW THREE LOAVES AT MIDNIGHT

For thirty years and more our Lord had been laying up materials for His future sermons. And He had started to collect His materials with something like this as one of His guiding principles: —

> What surmounts the reach
> Of human sense, I shall delineate so,
> By likening spiritual to corporal forms,
> As may express them best; though what if Earth
> Be but the shadow of Heaven, and things therein
> Each to other like, more than on Earth is thought?

Our Lord knowing that to be the case, and taking that for one of His guiding principles in His preaching, it came about that what we call His parables, were, in reality, not so much parables of His at all, as they were His observations of human life, and His experiences of human life, with His divine intuitions of grace and truth irradiating and illuminating them all. In our artificial and superficial way we think of our Lord as making up His parables as He went on with His sermons, and throwing them in just as they occurred to Him at the moment. But that was not His way of preaching at all. His way of preaching, and of preparing for His preaching, was a far better way than that. For, not seldom His parables were His own personal experiences, and His own immediate observations, collected and laid up in His mind and in His memory and in His heart, and to be afterwards worked up into His sermons. As we find them worked up with all the freshness and impressiveness and authority that personal experience always gives to preaching, whether that preaching is our Lord's own incomparable preaching, or such poor preaching as our own.

Our Lord, says the evangelist, was praying in a certain place. Our Lord was always praying, and in every place, and the evangelist knew that quite well. But he is a practised and a skilful writer, and what he here writes is written, every word of it, with an intended purpose. The evangelist here gives his readers this report of that day just as he had received it from an eye and ear witness of the occurrences of that day, and he introduces this most important narrative with a certain studied circumstantiality of style. There had been something quite out of the ordinary in our Lord's private devotions that day. He had been much longer absent from His disciples that day than was His wont. And, besides, when He joined them again there was something about Him that specially arrested the attention of one of His disciples. Whoever he was, that disciple went up to his Master and said to Him, Lord, teach us to pray, as Thou Thyself so often prayest. And thus it was that that happy disciple, whoever he was, got on the spot, "Our Father, which art in heaven," as his Master's answer to his request. A great reward to him and to us for his holy boldness, and for his timeous petition that day. And not the Lord s Prayer only; but that richly-favoured disciple got for himself and for his fellow-disciples and for us also, what we call the parable of the friend at midnight. Our Lord not only taught His disciples that prayer of prayers that day but—to enforce the lesson, He told them a story out of His rich treasure-house of such stories; a story that has all the freshness, and all the lifelikeness, and all the pointedness, of a personal experience. "Which of you," He said, turning to the twelve, "shall have a friend, and shall go to him at midnight, and shall say unto him, Friend, lend me three loaves. For a friend of mine on his journey has come to me, and I have nothing to set before him?" Now there is only too good ground for believing that the carpenter's house was one of the poorest houses in all Nazareth and Capernaum. Sickness, death, suretyship, losses in business, and trouble upon trouble of every kind, had overtaken Joseph's household, till, with all their industry, and all their frugality, his household would seem to have been poor beyond any of their kindred or any of their acquaintances. So much so, that nothing is more likely than that Joseph had oftener than once undergone the very indignity that is here so feelingly described. And not Joseph only, but He who here tells this touching story was found under Joseph's roof as one of his sons, and all His days on earth He was one of the poorest of men. No. Depend upon it, He did not make up the parable of the importunate poor man at midnight. He did not need to make it up. He was Himself in all points made like that poor and importunate man. Poor and importunate, not for Himself, but for men poorer than Himself who had thrown themselves upon Him. Our Lord was an experimental preacher. Just as He was and is an experimental priest.

It is a most pathetic, but at the same time a most amusing, story. It has been said sometimes that our Lord never laughed. Perhaps not. But we both laugh and weep at once over this scene as He here sets it before us. The well-supped churl is folded up in his warm bed and is just falling asleep, when a knock comes to his door so loud that it wakens the very dogs in the street. And then his angry denial is only answered with louder and louder knocking. Till we see that the well-fed and warmly laid down householder is completely at the mercy of that dreadful neighbour of his at the door. His very love for his bed lays him open to every knock that resounds through his well-supped and well-bedded house. I tell you I cannot rise! he shouts. Ay, but he will have to rise if the man at the door only holds on. Let him only hold on knocking loud enough and long enough, and as sure as that householder loves his warm bed, so sure will the traveller in the other house get his supper. And not three loaves only. But once he is out of bed the sleepy man thrusts more loaves on the knocking man than he wants. His love for his bed makes him afraid that this noisy neighbour of his may come back again before the night is over. How many travellers did you say had come to you? And how many loaves will they need? Three? Take four. Take six. Oh, no, says the petitioner, three will do. Take four, at any rate, says the half-naked and generous-hearted householder. Take as many as you can carry, lest you should have to come back again. And he loads the man at the door with an armful of his best bread. Good-night! And he shuts his door and returns to his bed, glad at any cost to get rid of such an untimeous and unceremonious neighbour.

"Importunity" cannot be called a bad rendering exactly. Only it is not by any means the best rendering of the original writing. Nor does it by any means bring out to us the whole intended instructiveness of the scene. We must not water down our Lord's words, even when they are too strong for our feeble digestion. What our Lord actually said was not importunity but "shamelessness." "I say unto you because of his shamelessness he will rise and give him as many as he needeth." Think shame, man! the passers-by exclaimed as they heard him making that so disgraceful noise in the midnight street. The neighbours also looked out of their windows and shouted "Think shame!" at him. And they were right. For it was nothing short of a shameless knocking that the determined man made. Indeed, it was the very shamelessness, that is to say, the lateness and the loudness, of the knocking, that was the success of it. To be shameless in that way and to that degree was the man's wisdom, and hence his utter shamelessness is our Lord's very point with His disciples and with us. Never mind who cries shame, says our Lord to us. Keep you on knocking, shame or no shame. Think shame, woman! the devil said to Santa Teresa. A woman at your time of life having to make such a confession. And presumptuously hoping for pardon for such shameless sins. Think shame! Or if you will still presume to pray for forgiveness, at any rate, wait a little. Do not go to God and you still reeking with such uncleanness. Wash in the holy water first. Perform a time of penance first. "The devil never so nearly had my soul for ever, as just after another fall of mine, and when he cried, For shame, O woman, for shame." These are her very identical words to us in this matter: "Never let any one leave off prayer on any pretence whatsoever; great sins committed, or any pretence whatsoever. I tell you again that the leaving off prayer after sin was the most devilish temptation I was ever met with."

Importunity, then, and shameless importunity, and that in midnight prayer, is the great lesson of this scripture. Indeed, the whole point of the story here told by our Lord turns upon the untimeousness of the hour when the knocking took place. The thing could never have taken place in the daytime. It is a story of midnight importunity, and it is told to teach us the great lesson of midnight and importunate prayer. Travelling, with all its accompanying incidents such as this, takes place mostly at night in the East, and importunate prayer in the West. And this lesson that our Lord gives us is quite as much to teach us to pray at night as it is to pray with importunity, and for excellent reasons. The Psalms, when we begin to attend to what we read and sing, are full of night, and midnight, and early morning, prayer. I was greatly struck, no longer ago than last night, with what I had never felt with such force before. I was reading the fifth and sixth verses of the sixty-third Psalm at family worship. I find that reading a single verse sometimes will impress our hearts at home more than a whole Psalm. Well, I was reading to them those two verses, and it occurred to me to turn them round and read the sixth verse first and then the fifth, in this way: "When I remember thee upon my bed, and meditate on Thee in the night watches; my soul, as often as I do that, is always satisfied again as with marrow and fatness." As much as to say—"When my soul thirsteth for Thee; when my flesh longeth for Thee; when my soul is like the man in the parable who had a hungry traveller in his house, and had nothing to set before him; then I remember the Lord. I remember His name and all that His name contains. I remember His merciful and gracious name, and I call like that loud-calling man upon His merciful and gracious name. I meditate and remember, and remember and meditate, and that in the night watches, till my soul is again satisfied as with marrow and fatness." The sixty-third Psalm is just the eleventh of Luke before the time. The eleventh of Luke is all in the Psalms. As soon as we get all the best teaching of the New Testament about prayer, we return and find it all ready in the Psalms. We would not have found it in the Psalms but for the New Testament; only, once we have the whole doctrine of New Testament prayer taught to us, we come to our full astonishment at David, then, and with David's Son, both teaching us to pray, we ourselves should surely come to some success and proficiency in prayer. With these, and with such a wealth of other experiences and testimonies and examples of praying men as we possess, and of praying men at night, we should surely learn to pray. Take this home with you from Father John of the Greek Church. "When praying at night," he says to his people, "do not forget to confess with all importunity, and sincerity, and contrition, those sins into which you have fallen during the past day. A few moments of importunate repentance, before you sleep, and you will be cleansed from all your iniquity. You will be made whiter than the snow. You will be covered with the robe of Christ's righteousness, and again united to Him. Often during the day I myself have been a great sinner, and at night, after importunate prayer, I have gone to rest washed and restored, and with the deepest joy and the most perfect peace filling my heart. How needful it will be for our Lord to come and save us in the evening of our life, and at the decline of our days! O save me, save me, save me, most gracious Lord, and receive me at the end of my days into Thy heavenly kingdom."

IX

THE IMPORTUNATE WIDOW

With all his ungodliness and with all his inhumanity, there was a widow in that city who brought the unjust judge to his senses. His boast within himself was that he neither feared God nor regarded man, but there was a widow in that city who made him both fear her and regard her. There were many widows who had adversaries in our Lord's land and day, and He must have known more than one of them. His own mother Mary may well have been one of them. Who knows but that she herself was this very widow with an adversary? Nothing is more likely. At any rate, whoever this widow was, by this time she was driven all but beside herself with adversity and oppression and robbery. She had spent all her living on daysmen and mediators, but the unjust judge was a companion of thieves and he would not hear her advocates. And, had it not been for her fatherless and fast-starving children, she would soon have been laid out of sight and out of hearing in her dead husband's forgotten grave. It was her orphaned and starving children that made their mother to be like a she-bear robbed of her whelps. Avenge me of mine adversary! She stood in the way of the unjust judge's chariot all day and cried out, Avenge me of mine adversary! She burst in upon the business of his court and cried, Avenge me of mine adversary! She stood under his window all night and cried out, Avenge me of mine adversary! And he would not for a while. But after that day when this wild woman suddenly sprang in upon him with a knife hidden away among her rags—after that day he said, Because this widow troubleth me, I will avenge her, lest by her continual coming she weary me! There is a tinge of blood in the original ink that is lost in the tame translation, because there was a gleam of blood in the widow's wild eye on that last day of her warning and appeal to the unjust judge. And the Lord said, Hear what the unjust judge saith. And shall not

God avenge His own elect which cry day and night to Him, though He bear long with them? I tell you that He will avenge them speedily.

Now it is not by any means every woman who has the making of a "widow indeed" in her. And it is not by any means every soul under sanctification who cries for victory over sin day and night. There are many—even gracious souls among us—to whose case this Scripture does not by any means answer. But there are some other souls who say unto their Lord as soon as He has spoken this about the widow and her adversary to them: Lo, now speakest Thou plainly, and speakest no parable. Now we are sure that Thou knowest all things, and needest not that any man should ask Thee: for by this we believe that Thou camest forth from God. Such souls are sure that He knows all things about them, at any rate; and by His knowledge of them and of their adversary they believe that He has come forth to them from God. And, like one who has come forth from God and who knows the secret things of God, He here announces to us who are God's elect among us, and who are not. Every elect soul, He says, is like that widow in that city. For every elect soul is poor, and downtrodden, and dispossessed, and desolate. Is, or ought to be. As that widow had an adversary who had done all that to her, even so, every soul, elect to a great salvation, has an adversary who has done all that to it, and far more than all that. I do not know, and I cannot tell you, the name of that widow's adversary in that city. But if you do not know I will tell you the name of the universal adversary of all God's elect in this city. It is sin. This widow had only one adversary, and so it is with the elect. You never hear from their lips a demand for vengeance against any adversary of theirs but one. And all elect souls have one and the same adversary. And this is as good to them all as the seal of their election, this, that their only and real adversary is sin. Now you would all like to be assured, would you not, that you are among God's elect? You would all like to get a glimpse, for a moment, into the book of God's decrees, so as to read your name there. But you do not need to climb up to heaven in order to make your election sure. Who is your adversary? Who makes your life a burden to you? Who persecutes and oppresses and impoverishes your soul day and night continually? Against whom is it that you, almost demented, cry without ceasing, Avenge you of your adversary? Sin is the spot of God's children. Sin, and the woe it works in the soul, is the seal of God's elect. Have you that spot? Have you that seal? Has your sin dispossessed you, and beggared you, and driven you beside yourself? Nevertheless, the foundation of God standeth sure, having this seal. Now, are you such? Look well into yourself and see. Among all your adversaries, who is it that drives you day and night to God, like this woman to the judge? Do you think that our Lord counts you up among His Father's elect? I think He does? I am sure He does, if your adversary that you cry to be revenged upon is sin.

Avenge me! the widow cries. Her heart is full of her great wrongs. Her heart is full of a great rage. Her heart is full of fire. And she here puts her hot words into our mouth. She teaches our sin-tortured souls how to pray. She says to us, Remember me. Imitate me. I got vengeance done at last on mine adversary. Take no rest until you have got vengeance done on yours. She being dead, yet speaketh. Let us imitate her. Let us call on God as she called on the judge. Let us dwell day and night before God on our great wrongs. Let us keep ever repeating before Him what we have suffered at our adversary's hands. Tell Him that it is past telling. Tell Him that you are beside yourself. Tell Him that all He can do to your adversary will not satisfy your fierce feelings. O sin! O sin! How thou has persecuted my soul down to the ground! How thou hast robbed and desolated my soul. How thou hast made my life a burden to me! How thou hast driven me sometimes beside myself with thy cruel and bitter bondage! How my soul sometimes seeks death to escape from thee! O thou foul and cruel tyrant, I will surely be revenged upon thee yet!

And He spake this parable unto them to this end, that men ought always to pray. Not once; not twice; not seven times; not a thousand times. But always till we are avenged of our adversary. We are not to pray against a besetting sin for a time, and then to despair and let it have its own way with us. We are to pray always. We are to pray on till we need to pray no longer. No sooner is one such prayer offered than we are to begin another. No sooner have we said, Amen! than we must say with our very next breath, O Thou that hearest prayer; to Thee shall all flesh come. No sooner have we risen off our knees than we must return to our knees. No sooner have we opened the door to come out of our closet than we must shut the door again, and return to our Father who seeth in secret. To whom else can we go? To whom else can we tell it all out, how our iniquities still continue to prevail against us?

Always, or as it is rendered in the seventh verse, day and night.

All day and all night; the first thing in the morning and the last thing at night. The first thing in the morning and then all the day. When you open your eyes, and before that, always say this, When I awake, I am still with Thee. When you rise off your bed always say, Awake, my soul, and with the sun thy daily stage of duty run. When you wash your hands and your face say, Wash Thou me, and I shall be clean. When you bathe your whole body say, There is a fountain filled with blood, and sinners plunged beneath that flood, lose all their guilty stains. When you dress yourself say, He hath clothed me with the garments of salvation, He hath covered me with the robe of righteousness. And then when you go forth to your day's work, say with David when he went forth to his day's work, On Thee do I wait all the day. What is your occupation? Whatever it is say as you again enter on it,The kingdom of heaven is like this, and that, more than on earth is thought. Are you a carpenter? say So was He. Are you a mason—say Other foundation can no man lay than that is laid. Are you a laundress? say His raiment was shining, exceeding white as snow; so as no fuller on earth can white them. Are you a cook? When you burn yourself, then say with Brother Lawrence, Who among us shall dwell with the devouring fire? Who among us shall dwell with everlasting burnings? And say with him also, Even the dogs eat of the crumbs. Are you a preacher? say Lest that by any means, when I have preached to others, I myself should be a castaway. Are you a physician? say Physician, heal thyself. And say Esculapius healed many, but at last he succumbed himself. And say at every patient's door with Sir Thomas Browne, Peace be to this house, and health from the God of their salvation. Are you a banker? say to yourself, Thou wicked and slothful servant, thou oughtest to have put my money to the exchangers, and then at my coming I should have received mine own with usury. And cast ye the unprofitable servant into outer darkness. Are you an aurist? say He that planted the ear, shall He not hear? Are you an oculist? say He that formed the eye, shall He not see? Do you own horses, or ride or drive, horses? say Be ye not as the horse, or as the mule, which have no understanding; whose mouth must be held in with bit and bridle. And are you not good at driving? Then say like the English clown: I have driven into the ditch, O Jesus Christ, take Thou the reins! When on the street you see a prisoner in the hands of his jailor, say There goes John Newton, but for the grace of God. No, it was when John Newton saw a scaffold that he said that. And, speaking of John Newton, if you are a shoe-black, say If only for the credit of Christ, I will be the best shoe-black in the parish. When you meet a funeral, take off your hat and say The sands of time are sinking. When you meet a marriage, say Behold, the bridegroom cometh! When the sun sets in the west, say There shall be no night in heaven. When you lay your head down on your pillow say, if only out of respect to your sainted mother, This night I lay me down to sleep, I pray the Lord my soul to keep. When you cannot sleep, say At midnight will I rise and praise Thee. And when you awake in the morning, say Nevertheless, I am still with Thee. And shall not God avenge His own elect, which cry day and night unto Him, though He bear long with them? I tell you that He will avenge them speedily.

There is a well-known system of medicine that, most paradoxically as one would think, for a cure prescribes a little more of that which caused the sickness. I do not know whether that is sound science, or whether it is what its enemies call it. That is not my field. But this is. And I am safe and certain to say that whether homœopathy is sound medicine or no, it holds in divinity, and especially in this department of divinity, unfainting prayer for sanctification. If you are fainting in prayer for sanctification I recommend and prescribe to you Samuel Hahnemann's dictum *similia similibus curantur*. Only not in small doses. The opposite of that. Small doses in prayer will be your death. The very thing that has caused your whole head to be sick, and your whole heart to be faint,—hitherto unanswered prayer, answered or unanswered, pray you on. The answer is not your business. It is importunate and unfainting prayer that is your only business. And, always, more and more importunate and unfainting prayer. *Similia similibus.* Mix up your medicine with every meal. Make your whole meal upon your medicine. Have it standing ready at your bedside all night. Take it the last thing at night and the first thing in the morning. And if you hear the hours striking all night, betake yourself to your sure febrifuge and sleeping draught. In plain words, when you faint in prayer for a holy heart continue all the more instant in that prayer. Pray always for a holy heart, with all prayer and supplication in the Spirit, and watch thereunto with all perseverance. The next time you feel your heart ready to faint in that kind of prayer, call to mind Who says this to you, and where He says it. This, that men ought always to pray against this adversary, and not to faint.

Nevertheless, when the Son of Man cometh, shall He find such prayer on the earth? I do not know. I cannot tell. The earth is too large for me to speak for it, and too far away from me. My matter is, shall He find such prayer in me? Shall He find me in my bed, or on my knees? Shall I be reading this parable of His for the ten thousandth time to keep my heart from fainting? Shall, Avenge me of mine adversary, be on my lips at the moment when the judgment-angel puts the last trump to his lips? And shall I be found of him on my knees, and with my finger on this scripture, when the trumpet shall sound, and I shall be changed?

X

THE PRODIGAL SON

A CERTAIN man had two sons. And the younger of them said to his father. Father, give me the portion of goods that falleth to me. And he divided unto them his living. And not many days after the younger son gathered all together, and took his journey into a far country, and there wasted his substance with riotous living. The country-bred boy had been told stealthy and seductive stories about the delights of city life. 'A young man with a little money,' he had been told, 'can command anything he likes in the great city. A young man who has never been from home can have no idea of the pleasures that are provided in the city for young men whose fathers have money. The games, the shows, the theatres, the circuses, the feasts, the dances, the freedom of all kinds; there is absolutely nothing that a young man's heart can desire that is not open to him who brings a good purse of money to the city with him.' All these intoxications were poured into this young man's imagination, and he was but too good a pupil to such instructions.

How long will my father live? he began to ask. How long will that old man continue to stand in my way? It is not reasonable that a young man should be kept so long out of what really belongs to him. It is not fair to treat a grown-up man as if he were still a child. "Father, give me the portion of goods that falleth to me." It was a heartless speech. But secret visions of sin will soon harden the tenderest heart in the world. *Cogitatio et imaginatio,* according to À Kempis, are the two first steps of a young man's heart on its way down to the pit. Keep a young man's thoughts and imaginations clean, and he is safe, and will be a good son. But once pollute, by bad books or bad companionships, a young man's mind and imagination, and nothing in this world will hold that young man back from perdition.

And not many days after the younger son gathered all together and took his journey into a far country, and there wasted his substance with riotous living. Let one who lived for a long time in that far country describe it. "A darkened heart is the far country. For it is not by our feet, but by our affections, that we either leave Thee or return to Thee. Nor did that younger son look out for chariots, or ships, or fly with visible wings, that he might go to the far country. Unclean affections, and a God-abandoned heart, that is the far country. This was the world at whose gate I lay in imagination, while yet a boy. And this was the abyss of my vileness when I was cast away from before Thine eyes. Who was so vile before Thee as I was? I was vile even to myself."

And when he had spent all, there arose a mighty famine in that land; and he began to be in want. "A mighty famine" is perfect English. It is one of those great strokes of translation that sometimes surpass the original. "A mighty famine" put a perfect picture of that far country before us. Now what chance, in the midst of a mighty famine, had a prodigal son who had already wasted all his substance with riotous living? What hope was there for him? What could a penniless spendthrift do? Till, covered with rags, and with all his bones staring till they could be counted, he threw himself upon a citizen of that country, and said:—'Only give me one crust-of-bread and water, and I will do anything you like to command me. I have a father at home, but that is far away. Oh, for my father's sake, and he will repay you, give me something to eat.' And he sent him into his fields to feed swine. "Did I see a boy of good make and mind, with the tokens on him of a refined nature, cast upon the world without provision, unable to say whence he came, or who were his family connections, I should conclude there was some secret connected with his history, and that he was one of whom, from one cause or another, his parents were ashamed." Such is Dr. Newman's picture of the human race, as it is fallen away from God, and gone into a far country.

"AND WHEN HE CAME TO HIMSELF"—Underline these words. Print these words in capitals. Engrave these words in letters of gold. For up till now sin has abounded, but henceforth grace is much more to abound. And already the abounding grace that the prodigal son is so soon to be met with, is beginning to drop from His lips Who here tells the prodigal's sad story. Look at the beautiful way in which the terrible truth is softened in the telling. Every word is so tenderly, and almost apologetically, chosen. You do not upbraid a son of yours when he is brought home to you safe and sound from the asylum. Whatever he may have said or done during his illness there, you refuse to listen to it. You say, My poor possessed child! You say, My son at that time was not responsible. And you shut your ears to all the heartless tales they tell about what he said and what he did when he was still beside himself. You rebuke his cruel accusers. You tell them that nobody reckons to a recovered man the things that would be reckoned and punished to an entirely sound-minded man. These grace-chosen words, "When he came to himself," already prepare us for the speedy return and complete restoration of this unhappy son, whose infirmity and affliction, rather than his sin and guilt, are the subject of his history as it is here told to us.

"But when he was yet a great way off, his father saw him." And we see him. Our Lord sees him, and He makes us see him. Look at him! Look how he runs! He runs like a man running for his life. He forgets his bleeding feet and his hungry belly. He outstrips everybody on the same road. He runs as he never ran before. But when he comes to the first sight of his father's house his strength suddenly fails him. He stands still, he sinks down, he beats his breast. He cries out as with an intolerable pain till the passers-by hasten on in fear. The man is possessed, one says to him. How long wilt thou be drunken? says another. But he sees them not. He hears them not. The only thing he sees is his father's house through his tears and his sobs. And all that any of the people in the fields or on the road could make out from him was always this: "Against thee, thee only, have I sinned, and done this evil in thy sight!"

And, then, all this long far-country time, his father's grey hairs were being brought down with sorrow to the grave. His father had never been the same man since the evil day when his son had left his father's door without kissing his father. He had ever since that day gone up and down his house a broken-hearted man. His very reapers had wept for him as they saw him walking up and down alone in his harvest fields. Every night also he sat and looked out of his window till the darkness fell again on all the land. And all through the darkness he listened all night for a footstep that never came. But, at last one day,—That is none other than my long-lost son! And when he was yet a great way off, his father saw him, and had compassion, and ran, and fell on his neck, and kissed him.

And now, among many other things, our Lord, I feel sure, would have us learn from this family history such things as this —The unspeakable evil of a mind early stained with images of sensual sin. This young man was at one time as innocent of this sin, and was as loyal to his father and mother, as are any of your sons or mine. But on a fatal day some bad man told him a bad story. Some one whispered to his heart some of the evil secrets of Satan's kingdom. And then, as the *Imitation* has it, there was first the sinful knowledge, and then there arose out of that a sinful imagination, a picture of the sin, and then the young sinner's heart took a secret delight in the knowledge and the vision, and then he sought for an opportunity, and the opportunity soon came. A bad companion will do it. A bad book will do it. A bad picture will do it. The very classics themselves will sometimes do it. It is being done every day in our bothies, and in our workshops, and in our schools, and in our colleges. A bad story will do it. A bad song will do it. A bad jest will do it. Indeed, it is in the very air that all our sons breathe. It is in the very bread they eat. It is in the very water they drink. They cannot be in this world and clean escape it. For myself, one of the saintliest men I ever knew once told me certain evil things, just out of the evil fullness of his heart, when I was not asking for them. Evil things that I would not have known to this day but for that conversation. Supply me with a knife deep enough and sharp enough to cut that corrupt spot out of my memory, and I will, from this moment, cast it out on the dunghill of the devil for ever—as we had, at last, to cut off and cast him. It was some one like my early friend who polluted that young man's imagination till nothing could keep him back from becoming the prodigal son of whom our Lord here tells us all these things for our warning and for our rebuke.

The very finest point in all this history full of fine points, is this,—"When he was a great way off, his father saw him, and had compassion on him." And there is nothing more true in our own history than just this, and nothing more blessed for us to be told than just this, that our Father also sees us when we are yet a great way off from Him, and has compassion on us. When we are just beginning to remember that we have a Father; when we are just beginning to repent toward Him; when we are just beginning to pray to Him; when we are just beginning to believe on Him, and on His Son Jesus Christ our Saviour; when we are still at the very first beginnings of a penitent, returning, obedient, pure, and godly, life; ay, when we are yet a great way off from all these things, our Father sees us, and has compassion on us, and comes to meet us. I do not know a sweeter or a more consoling scripture anywhere than just this,—"When he was yet a great way off." For, what grace is in that! What encouragement, what hope, what comfort, what life from the dead is in that! Blessed be the lips that told this whole incomparable story, and added to it these words of gold—"a great way off."

And, then, to sum up. This whole story, in every syllable of it, has its exact and complete fulfilment in ourselves every day. A prince of Scripture exposition holds it to be doubtful whether our Lord intends under this family story to set forth the first conversion of a great sinner, or the repeated restoration of a great backslider. But the truth is, our Lord intends to set forth both; and much more than both. For not one, nor two, nor three, but all the steps and all the stages of sin and salvation in the soul of man, are most impressively and most unmistakably set before us in this masterpiece of our Master. From the temptation and fall of Adam, on to the marriage supper of the Lamb—all the history of the Church of God, and all the experiences of the individual sinner and saint, are to be found set forth in this most wonderful of all our Lord's histories. John Howe warns us that we must not think it strange if all the requisites to our salvation are not to be found together in any single passage of Holy Scripture. But, on the other hand, I will take it upon me to say that all the incidents and all the experiences of this evangelical history are to be found together in every soul of man who is under a full and perfect salvation. In a well-told story like this, all that the prodigal son came through, from first to last, must of necessity be set forth in so many successive steps and stages: the one step and stage following on the other. But that is not at all the case in the actual life of sin and grace in the soul. The soul is such that it is passing through *all* the steps and stages of sin and salvation at one and the same time. Some of the steps and stages of sin and salvation may be more present and more pressing at one time than at another time, but they are all somewhere or other within the soul, and are ready to spring up in it. We speak in our shallow way about the Apostle Paul being for ever out of the seventh of the Romans and for ever into the eighth. But Paul never spoke in that superficial fashion about himself. And he could not. For both chapters were fulfilling themselves within their profound author: sometimes at one and the same moment. Sometimes the old man was uppermost in Paul, and sometimes the new man; sometimes the flesh, and sometimes the spirit; sometimes the law and sin and death had Paul under their feet, and sometimes he was more than a conqueror over all the three. But, all the time, all the three were within Paul, and every page he writes, and every sermon he preaches, shows it. And so it is with ourselves, so far as this history, and so far as Paul's history, is our history. For, like the prodigal son, we are always having lewd stories told us about the far country. We are always dreaming of being at liberty to do as we like. We are always receiving our portion of goods, and we are always wasting our substance. We are always trying in vain to fill our belly with the husks that the swine do eat. And we are always arising and returning to our Father's house. In endless ways, impossible to be told, but by all God's true children every day to be experienced, every step and every stage of the prodigal's experience, both before he came to himself, and after it, is all to be found in the manifold, boundless, all-embracing, experience of every truly gracious heart. In His unsearchable wisdom, God has set both the whole world of sin, and the whole world of salvation, in every truly renewed heart. And that, not in successive and surmounting steps and stages, but at one and the same time. And that accumulating, complex, and exquisitely painful state of things, will go on in every truly regenerate heart, till that day dawns when the greatest prodigal of us all, and the saddest saint of us all, shall begin to be merry.

XI

THE MUCH FORGIVEN DEBTOR AND HIS MUCH LOVE

We will sometimes ourselves be like Simon the Pharisee. We will sometimes invite a man to come to take a meal with us when we do not really mean it. We were in a warm mood of mind at the moment when we asked him to dine or sup with us. We met him in circumstances such that we were led into giving him the invitation when we did not really intend it. So much so that when the man comes we had quite forgotten to expect him, and we can scarcely hide our vexation at the sight of him. Now it was something not unlike that with Simon the Pharisee that night.

We must put out of our mind all our modern ideas and all our sound doctrines about our Lord. It is not easy for us to do that, but we will never read a single page of the four Gospels aright, unless we go back in imagination to the exact circumstances of that extraordinary time. We must accustom ourselves to return to those early days when our Lord was still half a carpenter of Nazareth, and half a preacher at the street corner. Some men holding Him to be a prophet come from God, and some holding that He was just Joseph's son gone beside Himself. It was in these circumstances that our Lord was sometimes invited to dine or to sup, His hosts sometimes forgetting that they had invited Him, and sometimes heartily wishing that He would not come, and, when He did come, positively not knowing what to do with Him. Such exactly was Simon's case. He had undoubtedly invited this so-called prophet to sup at his house that night. But when He came at the hour appointed, Simon was wholly occupied with looking after much more important people. When we arrive at any man's door on his distinct invitation and see that we are not expected; when nobody knows us or pays any attention to us; when the head of the house sees us quite well, but has not so much as a moment or a nod or a smile to spare to us,—it is all we can do not to put on our hat and go away home again. And if we do go in and sit down at his table, we are in a most sour and unsocial state of mind all the evening. But Simon's neglected Guest was quite accustomed to that kind of treatment. Every day He put up with incivility, and said nothing. No insult ever angered Him. No openly exhibited or plainly intended slight ever embittered Him. And thus it was that He went in and sat down at Simon's supper-table that night, with a quiet mind and an affable manner, and was the best of neighbours to all who sat near Him.

But who and what is this? For, behold a woman in the city, which was a sinner, when she saw that Jesus sat at meat in the Pharisee's house, brought an alabaster box of ointment, and stood at His feet behind him weeping, and began to wash His feet with tears, and did wipe them with the hairs of her head, and kissed His feet, and anointed them with the ointment. Now, when the Pharisee which had bidden Him saw it, he spake within himself, saying, This man, if He were a prophet, would have known who and what manner of woman this is that toucheth Him: for she is a sinner. 'I have made a great mistake,' said Simon within himself. 'I am always far too precipitate with my invitations. I might have known better. What a scene! I will never hear the end of it. I will never forgive myself for it. I should never have had him across my doorstep. I was warned against him and his followers, and I see now that they who so warned me were right. Whatever he is, he is not a prophet.

If he were a prophet he would at once have put a stop to this scandalous scene.'

Simon, I have somewhat to say unto thee. And he saith, Master, say on. There was a certain creditor which had two debtors: the one owed five hundred pence, and the other fifty. And when they had nothing to pay, he frankly forgave them both. Tell Me, therefore, which of them will love him most? Simon answered, and said, I suppose that he to whom he forgave most. And He turned to the woman, and said unto Simon, Seest thou this woman? I entered into thine house, thou gavest me no water for My feet: but she hath washed My feet with tears, and wiped them with the hairs of her head. Thou gavest Me no kiss: but this woman, since the time I came in, hath not ceased to kiss My feet. My head with oil thou didst not anoint: but this woman hath anointed My feet with ointment. Wherefore I say unto thee, her sins, which are many, are forgiven; for she loved much: but to whom little is forgiven, the same loveth little.

From that scene, then, at Simon's supper-table, we are to learn this to-night. The less forgiveness, the less love: the more forgiveness the more love: no forgiveness at all, no love at all: but, nothing but forgiveness, then nothing but love. And then love is always love. Love, in short, is always like that woman. If you would see love at its very best, just look at that woman. Simon, being neither a publican nor a sinner, had needed so little forgiveness that he had not love enough to provide his Saviour with a basin and water wherewith to wash His feet. Simon had neither love enough, nor anything else enough, to teach him good manners. I am afraid for Simon. For, even a very little forgiveness, even fifty pence forgiven, even five pence, even five farthings, would surely have taught Simon at least ordinary civility. When I see any man among you hard and cruel to another man, discourteous and uncivil, not to say intentionally and studiously insolent, I say to myself, either that man has not yet been forgiven at all, or he has been forgiven so little that he does not feel it any more than a stone. The truth is, grant forgiveness enough and you will soon convert the greatest churl among you to be the most perfect gentleman among you Nothing else will do it, but forgiveness enough will do it. Grant forgiveness enough, and love enough, and you will have all considerateness, all civility, all generosity, all gratitude, springing up in that man's heart. Would you have a true gentleman for a friend, or for a lover, or for a husband, or for a son? Then manage, somehow, to have him brought to Simon's Guest for a great forgiveness, and the thing is done.

This, then, was the whole of Simon's case. He called our Lord Master, in as many words. He had our Lord at his table that night; but, all the time, he loved our Lord very little, if any at all. In other words, Simon had been forgiven by our Lord very little, if any at all. Simon did not need much forgiveness, if any at all, and in that measure Simon's case was hopeless. Simon, in short, was a Pharisee, and that explains everything concerning Simon. I know nothing more about Simon than I read in this chapter. I know nothing of his past life. I suppose it was, touching the righteousness which is in the law, blameless. But, blameless or no, I am sure of this about Simon, that the holy law of God had never once entered Simon's heart. All Simon's shameful treatment of our Lord, and all his deep disgust at that woman, and all his speeches to himself within himself, all arose from the fact that the holy law of God against all kinds of sin and sinners, and especially against himself, had not yet begun to enter Simon's hard heart. My brethren, to make the holy law of God even to begin to enter your hard heart would be the greatest service to you that any man could do to you. Only, no man can do you that service. No mere man, as the Catechism says, but that Man only who sat that night at Simon's supper-table and said to him,—"Simon, I have somewhat to say unto thee." Your minister may preach to you till he is old and grey-headed, but he will be to you as one that plays on an instrument; you will not take him seriously. You will pay no attention to him, till after the law enters. And just to the depth and to the poignancy with which the law of God enters your sinful heart, just in that measure will you possess in your broken heart a great or a small forgiveness, and will manifest before God and man a great or a small gratitude. Let no true preacher then be browbeaten by all the Pharisees in the world from labouring to make the law enter the innermost hearts of his people: both the law legal, and the law evangelical.

Then they that sat at meat with Him began to say within themselves, Who is this that forgiveth sins also? He and they had up till now been talking in the most friendly way together as they ate and drank. They had been talking over the latest news from Rome and Jerusalem: over the gossip of the town: over the sudden deaths of last week, and over the foul and fair weather of last week: when, suddenly, their talk was cut short by the unaccountable conduct of that woman. Some of them who sat at meat with Him had for months past been much exercised in their minds about Him. At one time they had thought one thing about Him, and at another time they had thought another thing about Him. Some could scarcely eat their supper for watching Him, how He ate, and how He drank, and how He talked, and all what He said and did. Till, when He spoke out, and told the story of the creditor and his two debtors, and then wound up the story with such a home-thrust at Simon, they wished themselves seated at another table. They wished that they were well home again. And then when His voice rose to a tenderness and a solemnity they had never heard in any man's voice and manner before, it was no wonder that they said within themselves, Who is this that forgiveth sins also?

Now, listen to this, my brethren. Listen, and receive this. That same Man who forgiveth sins is here also. Here, at this moment, in this House. And He is here on the same errand. He is here seeking and saving sinners. Come to His feet then as that sinful woman came. Come if you are as unspeakably vile as she was, and with the same unspeakable vileness. Come if she is your sister in sin. Up till to-night a Pharisee like Simon; or up till to-night a harlot like this woman; equally come. And come all the more quickly. This woman was on her way to throw herself into the pond when she heard our Lord preaching one of His sermons of salvation: and before He had done with His sermon she was at His feet. Come even if you are intending to take your own life to-night. A woman once had the arsenic bought on a Saturday, when she said to herself that she would go once more to the church before she took it. The text that morning was this: What profit is there in my blood? She told me her whole story long afterwards. Come if you have the arsenic in your pocket. Come and cast it at His feet.

And then He will have in you the wages for which He worked; for how you, for one, will love Him! Jesus Christ is not easily satisfied with love; but He will be satisfied, and to spare, with your love. And every day on earth will add coals of fire to your love to your Redeemer. And no wonder. For He will have to say to you ten thousand times this same thing: Thy sins, which are still many, are all forgiven thee. Again, and again, and again, He will have to say it, for, having begun to say it to you, He will say it to you to the end. Thy faith hath saved thee, go in peace, He will say.

Samuel Rutherford was wont to set this riddle of love to the old saints in Anwoth: Whether they would love their Saviour more for their justification or for their sanctification? And some said one thing and some said another thing. And some wary old ones said both things. Oh yes! What a love, passing all earthly love, will He be loved with to all eternity! By some men and some women, that is. All His redeemed will love Him, but some will love Him more than these. To have been frankly forgiven such a fearful debt, and then, as if that were not enough, to have been washed whiter than the snow, and from such unspeakable pollution. Tell me, therefore, which of them will love Him most? I suppose that they to whom He forgave most. Yes; but what about those to whom He did both? Both frankly forgave them their fearful debt; and also, though their sins were as scarlet: though they were

From scalp to sole one slough and crust of sin,

made them as white as snow; and though they were red like crimson, made them to be as wool. Let Rutherford take that woman for his answer. For no better answer will ever be given to his riddle of love in this world. Behold, a woman in the city, which was a sinner, brought an alabaster box of ointment, and stood at His feet behind Him weeping, and began to wash His feet with tears, and did wipe them with the hairs of her head, and kissed His feet, and anointed them with the ointment. Wherefore I say unto thee, her sins, which are many, are forgiven; for she loved much.

When I stand before the throne,
Dressed in beauty not my own
When I see Thee as Thou art,
Love Thee with unsinning heart,
  Then, Lord, shall I fully know,
  Not till then how much I owe.

Chosen not for good in me,
Wakened up from wrath to flee,
Hidden in the Saviour's side,
By the Spirit sanctified,
  Teach me, Lord, on earth to show,
  By my love, how much I owe.

XII

THE TEN VIRGINS

EVERYTHING that our Lord saw on the earth immediately made Him think of the kingdom of heaven. Our Lord was of that angel's mind who said to Adam,—'What if earth be but the shadow of heaven, and things therein each to other like, more than on earth is thought.' And thus it was that when our Lord and His disciples were called to that marriage where the original of this parable took place, as soon as He saw the five wise virgins admitted to the marriage, and the five foolish virgins shut out, He turned to the twelve and said,—The kingdom of heaven is just like that. It would have been well, and we would have been deep in their debt, had some of the twelve said to their Master at that moment: Declare to us the parable of the ten virgins also. It would have been a great assistance to us if, over and above the parable itself, we had possessed our Lord's own exposition of it. For, who and what are the ten virgins, and why are they so called? Why are they exactly ten, and why are they so equally divided into five and five? What are their lamps also, and what are their vessels with their lamps, and what is the oil that the wise had, and that the foolish had not? What does the tarrying of the bridegroom mean, and what the slumbering and sleeping of the whole ten? And then who are they that make the midnight cry, Behold the bridegroom cometh? And then the hurried trimming of the lamps, with the going out of the lamps of the foolish,—what is the meaning of all that? The request of the foolish for a share of the oil of the wise, with the refusal of the wise to part with any of their oil,—what are the spiritual meanings hidden under all that? And specially, who sell the oil, and where do they sell it, and at what price? And then the shutting of the door? And then what it is to be ready—as well as what it is to watch, and when we are to watch, and where? It would have been an immense service done to us all had the disciples petitioned their Master for His own authoritative answer to all these questions. As it is, we are left to our own insight into the things of the kingdom of heaven, and to our own experience of its mysteries, to find out for ourselves and for others the true key to this parable.

The wisdom, whatever it was, of the five wise virgins is, plainly, the main lesson set to be learned out of this whole parable. All the rest of its lessons, however good and however true, are subordinate to that. All the rest is, more or less, the framework and the setting of that. Other lessons, more or less essential, more or less interesting, and more or less instructive, may be extracted out of this remarkable parable, but its supreme and commanding lesson is the richly rewarded wisdom of the five wise virgins. They that were foolish took their lamps, and took no oil with them. But the wise took oil in their vessels with their lamps.

Now if you would fain know what, exactly, this oil is of which so much is made in this parable, this oil the possession of which made the five virgins so wise, just look into your own heart for the answer to that. What is it that makes your heart to be so dark, and so sad, and so unready, sometimes? Why is there so little life and light and joy in your heart? Why is your religious experience so flat and so stale, when it should be as full of gladness as if your whole life were one continual making ready for your marriage? What is really the matter with you and with your heart? In plain English, and in few words, it is the absence from your heart of the Spirit of God. It is God's Holy Spirit Who makes God Himself to be so full of Life and Light and Blessedness. It is God's Holy Spirit Who makes our Lord Himself what He always is, and what He always says and does. The fruit of the Holy Spirit in God and in man, on earth and in heaven, is love, joy, peace, long-suffering, gentleness, goodness. Now, that is the whole of the matter with us all. It is the lack of the Spirit of God that makes all of us to be the lump of darkness and death that we are. If we had God's Holy Spirit shed abroad in our heart we would make every house in which we live, and every company into which we enter, like a continual marriage supper. Our very face would shine with heavenly light, and we would shed abroad life and love and beauty everywhere we go. No question, then, what this oil is, nor why we are such children of the day when we have it, and are such children of the night when we have it not. Fix this firmly in your mind, that the Holy Ghost is this light-giving and life-giving oil, and you will have in that, not only the true key to this whole parable, but at the same time the true key to all your own light and darkness also.

"Not so: lest there be not enough for us and you: but go ye rather to them that sell, and buy for yourselves." You go to the oil-sellers when your oil is done, and when the long and dark nights are coming on. And, in the very same way, you must go to God for the Holy Spirit. God the Father is the real seller of this Holy Oil. The Holy Ghost proceeds from the Father. The Son Himself had the Holy Ghost, not of Himself, but of the Father. When the night fell the wise virgins had the oil already in their vessels. They had been at the oil-sellers in good time, and before the darkness fell. Go you in good time also. Be beforehand with the darkness. Have the Holy Ghost already in your heart, and then you will not walk in darkness, nor be shut out into the darkness, however suddenly the Bridegroom may come.

And then this is the remarkable law of this oil-market. "What things soever ye desire, when ye pray, believe that ye receive them, and ye shall have them." That is to say, as soon as in prayer you ask the Father for the Holy Spirit, immediately believe that your prayer is answered. Immediately begin to live in the Spirit. Immediately begin to walk in the light. Do not put off walking in the light till you feel your heart full of light and love and joy and peace and all such holy illumination. But begin at once to live in the Spirit, and He will begin to live in you. As soon as you begin to ask for the Spirit of love and joy and peace to be shed abroad in your heart, begin yourself to shed that Spirit abroad in all your life. Let all your words and deeds, let all your moods of mind, and all your affections of heart, be full of love and joy and peace, and He will not fail to work in you to will and to do of His good pleasure. This is a most wonderful oil, and a most wonderful oil-market, and a most wonderful oil-merchant! Go all of you to Him who sells, and buy for yourselves, and you will soon be wiser in this divine marketry than all your teachers. Were I to enter on all the times, and all the places, when and where, this holy oil is bought and sold, I would have to say of it that there is no time and no place when and where you may not buy this oil. At the same time there are special seasons, and special spots, when and where, as a matter of experience, that oil is specially dispensed to all buyers. Olive oil, and all other kinds of oil, are to be bought in the oil-shops. And the Holy Ghost is best to be bought, is only to be bought, in secret prayer. Oil merchants advertise their oil; its qualities and its prices and where their place of business exactly is. And here is a copy of the heavenly advertisement: "Ask, and it shall be given you; seek, and ye shall find; knock, and it shall be opened to you. For how much more shall your Heavenly Father give the Holy Spirit to them that ask Him." And again: "But thou, when thou prayest, enter into thy closet, and when thou hast shut thy door, pray to thy Father which is in secret, and thy Father which seeth in secret, shall reward thee openly." Could anything be clearer? Could anything be plainer? A wayfaring man, though a fool, could not miss where this oil is to be had. "What," demanded his Master, in shame and pain at Peter's sloth and indifference in this very same matter, "What, could ye not watch with Me one hour?" Watch and pray for the Holy Spirit, He means. For it was just this heavenly oil that Peter needed above all things that dark and sudden midnight. And had Peter but spent that one hour with Him who hears prayer and thus sells His oil, he would have played a far better part all through the still thicker darkness of to-morrow and to-morrow night. It is still the old story, my brethren. There is no getting past the old story. You had better yield and surrender at once. That "hour" of prayer, which is now so haunting you, will never all your days let you alone. It will follow you wherever you go and whatever you are doing. Not till the door is shut will that secret "hour" of prayer give over pursuing you. Not till it ceases pursuing you and says, Sleep on now, and take your rest!

Though it is literally true that this holy oil is to be had for the asking, at the same time, and as a matter of fact, what amounts to a tremendous price has to be paid down for it. As Seneca says, "Nothing is so dear as that which is bought by prayer." A man may buy oil for his household lamps to last him for a whole winter, and yet may not be sensibly the poorer for his purchase. He may pay his oil bill, and yet have plenty of money left wherewith to buy wine and milk for himself and for his family. But not in this oil-market. To buy the Holy Spirit is as costly to a sinner as buying Christ Himself and all His righteousness. And you know how penniless that purchase left Paul. Indeed, ever since Paul's day the price of Christ and His righteousness has been a proverb of impoverishment in the Church of Christ. And had the apostle been led to tell us how much he had to lay down to win the Holy Spirit, it would just have been the same all-impoverishing story over again. Not one penny had Paul left. Not one farthing. And so is it with every man who once really enters this same oil-market. If you do not follow my argument, just take an hour to-night in that market for yourself, and tell me to-morrow morning how you get on in it. Tell me how much you have left to call your own after you have once bought this priceless oil. See what it will cost you so much as to enter this oil emporium. There are some places of sale, bazaars and such like, where a great income is made just by the entry-money. Tell me how much is demanded of you before you are able to shut your door upon God and yourself alone to-night, not to speak of what He will charge you for the oil after you are in. You will see how everything you have hitherto valued will have to go. No wonder that only the half of the ten virgins had the heart to make the impoverishing purchase. For my part, I often wonder there were so many.

Our Lord does not explicate, point by point, all this parable to us, but He is most emphatic, and even alarming, in His application of it. Watch, therefore, He warns us, for ye know neither the day nor the hour wherein the Son of Man cometh. He may be here, and your time may be at an end any moment. And then, it takes far more time than you would think to buy this oil and to have it always ready. Even to get well into the place where this oil is sold takes time. To get your money ready takes time. To get your vessel well filled takes time. And to make due allowance for all the obstacles and accidents by the way, and for all the unforeseen interruptions and delays in the market,—all that, taken together, takes up more time than any one would believe beforehand; immensely more time and trouble than any one would believe who has not gone through it all. And thus it is that our Lord is always pleading with us to give an hour to it every night. Better too much time, He argues with us, than too little. You may get through the transaction quicker than some others, He admits. But then there is this also, that it may turn out to take much more in your case than you have left to give it.

And, once more, watch, for the wisest are sometimes to be found playing the fool, like the foolish, in this tremendously precarious matter. The five wise virgins slumbered and slept when they should have been employing their spare time in trimming their lamps, and in keeping both themselves and their fellows awake and ready. And had it not been that they were, all the time, much wiser than they seemed to be, they would have been shut out with the rest. But as it turned out they had oil, all the time, in their vessels with their lamps. And that made all the difference when the bridegroom came so suddenly. Now, where and how, will the same difference come in among ourselves? It will come in, and you will see it, this very night, and in this very way. To-night some here will hasten home as soon as the blessing is pronounced. They will try to escape their talkative neighbours at the door. All the time of supper and prayers at home they will be hiding this terrible parable in their hearts. And then when the house is quiet, the true business of this whole day will begin with those wise men. I have told you before, but not once too often, of a Sabbath night I once spent long ago in the Alrick with old John Mackenzie. After supper and prayers I petitioned for another half-hour's reading of the notes he had preserved of Dr. John Duncan's Persie sermons. "Pardon me," said the old saint, "but we always take our candles immediately after prayers." The difference will be that the foolish among us will sit to-night and talk and talk till they extinguish this parable and all its impressions clean off their minds and their hearts, while the wise among us will take their candles.

XIII

THE WEDDING GUEST WHO SAT DOWN IN THE LOWEST ROOM

It is my deliberate opinion that this wedding guest who sat down in the lowest room was none other than our Lord Himself. I think I see enough to justify me in believing that this parable was no parable but was an actual experience of our Lord Himself. I feel as sure as if I had seen Him do it, that He sat down in the lowest room when He entered that supper chamber. The two sons of Zebedee chose out the chief rooms for themselves, their mother encouraging them to do it. Go up yonder, she said. There are two seats at the head of the table, go up at once and take them. And they went up, their mother pushing them up. But Mary and her Son sat down at the foot of the table. The more I imagine myself present at that marriage, the more convinced I became that our Lord was that humble-minded man Himself. At any rate, whether our Lord only invented and composed this parable, or actually Himself experienced it, at any rate, it has all been performed by Him and fulfilled to Him by this time, in every jot and tittle of it, first in His earthly life, and then in His heavenly life. For did He not sit down in the lowest room in the over-crowded inn? And as His birth was so was His whole life on earth down to the end of His life in the lowest of all this earth's low rooms. Till a Voice came from the head of the table, which said to Him, Friend, come up higher. And now, as this parable says,

He has worship in the presence of them that sit at meat with Him. Yes; I for one am to delight myself, and impress myself, and instruct and rebuke myself, with believing that our Lord's whole life, and now His whole heavenly life, was all enacted, in small, at that wedding supper to which He was called and with Him His twelve disciples.

"A new commandment give I unto you," said their Master to His disciples at the last supper of all. But at this present supper now spread before us He gives both His disciples and us this new commandment of His also. "When thou art bidden of any man to a wedding, go and sit down in the lowest room." And then, like the Shorter Catechism, He annexes His reasons, which, when drawn out, are such as these. No man can ever say to you, Give this man place; no man can ever say to you, Sit lower down, if you have already chosen for yourself the lowest seat. No man can humiliate you and clothe you with shame if you are always clothed with humility. But on the other hand, if you are always and everywhere exalting yourself: if you are always scheming for yourself, and are always choosing out the best seats for yourself, depend upon it you are laying up shame and humiliation for yourself. If you are constantly pluming yourself on your own performances, and on your high deservings of praise and what not at all men's hands, depend you upon it your humiliation will not tarry. You will be disappointed, superseded, over-looked, over-stepped, and over-ridden, absolutely every day. It will seem to you, and not without good grounds, as if all men were in one plot against you, for so they are. If they can help it, you shall with shame begin to take the lowest room. But if I were you, I would outwit them. I would lay this wise commandment of our Lord's to my heart if I were you, till I had completely outwitted them. When you are next bidden to anything, begin to sit down in the lowest room; yes, in the very lowest room you can get. Begin at once to humble yourself everywhere, and in everything. Put on the sack-cloth of humility immediately and always. Set less and less store by your own talents, attainments, performances, and deserts; and set more and more store by all other men's talents, deserts, and performances. Pooh-pooh your own heart when it says to you,—What a grand man you are! When it says to you,—What a grand sermon that is you have just preached! What a grand book that is you have just published! What a grand run in the race-course that was with all men's eyes upon you! And what a grand leap that was leaving all your rivals far behind you! Turn upon your puffed-up heart and tell it that nobody is thinking about your grand sermons, or your grand books or your grand runs, or your grand leaps; nobody but yourself. Only, all your competitors in preaching and in leaping, *they*, indeed, are thinking almost as much, and almost as often, about you as you are about yourself. Only, in a very different way. And in a way that, if you knew it, would make you take down your top-sail, as Samuel Rutherford says. My friends, expect nothing for yourselves and you will not be disappointed; demand nothing for yourselves and you will be continually surprised how praise and promotion will pour in upon you, and that at the most unexpected times and from the most unexpected people. How does Jupiter occupy himself on Olympus? asked Chilo at Æsop. In humbling the high, was Æsop's answer, and in lifting up the low. Just as Peter has it, who was present at that supper-table. "Yea, all of you be clothed with humility; for God resisteth the proud, and giveth grace to the humble."

Only, there is humility and humility. And the best kind of humility is that kind which Thomas Shepard, so far as I know, was the first to call "evangelical humility." Jonathan Edwards has now made this borrowed phrase famous in some of the golden pages of his *Religious Affections*. Hear then, what this master in Israel says:—"Evangelical humility is the sense that a Christian man has of his own utter insufficiency, utter despicableness, and utter odiousness: with an always answerable frame of heart. This humility is peculiar to the true saints. It arises from the spirit of God implanting and exercising supernatural and divine principles: and it is accompanied with a sense of the transcendent beauty of divine things. And then, God's true saints all more or less see their own odiousness on account of sin, and the exceedingly hateful nature of all sin. The very essence of evangelical humility consists in such humility as becomes a man in himself exceeding sinful but now under a dispensation of grace. It consists in a mean esteem of himself, as in himself nothing, and altogether contemptible and odious. This indeed is the greatest and the most essential thing in true religion." My brethren, you will not be long troubled with *that* guest choosing out the chief rooms for himself. If you have all the chief rooms to yourselves, and to your children, frequent those feasts, and engineer to get your children invited to those feasts, to which none but Thomas Shepard's disciples are invited.

Parents are terribly perplexed at present as to what is the proper education for their children; and for their sons especially.

Shall they take the ancient or the modern side of the University? Shall it be the classics, and almost nothing else, as was the old way? Or shall it be a commercial education almost exclusively? And one adviser advises the one way, and another adviser advises the other way, till many anxious parents are driven distracted. Whichever side you determine on, be sure that your sons take Moral Philosophy in the curriculum. If it is Latin and Greek, and the old culture, that you decide on, be sure they take Æsop with it as above. Or if it is a military or a commercial education, still take Æsop as above, even if it is only in translation. Whether they are to be men of all literature, or men of one book only, and that the ledger, see to it that they mix all their books with humility. That will make your sons true gentlemen, whichever side they take in education. And that will make your daughters true ladies, whatever school and college, whatever course you decide on for them. Housewifery, like their mothers and their grandmothers, or a degree, like their fathers and their brothers. I will not quarel with your choice for them if only you mix it well with humility. If your sons have the head and the heart to read Shepard and Edwards—and it will need all the head and all the heart you can give them to read those two masters—then I will prophesy your sons' prosperity from either culture; the ancient or the modern. And if you bring up your daughters to respect the servants and to share their work; to rise early in the morning, to make their own beds, to decorate their own rooms, and to brush their own boots, then they can add University degree to that with the applause of all men, both young and old. If they are but popular downstairs, I will read their names in the *Scotsman* and *The Times* with a pride almost as much as your own. Only begin their education while they are yet infants; or, at any rate little children. It so happens that just as I am composing these lines for you I have come in our morning worship on this children's hymn for your children and mine:—

Day by day the little daisy
  Looks up with its yellow eye,
Never murmurs, never wishes
  It were hanging up on high.

And the air is just as pleasant,
  And as bright the sunny sky,
To the daisy on the footpath
  As to flowers that bloom on high.

God has given to each his station;
Some have riches and high place,
Some have lowly homes and labours;
All may have His precious grace.

"All our humility on earth will come to its head in heaven," says Samuel Rutherford. Till the only difficulty at the Marriage Supper of the Lamb will be to get the chief rooms at that Supper to be filled with their proper guests. It will be somewhat like that Highland Communion at which I was present. Friends, come up higher! the minister pled with his people. But with all his authority, and with all his promises and pleas, he could not overcome his people's shame and pain of heart that day. And all the assisting minister could do, with all his fresh promises and pleas and encouragements, it was long before the Lord's Table was even half filled that day. And so, somewhat, will it be with ourselves at the Lord's Table above. Our eyes will seek for them, and, as soon as we enter the supper-room, we will see men and women already seated there, the sight of whom will so awaken and inflame our old sin and shame, that we will turn to flee: only, by that time, escape will be impossible, for the door will be shut. The sight of the Table and of Him who sits at the head of the Table, and of some of the guests already in their seats there, and a thousand other things, will all rush in upon us till we shall fall down as dead. "And he laid His right hand upon me, saying unto me, Fear not: I am the first and the last. I am He that liveth and was dead, and, behold, I am alive for evermore, Amen: and have the keys of hell and of death." Friend! He will say to us, as He lifts us up in glory as He used to do in grace. Friend! and this word of His will at once revive us. And we will sit down humbly just where He seats us. No one else will have taken our place. Wherever at His Table our place is it will be ours alone, and no stranger will intermeddle with it. And, to borrow a word from this night's scripture, it will be with shame that we will sit down in the place prepared for us. Only, it will be with a sweet, holy, heavenly, blessed and beatific shame. Friend! He will say, go up higher. Then shalt thou have worship in the presence of them that sit at meat with thee. For whosoever exalteth himself shall be abased; and he that humbleth himself shall be exalted.

XIV

THE BIDDEN TO THE GREAT MARRIAGE SUPPER AND SOME OF THEIR EXCUSES

You are all bidden to this great marriage supper. The invitations sent out to our marriage suppers have to be limited to the more intimate friends of the bride and the bridegroom. Our largest houses would not hold the half of the friends we would like to see with us on such happy occasions. But there is no such limitation here. You are all bidden to this marriage. And the only limitation to-night lies entirely with yourselves. What, then, is your answer to be to-night?

This is a most extraordinary marriage and marriage supper. And therefore you must not measure what is now to be said about this marriage by what you have seen or heard of the marriages of this world. For there are far better worlds than this world, and there are far better marriages than this world has ever seen. Indeed, this marriage that is in your offer to-night is the only real and true and perfect marriage that has ever been made in this or in any other world, or that ever will be made. You have been dreaming about marriages all your days, but a marriage like this has never entered your most extravagant imaginations. For this is nothing less than the marriage of the Eternal Son of God with your own immortal soul. You, sitting there, are the bride, and Jesus Christ is the Bridegroom. And the Father of the Bridegroom has His heart so much set upon this marriage that he has sent His servant to-night to say to you that all things are now ready. Some of our marriages take a long time to get all things ready. And this great marriage has not by any means been made ready in a day. This marriage was actually proposed and planned for and the preparations began to be made for it before the foundations of this world were laid. You like to read and hear about marriages, and the arranging of marriages, and how the course of true love did, or did not, run smooth. Well, I, like you, have read many love romances in my day, and have delighted in them in my day; but this great love, and the sometimes smooth, and sometimes stormy, course it has had to run, quite out of sight eclipses all other romances to me now. So much so, that I have for long wholly given up reading anything else except about this everlasting love. But this is the immediate and the main point that all things are ready now. All things that the bride needs to make herself ready are ready now. And all things that the Bridegroom needs are ready now. The Father is ready to receive you. The Son stands ready to be for ever united to you, and to have you united to Him. And the Holy Ghost stands beside the Son ready, and book in hand like the minister, to pronounce you the Lamb's wife. And it only remains for you to say yes, or no. It only remains for you to say that your heart within you is as the chariots of Amminadib in the Song of Solomon, and your marriage is consummated, or will be consummated immediately.

This very same message and invitation was once sent to a congregation of people just like yourselves; and they all, with one consent, began to make excuse. We can scarcely believe it about them, but it must be true, else it would not be recorded against them to all time, as it is here recorded. Come, said the servant to those that were bidden: Come, for all things are now ready. But they all, with one consent, began to make excuse. The first said unto the servant, I have bought a piece of ground, and I must needs go to see it; I pray thee have me excused. And another said, I have bought five yoke of oxen, and I go to prove them; pray thee have me excused. Another said, I have married a wife, and therefore I cannot come. You are sometimes like that yourselves among the dinner and supper invitations of our own city. You hear with apprehension sometimes of certain dinners and suppers that are soon to come on. Your hearts are not in those intended entertainments, and you would give anything not to be invited to them. And when you are invited you are at your wits' end how to answer so as not to give an unpardonable offence. You sit at your desk and you bite your pen over your excessively difficult answer. You try one form of answer and you tear it up; the lie is too transparent. "Thank you," you at last answer, "but I have an engagement already on my hands for that very evening. I have done my best to get out of it, but it is impossible." Or you try this—A friend of yours, that you have not seen for many years, has offered you a visit on that evening on his way through the city and you cannot put him off; or, you have a most important meeting down for that evening and for that hour, at which, indeed, you are already advertised to take the chair. 'Accept my most sincere apology,' you add, 'and convey my best respects to your honoured guest.' The dinner belongs to another political, or ecclesiastical, or civic, party than that to which you belong.

There are old sores in your mind against your proposed host as well as against some of the guests who are sure to be there. In short, you cannot and you will not go. Even at the risk of your absence being misunderstood, and taken in ill part, you will not go. 'We will not trouble him again,' say the host and the hostess to one another over your transparent subterfuge; 'he will come the next time he is asked to any dinner of ours.'

Those were clever enough excuses that your predecessors in Israel made. Indeed, they were entirely true excuses, rather than merely clever. For the real truth was they had no heart for that invitation. All their treasure, and consequently all their heart, was elsewhere. The first man's treasure was his newly-bought piece of ground. The second man's treasure was his five yoke of oxen. While the third man had the best treasure and the best excuse of all. For he had a young wife at home, and the dinner was never dressed that would draw him away from her side so soon. Now what is your excuse to-night? You have an excuse that you have sent up as your answer before now; often before now. Is it to be the same excuse and answer to-night again? It is as if an angel had come straight from heaven to you with an invitation addressed to you in his hand. There he is, standing in the passage at the end of your pew. Yes, there he is. It is not the first time I have seen him standing impatiently there. But to-night it may be the last time. When he goes home to-night empty again his Master may well be so angry this time that He may swear that your invitations shall be no longer. 'He is joined to his ground, and to his oxen, and to his wife—let him alone.' And, then, what will all these things do for you against the anger of Almighty God, and against the wrath of the Lamb? Whereas, say Yes! and all things are yours, and you are His and He is God's. Wait one moment, then, O impatient angel: wait, just wait one moment! And then speed up with your answer to your Lord.

But even that sufficient danger and disaster is not all. There are more men involved in your salvation or damnation than yourselves. Your ministers are almost as much involved as you are. O light-hearted students, go and make your piece of bread in some much safer calling. For God lays this same awful order on all His ministers,—Go, He says, and compel them to come in. Compel is His very word. That is your minister's ordination oath, and if you are lost: if you go on to the end making excuses and refusals, your lost eternity will be at your minister's door, as well as at your own. Your minister must compel you therefore, if he is not to be involved in your ruin. 'Did you do all that it was commanded you to do?'—it will demanded of him on that day! 'You knew quite well that that man there, and that woman there, were no more saved than were the seats they sat on, and what did you do? Did you let them fall asleep while you delivered my message to them? Did you tell them plainly how it would end with them? Or were you afraid to offend them, and lose their approval and their patronage? Did you demand of them every Sabbath day what provision they had made against death and judgment? Did you preach every sermon of yours as if it were your last and their last? And as if you and they might be summoned before the great white throne at the end of your sermon? Did you compel them to see that there were only two things possible before them—the right hand or the left: heaven or hell: the wrath of the Lamb, or His everlasting love? If you did all that, then you are clear of their blood. But if you did not do all that, and that continually, you are no minister of mine.' O men and women! Be not so inhuman as to drag down your minister with yourselves. Say, at any rate, to God's angel that your minister is not to blame. Say to him that your minister did all that mortal man could do. Say to him that your minister's hands are pure of your blood, and that you alone are without excuse.

This parable, it is much to be feared, will have a very visible fulfilment in this house during the next fortnight. For this day fortnight the marriage supper of the Lamb is to be made ready here. And from to-night onward this call will go forth to all this congregation,—The Lord's Supper is again made ready. Come and partake of it. Prepare yourselves in the ways appointed you, and then come to the Lord's Table. But when the two days of special preparation are come, what will we see here? We will see the church on the Thursday evening, and on the Saturday afternoon, not one-fourth full: till your ministers will be ashamed to have brought two of God's servants to preach to your empty pews. So many intending communicants will, with one consent, begin to make excuse. One will say, The hour is so late. Another will say, The weather is still so unsettled. Another will say, Those services are getting antiquated and out of date and so few people attend them. Another will say, To tell the truth I had wholly forgotten about the communion, and my wife and I have a dinner-party in our house that evening. Another will say, The young people are at their lessons on Thursday night, and they need fresh air on Saturday afternoon, and are away out of the town on their bicycles. And then the ministers and the elders will get such refreshment and such a preparation from those two services that they will look round and will say to themselves: —Oh, why were so and so not here? What a blessing they have lost. What can they have got elsewhere to make up to them for the loss of such a preparation-service as this has been? And then those who so excused themselves on the Thursday and the Saturday will come up so unprepared on the Sabbath that when the King comes in to see the guests it will be impossible for Him to wink at the state of matters between Him and many who will intrude themselves that day. Till in very faithfulness He will say to them, Friend, how camest thou in hither not having a wedding garment? But be not speechless to-night. Come to-night. Say yes to-night. For all things are now ready, wedding garment and all.

XV

THE MAN WHO HAD NOT ON A WEDDING GARMENT

SUPPOSE this. Suppose you were commanded to sup with King Edward the Seventh on this day week. Then what else than that command would you think about all the intervening six days and six nights? I feel sure you would think about nothing else. The great invitation, and the coming supper in the king's palace, would never be out of your thoughts for a moment. You would discourse about your high honour all day, and you would dream about it all night. But at the same time, you would rejoice at the prospect with trembling. And you would do this. You would seek out those in this city who had sometimes been at court. You would apply to those ministers, or other highly honoured men, who had dined or supped with the late Queen, his Majesty's mother, and you would beseech them to tell you all about the palace and its royal rules and regulations. You would interrogate them about a thousand things, from the way in which you should reply to such a command, down till you were safely back again in your own house. You would be in such mortal terror lest in your inexperience and ignorance you should fall into some awful mistake. You have never been much in good society, not to say in such society as a crowned head keeps, and it would not be to be wondered at if you scarcely slept with anxiety till it was all over and you were safely home again. And if there was any book of palace etiquette and court ceremonial to be had for love or money, you would sit up all night over it; you would set your very Bible aside night after night in order to give all your mind to the Court Guide. Your Bible could wait, but not your preparation for the great event of your life. And if in studying its directions you came on any expressions and descriptions you did not understand, you would go back again to the king's chaplain rather than risk the smallest misunderstanding or mistake. And if you could accuse yourself of neglecting the very utmost precaution, and thus fell into some disgraceful blunder at court, you would never forget it, and you would never forgive yourself, to your dying day. And who would blame you for all that solicitude? Who would say that you were anxious over much? We would all envy you for your high honour, but we would all be thankful that we had not to go through your ordeal. And as often as we thought of your certainty to make some terrible mistake, we would say to ourselves —Better him than me.

Intending communicants! Your own hearts have already interpreted to you what I have been driving at all this time. For this day seven-night you are all commanded to be ready to present yourselves before your Lord in His Father's house. Now what are you intending to do all this week with a view to the Lord's Supper? With whom do you intend to take counsel? Do you know, in all your circle of acquaintances, any one you feel sure is at home in such matters? What books will you read this week, and what books will you judge it impertinent, and unseasonable, and unbecoming, to read this week? How do you intend to lay out your nights especially? In short, what steps do you intend to take to secure and guard yourself against some awful slip or oversight when you are ushered into the King's presence? Have you any plan? Have you any programme? Six days and six nights look a long time in which to prepare. But they will all be past and gone before you know where you are. For one thing, I have a great faith myself in the proper books. I shall owe my own soul, if it is saved at last, to the proper books. And if your soul is lost at last that catastrophe will be accounted for largely by your persistent reading of unseasonable and unbecoming books, and especially in the night-watches of the communion week. Some intending communicants will do something like this. To-morrow night they will take time and will read again all about the institution of the Passover in Israel, and they will apply all the lessons of the Passover to their own hearts. and to their own lintels and side-posts. On Tuesday night if you went in on them late you would find them deep in the Fifty-first Psalm. And on Wednesday night deep in the Fifty-third of Isaiah. On Thursday we used to have all the shops shut, and all the churches open; and we still have our communion books, if we choose, that no one can shut as they have shut the churches. And all Thursday night they will be still deeper in the arrest and the trial and the cross of their Redeemer. What else, in the name of sin and salvation, would you expect to find them reading on such a night and in such a week! And all the week they will have among their choicest books some classic on the communion, say like Robert Bruce, and they will work their soul-saving way through that great book again. Robert Bruce's book is not in the circulating library, and it is too dear for you who are laymen to be expected to buy it. But if there is any divinity student here who hopes one day to be a good minister of Jesus Christ, let him get his hands somehow or other on Bruce before to-morrow night, and master one of "that stately Presbyterian divine's" sermons on the Sacrament every night all the week. I have not read Bruce so often, I am ashamed to say, as Jowett had read Boswell. But I read him for the first time forty years ago, and I read him again last week. And in the strength of many readings of that great Edinburgh preacher I will venture this prophecy that if you begin Bruce at this communion, you will still be reading him forty years after this, and you will be liking him better and better at every returning communion in your history,—a sure mark of a masterpiece.

But with all that, you must not sit at home and read your Bible and Bruce on the Sacraments all the week, and do nothing else. "Therefore we must," says Jeremy Taylor, "before every communion especially, remember what differences or jealousies are between us and any one else, and recompose all such disunions, and cause right understandings between each other. Offering to satisfy whom we have injured, and to forgive those who have injured us." And so on, in his heart-searching and eloquent treatise. As for instance. One of our own elders on the Sabbath before one communion heard a sermon on the text, "Leave thy gift before the altar, and go thy way: first to be reconciled to thy brother, and then come and offer thy gift." Now that elder had long ago had a miserable quarrel with a man in the same profession as his own, and whose office was in the same street as his own. And on the Monday before the communion, as if it were to-morrow, he left his own office-door and crossed the street and rang his enemy's bell. He felt, as he told me himself, that he would almost as soon have faced a lighted cannon as rung that bell. But he did it. And when he stood before his old foe he did not speak. He only held out his hand. The two estranged men looked at one another. They shook hands and parted without words. But a load of anger and hatred and wickedness that had lain like a mill-stone on both their hearts was from that moment removed. And the two men came to the table next Sabbath reconciled to God and to one another. Will you do the same preparatory act to-morrow forenoon? Or still better, will you do it to-night on your way from the House of God?

And then when the communion day dawns this day week, rise early. Be like Moses that morning when he was hidden in the cleft rock, and when he first heard the Name of the Lord. And have something suitable in your mind the last thing on Saturday night that you are to say the first thing on Sabbath morning. Have this: When I awake I am still with Thee. Or this: I shall be satisfied when I awake with Thy likeness. Or this: This is the day the Lord hath made. Or this: He was delivered for our offences, and was raised again for our justification. Or this: Bless the Lord, O my soul, and forget not all His benefits. And then finish up with this: I will take the cup of salvation, and call upon the name of the Lord. And, all the morning hours, let your mind go back to that first Lord's day morning. Think you see Mary Magdalene while it is yet dark. Think you hear what she says to her Risen Lord, and what He says to her. Go through their dialogue with them. And open and read the journey to Emmaus, and think you are one of them, till your heart burns within you. And be up here in good time. We will have the doors open in good time. Come so as to have a quiet half-hour to yourself. Do not come late and agitated with getting ready. Have a good half-hour to read and think and pray. And enter at once into the stream of psalms and hymns and spiritual songs, and make melody in your heart to the Lord. Follow the action-sermon with your whole attention. Miss nothing that is said. I think it will suit you next Sabbath. And then at the table rise to your best faith, and to your best love. And if your heart has resisted all the preparations of the week and you are ready to sink into the earth when the elders bring forward the elements, then give vent to your heavy heart in such ejaculations as this: I am not worthy, Holy Lord. And this: Then will I to thine altar go. And this: Just as I am. And this: Cleft for me. And then when the King comes to see the guests He will find you singing in your heart to Him and to yourself this acceptable song:—

O let the dead now hear thy voice:
Now bid thy banished ones rejoice,—
Their beauty this, their glorious dress,
Jesus, Thy blood and righteousness.

And then take a moment or two at the Table to pray for those who are as dear to you as your own soul. For those you love as Christ has loved you. And, after your own flesh and blood, then for those you love almost as much, your choicest and most select friends. And wind up with the man you were reconciled to last week. For that is the best friendship, and that is the surest reconciliation, that is sanctified and sealed at the Lord's Table.

And then, when your Saviour says to you after supper, Know you what I have done to you? you will have your answer ready. My blessed Lord, you will say, I know only too well what Thou hast done for me. I doubt, in all Thy great doings for sinners, if ever Thou hast done for mortal man what Thou hast done for me. Many men call themselves the chief of sinners; but I know, and Thou knowest, better than that. If I do not know all Thou hast done for me, keep the full knowledge of it back till I am able to bear it. For I am not able to bear any more to-day. Oh! the past, the past! you will cry in your agony of remorse mingled with faith and love. For you see your past sins and your present sinfulness at every returning communion blacker and blacker. Yea, Lord, Thou hast redeemed me. Thou hast substituted Thyself for me. Thou hast borne my sins in Thine own body on the tree. Thou hast come after me, and Thou hast been full of unparalleled long-suffering with me. Thou has endured me far past all other men. No man has provoked Thee to the uttermost as I have done. And yet, you will say,—I am not in hell, but at the Lord's Table!

And then, with all that possessing your heart, you will go home from the Lord's Table a new creature. You will go home at peace with God and with your own conscience through the sin-atoning death of the Son of God. At peace also with all men, and full of love and prayer for all men. And you will henceforth walk with a far more perfect heart before your house at home. And you will henceforth possess your heart with a holy patience among all the crooks in your lot, and under all the crosses that God sees good to lay upon you. And amid all these things you will henceforth be one of the most watchful, and prayerful, and humble-minded, and easy to live with, of men. A miracle to yourself, and a wonder to many. From one day to another living for nothing else so much as to perfect holiness in the fear of God. And God every day more and more perfecting in you what

He has begun in you, till the day of Christ. Till that day, that is, when He shall come in to see the guests, and to go no more out.

XVI

THE PHARISEE

DR. PUSEY has said somewhere that a Pharisee was just a Jew with divine light but without divine love. And that saying of Dr. Pusey's is just the thirteenth chapter of 1st Corinthians put into an epigram. Paul was once a Pharisee himself, and in the beginning of that famous chapter to the Corinthians he describes himself as a Pharisee to perfection. Every finished Pharisee, he tells us, had not the tongue of a man only, but the tongue of an angel. In some instances the Pharisee had the gift of prophecy also, and could understand all mysteries, and all knowledge. There had been Pharisees known to Paul who had a faith that could actually remove mountains. While others again had been known not to give a tenth only of all that they possessed, but who positively bestowed all their goods to feed the poor. While some went the awful length of giving their very bodies to be burnt. Our hearts bleed for the Pharisees. Our hearts bleed within us for men who could do and endure all that, and yet after all that were complete castaways from the kingdom of heaven. Who then, my brethren, can be saved?

In answer to that staggered exclamation of ours, the Apostle, who was one of them and one of the very best of them, goes on to accuse the Pharisees with such unanswerable accusations as these. With all that, says the Apostle, the finished Pharisee was wholly without love in his heart. To come to particulars and instances of that, says the Apostle. The true Pharisee entirely lacked large-heartedness and brotherly-kindness, he entirely lacked appreciation and admiration for other men. He vaunted about himself in everything, he was puffed up with himself in everything. He took no pleasure in hearing other men praised for their talents, or for their performances, or for their conduct, or for their character. The true Pharisee took no pleasure in the pure truth about other men. Nay, he had no better pleasure than in all unjust judgments and in all harsh censures concerning all other men. When he heard a back-biter he delighted in him, and he was a partaker with busybodies. He wholly lacked liberality of mind and hospitality of heart. He wholly lacked trust and hope and love. In Dr. Pusey's short and sharp way of it the true Pharisee of our Lord's day had plenty of divine light in his head, only he was wholly lacking in divine love in his heart.

But let us go back again upon some of the Pharisee's good points. And that not only for his sake but for our own sakes. For the better a man the Pharisee was the more solemnising will his history and his character and his condemnation be to us. If the Pharisees had been out and out bad men, their condemnation would not have been so startling and so solemnising to us as it is. Now when you study your New Testament well you will see how much there is to be said in behalf of the Pharisees. Compared with the Sadducees, for instance, the Pharisees were men of a high religious character. They loved the Bible. They knew the Bible by heart. They sanctified the Sabbath day. None of you better. They observed the Fast days, and all the other church ordinances, with what we would call a Puritan scrupulosity and self-denial. In short, all the best people in Israel in our Lord's day belonged to the party of the Pharisees.

But, with all that, the Pharisee was all wrong in his heart. The true Pharisee's heart was not a broken heart; and thus it was that nothing was right that the Pharisee ever said or did. This sounds a hard saying that nothing was right he ever said or did, but it is the simple truth. In one of the most powerful of his Roman Catholic sermons, entitled "The Religion of the Pharisee," Dr. Newman brings out this about a Pharisee's unbroken heart in his own incomparably powerful and impressive way. I will not water down the passage, but will give you the enjoyment and the profit of it just as it stands. "The characteristic mark of the religion of Christ," he says, "is a continual confession of sin, and a continual prayer for mercy. What is peculiar to our divine faith, as to Judaism before it, is this, that confession of sin enters into the idea of its highest saintliness, and that its pattern worshippers, and the very heroes of its history, are only, and can only be, and cherish in their hearts, the everlasting memory that they are, and carry with them into heaven the rapturous avowal of their being, restored transgressors. Such an avowal is not simply wrung from the lips of the neophyte, or of the lapsed; it is not the cry of the common run of men alone, who are buffeting with the surge of temptation in the wide world; it is the hymn of saints, it is the triumphant ode sounding from the heavenly harps of the Blessed before His throne, who sing to their Divine Redeemer,

Thou wast slain, and hast redeemed us to God in Thy blood, out of every tribe, and tongue, and people, and nation. And what is to the saints above a theme of never-ending thankfulness is, while they are yet on earth, the matter of their perpetual humiliation. Whatever be their advance in the spiritual life, they never rise from their knees, they never cease to beat their breasts. So it was with St. Aloysius, so it was with St. Ignatius, so it was with St. Philip Neri who, when some one praised him, cried out, Begone; I am a devil, and not a saint! And who, when going to communicate, would protest before his Lord that he was good for nothing but to do evil. Such utter self-prostration, I say, is the very badge and token of the servant of Christ; and this indeed is conveyed in His own words when He says, I am not come to call the righteous, but sinners to repentance. And it is solemnly recognised and inculcated by Him in these words: Every one that exalteth himself shall be abased, and every one that abaseth himself shall be exalted. Could contrast be greater than between that and this? God I thank Thee that I am not as other men are, or even as this publican. I fast twice in the week, I give tithes of all that I possess. No; contrast could not further go than that between the true penitent, and the true Pharisee."

The very name that the Pharisee took to himself condemned him to his face. To be a "Pharisee" was to be a self-selected and a separated man. Now, while all good and true men must sometimes, at whatever cost, separate themselves from all bad men, and from all bad causes among bad men, at the same time, all good and true men will make the separation with great humility, and will make it as short as possible. They will not flaunt abroad their separation like a flag. They will not lay their separation like a foundation stone, and they will not build their church upon it. Now that is just what this true Pharisee was doing in the temple all that day when our Lord discovered him and denounced him. He was flaunting his flag of superiority and separation in the face of God and man. He was taking up his stance on this standing-ground before God and man, that he was so much better than all other men. He must be correctly reported, and if he is, he here puts all other men on one side, and separates himself from them all, and thanks God for it. 'Stand by,' he says to every other worshipper in the temple. 'Come not near to me; for I am holier than thou.' You have the true Pharisee in all ages, and out of his own mouth, in that speech of his. You have here that detestable spirit of sectarianism and schism that tore to pieces the Church of God in Israel, and that is tearing to pieces the Church of Christ to this day. Wherever you see any man, high or low, great or small, dwelling continually on his superiority over all other men, and on the superiority of his church over all other churches, there speaks the true Pharisee. Especially when you see him labouring by tongue or pen or purse to keep open the running sores in the Body of Christ, to dwell upon those sores, to exasperate them, to spread them, and to perpetuate them.

Now, to apply all that to the topic of this day—Christian Unity—and to our own part in the topic of this day.

To begin with, if we are ever to take any true part in healing the grievous wounds in the Body of Christ, we must first of all have clean hands ourselves; that is to say, we must have clean hearts; that is to say, we must have broken, humble, contrite hearts. What kind of a healer would he be who came to you to bind up your wounds with his hands all dropping with all manner of taint or infection? You would say to him, Physician, heal thyself. And we must all look to ourselves before we begin to bind up the Body of Christ. It is our universal and incurable self-love and self-righteousness that is the real root of all our sectarianisms and schisms and controversies, whether those controversies are carried on by the tongue or by the pen or by the sword. It is our pride and our self-idolatry; it is our contempt and scorn of all other men; it is not our love of truth, so much as our love of ourselves, that is the real cause of all our contentions and controversies. Paul was a tremendous Churchman and a tremendous sectarian controversialist as long as he was a Pharisee: that is to say, as long as his heart was unbroken. But look at him after he was born again and had become a new creature. What a contrast to his former self! What humility, what condescension, what geniality, what courtesy, what catholicity, what universal loving-kindness; in short, and in modern language, what a Christian gentleman! Coleridge says that while Luther was not perhaps such a perfect gentleman as Paul, he was almost as great a genius. And Luther gives us a taste both of his genius and of his gentlemanliness also in what he says about Paul after Paul had ceased to be a Pharisee. "Paul was gentle, and tractable, and peaceable, in his whole Christian life. Paul was meek, and courteous, and soft-spoken. Paul could wink at other men's faults and failings, or else he would expound them to the best. Paul could be well contented to yield up his own way, and to give place and honour to all other men, even to the froward and the intractable." So speaks of Paul the most Paul-like man of the modern world. And an English gentleman, if ever there was one, has said of Paul in more than one inimitable sermon: "There is not one of those refinements and delicacies of feeling that are the result of advanced civilisation, nor any one of those proprieties and embellishments of conduct in which the cultivated intellect delights, but Paul is a pattern of it. And that in the midst of an assemblage of other supernatural excellences which is the characteristic endowment of apostles and saints." But then every fibre of that, if you search down deep enough for it, you will find it all rooted in such a soil as this: "Putting me into the ministry: who was before a blasphemer, and a persecutor, and injurious." And still more in this: "O wretched man that I am! who shall deliver me from the body of this death?" That is the true temper of Church unity, even as the Pharisee's prayer is the true temper of all separation and sectarianism and laceration of the Body of Christ. Only set the chief of sinners, and with broken hearts, as the earthly heads and leaders of all your churches, and the days of debate and division and separation are from that day doomed.

As you are my witnesses I am always beseeching you to work together with God in driving out of your hearts the seven devils of prepossession, and prejudice, and partyspirit, and narrowmindedness, and narrowheartedness. And that by reading the very best books, and especially reading the very best of your enemy's books. I will repeat to you what I took it upon me to say on this subject last May in the General Assembly of the Church of Scotland. I had the honour, I told them, and the happiness, to be one of Dr. John Duncan's students, that so catholic genius and true saint, and among the many lessons of truth, and grace, and genius, and rare Christian wisdom, he taught his students I always remember this. "If," he said, "I met a man from New England, I would say to him, Read the Marrow Men; and if met a Marrow Man, I would say, Read the New Englanders." And, though I almost owe my soul to the great Puritans, yet, acting on Dr. Duncan's advice, I have read Hooker, the great opponent of the Puritans, till I have come to see that in many of their contentions Hooker was in the right, and Travers in the wrong. And this very morning, I told them, I counted seven very different authors all standing most amicably on my desk. There was Hooker at their head with his *Polity,* there was John Donne with his Sermons, there was Edwards with his *Affections,* there was Newman with his *Grammar,* and there was Dante, with his *Banquet.* I had been making a banquet for my classes out of them all, and there they stood, not excommunicating one another any more, but rather supplementing, and supporting, and assisting, one another, and me. And not only do all those authors agree on my desk to-day, but they all agree themselves now where they now are. They are all reading one another's books now with an open mind and with an open heart. They are all blaming their own past prejudices now, they are all ashamed of all their past party spirit now. They are all rejoicing in their neighbour's truth now, and in his prosperity, and in his fame. In the pulpit of the Heavenly Temple the forenoon no longer speaks Canterbury, and the afternoon Geneva. And not only the great masterpieces of the past, but to read the periodicals and the newspapers of other churches than your own will reward you, and that not only with information that you will not get elsewhere, but with a wider sympathy, a more catholic, and a more liberal and generous temper. And that will be Christian unity accomplished already, as far as you are concerned. That will be heavenly already, with its love and its peace, descended into you.

And on the other hand shun controversial literature of all kinds, unless you are very far advanced in all knowledge and in all love. If controversial literature must be written and read, I doubt if you are the man either to write it or to read it. You are not, unless your heart is far more full of love and its fruits than most men's hearts are. Richard Baxter, you must admit, has purchased a right and a title to speak to us all on this matter now in hand. "Another fatal hindrance to a heavenly walk and conversation," he says, "is our too frequent disputes. A disputatious spirit is a sure sign of an unsanctified spirit. They are usually men least acquainted with the heavenly life who are the most violent disputers about the circumstantiality of religion. Yea, though you were sure that your opinions were true, yet when the chiefest of your zeal is turned to these things, the life of grace soon decays within. I could wish you were all men of understanding and ability to defend every truth of God; but, still, I would have the chiefest truth to be chiefly studied, and no truth to shoulder out the thought of eternity. The least controverted truths are usually the most weighty and of most necessary and frequent use to our souls." So testifies to us the seraphic author of the *Saint's Rest*. And, to wind up with, listen to a very different voice from that of Richard Baxter. Listen to what Homer says, who though dead yet speaketh through the mouth of Æneas to Achilles: —

> Long in the field of words we may contend,
> Reproach is infinite, and knows no end,
> Arm'd, or with truth or falsehood, right a wrong:

So voluble a weapon is the tongue,
Wounded we wound; and neither side can fail,
For every man has equal strength to rail.

The God of peace did not leave Himself without a witness wherever even a Homer sang his immortal *Iliad*.

XVII

THE PUBLICAN

OUR Lord was teaching and healing daily in the temple. And among the multitudes who came and went while He was so employed He paid special attention to a Pharisee and a publican. The Pharisee came up to the temple not caring who saw him or who heard him when he was at his prayers. He had nothing to say in his prayers of which he had any reason to be ashamed. Whereas the publican stood afar off, and would not lift up so much as his eyes to heaven. But all the same, there was One teaching and healing in the temple that day who not only saw both the Pharisee and the publican, but who, without listening, heard them both pray, and read all that was in both their hearts. He needed not to leave His seat where He was teaching and healing, because at all that distance, and notwithstanding all that surging multitude, He knew in Himself what those two men were thinking and what they were saying. For,—I am He that searcheth the reins and the hearts. And I will give to every one of you according to your works.

The Pharisee need not detain us long. He is no deep study to us. He is familiar to us. We have him among ourselves. There are multitudes like him among ourselves. At the same time, would that there were more men like him among ourselves. For he was a blameless man. He was a man of a spotless life. He was an upright man in all his dealings with other men. He was a cornerstone of the city. He was a pillar of the temple. There was no one in the temple that day who did not do him obeisance as he passed by. He was admired, and honoured, and praised, of all men. Yes. Would that that there were more men like him in all our cities and in all our temples also.

It is the publican who is here brought forward by our Lord for our special learning. The publican is discovered to us for our very closest study. His name is familiar to us, but not his state of mind. There were few men of his state of mind in his day, and they are not many in our day. God be merciful to me a sinner! was what the publican beat his breast and said. *The* sinner! that was, in exact terms, what he felt and what he said. *The* sinner,—as if there was no other sinner in existence but himself. The publican was as possessed with his sinfulness as the Pharisee was possessed with his righteousness. The Pharisee thought that no other man in all the world was at all his equal in his righteousness, and that was exactly what the publican thought about himself in his sinfulness. The publican felt utterly alone in the temple that day. He felt utterly alone in the whole world every day. And the definiteness of the word that he instinctively used about himself—*the* sinner, is to this day the best possible test of the state of mind of all who either read this parable or speak about it. Coleridge, when he is writing in one place about Santa Teresa, lapses for once into a stupidity that is unaccountable in a man of such spiritual insight and such spiritual sympathy. The saint had been speaking to herself in her Journal, and that in the very same terms in which the publican spoke about himself in the temple, and in the very same terms in which Paul speaks about himself in his first Epistle to Timothy, when the great critic breaks out upon her for her insincerity and her extravagant language in a way very distressing to his admirers to read, and very unlike himself. Were it not such an exception to his usual insight and sympathy, I would be tempted to say that such a censure of such a saint is, to my mind, and I think I have the mind of Christ, a far worse sign of Coleridge than all the opium he ever ate, and all the procrastinated work he died and left unfinished. It was not that the publican was, speaking coarsely, the absolutely most immoral man in all the city. It was not that Paul was, stupidly speaking, actually the chiefest of all the actual sinners of his day. It was not that Santa Teresa was the very worst and wickedest woman in all Spain in her day. But to put this truth about them all in a somewhat homely way, it was something not unlike this. I have good reason to believe that other men than myself have suffered from toothache and rheumatism. Only, I have never had the actual and personal experience of any man's excruciating pain but my own. And indwelling and secret sinfulness is the toothache, and the neuralgia, and the cancer, and the accumulated and exasperated agony, of each spiritual man's own soul. It was not what the publican had actually and openly done that festered like hell-fire in his heart and conscience, it was what he himself inwardly was, and inwardly was to himself alone. The heart knoweth its own bitterness, he would have said to Coleridge writing far too flippantly about Teresa. It was because Solomon's prayer, offered long ago at the dedication of the temple, was fulfilled in the publican. Which, said Solomon, shall know every man the plague of his own heart, and shall spread forth his hands toward this house. The whole of the publican's case is explained beforehand in that one profound petition of Solomon's prayer. O poor publican! O publican to be pitied both of God and man! God be merciful to all men everywhere and in every day who know the plague of their own heart!

Why did our Lord not say sanctified? Or, still better, why did He not say both justified and sanctified? Why did He confine Himself to justified? It was sanctification that the publican needed even more than justification, and our Lord knew that quite well. Whereas, He only said that this man went down to his house justified. Justification was but the half of the publican's prayer, and it was not the most poignant and most pressing half. For, if he is only justified to-day he will be back to the temple to-morrow nothing better of having been justified but rather worse. If our Lord in His great mercy to the publican's misery had only said sanctified what a happy worshipper the publican would have been from that day! And what a happy house he would have had at home from that day! Now, why did our Lord not say the word? Why did He not both say it and do it to this poor wretch on the spot? He would need to have a good reason to show why He did not say sanctified. And no doubt He will have a good reason to show when He is judged. Though it is not always easy for us to see what His reason can be. Perhaps He tried to say sanctified that day in the temple and could not. Who can tell but that He was so carried away with pity for the poor publican that He said Father, if it be possible, let us send this miserable man to his house sanctified? And perhaps He had to submit and say, Thy will be done. For justification is an immediate act of the Father's free and sovereign grace. An act, on the spot, of God's own mind and heart and holy will. And therefore the publican went down to his house only justified. Whereas, sanctification is "an exceedingly complex work," as John Wesley used to call it. God is sending sinful men down to their own houses justified every day, but not sanctified. It takes a long lifetime, in most cases, to sanctify a sinner; and at the end it is the miracle of all miracles to the old sinner himself that he is ever sanctified. Both are miracles. Both justification and sanctification. Samuel Rutherford used to pose the saints of his day with this dilemma, which of the two miracles they will wonder most at to all eternity, their justification or their sanctification? For what is justification? Justification is an act of God's free grace, wherein He pardoneth all our sins, and accepteth us as righteous in His sight, only for the righteousness of Christ imputed to us, and received by faith alone. And what is sanctification? Sanctification is the work of God's free grace, whereby we are renewed in the whole man after the image of God, and are enabled more and more to die unto sin, and live unto righteousness. And, as many of yourselves know, it takes many a visit to the temple, and many a far-off stand in the temple, and many a penitent prayer both in the temple and in your own house, and many a beat of the breast everywhere, before the exceedingly complex work of sanctification can be safely said to be begun in you, not to say finished in you.

Now, on this whole scene I will make this one more observation, and so close. You are not to suppose that this was the first time, much less the one and the only time, those two men had come up in that way to the temple to pray. You may depend upon it the Pharisee never neglected public worship, and by this time neither did the publican. And the oftener the Pharisee went up to the temple the more he went down to his house despising others. Whereas, on the other hand, the oftener the publican went up the more poignant was the pain in his breast. For if he went down every Sabbath day justified, as he did, the more all the next week he loathed himself in his own sight for his iniquities and for his abominations. And that went on till at last God was merciful to him, and took him up to the heavenly temple where he was at last both sanctified and glorified as well as justified. He had often fallen back in the agony of his heart on such Scriptures as this: "As for me, I will behold Thy face in righteousness; I shall be satisfied when I awake with Thy likeness." But with that, and with many more Scriptures like that, to alleviate his agony, he had often charged God foolishly for the length and the depth of his misery. But when the shore was won at last, no more he grudged the billows past. For by that time he was like the prisoner in Plutarch who received a chain of gold with as many links in it, and each link as heavy, as had been that chain of iron, bound with which he had lain so long in prison for his exiled sovereign's sake. And you must learn not to grudge or repine at your lifelong visits to this temple in search of sanctification. The thing you so unceasingly seek is not here. At the same time, this is the way to it. And, meantime, you will every Sabbath day go down to your house at any rate justified. And while falling infinitely far short of a finished sanctification, you will find here many incidental blessings that will help to keep your heart from wholly fainting, till to you also it will be said, O thou sinner of all sinners, be it unto thee in this matter of sanctification also, even as thou wilt. And then for all your shame you shall have double, and for confusion you shall rejoice in your portion, therefore in that land you shall possess the double, everlasting joy shall be unto you.

XVIII

THE BLIND LEADERS OF THE BLIND

ALL the same, the Scribes and Pharisees were quite right, as they often are. And our Lord's disciples were wholly in the wrong, as they often are. The disciples had no business to sit down to eat with unwashen hands, and the Scribes and Pharisees were only doing their bounden duty in entering their protest against such disorderly conduct. Moses never sat down to eat till he had washed both his hands and his feet. And the Scribes and Pharisees sat in Moses' seat for the very purpose of seeing to it that the great law-giver was obeyed and imitated in all things great and small that he had ever said and done. But, indeed, Nature herself should have taught the disciples to observe ordinary decency in all their habits at table, as well as everywhere else. And, though the complainers could not know it, they had our own John Wesley with them also. For Wesley was wont to preach this high doctrine of Moses, and of Nature herself, to the people called Methodists, this high doctrine of his, that cleanliness is next to Godliness. And, more than all that, the Scribes and Pharisees had the Master of the disciples so far with them. If the beam had not been in their own eye He would have been wholly with them in pulling this mote out of the eyes of His disciples. You are quite right, He as good as said to the complainers. You are only doing your duty in what you say to My disciples. At the same time, why do you get yourselves into such a wicked temper about it? And why is it that you come down all the way from Jerusalem to do nothing else but to find fault about such matters as the washing of hands, and feet, and cups, and pots, and tables? Have you no washing to do yourselves at home? Wash your own hearts, you hypocrites.

And with that He turned on them in a way that made Peter interpose and reprove Him. 'It is not safe; it is not wise,' said Peter, 'to speak to the authorities in that way. Such language will be sure to bring sharp reprisals on us all one day.' But instead of the timidity and the restraint the disciples would have had their Master observe to those men of such power, He all the more went on with some of the most plain-spoken words He ever uttered. "They be blind leaders of the blind. And if the blind lead the blind, both shall fall into the ditch." Till Peter's prophecy at last came true. And till His enemies took the most terrible reprisals on Peter's Master for His heart-searching eye and for the fearlessness of His speech.

Now, the great value of this passage to us lies in this, that we have two classes of preachers here set before us for our learning. We have those teachers and preachers who are wholly taken up with the outside of things; with cups, and pots, and pans, and tables, and beds, as this passage has it. And on the other hand, we have our Lord who passes by all these things in order that He may get at once at the hearts of men. And it is a most fearful picture that our Lord here gives us of the hearts of men, and of the work that He and His successors in the Christian ministry have to do in the hearts of men. "For from within, out of the hearts of men, proceed evil thoughts, adulteries, fornication, murders, thefts, covetousness, an evil eye, blasphemy, pride, foolishness." No wonder young Newman said that amid all his wine-parties, and all his musical evenings, and all his readiness and eagerness to join in any merriment, he was shuddering at himself all the time.

Generalia non pungunt. No. But there are no pointless generalities in our Lord's preaching. His preaching is quick and powerful, and sharper than any two-edged sword, piercing even to the dividing asunder of soul and spirit, and is a discerner of the thoughts and intents of the heart. Neither is there any creature that is not manifest in His sight; but all things are naked and opened to the eyes of Him with whom we have to do. "In the department of Christian morality," says John Foster, "many of our most evangelical preachers are greatly and culpably deficient. They rarely, if ever, take up some one topic of moral duty, such as honesty, veracity, impartiality, good temper, forgiveness of injuries, improvement of time, and such like, and investigate the principles, and the rules, and the discriminations, and the adaptations, of such things. There is little, nowadays, of the Christian casuistry found in many of our old divines. Such discussions would cost labour and thought, but they would be eminently useful in setting people's judgments and consciences to rights." And Robert Hall, in an ordination charge addressed to a young minister, says "Be not afraid of devoting whole sermons to particular parts of moral conduct and religious duty. Sometimes dissect characters, and describe particular virtues and vices. Point out to your people, and with unmistakable distinctness, both the works of the flesh and the fruits of the Spirit." John Jamieson of Forfar, for one, would have satisfied both John Foster and Robert Hall. For, long before their day, he had preached and published fifty most powerful sermons on our Lord's present text, treating the text as our Lord returned to it and treated it continually in His sermons, and as Foster and Hall demanded that it should be treated in every pulpit worth the name. And even after those two clear-eyed volumes of heart-searching sermons, Jamieson is bold to assert that every hearer and reader of his, who knows the plague of his own heart, will admit that the half of the shame and the pain and the wretchedness and the downright misery of his heart has not yet been told him. And those fifty Gennesaret sermons delivered in Forfar dug the deep foundations on which more than a hundred years of great preaching has been laid in Forfar, and is being laid in that privileged town down to this day. Would that every pulpit in Scotland had such Christian casuistry in it, and such unmistakable distinctness! But, then, that would not only cost the preacher labour and thought, as Foster admits, but, like the poet, such preachers would have to cease biting their pens for arguments and eloquence, and would have to look into their own hearts for all the arguments and all the eloquence of their sermons. It is the Spirit that quickeneth both you and your preaching, our Master is always saying to us preachers. And it is when our hearts are quickened to see in our own hearts all that He sees in them, it is then, and only then, that we shall be able to deal as He would have us deal, and as John Foster and Robert Hall would have us deal, and as John Jamieson actually did deal, with the hearts of his hearers. The Scribes and the Pharisees had eyes enough to preach against adultery and murder when these things once came out of the hearts of the people; but they were as blind as moles to the real roots of these things, as well as to the kindred roots of pride, and covetousness, and envy, and deceit, of which their own hearts, and the hearts of all their blinded hearers, were full. And these are the things that truly defile a man—evil thoughts, covetousness, deceit, an evil eye, and such like.

Are ye so without understanding also? demanded their Master

of His still ignorant disciples. Without understanding, that is, of what it is that really defiles a man, and where it comes from. It is bad enough to have some secret and deadly disease about you. But to have your physician stark ignorant of what is the matter with you, and how to treat you, that is simply despair and death to you. I was once summoned to a deathbed around which stood three of the most eminent doctors in the city. Surely it is not come to that, I said, as the dying man sent for me to bid me good-bye. It need not come to that, said the three doctors, if he would only rouse himself and determine not to die. You will see! said the dying man, smiling to me. He felt the hand of death on him, but his doctors were stark blind to what he felt, and why he felt it. They were without understanding, and so he was in his grave before the week was at an end. Tragedies like that will occur sometimes even with the best physicians, but such tragical cases are of every day occurrence with us ministers. The diseases of our patients are so deep down in their hearts, and we are so blind to our own hearts, and to the diseases of our own hearts, that such blood-guilty deaths take place with us every day. In the plain-spoken words of this very Scripture, we attend too much to the outside of things; to pots, and pans, and tables, and beds, and too little to our own hearts and the hearts of our hearers.

When the Pilgrim was making his progress through the valley of the shadow of death, his rare biographer tells us some things about the pilgrim's experiences that always speak home to my heart. About the middle of the valley was the mouth of hell, and it stood also hard by the wayside. Also he heard doleful voices, and rushings to and fro, so that sometimes he thought he should be torn to pieces, or trodden down like the mire in the streets. Just when he was come over against the mouth of the burning pit, one of the wicked ones got behind him, and stept up closely to him, and whisperingly suggested many grievous blasphemies to him, which he verily thought had proceeded from his own heart. When Christian had travelled in this disconsolate condition for some considerable time, he thought he heard a voice of a man, as going before him, saying, Though I walk through the valley of the shadow of death, I will fear no evil, for Thou art with me. Now, this Scripture at present open before us has much the same effect on me as that voice in the valley of the shadow of death had upon Christian. For, as from that voice he gathered that some one who feared God was in that valley as well as himself; so, from this scripture I gather that He who here searches the hearts of men, knows my heart down to the bottom, with all its wickedness, and all its wretchedness, and all its possession of the devil. Speaking only for myself in all these matters, but speaking honestly for myself, I confess to you that I find far more comfort just in this dreadful discovery of the hearts of men, and of my own heart, than I find in far more ostensibly evangelical scriptures. To me this awful scripture is as cheering sometimes as was the voice of that as yet unseen man in the valley of the shadow of death. And for much the same reason. I told you about the three doctors and their fast-dying patient. Now, he died of sheer despair because his disease was so much deeper than his doctors' diagnosis. Had those three doctors put their finger on the deadly spot, and said, thou ailest here and here; and thou ailest with this kind of agony and that,—then that dead man would have been back at his work within a week. But as it was he was in his grave before the next Sabbath day dawned. And it is just because my great Doctor, Jesus Christ, puts His Divine finger straight on this agony of mine and that: it is this that makes me turn away from every other practitioner of the heart, and say to Him, To whom can I go but to Thee! And it is this same thing that makes me always go away back to John Bunyan, and to the other great specialists of his deep and true school. Almost all the doctors who stand round my bed in these days seem to me to be far too much taken up with the outside of things; while, all the time, I am dying of a heart like the pilgrim's heart, and like this same heart that Christ here lays bare to His apostles and to the people. And thus it is that my Master's so perfect diagnosis of me, even before He has begun to prescribe to me, is already such a message of hope to me. The seventh of Mark, as well as the seventh of Romans, and the *Pilgrim's Progress,* and John Owen, and all the rest of that great heart-searching kind, all make me glad, and for these reasons: First, because I gather from them that some who feared God were in this valley as well as myself. Second, for that I see that God was with them, though in that dark and dismal state, and why not with me? And, third, that I shall have them for my company all the rest of my way.

And when He had called all the people unto Him He said unto them, Hearken unto Me, every one of you, and understand. And, every one of you people here to-night, hearken and understand all that He here says to you about your own hearts, every one of you. And then understand this also, that they that be whole need not a physician, but they that are sick. And, every one of you, understand with me also, and act with me. And act with me in this way. His discovery to me of the state of my own heart only the more entitles me and encourages me to take my heart to Him, and to claim at His hands all His skill in such hearts as mine, and all His instruments for them and all His remedies for them. It is my part to hear and to understand what He here says to me about myself, and then it is His part to heal me. And I warn Him, and I take all you people for witnesses, that I will give Him no rest till my heart is as clean and as whole as His own.

XIX

THE RICH MAN AND LAZARUS

At table one day Dr. Luther was asked whether he took the story of the rich man and Lazarus for a parable, or for an actual fact. The Reformer replied that to his mind the opening passage at any rate is evidently historical. The description of the rich man is so life-like. There is his dress, and his table, and his five brothers all following in his footsteps. And then the painful picture, as if it also had been taken from the life, of a certain well-known beggar with his sores, named Lazarus. Yes, said Luther, I do think our Lord must have known the rich man and Lazarus in Galilee, or in Samaria, or in Judea.

Now, whether it is pure history, or pure parable, or founded on fact, this tremendous Scripture is equally true and is equally solemnising to us, since it comes straight to us from our Lord's own lips. And our main errand here this evening is to enquire in His temple just what lessons our Lord would have us all to learn and to put in practice out of this terrible story.

The very first thing, as I think, that we are to see clearly in this scripture is this, that the rich man is not in hell simply and wholly because he had starved Lazarus to death. I used to read this parable so superficially as to think that the rich man is where he is altogether because of his starvation of Lazarus. But I see now that our Lord nowhere says so. No. Let the full story be told even about a man in hell. Let him get all the advocacy, and all the exculpation, and all the palliation, possible. No; it is nowhere said that Lazarus died of this rich man's neglect. Not at all. On the other hand, the crumbs that were sent out to Lazarus must, as I think, have been much more than mere crumbs. They must have been both many and large and savoury crumbs, as I think, else Lazarus would not have been laid so regularly and so long at that gate. Those who carried Lazarus to that rich man's gate every morning did so, as I think, because they had found out by experience that this was the best gate in all the city at which to lay Lazarus down. They must have tried all the other gates in the city, but they always came back to this gate.

It is quite true, the rich man might have done much more for Lazarus than he did. For instance, he might have fitted up one of his many out-houses for Lazarus to live in; or he might have arranged for a weekly pension to be paid to the incurable pauper in his own hovel; he might even have sent his own physician to report to him as to the symptoms and the progress of Lazarus's sores. But he did not do any of these gracious actions to Lazarus. At the same time he did not issue an angry order that the putrifying corpse, called Lazarus, must no more pollute the air before the door of his mansion. He might have given orders to his servants that that disgusting carcass was to be carted away for ever from out of his sight. But it is not said that he was so hard-hearted as that. He is in hell, indeed, but he is not in hell for that; his hell would have been both deeper and hotter than it is, if he had said and done all that against Lazarus. For you must know that there are degrees in hell as there are in heaven; there are depths and deeper depths there; and there are hotter and hotter beds there; and with less and less water to cool tormented tongues. And that being so, this rich man might have been even worse than he is, as He here tells us, who has the key of hell and of death in His hands.

Both our Bible and our daily life are full of the real lesson of this scripture—the great danger of great riches to the rich man's immortal soul. Every day we see great riches simply ruining their possessors' souls both for time and eternity. Rich men are so tempted to become high-minded, proud-spirited, arrogant, imperious, selfish, forgetful, and cruel. Rich men get their own way from everybody, and there is nothing in this world so bad for a man as just to get his own way in everything and from everybody. All men yield to a rich man. All men prostrate themselves before a rich man. He speaks when he pleases, and he is silent when he pleases. All are silent when he speaks and wait till he has finished what he has to say. He will not bear to be contradicted or corrected, and all men learn to leave him alone. A rich man would need to be a very good man before his riches come to him, and then he would both know the temptations that lie in his riches and would strive successfully against those temptations. And if he is not a truly good man before he is a rich man; if he is not a meek, modest, humble-minded, considerate Christian gentleman before he is a rich man, a thousand to one he never will become a gentleman after he has become rich. At the same time, while all that is true, great riches are sometimes great stepping-stones to a high place in heaven; that is to say, when they are in the possession of a man whose treasure does not lie in his riches. To go no further than Abraham in the history now open before us. Abraham was a very rich man. One of the finest chapters in all the Old Testament turns upon Abraham and his great riches. So rich was Abraham that his mere overflow was quite enough to make Lot his nephew a rich man also. Only, though Abraham in his generosity could make Lot a rich man, he could not make him a gentleman. Abraham might have turned upon Lot and might have said to him that every horn and hoof that Lot possessed he possessed through his uncle's liberality. But what did Abraham as a matter of fact say? He said these immortal words to Lot. "Let there be no strife, I pray thee, between me and thee, and between my herdsmen and thy herdsmen; for we be brethren. Is not the whole land before thee? Separate thyself, I pray thee, from me: if thou wilt take the left hand, then I will take the right: or if thou depart to the right hand, I will go to the left." What a Christian gentleman was Abraham, and that too such a long time before the day of Christ! And what an abominable mind his nephew in his greed exhibited! And the root of the whole contrast lay in this. Abraham had begun life believing God. He had sought first the kingdom of God and His righteousness, and all those flocks and herds were added to him. And with them there was also added an ever humbler, an ever nobler, and an ever-heavenlier, mind. Once get Abraham's humble, noble, heavenly, mind, and then set your heart upon making riches as much as you like. For the good that you will then be able to do all your days, both to yourself and to all other men, will be simply incalculable.

But it is time to pass the great gulf, our Lord leading us across it, in order to learn from Him some of the great lessons that He here sets us to learn, both in heaven and in hell. And first in heaven. Well, Lazarus who now lies in Abraham's bosom, had his own temptations as he lay at the rich man's gate. And had he yielded to those temptations he would not have been where he now is. He would have been where the rich man now is. Lazarus's temptations were to be embittered, and to repine, and to complain, and to find fault with God and man. Lazarus had

Asaph's temptations over again and the Seventy-third Psalm may have helped Lazarus to overcome his temptations. "As for me," said Asaph, "my feet were almost gone: my steps had well-nigh slipped. For I was envious at the foolish, when I saw the prosperity of the wicked. For their eyes stand out with fatness: they have more than heart could wish. Therefore his people return thither: and waters of a full cup are wrung out to them. For all the day have I been plagued, and chastened every morning." And like Jeremiah also, Lazarus would remember the sins of his youth, and then he would lament in this manner—"Wherefore doth a living man complain, a man for the punishment of his sins? He sitteth alone and keepeth silence. He putteth his mouth in the dust if so be there may be hope." And then, since he had been brought up to read and remember his Bible, he would call this out of Micah to mind. " I will bear the indignation of the Lord, until He plead my cause, and execute judgment for me." Which He did one day. For one day when the rich man's servant took out his morning crumbs to Lazarus he was nowhere to be found. For just when the previous night was at its darkest, and just before the dawn, the angels came down and carried Lazarus up into Abraham's bosom.

Perhaps the most terrible piece of pulpit rhetoric that ever fell from any preacher's lips is to be found in one of Newman's Catholic sermons. I had intended to quote it at this point but I feel now that I dare not. It is too terrible. It is literally true, but you would turn sick under it. For it describes what every lost sinner will say and do when he comes to himself too late before the judgment-seat of Christ. Just think for yourself what you will say and do if you come to yourself for the first time there. Well, that is Newman's terrible sermon. And then he goes on with his fearful satire to give us the conversations about this and that lost soul that go on in every mourning coach on the way home from every such rich man's funeral. But, terrible as Newman's pulpit can be, there is no pulpit anywhere with the concentrated terror of our Lord's pulpit when as here He takes us and lays our ears against the door of hell. The rich man also died, and was buried. And in hell he lift up his eyes, being in torments, and seeth Abraham afar off, and Lazarus in his bosom. And he cried, and all hell heard him, Father Abraham, have mercy on me, for I am tormented in this flame. And all hell listened till it heard Abraham's answer. And Abraham said, Son, remember! And the smoke of their torment went up, as never before, when they all began to remember.

It is hell on earth already when any sinner begins to

remember. Myself am hell! cried Satan when he began to remember. And we are all Satan's seed in that. We simply could not continue to live if we did not manage, one way or other, to forget. When God comes and compels us to remember, what a tornado of despair overwhelms our hearts till we manage again to forget. Now, as you would not lie down in hell, Son, remember! Relieve God of His strange work, and remember. Set your past sins in order before yourself from time to time. Take the remorseful work out of God's hand and take it up into your own hand. Go back and remember. Go back to that day. Go back to that night. Go back to that hour and power of darkness. Remember those who are now in hell and who were once your companions in sin. Remember that man. Remember that woman. Remember all that they remember about you. We sometimes speak of the book of memory. Read often in it, especially in the blackest pages of it. "I have no books, but I have myself," said a great genius and a great saint. Well, you may not have many books, but you all have one book. It is a great book. It is a tragic book. It is such a book that there is no other book like it to you for terror and for horror. And then it is all true. It is no romance. It is no invention. For it is the literal record of your own past life. Return often to that book. Hold daily readings in that book.

There are many more lessons in this terrible scripture. But there is one lesson specially intended, as I think, for us who are ministers. This lost soul seems to have had no hope for his five brothers if they were left alone with the minister he had been wont to meet with at his father's table, and had been wont to hear preaching on Sabbath. In hell he seems to have come to be of the mind of our forefathers who magnified the reading, but "especially the preaching, of the word." That is to say, he became a Puritan in his appreciation of earnest preaching, when it was too late. He admitted that his five brothers had the Prayerbook and the Bible. 'But so had I,' he said. 'Only, I never opened them. I did not understand them. And none of the young fellows who dined and danced in our house ever once opened their Bible any more than I did. Among my father's servants we had a man in black who read prayers morning and night: but I seldom was present, and when I was present, I always fell asleep. Nobody paid any attention to his dronings. He never spoke to me alone. Nor did my father nor did my mother. Nobody ever took me and told me that the wages of a life like mine would be paid me in this place of torment. Else, if they had, do you think I would have been where I now am! O Father Abraham: pity my brothers, and send and deliver them from those dumb dogs that eat and drink till they cannot bark.'

A lesson from hell—as it seems to me—how to read, and how to teach, and how to preach; especially how to preach. 'Put a *testimony* into it,' he says to us toothless preachers. "Testify" is his very word to us from hell. 'Show your people that you believe it, if no one else does. Especially, speak straight out to your young men; they are open and honest. They will believe you, and will honour you, and will through you escape this place of torment.' "Testify!" and again he says—"Testify!"

Son, remember, testified Abraham, that thou in thy lifetime receivedst thy good things, and likewise Lazarus evil things. Now, my sons and my daughters, what are your good things? And what are your evil things? What is your treasure? And where is it? On what is your heart set day and night? When you pray to your Father in secret, for what do you most importunately and unceasingly ask? Child of God, I will answer for you. I know what your evil things are, and what are your good things. Just go on in that mind. Just go forward in that pursuit. And some day soon—the day is at the door—the same angels that carried up Lazarus to Abraham's bosom will come and carry you up to be for ever with the Lord, and to be for ever like Him. And, till they come, make this your song every morning and every night and the whole of every day and every night—

God is the treasure of my soul,
The source of lasting joy;
A joy which want shall not impair,
Nor death itself destroy.

XX

THE SLOTHFUL SERVANT WHO HID HIS LORD'S MONEY

HAD we been with our Lord on the Mount of Olives that day, this parable would have ended far differently from the way we would have expected it to end. As we heard the servant with the five talents introduced, and then the servant with the two talents, and then the servant with the one talent, we would have felt sure that some very severe things were soon to be said about the greatly gifted among men, and the continually prosperous. All our sympathies would have been with that under-estimated and overlooked servant who had only one talent entrusted to him. And at the beginning of this parable we would have felt sure that before it closed the Divine Preacher would take the side of the despised and untalented servant, and would say some of His severest things about the rich, and about the great, and about those who were full of all manner of prosperity. But we would have been disappointed in our expectations. We would soon have seen that our Lord's thoughts are not our thoughts about such men and such matters. The talented and the privileged and the prosperous in life are always the few and not the many. It is the untalented and the unsuccessful and the obscure and the overlooked who are always the multitude. And it is to the multitude, and to the peculiar temptations of the multitude in the matter now in hand, that our Lord here speaks.

The servant with the one talent started on his stewardship with a great grudge at his master. He is a hard master, said that sullen servant in his heart. At any rate, he has been a hard master to me. He felt himself to be as good a man and as deserving as any of his fellow-servants, and he may very well have been in the right in so thinking and in so saying. And here was he treated in this hard and cruel manner. No wonder he was soured at his heart with the treatment he had got. No wonder that he took up his one talent with a scowl, and cast it into a hole of the earth with disgust, saying as he did so that a harder or a more unjust master no honest servant ever had. Those five talents, and those two talents, and then that one talent, all rankled in his heart, till he was the most embittered and resentful and rebellious of men.

When Ouranius first entered holy orders he had a great haughtiness in his temper. The rudeness, ill-nature, or perverse behaviour, of any of his flock used at first to betray Ouranius into impatience. At his first coming to his little village, it was as disagreeable to him as a prison, and every day seemed too tedious to be endured in so retired a place. He thought his parish was too full of poor and mean people, that were none of them fit for the conversation of a gentleman. This put him upon close application to his studies. He kept much at home, writ notes upon Homer and Plautus, and sometimes thought it hard to be called to pray by any poor body's bedside when he was just in the midst of one of Homer's battles. The slothful servant was the father of Ouranius.

This servant who hid his talent in the earth was the father of that young Highland minister also who hid his sermon in the snow. His history was this. A city congregation was looking out for a colleague and successor to their old minister. They had heard of a preacher of great promise in a remote locality, but before they would commit themselves to him they sent four of their number to hear him in his own pulpit. It was mid-winter and a great snow-storm came on that Saturday night. The ambitious and not unfaithful young minister had his sermon all ready, but as there would be a small congregation that snowy morning he would not throw away his whole week's work on such a handful, and so he left his sermon at home. When he entered the pulpit it was too late now when he saw a seatful of city-looking men in the far end of the empty church. And the explanation he stammered out to them did not mend matters. Till it is to be feared that his Master's prophecy at the end of this parable was, some of it, fulfilled in that manse that Sabbath night. He had for long been ambitious of the city, and he had a sharp punishment that day for despising his small congregation; for hiding his talent at home because there would not be enough people to appreciate it.

This servant who hid his lord's money was the father also of all those ministers among us who will not do their ordained work because they have so little to do. Their field is so small that it is not worth their pains taking off their coat to gather out the stones, and to weed out the thorns, and to plough up the fallow ground, and to sow in their too small pulpit and pastorate the seed of the kingdom of heaven. If they had as large a field as that five-talented fellow-servant of theirs; if they had a city pulpit; if they had a people of education and intelligence, they would prepare for the Sabbath in a very different fashion from what they do. But as it is, what is the use? He was the father of all those probationers also who stand idle till they are settled. Once they are settled and married they will lay out their days, and read the best, and rise in the morning, and preach every Sabbath to the top of their ability. You will see if they will not. But a probationer with an unsettled mind cannot work in that way. He is here to-day and there to-morrow, and he has no heart to tackle a serious task of any kind. Indeed what can he do but wait on and on for a call? With all those drawbacks, two probationers rise up before me who had another father than this wicked and slothful servant. The one of them did this among other things all his probationer time. When he preached in a vacancy, or for a friend, as he was preaching it, for the first time he found out the faults of his sermon. He found out the loose links that were in it: the want of a beginning and a middle and an end there was in it; the want of order and proportion there was in it; the want of march, and of progress, and of coming to a head there was in it; and the many other faults of all kinds there were in it. And on Monday morning the first thing he did. while the shame and the pain of his bad work were still in his heart, he rose and took his sermon to pieces, re-arranged it in the light of yesterday, re-wrote it from beginning to end, and preached it again next Sabbath, a completely new creation, and a conscientious, a living, and a life-giving, message. Newman re-wrote all his sermons three time over, and one of his best-written books he re-wrote five times. And that probationer did that again and again and again till he not only made his first sermons perfect, but, better than that, by that fidelity and by that labour he worked his whole mind into a methodicalness, and into an order, and into a clearness, and into a consecutiveness, and into other high qualities, that have all combined to make him one of the foremost preachers of our day. The other probationer who rises up before me executed editorial and other work during that same period of his life: work which stands on all our shelves a quarry of resource to us, and a monument of honour to him. And at the same time he began to lay up those immense stores of reading and writing that make his every sentence to-day a model of fullness, and clearness, and finish.

The unprofitable servant was the father of Clemens, and Fervidus, and Eugenia also. For Clemens is always proposing to himself what he would do if he had a great estate. He would outdo all the charitable men that have gone before him; he would retire from the world; he would have no equipage; he would allow himself only necessaries, in order that widows and orphans, the sick and distressed, might find relief out of his estate. Come to thy senses, Clemens. Do not talk what thou wouldst do if thou wert an angel, but consider what thou canst do as thou art a man. Make the best use of thy present state. Remember the poor widow's mite, Clemens. You will find Clemens in the Law gallery also. Fervidus, again, is only sorry that he is not in holy orders. He is often thinking what reformation he would make in the world if he was a priest or a bishop. He would then have devoted himself wholly to God and religion, and have had no other care but how to save souls. But do not believe yourself, Fervidus. For why do you neglect as you do those whose priest and bishop you already are? You hire a coachman to carry you to church, and to sit in the street with his horses whilst you are attending divine service. You never ask him how he supplies the loss of divine service, or what means he takes to preserve himself in a state of piety. And so on, Fervidus, through all your un-Christian life. Eugenia, again, is a good young woman, full of pious dispositions. She is intending if ever she has a family to be the best mistress of it that ever was. Her house shall be a school of religion, and her children and servants shall be brought up in the strictest practice of piety. She will spend her time in a very different manner from the rest of the world. It may be so, Eugenia. The piety of your mind makes one think that you intend all this with sincerity. But you are not yet the head of a family, and perhaps never may be. But, Eugenia, you have now one maid. She dresses you for church, you ask her for what you want, and then you leave her to have as little religion as she pleases. You turn her away, you hire another, she also comes, and after a time goes. You need not stay, Eugenia, to be so extraordinary a person. The opportunity is now in your own hands. Your lady's maid is your family at present. She is under your care. Be now that religious governess that you intend to be. Teach her the catechism, hear her read and exhort her to pray. Take her with you to church, and spare no pains to make her as holy and devout as yourself. When you do this much good in your present state, then you are already that extraordinary person you intend to be. And, till you thus live up to your present state, there is but little hope that the altering of your state will alter your way of life. Eugenia also, you will all see, is one of his daughters who said: If I had had five talents committed to me, or even two, I would have traded with the same and made them other five talents and other two.

But let Eugenia be done at once and for ever with such a father. Let Eugenia be born again till she has her Father in heaven, not in name only, but in deed and in truth. Come out this week to Fountainbridge, Eugenia. In our mission district in Fountainbridge you will find a prepared scope for all your talents of every number and of every kind. There are hundreds of girls out there who sorely need just such a friend as you could be to them. They need above everything else an elder sister and a more talented sister just like you. Solitary girls in lodgings have a hard fight of it to keep their heads above water. Poor girls starved to death for want of some one to love them, and befriend them, and counsel them, and encourage them in virtue and godliness. You may not have many talents, you may not be rich, you may not be very clever, or very far on yourself in the best things, but you are better off, a thousand times, than those poor sisters of yours out there. And you can speak to them, and know their names, and tell them your name, and go sometimes to see them. At your very poorest and very least talented you can teach two or three neglected children for an hour every Sabbath day. You can take them down to the water-side on a Saturday. You can take them home to a little tea-party every week or two. You can give them little books to read, and make them tell you what they have read, and better and better books as they grow up. Good books for children are so cheap nowadays that you do not need to be rich in order to have a delightful little library provided for every poor girl's lodgings, and for every Sabbath-school child's mother's house. Come out and make a beginning with your one talent this very week. We are all making a beginning again this very week in that famous old field so well known to your forefathers and foremothers in such noble work. Let Clemens, and Fervidus, and Eugenia all come. Let the five-talented and the two-talented, and the one-talented, and the no-talented at all, come. For there is a field for all in Fountainbridge, and many a Well done, good and faithful servant! will before long be purchased there again, as in days gone by. Come away then, O servant of God with the one talent! Come and light a lamp, like Samuel. Come and keep a door, like David. Come and give two mites, like the poor widow. Come and give a cup of cold water in the name of a disciple. For,

Little drops of water,
  Little grains of sand,
Make the mighty ocean
  And the pleasant land.

Little deeds of kindness,
  Little words of love,
Help to make earth happy,
  Like the heaven above.

XXI

THE UNMERCIFUL SERVANT

If you had been destined by your parents to be a minister, and if at twelve years old you had come to the same decision yourself, from that day you would have begun to think continually about your future office, and you would every day have done something to prepare yourself for your future office. You would have made it your custom every Sabbath day to go up to the sanctuary both to hear and to ask questions about the Word of God, in the reading and preaching of which your whole life was to be spent. Even if your teachers had not shown you the way you would have found out your own way of reading the Word of God, and meditating upon it, and employing, not your memory only, but your pen and ink also, in order to store up your observations and your readings and your meditations against the time to come. You would have been like Apelles the painter who never passed a day without drawing at least one line and filling it in. *Nulla dies sine linea,* was all that artist's secret, and it was all his advice to his privileged apprentices. And all your days you would have attributed any success of yours to that teacher who first printed that proverb on your young conscience, and at the same time showed you how to perform it. Now, *mutatis mutandis,* that is to say, after making all the necessary changes, that was our Lord's exact case till He began to be about thirty years of age. And thus it was that, having been made in all things like unto His brethren, He both observed, and read, and meditated, and laid up, the greatest treasures of grace and truth against the day of His showing to Israel. And thus it was that, in all His ministry, He was never once taken unawares or unprepared. Give Him suddenly any Old Testament text to open up and He was ready on the spot to do it. Set Him any intricate question, whatever your motive might be, and immediately you got your answer. As for instance in the case now before us. When Peter came to Him and said, Lord, how oft shall my brother sin against me, and I forgive him? His Master that moment recalled that Roman procurator to mind whose case had been the conversation and congratulation of all Galilee in years now long past. And how well that case fitted into the kingdom of heaven for one parable of that kingdom, all the world has seen ever since that day on which our Lord gave that procurator's case as His answer to Peter's complaint.

Peter, for a long time, was a most interfering and offensive disciple. Peter was continually running up against all other men. He was always both giving offence and taking offence. He was always inflicting wounds and receiving the same. When Peter was converted from all that he splendidly strengthened his brethren. But during the process of his conversion, and till it was perfected, he both caused himself many stumbles and many falls, and was the cause of many such things to his fellow-disciples. What the exact matter was at that moment we are not told. Only, we have Peter coming with this remonstrance to his Master—How oft shall my brother sin against me, and I forgive him? till seven times? Jesus saith unto him, I say not unto thee until seven times: but, until seventy times seven. And then He told Peter the story of that Roman officer who is now known to all time as the Unmerciful Servant. And in this so apposite story, our Lord was like a scribe, as He says Himself, which is instructed unto the kingdom of heaven, which bringeth forth out of his treasure things new and old. And then after telling Peter and all the Twelve this story of Cæsar and his degraded and imprisoned procurator, our Lord added this application to the story—So likewise shall My Heavenly Father do also unto you, if ye from your heart forgive not every one his brother their trespasses.

Now, we are all to learn from this scripture, as we have all learned it already from our own experience, that Almighty God has His reckoning times with all His servants, even in this life. He is to have a great, a universal, and an irrevocable, reckoning time with all men at the end of this life; but the first point in this parable is this, that He has preliminary and preparatory reckoning times in which He begins to take account of His servants even in this world. Cæsar would take account of his servants, says our Lord. Now the best way to understand this is to look back at our past lives. Unless, indeed, we have all along been let alone of God, as is sometimes the case. But, no doubt, those reckoning times have, by God's special grace to us, come already to some of us. When Dr. Chalmers's reckoning time first came to him he was a greatly gifted, but as yet an utterly unprofitable, servant. It came to him in his brother George's illness and death; and then it came back again to him in his own long, and all but fatal, illness. It came to that young communicant I told you about, when her mother died. And it came to that other young communicant when—"I was engaged to be married, sir, and she died." I have one time, especially, ever before me, when my own reckoning time once came to me. And ever since that time I see myself in this chapter as in a glass. This chapter always reads to me like a literal prophecy of myself. How did your reckoning time come to you? What was it that brought your debt to a head? What was it that brought you up to God's judgment seat before the time? What great trespass was it of yours? What great accumulation of debt was it of yours? And did you do like this Galilean procurator? Did you fall down and worship God and appeal to His patience? Did you promise to pay all the debt if only He would let you have sufficient time in which to pay it? Did you swear to Him that you would never commit that great trespass again? Did you engage also that you would watch, and pray, and would crucify your flesh, with its affections and lusts, if only He would not deliver you to the tormentors. And how did it all end? Or, has it all ended yet?

But the same servant went out, and found one of his fellow-servants which owed him an hundred pence; and he laid his hands on him and took him by the throat, saying, Pay me that thou owest. Now we are such, and our fellow-servants are such, that they are continually running into all kinds of debt to us, and to all depths of debt. Our brother is like Peter's brother, in that he is sinning against us seven times every day. Partly through his offensiveness and injuriousness, and partly through our imagining all kinds of offences and injuries at his hand, the most immense debts are being run up between us. Seven things in a single day, sometimes, will come between us and our brother. He forgot us. He overlooked us. He preferred some one else to us. He acted on his own intelligence, and judgment, and conscience, in some matter in which we had the insolence and effrontery to dictate to him. He got some promotion, or some praise, that we had not friendship enough to him to stomach. He was more talked about than we were. He carried his custom to another shop than ours. We wrote a book, we preached a sermon, we made a speech, we sang a song, and he did not praise us to the top of our bent. Say, how often shall my brother sin against me in such ways as these, and I forgive him? No, I cannot do it. I have tried it, and I cannot do it. From the heart to forgive debts like these no, never, I cannot do it. And dost Thou actually expect it of me? Or, is this only another economy of Thine? At any rate, it cannot be done. It has never been done, and it never will be done, so as to justify my Heavenly Father in forgiving me my trespasses. If He suspends my forgiveness on my forgiving such trespasses as these—who shall be saved? Not one. No, not one. Not I, at any rate. "Do you think it will ever be possible to construct an instrument to discover and to exhibit our thoughts against our neighbour?" asked a *Pall Mall* interviewer at Mr. Edison, the great American inventor. "Such an instrument is possible," returned Edison. "But what then? Every man would flee from the face of his neighbour, and would flee to any shelter." So he would. And so he does seventy times every day. As Peter afterwards said, Lord to whom shall I flee but unto Thee? Who shall shelter me and my unforgiving heart but Thee! Who can justify a man like me, both now and at the last account, but Thee and Thy Heavenly Father in Thee! Likewise also say all His disciples. As well ask us to cast Arthur's Seat into the sea.

I feel sure you all say the Lord's Prayer every night before you sleep. Well, how do you do when you come to the fifth petition, which is this—And forgive us our debts, as we forgive our debtors? Dr. Chalmers confesses in one place that he did not feel that dreadful sense of sin and guilt which so overwhelmed Halyburton every night. There are some advantages, you see, in not having such an overwhelming sense of sin as Halyburton had. For one thing, you get sooner to sleep every night, and you get your sleep more unbroken with dreams of the coming day of account. Amen! stuck in my throat, says Macbeth. And Amen stuck many a night in Halyburton's throat over the fifth petition. His brother in St. Andrews had trespassed against him that day. He had outrun him in some race. He had outbidden him in some market. He had damned Halyburton's sermon with faint praise. He had just hinted a fault, and had hesitated dislike. He had been reported to Halyburton as having sneered at the scholarship and the style of Halyburton's first publication. He had trespassed against Halyburton that day in a way that Halyburton has not the courage to set down in black and white in his diary that night, and therefore he could neither say Amen, nor get to sleep. But Chalmers got his fill of Halyburton's sense both of the guilt and the pollution of sin, long before he went so suddenly to his last account, as we see in this mathematical illustration of it: —"The wider the diameter of light, the larger the circumference of darkness." And in this "far ben" entry of it: —"What would I do if God did not justify the ungodly!"

There is a fine touch in this ancient history that must not be neglected. When the fellow-servants of this unmerciful servant saw him so forget his own ten thousand talents as to take his hundred-pence debtor by the throat and cast him into prison, they were both sorry and angry, and went and told their Lord what had taken place. It was an excellent saying of one of the seven wise men of Greece, who, when he was asked what would rid the world of injuries, answered: —"When the bystanders shall resent an injury as keenly as he does who suffers the injury." Now those fellow-servants did that, and their resentment is told us in order that we may imitate them in their resentment. That would largely banish all injury from among ourselves, if we would all do what that wise man of Greece advised, and what those fellow-servants actually did If we would put ourselves in the places of the men who are injured unjustly by their wicked neighbour. When we read or hear of any man being wickedly attacked by tongue or by pen, ten to one all the offender's fault has been that he has disappointed, or offended, or crossed the self-love, and the self-interest, of that revengeful and implacable man. And that, often in the utmost innocence, and even in the most absolute righteousness. Ten to one the root of the wicked treatment is nowhere else but in the wicked heart of that mortally offended, unforgiving, and revengeful man. Keep well in mind, my brethren, what the wise man said, when you see any man or any cause truculently attacked by tongue or by pen. Resent the injury as if it were done to yourself, and that will somewhat help to rid the world of all such injuries, and of all such injurious men. At any rate, be you not such injurious men yourselves. Forgive, and you shall be forgiven. For with the same measure that you mete withal, it shall be measured to you again.

XXII

THE UNPROFITABLE SERVANT

ACCORDING to some ancient authorities Bartholomew was a nobleman of Galilee before he was a disciple of Christ. Not many mighty, not many noble, were called; but Bartholomew was called as if to show that no class of men is shut out from the discipleship and the apostleship of Christ and His church. Bartholomew was a sort of gentleman-farmer, and, like Matthew the publican, he made a supper to his neighbours before he finally parted with his patrimonial estate. And it was while they were all sitting at supper that this incident, so it is supposed, took place, and this conversation that completed the incident. One of Bartholomew's men-servants came in from the field, put off his everyday clothes, girded himself with a waiting garment, and then served the table till his master and all his master's guests had risen from their supper. Are you not much too tired? said Peter sympathetically to the servant. Are you not doing two men's work? And besides, you must be faint by this time with hunger. O no! said Bartholomew's serving-man smiling, I am only doing my bounden and delightful duty in waiting on my good master, and on his honoured guests. And then I will sit down to my own excellent supper immediately. "Hear ye what this so exemplary servant saith," said their Master to the twelve, "Verily, I say unto you, Wheresoever this gospel shall be preached in the whole world, there shall also this, that this man has said and done, be told for a memorial of him."

Our Lord applied that incident in its first intention to the twelve. Their Master was teaching and training the twelve by everything that happened every day to Him and to them. In order to teach and to train the twelve for their fast-coming work, their Master found tongues in trees, books in the running brooks, sermons in stones, and this great lesson in Bartholomew's ploughman-waiter. The twelve had this lesson taught them first, and, after them, all their successors are taught the same lesson, down to this day. That willing-minded, many-handed, ploughing-man is a pattern to all preachers and pastors to the end of time. For he worked for Bartholomew in season, out of season. He made more work for himself when all his proper work was done. One day, so Hermas tells us in his ancient history, when this servant was commanded by his master to run a paling round a vineyard, he not only ran the paling round the vineyard, but he dug a ditch round the same vineyard, and then he gathered the stones and the thorns out of it; and such things he did always, till, when Bartholomew became a disciple, he left one whole farm, with its full plenishing on it, as a bequest to this ploughman as if he had been his own son and true heir. He is a fine pattern for all ploughmen and for all feeders of their masters' cattle; but he is a perfect prototype to all preachers and pastors especially. Every single syllable of this scripture is a study for us who are ministers. Whatever other men may make or may not make of this fine scripture, no minister can possibly miss or mistake its meaning for him, or get away from Christ's all-seeing eye as he reads it. Christ sets every minister before this ministerial looking-glass, in order that in it he may see what manner of minister he now is, and may forecast what his place is likely to be when his Master sets His supper, and Himself serves it, for all His ploughmen and for all His vine-dressers. Only, far better have ten ploughmen's work to do than one minister's work. A ploughman may finish his tale of furrows, and may then give his fellow-servant a hand in feeding his master's cattle, and may then take another and a willing hand in the work of the house, after which he will sit down to his supper with a sense of satisfaction over his hard day's work. But I defy any apostle of Jesus Christ ever to have that ploughman's good conscience. And much less any successor of an apostle. If you have been bold enough to be numbered among the true successors of the apostles you have taken up a task that makes self-satisfaction for ever impossible to you. You may write your sermon over and over again as often as Dr. Newman wrote his masterpieces; but as long as you have not torn it up "fiercely," and written it yet again, you will preach it on Sabbath with such jolts and jars in it as will make you blush and stagger before your people. And you may visit your dying parishioners every afternoon, and your sick, and aged, and infirm, every ten days, but you will never be able to say this ploughman's grace over your supper all the days and nights of your pulpit and pastoral life. For, "the wider the diameter of light," as Dr. Chalmers demonstrated to Dr. Hanna's parishioners on a blackboard at Skirling,—"the larger the circumference of darkness."

Our Lord tells all His true ministers to say every night that they are unprofitable servants, and they all say it. But at the same time He solemnly warns all His so-called ministers that He will irrevocably pronounce this very sentence at the last day against some of them. "Cast ye that slothful and unprofitable servant into outer darkness: there shall be weeping and gnashing of teeth." I was told about such a threatened minister of Christ and of His Church in Scotland only last night. He got a good congregation committed to his charge when he was ordained. But at the present moment he has neither Sabbath School, nor Prayer Meeting, nor Bible Class nor Endeavour Society, nor Band of Hope, and as for his pastoral work, an old man died the other day, not many stonecasts from the manse, who had not seen his minister for two years. Would any institution set up among man but the Church of Christ endure a scandal like that? Would the army endure it? Or a bank? Or a railway? But let us not despair of any man. Even John Mark once ran away from his work. And yet, long after Paul had denounced and deposed him, we have the Apostle actually saying, Take Mark and bring him with thee, for he is profitable to me for the ministry. John Mark's whole story is told first in the Acts, and then in the Epistles, just to guide and encourage the Church in all her dealings with all such unprofitable ministers as Mark once was. And by far the best way of dealing with all our unprofitable ministers would be to induce and enable them to visit Bridge-of-Allan, or Dunblane, or Perth, or Keswick, or Mildmay. "We've gotten a minister noo!" said an old elder to me after his hitherto unprofitable minister had been induced and enabled to make such a visit. Or send him a Life of Wesley, or of Whitefield, or of Boston, or of Chalmers, or Spurgeon. Or perhaps better than all that, get an evangelist on fire to spend a week with him in his parish. "Demas apostatises," says Bengel, "but Mark recovers himself." If you have the means and the opportunity, help your Mark in these ways to recover himself, and he may live to write a gospel for you before all is done.

But all the time, though this character-sketch is intended by our Lord for us ministers in the first place, it is not intended for us only. Our Lord's true people are all ministers in their own measure, as Moses prayed they might all be. You are all true and direct successors of the disciples and the apostles. And, minister or people, a ploughman or a feeder of cattle, putting up palings, digging ditches, gathering out stones, or hewing up thorns, when you have done all, end all, as Bartholomew's ploughman ended his long and arduous day's work. End it all with his proverb in your mouth, and in your heart. For be sure of this, that he of God's servants who thinks that he has fully finished and done what he was commanded to do, that man neither knows his Master, nor his Master's commands, nor does he know the a, b, c, of true knowledge about himself. Well may Paul ask, Where is boasting then? And well may he answer himself, It is excluded. And there can be no better mark of the mind and heart of a true and an accepted servant of God than just that he says in his mind and in his heart, after every new and better service of his, that he is the most unprofitable of all God's servants. "The more," says Newman in one of his thrice-written sermons, "any man succeeds in regulating his own heart, the more he will discern its original bitterness and guilt." And all who are engaged in regulating their own heart—which is our Master's whole commandment—will subscribe to what the great preacher says about that. We are fresh in the classes from Chalmers, and Spurgeon, and Foster, and the Wesleys, and Whitefield, and we found them all subscribing to Newman and to Bartholomew's ploughman. But not one of them all is so much to my own remorseful taste in this matter, as is Thomas Shepard, the Pilgrim Father. Not one of them—passionate as some of them are—is passionate enough for me, till I come to the author of *The Ten Virgins*. Shepard is the most heart-broken, and the most heart-searching, and the most pungently profitable, of all God's heart-ploughing servants to me.

At the same time, while all that is true, and not even Shepard has told the half of the truth, there is another side to all that. And I have never seen that other side so well put as in Marcus

Dods of Belford's *Incarnation of the Eternal Word.* "A Book," says the noble-minded and generous-hearted Chalmers, "of great mental wealth and great mental vigour, rich in scholarship, and of a massive and an original power." John Foster demands more case-preaching in our evangelical pulpits, and Marcus Dod's case-page is exactly what Foster wants. And I refer to that page because it so restores the true balance of evangelical and experimental truth in this matter now in hand. It sometimes happens, says Dods, that the true Christian is so far from boasting of himself that he goes much too far in the opposite direction. He dwells far too much upon the defects of his services, or upon some impropriety of motive that had mingled with them. He feels the very acutest anguish over his best and his holiest performances. But there is often a certain taint of self-righteousness in all that. For such a sufferer not seldom forgets to give the atonement, and the intercession of his great High Priest for him, their true and their full place. He will not take rest nor peace of mind short of the most absolute perfection in his services, leaving no room for the rest and the peace that Christ offers, and Himself is, to all His true-hearted servants. You admit and believe that your services are accepted of God in and through the merit of Christ alone. And yet you are inconsolably distressed because you still detect imperfections in them, and you fear that both you and your services will be for ever cast out of God's presence. Now what is that but making Christ of none effect as your High Priest? What is that but making Him die, and rise again, and intercede for you, in vain? "I have found," says this eminent theologian and evangelical preacher, "this mode of reasoning successful in enabling the mourner to detect the source of his causeless sorrows, and to recover that peace of mind which results from a simple and unhesitating reliance upon our great High Priest, for the pardon of all our sins, and for the acceptance of all our services."

Now, it is all this that explains Paul, and justifies Paul, and makes Paul our greatest evangelical example, where he says with such assurance of heart,—"I have fought a good fight, I have finished my course, I have kept the faith." The best fight Paul ever fought was not with wild beasts at Ephesus, but it was with his own self-righteous heart. It was fought that he might be found in Christ, with all his ever-increasing self-discovery and self-condemnation. And it is his profound grasp of the evangelical faith, that enables Paul so to assure us also that if we only look to Christ alone as our righteousness, and "love His appearing," we shall have our crown of righteousness given to us also at that great day. To be the most unprofitable of servants in our own eyes; to sink into the dust every night speechless with shame and pain over another all but lost day; and at the same time to lie down to sleep accepted in the Beloved,—that is truly to fight the good fight of faith, and to fight it with the whole armour of God: that is really and truly to keep the faith of the gospel till we shall hear our Master's voice saying over us also,—Well done, thou good and faithful servant! Enter thou into the joy of thy Lord.

XXIII

THE LABOURER WITH THE EVIL EYE

ÆSOP'S dog in the manger, and our Lord's labourer with the evil eye, are two companion portraits. Æsop's famous fable taught the very same lesson in ancient Greece that our Lord's present parable taught to Israel in His own day, and still teaches to Christendom in our day.

But before we come to that, there are one or two preliminary lessons that we are intended to learn from the very framework, so to call it, of this parable. And to begin with, let us look well at this unheard-of husbandman. For the like of this husbandman has never been seen before nor since in Galilee, nor in Jewry, nor in Samaria, nor anywhere else. This singular husbandman plants and reaps his vineyard less for the sake of his vines, than for the sake of his vinedressers. This so altruistic husbandman, as we would call him, occupies his vineyard not at all for his own advantage, but for the sole advantage of his labourers. Their well-being is better to him than all the wine they will ever produce. Indeed, and to let out the whole truth at once, this husbandman is a perfect portrait of God the Father, drawn by the skilful and loving hand of God the Son. My Father is the husbandman, says our Lord in another parable. And it must be so here also. For no other husbandman in all the world ever went out at all hours of the day to hire his labourers, and at the same wages. No other husbandman could afford to pay for one hour's work in the evening of the day as much as he pays for the burden and heat of the whole day. No; this husbandman's portrait is no pure invention of our Lord's sanctified genius, as some of His other portraits are. There is no original stroke of our Lord's holy and fruitful imagination. This is as real and as genuine a likeness as is the likeness of the snarling labourer himself. Only, the snarling and snapping labourer is a likeness taken from this envious and spiteful earth. Whereas this husbandman is the speaking likeness of Heavenly Love. My Father is the husbandman.

"Which went out early in the morning to hire labourers into his vineyard." Ah, me! With what a sharp stroke does that incidental-looking statement come home to those of us the morning of whose days is now long past! For we remember well how God came to us early in our life, and before we had as yet hired ourselves out to other masters. O young people, if you would only believe it! If we could only put our old hearts into your young bosoms! How fast you would fall in with the husbandman's earliest offer! And what a life of blows, and starvation, and all kinds of cruel usage, would you thus escape! Satisfy our children, O Lord, early with Thy mercy, that they may rejoice and be glad in Thee all their days.

But of all the hours of this husbandman's labourer-hiring days it is His eleventh hour that comes most home to my own heart. It is His eleventh hour that makes all of us old men to exclaim —Who is a God like unto Thee! Whether any young people will be won to God through this scripture to-night, I do not know. But I will answer for some of the old. For He came to us also at the first hour of the day, and at the third hour of the day, and at the sixth hour, and at the ninth hour. But if He will take us at the eleventh hour, we are His on the spot. The holy child Samuel, and many more early-called, and early-employed, children of God have had their own long and happy lives of rewarded labour. But the thought of all such holy and happy labourers is a positive hindrance and stumbling-block to us. All such wise and good men are a rebuke to us rather than an encouragement. It is the thief on the cross who, of all saved men, is our especial example. The thief on the cross was the great eleventh-hour labourer of our Lord's day, and we come into the vineyard with him. At the end of our evil life we come with him. When the sins of our youth, and all our sins, have found us out we come with him. When the wages of our life-long service of sin has become death to us also we come with him. When this mocking taunt is thrown in our teeth,—What fruit have ye now of those things of which ye are now ashamed? we come with him. Those who are still in the early morning of their days have never heard of the thief on the cross. They have never once read his so heart-encouraging history. It is not yet written for their learning. Not till they are as old as we are will they be able to read the thief's so heartening history as we read it. But it is now the eleventh hour with us as it was with him, and we come with him. Since God takes the bitterest dregs of our sinful lives, and, like this husbandman, pays so altruistically for them, we come. Take us, O God; O do Thou take us. And where our sin has abounded, let Thy grace much more abound.

Is thine eye evil? said the good husbandman to the murmuring labourer. Now, an "evil eye" is just our old Bible English for the Latin word "invidia." Is thine heart so selfish and so envious as that? was what our Lord said to this man who could not enjoy his wages for grudging and growling at his neighbour's wages. Æsop's dog in the manger had his own bone, and he did not deny that it was both a big and a sweet bone. But he was such a hound at heart that he could not see his master's ox beginning to munch his bottle of straw in his manger without snarling and snapping at him. And no more did this dog of a labourer complain that his wages were not quite enough for all the work he had done. All his unhappiness lay in this that his neighbour had so much wages to take home with him that night to his happy wife and children. He did not complain that he was underpaid himself. All his misery came from this, that his fellow-servant was so much overpaid. Both Æsop's dog, and our Lord's dog-like labourer, were sick of that strange disease,—their neighbour's health. This wretched creature was so full of an evil eye that every one must have seen it. Even if he had held his peace every one must have seen his evil heart running out of his eye. Even if you were a perfect stranger to me; even if I had never seen you before, I would undertake to tell to all men the name of the man you both envy and hate, if I were near enough to see your eye when your rival is being praised and rewarded in your presence. Nay, I would know it from the very tone of your voice; aye, from the very cough in your throat. For envy, like love, will out. And, as our Lord is always saying to us, it will out at the eye. "As to the motive of those attacks on Goethe," says Heine, "I know at least what it was in my case. It was my evil eye." Now, who is your Goethe? Who is your fellow-labourer in your special line of life? "Potter envies potter," says Aristotle. Who is your companion-potter? And do you have the self-knowledge that even poor Heine had, to say to yourself every day—'As for these dislikes, and aversions, and antipathies, that I feel in my heart; as well as for these depreciations and contempts that pass continually through my tongue and my pen; I know what their motive is in my case at least, it is in my own evil eye.'

Envy so parched by blood, that had I seen
A fellow man made joyous, thou hadst mark'd
A livid paleness overspread my cheek.

Such harvest reap I of the seed I sow'd.
O man, why place thy heart where there doth need
Exclusion of participants in good?

If he is rightly reported, a Greek commentator who bears a great name makes a very shallow remark at this point. He says that it is difficult for him to believe that any man who is really within the kingdom of heaven himself, and is in its service, and is receiving its rewards, could have an evil eye at another man for his work and for his wages in that kingdom. A more stupid remark never fell from an able man's pen. A more senseless and self-exposing annotation was never made. A young friend of Mr. George Meredith's once came to him in an agony of pain and shame. "This is too bad of you!" he cried. "Willoughby is me!" "No, my dear fellow," said the great writer, "Willoughby is all of us." And in like manner, instead of it being difficult to believe that there was ever such a dog in the manger as this murmuring labourer, we are all such dogs, and he who does not know and confess it—the shell is yet on his head. Yes, Willoughby is all of us. The truth is, an evil eye, like the labourer's evil eye, is not only in all our hearts, but it is the agony of every truly good man's heart that it is so: it is very hell itself to every truly good man's heart that it is so: to every man's heart who is so much as even beginning to know what true goodness really is. Instead of there being no envy among the disciples of Jesus Christ, and among those who labour in His Father's vineyard, as this stupid old annotator would have us believe; instead of that, the true hellishness of envy is never tasted by any man till he is far up in the kingdom of heaven, and is full of its mind and spirit. Dante was far up on his way to Paradise when the fine dialogue on envy and on love took place. Dante sounds his deepest depths in his heart-searching cantos on envy, even as his most seraphic flights are taken in his cantos on love.

"Behold we have forsaken all, and followed Thee; what shall we have therefore?" That miserable speech of Peter's, which gave occasion to this parable, utterly vitiated all Peter's work for his Master, however hard he had worked, and however much he had forsaken for his Master's cause. For it is yet another of the absolute principles of this noble vineyard that it is *motive* in its labourers that counts with its Master. It is motive alone that counts with Him, far more than strength, or skill, or early morning promptitude and punctuality, in His labourers. Unless all these admirable qualities are informed and animated by the right motives, they all go for next to nothing in this so singular and so spiritual vineyard. "An unexamined life is no true life at all," Socrates kept saying continually, as he both examined his own motives every day and set all other men on the daily examination of their own motives. We know from Peter's own mouth what his motive had been in his discipleship up till now. And Peter's shame is told us here that we may see our own shame in our own motives also and up till now. Why, then, do I do this and that work in the vineyard? Why do I study? Why do I preach? Why do I visit the sick and dying? Why am I an elder? Why am I a deacon? Why do I subscribe to this fund and that? Why am I a Sabbath-school teacher? And why am I a member of this church rather than of that? It is our mean and self-seeking motives that lurk so unexamined in our hearts that make us all so many dogs in the manger, and so many envious and murmuring labourers in the vineyard. And as it was at Peter and his miserable motives that his Master levelled this parable, so it is at us and at our miserable motives, and at the miserable envies and jealousies that spring out of our miserable motives, that He levels this same parable in this house to-night.

And now in summing up our Lord adds this noble lesson to all His other noble lessons in this noble and ennobling scripture. Many are called, he adds, but few are chosen. Take them all together, He says; take those called at the first hour of the day, and those called at the third hour, and those called at the ninth hour, and those called at the eleventh hour—when they are all counted up—many are called. But, with all that, the chosen men; the truly choice spirits even among the men who are called; the men who are sincere and single in their motives; the men who are full of humility about themselves, and about their work, and about their wages; the men who are so full of brotherly love that they have no evil eye left at their brother's good work or good wages, but who rather rejoice in all the good things that fall to their brother-labourer's lot—such men are not many even in the vineyard of heaven itself. There are many in that vineyard who say with Peter—What shall we have, therefore? But they are few who work at all hours of the day, and still receive their wages at night with pain and shame, and say to themselves that they are the most unprofitable of all their fellow-servants. They are the few, even among God's true servants, who continually look on all they receive and possess as so many proofs of His singular and unparalleled grace and goodness to themselves. They are the few who so think and so feel and so speak; but, then, they are the very finest and the very choicest of all His saints. They are the elect of His elect. Their true place on earth is in such a noble vineyard as this, and they are the true servants of such a noble Master as this. My brethren, at whatever hour you enter this vineyard, early or late, work all your days in this fine and noble spirit. So work for your Master, and so love your neighbour as yourself, that you may be found at last, not only among the many called, but among the few chosen.

XXIV

THE CHILDREN OF CAPERNAUM PLAYING AT MARRIAGES AND FUNERALS IN THE MARKET-PLACE

It is the market-place of Capernaum and it is the cool of the day. The workmen and the workwomen of the town are sitting in the shade after the work of the day is over, and the children having been released from school, are boisterously engaged in their evening games. 'Come,' cries a leading boy, 'Come and let us have a marriage. This here will be the bride's house, and I will be the bridegroom, and we will all get our lamps lighted, and we will go to the bride's house to bring her home to my house.' 'No,' shouts another. 'No. We had a marriage yesterday, when you were the bridegroom. Let us have a funeral to-day. And I will be the dead man, and you and you and you will take me up and carry me out of the gate, and all the rest will come out after us lamenting and mourning and weeping.' But the bridegroom would not have a funeral, and the dead man would not have a marriage, till a quarrel rose, and till their fathers and mothers had to separate their children and take them home. And till One who had sat in the market-place and had seen it all, arose and went out into the hill-country and was all that night alone and in prayer. And as He looked on Capernaum He wept and said. "And thou, Capernaum, whereunto shall I liken thee, but to thine own children playing in the market-place, and calling to their fellows, and saying—We have piped unto you, and ye have not danced: we have mourned you, and ye have not lamented."

The childhood shows the man,
As morning shows the day,—

sings Milton about the childhood of our Lord. And that childhood scene in the market-place of Capernaum already shows the coming manhood and womanhood of those contending children. And it shows, not their childhood and manhood and womanhood alone, but our own childhood and manhood and womanhood also. The self-will and the bad humour and the obstinacy and the fault-finding of those Capernaum children in the market-place, and of their parents in the synagogue, are all held up before us in this glass of God, looking into which we are instructed to see, not our own children only, but our grown-up selves also. Just because a marriage was proposed by one playfellow his neighbour would not have a marriage. He would have a funeral. His little wilful heart at once rose up within him to resist his neighbour's proposal. He would have a funeral that day and in nothing but a funeral would he take any part. The marriage game was surely a far more delightful game than the funeral game. But it was not delight that he was now set upon; it was his own will and his own way. "The cause is in my will," said Cæsar. "I will not come. Let that be enough to satisfy the senate." And it was enough that this little Cæsar of Capernaum said that he would not have a marriage but a funeral. Immense libraries have been written, first and last, on the will: and that by our very ablest and very best men. But behind Cæsar's will in Rome, and behind this little tyrant's will in Capernaum, no philosopher or theologian of them all has ever been able to go. We see self-will every day and we taste the bitter fruits of it every day. But why the human will should be so incurably evil, that is past the wit of our wisest men to find out. An evil will is the true mystery of iniquity, till the whole world is one huge market-place of Capernaum, and all owing to your evil will and mine. I will not play with you unless I get my own will and way in everything. And you will not play with me unless you get your own will and way in everything. "He is a very nice man when he gets his own way," said one of yourselves the other day when he was praising one of yourselves. And Elizabeth, as we are told, was a very nice queen when her bishops tuned their pulpits to keep time to her dancing. But when they tuned their pulpits to the truth she showed herself a very virago. She would play at churches with them every day, and all day, if they would but play to please her. But if they did not, they would know the consequences. To how many things, both in the church and in state, and both at home and at play, has Cæsar given us the one true and complete key—"The cause is in my will. Let that satisfy the senate."

It was the mother of the dead man of last night who came

with her son in her hand to our Lord as He was preparing to preach in the market-place next morning. 'Master,' she said, 'I saw all Thy sorrow and shame over my son last night. I watched Thee all the time and I knew all that was in Thy thoughts about him. But they were not such sad thoughts as mine were. And now I have brought my little son that Thou mayest lay Thy hand upon him and make him a new heart. And if not, I would rather he had never been born; I would rather see him a dead man indeed, and carried out of the city on his dead bier, than live to see him grow up as he began last night.' And Jesus had pity on her. And He laid His hand on her little son's head, and said, 'Blessed be the son of such a mother. For of such mothers, and of the sons of such mothers, is the kingdom of heaven.

They that have my Spirit,
These, said He, are mine.'

Now my brethren, if you and I have grown up, and are growing old, without having been blessed of God with a new heart: that is to say with a gentle, humble, meek, affable, and complying heart: if we are come to manhood and womanhood with a hard and stony heart: a proud, self-willed, obstinate, despotic, and tyrannical heart still within us—how is it all to end? and when? and where? We cannot be content, surely, to go on and on with such an evil heart within us, making ourselves miserable, and making all who have to do with us miserable also. And if the New Testament is true; if we suddenly die with such a heart still in us, it will be to be devils for ever ourselves, and the play-fellows of devils for ever. If we are hardening our hearts against God and man, and are set on having our own will in everything; if we go about tyrannising over everybody, and making every-body suffer from our insolent temper, what is there in death, or after death, to give such as we are a new heart? There are abund-ance of promises in death and after to the meek, and to the sweet, and to the submissive, and to the self-surrendering, and to the self-sacrificing. But I have not found any such promises and con-solations to the high-minded, and the sour-tempered, and the quarrelsome, and the self-asserting—have you? I have met with not a few warnings and threatenings and divine denunciations against such, both in this world and in the world to come. And you must have met with the same. And to all such among you, amid scenes of misery caused by your wicked temper and your tyranny, your own conscience must have told you to your face that you are the man. Now what are you doing to alter that? Or are you doing anything? And are you content to go on as you are, with such a heart as yours and you taking no step to mend it? Yes, what step are you taking to mend it? For even if you came to Him to whom the Capernaum mother came, He would only say to you what He said to her, and what He said to her far-off fathers and mothers through His servant Ezekiel. "Repent," He will say to you, "and turn yourselves from all your transgressions; so your iniquity will not be your ruin. Cast away from you all your transgressions, whereby ye have transgressed, and make you a new heart, and a new spirit, for why will you die? For I have no pleasure in the death of him that dieth, saith the Lord God; wherefore turn yourselves, and live ye." Come away then, and let us look at some of the times and the places when and where you must set about making yourselves a new heart; that is to say, a broken, contrite, chastened, tender, yielding, companionable, heart.

" How shall a man like me ever become of an affectionate and companionable temper?" asks Epictetus, the Stoic professor, at his students in his lecture-room in Nicopolis. And this is the answer he gives himself in their hearing. I take his answer out of the notebook of one who was present. And I take Epictetus because our Lord said, "And thou, Capernaum; they shall come from the east and the west, and shall sit down in the kingdom of heaven, while many of the children of the kingdom, such as thou and thy children are, shall in nowise enter into it." "How," asks the old Stoic, "shall a man like me ever become of a truly noble and divine disposition?" And he answers himself in this way. "Every man is improved by the corresponding acts. The carpenter is improved by the acts of carpentry. And the orator is improved by the acts of oratory. But if a carpenter slovens over his work he will never become a good carpenter. And if an orator does not speak better and better every time he rises to his feet he will soon be hissed out of the pulpit. And in religion and morals it is the same very thing. Thus, modest actions preserve and improve the already modest man, and immodest actions destroy him. Shamelessness strengthens the shameless man, faithlessness the faithless man, abusive words the abusive man, angry words and angry acts make the man more and more a man of anger, and avaricious acts end in making a man a miser." And the great Stoic has line upon line, and precept upon precept to his scholars in this all-important matter. For in another page of Arrian's notebook I come upon this—"Every habit and faculty is maintained and increased by the corresponding actions. The habit of walking by walking, and the habit of running by running. If you would be a good reader, read; if a good writer, write. Lie down ten days and then attempt a long walk, and you will see how your power of walking has gone from you. Generally, then, if you would make anything a part of your character, practise it. When you have been again angry to-day, you have not only been angry to-day, but you are all that the more open to anger to-morrow. Till to-day's anger, and to-morrow's anger, and the next day's anger, will all unite to make you an absolute savage to all who live near you. But if you wish not to be such a savage, do not do the acts of a savage, but the acts of a gentleman. Do not feed your savage temper by savage words and savage actions. Keep your bad temper in hand, till you can count the days on which you have not been angry. I used to be in a passion every day at something or somebody, now every second day, then every third, then every fourth day. But if you have intermitted thirty days without an explosion of anger, make a thanksgiving sacrifice to God. If you escape for two or three months, be assured that you are in a very good way. Great is the combat, divine is the work; it is for freedom, it is for happiness, it is for holiness. Remember God, and go on." So far Epictetus.

Are you then a self-willed, proud-hearted, intolerant, and tyrannical man? Or are you a virago of a woman? And would you be a gentleman and a gentlewoman? Epictetus has told you the way to-night. Butler has told you the same way in your own tongue, but Epictetus was beforehand by two thousand years. Gentlemanly acts will end in making you a gentleman, and nothing else will. No man was ever born a gentleman; no mere man. But multitudes have made themselves gentlemen and gentlewomen. And that on the Epictetus-principle of acts, habits, character. The next time, then, that opinions and proposals differ where you are concerned, seize you this assurance, that God Himself has brought about that difference of opinion, and those conflicting proposals, with His eye set on you. Opinions and proposals are nothing to Him: but you, and your moral character, and your Christian conduct are everything to Him. To-night yet, and before you have slept this scripture of His off your mind, and to-morrow, to a certainty, two opinions and two proposals will be tabled before you, and that in order to put it to the proof if you have paid any attention to-night. In order to see if your visit to the playground of Capernaum, and to the mountain of prayer above Capernaum, has done you any good. Be you ready. Be you prepared. Play you the man that moment. If it is a marriage that is proposed, put yourself at their disposal. Say that you will undertake to see the registrar and the minister. Do not mention the other engagements you had made for that week and that day. But put them all off till you have seen this marriage carried smoothly and sweetly through. And after you have seen them away to their honeymoon, you will be far happier in your lonely lodging than if you had been the bridegroom himself. Do it and see! At any rate, there will be better than bridegroom-joy in heaven over you because this playground of Capernaum has not been lost upon you to-night.

XXV

THE SAMARITAN WHO SHEWED MERCY

A CERTAIN man went down from Jerusalem to Jericho, and fell among thieves, which stripped him of his raiment, and wounded him, and departed, leaving him half dead. And by chance there came down a certain priest that way; and when he saw him, he passed by on the other side. And likewise a Levite, when he was at the place, came and looked on him, and passed by on the other side. But a certain Samaritan, as he journeyed, came where he was; and when he saw him, he had compassion on him, and went to him, and bound up his wounds, pouring in oil and wine, and set him on his own beast, and brought him to an inn, and took care of him. And on the morrow, when he departed, he took out two pence, and gave them to the host, and said unto him, Take care of him: and whatsoever thou spendest more, when I come again, I will repay thee.

"And, by chance, there came down a certain priest that way," says our Lord, telling the story after the manner of men. He knew better than any one that there is nothing left to "chance" in this world; not even the fall of a sparrow; not even a hair of our head. "It will be obvious to the intelligent reader," says Thomas Boston's son in editing his father's priceless *Autobiography,* "that the radical principle upon which this narration is founded, is that *God hath preordained whatsoever comes to pass.* This principle the author believed with all his heart, it was often an anchor to his soul, and every minister of the Church of Scotland is bound, by his subscription and ordination vows, to maintain it. This, kept in view, will account for the author's ascribing to an over-ruling Providence many incidents, which some may think might be resolved into natural causes." I do not know what, all, this priest's ordination vows may have been. But I am quite sure that if any one had asked him in the temple yesterday saying, Master, what shall I do to inherit eternal life? He would have answered him, Thou shalt love the Lord thy God, with all thy heart, and with all thy soul, and with all thy strength, and with all thy mind; and thy neighbour as thyself. But the pity with this priest was, that as soon as he got his temple duties over yesterday, he forgot all that about his neighbour till he put on his gown again next Sabbath morning in Jericho. And thus it was that he was on his way down to Jericho that day when, by chance, he came on a half-dead man on the way-side. Being a temple priest, he should have said to himself as he set out on his journey,—

> The Lord shall keep thy soul: He shall
> Preserve thee from all ill.
> Henceforth thy going out and in
> God keep for ever will.

And then he should have been making the "bloody pass" safe to himself and to others by singing to himself,—

> Shew me thy ways, O Lord:
> Thy paths O teach thou me:
> And do thou lead me in thy truth,
> Therein my teacher be.
>
> For thou art God that dost
> To me salvation send,
> And I upon thee all the day
> Expecting do attend.

But not setting out in that way, and not singing to himself in that way, the priest missed his chance of salvation and of eternal life,—for that day at any rate.

The Levite who followed him would seem, for one thing, to have had somewhat more curiosity than the priest, and to have come all that the nearer that day to eternal life. The priest saw enough at the first glance to suffice and satisfy him: but the Levite stopped and went to the side of the road and looked at the half-murdered man, but that one look was enough for him also, for he also passed by on the other side. If the half-dead man's eyes were not entirely torn out by the thieves, and if he was able to open his eyes for a moment as he heard the coming footsteps, how his heart must have beat back to life again at the sight of the priest and the Levite. When a beggar at one of our road-sides sees a minister coming along with his black clothes and his white neckcloth, the poor wretch feels sure that he will not be passed by this time without a kind word at any rate. But his disappointment is all the more when the man of God looks the other way and passes by in silence on the other side.

Now, nobody who knew what the Samaritans were would have wondered at one of them setting out on a journey any morning and every morning without a Psalm, and then coming "by chance" on this man and that, all the day, and passing them by without a thought. But however he set out, psalm or no psalm, and however this Samaritan was occupied as he rode down the Jericho-pass, as God would have it, Behold, there is a half-dead Jew lying in the ditch at the roadside. Were ever any of you as full as you could hold of mortal hatred at any enemy of yours? At any enemy of your church or your country? Were you ever in such a diabolical state of mind at any man, or at any race of men, that it would have made you glad to see him lying wounded and half dead? Well, that was the way that the Jews and the Samaritans felt to one another in our Lord's day. They had nothing short of your mortal hatred at one another. And, had that been a half-dead man of Samaria, it would have been nothing wonderful to see the Samaritan traveller doing all that to his fellow-countryman. But to do it to a Jew,—that is why this Samaritan's name is so celebrated in heaven. What do you think would be the thoughts of the half-dead Jew as he saw his own temple-kinsmen passing by on the other side, and then saw this dog of a Samaritan leaping off his mule? What would he think and say all night as he saw this excommunicated Samaritan lighting the candle to pour oil and wine into his wounds and watching all night at his bedside? That Samaritan mule hobbling down the Jericho-pass with that half-dead burden on its back always reminds me of Samuel Johnson hobbling along to Bolt Court with the half-dead street-walker on his back and laying her down on old Mrs. Williams's bed to nurse her back to life. The *English Dictionary* has long been superseded, and it is only one enterprising student of the best English literature here and there who goes back to *The Lives of the Poets*. But that immortal picture of that midnight street in London, and that immortal picture of that bloody pass of Adummim, will be sister portraits for ever among the art-treasures of the new Jerusalem. And if you love your neighbour as yourself in this city, as this Samaritan and Dr. Johnson did in Jericho and in London, you will yet see those two portraits and the originals of them with your own eyes, in the art-galleries of the heavenly country.

Then said Jesus to the lawyer, Go, and do thou likewise. But he, willing to justify himself, began, lawyer-like, to raise speculative and casuistical questions, instead of immediately setting about to do his duty. "Thou shalt love thy neighbour as thyself." 'Yes,' said the man of law, 'but who is my neighbour? Distinguish, and clear up to me who, exactly, my neighbour is,' said this subtle casuist. My brethren, all men are your neighbours. Absolutely all men. Absolutely every man. But more immediately every stripped, and wounded, and half-dead, man. And still more, every enemy of yours. Yes, absolutely every man. For, who is so unrobbed, and so unwounded, and so full of life and love, as not to stand in need of your brotherly love, and of every kind of life-giving office at your hands? Who is there on the face of this earth who does not need, and will not welcome, the oil and the wine of your loving kindness poured into his many wounds? No man. No woman. It is not only in the bloody pass of Adummim and on the midnight street of London that your neighbours are to be come on wounded and half-dead: they are to be found everywhere. Many who have their own beasts to ride upon, and who are quite able to pay their own bill to the inn-keeper and your bill also: many such stand in as much need of your love and your services of love as did that half-dead Jew on the road to Jericho. A kind thought, a kind look, a kind word, a kind deed; carry about that oil and that wine with you, and you will not lack wounded and half-dead men and women to bless the day on which they first saw your face and heard your voice.

But some lawyer here, willing to justify himself, will stand up to tempt me, and will demand of me whether I mean to deny all my late sermons on the Romans? And to teach to-night that this Samaritan was justified before God simply because of this good deed of his? I quite admit that both our Lord, and His Apostle, sometimes teach economically, and paradoxically, and one-sidedly even, on occasion. All the same,—go you and do you as this good Samaritan did. And if death and judgment overtake you walking beside your mule on the way to the inn at Jericho: or if your Lord summons you to give in your account when you are up smoothing the pillow of a half-dead enemy of yours; I would far rather take your chance of eternal life than if death and judgment overtook you still debating, however Calvinistically, about your evangelical duty. Yes: Go at once to-night and do likewise.

Spurgeon says somewhere that wherever his text is, and whatever his text is, he will find his way, somehow, to Jesus

Christ before he leaves his text. Now it is not to go far from this text to go to Him who is The Good Samaritan indeed. It has been said to Goethe that, like this priest and this Levite, he kept well out of sight of stripped, and wounded, and half-dead, men. I hope it is not true of that great intellectual man. At any rate it is not true of Jesus Christ. For He comes and He goes up and down all the bloody passes of human life, actually looking for wounded and half-dead men, and for none else. Till He may well bear the name of The one and only entirely Good and True Samaritan. They are here to whom He has said it and done it. "When I passed by thee, and saw thee wounded and half dead, I said unto thee when thou wast in thy blood, Live; yea, I said unto thee when thou wast in thy blood, Live. Now when I passed by thee, and looked upon thee, behold, thy time was a time of love. Then washed I thee with water, and I anointed thee with oil." And we ourselves are the proof of it. That we are here to-night, in the land of the living and in the place of hope, is the sufficient proof of it. We are as it were in the inn of Jericho to-night. But to-morrow He will come back and will repay whatever they are to-night spending here upon us. And as soon as we are able to be removed He will come and take us home with Him, for a greater and a better and a bigger-hearted than the best Samaritan is here. He will take us to that land with Him where no man falls among thieves and where they rob not nor wound nor leave a man half-dead. Go, said His Father to Him, and love Thy neighbour and Thine enemy as Thyself. And instead of wishing to justify Himself; instead of saying, But who is My neighbour—you know what He said, and what He did, and to whom He said it and did it. And we who were in the bloody pass, and were stripped, and wounded, and half-dead, we are the proof of it, and will for ever be the proof and the praise of it.

And now, my brethren, is it not a cause of the profoundest praise and thanksgiving to Almighty God that peace has come, and that there is not a man on the face of the whole earth that we any more wish to see wounded and half-dead? And must it not be a sweet thing to our King to think about on his bed, and to all his Royal House, that he has no enemy now to his throne and sceptre and crown in all the wide world. And that is so, because He, The Good Samaritan, is our peace, Who hath made both one, and hath broken down the middle wall of partition between us: having abolished in His flesh the enmity; for to make in Himself of twain one new man, so making peace. And that He might reconcile both unto God in one body by the

Cross, having slain the enmity thereby. For through Him we both have access by one spirit unto the Father; through Jesus Christ, in whom all the building fitly framed together groweth unto an holy temple in the Lord, in whom ye also are builded together for an habitation of God through the Spirit.

XXVI

MOSES ON THE NEW TESTAMENT MOUNT

THE Sermon on the Mount is the last sermon of Moses that has come down to us. It is the last sermon and it is the best of that great lawgiver. In this last sermon of his we have Moses rising above himself and stretching himself beyond himself. But all the time, and with all that, this is still Moses. The mouth, indeed, is the mouth of a far greater than Moses, but the hands and the heart are still the hands and the heart of the old lawgiver. For as we sit under this sermon we soon find that we are still in the hands and the heart of the law. The law is at its most spiritual indeed; the law is at its most holy and just, and good indeed, in the Sermon on the Mount. But the very spirituality of its holiness only serves to make our condemnation under it all the more hopeless, and our death at its hands all the more certain and inexorable. Till we cry out under this sermon, as the murderers of his Master cried out under Peter's sermon—Men and brethren, what shall we do? The eight beatitudes with which this sermon begins are undoubtedly very beautiful. There is no denying that. That is to say they are very beautiful to him who finds himself in a position to claim them as his due, and to possess them and to expatiate upon them. But let him who has tried with all his might to purchase them and to claim them, let him tell us what he thinks of their beauty and what effect their beauty always has upon his heart and upon his conscience. Orion and the Pleiades are very beautiful, he will tell you. But he will tell you also that he will sooner hope to build his house up among their sweet influences, than he will hope to possess the beatitudes of the Sermon on the Mount by anything he can ever suffer or perform or attain. The pole-star is not so far out of his reach, he will tell you, as is the nearest to him of those beautiful, but heart-breaking, beatitudes of the Sermon on the Mount. I do not know how it is in this matter with you. But I will tell you frankly how it is with me. Ever since

I first saw something of their terrible spirituality, I cannot bear to read so much as one single beatitude, or indeed any other sentence in this sermon, till I have again strengthened my heart with the Epistle to the Romans. To me the Epistle to the Romans is the true foundation-stone, corner-stone, and cope-stone, of the whole New Testament. Nay, its bold-hearted author is bold enough to take his Epistle to the Romans, and his Epistle to the Galatians, and to lay them away up before and underneath even the Book of Genesis itself. And as often as I read again his so ancient and so unanswerable argument, I forthwith feel that I hold in my hand, not only the true key to all the promises and prophecies and types and emblems of the Old Testament; but what is far better to me, I hold in my hand the true and only key to let me out of that dungeon of despair into which Moses again shuts me, as often as I read any of his sermons, and forget my Romans and my Galatians. I can walk at liberty around Mount Sinai itself; I can climb to the very top of its most threatening precipices, and can look down over them to their very bottom, if I have Paul as my mountain guide to lean upon, and his Romans to direct me and to encourage me.

Luther—"not such a perfect gentleman as Paul, perhaps, but almost as great an evangelical genius,"—Luther labours with all his might, and it is not little, to keep Moses in his right place and not to let him move out of his right place, no, not by so much as one single inch, or, rather, out of his three right places. The first of Moses' right places is what the Reformer calls his political place. That is to say, the place from which the great lawgiver issues his laws for the good government of states and cities and households. Moses' second place is that of a universal prosecutor and accuser of all men; for out of his second place he convicts all men of sin and death and shuts all men's mouths. And his third right place, according to Luther, is to be an overseer and task-master of all wise and safe housebuilding, as in the text. Now come and let us take this approved housebuilder to-night, and let us address ourselves to learn some communion-evening lessons from him, and from Moses, and from Paul.

Well then, let it be remarked and remembered that the first praise that is given to this wise housebuilder is this, that he digged deep down for a foundation before he began to build his house. And this sermon which leads up to him, digs deep down also, if ever sermon did. As you will see if you will but walk over the ground it covers and with your eyes open. Take, to begin with, that hunger and thirst after righteousness to which the fourth beatitude is attached, and you will see what a deep and central shaft that sinks into your own soul. Then take all kinds of purity of heart, and that is, as you must confess, another very deep and very secret shaft. And take your demanded reconciliation to your offended brother, before you need seek for your reconcilation to your offended God, and that, you must allow, is not surface work. Neither is the command to do good to the men who hate you and despitefully use you. Now all that is what this sermon describes as digging deep. And one of our very first lessons from all that should surely be that as this sermon digs so deep, so should all sermons do. The true worth to us of every sermon is not its learning, or its eloquence, but its depth: the depth of him who preaches it, and the depth of them who hear it. Thomas Goodwin, whose depth has drawn me to him all my days, has this passage on this subject. "By this digging deep I do not mean deep terrors, for it is not necessary that all kinds of earth should be digged out with iron pickaxes. God uses such tools to none but hard earth only. Very small spades and shovels suffice to dig up and empty out some men. Only, all men must be dug up and emptied out somehow. All men must be emptied out by a spiritual insight into their true estate, and made to see down to the bottom of their own hopelessly evil hearts. And must be made to confess their utter inability to build a single stone of a safe house for themselves, except out of and then upon that Rock which is Christ."

There is no saying of His in all this sermon of His that is more deep-digging and fundamental than what our Lord here says to us about much secret prayer. For there is nothing that we scamp and skim over more than just much secret prayer. The Preacher of this sermon had all His own days dug deep, and had laid the foundations of His own house deep, in continual and unceasing secret prayer. And He went on doing that till the time came when He Himself was to be likened to a wise man. For all that night in the garden of Gethsemane He was still digging deep, and was making absolutely sure that His house was founded on God His Father, and on Him alone. And it was so, that when the rain descended, and the floods came, and the winds blew and beat upon that house all that night, it fell out: for it was founded on a Rock. And had Peter taken his Master's advice and example all his days, and even that one night, his house would not have fallen with such a sad fall, all that night and all next day. Do this deep saying of Christ yourselves, O all you communicants of to-day! For there are clouds rising that will soon burst on your house also, and if it is not dug deep with much secret prayer, you may depend upon it, great will be the fall of it.

And now as you go over all this deep-dug ground, what do you say to all these sayings of His about meekness, and about hunger after righteousness, and about purity of heart, and about peacemaking, and reconciliation to your offended brother, and about cutting off your right hand, and plucking out your right eye, and about loving your neighbour as yourself, and about closet prayer, and about laying up treasure in heaven, and about seeking first the kingdom of God and His righteousness, and about judging not, that you be not judged, and about entering in at the strait gate—what do you say to all these sayings of His who came not to destroy the law but to fulfil it, and to have it fulfilled in you? What do you really think and feel about the whole of this Sermon of His on the Mount? Babes at the breast; preachers and writers with the shell on their heads, chatter their praises of the Sermon on the Mount, and incessantly advertise us that all their New Testament, and all their creed, and all their catechism, are summed up in the Sermon on the Mount. My brethren, you know better. You have dug deeper. The law of God has been dug deeper than that into your understanding you, and Moses with his two-edged sword in his hand, as never before. "By the law is the knowledge of sin." And by this deep law of wise house-building all your foolish building is discovered and denounced to you. Just try your hand at a truly spiritual house, and see. Take—"Blessed are the meek; for they shall inherit the earth." And begin at once to found deep, and to build up, your spiritual house. Begin to live a life of meekness. Study humility. Keep ever before your eyes the many and deep reasons there are why you should be the meekest and the humblest-minded of men. Set yourself with all your might to put up with all injustice, and all ill-usage, and all contempt, and all neglect on all hands. Suffer long and be kind. And your house will rise, for a time, on that foundation, till one day a storm will come. One dark day the rain will descend and the floods will come, and the winds will blow and beat upon your house of meekness, till it will fall, and will bury you under it. Another will attempt his house on this foundation, "Judge not, that you be not judged. For with what judgment you judge, you shall be judged; and with what measure you mete, it shall be measured to you again." Begin to lay judgment to the line, and righteousness to the plummet, and tell me how long your refuge lasts you. and your heart and your conscience. Yes, this is very Moses to And so on, through all the foundations laid on Sinai.

Yes. This whole sermon is still Moses and his two tables of stone, rather than Jesus Christ and His Cross and Righteousness. Literally, no doubt, Jesus Christ did preach this sermon. Nobody disputes that. But then, the real truth is, that it is not Christ's preaching that proves Him to be the true Christ to you at all; it is not His sermons but His Cross that is the sure proof of that to you: and His Cross is still a far way off. We have far greater preachers of Christ in the New Testament Church than Christ was Himself. It was not yet the time for any one fully to preach Christ. As He said Himself to His mother at the marriage of Cana—My time is not yet come. The truth is—I will say it for myself, if you will not let me say it for you—unless far other sermons than the Sermons on the Mount had been preached in the New Testament Church it had been better for me I had not been born. But for Paul's preaching of Christ, I, for one, would be of all men the most miserable. 'Far greater and far better sermons than mine shall be preached,' He said, 'because I go to the Father. I have yet many things to say unto you, but you cannot bear them now. Howbeit, when He, the Spirit of truth, is come, He will guide you into all truth. He shall glorify me; for He shall receive of mine, and shall show unto you."

Wherefore then serveth the Sermon on the Mount? you will demand for me; to which demand of yours Paul will answer you. "It was added because of transgressions, till the seed should come to whom the promise was made. Is the law then against the promises of God? God forbid; for if there had been a law given which could have given life, verily righteousness should have been by the law. But the Scripture hath concluded all under sin, that the promise by faith of Jesus Christ might be given to all them that believe." In other words—The Sermon on the Mount sets forth, as never before nor since, a splendid exhibition of the majestic and noble righteousness, as well as the exquisitely inward spirituality, of God's holy law. And this sermon commands all men, and more especially all men of a spiritual mind, to keep looking at themselves continually in this glass that Christ Himself here holds up before them. Holds up with His own hands before them in order that they may see, and never for a moment forget, what manner of men they still are. And then His redeeming death being accomplished, and Paul being raised up to preach the true, and full, and complete, and final Gospel; and after we have heard and believed that Jesus Christ is made of God to us wisdom, and righteousness, and sanctification, and redemption, we now return to the Sermon on the Mount to see in all its beatitudes and in all its commandments what manner of persons we ought to be in all holy conversation and godliness.

XXVII

THE ANGEL OF THE CHURCH OF EPHESUS

You are not to think of an angel with six wings. This is neither a Michael nor a Gabriel. I cannot give you this man's name, but you may safely take it that he was simply one of the oldest of the office-bearers of Ephesus. No, he was no angel. He was just a chosen and faithful elder who had begun by being a deacon and who had purchased to himself a good degree, like any one of yourselves. Only, by reason of his great age and his spotless character and his outstanding services, he had by this time risen till he was now at the head of what we would call the kirk-session of Ephesus. By universal acclamation he was now the "president of their company, and the moderator of their actions," as Dr. John Rainoldes has it. This angel, so to call him, had grown grey in his eldership and he was beginning to feel that the day could not now be very far distant when he would be able to lay down his office for ever. At the same time, it looked to him but like yesterday when he had heard the prince of the apostles saying to him those never-to-be-forgotten words—"Take heed to thyself, and to all the flock over which the Holy Ghost hath made thee an overseer, to feed the flock of God, which He hath purchased with His own blood." And, with many mistakes, and with many shortcomings, this ruling and teaching elder of Ephesus has not been wholly unmindful of his ordination vows. In short, this so-called angel of the Church of Ephesus was no more an actual angel than I am. A real angel is an angel. And we cannot attain to a real angel's nature, or to his office, so as to describe such an angel aright. But we understand this Ephesus elder's nature and office quite well. We see his very same office every day among ourselves. For his office was just to feed the flock of God, as Paul has it. And again, as James has it, his office was just to visit the widows and orphans of Ephesus in their affliction, and to keep himself unspotted from the world of Ephesus. And he who has been elected of God to such an office as that in Ephesus, or in Edinburgh, or anywhere else, has no need to envy the most shining angel in all the seven heavens. For the most far-shining angel in the seventh heaven itself desires to look down into the pulpit and the pastorate of the humblest and obscurest minister in the Church of Christ. And that because he knows quite well that there is nothing for him to do in the whole of heaven for one moment to be compared with the daily round on this earth of a minister, or an elder, or a deacon, or a collector, or a Sabbath-school teacher.

Now, there is nothing so sweet, either among angels or among men, as to be appreciated and praised. To be appreciated and praised is the wine that maketh glad the heart of God and man. And the heart of the old minister of Ephesus was made so glad when he began to read this Epistle that he almost died with delight. And then as His all-seeing and all-rewarding way always is, His Lord descended to instances and particulars in His appreciation and praise of His servant. 'I know thy works. I chose thee. I gave thee all thy talents. I elected thee to thy charge in Ephesus. I ordained thee to that charge, and my right hand hath held thee up in it. Thou hast never been out of my mind or out of my eye or out of my hand for a moment. I have seen all thy work as thou wentest about doing it for me. It is all written before me in my book. All thy tears also are in my bottle.'

We have an old-fashioned English word that exactly sets forth what our Lord says next to the angel of Ephesus. 'I know all thy painlessness also,' He says. It is a most excellent expression for our Master's purpose. No other language has produced so many painful ministers as the English language, and no other language can so well describe them. For just what does this painfulness mean? It means all that is left behind for us to fill up of His own painful sufferings. It means all that tribulation through which every true minister of His goes up. It means cutting off now a right hand and plucking out now a right eye. It means taking up some ministerial cross every day. It means drinking every day the cup of the sinfulness of sin. It means to me old Thomas Shepard more than any other minister that I know. "Labour," as our bloodless version has it is a far too dry, a far too wooden, and a far too tearless, word, for our Lord to employ toward such servants of His. Depend upon it He will not content Himself with saying "labour" only. He will select and will distinguish His words on that day. And to all who among ourselves have preached and prayed and have examined themselves in and after their preaching and praying, as it would seem that this angel at one time did, and as Thomas Shepard always did, their Master will signalise and appreciate and praise their "painfulness" in their own so expressive old English, and they will appreciate and appropriate His so suitable word and will appreciate and praise Him back again for it.

His patience is another of the praises that his Master gives to this once happy minister. I do not suppose that the angel of Ephesus counted himself a specially happy man when, all unthought of to himself, he was laying up in heaven all this eulogium upon himself and upon his patience. But all the more, with such a suffering servant, his Master held Himself bound to take special knowledge of all that went on in the Church of Ephesus. And to this day and among all our so altered circumstances, patience continues to take a foremost place in the heart and in all the ministry of every successor of the true apostleship. Nay, patience was not only an apostolic grace, it was much more a Messianic grace. Patience was one of the most outstanding and far-shining graces of our Lord Himself as long as He was by far the most sorely tried of all His ministers. And He has all men and all things in His hands to this day that He may so order all men and all things as that all His ministers shall be put to this school all their days, as He was put all His days by His Father. The whole of every minister's lot and life is divinely ordained him so as to win for him his crown of patience, if he will only listen and believe it. "I know all thy patience," said our Lord to the angel of Ephesus.

I do not the least know who or what the Nicolaitans of Ephesus were, and no one that I have consulted is any wiser than I am, unless it is Pascal. And Pascal says that their name is equivocal. When that great genius and great saint comes upon the Nicolaitans in these Epistles, he has an original way of interpretation all his own. He always interprets this name, so he tells us, of his own bad passions. And not the Nicolaitans of Ephesus only; but the Egyptians, and the Babylonians, and as often as the name of any "enemy" occurs in the Old Testament, and it occurs in the Psalms continually, that so great and so original man interprets and translates them all into his own sinful thoughts and sinful feelings and sinful words and sinful actions. That is I fear a far too mystical and equivocal interpretation for the most of us as yet. To call the Nicolaitans of Ephesus our own wicked hearts, is far too Port-Royal and puritan for such literalists as we are. Only, as one can see, the minister of Ephesus would be swept into the deepest places, and into the most spiritual experiences, both of mysticism and of puritanism before their time, as often as he set himself, and he must surely have henceforth set himself every day of his life, to hate the deeds of the Nicolaitans, whoever they were, and at the same time to love the Nicolaitans themselves. To a neighbour minister in the same Synod our Lord sends a special message about the sharp sword with the two edges. And it would need all the sharpness of that sword and all its edges to divide asunder the deeds of the Nicolaitans from the Nicolaitans themselves in their minister's heart. To divide them, that is, so as to hate their evil deeds with a perfect hatred, and at the same time to love the doers of those deeds with a perfect love. The name Nicolaitan is equivocal, says Pascal.

A *litotes* is a rhetorical device by means of which far less is said than is intended to be understood. A true *litotes* has this intention and this result that while, in words, it diminishes what is actually said, in reality, it greatly increases the effect of what is said. What could be a more condemning charge against any minister of Christ than to tell him in plain words that he had left his first love to his Master and to his Master's work? And yet, just by the peculiar way in which that charge is here worded, a far more sudden blow is dealt to this minister's heart than if the charge had been made in the plainest and sternest terms. To say "nevertheless I have somewhat against thee" to say "somewhat," as if it were some very small matter, and scarcely worth mentioning, and then suddenly to say what it is, that, you may depend upon it, gave a shock of horror to that minister's heart that he did not soon get over. You would have thought such a minister impossible. Had you heard his praise so generously spread abroad at first both by God and man you would have felt absolutely sure of that minister's spiritual prosperity and praise to the very end. You would have felt as sure as sure could be that behind all that so immense activity and popularity there must lie hidden a heart as full as it could hold of the deepest and solidest peace with God; a peace, you would have felt sure, without a speck upon it, and with no controversy on Christ's part within a thousand miles of it. But the ministerial heart is deceitful above all other men's hearts. And these shocking revelations about this much-lauded minister have been recorded and preserved in order that all ministers may see themselves in them as in a glass. Now, there is not one moment's doubt about when and where all this terrible declension and decay began to set in. His Master does not say in as many words just when and where matters began to go wrong between them two. But that silence of His is just another of His rhetorical devices. He does not tell it from the housetops of Ephesus, as yet. But the minister of Ephesus knew quite well, both when and where his first love began to fail and he to fall away. He knew quite well without his Master's message about it, that all this declension and collapse began in the time and at the place of secret prayer. For, not this Ephesus minister only, but every minister everywhere continues to love his Master and his Master's work, ay, and his Master's enemies, exactly in the measure of his secret reading of Holy Scripture and his secret prayerfulness. Yes, without being told it in as many words I am as sure of it as if I had been that metropolitan minister myself. You may depend upon it; nay, you know it yourselves quite well, that it was his habitual and long-continued neglect of secret prayer. It was from that declension and decay that his ministry became so undermined and had come now so near a great catastrophe. 'With all my past praise of thee, I give thee this warning," said that Voice which is as the sound of many waters, 'that unless thou returnest to thy first life of closet communion with Me, I will come to thee quickly and will remove thy candlestick out of its place. I gave thee that congregation when I might have given it to another. And I have upheld thee in it, and have delivered thee out of a thousand distresses of thine. But thou hast wearied of me. Thou hast given thy night watches to other things than a true minister's meditation and prayer for himself and for his people. And I will suffer it at thy hands no longer. Remember from whence thou hast fallen, and repent, and do the first works.'

And now with all that in closing take this as the secret prayer of the angel of Ephesus the very first night after this severe message was delivered to him. 'O Thou that holdest the stars in Thy right hand, and walkest in the midst of the seven golden candlesticks. Thou hast spoken in Thy mercy to me. And thou hast given me an ear to hear Thy merciful words toward me. Lord, I repent. At Thy call I repent. I repent of many things in my ministry in Ephesus. But of nothing so much as of my restraint of secret prayer. This has been my besetting sin. This has been the worm at the root of all my mistakes and misfortunes in my ministry. This has been my blame. O spare me according to Thy word. O suffer me a little longer that I may yet serve Thee. What profit is there in my blood? Shall the dead hold communion with Thee? Shall the grave of a castaway minister redound honour to Thee? Restore Thou my soul. Restore once more to me the joy of Thy salvation, then will I teach transgressors Thy ways, and sinners shall be converted to Thee. The sacrifices of God are a broken spirit; a broken and a contrite heart, O God, Thou wilt not despise. Do good in Thy good pleasure unto Zion; build Thou the walls of Jerusalem.'

XXVIII

THE ANGEL OF THE CHURCH IN SMYRNA

IF Polycarp was indeed the angel of the Church of Smyrna, then we know some most interesting things about this angel over and above what we read in this Epistle addressed to him. All John Bunyan's readers have heard about Polycarp. "Then said Gaius, is this Christian's wife and are these his children? I knew your husband's father, yea, also, and his father's father. Many have been good of this stock. Stephen was the first of them who stood all trials for the sake of the truth. James was another of the same generation. To say nothing of Peter and Paul, there was Ignatius, who was cast to the lions. Romanus, also, whose flesh was cut to pieces from his bones. And Polycarp, that played the man in the fire." You possess Polycarp's whole history in a nutshell in that single sentence of John Bunyan about him. And if you but add that one sentence to this Epistle you will have a full-length and a perfect portrait of the angel of the Church of Smyrna.

Polycarp was born well on in the first century. And it must have been a matter of constant regret to Polycarp that he had not been born just a little earlier in that century so as to have seen his Lord with his own eyes and so as to have heard Him with his own ears. But as it was, Polycarp was happy enough to have been born, and born again, quite in time to enjoy the next best thing to seeing and hearing his Saviour for himself. For Polycarp was a disciple of the Apostle John, and he must have often heard the Fourth Gospel from John's lips long before it had as yet come from John's pen. And that was surely a high compensation to Polycarp for not having seen and heard the Divine Word Himself. And then we are very thankful to possess a circular-letter which the elders of the Church of Smyrna sent round to the Seven Churches telling the brethren everywhere how well their old minister had played the man in the fire. After narrating some remarkable incidents connected with Polycarp's apprehension the circular-epistle proceeds: —

"When Polycarp was brought to the tribunal the pro-consul asked him if he was Polycarp. Have pity on thy great age, said the humane Roman officer. Swear but once by the fortunes of Cæsar. Reproach this Christ of thine with but one word, and I will set you free. "Eighty-and-six years," answered Polycarp, "I have served Jesus Christ, and He has never once wronged or deceived me, how then can I reproach Him!" And then as some of the executioners were binding the aged saint, and others were lighting the fire, certain who stood by took down this prayer from his lips: "O Father of Thy well-beloved Son Jesus Christ. I bless Thee that Thou hast counted me worthy of this day and of this hour. I thank Thee that I am permitted to put my lips to the cup of Christ. And I thank Thee for the sure hope of the resurrection and for the incorruptible life of heaven. I praise Thee, O Father, for all Thy soul-saving benefits. And I glorify Thee through our eternal High-Priest, Jesus Christ, through whom, and in the Holy Ghost, be glory to Thee, both now and ever, Amen." Eleven brethren from the Church of Philadelphia suffered with Polycarp, but he is famous above them all; the very heathen venerate his name. He was not only an eminent teacher and an illustrious martyr, but in all he did he did it out of a truly apostolical and evangelical spirit. Polycarp suffered his martyrdom on the great Sabbath, at the eighth hour of the day. I, Pionius, have transcribed and posted this letter to all the Churches round about. So may our Lord gather my soul among His elect, Amen."

Apostolical, evangelical, and most illustrious, martyr, as Polycarp proved himself to be at the last yet, when he began his ministry in Smyrna he was a man of like fears and flinchings of heart as we are ourselves. You may depend upon it, Polycarp was for a long time in as great bondage through fear of death as any of yourselves. And every syllable of this Epistle is the proof of that. His Master dictated every syllable of this Epistle with the most direct and the most pointed bearing on Polycarp and on his ministry in Smyrna. Every iota of this Epistle shows us that it was addressed to a minister who was at that time of a timid heart and one whose continual temptation it was to flinch and flee. The very name that Polycarp's Master here selects for Himself in writing to Polycarp spoke straight home to Polycarp's trembling heart. "These things saith He which was dead and is alive." Polycarp was in constant danger of death and in constant fear of death. But after this Epistle, and especially after that opening Name of His Master, Polycarp became another man and another minister. Till this was Polycarp's song every day till the day when he played the man in the fire—

> Death! thou wast once an uncouth, hideous thing!
> But since my Master's death
> Has put some blood into thy face,
> Thou hast grown sure a thing to be desired
> And full of grace!

We found the *litotes* device in the first of these Seven Epistles, and we find here the *parenthesis* device in the second of the Seven. When the Spirit speaks to the Seven Churches He does not despise to make use of the rhetorician's art. He recognises and sanctifies that ancient accomplishment by His repeated employment of it, and in His repeated employment of it He gives us so many lessons in our employment of it. "The parenthesis is the delight of all full minds and quick wits." Now though these exact words have never before been applied to Him whose Epistle to Polycarp we are now engaged upon; at any rate, we may surely go on to apply these so expensive words to His so-talented amanuensis. And this full-minded and quick-witted parenthesis comes in here in this way. Polycarp's poverty was one of his many trials and temptations as the minister of Smyrna. And just as the ever-present image of his Divine Master's death and resurrection nerved Polycarp to overcome all fear of his own death, so in like manner his poverty is here put to silence for ever by this parenthesis, ("but thou art rich"). And not only have we a parenthesis here, but a paradox as well. And both of these rhetorical devices are demanded here in order to give utterance to the fullness of the mind and the quickness of the wit both of the true Author of this Epistle and of the highly privileged amanuensis of it. So he was. Polycarp was both poor and at the same time rich. As many of his best successors in the ministry still are. They are almost as poor as he was as far as gold and silver go. But they are even richer than he was in many things that gold and silver cannot command. For one thing, they are far richer than Polycarp could possibly be in the riches of the mind. They are surpassingly rich in so far as they possess the talents and the trainings and the tastes of cultivated and refined Christian scholars. Money is greatly coveted because it gives its possessor the entrance into the best society of the day. But a well-educated and a well-read minister has entrance not only into the very best society of his own day, but of every day, and he will deign to enter no society of any day but the very best. He keeps company with the aristocracy only. Again, riches are to be desired for what they enable their possessor to be and to do and to enjoy. Riches enable their possessor to the true enjoyment of life, to the true use of life, to true power in life, and to the opportunity and the ability of attaining to the true end of life. Unchallengeably, riches in the right owner's hand immensely assist in the attainment of all these high ambitions. But sure I am, there is no class of men among us who are so rich in all these respects as just our well-educated, well-read, hard-working, absolutely-devoted, ministers. No doubt the parenthesist had in his eye Polycarp's riches toward God exclusively. But had he written in our day he would certainly have extended his arms to embrace a poor minister's few but fit books, and his select friendships, as well as many other things that go to alleviate and even to make affluent his remote and arduous life. Money brings troops of friends also, so long as it lasts. But when Polycarp was robing for presentation at Court, so Pionius tells us, his young men would not let him so much as touch his own shoe-latchet. Now you may have your shoes put on and taken off for money, but you cannot have them tied with heart-strings, as Polycarp's shoes were tied that day.

Malicious and abusive language was another of Polycarp's tribulations. I have not enough ancient Church History to be able to inform you just what outlets they had for their malice in that sub-apostolic day. We have Letters to the Editor among the resources of our civilisation. And neither do I know beyond a guess just what Polycarp did when he was again ill-used by the tongues and pens of his day. But if you will hear it I will tell you what Santa Teresa did. And it is because she did what I am to invite you to do, that I for one entirely, and with acclamation, acquiesce in her canonisation. "After my vow of perfection I spoke not ill of any creature, how little soever it might be. I scrupulously avoided all approaches to detraction. I had this rule ever present with me, that I was not to wish, nor assent to, nor say such things of any person whatsoever, that I would not have them say of me. Still, the devil sometimes fills me with such a harsh and cruel temper; such a spirit of anger and hostility at some people, that I could eat them up and annihilate them. At the same time, concerning things said of myself in detraction, and they are many, and are very prejudicial to me, I find myself much improved. It is a mark of the deepest and truest humility to see ourselves condemned without cause, and to be silent under it. Indeed, I never heard of any one speaking evil of me, but I immediately saw how far short he came of the full truth. For, if he was wrong or exaggerated in his particulars, I had offended God much more in other matters that my detractor knew nothing about. O my Lord, when I remember in how many ways Thou didst suffer detraction and misrepresentation, I know not where my senses are when I am in such haste to defend and excuse myself. What is it, O Lord? what do we imagine to get by pleasing worms like ourselves, or being praised by them! What about being blamed by all men, if only we stand at last blameless before Thee." The slander of the synagogue of Satan in Smyrna was not met, I am sure, with a mind more acceptable to the First and the Last than that.

The last thing that He which was dead and is alive said to Polycarp was this mysterious utterance of His, "Thou shalt not be hurt of the second death." Did Polycarp fully understand that assurance, I wonder? Do you fully understand it? At any rate, you understand what the first death is. In our first death our souls will leave our bodies, and then corruption will so set in upon our dead bodies that those who loved us best will be the first to bury us out of their sight. Now, whatever else and whatever beyond that the second death is, it begins with God leaving our souls. God is the soul of our souls. He is the life, the strength, the support, the light, the peace, the fountain, of all kinds of life in soul and body. And when He leaves our souls that is the beginning of the second death. Only, God does not, properly speaking, leave the soul. He is driven out of the soul. In spite of all that God could do, in spite of all that love and grace and truth could do, the lost soul has banished God for ever out of itself. It has insulted and despised God in every way. It has trampled upon Him in every way. It has shut its door in His face ten thousand times, and has taken in and has held revels with his worst enemies. Had Polycarp feared death more than he feared Him who was now alive; had he feared the fires in the market-place of Smyrna more than the fires that are not quenched; had he deserted his post in Smyrna because of its difficulties; had his soul soured at God and man because of his poverty; when he was reviled, had he reviled back again; when he suffered, had he threatened; and had he reproached Christ when he was bribed with his life so to do,—Polycarp is here told plainly that he would have died the second death with all that it involves. But as it was, he died neither the first death nor the second. Polycarp was changed, rather than died. Polycarp had such a Master that He died both deaths for His servant. It was not for nothing that He said to Polycarp that He was once dead but is now alive. For He was dead with both deaths for Polycarp. It was when He was hurt of the second death for

Polycarp that, under the soreness of the hurt, He cried out first in the garden, and then on the Cross. Have we not seen that in the second death the soul is forsaken of God? And was He not forsaken till Golgotha for the time was like Gehenna itself to Him? He that hath an ear, let him hear what the Spirit saith to the Churches: He that overcometh shall not be hurt of the second death. I will ransom them from the power of the grave. I will redeem them from the fear of death. O death, I will be thy plague. O grave, I will be thy destruction.

XXIX

THE ANGEL OF THE CHURCH IN PERGAMOS

IN his beautifully-written but somewhat superficial commentary, Archbishop Trench says that there is a strong attraction in these seven Epistles for those scholars who occupy themselves with pure exegesis. And that strong attraction arises, so the Archbishop says, from the fact that there are so many unsolved problems of interpretation in these seven Epistles. Now, I am no pure exegete and those unsolved problems of pure exegesis have little or no attraction for me. My irresistible attraction to these seven Epistles lies in this that they are so many looking-glasses, as James the Lord's brother would say, in which all ministers of churches everywhere to the end of time may see themselves, and may judge themselves, as their Master sees them and judges them. Another thing that greatly attracts our commentators to Pergamos is the intensely interesting and extraordinarily productive field of pagan antiquities that Pergamos has proved itself to be. Pergamos was the most illustrious city in all Asia. It was a perfect city of temples. Zeus, Athene, Apollo, Dionysus, Aphrodite, Æsculapius, were all among the gods of Pergamos, and all had magnificent shrines erected and administered to their honour. Here also Galen the famous physician was born. Pergamos possessed a library also that rivalled in size and in value the world-renowned library of Alexandria itself. Two hundred thousand volumes stood entered on the catalogue of the public library of Pergamos. Our well-known word "parchment" is derived to us from the stationers' shops of Pergamos, and so on. Whether the minister of Pergamos found all that heathen environment as full of delight and edification to himself, and to his proselyte people, in his day as it is to us in our day, is another matter. But of the deep interest and the great delight that all these things have to us there can be no doubt. For the most of our expositors spend both their time and our time in little else but in telling and hearing about the antiquities of Pergamos. But with all those intellectual and artistic attractions filling every part of his parish, after the minister of Pergamos had this Epistle sent to him, all the rest of his days in Pergamos he would have neither time nor thought nor taste for anything else but for this, that Satan had his seat in Pergamos.

It was to bring home the discovery of this fearful fact to the minister of Pergamos that was the sole object of this startling Epistle to him; just as his receiving of this Epistle was the supreme epoch and the decisive crisis of his whole ministerial life. And no wonder. For to be told, and that on such absolute authority, that while Satan had his colonies and his dependencies and his outposts in Ephesus, and in Smyrna, and in Thyatira, yet that his very citadel and stronghold was in Pergamos,—that must have been an awful revelation to the responsible pastor of Pergamos. Pergamos is Satan's very capital, said this Epistle to the overwhelmed minister of Pergamos. It is the very metropolis of his infernal empire. All his power for evil, both against God and man, is concentrated and entrenched in Pergamos. "London is a dangerous and an ensnaring place," writes John Newton in his *Cardiphonia*. "I account myself happy that my lot is cast at a distance from it. London appears to me like a sea, wherein most are tossed by storms, and many suffer shipwreck. Political disputes, winds of doctrine, scandals of false professors, parties for and against particular ministers, fashionable amusements, and so on. I often think of the difference between London grace and country grace. By London grace, when genuine, I understand grace in a very advanced degree. The favoured few who are kept alive to God, simple-hearted and spiritually-minded, in the midst of such deep snares and temptations, appear to me to be the first-rate Christians of the land. Not that we are without our trials here. The evil of our own hearts and the devices of Satan cut us out work enough. My own soul is kept alive, as it were, by miracle. The enemy thrusts sore at me that I may fall. In London I am in a crowd of temptations, but in the country there is a crowd of temptations in me. To what purpose do I boast of retirement, when I am myself possessed of Satan's legions in every place?

My mind, even at Olney, is a perfect puppet-show, a Vanity Fair, an absolute Newgate itself."

John Newton is one of the three best commentators I have met with on this Epistle. John Newton, and James Durham, and Miss Rossetti. And what so greatly interests those three commentators in Pergamos is this, that they see from this Epistle to the minister of Pergamos that Satan really had his seat in that minister's own heart, just as that same seat is in their own heart. No other antiquity in Pergamos has any interest to James Durham at any rate, but that antique minister's heart in Pergamos. For Satan, if he is anything, is a spirit. And if he has a seat anywhere in this world it is in the spirits of men. Satan dwells not in temples made with hands, either in Pergamos, or in Olney, or in Edinburgh, but only in the spirits of men; and, most of all, in the spirits of ministers, as this Epistle teaches us, and as all the best commentators tell us it teaches us. And the reason of that so perilous pre-eminence of ministers is plain. Ministers, if they are real ministers, hold a kind of vicarious and representative position both before heaven and hell, and the swordsmen and archers of both heaven and hell specially strike at and sorely wound and grieve all such ministers. Satan is like the King of Syria at the battle of Ramoth-Gilead. For before that battle the King of Syria commanded his thirty-and-two captains that had rule over his chariots, saying, "Fight neither with small nor great save only with the King of Israel." And Satan is right. For let a minister but succeed in his own battle against Satan, let a minister but "overcome," as our Lord's word is in every one of these ministerial Epistles, and his whole congregation will soon begin to share in the spoils of their minister's victory.

Thus Satan trembles when he sees
A minister upon his knees.

O poor and much-to-be-pitied minister! With Satan concentrating all his fiery darts upon you, with the deep-sunken pillars of his seat not yet dug out of your hearts, with all his thirty-two captains fighting day and night for the remnants of their master's power within you, and all the time, a far greater than Satan running you through and through with that terrible sword of His till there is not a sound spot in you—O most forlorn and afflicted of all men! O most bruised in your mind, and most broken in your heart, of all men! Pity your ministers, my brethren, and put up with much that you cannot as yet understand or sympathise with in them. And never for a day forget to pray for them in secret, and by name, and by the name of their inward battle-field. Do that, for your ministers have a far harder-beset life than you have any idea of; with both heaven and hell setting on them continually and to the last drop of their blood. May my tongue cleave to the roof of my mouth before I say a single word to turn any young man away from the ministry, who is called of God to that awful work. At the same time, let all intending ministers count well the cost lest, haply, after they have laid the foundation and are not able to finish, both men and devils shall point at them and say, this minister began to build for himself and for his congregation, for eternity, but come and see the ruin he has left! Count well, I say again, whether or no you are able to finish.

A single word about "Antipas my faithful martyr" in Pergamos. "It is difficult," complains the commentator mentioned in opening, "to understand the silence of all ecclesiastical history respecting so famous a martyr as Antipas." But faithful martyrs are not surely such a rarity, either in ancient or in modern ecclesiastical history, that we need spend much regret that we are not told more about one out of such a multitude. At any rate, we have a pretty long roll of well-known names in our own evangelical martyrology, and the cloud of such witnesses is by no means closed in Scotland. Whether this Antipas was a martyred minister or no, I cannot tell. Only there are many martyred ministers in our own land and Church whose names are as little known as the bare name of Antipas. Only, the silence and the ignorance and the indifferences of earth does not extend to heaven. The silence and the ignorance and the indifference of earth will only make the surprise, both of those ministers and of their persecutors, all the greater when the day of their recognition and reward comes. "Then shall the righteous man stand before the face of such as have afflicted him, and have made no account of his labours. When they see it they shall be troubled with terrible fear, and shall be amazed at the strangeness of his salvation, so far beyond all they had looked for. And they, repenting and groaning for anguish of spirit, shall say within themselves—This was he whom we had sometimes in derision, and made a proverb of reproach. We fools counted his life madness, and his end to be without honour. But now he is numbered among the children of God, and his lot is among the saints!" For then shall be fulfilled that which is written, To him that overcometh will I give to eat of the hidden manna. And I will give him a white stone, and in the stone a new name written, which no man knoweth saving he that receiveth it.

This new name which no man knoweth saving he that receiveth it is plain. This is no unsolved problem of interpretation. For, a name in Scripture is always just another word for a nature. That is to say, for the very innermost heart and soul of any person or any thing.

> I named them as they passed, and understood
> Their nature; with such knowledge God endued
> My sudden apprehension,

says Adam to the angel. And a new name is always given in Scripture when a new nature is imparted to any person or to any thing. And so will it be beyond Scripture when that day comes to which every scripture points and promises, and for which every holy heart yearns and pants and breaks. That day when He which hath the sharp sword with two edges shall make all His redeemed to be partakers of His own nature; whose nature and whose name is Love. And just as no man knoweth the misery of that heart in which Satan still has his seat but the miserable owner of that heart, so only God Himself will know with them the new name that He will give to His holy ones on that day. As every sin-possessed heart here knows its own bitterness, so will every such heart alone know its own unshared sweetness in heaven, and no neighbour saint nor serving angel will intermeddle with things that are beyond their depth. And ministers especially. When they have overcome by the blood of the Lamb; when their long campaign of sanctification for themselves and for their people has been fought out and won; a new name will be given to every such minister that he alone will know and understand, and that, as Adam said, by a sudden apprehension. When we are under our so specially severe sanctification here—

> Not even the tenderest heart, and next our own,
> Knows half the reasons why we smile or sigh,

and much more will it be so in the uninvaded inwardness and uniqueness of our glorification. No man knows the hardness and the blackness of a sinful heart but the unspeakably miserable owner of it, and no man knows the names he calls himself continually before God, but God who seeth and heareth in secret. And, as a consequence and for a recompense, no man shall see the whiteness of the stone, or hear the newness of the name written in that stone, saving he that receiveth it. For your shame ye shall have double; and for confusion they shall rejoice in their portion; therefore in their land they shall possess the double; everlasting joy shall be unto them. He that hath an ear, let him hear what the Spirit saith unto the churches, and unto the ministers of the churches.

XXX

THE ANGEL OF THE CHURCH IN THYATIRA

READ the first three chapters of Hosea and this Epistle to the angel of the Church in Thyatira together, and substitute the *dura lectio*, the hard reading, "thy wife," for the easy reading, "that woman" in the twentieth verse, and it will be seen at once that the angel of the Church in Thyatira is just the prophet Hosea over again. Very much the same scandal and portent that Hosea and his house were in Israel; nay, almost more of a scandal, has the house of the angel of the Church in Thyatira been in Christendom. Our classical scholars have a recognised canon of their own when they are engaged on their editorial work among old and disputed manuscripts; a canon of criticism to this effect that the more difficult to receive any offered reading is the more likely it is to be the true reading. Nay, the more impossible to receive the offered reading is the more certain it is to have stood in the original text. And this so paradoxical-sounding, but truly scientific, principle of our great scholars, has been taken up by some of our greatest expositors and preachers, and has been applied by them to the exegetical and homiletical treatment both of Hosea's household history in the Old Testament, and of this so similar household history in the New Testament. And, indeed, as if it were to forewarn us, and to prepare us for some impossible-to-be-believed disclosures in Thyatira, our Lord introduces Himself to the minister of Thyatira and to us under a name that He has not taken to Himself in the case of any of the other seven ministers of the Seven Churches. Only the very greatest and very grandest of the classical tragedies ever dared to introduce and endure the descent and the intervention of a god. Now Thyatira at this crisis in her history is a great and grand tragedy like that. For our glorified Lord puts on His whole Godhead when He comes down to deal with this tragical minister in Thyatira and with his tragical wife and children. These things saith the Son of God, and He armed with all the power and clothed with all the grace of the Godhead. The Son of God who has His eyes like unto a flame of fire wherewith to search to the bottom all the depths of Satan that are in Thyatira. That is to say, to search to the bottom the reins and the heart of the minister of Thyatira, and the reins and the hearts of all his household, and of all his people. And then His feet are like fine brass wherewith to walk up and down in Thyatira, till He has given to the minister of Thyatira and to his house and to all the rest in Thyatira according to their works. Neither let a god interfere, unless a difficulty should happen worthy of a god descending to unravel; nor let a fourth person be forward to speak, is the advice of Horace to all his young dramatists.

It was not the schools of the prophets in Israel that made Hosea the great and original and evangelical prophet that he was. It was his life at home that did it. It was his married life that did it. It was his wife and her children that did it. We would never have heard so much as Hosea's name had it not been for his wife and her children. At any rate, his name would not have been worked down into our hearts as it is but for his awful heart-break at home. And so it was with the minister of Thyatira. We might have heard that there was a certain minister in that ancient city in the days of the Revelation, but this so terrible Epistle would never have been written to him or transmitted to us but for his household catastrophe—a catastrophe so awful that it cannot be so much as once named among us. His Divine Master would have known all the good works of His servant in Thyatira, but He would not have been able to say that the last of those good works of his were so much better than his first works, had it not been for that terrible overthrow in his house at home. The minister of Ephesus had left his first love to God and to God's work because he was so happy in the love of his wife and children. But his co-presbyter in Thyatira had never known what the love of God really was till all his household love had decayed, and had died, and had been buried, and had all turned to corruption and pollution. Both the prophet Hosea in the Old Testament and this apostolical minister in the New Testament had come to see that when any man is called of God to this work of God, all he is and all he has, all his talents, all his affections, all his possessions, all his enjoyments, his very wife and children, must all be held by him under this great covenant with God, that they are all to be possessed and enjoyed and used by him, in the most absolute subordination to his ministry. And all the true successors of those two typical men have at one time or other, and in one way or other, to make this same great discovery and have to submit themselves to this same sovereign necessity.

Marriage or celibacy, an helpmeet or an hindrance, children or childlessness, good children or bad, health or sickness, congregational prosperity or congregational adversity, and all else; absolutely and without any reserve *everything* must come under that great law for all men, but a thousand times more for all ministers; that great law which the greatest of ministers has thus enunciated:—"For we know that all things work together for good to them that love God, to them who are the called according to His purpose." Hosea learned at home, and all the week, that new sensibility to sin, that incomparable tenderness to sinners, and that holy passion as a preacher, with all of which he carried all Israel captive Sabbath after Sabbath, and so did his antitype in Thyatira. His antitype, the minister of Thyatira, was a fairly good preacher before he had a household, but he became an immeasurably better preacher as his household life went on and went down to such depths as it did. As many as had ears to hear in Thyatira they could measure quite well by the increasing depth of his preaching and his prayers the increasing depths of Satan through which their minister was wading all the week. We have never had deeper-wading preachers than Jonathan Edwards and Thomas Boston, and never since the garden of Eden has there been two ministers happier at home than they were. And it is very happy for those of us who are ministers to see also that the two happiest homes in all New England and in all old Scotland were also the homes of two such deep and holy and heavenly-minded and soul-winning preachers. But they were not without this same universal and indispensable training in sin and sorrow. Only they got their training in those things in other ways than in shipwrecked homes. With all their happiness in their wives and children, the author of the *Religious Affections*, and the author of the *Crook in the Lot* and the *Autobiography*, had not their sorrows to seek. Some of the sorrows that sanctified them and taught them to preach so masterfully all their readers see and know, while some of his most constant and most fruitful sorrows the closest students of Boston have been absolutely beat to find out. But it is enough for us to be sure that such noble sorrows were there though the deepest secrets of the manse of Ettrick then were, and still are, with the

Lord. And thus it is that with two such enviable households as were the households of Edwards and Boston, those two ministers also in their own ways are another two outstanding illustrations of Luther's great pulpit principle—'Who are these so incomparable preachers, and from what divinity hall did they come up? These are they who climbed the Gospel pulpit out of great tribulation, and have washed their robes and made them white in the blood of the Lamb.

Though you are not ministers you must know quite well how the same thing works out in yourselves. You are not ministers, and therefore it is not necessary that you should be plunged into such depths of experience as your ministers are plunged into continually if they are to be of any real use to you. But you are hearers, and good hearing is almost as scarce, and almost as costly to the hearer, as good preaching is to the preacher. To hear a really good sermon, as it ought to be heard, needs almost as much head and heart, and almost as much blood and tears, as it needs to preach a really good sermon.

> A jest's prosperity lies in the ear
> Of him that hears it, never in the tongue
> Of him who makes it.

Yes; but a sermon's prosperity lies in both the tongue of the preacher and the ear of the hearer. And a sermon's true prosperity is purchased by both preacher and hearer at more or less of the same price.

There is still left one more of those cruxes of interpretation that had almost turned me away from this Epistle to the minister of Thyatira altogether. And it is this: "He that overcometh, and keepeth my works to the end, to him will I give power over the nations. And he shall rule them with a rod of iron; as the vessels of a potter shall they be broken to shivers; even as I received of my Father. And I will give him the morning star." What a strange promise to make to a minister,—a rod of iron! Yes, this is just one more of those scripture-passages of which Paul once said that the letter killeth, but the spirit giveth life. For the letter here had almost killed out all my hope in this passage till a gleam of the Spirit came to light me into it and to light me through it. "He that overcometh" is just that minister who meets all the temptations and trials of life, at home and abroad, with more and more clarity, and with more and more faith, and with more and more patience, as long as there is a hard heart in his house at home or in his congregation abroad. It is just to the minister who so overcomes his own passions in his own heart first, that his Master will give power to break in shivers the same passions in all other men's hearts, as with a rod of iron. By his charity and by his patience, by these two rods of iron, especially, any minister will overcome as the angel of the Church in Thyatira at last overcame. All the iron rods in the world would not have broken men's hard hearts as that reed broke them, that our Lord took so meekly into His hand when the soldiers were mocking and maltreating Him. And if you just strike with all your might, and with that same rod, all the hard hearts that come near you, you will soon see how they will all go to shivers under it. Till for your reward your Master will give to you also the morning star. That is to say, when many other ministers that sleep in the dust of the earth shall awake, some to everlasting life, and some to shame and everlasting contempt, they that be wise shall shine as the brightness of the firmament; and they that turn many to righteousness as the stars for ever and ever.

XXXI

THE ANGEL OF THE CHURCH IN SARDIS

THEMISTOCLES, Plutarch tells us, could not get to sleep at night so loud was all Athens in the praises of Miltiades. And the ministers of the other six churches in Asia were like Themistocles in the matter of their sleep, so full were all their people's mouths of the name and the renown of the minister of Sardis. When he went to the communion-seasons at Ephesus and Smyrna and Pergamos and Thyatira, for years after the captivated people could tell you his texts and at every mention of his name they would break out about his preaching. His appearance, his voice, his delivery, his earnestness and impressiveness, and his memorable sayings, all contributed to make the name of the minister of Sardis absolutely a household word up and down the whole presbytery. Now it was after some great success of that pulpit kind; it was immediately on the back of some extravagant outburst of his popularity as a preacher, that his Master could keep silence no longer toward the minister of Sardis. In anger at him, as also at those who so puffed him up; both in anger and in love and in pity, his Master sent to His inflated servant this plain-spoken message and most solemn warning. 'Thou hast a great name among short-sighted men. Thou hast much praise before men, but not before God. All men think well of thee, but not God. All thy great sermons are so much sounding brass before God. And what is not already spiritually dead in thee is ready to die, and will soon be for ever dead, unless thou dost become a new manner of minister, not before men, but before God."

"Of all men in the world," says James Durham, "ministers are most obnoxious to this tentation of vanity. And that because most of their appearances are before men, and that in the exercise of some gift of the mind which is supposed to hold forth the inward worth of a man more than any other gift. Now when this meeteth with applause, that applause has a great subtility in its pleasing and tickling of them, and is so ready to incline them to rest satisfied with that applause." Durham is right in that. For praise and popularity is the most dangerous of all drugs to a minister. Dose a minister sufficiently with praise, and you will soon drown his soul in perdition, if God does not interpose to save him. He is as happy as a king all that day after a sufficient draught of your soul-intoxicating praise. He is actually a sanctified and a holy man all the rest of that day. His face shines on all the men he meets that day. He loves all the men he meets. He even walks with God all that day. But you must give him his dram again on his awaking to-morrow morning, else as soon as he has slept off his debauch he will be a worse man and more ill to live with than he was before. To him who lives on praise all the world is as dark as midnight and as cold as mid-winter to him when he cannot get his praise. The wings of an angel sprout in his soul as long as he gets enough praise, but he is as good as in his grave when he opens his mouth wide and you do not fill it. It is true that is a very weak mind which values itself according to the opinion and the applause of other men. But then it is well known that God chooses the weakest of men to make them His ministers. For many reasons He does that, some of which reasons of His all His ministers know, and some of which reasons the wisest of them have not yet found out. "It were vain," says one of the wisest of ministers, "to pretend that I do not feel in me that mean passion that can be elated by applause, and mortified by the contrary; but there is nothing under heaven that I more sincerely and totally despise, and nothing which ever makes me so emphatically despise myself. I feel it infinitely despicable at the very moment the passion for praise is excited, and I hope by degrees, as time goes on, to be substantially delivered from it. I have a thousand times been astonished that this mean passion of mine should not have been completely extirpated by the sincere and deliberate contempt I have long entertained for human opinion. Opinion, I do not mean, as regarding myself, but as regarding any other person, or any other book. To seek the praise that comes from God only, is the true nobleness of character; and if a due solicitude to obtain this praise were thoroughly established in the soul, all human notice would sink into insignificance, and would vanish from our regard." By the end of his ministry the angel of Sardis will subscribe to every syllable of John Foster. But he is a long way from that as yet, and he will need to have some plain words told him about himself, and about his ministry, before he comes to that.

For one thing, admitting and allowing for all the good work His servant did, I have found it far from perfect, his Lord says. But perfection in the work of the ministry at Sardis or anywhere else is quite impossible; and thus it is that when we look closer into our Lord's words we find that it was not so much absolute perfection that his Master demanded, as ordinary honesty, integrity, and fidelity. What He really said was this, "I have not found thy work at all filled up on its secret and spiritual and God-ward side. On its intellectual and man-ward side I have nothing to complain about—but not before God." You see the state of the case yourselves. No man can long command pulpit popularity without hard work. And it is not denied that this minister paid for his popularity with very hard work. He was a student. He took off his coat to his sermons. He wrote them over and over again till he got them polished to perfection. And his crowds of polished people were his reward. But while doing so much of that kind, and no man in all Asia doing it half so well, at the same time he left a whole world of other things not done. Milton did all his work from his youth up under his great Taskmaster's eye. And so did the minister of Sardis. Only his taskmaster was the great crowds that hung on his elaborated orations. Take away the eyes and the ears of those captivated crowds and this thrilling preacher was as good as dead. "Dead," indeed, is the very word that his Master here so bitterly charges home upon him. "Thou hast a name that thou livest, and art dead." His preaching was all right. None of his neighbour ministers, not the most accepted of God and the most praised of God of them all, could preach half so well. His preaching was perfect; but his motives in it, his aims and his ends in it, the sources from which he drew his pulpit inspiration, his secret prayers both before his sermons were begun, and all the time they were under his hand, and while they were being delivered, and still more after they were delivered,—in all these things,—"thou hast a name that thou livest, and art dead." 'Be watchful, and strengthen these things,' said his Master to him. 'It is good to study, only strengthen it with much faith and with much prayer before God. It is good to give thyself to reading, only read and write in the presence of God. It is good to bring up thy very choicest work to these great congregations of thine, only seek their salvation in every sentence of thy sermons. It is good to take captive with thy wonderful eloquence the attention and the admiration of these crowds, only do so in order to take their hearts captive, not to thyself as heretofore, but to Me henceforth. Strengthen, I say unto thee, the things that remain and are ready to die. And above all else, and with a view to all else, and as a means to all else, strengthen thy closet-prayer before God. Strengthen it in the length of it, and in the breadth of it, and in the depth of it, and in the height of it. Strengthen it in the time you take to it, in the intensity you put into it, and in the way you work it up into your sermons, both in their composition, and in their delivery, and in the way you continue to wait and to pray after your sermons; to wait, that is, not for the applause of the hearers, but for their profit and My praise.'

And his heart-searching Master still proceeds with His pastoral counsels to this minister of His, very unwilling to give him over to the decay of soul into which he has fallen. "Remember how thou hast received, and heard, and hold fast, and repent." As if He were to say to some such minister among ourselves—'Remember thy conversion, and the spirit of truth and love that was instilled into thee, and that made thee turn into this ministry of Mine. Remember thy college days, and the high hopes and generous vows made to Me in those days. Remember also how I delivered thee when in thy deep distresses thou didst call on Me, and what communings and confidences used to go on between us. Remember thy ordination day, and the laying on of the hands of the presbytery, and the way thy heart swelled within thee as they pronounced and enrolled thee a minister of Mine.' Yes, even to call such things to remembrance, my brethren, will work together with the seven Spirits that are in Christ's right hand, and with many other things, to set a fallen-down minister on his feet again, and to give him a new start even after he is as good as dead and deposed in the sight of God. Ay, such remembering and such repenting will yet save this all but lost minister of Sardis, and it will save some ministers among ourselves who are quite as far gone as he was. And as he was saved through this Epistle, so will they; and like him they will yet receive the heavenly reward that is here held out to us all by Him who has the seven Spirits of God and the seven stars.

The last thing of the nature of a threat that is addressed to the minister of Sardis is this, "If therefore thou shalt not watch, I will come on thee as a thief, and thou shalt not know what hour I will come upon thee." There is a certain note of terror in that warning which is here addressed to all ministers, the most watchful, the most prayerful before God, and the best. And yet, no; for perfect love casteth out all such terror; perfect love to Christ, and to His work, and to His coming, delivers them who through fear of His coming have all their days been subject to terror. If I love you you cannot come too soon to me. And the more unexpected your coming is to my door the more welcome will you be to me. If I am watching and counting and keeping the hours till you come, you cannot come on me as a thief. Christ could not come on Teresa as a thief as long as she clapped her hands for His coming every time her clock struck. He cannot come too soon for me if I am always saying to myself —why tarry the wheels of His chariot? If my last thought before I sleep is about you I will be glad to see your face and hear your voice the first thing in the morning. When I awake I am still with Thee. The name of that chamber was Peace, and its window opened to the east. And every night after he received and read this Epistle, the minister of Sardis always slept in that chamber till the sun-rising.

And now that the tide is beginning to turn in this Epistle, and in this minister's heart and life, this so unexpected word of encouragement and comfort is spoken to him, "Thou hast a few names even in Sardis which have not defiled their garments: and they shall walk with Me in white: for they are worthy." It was with the minister of Sardis somewhat as it was with Thomas Scott when he was first awaking to his proper work. Scott in his youth had been ambitious to be an author, but he was now beginning to see that preaching was second to nothing on the face of God's earth; and that it had praise of God as nothing else had when it was well done. Scott's preaching was not yet well done by a long way, but it was far better than it once was. And one of the best proofs of its improvement was this, that his parishioners began to come to ask guidance from him in the things of their souls. But at that stage Scott had put all he knew into his sermons and he had little to add as pastoral counsel to his inquiring parishioners. And it would be something like that in Sardis. Some of his people had somehow been kept in life all through their minister's declension and death. There is nothing more surprising and touching than to see how a tree will sometimes cling round a rock and will suck sap and strength out of a cairn of stones. "How do you manage to keep yourself alive, then?" I asked an old saint who is in a case not unlike those few names in Sardis. "O," she said, "I have an odd volume of Spurgeon's Sermons, and I have a son at the front." I did not ask her, but I suppose she meant that the thought of her son in his constant danger made her life of intercessory prayer in his behalf perfect before God, and all Spurgeon's readers will bear her out about his sermons. Even in Sardis, their sons in constant peril, and a volume of some first-century Spurgeon, kept alive those few names all those years that their minister was dead.

And then to put the copestone on this far-shining case of a minister's recovery, and to send him back to his work till, like his much-tried neighbour in Thyatira, his last years should be far better than his first, this splendid seal was set on his second conversion—"to him that overcometh, the same shall be clothed in white raiment: and I will not blot his name out of the book of life, but I will confess his name before my Father and before His angels." It will be on that day to the minister of Sardis like that great day when Joshua stood before the angel of the Lord and Satan stood at his right hand to resist him. Satan will resist him and will tell to his face how he sought his own things in the early days of his ministry and not the things of his people or of his Master. How he swelled with vanity in the day of his vanity. How his own name was in every thought of his and nothing else but his own name. Only let his name be blazoned abroad, Satan will say, and he was happy and all about him were happy. And so on, till Christ will stop the accuser's mouth, and will confess His servant's name. The Lord rebuke thee, O Satan; even the Lord that hath chosen Jerusalem rebuke thee; is not this a brand plucked out of the fire? And he answered and spake unto those that stood before him, saying, Take away the filthy garments from him. And unto him he said, Behold, I have caused thine iniquity to pass from thee, and I will clothe thee with change of raiment. And I said, Let them set a fair mitre upon his head. So they set a fair mitre upon his head, and clothed him with garments. And the angel of the Lord stood by.

XXXII

THE ANGEL OF THE CHURCH IN PHILADELPHIA

If James Durham had lived in Kirriemuir in Disruption days he would to a certainty have said that very much what Daniel Cormick was in the presbytery of Forfar, that the angel of Philadelphia was among the seven churches in Asia. No minister all round about had less strength of some kinds than Daniel Cormick: but, then, like the angel of Philadelphia, by universal consent, he was by far the holiest man of them all and by far the most successful minister of them all. Mr. Cormick used to say in his humility that had it not been for the liberality of Lady Fowlis he would never have got to College at all, and that had it not been for the leniency of some of his professors he would never have got the length of being a minister. Be that as it may, it will be to the everlasting salvation of many that Daniel Cormick was ever sent to College, was carried through his studies, and was ordained a minister. When I was a lad in Kirriemuir our minister's name was wide-spread and dear to multitudes, not so much for his pulpit gifts, as for his personal and pastoral graces. The delightful stories of Mr. Cormick's unworldliness of mind, simplicity of heart, and beauty of character, crowd in upon me at this moment till I can scarcely set them aside. And it was such things as these in Daniel Cormick that far more than made up for the fewness of the talents his Sovereign Master had seen good to commit to the stewardship of His servant. I see myself standing in the passage all through the forenoon and afternoon services, the church was so full. I see Dr. Mill in his crowded pew, a much-honoured man, who largely shared in his minister's saintliness. And there sits Mr. Brand, the banker and writer, whose walk and conversation, like the same things in Dr. Mill, influenced and edified the whole town and country round about. Mr. Brand's copy of Halyburton's *Memoirs,* with his name and my mother's name on it in his own handwriting, is always within reach of my chair, and I am sure I have read it at least as often as Dr. Jowett said to Lady Airlie he had read Boswell. And dear old heavenly-minded, if somewhat sad-hearted, Duncan Macpherson, the draper. A saint if ever I knew one; if, perhaps, a little too much after the type of Mr. Fearing and Mr. Weteyes. There never was a kirk-session in Kirriemuir or anywhere else like David Cormick's kirk-session, and the pillars of it were almost all and almost wholly of their minister's own quarrying and hewing and polishing and setting up. When David White of Airlie became awakened to see what he was, and what a minister ought to be, he sought out Daniel Cormick for his counsellor. As Walter Marshall sought out Thomas Goodwin, and as Thomas Scott sought out John Newton, so did David White sit at Daniel Cormick's feet. The two ministers used to tryst to meet in the woods of Lindertis, where they strolled and knelt and spent hours and days together, till Mr. Cormick was honoured of God to lead one of the ablest men I ever knew into that grace in which he himself stood with such peace and such assurance of faith. To Mr. Cormick's kind and winning ways with children I can myself testify. Is *James Laing: A Lily Gathered,* still in circulation in Dundee? I well remember that red-letter day to me when Mr. Cormick took me to his lodgings with him and gave me that little book to take home with me. But I am wandering away from my proper subject before I have even begun it. I am taking up too much time with Daniel Cormick, deserving of it all as he is. The angel of the church in Philadelphia could not be more deserving. It was James Durham, in the way he speaks about "the little strength" of the angel of Philadelphia, that led me back to speak of Daniel Cormick with all this love and reverence and thankfulness.

If his Sovereign Master allowed to the minister of Philadelphia but little strength of intellect, as James Durham in his profound commentary holds it was, and but little learning; then, what he lacked on the mere mental side was more than made up to him on the moral and spiritual side. And that wisest by far of all the seven ministers in Asia soon found out where his true strength lay and threw himself with all his weakness upon his true strength. William Law complains with all his incomparable scorn that so much of the ministers of his day spent so much of their time and strength in the pulpit on such subjects as the seasons and the directions of the wind called Euroclydon, and on the times when the Gospels were writ. Now Daniel Cormick had not that temptation, for he possessed none of its literature, and even had he lived in our so-learned day and possessed all the learned apparatus of our day, he would not have given way to our temptations in his pulpit. "You, brethren," said Andrew Bonar in Daniel Cormick's funeral sermon, "are witnesses that in all his ministry your pastor ceased not to preach in public, and from house to house, repentance towards God, and faith towards our Lord Jesus Christ. His first sermon after his ordination was on this great text: 'Be ye reconciled to God.' And was not that commencement truly characteristic of Mr. Cormick's whole ministry among you? For, whatever subject he handled he failed not to arrive at sin and salvation before he left it. And such was the unction of his words that even when he was not exhibiting very intellectual views of the text, still his personal affection in setting forth the subject was always felt to be refreshing and quickening."—And this Epistle pays the same praise to the minister of Philadelphia for the way he preached his Master's name, and his Master's name only, in every sermon of his. I have myself, to my confusion of face I confess it, wasted many a precious hour in this pulpit on Euroclydon, and on the times when the Prophets, and the Psalms, and the Gospels, were writ. But I am beginning now to number my days, and I am, as you must witness, turning my own attention and yours far more to the name of Jesus Christ, in imitation of the minister of Philadelphia. Now, what is His name? and what is His Father's name? if you have begun to learn those great names from me and with me? For we ministers should preach the name of the Father and the name of the Son far more than we do. And you, our people, should read far more than you do read, both in your Bible and in other books, on those so foundation and so fruitful subjects. Just what a name is, what its root is, and where this and that name of the Father, and the Son, and the Holy Ghost were first heard; these inquiries, as Clement says, breed great light in the souls both of preachers and hearers. To turn up and read continually the very chapter where God first gave His full and true name to Moses, and then to trace that name and see that once it was given to Israel there is little or nothing else in the whole of the Old Testament but that name. And then to see how the Father's name gives place to the Son's name in the New Testament,—all that breeds great light in the soul, as Clement says. Even with as little strength as there was in Philadelphia and Kirriemuir, a minister will win great praise, both from God and from God's people, if he keeps close to God's word and more and more holds up God's name.

Tentatio, meditatio, oratio, were Luther's three indispensable qualifications for a minister. Now we gather that the minister of Philadelphia had quite a special training in the school of temptation. We hold far too coarse ideas about temptation. We think of temptation as if it were for the most part to whoredom and wine. But the temptations that make a minister after Luther's own heart are as far as the poles asunder from such temptations as these. The holier and the more heavenly-minded a minister is, the more he lays himself open to a life of unspeakable temptation. With every new advance in holiness, with every new progress in the knowledge of God and of himself, with every deeper and deeper entrance of the exquisitely holy law and spirit of God into his heart and conscience, a minister's temptations multiply upon him, till he feels himself to be the most beset, behind and before, of all beset men that dwell upon the earth. And there is good reason for that. For if a minister is to be a real minister; if he is to know, as by the best and the latest science, all the diseases and all the pains in the souls of the saints who are in his ward, of necessity he must have been they have all been made to meet in him. O, wretched man that taken through all those spiritual experiences himself; of necessity he is! before he is fit to feel for and to prescribe to like wretched men with himself. And that is the reason why He who was Himself made perfect through temptation has specially promised that He will keep His ministers in the hour and power and crisis of their temptations, as He was kept in the hour and power and crisis of his own. Tentatio, meditatio, oratio. Oratio especially. Now, there was one special kind of prayer that Daniel Cormick was greatly noted for among those who were intimate with him. All ministers pray much and earnestly before preaching. And the reason is, they are so afraid that they may not do so well to-day. The minister of Sardis, who never prayed at any other time in all the week, to be called prayer, was always in real anxiety and earnestness before he entered the pulpit, because he had such a name for preaching to keep up. And so it is still with all who are like him. They are so afraid that they may forget or displace things, or in other ways disappoint your expectations, that they pray with all their heart till God, according to His promise, hears them and carries them through again without a stumble. The difference with Daniel Cormick was that he would get, now Robert M'Cheyne, and now Andrew Bonar, and now John Baxter, to pray both with him and for him *after* his preaching. As I remember Thomas Shepard also always did: and as, I feel sure, the angel of Philadelphia also did. The "honest weak ministers," that they all three were, as James Durham, that honest but not weak minister, in his incomparable commentary calls them.

"Behold, I come quickly: hold fast that thou hast, that no man take thy crown," said He that is holy, He that is true, to this minister of His. As if He had said, "Hold fast by thy temptations, and thy meditations, and thy prayers both before and after preaching. And hold fast also by My name, and by all that is due to My name in thine office, as well as in thine own soul. Let no man take thy crown in that matter. Be suspicious, be jealous, of all men. Let no man invade on thy work. Give up not an atom of thy work thou canst by any possibility perform thyself. Never weary for one moment in thy well-doing. Let not thy hand for one moment become slack. Do not let thyself lie down to die till all thy work is fulfilled and finished. For if thou dost so die, then thy successor in Philadelphia will take thy crown which I had intended for thee." As John Newton took Thomas Scott's crown as long as Scott neglected his dying parishioners till they sent for Newton. And as ministers' crowns are dropping off their heads in every parish all round about for any ambitious man to pick them up and put them on. Any one, that is, who will visit such and such a sick-bed, and read a Psalm there, and after it one of the Pilgrims' crossings of the Jordan. Hold fast, O all you ministers and elders and nurses and doctors! Hold fast as Dr. Mill held fast at so many death-beds in and around Kirriemuir, till he stole some shining gems even out of Mr. Cormick's crown. Hold fast lest some aspiring man run off altogether with the crown your Master had at one time intended for you. If it took a man like Daniel Cormick all his might to keep his crown from being all stolen from him, what chance, think you, have the most of us ministers?

But look up! Who is that glorified saint shining as the brightness of the firmament, and as the stars for ever and ever? That is the angel of the Church that once was in Philadelphia. That is he, built in for ever as a "pillar" in the heavenly temple to go no more out. He was such a true pillar on earth that the whole of the seven Churches in Asia were strengthened and upheld by means of him. And now he is set in the very midst of the city of God which is new Jerusalem. And, behold, with the name of his God also written upon him, so that all men can read that name on him, as they pass by. Had the name of his God been strength of understanding, or depth and power of mind, or stores of learning, or an eloquent tongue; had it pleased God to save His people by dialectics, then that pillar had not borne as he now bears the name of his God. But God's nature is not like to ours. For we read in letters of gold God's glorious nature and name, and it is this,—the Lord; the Lord God, merciful and gracious, long-suffering, and abundant in goodness and truth, keeping mercy for thousands, forgiving iniquity and transgressions and sins. And that name was taken up with such Paul-like determination, and was so preached in Philadelphia and nothing else was preached, till both the preacher and the people knew none other name. Like preacher, like people. That preacher of Philadelphia fed his people on the finest of the wheat till it became bone of their bone and flesh of their flesh, and till God's great name came out in letters of light all over their foreheads, and was written in works of love all over their lives. What a comfort to the most of us ministers! For the most of us ministers must always be far more like the minister Philadelphia with his little strength than like the minister of Sardis with his great name. For ye see your calling, brethren, how that not many wise men after the flesh, not many mighty, not many noble are called. But God hath chosen the foolish things of the world to confound the wise; and God hath chosen the weak things of the world to confound the things that are mighty. That, according as it is written, He that glorieth, let him glory in the Lord.

XXXIII

THE ANGEL OF THE CHURCH OF THE LAODICEANS

THE Archippus who is so remonstrated with in the Epistle to the Colossians concerning his neglected ministry, may very well have lived on to be the lukewarm angel of the Church in Laodicea. As a matter of fact, there is both internal and external evidence that the angel of the Church in Laodicea was none other than this same inculpated Archippus now grown old in his unfulfilled ministry. And if the external evidence had only been half as strong as the internal the identity of those two unhappy men would have been proved to demonstration. It is much more than a working hypothesis then, the assumption that this angel now open before us is none other than young Archippus at last grown grey in neglect of his work and in ignorance of himself. Archippus was still to all intents and purposes a young minister when this message was sent to him from the aged Apostle, "Say to Archippus, take heed to the ministry which thou hast received in the Lord, that thou fulfil it." But instead of taking that timeous reproof to heart,

Archippus had gone steadily down in his declension and decay till he had this last reproof addressed to him, and which has been a last reproof to so many ministers and their people since his day and down to our own day.

The English language has inherited one of its most contemptuous and denunciatory epithets from this Epistle to this lukewarm minister and his lukewarm church. We call a man a Laodicean. We have no other single word that so graphically describes a certain detestable type of human character. "I know thy works, that thou art neither cold nor hot. I would thou wert cold or hot. So then because thou are neither cold nor hot, I will spue thee out of my mouth." That is plain-spoken enough and in few words. But ever since this so scornful Epistle was written, all that, and more than all that, has been collected up into this one supremely scornful word,—thou art a Laodicean! And thus it is that to all time the angel of the Church in Laodicea will stand forth as the spiritual father of all such spiritual sons. Archippus will stand at the head of a long apostolic succession that has descended from his ancient diocese into all the churches: Episcopal, Presbyterian, and Independent. And this Epistle now open before us is a divinely fashioned looking-glass, as James the Lord's brother would have called it, in which all Laodicean ministers and people are intended to see themselves.

"Because thou sayest, I am rich and increased with goods, and have need of nothing." But Archippus with all his stark stupidity could never by any possibility have said that. He was not such an absolute idiot as actually to say that. No, not in so many words. No minister ever, out of Bedlam, said that in so many words. No. But at the same time by the very Scriptures he read and expounded to his people, as well as by the Scriptures he did not read; by the very psalms and hymns and spiritual songs he sang, and did not sing; but especially by his prayers, Archippus all his days sealed down his people in the same deadly ignorance in which he lay sealed down himself. And indeed it is just of this deadly ignorance of himself that his Master here so scornfully speaks. "Thou knowest not that thou art wretched, and miserable, and poor, and blind, and naked." On the margin of a copy of Thomas Adams' *Private Thoughts* now preserved among the treasures of the British Museum, Coleridge has written these pencilled lines: "For a great part of my life I did not know that I was poor, and naked, and blind, and miserable. And even after I did know that, I did not feel it aright. But I thank God I feel it now somewhat as it ought to be felt. Stand aside, my pride, and let me see that ugly sight, myself. I have been deceived all my life by sayings of philosophers, by scraps of poetry, but most of all by the pride of my own heart, into an opinion of self-power, which the Scriptures plainly tell me, and my repeated failures tell me, that I possess not. It is the design of the religion of Jesus Christ to change men's views, to change their lives, and to change their very tempers. Yes. But how? By the superior excellence of its precepts? By the weight of its exhortations, or by the promise of its rewards? No. But by convincing men of their wretchedness, and guilt, and blindness, and helplessness. By inculcating the necessity of the remission of sin, and the necessity of supernatural light and assistance, and by promising to the penitent sinner, and by actually conveying to him, these evangelical blessings." Well might Charles Lamb say, "Reader! lend thy books to S. T. C., for he will return them to thee with usury, He will enrich them with his annotations, and thus tripling their value. I have had experience, and I counsel thee. Shut not thy heart, nor thy library, against S. T. C."

Among all the terrible things here threatened against this miserable minister of Laodicea, his "nakedness," and " the shame of his nakedness," is surely the most terrible. There is nothing that is more terrible to the heart of man than shame. Shame and contempt, as a parallel passage in the Old Testament has it. Shame and contempt are far worse to face than death itself. When we speak of shame, in our shallow and superficial way we usually think of the shame of a naked body. But there is no real shame in that. When the Bible speaks of shame it is always of the infinitely more terrible shame of a naked soul. Take away the terrible shame of a naked soul and there is no shame at all in the nakedness of the body. But once strip a soul naked, and death is its only refuge and hell its only hiding-place. Take it home to yourselves and see. Suppose your innermost soul laid absolutely bare to us who are your friends and neighbours. Suppose your most secret thoughts about us told to us from the housetops. Suppose all your malicious thoughts about us told, and all your secret hatred of us, and all your envy of this man and that man, naming him, and for what. Suppose it, if you dare for one moment to suppose it, the whole bottomless pit of your evil heart laid bare. Now all that is the threatened case of this miserable creature here called an angel. Indeed his case is far worse than yours; unless, indeed, like him you are a minister. For he will have all the shame that you will have, and, over and above all that, being a minister he will have the special shame and the special contempt and the special revenge both of God and man to bear, and that, if the prophet is right, to everlasting. It is the awful forecast of all this to Archippus that makes his Master's heart to relent once more and to address to him this last-trumpet Epistle. "I counsel thee to buy of Me gold tried in the fire, that thou mayest be rich; and white raiment, that thou mayest be clothed, and that the shame of thy nakedness do not appear; and anoint thine eyes with eyesalve, that thou mayest see." It was this same salvation offered to all such ministers as Archippus in the Old Testament, that made Micah exclaim at the end of his ministry, Who is a God like unto Thee!

And then there is this evangelical invitation to crown all. "Behold, I stand at the door and knock. If any man hear My voice, and open the door, I will come into him, and will sup with him, and he with Me." This, I feel quite sure, is a reminiscence of what had often happened to Him who here speaks. For He was often that He had not where to lay His head. He was often that He had to stand at the door and knock. The parable of the friend at midnight was not so much a parable after all. He must often have been that poor and importunate man Himself. For if He hungered on His way to the city, much more must He have hungered and thirsted and been nigh unto fainting, on His way out of the city. And at such times of temptation, Satan would say to Him—'If thou be the Son of God, command these stones to become bread, and command the wayside streams to run with wine and milk.' But He would say to Satan—'Neither have I gone back from the commandment of His lips: I have esteemed the words of His mouth more than my necessary food.' And so saying He entered a certain village, and knocked at the door. And the man from within answered, "Trouble me not; the door is now shut, and my children are with me in bed, I cannot rise and let thee in." But in the next street there was a lamp still burning, and a voice from within answered, "Come in, Thou Blessed of the Lord." And they supped together that night. When you next think you hear His knock, rise off your seat, rise off your bed even, and open the door. Yes: go and actually open the door. Think to yourself that He is actually in the street, and is actually, and in the body, standing at your door. This is the sacrament night. And it will be a sacramental action to go and actually open your room door or your street door late and alone to-night. Imagine to yourself that you see Him dim in the darkness of the night. Put out your hand into the darkness. Lead Him in. Set a seat for Him. Ask Him when and where He broke His fast this morning. Ask Him where He has been all day, and going about and doing what good. Tell Him that you are sure He has not had time so much as to eat. And set the best in your house before Him, and He will come in and will sup with you, and you with Him. Believe and be sure that He is in this city to-night. Believe that and it will make you to be on the watch. Do not put off your coat, do not wash your feet, till you have opened the door to Him. Sit up for Him. Expect Him. Set your candle in your window. Have your door standing already ajar. And even if you should again and again be deceived and disappointed: even if again and again you should mistake some other sound in the street for His footstep, do not despair of His coming. Do not shut the door whatever you do. Far better a thousand such mistakes through overwatchfulness than to be dead asleep when at last He comes. And besides, who can tell, He may not have eaten a morsel or drunk a drop in all the city this day,—all these communion-tables notwithstanding. And would it not be wonderful if all the entertainment He is to get in this city this whole day still awaits Him in your house this night. And then there is this; whosoever or whatsoever you are, let nothing debar you from supping with Christ to-night. You may not have been at our table to-day. We lay down rules and restrictions as to who shall, and who shall not, sup with Him in this house. But, all the time, He is the Master, and He can lift off all our restrictions, even when they are quite right in us to lay them down, and He can and He will sup when and where and with whom He pleases. And these are His own undoubted words about this night that is yet before Him and before you and before us all. These words: "If *any* man hear My voice, and open the door,"—communicants, He means, or non-communicants; members or adherents; young or old; minister or elder; especially any minister. For as He stood that night at Archippus's door in Laodicea, so will He stand at all ministers' doors in Edinburgh this night. And, all the more, if they are all asleep, have you your lamp still burning on your window-sill for Him. And you will be able to tell us to-morrow how your heart burned as He supped with you and you with Him. For it was a proverb in Athens that they were always well in health, and full of all sweet affability all next day, who had supped last night with Plato.